Book 1

PhonicsWorks™
Lesson Guide Advanced

K12

Book Staff and Contributors

Kristen Kinney *Senior Content Specialist*
Lenna King, Amy Rauen *Instructional Designers*
Mary Beck Desmond *Senior Text Editor*
Jill Tunick *Text Editor*
Suzanne Montazer *Creative Director, Print and ePublishing*
Sasha Blanton *Senior Print Visual Designer*
David Batchelor, Carol Leigh *Print Visual Designers*
Kim Barcas, Stephanie Williams *Cover Designers*
Amy Eward *Senior Manager, Writers*
Susan Raley *Manager, Editors*
Deanna Lacek *Project Manager*

Maria Szalay *Senior Vice President for Product Development*
John Holdren *Senior Vice President for Content and Curriculum*
David Pelizzari *Vice President, Content and Curriculum*
Kim Barcas *Vice President, Creative*
Laura Seuschek *Vice President, Instructional Design and Evaluation & Research*
Aaron Hall *Vice President, Program Management*

Lisa Dimaio Iekel *Production Manager*
John Agnone *Director of Publications*

Credits

About K12 Inc.

K12 Inc., a technology-based education company, is the nation's leading provider of proprietary curriculum and online education programs to students in grades K–12. K12 provides its curriculum and academic services to online schools, traditional classrooms, blended school programs, and directly to families. K12 Inc. also operates the K12 International Academy, an accredited, diploma-granting online private school serving students worldwide. K12's mission is to provide any child the curriculum and tools to maximize success in life, regardless of geographic, financial, or demographic circumstances. K12 Inc. is accredited by CITA. More information can be found at www.K12.com.

978-1-60153-148-3

Printed by Quad Graphics, Versailles, KY, USA, March 2012, Lot 032012

Contents

Ending Consonant Blends –nd, –ft, –lk, and –ct

Ending Consonant Blends –lp and –lt

Ending Consonant Blends –mp and –sp

Ending Consonant Blends –sk, –st, –nt, and –nch

Beginning Consonant Blends *bl–*, *cl–*, *fl–*, *gl–*, *pl–*, and *sl–*

Beginning Consonant Blends *br–*, *cr–*, *dr–*, *fr–*, *gr–*, *pr–*, and *tr–*

Beginning Digraph Blends *shr–* and *thr–*

Beginning Consonant Blends *sc–*, *sp–*, *st–*, *sw–*, *sk–*, *sm–*, *sn–*, and *tw–*

Beginning Consonant Blends *spr–*, *str–*, *squ–*, *scr–*, and *spl–*

Words Ending in *–ank*, *–ink*, *–onk*, and *–unk*

Words Ending in *–ang*, *–ing*, *–ong*, and *–ung*

Silent *e* Spellings for Sounds /ā/, /ī/, /ō/, and /ē/

Silent *e* Spellings for Sounds /ū/ and Long Double *o*

Sounds /ar/ & /or/, Beginning Blends, and Silent *e* Spellings

Introduction

This book provides the following information for K[12] PhonicsWorks:

- About K[12] PhonicsWorks
- Lesson Guide
- Activity Book
- Assessments Book
- PhonicsWorks Readers
- PhonicsWorks Online

The Lesson Guide contains detailed lesson plans for each day and is organized by unit. The lesson plans are placed in the order in which you will use them. Activity Book and Unit Checkpoint Answer Keys are included for you in the lesson plans.

The Activity Book supplements the Lesson Guide and provides an opportunity for students to do some work on their own. While many of the Activity Book pages can be completed independently, we recommend that you provide instruction and guidance (for instance, reviewing the instructions and sample task together) as necessary.

Note that the pages in the Lesson Guide and the Activity Book are also available online in the Materials list. The online version will match the book version unless it has an "update" label.

K¹² PhonicsWorks™ Program Overview

Reading is the most important skill for success in school and society.
— SUSAN L. HALL AND LOUISA C. MOATS, *STRAIGHT TALK ABOUT READING*

Introduction

You *can* teach your child to read!

The K¹² PhonicsWorks™ program is based on the best current research and years of firsthand experience. K¹²'s approach is—

- ► Explicit; lessons directly address relationships between sounds and letters.
- ► Systematic, lessons build logically, sequentially, and step by step.
- ► Multisensory; lessons engage students in a variety of visual, auditory, and tactile activities.

The PhonicsWorks program is organized into two parts—Basic and Advanced— typically completed over the course of two grades. When combined with instruction in literature (such as K¹² Language Arts Literature and Comprehension program for Kindergarten and K¹² Language Arts program for Grade 1), PhonicsWorks offers a comprehensive and balanced approach to help students acquire the critical skills and knowledge required for reading and literacy.

General Objectives

PhonicsWorks is designed to help students achieve these important goals:

- ► Recognize the relationship between sounds and letters.
- ► Blend sounds represented by letters into words.
- ► Read and spell longer, unfamiliar words by breaking them into syllables.
- ► Read grade-level text with fluency (appropriate speed and accuracy).
- ► Read "sight words" (high-frequency words such as *said* or *was*; many of these words do not follow the patterns that have been taught).

Before You Begin

Before you get started, familiarize yourself with the PhonicsWorks program.

Standard Curriculum Materials (K¹² Supplied)

PhonicsWorks Advanced includes the following materials:

- ► *K¹² PhonicsWorks* DVD training video
- ► K¹² PhonicsWorks Basic Kit
- ► *K¹² PhonicsWorks Readers Advanced*
- ► *K¹² PhonicsWorks Advanced Lesson Guide Book 1* and *Book 2*
- ► *K¹² PhonicsWorks Advanced Activity Book*
- ► *K¹² PhonicsWorks Advanced Assessments Book 1* and *Book 2*
- ► Online activities

PhonicsWorks Advanced includes all of the materials in the Basic course, as well as an Advanced Tile Kit.

Additional Materials (Learning Coach Supplied)

You will need to have the following materials on hand, which are labeled "Also Needed" in offline and online Materials lists:

- 3½ x 5-inch index cards
- Index card file box
- Black, nontoxic marker
- Dictation notebook (either loose-leaf paper in a binder or a spiral-bound notebook)
- Pencils
- Folder with loose-leaf paper (for portfolio materials and notes on student progress)

Prepare in Advance

When it's time to begin instruction, you will be well prepared if you take the time to *watch the video, read the lesson plans, and practice using the Tile Kit.* The *K¹² PhonicsWorks* DVD introduces the PhonicsWorks program, shows you how to use the Tile Kit, and explains teaching procedures.

Sounds and Letters: Basics of Phonics

Printed words are made up of letters that represent sounds. When we read words, we turn the letters into their corresponding speech sounds.

Consider the word *cat*, which has three letters:

c a t

The word *cat* also has three speech sounds, or phonemes (FO-neemz), which are written as follows:

/k/ /ă/ /t/

You will notice that sounds are written within slashes that we call *sound boxes*. The *K¹² PhonicsWorks* DVD provides a guide to pronouncing basic phonemes in the English language.

Let's look at one more word. Consider the word *boat*, which has four letters:

b o a t

Although the word *boat* has four letters, it has only three sounds:

/b/ /ō/ /t/

Over the course of the PhonicsWorks program, students will learn the following relationships between sounds and letters:

- Some sounds are represented by only one letter. For example, the sound /m/, as in <u>m</u>ouse, is almost always spelled with the letter *m*.
- Some sounds are represented by a combination of letters. For example, the sound /ch/, as in <u>ch</u>ip, is almost always spelled with the letters *ch*.
- Some sounds can be spelled more than one way. For example, the sound /k/ can be spelled *c*, as in <u>c</u>at; *k,* as in <u>k</u>ite; or *ck*, as in chi<u>ck</u>. The long o sound, /ō/, can be spelled *o*, as in n<u>o</u>; *oa*, as in b<u>oa</u>t; *oe*, as in t<u>oe</u>; *ow*, as in sn<u>ow</u>; and *o-e*, as in h<u>o</u>m<u>e</u>.

Course Instruction Guide

Number of Lessons

K[12] PhonicsWorks covers a total of 360 lessons: 180 in the Basic course and 180 in the Advanced course. Lessons are organized into groups of five lessons. Every fifth lesson presents online review activities and an assessment.

Lesson Time

These lesson times are estimates. You and students might take more or less time per lesson. Feel free to split the lessons into smaller segments and provide breaks for students as needed.

- ▸ **Basic:** 180 lessons; 30 minutes offline, 20 minutes online
- ▸ **Advanced:** 180 lessons; 30 minutes offline, 20 minutes online during the first semester and 20 minutes offline, 20 minutes online during the second semester.

Working Offline and Online

In the printed Lesson Guide, you will find step-by-step guidance for the offline portion of each lesson. These direct, explicit, and systematic lessons help students build a strong foundation of letter–sound knowledge. After the offline portion of the lesson is finished, students are ready to work independently online to reinforce, through engaging review and practice, the core lesson content. Some students may benefit from a short break between the offline and online portions of each lesson.

PhonicsWorks Basic Program: Lesson Guide Components

Unit Overview and Lesson Overview

Each new unit begins with a Unit Overview to help you understand the topics to be covered in the unit. A unit covers five days of instruction. Each day, the first page of the lesson plan indicates the materials; objectives; and any advance preparation, keywords, or Big Ideas you will need to be familiar with before you begin teaching.

Sight Words

Typically, students learn three new sight words every other week. Do not worry if students are unable to master all of the words for the week, because later lessons provide many opportunities to review them.

It is recommended that students work on no more than five sight words at a time. For example, if students master two of the three words for a given week, it is fine to add the third word to the following week's list, for a total of four words. However, if students are unable to master all three of the words, do not add all three to the following week's words.

Preparing sight word cards: You will need two sets of sight word cards to complete the Sight Words activities. One set of cards is supplied in your PhonicsWorks Kit. For the second set, you may either create your own using index cards or print a set from the online lesson and cut them into cards. If you create a set using index cards, you will need 3½ x 5-inch index cards and the list of words found in this section of the program overview. Use a bold black marker and print each word in neat, large, lowercase letters. Keep the two sets of cards somewhere convenient. As you work through the Phonics lessons, you will gradually add these cards to the file box (sight words box).

Here are the sight words in the Basic course:

- the, and, is
- on, to, in
- it, he, was
- says, have, with
- where, from, there
- that, of, put
- two, they, both
- you, went, we

- what, their, want
- said, your, so
- who, see, or
- for, she, her
- does, why, one
- were, my, are
- Mr., Mrs., Dr.

Get Ready

These activities help students review previously taught sounds and letters, and reinforce skills and concepts from earlier lessons.

Learn

In this section of the lesson, new concepts are introduced and practiced through a variety of multisensory activities, including the following:

- Listening to sounds in words
- Manipulating letter tiles
- Completing Activity Book pages with fun written activities
- Writing words and sentences that you dictate

In the first eight units, students practice phonological awareness. Phonological awareness is the ability to recognize and distinguish sounds of speech in language. We learn to speak before we learn to read; we learn to hear sounds before we learn which letters represent those sounds. Accordingly, in the first eight units of PhonicsWorks Basic, students focus on phonological awareness activities, distinguishing and manipulating sounds. Activities include Sound Chains; Finger Stretching; and Head, Waist, Toes.

Be patient. Do these activities thoroughly and well. Research has shown that explicit phonological awareness instruction leads to better reading.

Try It

This section of the lesson asks students to apply their new knowledge of a concept in a variety of ways. They may be asked to read from a PhonicsWorks Reader, write words or sentences in a Dictation activity, or complete an Activity Book page.

- **PhonicsWorks Readers:** The K[12] PhonicsWorks Readers are "decodable readers" with a carefully controlled vocabulary almost exclusively made up of letter–sound patterns and sight words students have already studied. Even though these stories are written in words students have studied, most beginning readers still need plenty of time to figure out the words. When students read the stories, you serve as a guide to help them when they have difficulty. The lessons offer detailed suggestions about how to help students read accurately and sound out challenging words.

Monitor progress: As students read, it is very important that you sit next to them and carefully observe their progress. Lesson plans provide instructions for taking notes while you listen to students read. These notes will help you decide which letters and sounds students still need to work on and which sight words are still difficult for them. You may want to keep a small notebook in which you can write the title of the reading assignment, the date, a list of skills students have mastered, and what they need to work on.

▸ **Dictation:** Early in the PhonicsWorks program, students will use letter tiles to create words dictated to them. As students' skills progress, students move to writing words and then sentences. It is important that you follow the instructions for Dictation as outlined in the Lesson Guide. Research indicates that these steps are the most effective for reinforcing students' letter–sound knowledge.

▸ **Activity Book Pages.** Students will complete two to four pages in each unit of PhonicsWorks. In most cases, after you have read the directions to students and observed them complete one or two examples, they may finish the page independently. Be sure to review students' completed work, making note of any letters and sounds they still need to work on and which sight words have yet to be mastered.

Online Overview

The last section of the Lesson Guide provides an overview of what students will accomplish during their online, independent review and practice of concepts taught to date. You may choose to sit with students during this time, but these activities were designed with plenty of audio and engaging animation to help them work independently.

Unit Checkpoint

Every fifth lesson in the PhonicsWorks program provides a Unit Checkpoint to help you determine how well students have learned the skills covered in the unit. On Unit Checkpoint days, students begin by spending time online completing review and practice activities. The activities provide a fun, interactive way to review concepts from the unit.

Unit Checkpoints and Answer Keys: You will find the Unit Checkpoint assessment pages in *K¹² PhonicsWorks Assessments*. You will find Answer Keys in the Lesson Guide. You can also print both the Unit Checkpoint pages and the Answer Key from the online lesson.

Please note: Throughout the PhonicsWorks program, the Lesson Guide for Unit Checkpoints contain test exercises that are not listed on students' Unit Checkpoint pages. This is not an error. The exercises printed only in the Lesson Guide are for you to assess students' listening skills. Please follow the directions and note students' verbal responses on the Unit Checkpoint page to use later when scoring the Checkpoint.

After you have scored the Unit Checkpoint, remember to ***return to the computer and enter the results***.

"Getting Stronger" Units

After the tenth unit of the Basic course, every other unit is called a "Getting Stronger" unit. These units are designed to strengthen students' skills through review and practice. If students are consistently scoring 100 percent on the Unit Checkpoints in prior units, you may choose to skip the Getting Stronger units. Before skipping the unit, have students take the Unit Checkpoint to make sure they have truly mastered the content. ***Please note: If you choose to skip these units, you will need to return to the computer and mark all the lessons in the unit as "completed."***

Should you skip ahead? Each student learns to read at his or her own pace. This variation is natural and is generally not a cause for concern. We have designed PhonicsWorks to meet the needs of a broad range of students, and we believe most students will benefit from working through all lessons in the program.

While some students might be able to skip some of the Getting Stronger lessons, most students will benefit from the review and practice. This practice helps ensure that they have thoroughly mastered early reading skills and that they are making progress toward achieving what cognitive psychologists call "automaticity." That is, they are on their way to becoming skilled readers who can automatically turn printed letters into their corresponding speech sounds without having to linger over individual letters and sounds. It's like reaching the point in math when students can quickly add and subtract mentally without having to count on their fingers, or in music when they can play "Twinkle, Twinkle, Little Star" on the piano without having to search for the notes.

Most students need repeated review and practice to achieve automaticity. When you come to the Getting Stronger lessons, however, you may feel that students have sufficiently mastered the skills taught in prior lessons. If they are consistently achieving perfect or near-perfect scores on the Unit Checkpoints and if you feel that they will not benefit from further review and practice, then you may skip the Getting Stronger lessons and move to the next unit.

Keep a Portfolio

To document students' progress, we recommend that you keep a portfolio of their work. You can compile a comprehensive portfolio by keeping all of the following items:

- The box of sight word cards
- Completed Activity Book pages and Dictation activities
- Your notes from Try It activities
- Completed Unit Checkpoint pages

PhonicsWorks Advanced Program: Lesson Components

In the Advanced course, lessons are presented much like the lessons in the Basic course (see above). The first four units of the Advanced course review the content of PhonicsWorks Basic, and the remaining units provide instruction in more advanced phonics concepts, such as blends, long vowels, and difficult spelling patterns.

	Semester 1	Semester 2
Offline (with a Learning Coach	30 minutes	15 minutes
Online (independent review & practice)	20 minutes	15 minutes

Sight Words

The first four units of the Advanced course cover the 45 sight words from the Basic course. During this time, students will work on approximately 12 words per week. As in the Basic course, two sets of sight word cards are required. One set can be found in your PhonicsWorks Kit, and you may either make the second set yourself using index cards or print the second set from the online lesson. Here are the other sight words for the Advanced course:

- too, walk, talk
- again, out, pull
- next, my, friend
- goes, anything, begin
- down, know, after
- mother, father, only
- even, look, gone
- love, very, some
- none, more, held
- would, could, should
- brother, sister, baby

- many, animal, while
- together, people, other
- above, here, move
- these, against, now
- every, neighbor, behind
- once, come, about
- please, follow, saw
- everything, under, whether
- nothing, over, almost
- children, write, number
- because, its, first

The Tile Kit:
Multisensory Instruction

PhonicsWorks lessons incorporate *multisensory* instruction. Lesson activities ask students to look, listen, touch, move, and speak.

The Tile Kit is at the core of this multisensory instruction. The Tile Kit contains letters and letter combinations that represent sounds. Students use the magnetized tiles to manipulate sounds and letters in fun activities that combine visual, auditory, tactile, and oral learning.

How to Use the Tile Kit

The Tile Kit is used for a variety of gentle, interactive procedures, such as "build words," "touch and say," and "word chains." Detailed instructions for these procedures are provided in the lessons. (You can also see the Tile Kit used in the *K¹² PhonicsWorks* DVD.) The more you use the kit, the less you will need to consult the instructions, although the instructions are always available for you to use.

The Tile Kit helps students understand how speech is represented in print. For example, consider how we use the tiles to build the word *chin*. When students first build the word *chin*, they will be guided to select three tiles:

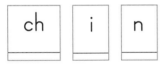

The single sound /ch/ is represented by two letters, *c* and *h*. Because those two letters are printed on a single tile, students get both visual and tactile reinforcement of the simple but important concept that two letters can represent one sound.

Basic Letter Tiles

In the PhonicsWorks Basic course, you receive the Tile Kit, which consists of a binder with pages for the Basic letter tiles. These tiles include the following:

▶ Color tiles
▶ All uppercase (capital) letters
▶ All lowercase letters (multiple tiles provided for each letter)
▶ Digraphs *sh*, *ch*, *th*, *wh*, *ph*, and *ck* and trigraph *tch* (multiple tiles provided for each)
▶ Common word endings –*s*, –*es*, –*ed*, –*ing*, –*er*, and –*est*
▶ Double letter endings –*ff*, –*ll*, –*ss*, –*zz*, and –*all*
▶ Basic punctuation marks: period, question mark, exclamation point, comma, and apostrophe
▶ Vowels printed in red (to provide a visual cue for identifying those letters)

Advanced Letter Tiles

In PhonicsWorks Advanced, you receive the PhonicsWorks Basic course Tile Kit and the Advanced letter tile pages, which include letter tiles with common spellings for sounds that can be spelled in more than one way. The pages are organized to group together the various letters or combinations of letters that represent one sound.

For example, in one section of the binder you will find the following tiles for the long *o* vowel sound:

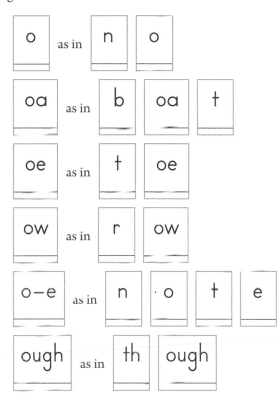

In another section you will find the following tiles to represent the consonant sound /j/:

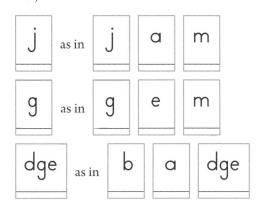

Here is the complete list of what you will receive (some tiles in multiples):

- All PhonicsWorks Basic tiles
- Word endings *ng, ang, ing, ong, ung*
- Word endings *nk, ank, ink, onk, unk*
- Long vowel sound /ā/: *a, e, ai, ay, eigh, a–e, ea*
- Long vowel sound /ē/: *e, e, ee, ea, ie, y, e–e*
- Long vowel sound /ī/: *i, e, ie, y, igh, i–e, y–e*
- Long vowel sound /ō/: *o, e, ow, oa, oe, o–e, ough*
- Long vowel sound /ū/: *u, e, u–e, ew, eu*
- Long double *o* sound (/o͞o/): *oo, e, u, ue, ew, u–e, ough*
- Short double *o* sound (/o͝o/): *oo, u, ou*
- Schwa sound: /ə/
- R-controlled vowels: *ar, or, er, ir, ur, ear, oar, ore*

My Accomplishments Chart

Research shows that rewarding students for quality work can increase their motivation. To aid you in rewarding students, you will receive a My Accomplishments chart and sticker sheet for use throughout the course. This chart gives students a tangible and concrete representation of their progress and accomplishments throughout the PhonicsWorks course (and other courses in which they may be enrolled), which they can proudly display and share with others. When students score 80% or above on a Unit Checkpoint, have them add a sticker for that unit to the My Accomplishments chart. Encourage students to set goals and watch their stickers accumulate. Verbally reinforce their progress to help them understand the connection between their own growing skill set and the My Accomplishments chart.

How to Correct Errors: "Accentuate the Positive"

All students will make mistakes as they learn to read. They may have to try repeatedly to grasp concepts that strike experienced readers as painfully obvious. When correcting mistakes, we need to remain patient and encouraging.

PhonicsWorks lessons suggest specific phrases for you to use when students make an error. These suggestions are meant to help make the experience of learning to read a positive one that focuses on success.

For example, imagine that you ask students to touch the letter *b* and they touch the letter *d*. You want to avoid a negative (and potentially discouraging) response such as, "No, that's not right. Try again." Instead, say, "You touched the letter *d*. This is the letter *b*. Touch this letter and say *b*." These words inform students that they did indeed touch a letter, and they serve as a reminder of the name of the letter touched. They also provide immediate and gentle guidance about how to give the right answer.

PhonicsWorks Keywords

accent – the emphasis, by stress or pitch, on a word or syllable. For example, in the word *garden*, the accent falls on the first syllable, *gar*.

base word – the part of a word that contains a prefix, suffix, or both. A base word can stand on its own.

blend – a combination of two or three consonants in which you hear the sound of each consonant; for example, the two letters *st* can each be heard in the word *stop*, and the three letters *str* can each be heard in the word *string*.

compound word – a word made from two smaller words (for example, *baseball*)

decode – the ability to translate written forms into their corresponding speech sounds. For example, students decode when they recognize that *d* represents /d/, *o* represents /ŏ/, *g* represents /g/, and therefore that combination of letters (*d-o-g*) is the word *dog*.

digraph – two letters together that make one sound. For example, the two letters *sh* in the word *fish* make one sound.

onset – the part of a word preceding the first vowel. For example, in the word *smart*, *sm* is the onset.

phonemes – the smallest units of sound. Phonemes are combined to make words.

phonological awareness – the ability to identify and manipulate sound parts in words. The ability to identify similar sounds in words, create rhyming words, and count syllables are all signs of phonological awareness.

rime – the part of a word that includes the first vowel and what follows it. For example, in the word *smart*, *art* is the rime.

schwa – an unstressed vowel indistinct in pronunciation, often similar to short *u*. In the word *garden*, the unstressed syllable *den* contains the schwa sound. In the word *alone*, the unstressed syllable *a* is the schwa sound. The schwa sound is represented by the symbol ə.

trigraph – three letters together that make one sound. For example, the three letters *tch* in the word *match* make one sound.

Look Back: Sound /ă/

Unit Overview

In this unit, students will
- ▶ Identify the short vowel sounds /ă/, /ŏ/, and /ŭ/.
- ▶ Review the letters of the alphabet.
- ▶ Identify beginning, middle, and ending sounds in words.
- ▶ Learn sight words.

Lesson Overview

Offline FOCUS: Sound /ă/ **30** minutes

Get Ready	Listen for Ending Sounds
	Face-Down Letters
	Sound Chains with Two Sounds
Learn	Look Back: Sound /ă/
Sight Words	Read Sight Words
Try It	Best Pick
	Dictation: Write Words

Online REVIEW: Sound /ă/ **20** minutes

Advance Preparation

Place lowercase letter tiles in alphabetical order on your whiteboard.

If you have not already done so, create **two sets** of the sight words on 3½ x 5-index cards (the list of words can be found in the Sight Words section of the Lesson Guide introduction). Use a bold black marker and print each word in neat, large, lowercase letters. Keep the two sets of cards somewhere convenient. As you work through the Phonics lessons, you will gradually add these cards to the file box (sight words box).

Big Ideas

- ▶ Phonological awareness activities deal with sounds only, not sounds and print.
- ▶ Sight word knowledge helps early readers read complete, grammatically correct sentences.

Materials

Supplied
- *K¹² PhonicsWorks Advanced Activity Book*, p. PH 1
- whiteboard, Learning Coach
- whiteboard, student
- Tile Kit

Also Needed
- sight words box
- dictation notebook

Keywords

alphabetic principle – understanding that letters and combinations of letters represent sounds

phonemic awareness – ability to identify and manipulate individual sounds in words; a subset of phonological awareness

phonics – the study of sounds and the letters that represent them

phonological awareness – ability to identify and manipulate sound parts in words

sight words – words that are taught and learned as whole words; the reader does not learn to sound out sight words

 **30 minutes**

FOCUS: Sound /ă/

Work **together** with students to complete offline Get Ready, Learn, Sight Words, and Try It activities.

Get Ready

Listen for Ending Sounds

Help students identify ending sounds.

1. **Say:** I am going to say a word. Your job is to listen for the last sound you hear in the word. Then you can tell me the last sound.

   ▸ For example, if I say *mop*, you will say /p/ because the last sound you hear in *mop* is /p/.
   ▸ Now it's your turn. Listen to the word I say. You repeat the word, and then tell me the last sound in the word.

2. Repeat the process, using the following words to help students recognize ending sounds:

   ▸ *fun* /n/
   ▸ *jam* /m/
   ▸ *cob* /b/
   ▸ *love* /v/
   ▸ *fell* /l/
   ▸ *loss* /s/
   ▸ *quiz* /z/

> **Objectives**
> * Identify ending sounds in words.
> * Identify letters of the alphabet.
> * Identify individual sounds in words.

Face-Down Letters

To help students learn to recognize the letters of the alphabet, have them practice identifying and naming letters. Grab your whiteboard with letters placed in alphabetical order.

1. Lay your whiteboard down on a flat surface and flip over the letter tiles *c*, *h*, *k*, *s*, *t*, and *w*.

2. **Say:** These letters are face down. We are looking at the back of them. Name each letter and then turn it over to see if you were right.

TIP If students miss any of the letters, have them turn over the missed ones and try again.

Sound Chains with Two Sounds

Play a game with color tiles to help students identify sounds that are the same and sounds that are different. Grab the color tiles from the Tile Kit.

1. Place the tiles on a table.

2. **Say:** I am going to make two sounds. If the sounds are the same, you'll pick out two tiles that are the same color and put them next to each other. If the sounds are different, you'll pick out two tiles that are different colors and put them next to each other. For example,

    ▸ When I make the sounds /mmm/ and /ēēē/, you'll pick out two tiles that are different colors because the two sounds are different. Remember, the two sounds I made were /mmm/, /ēēē/.
    ▸ Now listen carefully to the next two sounds: /mmm/, /t/. The first sound— /mmm/—stayed the same, but the second sound changed from /ēēē/ to /t/. To show that the second sound changed, you will change the second color tile to a tile of a different color.

3. Say each pair of sounds. Have students pick out and place tiles to indicate whether the sounds are the same or different. Note that students should **not** choose two new tiles for each pair of sounds; they should begin with two tiles and replace those tiles as necessary throughout the "chain."

    ▸ /d/, /t/
    ▸ /d/, /d/
    ▸ /n/, /d/
    ▸ /s/, /d/
    ▸ /f/, /d/
    ▸ /f/, /f/
    ▸ /ŏ/, /f/
    ▸ /ŏ/, /s/
    ▸ /h/, /s/

TIP If you have not done so already, watch the *K¹² PhonicsWorks* DVD, which models using color tiles.

Learn

Look Back: Sound /ă/

Help students recognize and use the short vowel sound /ă/. It's important that you explain this as closely as possible to what you see below.

1. Place lowercase letter *a* on students' whiteboard.

2. **Say:** Today we are going to review the short vowel sound /ă/, as in *apple*. Say /ă/. The sound /ă/ will be spelled by the letter *a* in almost all of the words we read during the next few weeks.

3. **Say:** The guide word for the sound /ă/ is *apple*. Say *apple*.

4. Pretend to hold an apple in your hand while you say the word *apple*.

5. **Say:** Whenever you can't remember the sound for /ă/, I will pretend to hold an *apple* to remind you that the sound for short *a* is the first sound in the word *apple*. Say /ă/ and touch the *a* letter tile as you say the sound.

6. Practice the sound and motion several times throughout the remainder of the lesson.

TIP For extra practice, repeat the sound and motion throughout the day.

> **Objectives**
> - Identify the letter, given the sound /ă/.
> - Identify the sound, given the letter *a*.
> - Identify and use the sound /ă/.
> - Identify individual sounds in words.

Sight Words

Read Sight Words

Help students learn the sight words *the, on, is,* and *and*.

1. Gather the sight word cards *the, on, is,* and *and*.

2. Show students the *and* card.

3. **Say:** This is the word *and*. We see this word so often that we want to be able to read and spell it quickly without thinking about it. Look closely at the word *and*. Spell the word *and* aloud. Take a picture of the word *and* in your mind. When you think you can spell *and* yourself, turn the card over and use your letter tiles to spell the word *and*. Check the card to see if you spelled the word *and* correctly. Read aloud the word you spelled with the letter tiles.

4. Place the card in students' sight words box.

TIP Sight words can be very difficult for some students. Let students work at their own pace and really master these words.

> **Objectives**
> - Read sight words.
> - Spell sight words.

Best Pick

Have students complete page PH 1 in *K¹² PhonicsWorks Advanced Activity Book* for more practice with the short vowel sound /ă/. First have students read each sentence aloud and circle the word that best completes it. Then have students write the word on the line and read the sentence again to be sure it makes sense.

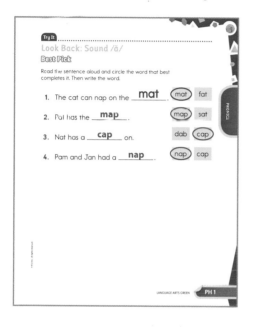

Dictation: Write Words

Have students practice identifying sounds and writing words.

1. Gather a pencil and the dictation notebook. Say the word *tab*. Then give these directions to students:

   ► Repeat the word.
   ► Write the word in your notebook.
   ► Read the word aloud.

2. When students have finished, write the following word on your whiteboard: *tab*.

3. Have them compare their answer to your correct version.

4. Repeat this procedure with the words *cat* and *pan*.

   ► If students make an error and don't see it, help them correct their mistake by having them finger stretch the sounds in the word they missed.
   ► If students are having difficulty selecting the correct letters or sounds, review those letters or sounds that are confusing them.
   ► If students have difficulty with first, middle, and last sounds, have them finger stretch the sounds in the word.

 **20 minutes**

REVIEW: Sound /ă/

Students will work online independently to

▸ Practice the short vowel sound /ă/.

Help students locate the online activities and provide support as needed.

Offline Alternative

No computer access? Have students point out and name things or words that contain the sound /ă/ (for example, *ax* and *cat*).

⭐ Objectives

- Identify the letter, given the sound /ă/.
- Identify the sound, given the letter *a*.
- Identify and use the sound /ă/.
- Identify individual sounds in words.

Look Back: Sound /ŏ/

Lesson Overview

≡ [Offline] FOCUS: Sound /ŏ/ — 30 minutes

Get Ready	Listen for Beginning Sounds
	Secret Sound
Learn	Introduce Finger Stretching
	Finger Stretching
	Look Back: Sound /ŏ/
Sight Words	Read Sight Words
Try It	Dictation: Write Words

🖵 [Online] REVIEW: Sound /ŏ/ — 20 minutes

Materials

Supplied
- whiteboard, Learning Coach
- whiteboard, student
- Tile Kit

Also Needed
- sight words box
- dictation notebook

Big Ideas

The ability to identify the individual sounds in words is a demonstration of phonemic awareness.

⟦ Offline ⟧ 🕙 minutes

FOCUS: Sound /ŏ/

Work **together** with students to complete offline Get Ready, Learn, Sight Words, and Try It activities.

Get Ready ....

Listen for Beginning Sounds

Help students identify beginning sounds.

1. **Say:** I'm going to say a word. Listen for the beginning sound. Then tell me the sound.

   ▸ For example, if I say *mop*, you will say /m/ because the first sound you hear in *mop* is /m/.

   ▸ Now it's your turn. Listen to the word I say. You repeat the word, and then tell me the first sound in the word.

2. Repeat the process, using the following words to help students recognize beginning sounds:

   ▸ *gum* /g/
   ▸ *jar* /j/
   ▸ *rat* /r/
   ▸ *zero* /z/
   ▸ *wall* /w/
   ▸ *mill* /m/
   ▸ *boss* /b/

Secret Sound

Say groups of words that begin with the same letter to help students recognize **beginning sounds** in words.

1. **Say:** I am going to say some groups of words. Listen for a secret sound at the beginning of each word. Then tell me what sound you hear at the beginning of each group of words.

2. Say each of the following groups of words. Have students identify the secret sound in each group.

   ▸ *edge, echo, Eskimo, ever* /ĕ/
   ▸ *lip, like, lend, little* /l/
   ▸ *inside, itch, igloo, if* /ĭ/
   ▸ *pat, pen, pig, pal* /p/
   ▸ *otter, onto, October, octopus* /ŏ/
   ▸ *yellow, yes, yesterday, yum* /y/
   ▸ *ugly, under, upset, upside down* /ŭ/
   ▸ *after, apple, alligator, add* /ă/

3. Repeat any groups of words for which students couldn't identify the secret sound. Have students repeat each word in that group. Then have them say what sound they hear at the beginning of each word.

Learn

Introduce Finger Stretching

Introduce students to the concept of finger stretching to represent the sounds in words.

1. **Say:** We can finger stretch the sounds in a word to count how many sounds there are in that word. Start by holding up your hand with your palm facing you and make a loose fist. Each time you say a sound in a word, extend a finger, starting with your thumb.

2. **Say:** Let's finger stretch the sounds in *mat*.

   ▶ Say the first sound in the word *mat*, /m/, and move your thumb out. Keep your thumb out.
   ▶ Say the second sound, /ă/, and move your index finger out. Keep your thumb and finger stretched out.
   ▶ Say the last sound, /t/, and move your middle finger out. Your fingers are stretched out; you have finger stretched the word *mat*.

3. **Say:** Let's count the number of sounds in the word *mat*.

   ▶ How many fingers are out? three
   ▶ How many sounds are in *mat*? three

4. **Say:** To finish finger stretching a word, put your fingers back into a fist and pull your fist toward your body as you say the word. When you finger stretch, you always say the word after you count the sounds with your fingers.

5. **Say:** Let's finger stretch the sounds in the word *mop*. Remember to extend a finger each time you say a sound.

   ▶ What is the first sound? /m/
   ▶ What is the second sound? /ŏ/
   ▶ What is the last sound? /p/

6. **Say:** Pull the sounds together by making a fist and pulling your fist toward your body while saying the word.

TIP Refer to the *K¹² PhonicsWorks* DVD for a demonstration of finger stretching.

Objectives
- Identify individual sounds in words.
- Identify the number of sounds within words.
- Identify the letter, given the sound /ŏ/.
- Identify the sound, given the letter *o*.
- Identify and use the sound /ŏ/.

Finger Stretching

Use finger stretching to help students identify individual sounds in words.

1. **Say:** Let's review finger stretching. In the word *cat*, the first sound is /k/, the middle sound is /ă/, and the last sound is /t/. I will finger stretch each sound as I say it. Then I'll say the word, while pulling my fist toward my body.

2. Finger stretch the word *cat* for students.

3. **Say:** I'm going to say words with several sounds in them. You'll say each word and then finger stretch it while you say each sound in the word.

4. Say the following words and have students finger stretch them. After they finger stretch each word, ask them the question for that word.

   ▸ *mad* /m/ /ă/ /d/   How many sounds are in the word? three
   ▸ *bag* /b/ /ă/ /g/   What is the last sound? /g/
   ▸ *bug* /b/ /ŭ/ /g/   What is the middle sound? /ŭ/
   ▸ *fog* /f/ /ŏ/ /g/   What is the first sound? /f/
   ▸ *not* /n/ /ŏ/ /t/   What is the middle sound? /ŏ/
   ▸ *odd* /ŏ/ /d/   How many sounds are in the word? two

Look Back: Sound /ŏ/

Help students recognize and use the short vowel sound /ŏ/.

1. Place lowercase letter *o* on students' whiteboard.

2. **Say:** Today we are going to review the short vowel sound /ŏ/, as in *octopus*. Say /ŏ/. The sound /ŏ/ will be spelled by the letter *o* in almost all of the words we read during the next few weeks.

3. **Say:** The guide word for the sound /ŏ/ is *octopus*. Say *octopus*.

4. Pretend that your hand is an *octopus* and your fingers are the tentacles. Walk the octopus from left to right as you say the sound /ŏ/.

5. **Say:** Whenever you can't remember the sound for /ŏ/, I will pretend my hand is an *octopus* to remind you that the sound for short *o* is the first sound in the word *octopus*. Say /ŏ/ and touch the *o* letter tile as you say the sound.

6. Practice the sound and motion several times throughout the remainder of the lesson.

TIP For extra practice, repeat the sound and motion throughout the day.

Sight Words

Read Sight Words

Help students learn the sight words *to*, *in*, *he*, and *it*.

1. Gather the sight word cards *to*, *in*, *he*, and *it*.

2. Show students the *to* card.

3. **Say:** This is the word *to*. We see this word so often that we want to be able to read and spell it quickly without thinking about it. Look closely at the word *to*. Spell the word *to* aloud. Take a picture of the word *to* in your mind. When you think you can spell *to* yourself, turn the card over and use your letter tiles to spell the word *to*. Check the card to see if you spelled the word *to* correctly. Read aloud the word you spelled with the letter tiles.

4. Repeat the activity with the remaining sight words.

5. Add the cards to students' sight words box.

TIP Sight words can be very difficult for some students. Let students work at their own pace and really master these words.

> **Objectives**
> - Read sight words.
> - Spell sight words.

Try It

Dictation: Write Words

Have students practice identifying sounds and writing words.

1. Gather a pencil and the dictation notebook. Say the word *pot*. Then give these directions to students:

   ▸ Repeat the word.
   ▸ Write the word in your notebook.
   ▸ Read the word aloud.

2. When students have finished, write the following word on your whiteboard: *pot*.

3. Have them compare their answer to your correct version.

4. Repeat this procedure with the words *bog* and *tag*.

   ▸ If students make an error and don't see it, help them correct their mistake by having them finger stretch the sounds in the word they missed.
   ▸ If students are having difficulty selecting the correct letters or sounds, review those letters or sounds that are confusing them.
   ▸ If students have difficulty with first, middle, and last sounds, have them finger stretch the sounds in words.

> **Objectives**
> - Write words by applying grade-level phonics knowledge.
> - Follow three-step directions.

 **20 minutes**

REVIEW: Sound /ŏ/

Students will work online independently to

▸ Practice the short vowel sound /ŏ/.

Help students locate the online activities and provide support as needed.

Offline Alternative

No computer access? Have students point out and name things or words that contain the sound /ŏ/ (for example, *mop* and *odd*).

Objectives

- Identify the letter, given the sound /ŏ/.
- Identify the sound, given the letter *o*.
- Identify and use the sound /ŏ/.
- Identify individual sounds in words.

Look Back: Sound /ŭ/

Lesson Overview

Offline — **FOCUS:** Sound /ŭ/ — **30** minutes

Get Ready	Review Consonant Sounds and Letters
	Review Vowel Sounds and Letters
Learn	Look Back: Sound /ŭ/
	Build Words
	Recognize Words and Syllables
Sight Words	Read Sight Words
Try It	By Sight
	Dictation: Write Words

Online — **REVIEW:** Sound /ŭ/ — **20** minutes

Materials

Supplied
- *K¹² PhonicsWorks Advanced Activity Book*, p. PH 2
- whiteboard, Learning Coach
- whiteboard, student
- Tile Kit

Also Needed
- sight words box
- dictation notebook

Advance Preparation

Place lowercase letter tiles in alphabetical order on your whiteboard.

Big Ideas

Letters are put together in a special, specific order to make words.

[Offline]   ⏱ 30 minutes

FOCUS: Sound /ŭ/

Work **together** with students to complete offline Get Ready, Learn, Sight Words, and Try It activities.

Get Ready ••

Review Consonant Sounds and Letters

Help students review the consonant letters and sounds of the alphabet. Grab your whiteboard with letters placed in alphabetical order.

1. **Say:** I am going to point to each consonant. Tell me the sound for the letter. Students should say the sound for each letter.

2. **Say:** This time, I am going to say the sound for each consonant. Repeat the sound and touch and say its letter. Students should touch each corresponding letter and say its name.

Review Vowel Sounds and Letters

Help students review vowel sounds and letters.

1. Place the following letter tiles on students' whiteboard: *a, e, i, o,* and *u,* plus any letters that are confusing.

2. **Say:** I am going to point to a letter. Tell me a sound for that letter.

3. **Say:** I am going to say a sound. Repeat the sound and touch its letter.

4. Point to some letter tiles two or three times, so students don't think that once they have named a sound they are finished with it.

5. Redirect students if they name the letter and not its sound.

   Say: You are right that the name of the letter is [incorrect letter]. We want the sound for this letter. What is the sound?

6. Redirect students if they name the sound incorrectly.

   Say: That is the sound of another letter.

7. Provide additional guidance if students touch the wrong letter tile during the review.

   Say: That is the letter tile for the sound [sound of incorrect letter tile]. We are looking for the letter tile for the sound [target sound].

8. If students touch the wrong letter tile again, point to the correct letter tile.

   Say: This is the letter tile for the sound [target sound]. Touch this letter tile and say its sound.

Learn ....

Look Back: Sound /ŭ/
Help students recognize and use the short vowel sound /ŭ/.

1. Place lowercase letter *u* on students' whiteboard.

2. **Say:** Today we are going to review the short vowel sound /ŭ/, as in *up*. Say /ŭ/. The sound /ŭ/ will be spelled by the letter *u* in almost all of the words we read during the next few weeks.

3. **Say:** The guide word for the sound /ŭ/ is *up*. Say *up*.

4. Point your finger up and move it from your waist to over your head as you say the word *up*.

5. **Say:** Whenever you can't remember the sound for /ŭ/, I will point my finger *up* to remind you that the sound for short *u* is the first sound in the word *up*. Say /ŭ/ and touch the *u* letter tile as you say the sound.

6. Practice the sound and motion several times throughout the remainder of the lesson.

TIP For extra practice, repeat the sound and motion throughout the day.

_____

Build Words
Help students use letters and sounds to build words.

1. Place the following letter tiles in the order shown at the top of students' whiteboard: *a, d, f, g, h, m, o, s, n, p, t, u,* and *x*.

2. Draw three horizontal lines across the middle of students' whiteboard to represent the sounds in a word.

3. **Say:** Let's use letters and sounds to build the word *map*.

4. Have students finger stretch the sounds in *map*.

5. Have students
   ► Identify the first, next, and last sounds in *map*.
   ► Choose the corresponding letter for each of the sounds.
   ► Move the letters to the correct lines on their whiteboard.

6. Guide students with these questions:
   ► What is the first sound in *map*? /m/
     Which line does the letter for that sound go on? the first one
   ► What is the next sound in *map*? /ă/
     Which line does the letter for that sound go on? the second one
   ► What's the last sound in *map*? /p/
     Which line does the letter for that sound go on? the last one

7. Have students touch and say the word.

8. Redirect students if they select the incorrect letter.

   Say: That sound is in the word [word], and it is the [first, second, third] sound. We want the sound [target sound].

   Continue until students select the correct letter.

Objectives
- Identify the letter, given the sound /ŭ/.
- Identify the sound, given the letter *u*.
- Identify and use the sound /ŭ/.
- Identify individual sounds in words.
- Identify the number of syllables in a word.

9. Repeat the activity to build the following words:

  ▸ *fox* /f/ /ŏ/ /ks/
  ▸ *sun* /s/ /ŭ/ /n/
  ▸ *not* /n/ /ŏ/ /t/
  ▸ *had* /h/ /ă/ /d/
  ▸ *gum* /g/ /ŭ/ /m/

Recognize Words and Syllables

Introduce the concept of syllables to students.

1. **Say:** When we talk, we make words by pushing air out of our mouths. Each push of air in a word is called a **syllable**. Each word has one or more syllables. You can think of syllables as chunks of words.

2. **Say:** Let's break some words into syllables.

  ▸ I'll say a word. I'll repeat the word.
  ▸ You'll say the word after me and you'll break it into syllables by saying the separate chunks of the word and tapping your fist on the table as you say each chunk.
  ▸ For example, I'll say *button*, and then I'll say it again.
  ▸ You will say *but / ton* and tap your fist on the table as you say each syllable.

3. Say each word and repeat it. Have students fist tap on the table as they say the syllables in each word.

  ▸ *morning morn / ing*
  ▸ *mistake mis / take*
  ▸ *gallop gal / lop*
  ▸ *chick chick*
  ▸ *traffic traf / fic*
  ▸ *tonsil ton / sil*
  ▸ *bird bird*

(TIP) Have students name items in the room and fist tap the syllables with you. For example, have them name and fist tap words such as *ta / ble* and *win / dow*. Challenge students to name and fist tap something with several syllables (for example, *tel / e / vi / sion*).

Sight Words

Read Sight Words

Help students learn the sight words *says*, *have*, *with*, and *was*.

1. Gather the sight word cards *says*, *have*, *with*, and *was*.

2. Show students the *says* card.

3. **Say:** This is the word *says*. We see this word so often that we want to be able to read and spell it quickly without thinking about it. Look closely at the word *says*. Spell the word *says* aloud. Take a picture of the word *says* in your mind. When you think you can spell *says* yourself, turn the card over and use your letter tiles to spell the word *says*. Check the card to see if you spelled the word *says* correctly. Read aloud the word you spelled with the letter tiles.

4. Repeat the activity with the remaining sight words.

5. Add the cards to students' sight words box.

(TIP) Sight words can be very difficult for some students. Let students work at their own pace and really master these words.

Objectives
- Read sight words.
- Spell sight words.

Try It

By Sight

Have students complete page PH 2 in *K¹² PhonicsWorks Advanced Activity Book* for more practice with recognizing and reading words by sight. Moving from left to right across the rows, have students read aloud for a total of one minute. When they get to the bottom of the page, have them start over. Students may want to place a bookmark under the row they are reading to help them stay on the correct row.

Objectives
- Read sight words.
- Read aloud grade-level text with appropriate automaticity, prosody, accuracy, and rate.
- Write words by applying grade-level phonics knowledge.
- Follow three-step directions.

Try It

Look Back: Sound /ū/

By Sight

Reading across the rows, see how many words you can read correctly in one minute. When you get to the bottom of the page, start over.

the	and	is	on	to
in	it	he	says	have
with	was	he	on	is
it	with	have	in	and
the	to	says	have	with

PH 2   LANGUAGE ARTS GREEN

Dictation: Write Words

Have students practice identifying sounds and writing words.

1. Gather a pencil and the dictation notebook. Say the word *tub*. Then give these directions to students:

   ► Repeat the word.
   ► Write the word in your notebook.
   ► Read the word aloud.

2. When students have finished, write the following word on your whiteboard: *tub*.

3. Have them compare their answer to your correct version.

4. Repeat this procedure with the words *got* and *man*.

   ► If students make an error and don't see it, help them correct their mistake by having them finger stretch the sounds in the word they missed.
   ► If students are having difficulty selecting the correct letters or sounds, review those letters or sounds that are confusing them.
   ► If students have difficulty with first, middle, and last sounds, have them finger stretch the sounds in words.

 **20 minutes**

REVIEW: Sound /ŭ/

Students will work online independently to

► Practice the short vowel sound /ŭ/.

Help students locate the online activities and provide support as needed.

Offline Alternative

No computer access? Have students point out and name things or words that contain the sound /ŭ/ (for example, *umbrella* and *gum*).

<aside>

Objectives

- Identify the letter, given the sound /ŭ/.
- Identify the sound, given the letter *u*.
- Identify and use the sound /ŭ/.
- Identify individual sounds in words.

</aside>

Look Back: Sounds /ă/, /ŏ/, and /ŭ/

Lesson Overview

[Offline] FOCUS: Sounds /ă/, /ŏ/, and /ŭ/ — 30 minutes

Practice	Review Consonant Sounds and Letters
	Review Vowel Sounds and Letters
	Search Sentences for Beginning Sounds
	Make Words from Syllables
Sight Words	Review Sight Words
	Use Words in Sentences
	Pick a Pair
Try It	Dictation: Write a Sentence

[Online] REVIEW: Sounds /ă/, /ŏ/, and /ŭ/ — 20 minutes

Materials

Supplied
- whiteboard, Learning Coach
- whiteboard, student
- Tile Kit

Also Needed
- sight words box
- dictation notebook

Advance Preparation

Place lowercase letter tiles in alphabetical order on your whiteboard.

Big Ideas

- Letters are put together in a specific order to make words.
- Words are put together in a specific order to make sentences.

[Offline] 30 minutes

FOCUS: Sounds /ă/, /ŏ/, and /ŭ/

Work **together** with students to complete offline Practice, Sight Words, and Try It activities.

Practice ••

Review Consonant Sounds and Letters

Help students review the consonant letters and sounds of the alphabet. Grab your whiteboard with letters placed in alphabetical order.

1. **Say:** I am going to point to each consonant. Tell me the sound for the letter. Students should say the sound for each letter.

2. **Say:** This time, I am going to say the sound for each consonant. Repeat the sound and touch and say its letter. Students should touch each corresponding letter and say its name.

Review Vowel Sounds and Letters

Help students review vowel sounds and letters.

1. Place the following letter tiles on students' whiteboard: *a, e, i, o,* and *u,* plus any letters that are confusing.

2. **Say:** I am going to point to a letter. Tell me a sound for that letter.

3. **Say:** I am going to say a sound. Repeat the sound and touch its letter.

4. Point to some letter tiles two or three times, so students don't think that once they have named a sound they are finished with it.

5. Redirect students if they name the letter and not its sound.

   Say: You are right that the name of the letter is [incorrect letter]. We want the sound for this letter. What is the sound?

6. Redirect students if they name the sound incorrectly.

   Say: That is the sound of another letter.

7. Provide additional guidance if students touch the wrong letter tile during the review.

   Say: That is the letter tile for the sound [sound of incorrect letter tile]. We are looking for the letter tile for the sound [target sound].

8. If students touch the wrong letter tile again, point to the correct letter tile.

   Say: This is the letter tile for the sound [target sound]. Touch this letter and say its sound.

Search Sentences for Beginning Sounds

To help students learn to recognize the **beginning sound** in a word, have them practice identifying a target sound.

1. **Say:** I'm going to say a beginning sound that is in a word. You will repeat that sound and the word. For example, the beginning sound is /d/, as in the word *dog*.

2. Have students say the target sound /d/ and the word *dog*.

3. **Say:** Now I will read a sentence. Repeat the sentence and tell me the word that has the same beginning sound as *dog*. The first sentence is, "I have a doll."

   ▸ What is the special beginning sound? /d/
   ▸ What is the word that has the special beginning sound? *doll*

4. Have students repeat the sentence and say the word.

5. Follow the same procedure with the words and sentences below to help students recognize beginning sounds in words.

   ▸ /m/, as in *map*   The toy belongs to me. *me*
   ▸ /f/, as in *foot*   Lisa filled the glass. *filled*
   ▸ /s/, as in *sit*   Take a seat. *seat*
   ▸ /g/, as in *go*   This gift is for you. *gift*

TIP If students don't name the correct word, repeat the sentence slowly, clearly pronouncing the beginnings of words. Remind them of the special beginning sound. If students continue to have difficulty, say two words from the sentence and ask them to choose the one with the target beginning sound.

Make Words from Syllables

Have students fist tap syllables and put them together to make words.

1. **Say:** I'm going to say some syllables. Your job is to repeat the syllables while fist tapping. Then tell me what word we make when we put all the syllables together.

2. **Say:** The syllables are *ti* and *ger*.

   ▸ Repeat the syllables while fist tapping each one.
   ▸ What word do you get when you put all the syllables together? *tiger*

3. Continue with all the words in the list.

  ▶ *can / yon canyon*
  ▶ *Fri / day Friday*
  ▶ *bas / ket / ball basketball*
  ▶ *mo / vie movie*
  ▶ *mu / sic music*
  ▶ *sam / ple sample*
  ▶ *fan / tas / tic fantastic*
  ▶ *ex / pert expert*
  ▶ *pen / man / ship penmanship*

TIP If students cannot put the syllables together to make a word, try compound words such as *streetcar, cowboy, raincoat, popcorn,* and so on. After students have mastered a few compound words, go back to the multisyllabic words for this exercise and try them again.

Sight Words

Review Sight Words

Help students learn to recognize sight words.

1. Gather all the sight word cards students have yet to master from their sight words box. Stack the cards on the table face down.

2. Have students pick up a word and read it to you.

3. If they read it quickly and correctly, put the card in one stack. If they hesitate or do not read the word correctly, put it in another stack. The second stack should have words that they will review again.

4. Take the stack of words that students read correctly and dictate each word to them. They may choose to either write the word or spell it aloud.

5. If students spell the word correctly, they have mastered the word. If they misspell the word, add it to the stack of cards to review again.

6. Chart students' progress on the back of each card.

  ▶ Divide the back of the card into two columns.
  ▶ Label the first column "Read" and the second column "Spell."
  ▶ Record the dates that students read or spell the word correctly. When students can read and spell the word correctly three times in a row, they have mastered the word. You may want to put a star or sticker on their card when they have mastered that word.

TIP Even if students can read and spell all the words correctly, it is still beneficial for students to review sight words. Choose as many additional words as you would like for each subsequent activity.

> **Objectives**
> - Read sight words.
> - Write sight words.
> - Spell sight words.

Use Words in Sentences

Help students use sight words in sentences.

1. Gather all the sight word cards students have yet to master from their sight words box. Spread the sight word cards on the table.

2. **Say:** Let's use sight words in sentences.

3. Have students

   - Touch each card and read the word on it.
   - Make up a sentence using the word.
   - Put the card in a pile after using the word in a sentence.
   - Go through the pile of cards and read each sight word again.
   - Spell each word.

TIP If students have difficulty with any of the sight words, place those word cards in a pile to review later in the week.

Pick a Pair

Play a card game with students for more practice with sight words.

1. Gather the sight word cards that students are reviewing. Choose two words and place the cards on the table.

2. Ask questions to help students identify each word. For example, if the words are *in* and *he*, you could ask, "Which word means *a boy*?" If the words are *on* and *is*, you could ask, "Which word is the opposite of *off*?"

3. Continue the activity until students identify all the words.

4. Take the stack of words that students read correctly and dictate each word to them.

5. Have students write each word or spell it aloud.

Try It ....

Dictation: Write a Sentence
Use sentences to help students identify individual sounds in words.

1. Gather a pencil and the dictation notebook. Say the sentence, *The cup went in the box*. Then give these directions to students:

   ▸ Repeat the sentence.
   ▸ Write the sentence in your notebook.
   ▸ Read the sentence aloud.

2. When students have finished, write the following sentence on your whiteboard: *The cup went in the box*.

3. Have them compare their answer to your correct version.

   ▸ If students make an error and don't see it, help them correct their mistake by having them finger stretch the sounds in the word they missed.
   ▸ If students are having difficulty selecting the correct letters or sounds, review those letters or sounds that are confusing them.
   ▸ If students have difficulty with first, middle, and last sounds, have them finger stretch the sounds in words.

Objectives
- Write words by applying grade-level phonics knowledge.
- Write sight words.
- Follow three-step directions.

〖 Online 〗 ⓴ minutes

REVIEW: Sounds /ă/, /ŏ/, and /ŭ/
Students will work online independently to

▸ Practice the short vowel sounds /ă/, /ŏ/, and /ŭ/.

Help students locate the online activities and provide support as needed.

Objectives
- Identify individual sounds in words.
- Identify short vowel sounds.

Offline Alternative

No computer access? Have students point out and name things or words that contain the sounds /ă/, /ŏ/, and /ŭ/ (for example, *actor, octopus,* and *munch*).

Unit Checkpoint

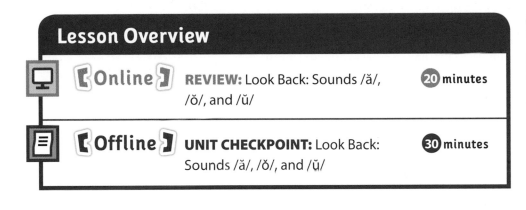

Lesson Overview

🖥	**【Online】** REVIEW: Look Back: Sounds /ă/, /ŏ/, and /ŭ/	**20** minutes
📄	**【Offline】** UNIT CHECKPOINT: Look Back: Sounds /ă/, /ŏ/, and /ŭ/	**30** minutes

【Materials】

Supplied

• *K¹² PhonicsWorks Advanced Assessments*, pp. PH 1–6

Objectives

- Identify and use the sound /ă/.
- Identify and use the sound /ŏ/.
- Identify and use the sound /ŭ/.
- Identify individual sounds in words.
- Given the letter, identify the most common sound.
- Given the sound, identify the most common letter or letters.
- Read sight words.
- Write sight words.
- Spell sight words.
- Read aloud grade-level text with approximate automaticity, prosody, accuracy, and rate.

【Online】 20 minutes

REVIEW: Look Back: Sounds /ă/, /ŏ/, and /ŭ/

Students will review the sounds /ă/, /ŏ/, and /ŭ/ to prepare for the Unit Checkpoint. Help students locate the online activities and provide support as needed.

[Offline] 30 minutes

UNIT CHECKPOINT: Look Back: Sounds /ă/, /ŏ/, and /ŭ/

Explain that students are going to show what they have learned about letters, sounds, and words.

1. Give students the Unit Checkpoint pages for the Look Back: Sounds /ă/, /ŏ/, and /ŭ/ unit and print the Unit Checkpoint Answer Key, if you'd like.

2. Use the instructions below to help administer the Checkpoint to students. On the Answer Key or another sheet of paper, note student answers to oral response questions to help with scoring the Checkpoint later.

3. Use the Answer Key to score the Checkpoint, and then enter the results online.

Part 1. Read Letters, and Word Parts Moving left to right, have students say the sounds of each letter or word part. Note any letter or word part students say incorrectly.

Part 2. Finger Stretching Say each word to students. Have them say each word and finger stretch the sounds. Note any words they finger stretch incorrectly.

19. *jam*	23. *top*
20. *log*	24. *sag*
21. *hug*	25. *rod*
22. *tub*	26. *wax*

Part 3. Dictation Say each word to students. Have them repeat and write the word.

27. *bad*	30. *lot*
28. *hut*	31. *rag*
29. *bog*	32. *tub*

Part 4. Writing Read each sentence to students. Have them repeat and write the sentence.

33. *Dad was not mad.*

34. *Gus says it is fun to run.*

Part 5. Read Aloud Listen to students read each sentence aloud. Note any words they read incorrectly.

Part 6. Say Letters Say each sound. Have students say the letter that makes that sound. Note any incorrect responses.

39. /ă/

40. /ks/

41. /s/

42. /d/

43. /w/

44. /h/

45. /j/

46. /ŏ/

47. /ŭ/

48. /k/

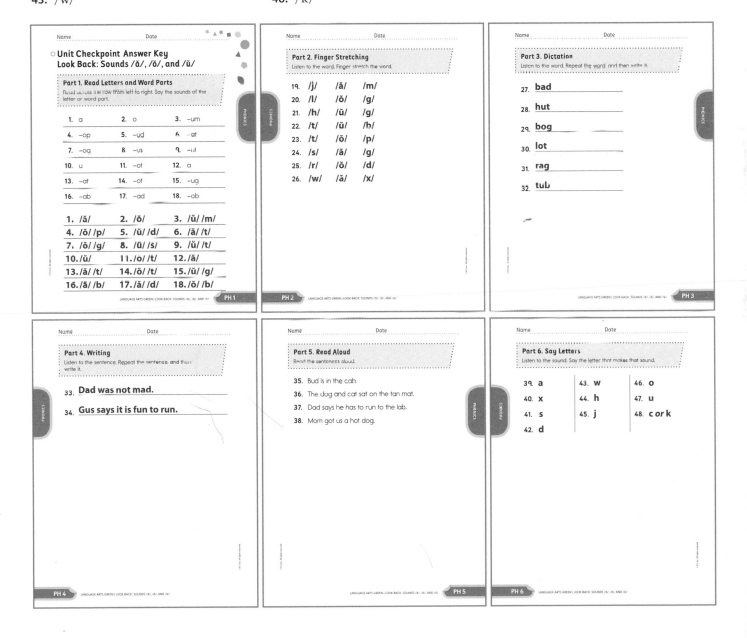

Look Back: Sound /ĭ/

Unit Overview

In this unit, students will
- Identify the short vowel sounds /ă/, /ĕ/, /ĭ/, /ŏ/, and /ŭ/.
- Review the letters of the alphabet.
- Identify beginning and ending sounds in words.
- Learn sight words.

Lesson Overview

[Offline] FOCUS: Sound /ĭ/ — **30** minutes

Get Ready	Listen for Short Vowel Sounds
Learn	Look Back: Sound /ĭ/
	Signal Middle Sounds
Sight Words	Read Sight Words
Try It	Word Quilt
	Dictation: Write Words

[Online] REVIEW: Sound /ĭ/ — **20** minutes

Materials

Supplied
- *K¹² PhonicsWorks Advanced Activity Book*, p. PH 3
- whiteboard, Learning Coach
- whiteboard, student
- Tile Kit

Also Needed
- sight words box
- dictation notebook

Keywords

sight words – words that are taught and learned as whole words; the reader does not learn to sound out sight words

[Offline] 30 minutes

FOCUS: Sound /ĭ/

Work **together** with students to complete offline Get Ready, Learn, Sight Words, and Try It activities.

Get Ready

Listen for Short Vowel Sounds

Help students identify the short vowel sounds /ă/, /ŏ/, and /ŭ/ in words.

1. **Say:** I am going to say a word. Your job is to listen for the **vowel sounds /ă/, /ŏ/, and /ŭ/** you hear in the word. Then you can tell me the vowel sound.

   ▶ For example, if I say *mop*, you will say /ŏ/ because the vowel sound in *mop* is /ŏ/.

   ▶ Now it's your turn. Listen to the word I say. You repeat the word, and then tell me the vowel sound in the word.

2. Repeat the process, using the following words to help students recognize vowel sounds:

   ▶ *cut* /ŭ/
   ▶ *pot* /ŏ/
   ▶ *hug* /ŭ/
   ▶ *sat* /ă/
   ▶ *nob* /ŏ/
   ▶ *fan* /ă/
   ▶ *wax* /ă/
   ▶ *Todd* /ŏ/
   ▶ *bun* /ŭ/

> **Objectives**
> - Identify short vowel sounds.
> - Identify individual sounds in words.

Learn

Look Back: Sound /ĭ/

Help students recognize and use the short vowel sound /ĭ/. It's important that you explain this as closely as possible to what you see below.

1. Place lowercase letter tile *i* on students' whiteboard.

2. **Say:** Today we are going to review the short vowel sound /ĭ/, as in *itch*. The sound /ĭ/ will be spelled by the letter *i* in almost all of the words we read during the next few weeks.

3. **Say:** The guide word for the sound /ĭ/ is *itch*. Say *itch*.

4. Pretend to scratch an itch on your arm while you say the word *itch*.

5. **Say:** Whenever you can't remember the sound for /ĭ/, I will pretend to scratch an *itch* on my arm to remind you that the sound for short *i* is the first sound in the word *itch*. Say /ĭ/ and touch the *i* letter tile as you say the sound.

> **Objectives**
> - Identify the letter, given the sound /ĭ/.
> - Identify the sound, given the letter *i*.
> - Identify and use the sound /ĭ/.
> - Identify middle sounds in words.

6. Practice the sound and motion several times throughout the remainder of the lesson.

(TIP) For extra practice, repeat the sound and motion throughout the day.

Signal Middle Sounds

Use a special signal to help students identify the **middle sounds /ă/, /ĭ/, /ŏ/, and /ŭ/** in words.

1. **Say:** I'm going to tell you a special sound to listen for. Repeat each word I say and make a special signal to tell me where the sound is. If the special sound is at the middle of the word, clap your hands. If the special sound is **not** at the middle of the word, just smile at me. For example,

   ▸ If I ask you to listen for /ă/ and I say the word *mat*, you'll repeat the word *mat* and clap your hands because *mat* has the sound /ă/ in the middle.
   ▸ If I say the word *pop*, you'll repeat the word *pop* and smile at me because *pop* has the sound /ŏ/, not /ă/, in the middle.

2. Say each sound and group of words. Have students make the special signal to identify the middle sound.

   ▸ /ĭ/: *pet, pin, kiss, sat, sip* clap: *pin, kiss, sip*
   ▸ /ŏ/: *fed, fog, fig, fun, not* clap: *fog, not*
   ▸ /ŭ/: *fun, gum, sod, pan, putt* clap: *fun, gum, putt*
   ▸ /ă/: *hot, hat, fit, nut, bat* clap: *hat, bat*

3. Redirect students if they name the sound incorrectly.

   Say: That is the sound of another letter. Think about the sound you hear in the middle of each word.

Sight Words

Read Sight Words

Help students learn the sight words *where, from, there,* and *that.*

1. Gather the sight word cards *where, from, there,* and *that.*

2. Show students the *where* card.

3. **Say:** This is the word *where.* We see this word so often that we want to be able to read and spell it quickly without thinking about it. Look closely at the word *where.* Spell the word *where* aloud. Take a picture of the word *where* in your mind. When you think you can spell *where* yourself, turn the card over and use your letter tiles to spell the word *where.* Check the card to see if you spelled the word *where* correctly. Read aloud the word you spelled with the letter tiles.

4. Repeat the activity with the remaining sight words.

5. Add the cards to students' sight words box.

(TIP) Sight words can be very difficult for some students. Let students work at their own pace and really master these words.

> **Objectives**
> • Read sight words.
> • Spell sight words.

Try It

Word Quilt

Have students complete page PH 3 in *K¹² PhonicsWorks Advanced Activity Book* for more practice recognizing words with the short vowel sound /ĭ/. Have students read each word in the quilt aloud and circle words that contain the sound /ĭ/. Have them read the sentence aloud and highlight words that contain the sound /ĭ/.

Dictation: Write Words

Have students practice identifying sounds and writing words.

1. Gather a pencil and the dictation notebook. Say the word *nib*. Then give these directions to students:

   ▸ Repeat the word.
   ▸ Write the word in your notebook.
   ▸ Read the word aloud.

2. When students have finished, write the following word on your whiteboard: *tab*.

3. Have them compare their answer to your correct version.

4. Repeat this procedure with the words *pit* and *him*.

   ▸ If students make an error and don't see it, help them correct their mistake by having them finger stretch the sounds in the word they missed.
   ▸ If students are having difficulty selecting the correct letters or sounds, review those letters or sounds that are confusing them.
   ▸ If students have difficulty with first, middle, and last sounds, have them finger stretch the sounds in words.

 **20 minutes**

REVIEW: Sound /ĭ/

Students will work online independently to

► Practice the short vowel sound /ĭ/.

Help students locate the online activities and provide support as needed.

Offline Alternative

No computer access? Have students point out and name things or words that contain the sound /ĭ/ (for example, *itch* and *fit*).

Look Back: Sound /ĕ/

Lesson Overview

Offline — **FOCUS:** Sound /ĕ/ — **30** minutes

Get Ready	Review Vowel Sounds and Letters
	Review Consonant Sounds and Letters
Learn	Look Back: Sound /ĕ/
Sight Words	Read Sight Words
Try It	Dictation: Write Words

Online — **REVIEW:** Sound /ĕ/ — **20** minutes

Materials

Supplied
- whiteboard, Learning Coach
- whiteboard, student
- Tile Kit

Also Needed
- sight words box
- dictation notebook

Keywords

phonics – the study of sounds and the letters that represent them

Advance Preparation

Place lowercase letter tiles in alphabetical order on your whiteboard.

Big Ideas

- Phonics teaches letter-sound correspondences.
- In order to learn how to read, one must understand the alphabetic principle: letters represent sounds, and there are rules for putting those letters together.

[Offline] ⏱ 30 minutes

FOCUS: Sound /ĕ/

Work **together** with students to complete offline Get Ready, Learn, Sight Words, and Try It activities.

Get Ready ···

Review Vowel Sounds and Letters

Help students review vowel sounds and letters.

Objectives
- Given the sound, identify the most common letter or letters.
- Given the letter, identify the most common sound.
- Identify short vowel sounds.

1. Place the following letter tiles on students' whiteboard: *a, e, i, o,* and *u,* plus any letters that are confusing.

2. **Say:** I am going to point to a letter. Tell me a sound for that letter.

3. **Say:** I am going to say a sound. Repeat the sound and touch its letter.

4. Point to some letter tiles two or three times, so students don't think that once they have named a sound they are finished with it.

5. Redirect students if they name the letter and not its sound.

   Say: You are right that the name of the letter is [incorrect letter]. We want the sound for this letter. What is the sound?

6. Redirect students if they name the sound incorrectly.

   Say: That is the sound of another letter.

7. Provide additional guidance if students touch the wrong letter tile during the review.

   Say: That is the letter tile for the sound [sound of incorrect letter tile]. We are looking for the letter tile for the sound [target sound].

8. If students touch the wrong letter tile again, point to the correct letter tile.

   Say: This is the letter tile for the sound [target sound]. Touch this letter and say its sound.

Review Consonant Sounds and Letters

Help students review the consonant letters and sounds of the alphabet. Grab your whiteboard with the letters placed in alphabetical order.

1. **Say:** I am going to point to each consonant. Tell me the sound for the letter. Students should say the sound for each letter.

2. **Say:** This time, I am going to say the sound for each consonant. Repeat the sound, and touch and say its letter. Students should touch each corresponding letter and say its name.

Learn

Look Back: Sound /ĕ/

Help students recognize and use the short vowel sound /ĕ/.

1. Place lowercase letter tile *e* on students' whiteboard.

2. **Say:** Today we are going to review the short vowel sound /ĕ/, as in *edge*. Say /ĕ/. The sound /ĕ/ will be spelled by the letter *e* in almost all of the words we read during the next few weeks.

3. **Say:** The guide word for the sound /ĕ/ is *edge*. Say *edge*.

4. Run your fingers slowly along the *edge* of the table while you say the word *edge*.

5. **Say:** Whenever you can't remember the sound for /ĕ/, I will run my fingers slowly along the *edge* of the table to remind you that the sound for short *e* is the first sound in the word *edge*. Say /ĕ/ and touch the *e* letter tile as you say the sound.

6. Practice the sound and motion several times throughout the remainder of the lesson.

TIP For extra practice, repeat the sound and motion throughout the day.

Objectives
- Identify the letter, given the sound /ĕ/.
- Identify the sound, given the letter *e*.
- Identify and use the sound /ĕ/.

Sight Words

Read Sight Words

Help students learn the sight words *of, put, two,* and *they*.

1. Gather the sight word cards *of, put, two,* and *they*.

2. Show students the *of* card.

3. **Say:** This is the word *of*. We see this word so often that we want to be able to read and spell it quickly without thinking about it. Look closely at the word *of*. Spell the word *of* aloud. Take a picture of the word *of* in your mind. When you think you can spell *of* yourself, turn the card over and use your letter tiles to spell the word *of*. Check the card to see if you spelled the word *of* correctly. Read aloud the word you spelled with the letter tiles.

4. Repeat the activity with the remaining sight words.

5. Add the cards to students' sight words box.

TIP Sight words can be very difficult for some students. Let students work at their own pace and really master these words.

Objectives
- Read sight words.
- Spell sight words.

Try It ....

Dictation: Write Words

Have students practice identifying sounds and writing words.

1. Gather a pencil and the dictation notebook. Say the word *pet*. Then give these directions to students:

   ► Repeat the word.
   ► Write the word in your notebook.
   ► Read the word aloud.

2. When students have finished, write the following word on your whiteboard: *pet*.

3. Have them compare their answer to your correct version.

4. Repeat this procedure with the words *Deb* and *Meg*.

   ► If students make an error and don't see it, help them correct their mistake by having them finger stretch the sounds in the word they missed.
   ► If students are having difficulty selecting the correct letters or sounds, review those letters or sounds that are confusing them.
   ► If students have difficulty with first, middle, and last sounds, have them finger stretch the sounds in words.

   TIP Remind students that the words *Deb* and *Meg* are proper nouns. Have them write each word with a beginning capital letter.

Objectives
- Write words by applying grade-level phonics knowledge.
- Follow three-step directions.

[Online] 20 minutes

REVIEW: Sound /ĕ/

Students will work online independently to

► Practice the short vowel sound /ĕ/.

Help students locate the online activities and provide support as needed.

___

Offline Alternative

No computer access? Have students point out and name things or words that contain the sound /ĕ/ (for example, *egg* and *bed*).

Objectives
- Identify the letter, given the sound /ĕ/.
- Identify the sound /ĕ/, given the letter *e*.
- Identify and use the sound /ĕ/.
- Identify individual sounds in words.

Look Back: Sounds /ă/, /ĕ/, /ĭ/, /ŏ/, and /ŭ/ (A)

Lesson Overview

[Offline] FOCUS: Sounds /ă/, /ĕ/, /ĭ/, /ŏ/, and /ŭ/ · **30** minutes

Practice	Review Consonant Sounds and Letters
	Review Vowel Sounds and Letters
Learn	Word Chains
Sight Words	Read Sight Words
Try It	To the Rescue
	Dictation: Write Sentences

[Online] REVIEW: Sounds /ă/, /ĕ/, /ĭ/, /ŏ/, and /ŭ/ · **20** minutes

[Materials]

Supplied
- *K¹² PhonicsWorks Advanced Activity Book*, p. PH 4
- whiteboard, Learning Coach
- whiteboard, student
- Tile Kit

Also Needed
- sight words box
- dictation notebook
- crayons

Keywords
decode – to take words apart
encode – to put words together

Advance Preparation

Place lowercase letter tiles in alphabetical order on your whiteboard.

Big Ideas

Phonics instruction combines phonological awareness and letter-name knowledge.

[Offline] 30 minutes

FOCUS: Sounds /ă/, /ĕ/, /ĭ/, /ŏ/, and /ŭ/

Work **together** with students to complete offline Practice, Learn, Sight Words, and Try It activities.

Practice

Review Consonant Sounds and Letters

Help students review the consonant letters and sounds of the alphabet. Grab your whiteboard with letter tiles placed in alphabetical order.

1. **Say:** I am going to point to each consonant. Tell me the sound for the letter. Students should say the sound for each letter.

2. **Say:** This time, I am going to say the sound for each consonant. Repeat the sound and touch and say its letter. Students should touch each corresponding letter and say its name.

> ### ⭐ Objectives
> - Given the sound, identify the most common letter or letters.
> - Given the letter, identify the most common sound.
> - Identify short vowel sounds.

Review Vowel Sounds and Letters

Help students review vowel sounds and letters.

1. Place the following letter tiles on students' whiteboard: *u, e, i, o,* and *u,* plus any letters that are confusing.

2. **Say:** I am going to point to a letter. Tell me a sound for that letter.

3. **Say:** I am going to say a sound. Repeat the sound and touch its letter.

4. Point to some letter tiles two or three times, so students don't think that once they have named a sound they are finished with it.

5. Redirect students if they name the letter and not its sound.

   Say: You are right that the name of the letter is [incorrect letter]. We want the sound for this letter. What is the sound?

6. Redirect students if they name the sound incorrectly.

   Say: That is the sound of another letter.

7. Provide additional guidance if students touch the wrong letter tile during the review.

   Say: That is the letter tile for the sound [sound of incorrect letter tile]. We are looking for the letter tile for the sound [target sound].

8. If students touch the wrong letter tile again, point to the correct letter tile.

   Say: This is the letter tile for the sound [target sound]. Touch this letter and say its sound.

Learn

Word Chains

Have students build words by adding and changing letters to help them recognize and use individual sounds in words.

1. Place the following letter tiles at the top of students' whiteboard: *a, b, c, e, h, k, m, n, o, p, s,* and *t.*

2. **Say:** I am going to build the first word in a chain. The word is *mop.*

   ▶ I will pull down the letters for the sounds /m/, /ŏ/, and /p/ to spell the word *mop.*

   ▶ I will touch and say *mop.* To change *mop* to *map,* I will think about what sound is changed from the word *mop* to *map.* I will need to replace the letter *o* with a letter *a.*

   ▶ Touch and say the word *map.* Now it's your turn to change *map* to *mat.* You can spell *mat* by making only one change. Touch and say the new word.

3. Redirect students if they select the incorrect letter for any sound.

   Say: That letter is for the sound [incorrect sound]. We want the letter for the sound [target sound]. What letter makes that sound? Answers will vary.

4. Redirect students if they name the sound incorrectly.

   Say: To change the word [first word] to [target word], we need the letter for the sound [target sound].

   Show students how to make the change. Have them touch and say the new word after they move the letters.

5. Follow this procedure to make the following words: *met, net, set, sat, sap, tap, map, cap, cop, mop.*

6. For every new word, have students add, replace, or remove only one letter.

   TIP If students struggle, review the sounds and letters that are confusing them.

Objectives
- Identify short vowel sounds.
- Given the sound, identify the most common letter or letters.
- Identify individual sounds in words.

Sight Words

Read Sight Words

Help students learn the sight words *both, you, went,* and *we.*

1. Gather the sight word cards *both, you, went,* and *we.*

2. Show students the *you* card.

3. **Say:** This is the word *you.* We see this word so often that we want to be able to read and spell it quickly without thinking about it. Look closely at the word *you.* Spell the word *you* aloud. Take a picture of the word *you* in your mind. When you think you can spell *you* yourself, turn the card over and use your letter tiles to spell the word *you.* Check the card to see if you spelled the word *you* correctly. Read aloud the word you spelled with the letter tiles.

Objectives
- Read sight words.
- Spell sight words.

4. Repeat the activity with the remaining sight words.

5. Add the cards to students' sight words box.

 Sight words can be very difficult for some students. Let students work at their own pace and really master these words.

Try It

To the Rescue

Have students complete page PH 4 in *K¹² PhonicsWorks Advanced Activity Book* for more practice identifying real from nonsense words. Have students read each word aloud and color the *real* words to find the path to the log.

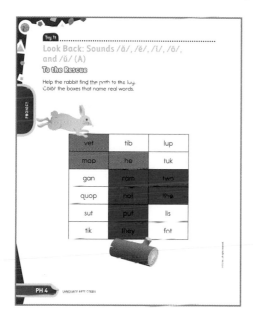

Dictation: Write Sentences

Use sentences to help students identify individual sounds in words.

1. Gather a pencil and the dictation notebook. Say the sentence, *The ten men can hum.* Then give these directions to students:

   ► Repeat the sentence.
   ► Write the sentence in your notebook.
   ► Read the sentence aloud.

2. When students have finished, write the following sentence on your whiteboard: *The ten men can hum.*

3. Have them compare their answer to your correct version.

4. Repeat this procedure with the sentence, *The cat sits on the mat.*

   ▸ If students make an error and don't see it, help them correct their mistake by having them finger stretch the sounds in the word they missed.
   ▸ If students are having difficulty selecting the correct letters or sounds, review those letters or sounds that are confusing them.
   ▸ If students have difficulty with first, middle, and last sounds, have them finger stretch the sounds in words.

 **20 minutes**

REVIEW: Sounds /ă/, /ĕ/, /ĭ/, /ŏ/, and /ŭ/

Students will work online independently to

▸ Practice the short vowel sounds /ă/, /ĕ/, /ĭ/, /ŏ/, and /ŭ/.

Help students locate the online activities and provide support as needed.

Offline Alternative

No computer access? Have students point out and name things or words that contain the short vowel sounds /ă/, /ĕ/, /ĭ/, /ŏ/, and /ŭ/ (for example, *jacket*, *men*, *pin*, *dog*, and *rug*).

> **Objectives**
> • Identify short vowel sounds.
> • Identify individual sounds in words.

Look Back: Sounds /ă/, /ĕ/, /ĭ/, /ŏ/, and /ŭ/ (B)

Lesson Overview

Offline **FOCUS:** Sounds /ă/, /ĕ/, /ĭ/, /ŏ/, and /ŭ/ — **30** minutes

Practice	Review Consonant Sounds and Letters
	Review Vowel Sounds and Letters
	Face-Down Letters
	Introduce Finger Stretching
Sight Words	Review Sight Words
	Use Words in Sentences
	Pick a Pair
Try It	Dictation: Write a Sentence

Online **REVIEW:** Sounds /ă/, /ĕ/, /ĭ/, /ŏ/, and /ŭ/ — **20** minutes

Materials

Supplied
- whiteboard, Learning Coach
- whiteboard, student
- Tile Kit

Also Needed
- sight words box
- dictation notebook

Advance Preparation

Place lowercase letter tiles in alphabetical order on your whiteboard.

[Offline] 30 minutes

FOCUS: Sounds /ă/, /ĕ/, /ĭ/, /ŏ/, and /ŭ/

Work **together** with students to complete offline Practice, Sight Words, and Try It activities.

Practice ·

Review Consonant Sounds and Letters

Help students review the consonant letters and sounds of the alphabet. Grab your whiteboard with letter tiles placed in alphabetical order.

1. **Say:** I am going to point to each consonant. Tell me the sound for that letter. Students should say the sound for each letter.

2. **Say:** This time, I am going to say the sound for each consonant. Repeat the sound and touch and say its letter. Students should touch each corresponding letter and say its name.

Review Vowel Sounds and Letters

Help students review vowel sounds and letters.

1. Place the following letter tiles on students' whiteboard: *a, e, i, o,* and *u,* plus any letters that are confusing.

2. **Say:** I am going to point to a letter. Tell me a sound for that letter.

3. **Say:** I am going to say a sound. Repeat the sound and touch its letter.

4. Point to some letter tiles two or three times, so students don't think that once they have named a sound they are finished with it.

5. Redirect students if they name the letter and not its sound.

   Say: You are right that the name of the letter is [incorrect letter]. We want the sound for this letter. What is the sound?

6. Redirect students if they name the sound incorrectly.

   Say: That is the sound of another letter.

7. Provide additional guidance if students touch the wrong letter tile during the review.

   Say: That is the letter tile for the sound [sound of incorrect letter tile]. We are looking for the letter tile for the sound [target sound].

8. If students touch the wrong letter tile again, point to the correct letter tile.

   Say: This is the letter tile for the sound [target sound]. Touch this letter tile and say its sound.

Face-Down Letters

To help students learn to recognize the letters of the alphabet, have them practice identifying and naming letters. Grab your whiteboard with letters placed in alphabetical order.

1. Lay your whiteboard down on a flat surface and flip over the following letter tiles so they are face down on the whiteboard: *a, d, f, m, q, s, t,* and *y.*

2. **Say:** These letters are face down. We are looking at the back of them. Name each letter and then turn it over to see if you were right.

(TIP) If students miss any of the letters, have them turn over the missed ones and try again.

Introduce Finger Stretching

Introduce students to the concept of finger stretching to represent the sounds in words.

1. **Say:** We can finger stretch the sounds in a word to count how many sounds there are in that word. Start by holding up your hand with your palm facing you and make a loose fist. Each time you say a sound in a word, extend a finger, starting with your thumb.

2. **Say:** Let's finger stretch the sounds in *rag.*

   ▸ Say the first sound in the word *rag,* /r/, and move your thumb out. Keep your thumb out.
   ▸ Say the second sound, /ă/, and move your index finger out. Keep your thumb and finger stretched out.
   ▸ Say the last sound, /g/, and move your middle finger out. Your fingers are stretched out; you have finger stretched the word *rag.*

3. **Say:** Let's count the number of sounds in the word *rag.*

   ▸ How many fingers are out? three
   ▸ How many sounds are in *rag*? three

4. **Say:** To finish finger stretching a word, put your fingers back into a fist and pull your fist toward your body as you say the word. When you finger stretch, you always say the word after you count the sounds with your fingers.

5. Have students finger stretch the following words. Remind them to say each word after finger stretching it.

   ▸ *tag* /t/ /ă/ /g/   What is the last sound? /g/
   ▸ *bug* /b/ /ŭ/ /g/   What is the vowel sound? /ŭ/
   ▸ *den* /d/ /ĕ/ /n/   What is the first sound? /d/
   ▸ *mat* /m/ /ă/ /t/   What is the last sound? /t/
   ▸ *sit* /s/ /ĭ/ /t/   What is the first sound? /s/

(TIP) Refer to the *K*[12] *PhonicsWorks* DVD for a demonstration of finger stretching.

Sight Words

Review Sight Words

Help students learn to recognize sight words.

Objectives
- Read sight words.
- Write sight words.
- Spell sight words.

1. Gather all the sight word cards students have yet to master from their sight words box. Stack the cards on the table face down.

2. Have students pick up a word and read it to you.

3. If they read it quickly and correctly, put the card in one stack. If they hesitate or do not read the word correctly, put it in another stack. The second stack should have words that students will review again.

4. Take the stack of words that students read correctly and dictate each word to them. They may choose to either write the word or spell it aloud.

5. If students spell the word correctly, they have mastered the word. If they misspell the word, add it to the stack of cards to review again.

6. Chart students' progress on the back of each card.

   ▸ Divide the back of the card into two columns.
   ▸ Label the first column "Read" and the second column "Spell."
   ▸ Record the dates that students read or spell the word correctly. When students can read and spell the word correctly three times in a row, they have mastered the word. You may want to put a star or sticker on their card when they have mastered that word.

TIP Even if students can read and spell all the words correctly, it is still beneficial for students to review sight words. Choose as many additional words as you would like for each subsequent activity.

Use Words in Sentences

Help students use sight words in sentences.

1. Gather all the sight word cards students have yet to master from their sight words box. Spread the sight word cards on the table.

2. **Say:** Let's use sight words in sentences.

3. Have students

   ▸ Touch each card and read the word on it.
   ▸ Make up a sentence using the word.
   ▸ Put the card in a pile after using the word in a sentence.
   ▸ Go through the pile of cards and read each sight word again.
   ▸ Spell each word.

TIP If students have difficulty with any of the sight words, place those cards in a pile to review again.

Pick a Pair
Play a card game with students for more practice with sight words.

1. Gather the sight word cards that students are reviewing. Choose two words and place the cards on the table.

2. Ask questions to help students identify each word. For example, if the words are *two* and *put*, you could ask, "Which word names a number?" If the words are *on* and *both*, you could ask, "Which word is the opposite of *off*?"

3. Continue the activity until students identify all the words.

4. Take the stack of words that students read correctly and dictate each word to them.

5. Have students write each word or spell it aloud.

Try It

Dictation: Write a Sentence
Use sentences to help students identify individual sounds in words.

1. Gather a pencil and the dictation notebook. Say the sentence, *The big red dog has a cup.* Then give these directions to students:

   ▸ Repeat the sentence.
   ▸ Write the sentence in your notebook.
   ▸ Read the sentence aloud.

2. When students have finished, write the following sentence on your whiteboard: *The big red dog has a cup.*

3. Have them compare their answer to your correct version.

4. Repeat this procedure with the sentence, *Tad got a big pet bug.*

   ▸ If students make an error and don't see it, help them correct their mistake by having them finger stretch the sounds in the word they missed.
   ▸ If students are having difficulty selecting the correct letters or sounds, review those letters or sounds that are confusing them.
   ▸ If students have difficulty with first, middle, and last sounds, have them finger stretch the sounds in words.

> **Objectives**
> • Write words by applying grade-level phonics knowledge.
> • Write sight words.
> • Follow three-step directions.

 **20 minutes**

REVIEW: Sounds /ă/, /ĕ/, /ĭ/, /ŏ/, and /ŭ/

Students will work online independently to

► Practice the short vowel sounds /ă/, /ĕ/, /ĭ/, /ŏ/, and /ŭ/.

Help students locate the online activities and provide support as needed.

Offline Alternative

No computer access? Have students point out and name things or words that contain the short vowel sounds /ă/, /ĕ/, /ĭ/, /ŏ/, and /ŭ/ (for example, *actor*, *elbow*, *itch*, *fog*, and *ugly*).

Objectives
- Identify individual sounds in words.
- Identify short vowel sounds.

Unit Checkpoint

Lesson Overview

🖥️ **[Online]** **REVIEW:** Look Back: Sounds /ă/, /ĕ/, /ĭ/, /ŏ/, and /ŭ/ — **20** minutes

📄 **[Offline]** **UNIT CHECKPOINT:** Look Back: Sounds /ă/, /ĕ/, /ĭ/, /ŏ/, and /ŭ/ — **30** minutes

[Materials]

Supplied
- *K12 PhonicsWorks Advanced Assessments*, pp. PH 7–12

Objectives
- Identify and use the sound /ă/.
- Identify and use the sound /ĕ/.
- Identify and use the sound /ĭ/.
- Identify and use the sound /ŏ/.
- Identify and use the sound /ŭ/.
- Identify short vowel sounds.
- Identify individual sounds in words.
- Given the letter, identify the most common sound.
- Given the sound, identify the most common letter or letters.
- Read sight words.
- Write sight words.
- Spell sight words.
- Read aloud grade-level text with appropriate automaticity, prosody, accuracy, and rate.

[Online] **20** minutes

REVIEW: **Look Back: Sounds /ă/, /ĕ/, /ĭ/, /ŏ/, and /ŭ/**

Students will review /ă/, /ĕ/, /ĭ/, /ŏ/, and /ŭ/ to prepare for the Unit Checkpoint. Help students locate the online activities and provide support as needed.

[Offline] 30 minutes

UNIT CHECKPOINT: Look Back: Sounds /ă/, /ĕ/, /ĭ/, /ŏ/, and /ŭ/

Explain that students are going to show what they have learned about letters, sounds, and words.

1. Give students the Unit Checkpoint pages for the Look Back: Sounds /ă/, /ĕ/, /ĭ/, /ŏ/, and /ŭ/ unit and print the Unit Checkpoint Answer Key, if you'd like.

2. Use the instructions below to help administer the Checkpoint to students. On the Answer Key or another sheet of paper, note student answers to oral response questions to help with scoring the Checkpoint later.

3. Use the Answer Key to score the Checkpoint, and then enter the results online.

Part 1. Read Words and Word Parts Moving left to right, have students say the sounds of each word or word part. Note any word or word parts the students say incorrectly.

Part 2. Finger Stretching Say each word to students. Have them say each word aloud and finger stretch the sounds. Note any words they finger stretch incorrectly.

16. *bed*   22. *mom*

17. *rib*   23. *nut*

18. *mug*   24. *ten*

19. *cob*   25. *quiz*

20. *tan*   26. *yes*

21. *dab*   27. *mix*

Part 3. Dictation Say each word to students. Have them repeat and write the word.

28. *rob*   31. *bit*

29. *men*   32. *cup*

30. *jam*   33. *yes*

Part 4. Writing Read each sentence to students. Have them repeat and write the sentence.

34. *The bug is on his leg.*

35. *That kid can run.*

Part 5. Read Aloud Listen to students read each sentence aloud. Note any words they read incorrectly.

Part 6. Say the Letters Say each sound. Have students say the letter that makes that sound. Note any incorrect responses.

41. /ŭ/

42. /ŏ/

43. /r/

44. /ă/

45. /ks/

46. /k/

47. /ĭ/

48. /ĕ/

49. /ŭ/

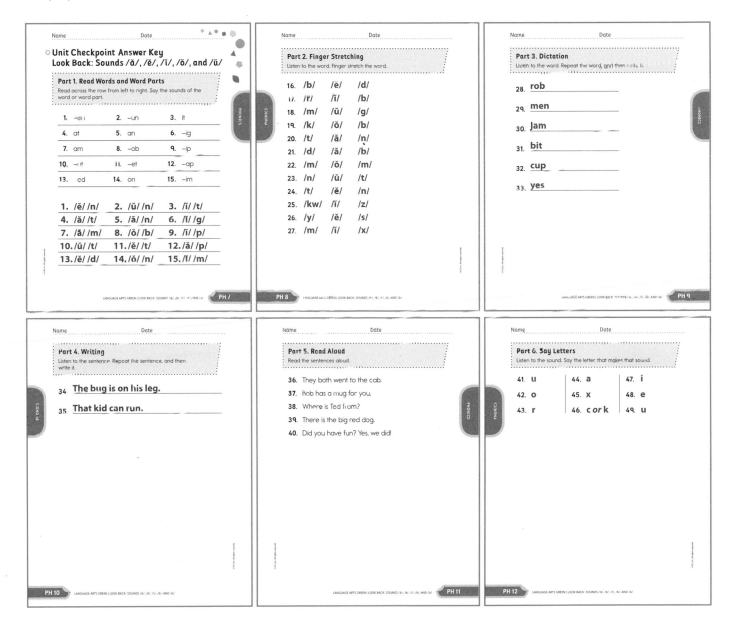

Name _____ Date _____

Unit Checkpoint Answer Key
Look Back: Sounds /ă/, /ĕ/, /ĭ/, /ŏ/, and /ŭ/

Part 1. Read Words and Word Parts
Read across the row from left to right. Say the sounds of the word or word part.

1. -en	2. -un	3. it
4. at	5. an	6. -ig
7. am	8. -ob	9. -ip
10. -it	11. -et	12. -ap
13. ed	14. on	15. -im

1. /ĕ/ /n/	2. /ŭ/ /n/	3. /ĭ/ /t/
4. /ă/ /t/	5. /ă/ /n/	6. /ĭ/ /g/
7. /ă/ /m/	8. /ŏ/ /b/	9. /ĭ/ /p/
10. /ŭ/ /t/	11. /ĕ/ /t/	12. /ă/ /p/
13. /ĕ/ /d/	14. /ŏ/ /n/	15. /ĭ/ /m/

LANGUAGE ARTS GREEN | LOOK BACK: SOUNDS /ă/, /ĕ/, /ĭ/, /ŏ/, AND /ŭ/   PH 7

Name _____ Date _____

Part 2. Finger Stretching
Listen to the word. Finger stretch the word.

16. /b/	/ĕ/	/d/
17. /r/	/ĭ/	/b/
18. /m/	/ŭ/	/g/
19. /k/	/ŏ/	/b/
20. /t/	/ă/	/n/
21. /d/	/ă/	/b/
22. /m/	/ŏ/	/m/
23. /n/	/ŭ/	/t/
24. /t/	/ĕ/	/n/
25. /kw/	/ĭ/	/z/
26. /y/	/ĕ/	/s/
27. /m/	/ĭ/	/x/

PH 8   LANGUAGE ARTS GREEN | LOOK BACK: SOUNDS /ă/, /ĕ/, /ĭ/, /ŏ/, AND /ŭ/

Name _____ Date _____

Part 3. Dictation
Listen to the word. Repeat the word, and then write it.

28. rob _____

29. men _____

30. Jam _____

31. bit _____

32. cup _____

33. yes _____

LANGUAGE ARTS GREEN | LOOK BACK: SOUNDS /ă/, /ĕ/, /ĭ/, /ŏ/, AND /ŭ/   PH 9

Name _____ Date _____

Part 4. Writing
Listen to the sentence. Repeat the sentence, and then write it.

34. The bug is on his leg. _____

35. That kid can run. _____

PH 10   LANGUAGE ARTS GREEN | LOOK BACK: SOUNDS /ă/, /ĕ/, /ĭ/, /ŏ/, AND /ŭ/

Name _____ Date _____

Part 5. Read Aloud
Read the sentences aloud.

36. They both went to the cab.

37. Bob has a mug for you.

38. Where is Ted from?

39. There is the big red dog.

40. Did you have fun? Yes, we did!

LANGUAGE ARTS GREEN | LOOK BACK: SOUNDS /ă/, /ĕ/, /ĭ/, /ŏ/, AND /ŭ/   PH 11

Name _____ Date _____

Part 6. Say Letters
Listen to the sound. Say the letter that makes that sound.

41. u	44. a	47. i
42. o	45. x	48. e
43. r	46. c or k	49. u

PH 12   LANGUAGE ARTS GREEN | LOOK BACK: SOUNDS /ă/, /ĕ/, /ĭ/, /ŏ/, AND /ŭ/

Look Back: Digraph *sh*

Unit Overview

In this unit, students will
- ▶ Identify and use the digraphs *sh* and *ch*.
- ▶ Review the double letter endings.
- ▶ Identify words that rhyme.
- ▶ Practice beginning, middle, and ending sounds.
- ▶ Learn sight words.

Materials

Supplied
- *K¹² PhonicsWorks Advanced Activity Book*, p. PH 5
- whiteboard, Learning Coach
- whiteboard, student
- Tile Kit

Also Needed
- sight words box
- dictation notebook

Lesson Overview

Offline FOCUS: Digraph *sh* **30** minutes

Get Ready	Simon Says
Learn	Double Trouble Letters
	Look Back: Digraph *sh*
Sight Words	Read Sight Words
Try It	Alphabet Addition
	Dictation: Write Words

Online REVIEW: Digraph *sh* **20** minutes

Keywords

digraph – two letters that represent one sound

Advance Preparation

Place lowercase letter tiles in alphabetical order on both your and students' whiteboards.

 **30 minutes**

FOCUS: Digraph *sh*

Work **together** with students to complete offline Get Ready, Learn, Sight Words, and Try It activities.

Get Ready ••

Simon Says

Play a game with students to help them recognize words that rhyme.

1. **Say:** We're going to play a Simon Says sound game. Listen carefully for words that rhyme with the Simon Says word. Today the Simon Says word is *ball.* Say *ball.*

   ‣ I'm going to say a word and do something. You will repeat the word.
   ‣ If the word rhymes with *ball,* you will copy the action I made.
   ‣ If the word doesn't rhyme with *ball,* then you will be still. We'll do two together.

2. Touch your nose as you say *call.*

3. **Say:** We both say *call* and touch our noses because *call* rhymes with *ball.*

4. Stomp your feet as you say *fuzz.*

5. **Say:** The word is *fuzz.* Repeat the word.

   ‣ We won't stomp our feet when we say *fuzz* because *fuzz* doesn't rhyme with *ball.*
   ‣ Let's begin. Remember, the Simon Says word is *ball.* The new word is *stall.*

6. Repeat the procedure with each word and action on the list.

   ‣ *stall,* clap your hands
   ‣ *whiff,* stick out your tongue
   ‣ *tall,* touch your nose
   ‣ *fall,* stand up
   ‣ *mess,* touch your ear

TIP Break each word into its onset and rime if students cannot tell which words rhyme. The **onset** is the part of the syllable before the first vowel sound. The **rime** part of the syllable is made up of the first vowel sound and any consonant sounds that follow it. For example, in *stall,* /st/ is the onset and *all* is the rime: /st/. . . *all.* . . *stall.*

> **Objectives**
> - Identify words that rhyme.
> - Identify and use ending –*ff.*
> - Identify and use ending –*ll.*
> - Identify and use ending –*ss.*
> - Identify and use ending –*zz.*

Learn

Double Trouble Letters

Use letter tiles and finger stretching to help students spell words that have two letters that are the same.

1. Along the right side of students' whiteboard, place the following tiles, with room to add other letters in front of them: *f f, l l,* and *s s*.

2. **Say:** You are going to spell the words I say. At the side of the whiteboard are the "double trouble" letters. Sometimes, at the end of words, the letters *f, l, s,* and *z* are doubled. I'll say a word that ends with double trouble letters. You will use the letters from my whiteboard to spell the words I say. The first word is *kiss.*

3. **Say:** Finger stretch the sounds in *kiss.*

   ▸ What is the last sound in the word *kiss*? /s/
   ▸ Touch the letters that make the last sound in the word.
   ▸ What letter makes the first sound in the word *kiss*? *k*
     Move that letter from my whiteboard to yours.
   ▸ What is the middle sound in the word *kiss*? /ĭ/
     Move the letter for that sound from my whiteboard to yours.
   ▸ Touch and say the word. Say and write the word.

4. Repeat the steps with the following words:

   ▸ *puff*
   ▸ *bill*
   ▸ *dull*
   ▸ *mass*
   ▸ *cuff*

Objectives
- Identify and use ending –*ff.*
- Identify and use ending –*ll.*
- Identify and use ending –*ss.*
- Identify and use ending –*zz.*
- Identify the letters, given the sound /sh/.
- Identify the sound /sh/, given the digraph *sh.*
- Identify and use the digraph *sh.*
- Identify individual sounds in words.

Look Back: Digraph *sh*

Help students recognize and use the digraph *sh*.

1. Place the *sh* tile on students' whiteboard and point to it.

2. **Say:** When we see *sh*, we read the sound /sh/. Touch the *sh* tile and say /sh/.

3. Have students touch the *sh* tile and say /sh/.

4. **Say:** Two letters that make one sound are called **digraphs**. It means that we write two letters to make that sound. Start looking and listening for words with /sh/ all around you.

5. **Say:** The sound for the digraph *sh* is /sh/, as in *ship*.

   ▸ Say /sh/ and touch the *sh* tile.
   ▸ Finger stretch the sounds in the word *ship*.
   ▸ Build the word *ship* with your letter tiles.
   ▸ Touch and say, and say and write, the word *ship*.

6. Continue this procedure with the following words:

   ▸ *shop*
   ▸ *shag*
   ▸ *shun*

Sight Words

Read Sight Words

Help students learn the sight words *what, their, want,* and *said*.

1. Gather the sight word cards *what, their, want,* and *said*.

2. Show students the *what* card.

3. **Say:** This is the word *what*. We see this word so often that we want to be able to read and spell it quickly without thinking about it. Look closely at the word *what*. Spell the word *what* aloud. Take a picture of the word *what* in your mind. When you think you can spell *what* yourself, turn the card over and use your letter tiles to spell the word *what*. Check the card to see if you spelled the word *what* correctly. Read aloud the word you spelled with the letter tiles.

4. Repeat the activity with the remaining sight words.

5. Add the cards to students' sight words box.

TIP Sight words can be very difficult for some students. Let students work at their own pace and really master these words.

Objectives
- Read sight words.
- Spell sight words.

Alphabet Addition

Have students complete page PH 5 in *K12 PhonicsWorks Advanced Activity Book* for more practice making words that contain the digraph *sh*. First have students add the parts of the word together to make a new word. Then have students write the word and read the word aloud.

> **Try It**
>
> **Look Back: Digraph *sh***
>
> **Alphabet Addition**
>
> Add the letters to make a word. Write the word, and then read it aloud.
>
> 1. b + ash = **bash**
> 2. sh + in = **shin**
> 3. f + ish = **fish**
> 4. c + ash = **cash**
> 5. sh + ip = **ship**
> 6. r + ush = **rush**
>
> Just for Fun
> Read the silly sentence.
> The red fish had a wish to shop.
>
> LANGUAGE ARTS GREEN   **PH 5**

Objectives

- Identify and use the digraph *sh*.
- Write words by applying grade-level phonics knowledge.
- Follow three-step directions.

Dictation: Write Words

Have students practice identifying sounds and writing words.

1. Gather a pencil and the dictation notebook. Say the word *wish*. Then give these directions to students:

   ► Repeat the word.
   ► Write the word in your notebook.
   ► Read the word aloud.

2. When students have finished, write the following word on your whiteboard: *wish*.

3. Have them compare their answer to your correct version.

4. Repeat this procedure with the words *shed* and *ash*.

   ► If students make an error and don't see it, help them correct their mistake by having them finger stretch the sounds in the word they missed.
   ► If students are having difficulty selecting the correct letters or sounds, review those letters or sounds that are confusing them.
   ► If students have difficulty with first, middle, and last sounds, have them finger stretch the sounds in the word.

 **20 minutes**

REVIEW: Digraph *sh*

Students will work online independently to

▸ Practice the digraph *sh*.

Help students locate the online activities and provide support as needed.

Offline Alternative

No computer access? Have students point out and name things or words that contain the sound /sh/ (for example, *shop* or *wish*). You might also ask students to spell words that contain the digraph *sh*.

Look Back: Digraph *ch*

Lesson Overview

[Offline] FOCUS: Digraph *ch*   30 minutes

Get Ready	Guess the Word
Learn	Look Back: Digraph *ch*
Sight Words	Read Sight Words
Try It	Dictation: Write Words

[Online] REVIEW: Digraph *ch*   20 minutes

[Materials]

Supplied
- whiteboard, Learning Coach
- whiteboard, student
- Tile Kit

Also Needed
- sight words box
- dictation notebook

[Offline] 30 minutes

FOCUS: Digraph *ch*

Work **together** with students to complete offline Get Ready, Learn, Sight Words, and Try It activities.

Get Ready ●

Guess the Word

Have students use word meaning and sentence structure to choose a word that best completes a sentence.

1. Write the following double-letter ending words on students' whiteboard: *buzz, miss, pass, off,* and *fell.* Make sure students know the meaning of all the words before you do this activity.

2. Have students underline the double letter endings in each word.

3. **Say:** We're going to play a guessing game. I'm going to read a sentence with a word missing. Your job is to look at the words on your whiteboard and decide which one is the right word to complete the sentence.

    ▸ Listen to this sentence: "When you are not here, I will _____ you."
    ▸ You will tell me what word makes sense in the blank of the sentence. This time the word would be *miss.*
    ▸ The complete sentence would be, "When you are not here, I will *miss* you." Now you try it.

4. Continue the procedure with the following sentences:

    ▸ *I stood by the flowers and heard the bees _____ . buzz*
    ▸ *I cannot reach the juice. Please _____ it to me. pass*
    ▸ *Last night snow _____ and covered everything. fell*
    ▸ *Turn the water _____ so we don't waste it. off*

> **Objectives**
> - Identify and use ending *–ff.*
> - Identify and use ending *–ll.*
> - Identify and use ending *–ss.*
> - Identify and use ending *–zz.*
> - Use context and sentence structure to determine meaning of words, phrases, and/or sentences.

Learn ●

Look Back: Digraph *ch*

Help students recognize and use the digraph *ch.*

1. Place the *ch* tile on students' whiteboard and point to it.

2. **Say:** When we see *ch*, we read the sound /ch/. Touch the *ch* tile and say /ch/.

3. **Say:** Two letters that make one sound are called **digraphs**. It means that we write two letters to make that sound. Start looking and listening for words with the sound /ch/ all around you.

> **Objectives**
> - Identify and use the digraph *ch.*
> - Identify the letters, given the sound /ch/.
> - Identify the sound /ch/, given the digraph *ch.*
> - Identify beginning sounds in words.

4. **Say:** The sound for the digraph *ch* is /ch/, as in *chin*.

   ▸ Say /ch/ and touch the *ch* tile.
   ▸ Finger stretch the sounds in the word *chin*.
   ▸ Build the word *chin* with your letter tiles.
   ▸ Touch and say, and say and write, the word *chin*.

5. Continue this procedure with the following words:

   ▸ *chop*
   ▸ *chap*
   ▸ *chum*

Sight Words

Read Sight Words

Help students learn the sight words *who, your, so,* and *see.*

Objectives
- Read sight words.
- Spell sight words.

1. Gather the sight word cards *who, your, so,* and *see.*

2. Show students the *who* card.

3. **Say:** This is the word *who*. We see this word so often that we want to be able to read and spell it quickly without thinking about it. Look closely at the word *who*. Spell the word *who* aloud. Take a picture of the word *who* in your mind. When you think you can spell *who* yourself, turn the card over and use your letter tiles to spell the word *who*. Check the card to see if you spelled the word *who* correctly. Read aloud the word you spelled with the letter tiles.

4. Repeat the activity with the remaining sight words.

5. Add the cards to students' sight words box.

TIP Sight words can be very difficult for some students. Let students work at their own pace and really master these words.

Try It ....

Dictation: Write Words

Have students practice identifying sounds and writing words.

1. Gather a pencil and the dictation notebook. Say the word *chin*. Then give these directions to students:

   ▸ Repeat the word.
   ▸ Write the word in your notebook.
   ▸ Read the word aloud.

2. When students have finished, write the following word on your whiteboard: *chin*.

3. Have them compare their answer to your correct version.

4. Repeat this procedure with the words *chat* and *much*.

   ▸ If students make an error and don't see it, help them correct their mistake by having them finger stretch the sounds in the word they missed.
   ▸ If students are having difficulty selecting the correct letters or sounds, review those letters or sounds that are confusing them.
   ▸ If students have difficulty with first, middle, and last sounds, have them finger stretch the sounds in words.

> ### Objectives
> - Write words by applying grade-level phonics knowledge.
> - Follow three-step directions.
> - Identify and use the digraph *ch*.

 **20 minutes**

REVIEW: Digraph *ch*

Students will work online independently to

▸ Practice the digraph *ch*.

Help students locate the online activities and provide support as needed.

Offline Alternative

No computer access? Have students point out and name things or words that contain the sound /ch/ (for example, *peach* and *chair*). You might also ask students to spell words that contain the digraph *ch*.

> ### Objectives
> - Identify and use the digraph *ch*.
> - Identify the letters, given the sound /ch/.
> - Identify the sound /ch/, given the digraph *ch*.
> - Identify individual sounds in words.

Look Back: Digraph *th*

Lesson Overview

[Offline] FOCUS: Digraph *th* — **30** minutes

Get Ready	Secret Sound
	Target Toss
Learn	Look Back: Digraph *th*
	all Aboard!
Sight Words	Read Sight Words
Try It	Finish the Job
	Dictation: Write Words

[Online] REVIEW: Digraph *th* — **20** minutes

[Materials]

Supplied
- *K¹² PhonicsWorks Advanced Activity Book*, p. PH 6
- whiteboard, Learning Coach
- whiteboard, student
- Tile Kit

Also Needed
- sight words box
- dictation notebook
- index cards (40)
- tape, masking
- household objects – small item, such as a key, button, or bean bag

Advance Preparation

Place letter tile *all* at the top of students' whiteboard. Place the following letter tiles under it: *th, b, c, f, h, m, t,* and *w.*

Go to Target Toss for the lists of double-letter ending words. Print the words in each word list on index cards, using one index card per word.

[Offline] 30 minutes

FOCUS: Digraph *th*

Work **together** with students to complete offline Get Ready, Learn, Sight Words, and Try It activities.

Get Ready

Secret Sound

Say groups of words that begin with the same letter to help students recognize **beginning sounds** in words.

1. **Say:** I am going to say some groups of words. Listen for a secret sound at the beginning of each word. Then tell me what sound you hear at the beginning of each group of words.

2. Say each of the following groups of words. Have students identify the secret sound in each group.

   ▸ *shop, shine, short* /sh/
   ▸ *top, tame, tiny* /t/
   ▸ *chase, chop, chin* /ch/
   ▸ *boy, baby, bin* /b/
   ▸ *very, van, village* /v/

3. Repeat any groups of words for which students couldn't identify the secret sound. Have them repeat each word in that group. Then have them say what sound they hear at the beginning of each word.

Objectives

- Identify beginning sounds in words.
- Identify and use ending *–ff.*
- Identify and use ending *–ll.*
- Identify and use ending *–ss.*
- Identify and use ending *–zz.*

Target Toss

Play a game with students to help them review double letter endings. The following word lists will be used in this game:

   ▸ **List 1** (/l/): *dull, bath, ball, catch, tall, fell, quell, toss, hill, pill*
   ▸ **List 2** (/f/): *tiff, Jeff, till, miff, buff, mess, cuff, whiff, biff, will*
   ▸ **List 3** (/s/): *lass, quack, boss, fuss, miss, kiss, less, mess, bass, gull*
   ▸ **List 4** (/z/): *fuzz, buzz, fizz, pass, fall, hitch, fuzz, rush, jazz, whack*

1. Gather the word cards you created for list 1 and organize the cards face up into a rectangular grid that measures approximately 1½ feet on one side and 1 foot on the other side. Make the grid on a tabletop or on the floor.

2. Gather a small household item such as a key, button, or bean bag.

3. **Say:** I am going to say an ending sound that is in a word. The first sound is /l/, as in *hull*. Try to toss this object onto a card that shows a word with the sound /l/, as in *hull*.

4. Have students toss the small object onto a card on the grid and read the word on the card where it lands.

5. Give students one point for each word that they land on and can read that contains the target ending sound.

6. Keep track of students' points. When they score five points, replace the cards in the grid with the cards from list 2.

7. Repeat the activity using the cards from lists 2 through 4.

TIP This game can be played outdoors. Just use chalk to make the grid on the sidewalk or driveway and write the words inside the boxes.

Learn

Look Back: Digraph *th*

Help students recognize and use the digraph *th*.

1. Place the *th* tile on students' whiteboard and point to it.

2. **Say:** Two letters that make one sound are called **digraphs**. It means that we write two letters to make a single sound. Start looking and listening for words with /th/ all around you.

3. **Say:** The digraph *th* makes two sounds instead of one. The sounds for *th* are /th/, as in *thin*, and /th/, as in *that*.

   ▸ Say /th/ and touch the *th* tile. Say /th/ and touch the *th* tile.
   ▸ Finger stretch the sounds in the words *thin* and *that*.
   ▸ Build the words *thin* and *that* with your letter tiles.
   ▸ Touch and say, and say and write, the words *thin* and *that*.

***all* Aboard!**

Help students practice identifying and making double-letter ending words that end with the letters *all*.

1. Gather students' whiteboard and point to the *all* tile.

2. **Say:** The letters on this tile spell the word *all*. Touch the tile and say the word *all*. Now I am going to build the word *pal*. Touch and say the sounds in *pal*. When we have one *l* after the letter *a*, we say /ă/, as in *pal*. But when we have two *l*'s after the letter *a*, we say /aw/, as in *all*.

3. **Say:** I am going to spell the word *ball* on your whiteboard. I will need only two tiles to do this: *b* and *all*. When I touch and say, I am going to say /b/.../all/.

Objectives

- Identify and use the digraph *th*.
- Identify the letters, given the sound /th/.
- Identify the letters, given the sound /th/.
- Identify the digraph *th*, given the sounds /th/ and /th/.
- Identify the sounds /th/ and /th/, given the digraph *th*.
- Identify the sound, given the letters *all*.
- Identify the letters, given the sound /all/.
- Identify individual sounds in words.

4. **Say:** Let's spell some words with the sound /all/ using the *all* tile. Use the tiles on your whiteboard to build the words as I say them. After you have spelled the word, touch and say, and say and write, the words.

5. Follow this procedure with the following words:

   ▸ *fall*
   ▸ *mall*
   ▸ *tall*
   ▸ *wall*
   ▸ *call*
   ▸ *hall*

6. Reinforce the idea that the letters *all* make the sound /all/.

7. **Say:** When we read the letters *a, l, l,* we pronounce them like the word *all.* When the double *l* follows the letter *a,* we don't say /ă/, as in *apple.* We say /all/, as in *tall.* The letter *a* has an unusual or odd sound in *tall,* so we call the letters and the sound for *all* **oddball** letters and sounds.

Sight Words

Read Sight Words
Help students learn the sight words *for, she, or,* and *her.*

1. Gather the sight word cards *for, she, or,* and *her.*

2. Show students the *for* card.

3. **Say:** This is the word *for.* We see this word so often that we want to be able to read and spell it quickly without thinking about it. Look closely at the word *for.* Spell the word *for* aloud. Take a picture of the word *for* in your mind. When you think you can spell *for* yourself, turn the card over and use your letter tiles to spell the word *for.* Check the card to see if you spelled the word *for* correctly. Read aloud the word you spelled with the letter tiles.

4. Repeat the activity with the remaining sight words.

5. Add the cards to students' sight words box.

TIP Sight words can be very difficult for some students. Let students work at their own pace and really master these words.

Objectives
• Read sight words.
• Spell sight words.

Try It

Finish the Job

Have students complete page PH 6 in *K¹² PhonicsWorks Advanced Activity Book* for more practice reading and writing words with the digraph *th*. First have students read each sentence aloud and have them choose a word from the box to complete the sentence. Then have students write the word and read the sentence aloud again.

> **Try It**
> **Look Back: Digraph *th***
> **Finish the Job**
> Choose a word from the box to complete the sentence.
> Write the word. Read the sentence aloud.
>
> | | |
> |---|---|
> | math | thin |
> | path | moth |
>
> 1. The pup is so __thin__!
> 2. Is this the __math__ quiz?
> 3. Josh is on the __path__ to the shop.
> 4. I have a net to get that __moth__.
>
> PH 6   LANGUAGE ARTS GREEN

Dictation: Write Words

Have students practice identifying sounds and writing words.

1. Gather a pencil and the dictation notebook. Say the word *math*. Then give these directions to students:

    ▸ Repeat the word.
    ▸ Write the word in your notebook.
    ▸ Read the word aloud.

2. When students have finished, write the following word on your whiteboard: *math*.

3. Have them compare their answer to your correct version.

4. Repeat this procedure with the words *that* and *ball*.

    ▸ If students make an error and don't see it, help them correct their mistake by having them finger stretch the sounds in the word they missed.
    ▸ If students are having difficulty selecting the correct letters or sounds, review those letters or sounds that are confusing them.
    ▸ If students have difficulty with first, middle, and last sounds, have them finger stretch the sounds in the word.

 **20 minutes**

REVIEW: Digraph *th*

Students will work online independently to

▶ Practice the digraph *th*.

Help students locate the online activities and provide support as needed.

Offline Alternative

No computer access? Have students practice the digraph *th*. Have them point out and name things or words that contain the sounds /th/ or /<u>th</u>/ (for example, *bath* or *them*). You might also ask students to spell words that contain the digraph *th*.

Objectives
- Identify and use the digraph *th*.
- Identify the letters, given the sound /th/.
- Identify the letters, given the sound /<u>th</u>/.
- Identify the digraph *th*, given the sounds /th/ and /<u>th</u>/.
- Identify the sounds /th/ and /<u>th</u>/, given the digraph *th*.
- Identify individual sounds in words.

Review Digraphs *sh*, *ch*, and *th*

Lesson Overview

⟦Offline⟧ FOCUS: Digraphs *sh*, *ch*, and *th* — **30** minutes

Practice	Secret Sound
	Make Up a Sentence
	Search Sentences for Ending Sounds
Sight Words	Review Sight Words
	Use Words in Sentences
	Pick a Pair
Try It	Dictation: Write Sentences

⟦Online⟧ REVIEW: Digraphs *sh*, *ch*, and *th* — **20** minutes

Materials

Supplied
- whiteboard, Learning Coach

Also Needed
- sight words box
- dictation notebook
- index cards (5)

Advance Preparation

For Make Up a Sentence, print each of the following words on index cards, using one index card per word: *there, shell, chill, toss,* and *went*.

Big Ideas

▸ Words written on a page represent words spoken or thought by someone.
▸ Letters are put together in a specific order to make words. Changing the order of the letters changes the word.
▸ Words are put together in a specific order to make sentences. Changing the order of the sentences changes the meaning of the sentence.

[Offline] 🕐 30 minutes

FOCUS: Digraphs *sh*, *ch*, and *th*

Work **together** with students to complete offline Practice, Sight Words, and Try It activities.

Practice ●●

Secret Sound

Say groups of words that begin with the same letter to help students recognize **beginning sounds** in words.

1. **Say:** I am going to say some groups of words. Listen for a secret sound at the beginning of each word. Then tell me what sound you hear at the beginning of each group of words.

2. Say each of the following groups of words. Have students identify the secret sound in each group.

   ▶ *edge, echo, Eskimo, ever* /ĕ/
   ▶ *lip, like, lend, little* /l/
   ▶ *inside, itch, igloo, if* /ĭ/
   ▶ *pat, pen, pig, pal* /p/
   ▶ *otter, onto, October, octopus* /ŏ/
   ▶ *yellow, yes, yesterday, yum* /y/
   ▶ *ugly, under, upset, upside down* /ŭ/
   ▶ *after, apple, alligator, add* /ă/

(TIP) If students can't identify the secret sound, have them listen while you say each word again and then have them repeat each word. Have students say what sound they hear in the middle of each word.

Make Up a Sentence

Help students practice writing sentences using familiar words.

1. Gather the word cards *there*, *shell*, *chill*, *toss*, and *went*.

2. Have students read all the words.

3. Have students choose a word and write it in a sentence in their dictation notebook. Help them with any words that are difficult for them by telling them the word, so that the flow of the sentence is not interrupted.

4. Continue to do this until students have selected all the words.

5. Have students read the sentences aloud.

> **Objectives**
> - Identify beginning sounds in words.
> - Identify ending sounds in words.
> - Identify individual sounds in words.
> - Read aloud grade-level text with appropriate automaticity, prosody, accuracy, and rate.
> - Write words by applying grade-level phonics knowledge.
> - Decode words by applying grade-level word analysis skills.

Search Sentences for Ending Sounds

Have students practice identifying **ending sounds** in words that are in a sentence.

1. **Say:** I'm going to say an ending sound that is in a word. You will repeat that sound and the word. The first sound is /k/, as in the word *luck*.

2. Have students say the target ending sound /k/ and the word *luck*.

3. **Say:** Then I will read a sentence. Repeat the sentence and tell me the word that has the same ending sound. The first sentence is, "Give me back the toy." Which word in the sentence has the special ending sound? *back*

4. Have students repeat the sentence and say the word.

   ▸ If students don't name the correct word, repeat the sentence and remind them of the target ending sound.
   ▸ If students have difficulty, say two words from the sentence and have them choose the one with the target ending sound.

5. Follow the same procedure with the words and sentences below to help students recognize ending sounds in words.

   ▸ /ch/ as in *rich*   Did Jim eat much? *much*
   ▸ /th/ as in *bath*   Ride your bike on the path. *path*
   ▸ /l/ as in *fall*   Ring the bell in the tower. *bell*
   ▸ /z/ as in *jazz*   Hear the bee buzz. *buzz*
   ▸ /sh/ as in *mesh*   Make a wish. *wish*

Sight Words

Review Sight Words

Help students learn to recognize sight words.

1. Gather all the sight word cards students have yet to master from their sight words box. Stack the cards on the table face down.

2. Have students pick up a word and read it to you.

3. If they read it quickly and correctly, put the card in one stack. If they hesitate or do not read the word correctly, put it in another stack. The second stack should have words that students will review again.

4. Take the stack of words that students read correctly and dictate each word to them. They may choose to either write the word or spell it aloud.

5. If students spell the word correctly, they have mastered the word. If they misspell the word, add it to the stack of cards to review again.

6. Chart students' progress on the back of each card.

   ▸ Divide the back of the card into two columns.
   ▸ Label the first column "Read" and the second column "Spell."
   ▸ Record the dates that students read or spell the word correctly. When students can read and spell the word correctly three times in a row, they have mastered the word. You may want to put a star or sticker on their card when they have mastered that word.

Objectives
- Read sight words.
- Write sight words.
- Spell sight words.

TIP Even if students can read and spell all the words correctly, it is still beneficial for students to review sight words. Choose as many additional words as you would like for each subsequent activity.

Use Words in Sentences

Help students use sight words in sentences.

1. Gather all the sight word cards students have yet to master from their sight words box. Spread the sight word cards on the table.

2. **Say:** Let's use sight words in sentences.

3. Have students

   ▸ Touch each card and read the word on it.
   ▸ Make up a sentence using the word.
   ▸ Put the card in a pile after using the word in a sentence.
   ▸ Go through the pile of cards and read each sight word again.
   ▸ Spell each word.

TIP If students have difficulty with any of the sight words, place those word cards in a pile to review later in the week.

Pick a Pair

Play a card game with students for more practice with sight words.

1. Gather the sight word cards that students are reviewing. Choose two words and place the cards on the table.

2. Ask questions to help students identify each word. For example, if the words are *or* and *one*, you could ask, "Which word names a number?" If the words are *on* and *but*, you could ask, "Which word is the opposite of *off*?"

3. Continue the activity until students identify all the words.

4. Take the stack of words that students read correctly and dictate each word to them.

5. Have students write each word or spell it aloud.

Try It

Dictation: Write Sentences

Use a sentence to help students identify individual sounds in words.

1. Gather a pencil and the dictation notebook. Say the sentence, *She and Chip both went to see the ship.* Then give these directions to students:

   ▸ Repeat the sentence.
   ▸ Write the sentence in your notebook.
   ▸ Read the sentence aloud.

2. When students have finished, write the following sentence on your whiteboard: *She and Chip both went to see the ship.*

3. Have students compare their answer to your correct version.

4. Repeat this procedure with the sentence, *The light is on.*

   ▸ If students make an error and don't see it, help them correct their mistake by having them finger stretch the sounds in the word they missed.
   ▸ If students are having difficulty selecting the correct letters or sounds, review those letters or sounds that are confusing them.
   ▸ If students have difficulty with first, middle, and last sounds, have them finger stretch the sounds in the word.

Objectives

- Write words by applying grade-level phonics knowledge.
- Write sight words.
- Follow three-step directions.

[Online] ⓴ minutes

REVIEW: Digraphs *sh*, *ch*, and *th*

Students will work online independently to

▸ Practice the digraphs *sh*, *ch*, and *th*.

Help students locate the online activities and provide support as needed.

Offline Alternative

No computer access? Review the digraphs *sh*, *ch*, and *th* with students. Have them point out and name things or words that contain the sounds /sh/, /ch/, /th/, and /<u>th</u>/ (for example, *shine*, *chain*, *thumb*, and *that*).

Objectives

- Identify and use the digraph *sh*.
- Identify and use the digraph *ch*.
- Identify and use the digraph *th*.
- Identify individual sounds in words.

Unit Checkpoint

Lesson Overview

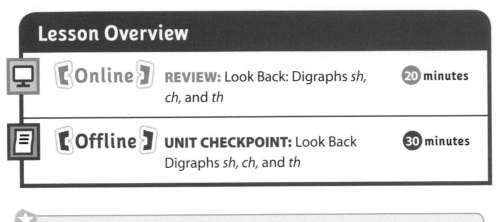

🖥	**[Online]**	**REVIEW:** Look Back: Digraphs *sh*, *ch*, and *th*	**20** minutes
📄	**[Offline]**	**UNIT CHECKPOINT:** Look Back Digraphs *sh*, *ch*, and *th*	**30** minutes

[Materials]

Supplied
- *K¹² PhonicsWorks Advanced Assessments*, pp. PH 13–18

Objectives
- Identify the sound /ch/, given the digraph *ch*.
- Identify the sound /sh/, given the digraph *sh*.
- Identify the sounds /th/ and /<u>th</u>/, given the digraph *th*.
- Identify the letters, given the sound /ch/.
- Identify the letters, given the sound /sh/.
- Identify the digraph *th*, given the sounds /th/ and /<u>th</u>/.
- Identify the sound, given the letters *all*.
- Identify the letters, given the sound /all/.
- Identify individual sounds in words.
- Identify short vowel sounds.
- Read sight words.
- Write sight words.
- Read aloud grade-level text with appropriate automaticity, prosody, accuracy, and rate.

[Online] **20** minutes

REVIEW: Look Back: Digraphs *sh*, *ch*, and *th*

Students will review the digraphs *sh*, *ch*, and *th* to prepare for the Unit Checkpoint. Help students locate the online activities and provide support as needed.

[Offline] **30** minutes

UNIT CHECKPOINT: Look Back Digraphs *sh*, *ch*, and *th*

Explain that students are going to show what they have learned about letters, sounds, and words.

1. Give students the Unit Checkpoint pages for the Look Back: Digraphs *sh*, *ch*, and *th* unit and print the Unit Checkpoint Answer Key, if you'd like.

2. Use the instructions below to help administer the Checkpoint to students. On the Answer Key or another sheet of paper, note student answers to oral response questions to help with scoring the Checkpoint later.

3. Use the Answer Key to score the Checkpoint, and then enter the results online.

Part 1. Read Letters and Word Parts Moving left to right, have students say the sounds of each letter or word part. Note any letters or word parts they say incorrectly.

Part 2. Finger Stretching Say each word to students. Have them say each word aloud and finger stretch the sounds. Note any words they finger stretch incorrectly.

16. *shut*	19. *thug*
17. *fizz*	20. *wish*
18. *bath*	21. *chat*

Part 3. Dictation Say each word to students. Have them repeat and write the word.

22. *bash*	25. *moth*
23. *ship*	26. *chop*
24. *then*	27. *wall*

Part 4. Writing Read each sentence to students. Have them repeat and write the sentence.

28. *Run to the shed.*

29. *Get that ball.*

Part 5. Read Aloud Listen to students read each sentence aloud. Note any words students read incorrectly.

Part 6. Say Letters Say each sound. Have students say the letter or letters that make that sound. Note any incorrect responses.

35. /ă/

36. /all/

37. /th/

38. /ŭ/

39. /ks/

40. /r/

41. /ĭ/

42. /ĕ/

43. /ŏ/

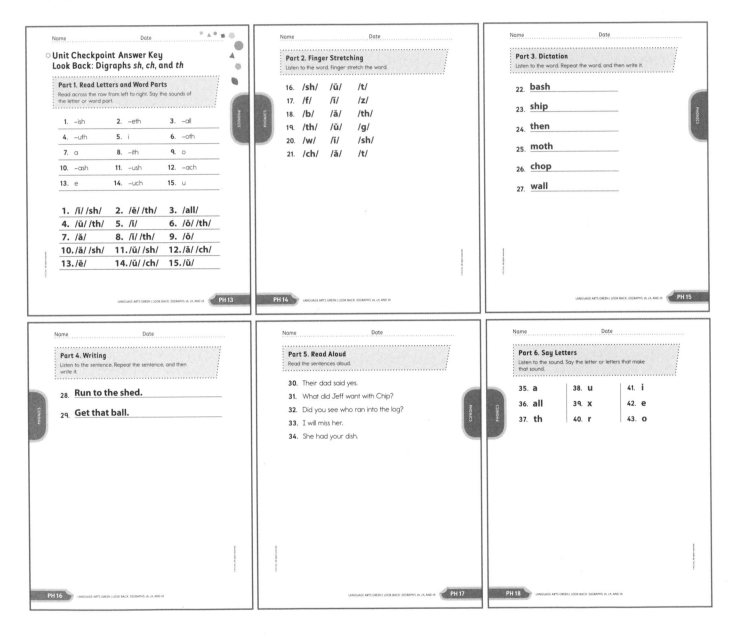

Name _____ Date _____

◇ **Unit Checkpoint Answer Key**
Look Back: Digraphs *sh*, *ch*, and *th*

Part 1. Read Letters and Word Parts
Read across the row from left to right. Say the sounds of the letter or word part.

1. –ish   2. –eth   3. –all
4. –uth   5. i   6. –oth
7. a   8. –ith   9. o
10. –ash   11. –ush   12. –ach
13. e   14. –uch   15. u

1. /ĭ/ /sh/   2. /ĕ/ /th/   3. /all/
4. /ŭ/ /th/   5. /ĭ/   6. /ŏ/ /th/
7. /ă/   8. /ĭ/ /th/   9. /ŏ/
10. /ă/ /sh/   11. /ŭ/ /sh/   12. /ă/ /ch/
13. /ĕ/   14. /ŭ/ /ch/   15. /ŭ/

LANGUAGE ARTS GREEN | LOOK BACK: DIGRAPHS *sh*, *ch*, AND *th*   PH 13

PH 14   LANGUAGE ARTS GREEN | LOOK BACK: DIGRAPHS *sh*, *ch*, AND *th*

Name _____ Date _____

Part 2. Finger Stretching
Listen to the word. Finger stretch the word.

16. /sh/   /ŭ/   /t/
17. /f/   /ĭ/   /z/
18. /b/   /ă/   /th/
19. /th/   /ŭ/   /g/
20. /w/   /ĭ/   /sh/
21. /ch/   /ă/   /t/

Name _____ Date _____

Part 3. Dictation
Listen to the word. Repeat the word, and then write it.

22. **bash** _____

23. **ship** _____

24. **then** _____

25. **moth** _____

26. **chop** _____

27. **wall** _____

LANGUAGE ARTS GREEN | LOOK BACK: DIGRAPHS *sh*, *ch*, AND *th*   PH 15

Name _____ Date _____

Part 4. Writing
Listen to the sentence. Repeat the sentence, and then write it.

28. **Run to the shed.** _____

29. **Get that ball.** _____

PH 16   LANGUAGE ARTS GREEN | LOOK BACK: DIGRAPHS *sh*, *ch*, AND *th*

Name _____ Date _____

Part 5. Read Aloud
Read the sentences aloud.

30. Their dad said yes.
31. What did Jeff want with Chip?
32. Did you see who ran into the log?
33. I will miss her.
34. She had your dish.

LANGUAGE ARTS GREEN | LOOK BACK: DIGRAPHS *sh*, *ch*, AND *th*   PH 17

Name _____ Date _____

Part 6. Say Letters
Listen to the sound. Say the letter or letters that make that sound.

35. a   38. u   41. i
36. all   39. x   42. e
37. th   40. r   43. o

PH 18   LANGUAGE ARTS GREEN | LOOK BACK: DIGRAPHS *sh*, *ch*, AND *th*

Look Back: Digraph *wh*

Unit Overview

In this unit, students will

- ▸ Identify and use the digraphs *wh* and *ck*.
- ▸ Identify and use the trigraph *tch*.
- ▸ Learn base words and the endings –*s* and –*es*.
- ▸ Review the double letter endings.
- ▸ Practice beginning, middle, and ending sounds in words.
- ▸ Learn sight words.

[Materials]

Supplied

- *K¹² PhonicsWorks Advanced Activity Book*, p. PH 7
- whiteboard, Learning Coach
- whiteboard, student
- Tile Kit

Also Needed

- sight words box
- dictation notebook
- index cards (11)

Lesson Overview

[Offline] FOCUS: Digraph *wh*   30 minutes

Get Ready	Scrambled Letters
	I Spy
Learn	Look Back: Digraph *wh*
	Add Ending –*s* to Base Words
	Add Ending –*es* to Base Words
	Choose Between Endings –*s* and –*es*
Sight Words	Read Sight Words
Try It	Sorting Day
	Dictation: Write Sentences

[Online] REVIEW: Digraph *wh*   20 minutes

Advance Preparation

For Choose Between Endings –*s* and –*es*, print each of the following words on index cards, using one index card per word: *pet, tack, duck, cab, fall, zip, rash, latch, dish, buzz,* and *loss*.

[Offline] 30 minutes

FOCUS: Digraph *wh*

Work **together** with students to complete offline Get Ready, Learn, Sight Words, and Try It activities.

Get Ready ....

Scrambled Letters

To help students learn the alphabet, have them practice identifying and naming letters.

1. Place the following letter tiles in random order on students' whiteboard: *b*, *k*, *m*, and *z*.

2. Have students arrange the letters in alphabetical order.

(TIP) Students may find this activity easier if they slowly sing "The Alphabet Song" to themselves as they work.

> **Objectives**
> - Identify letters of the alphabet.
> - Identify individual sounds in words.

___

I Spy

Have students name and use common objects to help them recognize individual sounds in words.

1. Explain to students that you will be playing I Spy and show them how to use the thumb and index finger to make a circle, simulating a spyglass.

2. **Say:** I say, "I spy, with my little eye, something that starts with the sound /l/." Your job is to guess what I spy. What I had in mind was the *lamp. Lamp* begins with the sound /l/.

3. Repeat Step 2 with a different object in the room.

4. **Say:** Are you ready to begin? I spy, with my little eye, something that starts with the sound [target sound]. Can you guess what it is?

5. After students have guessed the object, repeat Step 4 until you have spied six objects, or until students tire of the game. Possible words to use are *hair, window, door, box, sheet, refrigerator, magazine, sink, carpet, bowl, mat, newspaper, towel, basket, key,* and *napkin.*

6. Redirect students if they name an object with an incorrect sound.

   Say: The sound that begins the word [word] is [sound]. We're looking for something that begins with the sound [target sound]. What is a word that begins with that sound? Now look around the room. What do you see that begins with that sound?

7. Narrow down the search to a certain part of the room if students become frustrated. If students continue to have trouble, narrow down the search to two objects.

   Say: What is the beginning sound of [target word]? What is the beginning sound of [another word]? Which one starts with the sound [target sound]?

Learn

Look Back: Digraph *wh*

Help students recognize and use the digraph *wh*.

1. Place the *wh* tile on students' whiteboard and point to it.

2. **Say:** Two letters that make one sound are called **digraphs**. It means that we write two letters to make that sound. Start looking and listening for words with /w/ all around you.

3. **Say:** The digraph *wh* makes the sound /w/ as in *wham*.

   ▸ Touch the *wh* tile and say /w/.
   ▸ Finger stretch the sounds in the word *wham*.
   ▸ Build the word *wham* with your letter tiles.
   ▸ Touch and say, and say and write, the word *wham*.

Add Ending –*s* to Base Words

Have students make new words by adding letters to base words.

1. Make the following words with letter tiles at the top of students' whiteboard: *top, fan, cat, bed,* and *chug*.

2. Place the following letter tile at the bottom of students' whiteboard: *s*.

3. **Say:** The word we start with can be called the **base word**. We can change the base word *top* to *tops* by adding an *s* to the end of the word. We can add the ending –*s* to other words to make them mean more than one.

4. **Say:** Point to the word *fan* and read the word. Try adding an *s* to the word *fan*. Now read the word.

   ▸ What is the base word, or the word we started with? *fan*
   ▸ What is the ending sound? /z/

5. **Say:** This time, the ending –*s* makes the sound /z/. When we add the ending –*s* to a base word, it can have the sound /s/ or /z/. You will have to listen carefully to the sound. It is important to remember that both sounds, /s/ and /z/, are always spelled –*s* in these words.

6. **Say:** The next word is *cat*. Now add *s* to the word *cat* and read the word.

   ▸ What is the base word? *cat*
   ▸ What is the ending sound? /s/

7. **Say:** The next word is *bed*. Now add *s* to the word *bed* and read the word.

   ▸ What is the base word? *bed*
   ▸ What is the ending sound? /z/

Objectives

- Identify the digraph *wh*, given the sound /w/.
- Identify the sound /w/, given the digraph *wh*.
- Identify ending sounds in words.
- Read, write, and spell words containing the ending –*s*.
- Read, write, and spell words containing the ending –*es*.

8. **Say:** The next word is *chug*. Now add *s* to the word *chug* and read the word.

   ▸ What is the base word? *chug*
   ▸ What is the ending sound? /z/

9. Reinforce the difference between a base word and the word with an *s*. Create the words *pet* and *pets* on students' whiteboard.

   ▸ Place one word directly below the other.
   ▸ Align the letters so students can see that both words contain the letters *p*, *e*, and *t*.

10. **Say:** Watch while I take away the *s* at the end of *pets*. Compare the two words. The words are the same. Both words say *pet*. Now put an *s* at the end of one word. Read the word. By putting an *s* at the end of *pet*, you've changed the word *pet* to *pets*.

Add Ending –*es* to Base Words

Have students make new words by adding letters to base words.

1. Make the following words with letter tiles at the top of students' whiteboard: *kiss*, *fizz*, *box*, *wish*, and *match*.

2. Place the following letter tile at the bottom of students' whiteboard: *es*.

3. **Say:** With some words, we can simply add –*s* to the end to make the word mean more than one. But for other words, we need to add –*es* to the end. Let's look at each of these words.

4. Read each word to students. Have students point to and name the end letter or letters. Explain that words that end in digraphs, or the letters *s*, *x*, and *z*, must have an –*es* added to the end to make the word mean more than one.

5. **Say:** Point to the base word *kiss*. To make *kiss* mean more than one, we need to add an ending to the base word. Add the –*es* letter tile to the end of the word to make the word *kisses*. This word has two syllables: *kiss* and –*es*. The base word is *kiss* and the ending is –*es*.

6. **Say:** We can add the ending –*es* to other words to make them mean more than one. The ending –*es* makes the sound /iz/.

7. **Say:** Point to the word *fizz* and read the word. Try adding an –*es* to the word *fizz*. Now read the word.

   ▸ What is the base word? *fizz*
   ▸ What is the ending sound? /iz/

8. Continue this procedure with the words *box*, *wish*, and *match*.

Choose Between Endings –s and –es

Help students learn how to choose between –s and –es at the end of words.

1. Gather the cards you prepared.

2. Have students fold a piece of paper in half to make two columns. Write s at the top of the first column, and es at the top of the second column.

3. **Say:** Some words use the ending –s and other words use the ending –es. Words that end with the letters s, z, x, tch, sh, or ch take the ending –es.

4. Give the index cards to students one at a time.

5. **Say:** I will show you a word card. Tell me whether the word takes the ending –s or –es.

   ▸ If the word takes an –s, write the word in the –s column. *pets, tacks, ducks, cabs, falls, zips,*
   ▸ If the word takes an –es, write the word in the –es column. *rashes, latches, dishes, buzzes, losses*

6. If students struggle, review the letters for the word endings that take –s or –es.

Sight Words

Read Sight Words

Help students learn the sight words *does, why,* and *one.*

1. Gather the sight word cards *does, why,* and *one.*

2. Show students the *does* card.

3. **Say:** This is the word *does.* We see this word so often that we want to be able to read and spell it quickly without thinking about it. Look closely at the word *does.* Spell the word *does* aloud. Take a picture of the word *does* in your mind. When you think you can spell *does* yourself, turn the card over and use your letter tiles to spell the word *does.* Check the card to see if you spelled the word *does* correctly. Read aloud the word you spelled with the letter tiles.

4. Repeat the activity with the remaining sight words.

5. Add the cards to students' sight words box.

TIP Sight words can be very difficult for some students. Let students work at their own pace and really master these words.

Objectives
- Read sight words.
- Spell sight words.

Try It

Sorting Day

Have students complete page PH 7 in *K¹² PhonicsWorks Advanced Activity Book* for more practice reading and writing words with digraphs. First have them read each word in the box. Then have students write each word in the proper column.

> **Objectives**
> - Read aloud grade-level text with appropriate automaticity, prosody, accuracy, and rate.
> - Write words by applying grade-level phonics knowledge.
> - Write sight words.
> - Follow three-step directions.

Dictation: Write Sentences

Use sentences to help students identify individual sounds in words.

1. Gather a pencil and the dictation notebook. Say the sentence, *When does the sun set?* Then give these directions to students:

   ▸ Repeat the sentence.
   ▸ Write the sentence in your notebook.
   ▸ Read the sentence aloud.

2. When students have finished, write the following sentence on your whiteboard: *When does the sun set?*

3. Have them compare their answer to your correct version.

4. Repeat this procedure with the sentence, *Are your mom and dad at the shop?*

   ▸ If students make an error and don't see, it help them correct their mistake by having them finger stretch the sounds in the word they missed.
   ▸ If students are having difficulty selecting the correct letters or sounds, review those letters or sounds that are confusing them.
   ▸ If students have difficulty with first, middle, and last sounds, have them finger stretch the sounds in the word.

 **20 minutes**

REVIEW: Digraph *wh*

Students will work online independently to

▶ Practice the digraph *wh*.

Help students locate the online activities and provide support as needed.

Offline Alternative

No computer access? Review the digraph *wh* with students. Have them point out and name things or words that begin with the sound /w/ (for example, *whistle* or *wheel*). You might also ask students to spell words that contain the digraph *wh*.

Look Back: Digraph *ck*

Lesson Overview

〔Offline〕 FOCUS: Digraph *ck*   30 minutes

Get Ready	Quick Sounds
	Draw a Picture
Learn	Look Back: Digraph *ck*
Sight Words	Read Sight Words
Try It	Dictation: Write Words

〔Online〕 REVIEW: Digraph *ck*   20 minutes

〔Materials〕

Supplied
- whiteboard, Learning Coach
- whiteboard, student
- Tile Kit

Also Needed
- sight words box
- dictation notebook
- index cards (9)
- crayons

Advance Preparation

For Draw a Picture, print each of the following words on index cards, using one index card per word: *ball*, *rash*, *cap*, *whip*, *pig*, *fish*, *sun*, *mop*, and *lip*.

[Offline] 🕘 30 minutes

FOCUS: Digraph *ck*

Work **together** with students to complete offline Get Ready, Learn, Sight Words, and Try It activities.

Get Ready •••

Quick Sounds

Help students name words that have the same **beginning sound**.

1. **Say:** I'm going to say a sound that begins a word. Your job is to think of as many words as you can that begin with that same sound. Let's see how many you can name. The first sound is /j/, as in *jump*. How many words can you say that begin with /j/?

   ▸ If students have trouble thinking of words, have them look around the room and find objects that start with that sound.

2. Continue this procedure with the following sounds:

   ▸ /t/, as in *toy*
   ▸ /b/, as in *ball*
   ▸ /v/, as in *vase*
   ▸ /ă/, as in *apple*
   ▸ /ĕ/, as in *edge*

   TIP You could get a book and find pictures of things that start with that sound.

> **Objectives**
> - Identify beginning sounds in words.
> - Decode words by applying grade-level word analysis skills.

Draw a Picture

Help students practice identifying words by having them draw pictures to match the word.

1. Gather the index cards you prepared.

2. Have students

   ▸ Choose a card.
   ▸ Read the word on the card.
   ▸ Draw a picture (in crayon) of the word on the back of the card.

3. After they have drawn as many cards as they want, have students label each picture.

   ▸ If students can't remember how to spell a word, have them look on the other side of the card.
   ▸ If students have trouble labeling the items, have them finger stretch the words with you first.

Learn

Look Back: Digraph *ck*

Help students recognize and use the digraph *ck*.

1. Place the *ck* tile on students' whiteboard and point to it.

2. **Say:** Two letters that make one sound are called **digraphs**. It means that we write two letters to make that one sound. Start looking and listening for words with /k/ all around you.

3. **Say:** The sound for the digraph *ck* is /k/, as in *duck*.

   ▸ Touch the *ck* tile and say /k/.
   ▸ Finger stretch the sounds in the word *duck*.
   ▸ Build the word *duck* with your letter tiles.
   ▸ Touch and say, and say and write, the word *duck*.

4. Continue this procedure with the following words:

   ▸ *lock*
   ▸ *back*
   ▸ *tick*

> **Objectives**
> - Identify and use the digraph *ck*.
> - Identify the letters, given the sound /k/.
> - Identify the sound /k/, given the digraph *ck*.
> - Identify ending sounds in words.

Sight Words

Read Sight Words

Help students learn the sight words *were*, *my*, and *our*.

1. Gather the sight word cards *were*, *my*, and *our*.

2. Show students the *were* card.

3. **Say:** This is the word *were*. We see this word so often that we want to be able to read and spell it quickly without thinking about it. Look closely at the word *were*. Spell the word *were* aloud. Take a picture of the word *were* in your mind. When you think you can spell *were* yourself, turn the card over and use your letter tiles to spell the word *were*. Check the card to see if you spelled the word *were* correctly. Read aloud the word you spelled with the letter tiles.

4. Repeat the activity with the remaining sight words.

5. Add the cards to students' sight words box.

TIP Sight words can be very difficult for some students. Let students work at their own pace and really master these words.

> **Objectives**
> - Read sight words.
> - Spell sight words.

Try It ....

Dictation: Write Words

Have students practice identifying sounds and writing words.

1. Gather a pencil and the dictation notebook. Say the word *pack*. Then give these directions to students:

    ▸ Repeat the word.
    ▸ Write the word in your notebook.
    ▸ Read the word aloud.

2. When students have finished, write the following word on your whiteboard: *pack*.

3. Have them compare their answer to your correct version.

4. Repeat this procedure with the words *chick* and *sock*.

    ▸ If students make an error and don't see it, help them correct their mistake by having them finger stretch the sounds in the word they missed.
    ▸ If students are having difficulty selecting the correct letters or sounds, review those letters or sounds that are confusing them.
    ▸ If students have difficulty with first, middle, and last sounds, have them finger stretch the sounds in the word.

> **Objectives**
> • Write words by applying grade-level phonics knowledge.
> • Follow three-step directions.

[Online] 20 minutes

REVIEW: Digraph *ck*

Students will work online independently to

▸ Practice the digraph *ck*.

Help students locate the online activities and provide support as needed.

Offline Alternative

No computer access? Review the digraph *ck* with students. Have them point out and name things or words that have the ending sound /k/ (for example, *pick* or *trick*). You might also ask students to spell words that contain the digraph *ck*.

> **Objectives**
> • Identify and use the digraph *ck*.
> • Identify the letters, given the sound /k/.
> • Identify the sound /k/, given the digraph *ck*.
> • Identify ending sounds in words.

Look Back: Trigraph *tch*

Lesson Overview

[Offline] FOCUS: Trigraph *tch* — 30 minutes

Get Ready	Sentence Scramble
Learn	Look Back: Digraph *tch*
	Sounds for Digraphs and Trigraphs
	Introduce Compound Words
	Build Compound Words
Sight Words	Read Sight Words
Try It	Copy Cat
	Dictation: Write Words

[Online] REVIEW: Trigraph *tch* — 20 minutes

[Materials]

Supplied
- *K¹² PhonicsWorks Advanced Activity Book*, p. PH 8
- whiteboard, Learning Coach
- whiteboard, student
- small whiteboards (2)

Also Needed
- sight words box
- dictation notebook
- index cards (10)

Keywords
compound word – a word made from two smaller words

Advance Preparation

For Sentence Scramble, print each of the following words on index cards, using one index card per word: *can, where, she, go, in, run, dash, up, the,* and *hill.*

Big Ideas

▶ The word *backpack* is a compound word, made from the two smaller words *back* and *pack.*
▶ The ability to break compound words into two smaller words is a demonstration of phonological awareness.
▶ The ability to put two small words together to form a compound word is a demonstration of phonological awareness.

⟦ Offline ⟧ **30** minutes

FOCUS: Trigraph *tch*

Work **together** with students to complete offline Get Ready, Learn, Sight Words, and Try It activities.

Get Ready ··

Sentence Scramble

Have students build sentences by rearranging words to help them learn the meaning of words and phrases.

1. Gather the index cards you prepared, a pencil, and the dictation notebook.

2. Place the index cards in front of students.

3. Point to each word and have students read it aloud with you.

4. Arrange three of the cards as follows: *can she go*.

5. Ask students if the words make sense and tell them that the words make an asking sentence.

6. Write the words as a sentence on students' whiteboard: *Can she go?*

7. Point out the capital letter and the question mark in the sentence.

8. Read the sentence together.

9. **Say:** I am going to mix these words back with the others. Choose some word cards and put them together to make a different sentence. Read the words in the order you put them.

   ▸ Does your sentence make sense? Is it an asking or a telling sentence?
   ▸ Now write the sentence. Be sure to start with a capital letter. Remember to put a period or a question mark at the end.

10. Return the words to the original group and repeat the steps so that students can create and write one or more sentences.

    ▸ If students struggle with choosing among the words, remove the words *where, in, dash, up, the,* and *hill* and repeat the procedure.

11. Help students if they have difficulty in arranging the words correctly to make a sentence.

12. **Say:** Read the sentence aloud. Does it make sense?

    Point to any word that seems out of place.

    ▸ What is this word?
    ▸ Find a word that would make better sense.
    ▸ Switch the words. Now read the sentence.
    ▸ Does it make sense now?

Objectives

- Read aloud grade-level text with appropriate automaticity, prosody, accuracy, and rate.
- Decode words by applying grade-level word analysis skills.
- Use context and sentence structure to determine meaning of words, phrases, and/or sentences.
- Identify complete sentences.

Learn

Look Back: Digraph *tch*

Help students recognize and use the trigraph *tch*.

1. Place the *tch* tile on students' whiteboard and point to it.

2. **Say:** Three letters that make one sound are called **trigraphs**. It means that we write three letters to make that one sound.

3. **Say:** The trigraph *tch* makes one sound instead of three. The sound for *tch* is /ch/, as in *pitch*. Touch the *tch* tile and say /ch/.

4. **Say:** The trigraph *tch* is always used at the end of a word or syllable, as in *match*.

   ▸ Finger stretch the sounds in the word *match*.
   ▸ Build the word *match* with your letter tiles.
   ▸ Touch and say, and say and write, the word *match*.

5. Repeat the procedure with the words *latch* and *itch*.

Sounds for Digraphs and Trigraphs

Help students practice identifying the sounds made by digraphs and trigraphs.

1. Place the following letter tiles on students' whiteboard: *sh, ch, ck, th, th, wh,* and *tch*.

2. **Say:** Let's review the six sounds for digraphs and the one sound for a trigraph.

3. Touch the tiles for *sh, ch, ck, th, th, wh,* and *tch* on students' whiteboard and say each sound. Repeat in random order several times.

4. Have students touch each letter tile and say the sounds. Do this several times.

Introduce Compound Words

Introduce compound words to students.

1. Make the following words on students' whiteboard: *bath* and *tub*.

2. **Say:** Today, we are going to learn how to put words we know together to make other words. You know what the word *bath* means. You know what *tub* means. Now we're going to put them together to make one word.

   ▸ Slide together the two words to make one word.

3. **Say:** I'll read the new word: *bathtub*. How many syllables are in the compound word *bathtub*? Underline each word and read the word.

Objectives

- Identify and use the trigraph *tch*.
- Identify the trigraph *tch*, given the sound /ch/.
- Identify and use compound words.

Build Compound Words

Help students practice identifying and making compound words.

1. Gather two small whiteboards and a dry-erase marker.

2. **Say:** Now we are going to build some **compound words**. Say the word *uphill*.

   ▸ How many syllables do you hear? two

3. **Say:** Each syllable in the word *uphill* is also a small word: *up, hill*. Together they make the compound word *uphill*.

4. **Say:** When we spell compound words, we will first spell each syllable on the small whiteboards. To build the word, I will write the first syllable, *up*, on one whiteboard. Next I will write the second syllable, *hill*, on the other whiteboard. Now I'll push the two whiteboards together next to one another and read *uphill*.

5. **Say:** Now it's your turn. Build the word *cannot*.

   ▸ First tap the syllables on the table.
   ▸ Spell the first syllable on one whiteboard.
   ▸ Spell the second syllable on the other whiteboard.
   ▸ Put the boards together and read the word.

6. Repeat Step 5 with the words *suntan* and *hatbox*.

Sight Words

Read Sight Words

Help students learn the sight words *Mr., Mrs.,* and *Dr.*

1. Gather the sight word cards *Mr., Mrs.,* and *Dr.*

2. Show students the *Mr.* card.

3. **Say:** This is the word *Mr.* We see this word so often that we want to be able to read and spell it quickly without thinking about it. Look closely at the word *Mr.* Spell the word *Mr.* aloud. Take a picture of the word *Mr.* in your mind. When you think you can spell *Mr.* yourself, turn the card over and use your letter tiles to spell the word *Mr.* Check the card to see if you spelled the word *Mr.* correctly. Read aloud the word you spelled with the letter tiles.

4. Repeat the activity with the remaining sight words.

5. Add the cards to students' sight words box.

6. Explain to students that, sometimes, instead of writing out an entire word or phrase, we use an abbreviation. An **abbreviation** is a shortened form of a word or phrase. Most abbreviations end with a period and are written in lowercase.

TIP Sight words can be very difficult for some students. Let students work at their own pace and really master these words.

> **Objectives**
> • Read sight words.
> • Spell sight words.

Try It

Copy Cat

Have students complete page PH 8 in *K¹² PhonicsWorks Advanced Activity Book* for more practice identifying words with similar meanings. Have them read each word aloud and choose a word from the box with the same meaning as the word in the list. Then have students write the word.

> **Try It**
>
> **Look Back: Trigraph** *tch*
>
> **Copy Cat**
>
> Read the word aloud. Choose a word from the box that has almost the same meaning. Write the word.
>
> | latch | quick | ill |
> |-------|-------|------|
> | shack | fetch | wish |
>
> 1. catch   **fetch**
> 2. sick   **ill**
> 3. shed   **shack**
> 4. rush   **quick**
> 5. want   **wish**
> 6. lock   **latch**
>
> PH 8   LANGUAGE ARTS GREEN

Objectives
- Identify and use compound words.
- Write words by applying grade-level phonics knowledge.
- Follow three-step directions.

Dictation: Write Words

Have students practice identifying sounds and writing words.

1. Gather a pencil and the dictation notebook. Say the word *cobweb*. Then give these directions to students:

   ► Repeat the word.
   ► Write the word in your notebook.
   ► Read the word aloud.

2. When students have finished, write the following word on your whiteboard: *cobweb*.

3. Have them compare their answer to your correct version.

4. Repeat this procedure with the words *suntan* and *backpack*.

   ► If students make an error and don't see it, help them correct their mistake by having them finger stretch the sounds in the word they missed.
   ► If students are having difficulty selecting the correct letters or sounds, review those letters or sounds that are confusing them.
   ► If students have difficulty with first, middle, and last sounds, have them finger stretch the sounds in words.

 **20 minutes**

REVIEW: Trigraph *tch*

Students will work online independently to

► Practice trigraph *tch*.

Help students locate the online activities and provide support as needed.

Offline Alternative

No computer access? Have students point out and name things or words that contain the trigraph *tch* (for example, *watch* or *pitch*). You might also ask students to spell words that contain the trigraph *tch*.

Objectives

- Identify the trigraph *tch*, given the sound /ch/.
- Identify ending sounds in words.

Look Back: Sounds, Letters, Vowels, and Digraphs

Lesson Overview

[Offline]	**FOCUS:** Sounds, Letters, Vowels, and Digraphs	**30** minutes

Practice	Search Sentences for Compound Words
	Match Compound Words
	Draw a Picture
	Finger Stretching
Sight Words	Review Sight Words
	Use Words in Sentences
Try It	Dictation: Write Sentences

[Online]	**REVIEW:** Sounds, Letters, Vowels, and Digraphs	**20** minutes

[Materials]

Supplied
- whiteboard, Learning Coach

Also Needed
- sight words box
- dictation notebook
- crayons
- index cards (26)

Advance Preparation

For Match Compound Words, print each of the following words on index cards, using one index card per word: *cat, nap, in, to, back, pack, up, hill, sun, tan, nut, shell, sun,* and *set.*

For Draw a Picture, print each of the following words on index cards, using one index card per word: *sunset, pigpen, bathtub, bathmat, cobweb, zigzag, hatbox, hilltop, backpack, bobcat, eggshell,* and *suntan.*

[Offline] 30 minutes

FOCUS: Sounds, Letters, Vowels, and Digraphs

Work **together** with students to complete offline Practice, Sight Words, and Try It activities.

Practice

Search Sentences for Compound Words

Help students recognize compound words in sentences.

1. Gather a pencil and the dictation notebook.

2. **Say:** I'm going to read some sentences. Listen for the compound word in the sentence.

   ► First repeat the sentence, and then tell me the compound word.
   ► For example, if I say the sentence, "My cat loves catnip," you will repeat the sentence and then say the word *catnip*, which is a compound word.
   ► Then you will write the compound word in your notebook, spelling one syllable at a time.

3. Read this sentence: *The pig is in the pigpen.*

   ► What word in the sentence is a compound word? *pigpen*
   ► Write the compound word, spelling one syllable at a time.

4. Follow the same procedure with the following words and sentences to help students recognize compound words:

   ► *We cannot go to the shop. cannot*
   ► *Stuff the mess in my backpack. backpack*
   ► *Put the hat in the hatbox. hatbox*

Match Compound Words

Help students practice making compound words.

1. Gather the index cards you prepared.

   ► Place the following words in one row: *cat, in, back, up, sun, nut,* and *sun.*
   ► Place the following words in another row under the first row: *nap, to, pack, hill, tan, shell,* and *set.*

2. **Say:** I'm going to make a compound word by matching a word from the top row with a word from the bottom row. The first word is [word from top row]. Now I'll find a word from the bottom row that makes this a compound word.

Objectives

• Identify and use compound words.

• Decode words by applying grade-level word analysis skills.

• Write words by applying grade-level phonics knowledge.

• Identify individual sounds in words.

3. **Say:** Now it's your turn. Choose a word in the top row. Next find a word in the bottom row that you can put with the first word to make a compound word.

4. If students do not understand the concept of compound words, give them the word *sun*. Then have them choose between the words *tan* and *hill*. Have them tell you which one, together with *sun*, makes a word they know.

5. Guide students who put together two words that do not make a compound word. Have them read the word aloud.

   Say: Does that word make sense, or is it a nonsense word?

6. Continue this procedure until students have used all the cards to make compound words.

Draw a Picture

Help students practice identifying compound words by having them draw pictures to match the word.

1. Gather the index cards you prepared.

2. **Say:** Let's read some more compound words.

   ► If you read it correctly the first time, put it in one stack.
   ► If a word takes you more than one try, put it in another stack.

3. Help students read the words from the stack of words that took them more than one try. Then have them select two words from this stack and draw a picture (in crayon) of each word on the back of the card.

(TIP) If students have trouble reading the words, have them break the word into syllables. Then help students finger stretch the sounds in each syllable.

Finger Stretching

Use finger stretching to help students identify individual sounds in words.

1. **Say:** Let's review finger stretching. In the word *and*, the first sound is the short vowel sound /ă/, the middle sound is /n/, and the last sound is /d/. I will finger stretch each sound as I say it. Then I'll say the word, while pulling my fist toward my body.

2. Finger stretch the word *and* for students.

3. **Say:** I'm going to say words with several sounds in them. You'll say the word and then finger stretch it while you say each sound in the word.

4. Say the following words and have students finger stretch them. After they finger stretch each word, ask them the question for that word.

- ▸ *zig* /z/ /ĭ/ /g/   What is the first sound? /z/
- ▸ *base* /b/ /ā/ /s/   What is the middle sound? /ā/
- ▸ *wide* /w/ /ī/ /d/   What is the vowel sound? /ī/
- ▸ *when* /w/ /ĕ/ /n/   What is the first sound? /w/
  What are the letters that make up the sound? *wh*
- ▸ *neat* /n/ /ē/ /t/   What is the middle sound? /ē/
- ▸ *buck* /b/ /ŭ/ /k/   What is the last sound? /k/
- ▸ *ship* /sh/ /ĭ/ /p/   What is the first sound? /sh/
  What are the letters that make up the sound? *sh*

TIP Refer to the *K¹² PhonicsWorks* DVD for a demonstration of finger stretching.

Sight Words

Review Sight Words

Help students learn to recognize sight words.

1. Gather all the sight word cards students have yet to master from their sight words box. Stack the cards on the table face down.

2. Have students pick up a word and read it to you.

3. If they read it quickly and correctly, put the card in one stack. If they hesitate or do not read the word correctly, put it in another stack. The second stack should have words that they will review again.

4. Take the stack of words that students read correctly and dictate each word to them. They may choose to either write the word or spell it aloud.

5. If students spell the word correctly, they have mastered the word. If they misspell the word, add it to the stack of cards to review again.

6. Chart students' progress on the back of each card.

- ▸ Divide the back of the card into two columns.
- ▸ Label the first column "Read" and the second column "Spell."
- ▸ Record the dates that students read or spell the word correctly. When students can read and spell the word correctly three times in a row, they have mastered the word. You may want to put a star or sticker on their card when they have mastered that word.

TIP Even if students can read and spell all the words correctly, it is still beneficial for students to review sight words. Choose as many additional words as you would like for each subsequent activity.

Objectives
- Read sight words.
- Write sight words.
- Spell sight words.

Use Words in Sentences

Help students use sight words in sentences.

1. Gather all the sight word cards students have yet to master from their sight words box. Spread the sight word cards on the table.

2. **Say:** Let's use sight words in sentences.

3. Have students

   ▸ Touch each card and read the word on it.
   ▸ Make up a sentence using the word.
   ▸ Put the card in a pile after using the word in a sentence.
   ▸ Go through the pile of cards and read each sight word again.
   ▸ Spell each word.

(TIP) If students have difficulty with any of the sight words, place those word cards in a pile to review later in the week.

Try It

Dictation: Write Sentences

Use sentences to help students identify individual sounds in words.

1. Gather a pencil and the dictation notebook. Say the sentence, *Mitch does not have his backpack.* Then give these directions to students:

   ▸ Repeat the sentence.
   ▸ Write the sentence in your notebook.
   ▸ Read the sentence aloud.

2. When students have finished, write the following sentence on your whiteboard: *Mitch does not have his backpack.*

3. Have them compare their answer to your correct version.

4. Repeat this procedure with the sentence, *Why were Mr. and Mrs. Tash up there?*

   ▸ If students make an error and don't see it, help them correct their mistake by having them finger stretch the sounds in the word they missed.
   ▸ If students are having difficulty selecting the correct letters or sounds, review those letters or sounds that are confusing them.
   ▸ If students have difficulty with first, middle, and last sounds, have them finger stretch the sounds in words.

> **Objectives**
> • Write words by applying grade-level phonics knowledge.
> • Write sight words.
> • Follow three-step directions.

[Online] ⓴ minutes

REVIEW: **Sounds, Letters, Vowels, and Digraphs**

Students will work online independently to

▸ Practice identifying and using sounds, letters, vowels, digraphs, and compound words.

Help students locate the online activities and provide support as needed.

___

Offline Alternative

No computer access? Have students point out and name things or words that contain the short vowel sounds /ă/, /ĕ/, /ĭ/, /ŏ/, and /u/; digraphs *wh* and *ck*; and the trigraph *tch* (example vowel sounds: *actor*, *elbow*, *itch*, *fog*, and *ugly*; example digraphs: *while*, *whim*, and *thick*; example trigraphs: *patch*, *fetch*). Have students practice compound words by taking turns naming and spelling compound words. You might also provide one syllable of a compound word and have students provide the missing syllable. (For example, if you say *base*, students might add *ball* to make *baseball*.)

Unit Checkpoint

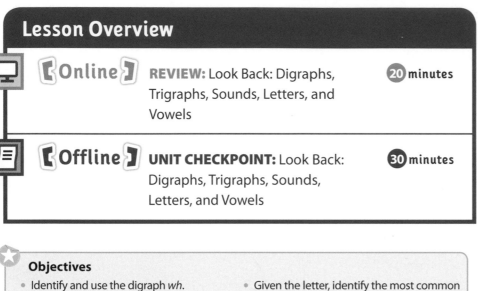

Lesson Overview

🖥	**⟦Online⟧**	**REVIEW:** Look Back: Digraphs, Trigraphs, Sounds, Letters, and Vowels	**20** minutes
📄	**⟦Offline⟧**	**UNIT CHECKPOINT:** Look Back: Digraphs, Trigraphs, Sounds, Letters, and Vowels	**30** minutes

⟦Materials⟧

Supplied

- *K¹² PhonicsWorks Advanced Assessments,* pp. PH 19–24

⭐ Objectives

- Identify and use the digraph *wh*.
- Identify and use the digraph *ck*.
- Identify and use the trigraph *tch*.
- Identify and use compound words.
- Identify individual sounds in words.
- Given the sound, identify the most common letter or letters.
- Given the letter, identify the most common sound.
- Read sight words.
- Write sight words.
- Spell sight words.
- Read aloud grade-level text with appropriate automaticity, prosody, accuracy, and rate.

⟦Online⟧ **20** minutes

REVIEW: Look Back: Digraphs, Trigraphs, Sounds, Letters, and Vowels

Students will review digraphs, trigraphs, sounds, letters, and vowels to prepare for the Unit Checkpoint. Help students locate the online activities and provide support as needed.

[Offline] ⏱ 30 minutes

UNIT CHECKPOINT: Look Back: Digraphs, Trigraphs, Sounds, Letters, and Vowels

Explain that students are going to show what they have learned about letters, sounds, and words.

1. Give students the Unit Checkpoint pages for the Look Back: Digraphs, Trigraphs, Sounds, Letters, and Vowels unit and print the Unit Checkpoint Answer Key, if you'd like.

2. Use the instructions below to help administer the Checkpoint to students. On the Answer Key or another sheet of paper, note student answers to oral response questions to help with scoring the Checkpoint later.

3. Use the Answer Key to score the Checkpoint, and then enter the results online.

Part 1. Read Words and Word Parts Moving left to right, have students say the sound of each word or word part. Note any words or word parts they say incorrectly.

Part 2. Finger Stretching Say each word to students. Have them say each word aloud and finger stretch the sounds. Note any words they finger stretch incorrectly.

13. *pitch*   15. *thatch*

14. *check*   16. *which*

Part 3. Dictation Say each word to students. Have them repeat and write the word.

17. *chums*   21. *riches*

18. *that*   22. *sacks*

19. *mashes*   23. *dutch*

20. *whip*   24. *shag*

Part 4. Writing Read each sentence to students. Have them repeat and write the sentence.

25. *She patches the hatbox.*

26. *Zack ran uphill so quick.*

27. *He cannot match them.*

Part 5. Read Aloud Listen to students read each sentence aloud. Note any words students read incorrectly.

Part 6. Say Letters Say each sound. Have students say the letter or letters that make that sound. Note any incorrect responses.

33. /ks/

34. /ch/

35. /d/

36. /sh/

37. /th/

38. /w/

39. /ŏ/

40. /ŭ/

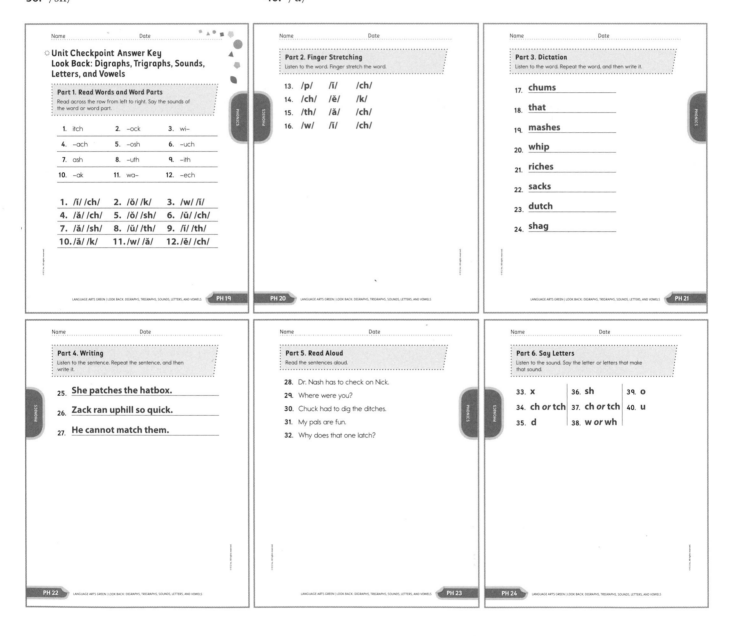

Name   Date

☼ **Unit Checkpoint Answer Key**
Look Back: Digraphs, Trigraphs, Sounds, Letters, and Vowels

Part 1. Read Words and Word Parts
Read across the row from left to right. Say the sounds of the word or word part.

1. itch	2. –ock	3. wi–
4. –ach	5. –osh	6. –uch
7. ash	8. –uth	9. –ith
10. –ak	11. wa–	12. –ech

1. /ĭ/ /ch/	2. /ŏ/ /k/	3. /w/ /ĭ/
4. /ă/ /ch/	5. /ŏ/ /sh/	6. /ŭ/ /ch/
7. /ă/ /sh/	8. /ŭ/ /th/	9. /ĭ/ /th/
10. /ă/ /k/	11. /w/ /ă/	12. /ĕ/ /ch/

LANGUAGE ARTS GREEN | LOOK BACK: DIGRAPHS, TRIGRAPHS, SOUNDS, LETTERS, AND VOWELS   **PH 19**

Name   Date

Part 2. Finger Stretching
Listen to the word. Finger stretch the word.

13. /p/   /ĭ/   /ch/
14. /ch/   /ĕ/   /k/
15. /th/   /ă/   /ch/
16. /w/   /ĭ/   /ch/

PH 20   LANGUAGE ARTS GREEN | LOOK BACK: DIGRAPHS, TRIGRAPHS, SOUNDS, LETTERS, AND VOWELS

Name   Date

Part 3. Dictation
Listen to the word. Repeat the word, and then write it.

17. chums
18. that
19. mashes
20. whip
21. riches
22. sacks
23. dutch
24. shag

LANGUAGE ARTS GREEN | LOOK BACK: DIGRAPHS, TRIGRAPHS, SOUNDS, LETTERS, AND VOWELS   **PH 21**

Name   Date

Part 4. Writing
Listen to the sentence. Repeat the sentence, and then write it.

25. **She patches the hatbox.**
26. **Zack ran uphill so quick.**
27. **He cannot match them.**

PH 22   LANGUAGE ARTS GREEN | LOOK BACK: DIGRAPHS, TRIGRAPHS, SOUNDS, LETTERS, AND VOWELS

Name   Date

Part 5. Read Aloud
Read the sentences aloud.

28. Dr. Nash has to check on Nick.
29. Where were you?
30. Chuck had to dig the ditches.
31. My pals are fun.
32. Why does that one latch?

PH 23   LANGUAGE ARTS GREEN | LOOK BACK: DIGRAPHS, TRIGRAPHS, SOUNDS, LETTERS, AND VOWELS

Name   Date

Part 6. Say Letters
Listen to the sound. Say the letter or letters that make that sound.

33. **x**	36. **sh**	39. **o**
34. **ch** *or* **tch**	37. **ch** *or* **tch**	40. **u**
35. **d**	38. **w** *or* **wh**	

PH 24   LANGUAGE ARTS GREEN | LOOK BACK: DIGRAPHS, TRIGRAPHS, SOUNDS, LETTERS, AND VOWELS

Ending Consonant Blend –nd

Unit Overview

In this unit, students will
- ► Identify the ending consonant blends –nd, –ft, –lk, and –ct.
- ► Review the letters of the alphabet.
- ► Learn digraph endings.
- ► Build words.
- ► Identify beginning, middle, and ending sounds in words.
- ► Learn sight words.

Lesson Overview

[Offline] FOCUS: Ending Consonant Blend –nd **30** minutes

Sight Words	Introduce Sight Words
Get Ready	Signal Ending Sounds
	Create Rhyming Words
Learn	Introduce the Ending Consonant Blend –nd
	Make More Words
Try It	New Beginnings
	Dictation: Write Sentences

[Online] REVIEW: Ending Consonant Blend –nd **20** minutes

Big Ideas
- ► Phonics is an integral part of a core, comprehensive reading program.
- ► In a consonant blend, each letter keeps its sound as the two sounds blend together.

Materials

Supplied
- *K¹² PhonicsWorks Advanced Activity Book*, p. PH 9
- whiteboard, Learning Coach
- whiteboard, student
- Tile Kit

Also Needed
- sight words box
- dictation notebook

Keywords

nonsense words – words that are phonetically decodable but carry no meaning; *Example:* The word *rog* carries no meaning, but it can be decoded: /r/, /ŏ/, /g/ rhymes with *dog*.

phonics – study of sounds and the letters that represent them

 **30** minutes

FOCUS: Ending Consonant Blend *–nd*

Work **together** with students to complete offline Sight Words, Get Ready, Learn, and Try It activities.

Sight Words

Introduce Sight Words

Help students learn the sight words *too*, *walk*, and *talk*.

1. Gather the sight word cards *too*, *walk*, and *talk*.

2. Show students the *too* card.

3. **Say:** This is the word *too*, as in "I ate too much candy!" We see this word so often that we want to be able to read and spell it quickly without thinking about it. Look closely at the word *too*. Spell the word *too* aloud. Take a picture of the word *too* in your mind. When you think you can spell *too* yourself, turn the card over and use your letter tiles to spell the word *too*. Check the card to see if you spelled the word *too* correctly. Read aloud the word you spelled with the letter tiles.

4. Repeat the activity with the remaining sight words.

5. Chart students' progress on the back of each card.

   ▸ Divide the back of the card into two columns.
   ▸ Label the first column "Read" and the second column "Spell."
   ▸ Record the dates that students read or spell the word correctly. When students can read and spell the word correctly three times in a row, they have mastered the word. You may want to put a star or sticker on their card when they have mastered that word.

6. Add the cards to students' sight words box.

TIP Sight words can be very difficult for some students. It's important to let students work at their own pace and really master these words, as they occur frequently in reading and writing.

TIP Students may notice that the letters *–lk* can sometimes look like a blend, but are not pronounced like one. **If students struggle with this**, have them finger stretch the sounds in the words *walk*, *talk*, *milk*, and *silk*. Point out that the words *walk* and *talk* have three sounds—the beginning sound, the middle sound /aw/, and the ending sound /k/. The *a* and the *l* work together to make the single sound /aw/. But the words *milk* and *silk* have four sounds—the beginning sound, the sound /ĭ/, the sound /l/, and the sound /k/. The letters *l* and *k* each say their own sound, making *–lk* a blend.

Objectives
• Read sight words.
• Spell sight words.

Get Ready

Signal Ending Sounds

Use a special signal to help students identify **ending sounds** in words.

1. **Say:** I'm going to tell you a sound, and then I'll say some words. Repeat each word I say and make a special signal to tell me where the sound is. If the special sound is at the end of the word, clap your hands. If the special sound is not at the end of the word, just smile at me. For example,

   ▸ If I ask you to listen for /s/ and I say the word *laughs*, you'll repeat the word *laughs* and clap your hands because *laughs* has the sound /s/ at the end.
   ▸ If I say the word *drum*, you'll repeat the word *drum* and smile at me because *drum* has the sound /m/, not /s/, at the end.

2. Say each sound and group of words. Have students make the special signal to identify the ending sound.

   ▸ /d/: *sad, send, bend, act, left* clap: *sad, send, bend*
   ▸ /n/: *rat, main, fun, sell, raft* clap: *main, fun*
   ▸ /l/: *mall, fill, sleep, gift, will* clap: *mall, fill, will*
   ▸ /z/: *jazz, buzz, find, fizz, round* clap: *jazz, buzz, fizz*

3. Redirect students if they name the sound incorrectly.

   Say: That is the sound of another letter. Think about the sound you hear at the end of each word.

Create Rhyming Words

Have students combine word parts and make words that rhyme.

1. **Say:** I'm going to break a word into two parts. Your job is to put the parts back together and say the word. For example, if the first part of the word is /j/ and the last part is /ill/, then you say *Jill*: /j/ . . . /ill/ . . . *Jill*.

2. **Say:** Next you'll add a new **beginning sound** to make a word that rhymes. For example, you'll use the same last part, /ill/, and add a new first sound, like /w/. The rhyming word is *will*.

3. Say the two word parts. Have students say the word the parts form. Have students add a new beginning sound to the last part of the word and make a rhyming word. Continue with this procedure until students have made all the words in the list.

   ▸ /w/ . . . /ill/ *will*; Possible rhyming words: *bill, pill, mill, fill*
   ▸ /r/ . . . /ift/ *rift*; Possible rhyming words: *sift, lift, gift*

Learn ••

Introduce the Ending Consonant Blend –nd

Help students recognize and use the ending consonant blend –nd.

1. Place the following letter tiles at the top of students' whiteboard: *a, b, d, e, i, n, s,* and *sh*.

2. Make the word *dish* and point to it.

3. **Say:** Touch and say this word.

    ▶ How many sounds are in the word? three
    ▶ How many letters are in the word? four
    ▶ The sound /sh/ at the end of this word has two letters but only one sound.

4. Make the word *and* and point to it.

5. **Say:** Touch and say the sounds in *and*.

    ▶ How many sounds are in the word? three
    ▶ How many letters are in the word? three
    ▶ We know that the *n* and *d* at the end of this word are called a **blend** because each letter keeps its own sound while the two sounds blend together.
    ▶ Where is the blend? at the end

6. Redirect students if they have difficulty with the consonant blend –nd.

    Say: The two letters *n* and *d* are often together at the end of a word. When they are together, they blend into the sounds /nd/, as in *band*. Can you say the word *band*? When you say *band*, don't stop between the last two sounds, /n/ and /d/. Try saying the word again.

7. Make the word *sand* and point to it.

8. **Say:** Touch and say the sounds in *sand*.

    ▶ How many sounds are in the word? four
    ▶ How many letters are in the word? four
    ▶ Where is the blend? at the end

9. Use the same procedure for the word *bend*.

10. Provide additional guidance if students have difficulty with blends. Take the last letter off the word students are struggling with.

    Say: I have taken the last letter off this word. Touch and say the word without the last sound. What sound do you make at the end of the word? Answers will vary.
    Say: Now I am going to put the last letter back on the word. Touch and say. Now what is the sound you make at the end of the word? What two sounds are heard in the blend at the end of the word? Answers will vary.

Objectives

- Identify and use the blend –*nd*.
- Identify ending sounds in words.
- Identify the number of sounds within words.
- Identify the new word when one sound is added to a word.

Make More Words

Have students make new words by adding and removing letters from words to make new words.

1. Place the following letters randomly on the bottom of students' whiteboard: *b, h, l, r, s, v,* and *z*.

2. Build the word *and* in the center of the board, with room to add a letter in front.

3. **Say:** When I put the letter *s* before the word *and*, I make the word *sand*. See how many new **real words** you can make by putting the letters on your whiteboard before the letters *and. land, hand, band*

4. **Say:** See how many **nonsense words** you can make. Answers will vary.

5. Repeat this activity with the word endings *end* and *–ond*.

Try It

New Beginnings

Have students complete page PH 9 in *K¹² PhonicsWorks Advanced Activity Book* for more practice making words that end with *–and* and *–ond*. First have students say the name of each picture and circle the beginning letter that completes the word. Then have students write the letter and read the word aloud.

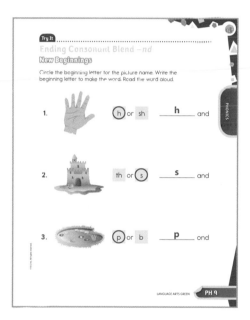

Objectives
- Identify and use the blend *–nd*.
- Read, write, and spell words containing the blend *–nd*.
- Write words by applying grade-level phonics knowledge.
- Write sight words.
- Follow three-step directions.

Dictation: Write Sentences

Use sentences to help students identify individual sounds in words.

1. Gather a pencil and the dictation notebook. Say the sentence, *We can run.* Then give these directions to students:

   ▸ Repeat the sentence.
   ▸ Write the sentence in your notebook.
   ▸ Read the sentence aloud.

2. When students have finished, write the following on your whiteboard:
   We can run.

3. Have them compare their answer to your correct version.

4. Repeat this procedure with the sentence, *Pam and Sam land.*

   ▸ If students make an error and don't see it, help them correct their mistake by having them finger stretch the sounds in the word they missed.
   ▸ If students are having difficulty selecting the correct letters or sounds, review those letters or sounds that are confusing them.
   ▸ If students have difficulty with first, middle, and last sounds, have them finger stretch the sounds in words.

 **20 minutes**

REVIEW: Ending Consonant Blend –*nd*

Students will work online independently to

▸ Practice the ending consonant blend –*nd*.
▸ Practice decoding text by reading a story.

Help students locate the online activities and provide support as needed.

Offline Alternative

No computer access? Have students point out and name things or words that contain the ending sound /nd/ (for example, *bend* or *pond*). You might also ask students to spell words that contain the ending consonant blend –*nd*.

> **Objectives**
>
> • Identify and use the blend –*nd*.
>
> • Identify ending sounds in words.
>
> • Read aloud grade-level text with appropriate automaticity, prosody, accuracy, and rate.
>
> • Decode words by applying grade-level word analysis skills.

Ending Consonant Blend –*ft*

Lesson Overview

Offline FOCUS: Ending Consonant Blend –*ft* **30** minutes

Sight Words	Sight Word Fun
Get Ready	Review Letter Names and Sounds
	Pairs of Ending Sounds
Learn	Introduce the Ending Consonant Blend –*ft*
	Word Chains
Try It	"Pat and Mr. Kim"

Online REVIEW: Ending Consonant Blend –*ft* **20** minutes

Advance Preparation

Place lowercase letter tiles in alphabetical order on your whiteboard.

Big Ideas

- Decoding occurs when one applies letter-sound knowledge in order to decipher printed words on a page.
- Students must decode automatically to become fluent readers.

[Offline] 🕥 minutes

FOCUS: Ending Consonant Blend –*ft*

Work **together** with students to complete offline Sight Words, Get Ready, Learn, and Try It activities.

Sight Words ··

Sight Word Fun

Help students learn the sight words *too*, *walk*, and *talk*, and up to two additional sight words they have yet to master.

1. Gather the sight word cards *too*, *walk*, and *talk*, and up to two additional sight word cards.

2. Choose one sight word card to begin.

   Say: Look at this word and take a picture of it in your mind. When you think you can spell the word yourself, turn the card over and use your letter tiles to spell the word.

3. After students spell the word, have them check the card to see if they spelled the word correctly.

   Say: Read aloud the word you spelled with the letter tiles.

4. Repeat the activity with the remaining sight words.

TIP Sight words can be very difficult for some students. Let them work at their own pace and really master these words.

> **Objectives**
> * Read sight words.
> * Spell sight words.

Get Ready ··

Review Letter Names and Sounds

To help students learn the sounds and letters of the alphabet, have them practice identifying and naming letters and sounds. Grab your whiteboard with letters placed in alphabetical order.

1. **Say:** All the letters of the alphabet are here. Say the name of each **consonant** you see. Touch the letter and say the sound it makes.

2. Redirect students if they name a letter incorrectly.

   ▸ Name the letter students missed.
   ▸ Have students touch the letter and say its name.
   ▸ Have students trace the shape of the letter with their finger on the brown side of their board, and have them say the letter's name as they trace the shape.
   ▸ If students name a letter incorrectly twice, point to the letter and tell them its name. Have them touch the letter and say its name.

> **Objectives**
> * Identify letters of the alphabet.
> * Identify ending sounds in words.

3. Help students if they name the sound incorrectly.

   Say: That is the sound for the letter [letter]. We are looking for the sound made by the letter [target letter].

Pairs of Ending Sounds

Help students recognize the difference between words that end with one sound or two sounds.

1. **Say:** Digraphs are two letters that make one sound. A blend is two letters, each of which keeps its own sound.

2. **Say:** I am going to say a pair of words. Repeat the pair of words I say and listen for the ending sounds. One word will end with a single digraph sound and the other will end with a consonant blend that has two sounds. When you hear a word with one ending sound, clap once. When you hear a word with two sounds that blend at the end, clap twice. For example,

   ▸ I will say *dish* and *pond*.
   ▸ You will repeat the word *dish* and clap once, since the word *dish* has one ending sound, /sh/.
   ▸ Then you will repeat the word *pond* and clap twice, since the word *pond* has two ending sounds, /n/ and /d/.

3. **Say:** Now it's your turn. The first pair of words is *wish* and *sand*. Students should repeat the words *wish* and *sand,* clapping once for *wish* and twice for *sand.*

   ▸ Which word has a blend? *sand*
   ▸ What two sounds make up the blend? /n/, /d/

4. Repeat Step 3 with the following pairs of words. Enunciate the words very clearly, pronouncing both sounds in the consonant blend words. Have students watch your mouth as you do so.

   ▸ *lend* and *sack lend,* /n/, /d/
   ▸ *bond* and *much bond,* /n/, /d/
   ▸ *rash* and *send send,* /n/, /d/

Learn

Introduce the Ending Consonant Blend –ft

Help students recognize and use the ending consonant blend –ft.

1. Place the following letters on students' whiteboard: *a, d, e, f, i, l, n,* and *t.*

2. Make the word *and* and point to it.

3. **Say:** Touch and say this word.

   ▸ How many sounds are in the word? three
   ▸ How many letters are in the word? three
   ▸ We know that letters *n* and *d* at the end of this word are called a blend because each of those letters keeps its own sound while the two sounds blend together.

4. Make the word *lift* and point to it.

5. **Say:** Touch and say the sounds in *lift.*

   ▸ How many sounds are in the word? four
   ▸ How many letters are in the word? fo ur
   ▸ Where is the blend? at the end
   ▸ We know that the letters *f* and *t* at the end of this word are called a blend because each of those letters keeps its own sound while the two sounds blend together.

6. Redirect students if they have difficulty with the consonant blend –ft.

   Say: The two letters *f* and *t* are often together at the end of a word. When they are together, they blend into the sounds /ft/, as in *loft.* Can you say the word *loft*? When you say *loft,* don't stop between the last two sounds, /f/ and /t/. Try saying the word again.

7. Make the word *left* and point to it.

8. **Say:** Touch and say the sounds in *left.*

   ▸ How many sounds are in the word? four
   ▸ How many letters are in the word? four
   ▸ Where is the blend? at the end

9. Follow the same procedure for the word *raft.*

10. Provide additional guidance to students who continue to have difficulty with blends. Take the last letter off the word students are struggling with.

    Say: I have taken the last letter off this word. Touch and say the word without the last sound. What sound do you make at the end of the word? Answers will vary.

    Say: Now I am going to put the last letter back on the word. Touch and say. Now what is the sound you make at the end of the word? What two sounds are heard in the blend at the end of the word? Answers will vary.

Objectives

- Identify and use the blend –ft.
- Identify ending sounds in words.
- Identify the number of sounds within words.
- Identify individual sounds in words.
- Identify the new word when one sound is added to a word.
- Identify the new word when one sound is changed in a word.

Word Chains

Have students build words by adding and changing letters to help them recognize and use individual sounds in words.

1. Place the following letters randomly at the top of students' whiteboard: *f, g, i, l, s,* and *t.*

2. **Say:** I am going to build the first word in a chain. The word is *if.*

   ▸ I will pull down the letters for the sounds /ĭ/ and /f/ to spell the word *if.*

   ▸ I will touch and say *if.* To change *if* to *ift,* I will think about what sound is added from the word *if* to *ift.* I will need to add the letter *t* to the end of the word *if.*

   ▸ Touch and say the word *ift. Ift* is a nonsense word. Let's make it a real word. Change *ift* to *lift.* You can spell *lift* by making only one change. Touch and say the new word.

3. Redirect students if they select the incorrect letter for any sound.

   Say: That letter is for the sound [incorrect sound]. We want the letter for the sound [target sound]. What letter makes that sound? Answers will vary.

4. Redirect students if they name the sound incorrectly.

   Say: To change the word [first word] to [target word], we need the letter for the sound.

   Show students how to make the change. Have them touch and say the new word after they move the letters.

5. Follow this procedure to make the following words: *gift* and *sift.*

6. For every new word, have students add, replace, or remove only one letter.

TIP If students struggle, review the sounds and letters that are confusing them.

Try It

"Pat and Mr. Kim"
Have students read "Pat and Mr. Kim" on page 1 of *K¹² PhonicsWorks Readers Advanced 1.*

   Students should read the story silently once or twice before reading the story aloud. When students miss a word that can be sounded out, point to it and give them three to six seconds to try the word again. If students still miss the word, tell them the word so the flow of the story isn't interrupted.

   After reading the story, make a list of all the words students missed, and go over those words with them. You may use letter tiles to show students how to read the words.

Objectives
- Read aloud grade-level text with appropriate automaticity, prosody, accuracy, and rate.
- Decode words by applying grade-level word analysis skills.

 **20 minutes**

REVIEW: Ending Consonant Blend *–ft*

Students will work online independently to

▸ Practice the ending consonant blend *–ft*.

Help students locate the online activities and provide support as needed.

Offline Alternative

No computer access? Have students point out and name things or words that contain the ending sound /ft/ (for example, *raft* or *left*). You might also ask students to spell words that contain the ending consonant blend *–ft*.

Ending Consonant Blend –*lk*

Lesson Overview

[Offline] FOCUS: Ending Consonant Blend –*lk* ⏱ 30 minutes

Sight Words	Sight Word Fun
Get Ready	Finger Stretching
Learn	Introduce the Ending Consonant Blend –*lk*
	Build Words
	Word Chains
Try It	Best Pick

[Online] REVIEW: Ending Consonant Blend –*lk* ⏱ 20 minutes

[Materials]

Supplied
- *K¹² PhonicsWorks Advanced Activity Book*, p. PH 10
- whiteboard, student
- Tile Kit

Also Needed
- sight words box

 **30** minutes

FOCUS: Ending Consonant Blend –*lk*

Work **together** with students to complete offline Sight Words, Get Ready, Learn, and Try It activities.

Sight Words

Sight Word Fun

Help students learn the sight words *too*, *walk*, and *talk*, and up to two additional sight words they have yet to master.

1. Gather the sight word cards *too*, *walk*, and *talk*, and up to two additional sight word cards.

2. Choose one sight word card to begin.

   Say: Look at this word and take a picture of it in your mind. When you think you can spell the word yourself, turn the card over and use your letter tiles to spell the word.

3. After students spell the word, have them check the card to see if they spelled the word correctly.

   Say: Read aloud the word you spelled with the letter tiles.

4. Repeat the activity with the remaining sight words.

TIP Sight words can be very difficult for some students. Let them work at their own pace and really master these words.

> **Objectives**
> - Read sight words.
> - Spell sight words.

Get Ready

Finger Stretching

Use finger stretching to help students identify individual sounds in words.

1. **Say:** Let's review finger stretching. In the word *mend*, the first sound is /m/, the next sound is /ĕ/, the third sound is /n/, and the last sound is /d/. I will finger stretch each sound as I say it. Then I'll say the word, while pulling my fist toward my body.

2. Finger stretch the word *mend*.

3. **Say:** I'm going to say words with several sounds in them. You'll say each word and then finger stretch it while you say each sound in the word.

> **Objectives**
> - Identify individual sounds in words.
> - Identify the number of sounds within words.

4. Say the following words and have students finger stretch them. After they finger stretch each word, ask them the question for that word.

- ▸ *rack* /r/ /ă/ /k/   How many sounds? three
- ▸ *pill* /p/ /ĭ/ /l/   How many sounds? three
- ▸ *gift* /g/ /ĭ/ /f/ /t/   How many sounds? four
- ▸ *fan* /f/ /ă/ /n/   How many sounds? three
- ▸ *band* /b/ /ă/ /n/ /d/   How many sounds? four
- ▸ *lift* /l/ /ĭ/ /f/ /t/   How many sounds? four
- ▸ *wax* /w/ /ă/ /ks/   How many sounds? three

TIP Refer to the *K¹² PhonicsWorks* DVD for a demonstration of finger stretching.

Learn

Introduce the Ending Consonant Blend *–lk*

Help students recognize and use the ending consonant blend *–lk*.

1. Place the following letters on students' whiteboard: *a, b, d, f, i, k, l, m, n, o, r, s,* and *t*.

2. Make the word *bond* and point to it.

3. **Say:** Touch and say this word.

   - ▸ How many sounds are in the word? four
   - ▸ How many letters are in the word? four
   - ▸ We know that letters *n* and *d* at the end of this word are called a blend because each of those letters keeps its own sound, while the two sounds blend together.

4. Make the word *raft* and point to it.

5. **Say:** Touch and say the sounds in *raft*.

   - ▸ How many sounds are in the word? four
   - ▸ How many letters are in the word? four
   - ▸ Where is the blend? at the end
   - ▸ We know that the letters *f* and *t* at the end of this word are called a blend because each of those letters keeps its own sound while the two sounds blend together.

6. Make the word *milk* and point to it.

7. **Say:** Touch and say the sounds in *milk*.

   - ▸ How many sounds are in the word? four
   - ▸ How many letters are in the word? four
   - ▸ Where is the blend? at the end

8. Redirect students if they have difficulty with the consonant blend *–lk*.

   Say: The letters *l* and *k* are often together at the end of a word. When they are together, sometimes they blend into the sound /lk/, as in *silk*. Can you say the word *silk*? When you say *silk*, don't stop between the last two sounds, /l/ and /k/. Try saying the word again.

9. Follow the same procedure for the words *silk* and *bulk*.

Objectives

- Identify and use the blend *–lk*.
- Identify ending sounds in words.
- Identify the number of sounds within words.
- Identify individual sounds in words.
- Identify the new word when one sound is added to a word.
- Identify the new word when one sound is changed in a word.

Build Words

Help students use letters and sounds to build words.

1. Place the following lowercase letter tiles in the order given at the top of students' whiteboard: *b, i, k, m, l, s,* and *u.*

2. Draw four horizontal lines across the middle of students' whiteboard to represent the sounds in a word.

3. **Say:** Let's use letters and sounds to build the word *milk.*

4. Have students finger stretch the sounds in *milk.*

5. Have students

   ▸ Identify the sounds in *milk.*
   ▸ Choose the corresponding letter for each of the sounds.
   ▸ Move the letters to the correct lines on their whiteboard.

6. Guide students with these questions:

   ▸ What is the first sound in *milk*? /m/
     Which line does the letter for that sound go on? the first one
   ▸ What is the next sound in *milk*? /ĭ/
     Which line does the letter for that sound go on? the second one
   ▸ What is the next sound in *milk*? /l/
     Which line does the letter for that sound go on? the third one
   ▸ What's the last sound in *milk*? /k/
     Which line does the letter for that sound go on? the last one

7. Have students touch and say the word.

8. Repeat the activity to build the following words: *bulk* and *silk.* /b/ /ŭ/ /l/ /k/ and /s/ /ĭ/ /l/ /k/

Word Chains

Have students build words by adding and changing letters.

1. Place the following letters at the top of students' whiteboard: *b, e, k, l, n,* and *s.*

2. **Say:** I am going to build the first nonsense word in a chain. The word is *el.*

   ▸ I will pull down the letters for the sounds /ĕ/ and /l/ to spell the word *el.*
   ▸ I will touch and say *el.* To change *el* to *elk,* I will think about what sound is added from the word *el* to *elk.* I will need to add the letter *k* at the end of the word *el.*
   ▸ Touch and say the word *elk.* Now it's your turn to change *elk* to the nonsense word *selk.* You can spell *selk* by making only one change. Touch and say the new word.

3. Redirect students if they select the incorrect letter for any sound.

   Say: That letter is for the sound [incorrect sound]. We want the letter for the sound [target sound]. What letter makes that sound? Answers will vary.

4. Redirect students if they name the sound incorrectly.

   Say: To change the word [first word] to [target word], we need the letter for the sound.

5. Follow this procedure to make the following words: *belk* and *nelk*.

6. For every new word, have students add, replace, or remove only one letter.

Try It

Best Pick

Have students complete page PH 10 in *K¹² PhonicsWorks Advanced Activity Book* for more practice with words that end with consonant blends. Have them read the sentence aloud and circle the word that best completes it. Then have students write the word and read the completed sentence aloud to determine if it makes sense.

Objectives
- Identify and use the blend –*lk*.
- Identify ending sounds in words.
- Read aloud grade-level text with appropriate automaticity, prosody, accuracy, and rate.

[Online] 🔟 20 minutes

REVIEW: Ending Consonant Blend –*lk*

Students will work online independently to

▸ Practice the ending consonant blend –*lk*.

▸ Practice decoding text by reading a story.

Help students locate the online activities and provide support as needed.

Offline Alternative

No computer access? Have students point out and name things or words that contain the ending sound /lk/ (for example, *hulk* or *folk*). You might also ask students to spell words that contain the ending consonant blend –*lk*.

Objectives
- Identify and use the blend –*lk*.
- Identify ending sounds in words.
- Read aloud grade-level text with appropriate automaticity, prosody, accuracy, and rate.
- Decode words by applying grade-level word analysis skills.

Ending Consonant Blend *–ct*

Lesson Overview

[Offline] FOCUS: Ending Consonant Blend *–ct* — 30 minutes

Sight Words	Sight Word Fun
Get Ready	Sort Ending Blend Sounds
Learn	Introduce the Ending Consonant Blend *–ct*
	Word Chains
Try It	"Jon and Jad"

[Online] REVIEW: Ending Consonant Blend *–ct* — 20 minutes

Materials

Supplied
- *K¹² PhonicsWorks Readers Advanced 1*, pp. 7–12
- whiteboard, student
- Tile Kit

Also Needed
- sight words box

Advance Preparation

Before students read "Jon and Jad," explain to them that the word *chalk* rhymes with the words *walk* and *talk*. If necessary, write all three words on students' whiteboard and have students identify each word.

 **30 minutes**

FOCUS: Ending Consonant Blend –ct

Work **together** with students to complete offline Sight Words, Get Ready, Learn, and Try It activities.

Sight Words

Sight Word Fun

Help students learn the sight words *too*, *walk*, and *talk*, and up to two additional sight words they have yet to master.

1. Gather the sight word cards *too*, *walk*, and *talk*, and up to two additional sight word cards.

2. Choose one sight word card to begin.

   Say: Look at this word and take a picture of it in your mind. When you think you can spell the word yourself, turn the card over and use your letter tiles to spell the word.

3. After students spell the word, have them check the card to see if they spelled the word correctly.

   Say: Read aloud the word you spelled with the letter tiles.

4. Repeat the activity with the remaining sight words.

   (TIP) Sight words can be very difficult for some students. Let them work at their own pace and really master these words.

> **Objectives**
> * Read sight words.
> * Spell sight words.

Get Ready

Sort Ending Blend Sounds

Have students practice making words by adding letters in front of ending consonant blends.

1. At the top of students' whiteboard, set up the blend tiles *ft*, *lk*, and *nd* as headings with room to add beginning letters to form words.

2. Under the blends, randomly place the following letter tiles: *a*, *e*, *g*, *i*, *l*, *m*, *o*, *r*, and *s*.

3. **Say:** I'm going to say some words to you. You will repeat the words after me and find the letters on your whiteboard that make the **ending sounds** and **beginning sounds** of the word. For example,

   ▸ If I say the word *sand*, you would say *sand*, find the letters that make the ending sound /nd/ on your whiteboard, and point to those letters.
   ▸ Then you will find the letters that make the sounds /s/ and /ă/, and move them in front of the letters *n* and *d* to make the word *sand*.
   ▸ Finally I want you to touch and say the word by saying each sound while running a finger under the word from the first letter to the last letter. Now you try it.

> **Objectives**
> * Identify ending sounds in words.
> * Identify beginning sounds in words.
> * Identify the new word when one sound is added to a word.

4. Use the following words. Pronounce the words very clearly, making sure that you pronounce both ending sounds in the consonant blend words. Have students watch your mouth as you do so.

   ▶ *land*
   ▶ *milk*
   ▶ *gift*
   ▶ *elk*
   ▶ *send*
   ▶ *left*
   ▶ *soft*
   ▶ *raft*
   ▶ *silk*

5. Have students use finger stretching if they form a word incorrectly.

   Say: Let's say the word, and then finger stretch the sounds in the word together. Now you try to finger stretch the sounds in that word. Look for the letter that makes each of the sounds we finger stretched, beginning with the first sound.

6. Redirect students if they are confused. Remove all of the letters from the board except for the ones forming the first word, *land*. Place the letters together to make *land*. Have students touch and say the letters that make the sounds for *land*.

   ▶ If students continue to be confused, scramble the letters on their whiteboard, placing the blend *nd* at the top of the whiteboard. Then go through the steps of the activity above, letting them show you how the sounds go together to form the word *land*.

Learn

Introduce the Ending Consonant Blend –*ct*
Help students recognize and use the ending consonant blend –*ct*.

1. Place the following letters on students' whiteboard: *a, c, d, f, i, k, l, n, p, s,* and *t*.

2. Make the word *land* and point to it.

3. **Say:** Touch and say this word.

   ▶ How many sounds are in the word? four
   ▶ How many letters are in the word? four
   ▶ We know that the letters *n* and *d* at the end of this word are called a blend because each of those letters keeps its own sound while the two sounds blend together.

4. Make the word *sift* and point to it.

Objectives
- Identify and use the blend –*ct*.
- Identify ending sounds in words.
- Identify the number of sounds within words.
- Identify the new word when one sound is added to a word.
- Identify the new word when one sound is changed in a word.

5. **Say:** Touch and say the sounds in *sift*.

   ▸ How many sounds are in the word? four
   ▸ How many letters are in the word? four
   ▸ Where is the blend? at the end
   ▸ We know that the letters *f* and *t* at the end of this word are called a blend because each of those letters keeps its own sound while the two sounds blend together.

6. Make the word *silk* and point to it.

7. **Say:** Touch and say the sounds in *silk*.

   ▸ How many sounds are in the word? four
   ▸ How many letters are in the word? four
   ▸ Where is the blend? at the end

8. Make the word *act* and point to it.

9. **Say:** Touch and say the sounds in *act*.

   ▸ How many sounds are in the word? three
   ▸ How many letters are in the word? three
   ▸ Where is the blend? at the end
   ▸ We know that the letters *c* and *t* at the end of this word are called a blend because each of those letters keeps its own sound while the two sounds blend together.

10. Follow the same procedure for the words *pact* and *fact*.

11. Provide additional guidance if students have difficulty with blends. Take the last letter off the word students are struggling with.

    Say: I have taken the last letter off this word. Touch and say the word without the last sound. What sound do you make at the end of the word? Answers will vary.
    Say: Now I am going to put the last letter back on the word. Touch and say. Now what is the sound you make at the end of the word? What two sounds are heard in the blend at the end of the word? Answers will vary.

Word Chains

Have students build words by adding and changing letters to help them recognize and use individual sounds in words.

1. Place the following letters randomly on students' whiteboard: *a, c, f, p, t,* and *t*.

2. **Say:** I am going to build the first word in a chain. The word is *ac*.

   ▸ I will pull down the letters for the sounds /ă/ and /k/ to spell the word *ac*.
   ▸ I will touch and say *ac*. To change *ac* to *act*, I will think about what sound is added from the word *ac* to *act*. I will need to add the letter *t* to the end of the word *ac*.
   ▸ Touch and say the word *act*. Now it's your turn to change *act* to *fact*. You can spell *fact* by making only one change. Touch and say the new word.

3. Redirect students if they select the incorrect letter for any sound.

   Say: That letter is for the sound [incorrect sound]. We want the letter for the sound [target sound]. What letter makes that sound? Answers will vary.

4. Redirect students if they name the sound incorrectly.

   Say: To change the word [first word] to [target word], we need the letter for the sound [target sound].

   Show students how to make the change. Have them touch and say the new word after they move the letters.

5. Follow this procedure to make the following words: *pact* and *tact*.

6. For every new word, have students add, replace, or remove only one letter.

"Jon and Jad"

Have students read "Jon and Jad" on page 7 of *K¹² PhonicsWorks Readers Advanced 1*.

Students should read the story silently once or twice before reading the story aloud. When students miss a word that can be sounded out, point to it and give them three to six seconds to try the word again. If students still miss the word, tell them the word so the flow of the story isn't interrupted.

After reading the story, make a list of all the words students missed, and go over those words with them. You may use letter tiles to show students how to read the words.

> **Objectives**
> - Read aloud grade-level text with appropriate automaticity, prosody, accuracy, and rate.
> - Decode words by applying grade-level word analysis skills.

[Online] ⓴ minutes

REVIEW: Ending Consonant Blend –*ct*

Students will work online independently to

▶ Practice the ending consonant blend –*ct*.

Help students locate the online activities and provide support as needed.

> **Objectives**
> - Identify and use the blend –*ct*.
> - Identify ending sounds in words.

Offline Alternative

No computer access? Have students point out and name things or words that contain the ending sound /kt/ (for example, *fact* or *duct*). You might also ask students to spell words that contain the ending consonant blend –*ct*.

Unit Checkpoint

Lesson Overview

🖥	**「Online 」**	**REVIEW:** Ending Consonant Blends –*nd*, –*ft*, –*lk*, and –*ct*	**20** minutes
📄	**「Offline 」**	**UNIT CHECKPOINT:** Ending Consonant Blends –*nd*, –*ft*, –*lk*, and –*ct*	**30** minutes

「Materials 」

Supplied

• *K¹² PhonicsWorks Advanced Assessments,* pp. PH 25–30

⭐ Objectives

- Identify and use the blend –*nd*
- Identify and use the blend –*ft*.
- Identify and use the blend –*lk*.
- Identify and use the blend –*ct*.
- Read, write, and spell words containing the blend –*nd*.
- Read, write, and spell words containing the blend –*ft*.
- Read, write, and spell words containing the blend –*lk*.
- Read, write, and spell words containing the blend –*ct*.
- Write words by applying grade-level phonics knowledge.

- Read instructional-level text with 90% accuracy.
- Identify individual sounds in words.
- Given the letter, identify the most common sound.
- Given the sound, identify the most common letter or letters.
- Read sight words.
- Write sight words.
- Read aloud grade-level text with appropriate automaticity, prosody, accuracy, and rate.

 **「Online 」** **20** minutes

REVIEW: Ending Consonant Blends –*nd*, –*ft*, –*lk*, and –*ct*

Students will review the ending consonant blends –*nd*, –*ft*, –*lk*, and –*ct* to prepare for the Unit Checkpoint. Help students locate the online activities and provide support as needed.

 **30 minutes**

UNIT CHECKPOINT: Ending Consonant Blends *–nd*, *–ft*, *–lk*, and *–ct*

Explain that students are going to show what they have learned about sounds, letters, and words.

1. Give students the Unit Checkpoint pages for the Ending Consonant Blends *–nd*, *–ft*, *–lk*, and *–ct* unit and print the Unit Checkpoint Answer Key, if you'd like.

2. Use the instructions below to help administer the Checkpoint to students. On the Answer Key or another sheet of paper, note student answers to oral response questions to help with scoring the Checkpoint later.

3. Use the Answer Key to score the Checkpoint, and then enter the results online.

Part 1. Read Words and Word Parts Moving left to right, have students say the sounds of each word or word part. Note any words or word parts they say incorrectly.

Part 2. Finger Stretching Say each word to students. Have them say each word aloud and finger stretch the sounds. Note any words they finger stretch incorrectly.

19. *soft*	23. *pitch*
20. *pond*	24. *gift*
21. *act*	25. *fact*
22. *silk*	26. *milk*

Part 3. Dictation Say each word to students. Have them repeat and write the word.

27. *bulk*	30. *elk*
28. *loft*	31. *sift*
29. *band*	32. *mend*

Part 4. Writing Read each sentence to students. Have them repeat and write the sentence.

33. *Dig in the soft sand.*

34. *Lift the jug of milk.*

Part 5. Read Aloud Listen to students read the sentences aloud. Count and note the number of words they read correctly.

Part 6. Say Letters Say each sound. Have students say the letter or letters that make that sound. Note any incorrect responses.

36. /ă/

37. /ĕ/

38. /ĭ/

39. /ŏ/

40. /ŭ/

41. /sh/

42. /w/

43. /th/

44. /ch/

45. /l/

46. /f/

47. /y/

48. /v/

49. /p/

50. /h/

51. /r/

52. /kw/

53. /ks/

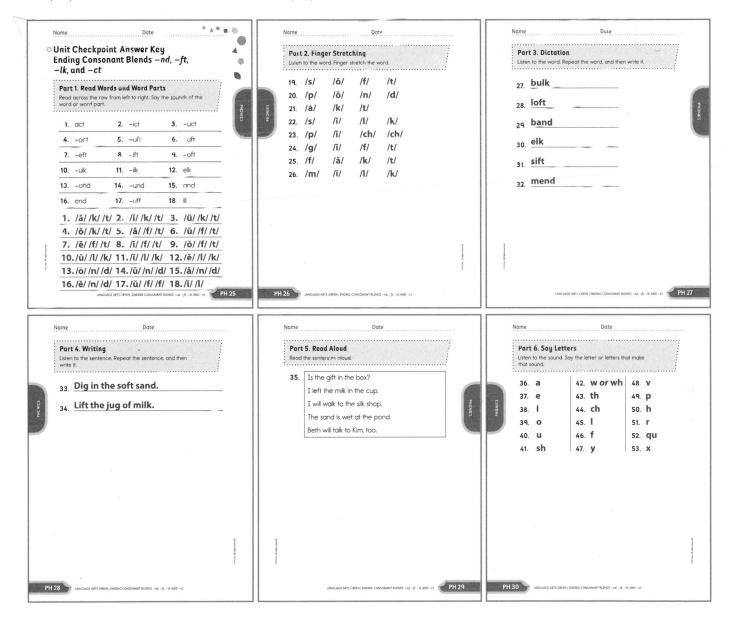

Introduce Ending Consonant Blend *–lp*

Unit Overview

In this unit, students will
- ▶ Review sight words.
- ▶ Review digraphs and the letters in the alphabet.
- ▶ Identify and say the ending consonant blends *–lp* and *–lt*.
- ▶ Distinguish between words that rhyme or sound different.
- ▶ Practice beginning, ending, and middle sounds.

Lesson Overview

🖹	**⟦Offline⟧** **FOCUS:** Introduce Ending Consonant Blend *–lp*	**30** minutes

Sight Words	Introduce Sight Words
Get Ready	Signal Ending Sounds
	Make Nonsense Rhymes
	Review the Ending Consonant Blend *–ct*
Learn	Introduce the Ending Consonant Blend *–lp*
Try It	Alphabet Addition
	Dictation: Write Sentences

🖥	**⟦Online⟧** **REVIEW:** Ending Consonant Blend *–lp*	**20** minutes

 **30 minutes**

FOCUS: Introduce Ending Consonant Blend –*lp*

Work **together** with students to complete offline Sight Words, Get Ready, Learn, and Try It activities.

Sight Words

Introduce Sight Words

Help students learn the sight words *again*, *out*, and *pull*.

1. Gather the sight word cards *again*, *out*, and *pull*.

2. Show students the *again* card.

3. **Say:** This is the word *again*. We see this word so often that we want to be able to read and spell it quickly without thinking about it. Look closely at the word *again*. Spell the word *again* aloud. Take a picture of the word *again* in your mind. When you think you can spell *again* yourself, turn the card over and use your letter tiles to spell the word *again*. Check the card to see if you spelled the word *again* correctly. Read aloud the word you spelled with the letter tiles.

4. Repeat the activity with the remaining sight words.

5. Chart students' progress on the back of each card.

   ► Divide the back of the card into two columns.
   ► Label the first column "Read" and the second column "Spell."
   ► Record the dates that students read or spell the word correctly. When students can read and spell the word correctly three times in a row, they have mastered the word. You may want to put a star or sticker on their card when they have mastered that word.

6. Add the cards to students' sight words box.

TIP Sight words can be very difficult for some students. Let them work at their own pace and really master these words.

Objectives
- Read sight words.
- Spell sight words.

Get Ready

Signal Ending Sounds

Use a special signal to help students identify **ending sounds** in words.

1. **Say:** I'm going to tell you some sounds to listen for, and then I'll say some words. Repeat each word I say and make a special signal to tell me where the sounds are. If the special sound is at the end of the word, clap your hands. If the special sound is **not** at the end of the word, just smile at me. For example,

   ▶ If I ask you to listen for the sound /nd/ and I say the word *sand*, you'll repeat the word *sand* and clap your hands because *sand* has the sound /nd/ at the end.

   ▶ If I say the word *drum*, you'll repeat the word *drum* and smile at me because *drum* has the sound /m/, not /nd/, at the end.

2. Say each ending consonant blend and group of words. Have students make the special signal to identify the ending sound.

   ▶ /nd/: *and, fly, toss, bend, hand* clap: *and, bend, hand*
   ▶ /ct/: *roof, shift, act, jump, fact* clap: *act, fact*
   ▶ /lk/: *silk, elk, dream, milk, chant* clap: *silk, elk, milk*
   ▶ /ft/: *run, raft, moon, shift, splash* clap: *raft, shift*

3. Redirect students if they name the sound incorrectly.

   Say: That is the sound of another letter. Think about the sound you hear at the end of each word.

Objectives
- Identify ending sounds in words.
- Identify and use the blend *–ct*.

Make Nonsense Rhymes

Help students identify **ending sounds** by having them make nonsense words.

1. **Say:** We're going to use word endings to make up **nonsense words**. First I will give you some ending sounds. Then I'll give you a nonsense word with those ending sounds. Your job is to tell me a nonsense word that rhymes with it. Let's do the first one. Remember, no real words are allowed!

2. **Say:** The first ending sound is /lk/. The nonsense word is *pilk*. Can you think of a nonsense word that rhymes with *pilk*? How about *jilk*?

3. **Say:** Let's do another one. The ending sound is /ft/. The nonsense word is *seft*. What is a nonsense word that rhymes with *seft*?

4. Repeat this procedure with the following sounds and words:

   ▶ /kt/ *dact*; Possible rhyming words: *nact* or *lact*
   ▶ /nd/ *nend*; Possible rhyming words: *kend* or *zend*
   ▶ /lk/ *hilk*; Possible rhyming words: *vilk* or *pilk*

Review the Ending Consonant Blend *–ct*

Help students recognize and use the ending consonant blend *–ct*.

1. Place the following letters on students' whiteboard: *a*, *c*, and *t*.

2. Make the word *act* and point to it.

3. **Say:** Touch and say this word.

   ▸ How many sounds are in the word? three
   ▸ How many letters are in the word? three
   ▸ The last sound, /ct/, at the end of this word is called a blend because each of the letters, *c* and *t*, keeps its own sound while the two sounds blend together.

Learn ....

Introduce the Ending Consonant Blend *–lp*

Help students recognize and use the ending consonant blend *–lp*.

1. Place the following letters on students' whiteboard: *e*, *h*, *l*, and *p*.

2. Make the word *help* and point to it.

3. **Say:** Touch and say this word.

   ▸ How many sounds are in the word? four
   ▸ How many letters are in the word? four
   ▸ The last sound, /lp/, at the end of this word is called a blend because each of the letters, *l* and *p*, keeps its own sound while the two sounds blend together.

4. Redirect students if they have difficulty with the consonant blend *–lp*.

   Say: The two letters *l* and *p* are often together at the end of a word. When they are together, they blend into the sound /lp/, as in *kelp*. Can you say the word *kelp*? When you say *kelp*, don't stop between the last two sounds, /l/ and /p/. Try saying the word again.

5. Make the word *yelp* and point to it.

6. **Say:** Touch and say the sounds in *yelp*.

   ▸ How many sounds are in the word? four
   ▸ How many letters are in the word? four
   ▸ Where is the blend? at the end

7. Provide additional guidance if students have difficulty with blends. Take the last letter off the word students are struggling with.

   Say: I have taken the last letter off this word. Touch and say the word without the last sound. What sound do you make at the end of the word? Answers will vary.

   Say: Now I am going to put the last letter back on the word. Touch and say. Now what is the sound you make at the end of the word? What two sounds are heard in the blend at the end of the word? Answers will vary.

Objectives

- Identify and use the blend *–lp*.
- Identify ending sounds in words.
- Identify the number of sounds within words.

Try It •••

Alphabet Addition

Have students complete page PH 11 in *K¹² PhonicsWorks Advanced Activity Book* for more practice making words that end with the letters *–lp*. First have students add the parts of the word together to make a new word. Then have them write the word and read it aloud.

> **Try It** ••••••••••••••••••••••••••••••••••
> **Introduce Ending Consonant Blend** *–lp*
> **Alphabet Addition**
>
> Add the letters to make a word. Write the word, and then read it aloud.
>
> 1. h + elp = __ **help**
> 2. y + elp = **yelp**
> 3. g + ulp = **gulp**
> 4. p + ulp = __ **pulp**
> 5. k + elp = **kelp**
>
> LANGUAGE ARTS GREEN   **PH 11**

Dictation: Write Sentences

Use sentences to help students identify individual sounds in words.

1. Gather a pencil and the dictation notebook. Say the sentence, *Gulp the milk.* Then give these directions to students:

   ▸ Repeat the sentence.
   ▸ Write the sentence in your notebook.
   ▸ Read the sentence aloud.

2. When students have finished, write the following sentence on your whiteboard: *Gulp the milk.*

3. Have them compare their answer to your correct version.

4. Repeat this procedure with the sentence, *Help Sam fix the van.*

   ▸ If students make an error and don't see it, help them correct their mistake by having them finger stretch the sounds in the word they missed.
   ▸ If students are having difficulty selecting the correct letters or sounds, review those letters or sounds that are confusing them.
   ▸ If students have difficulty with first, middle, and last sounds, have them finger stretch the sounds in words.

 **20 minutes**

REVIEW: Ending Consonant Blend –*lp*

Students will work online independently to

► Practice the ending consonant blend –*lp*.
► Practice decoding text by reading a story.

Help students locate the online activities and provide support as needed.

Offline Alternative

No computer access? Have students point out and name things or words that contain the ending sound /lp/ (for example, *help* or *pulp*). You might also ask students to spell words that contain the ending consonant blend –*lp*.

> **Objectives**
> - Identify and use the blend –*lp*.
> - Identify ending sounds in words.
> - Read aloud grade-level text with appropriate automaticity, prosody, accuracy, and rate.
> - Decode words by applying grade-level word analysis skills.

Practice Ending Consonant Blend –*lp*

Lesson Overview

[Offline] **FOCUS:** Practice Ending Consonant Blend –*lp* — **30** minutes

Sight Words	Sight Word Fun
Get Ready	Search Sentences for Ending Sounds
	Quick Sounds
	Sort Blends
	Guess the Word
	Place That Name
Try It	"Pam and the Kelp"
	Dictation: Write Words

[Online] **REVIEW:** Ending Consonant Blend –*lp* — **20** minutes

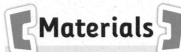

Materials

Supplied
- *K¹² PhonicsWorks Readers Advanced 1*, pp. 13–18
- whiteboard, student
- Tile Kit

Also Needed
- sight words box
- dictation notebook
- index cards (15)
- tape, clear

Advance Preparation

For Sort Blends, print each of the following words on index cards, using one index card per word: *help, yelp, gulp, pulp, rack, pass, sand,* and *milk.*

For Place That Name, print on index cards the names of seven items that may be located nearby, using one index card per word. Be sure the words are words that students can read independently, such as *milk, dog, cat, pen, dish, sack,* or *fan.*

 **30 minutes**

FOCUS: Practice Ending Consonant Blend *-lp*

Work **together** with students to complete offline Sight Words, Get Ready, and Try It activities.

Sight Words

Sight Word Fun

Help students learn the sight words *again*, *out*, and *pull*, and up to two additional sight words they have yet to master.

1. Gather the sight word cards *again*, *out*, and *pull*, and up to two additional sight word cards.

2. Choose one sight word card to begin.

   Say: Look at this word and take a picture of it in your mind. When you think you can spell the word yourself, turn the card over and use your letter tiles to spell the word.

3. After students spell the word, have them check the card to see if they spelled the word correctly.

   Say: Read aloud the word you spelled with the letter tiles.

4. Repeat the activity with the remaining sight words.

TIP Sight words can be very difficult for some students. Let them work at their own pace and really master these words.

> **Objectives**
> * Read sight words.
> * Spell sight words.

Get Ready

Search Sentences for Ending Sounds

Help students recognize the **ending sounds** in a word used in a sentence.

1. **Say:** I'm going to say an ending sound that is in a word. You will repeat the sound and the word. For example, the ending sound is /kt/, as in the word *fact*.

2. Have students say the target sound /kt/ and the word *fact*.

3. **Say:** Then I will read a sentence. Repeat the sentence and tell me the word that has the special ending sound. The first sentence is, "Pam and Ross like to act."

   ► What are the special ending sound? /kt/
   ► What is the word? *act*

4. Have students repeat the sentence and say the word.

> **Objectives**
> * Identify ending sounds in words.
> * Identify beginning sounds in words.
> * Identify and use the blend *-lp*.

5. Redirect students if they don't name the correct word.

   ▸ Have them repeat the sentence slowly, clearly pronouncing the endings of words.
   ▸ Remind them of the special ending sound.

6. Follow the same procedure with the words and sentences below to help students recognize ending sounds in words.

   ▸ /ft/, as in *loft*; *Move to the chair on your left. left*
   ▸ /lk/, as in *milk*; *Did you see the elk? elk*
   ▸ /nd/, as in *send*; *Do those words blend together? blend*
   ▸ /lp/, as in *help*; *John took a big gulp of water. gulp*

TIP If students still have difficulty, say two words from the sentence and have them choose the one with the target ending sounds.

Quick Sounds

Help students name words that have the same **beginning sound**.

1. **Say:** I'm going to say a sound that begins a word. Your job is to think of as many words as you can that begin with that same sound. Let's see how many you can name. The first one is /f/, as in *find*. How many words can you say that begin with /f/?

2. Continue this procedure with the following sounds:

   ▸ /d/, as in *doll*
   ▸ /sh/, as in *ship*
   ▸ /m/, as in *mat*
   ▸ /kw/, as in *queen*

TIP If students have trouble thinking of words, have them look around the room and find objects that start with that sound. You can also get a book and find pictures of things that start with that sound.

Sort Blends

Help students identify words that have the **ending sound /lp/**.

1. Gather the index cards you prepared and place them in random order in front of students.

2. **Say:** Some of these words have the sound /lp/ at the end. Your job is to find those words and make a pile of them.

   ▸ First touch and say each word.
   ▸ Then put the cards ending with /lp/ in a pile.

TIP To extend this activity, scramble the cards when students have finished and then read the words to students. Have them put their hands on their heads when they hear a word with the blend /lp/ at the end.

Guess the Word

Have students use word meaning and sentence structure to choose a word that best completes a sentence.

1. Write the following words on students' whiteboard: *help, yelp, gulp,* and *pulp.* Make sure students know the meaning of all the words on their whiteboard before you do this activity.

2. Have students underline the ending consonant blend *–lp* in each word.

3. **Say:** We're going to play a guessing game. I'm going to read a sentence with a word missing. Your job is to look at the words on your whiteboard and decide which one is the right word to complete the sentence.

   ▸ Listen to this sentence: "When I left my dog alone, he began to bark and _____ ."

   ▸ Next you will tell me what word makes sense in the blank of the sentence. This time the word would be *yelp.*

   ▸ The complete sentence would be, "When I left my dog alone, he began to bark and *yelp.*" Now you try it.

4. Continue the procedure with the following sentences:

   ▸ *When I can't reach something up high, I ask my tall friend for _____ . help*
   ▸ *That orange juice has a lot of _____ in it. pulp*
   ▸ *Judy had a big _____ of milk. gulp*

Place That Name

Play a game with students to help them identify names of common objects.

1. Gather the index cards you prepared with names of nearby objects and place them face down in one pile.

2. **Say:** We're going to play a game called Place That Name.

   ▸ First you will choose a card and read the word on it. Then you will find that object nearby and tape the card to it as a label, or tell me where the object is.
   ▸ I'll try first. Choose a card from the pile and read the word.

3. **Say:** I know where there is a [word on the card]. Let's put a label on it.

   ▸ It's your turn. Choose a card and read it to me.
   ▸ Now find that object and tape the card to it.

4. Repeat Step 3 until students have used all the cards. Remind them that all of the objects are somewhere nearby.

TIP If students stumble over any words, have them touch and say the words. Touch and say these words along with them.

Try It ●

"Pam and the Kelp"

Have students read "Pam and the Kelp" on page 13 of *K¹² PhonicsWorks Readers Advanced 1*.

Students should read the story silently once or twice before reading the story aloud. When students miss a word that can be sounded out, point to it and give them three to six seconds to try the word again. If students still miss the word, tell them the word so the flow of the story isn't interrupted.

After reading the story, make a list of all the words students missed, and go over those words with them. You may use tiles to show students how to read the words.

Dictation: Write Words

Have students practice identifying sounds and writing words.

1. Gather a pencil and the dictation notebook. Say the word *help*. Then give these directions to students:

   ▸ Repeat the word.
   ▸ Write the word in your notebook.
   ▸ Read the word aloud.

2. When students have finished, write the following word on your whiteboard: *help*.

3. Have them compare their answer to your correct version.

4. Repeat this procedure with the words *gulp* and *fact*.

   ▸ If students make an error and don't see it, help them correct their mistake by having them finger stretch the sounds in the word they missed.
   ▸ If students are having difficulty selecting the correct letters or sounds, review those letters or sounds that are confusing them.
   ▸ If students have difficulty with first, middle, and last sounds, have them finger stretch the sounds in words.

> **Objectives**
> - Read aloud grade-level text with appropriate automaticity, prosody, accuracy, and rate.
> - Decode words by applying grade-level word analysis skills.
> - Write words by applying grade-level phonics knowledge.
> - Follow three-step directions.

【Online】 ⑳ minutes

REVIEW: Ending Consonant Blend *–lp*

Students will work online independently to

▸ Practice the ending consonant blend *–lp*.

Help students locate the online activities and provide support as needed.

> **Objectives**
> - Identify and use the blend *–lp*.
> - Identify ending sounds in words.

Offline Alternative

No computer access? Have students point out and name things or words that contain the sound /lp/ (for example, *gulp* or *kelp*). You might also ask students to spell words that contain the sound /lp/.

Introduce Ending Consonant Blend –*lt*

Lesson Overview

Offline **FOCUS:** Introduce Ending Consonant Blend –*lt*   **30** minutes

Sight Words	Sight Word Fun
Get Ready	Name Letters and Sounds
	Review the Ending Consonant Blend –*lp*
Learn	Introduce the Ending Consonant Blend –*lt*
	Create Rhyming Words
Try It	Go Fish!
	Dictation: Write Sentences

Online **REVIEW:** Ending Consonant Blend –*lt*   **20** minutes

Materials

Supplied

- *K¹² PhonicsWorks Advanced Activity Book*, p. PH 12
- whiteboard, Learning Coach
- whiteboard, student
- Tile Kit

Also Needed

- sight words box
- dictation notebook
- crayons

Keywords

onset – the part of a word preceding the first vowel; in the word *smart, sm–* is the onset

rime – the part of a word that includes the first vowel and what follows it; in the word *smart, –art* is the rime

Advance Preparation

Scramble lowercase letter tiles on your whiteboard.

 **30** minutes

FOCUS: Introduce Ending Consonant Blend –*lt*

Work **together** with students to complete offline Sight Words, Get Ready, Learn, and Try It activities.

Sight Words

Sight Word Fun

Help students learn the sight words *again*, *out*, and *pull*, and up to two additional sight words they have yet to master.

1. Gather the sight word cards *again*, *out*, and *pull*, and up to two additional sight word cards.

2. Choose one sight word card to begin.

   Say: Look at this word and take a picture of it in your mind. When you think you can spell the word yourself, turn the card over and use your letter tiles to spell the word.

3. After students spell the word, have them check the card to see if they spelled the word correctly.

   Say: Read aloud the word you spelled with the letter tiles.

4. Repeat the activity with the remaining sight words.

   TIP Sight words can be very difficult for some students. Let them work at their own pace and really master these words.

> **Objectives**
> * Read sight words.
> * Spell sight words.

Get Ready

Name Letters and Sounds

Have students play a game to become familiar with the letters of the alphabet and digraphs. Grab your whiteboard with the scrambled letters.

1. Place the digraph tiles *ch*, *sh*, *th*, and *wh* at the bottom of your whiteboard.

2. **Say:** We're going to play a game. All of the letters of the alphabet and the digraphs are on my whiteboard. We will put the letters in alphabetical order, and then do the same with the digraphs. For each one, we will touch the tile, say the name of the letter or letters, say the sound the letter or letters make, and then say the name of something that begins with that sound.

3. Help students put the letters in order and then touch the letter *a*.

4. Have students answer these questions:
   ▶ What is the name of this letter? *a*
   ▶ What sound does the letter make? /ă/ or /ā/
   ▶ What is something that begins with this sound? *apple* or *ape*

> **Objectives**
> * Identify letters of the alphabet.
> * Given the letter, identify the most common sound.
> * Identify and use the blend –*lp*.
> * Identify ending sounds in words.

5. Take turns with students until you have touched all the letters and the digraphs.

TIP If students have trouble remembering what letter comes next in the alphabet, have them sing "The Alphabet Song" up to that point.

Review the Ending Consonant Blend –*lp*

Help students recognize and use the ending consonant blend –*lp*.

1. Place the following letters on students' whiteboard: *e*, *h*, *l*, and *p*.

2. Make the word *help* and point to it.

3. **Say:** Touch and say this word.

> ▸ How many sounds are in the word? four
> ▸ How many letters are in the word? four
> ▸ The last sound /lp/ at the end of this word is called a blend because each of the letters, *l* and *p*, keeps its own sound while the two sounds blend together.

Learn ••

Introduce the Ending Consonant Blend –*lt*

Help students recognize and use the ending consonant blend –*lt*.

1. Place the following letters on students' whiteboard: *b*, *e*, *f*, *l*, and *t*.

2. Make the word *belt* and point to it.

3. **Say:** Touch and say this word.

> ▸ How many sounds are in the word? four
> ▸ How many letters are in the word? four
> ▸ We know that the letters *l* and *t* at the end of this word are called a blend because each of those letters keeps its own sound while the two sounds blend together.

4. Make the word *felt* and point to it.

5. **Say:** Touch and say the sounds in *felt*.

> ▸ How many sounds are in the word? four
> ▸ How many letters are in the word? four
> ▸ Where is the blend? at the end
> ▸ We know that the letters *l* and *t* at the end of this word are called a blend because each of those letters keeps its own sound while the two sounds blend together.

6. Redirect students if they have difficulty with the consonant blend –*lt*.

Say: The two letters *l* and *t* are often together at the end of a word. When they are together, they blend into the sound /lt/, as in *felt*. Can you say the word *felt*? When you say *felt*, don't stop between the last two sounds, /l/ and /t/. Try saying the word again.

> **Objectives**
> - Identify and use the blend –*lt*.
> - Identify ending sounds in words.
> - Identify the number of sounds within words.
> - Identify a word when given the onset and rime.
> - Identify the new word when the onset changes.
> - Identify beginning sounds in words.
> - Produce rhyming words.

7. Make the word *pelt* and point to it.

8. **Say:** Touch and say the sounds in *pelt*.

   ▸ How many sounds are in the word? four
   ▸ How many letters are in the word? four
   ▸ Where is the blend? at the end

9. Provide additional guidance if students have difficulty with blends. Take the last letter off the word students are struggling with.

   Say: I have taken the last letter off this word. Touch and say the word without the last sound. What sound do you make at the end of the word? Answers will vary.

   Say: Now I am going to put the last letter back on the word. Touch and say. Now what is the sound you make at the end of the word? What two sounds are heard in the blend at the end of the word? Answers will vary.

Create Rhyming Words

Have students combine word parts and make words that rhyme.

1. **Say:** I'm going to break a word into two parts. Your job is to put the parts back together and say the word.

   ▸ For example, if the first part of the word is /s/ and the last part is /ilt/, then you'll say *silt*.
   ▸ Next you'll add a new **beginning sound** to make a word that rhymes. For example, you'll use the same last part, /ilt/, and add a new first sound, like /w/. The rhyming word is /w/ . . . /ilt/ . . . *wilt*.

2. Have students add a new beginning sound to the last part of each word below to make rhyming words.

   ▸ /kw/ . . . /ilt/ *quilt;* Possible rhyming word: *built*
   ▸ /b/ . . . /elt/ *belt;* Possible rhyming word: *pelt*
   ▸ /m/ . . . /elt/ *melt;* Possible rhyming word: *felt*

Try It

Go Fish!

Have students complete page PH 12 in *K¹² PhonicsWorks Advanced Activity Book* for more practice with the ending consonant blend *–lt* and digraphs. Have students read each word aloud. Then have them color the fish that have the blend *–lt* yellow and the fish that have a digraph pink.

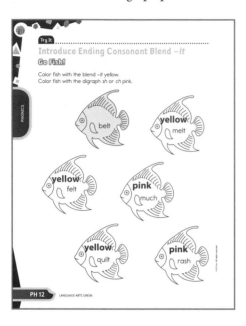

<table>
</table>

Objectives

- Identify and use the blend *–lt*.
- Write words by applying grade-level phonics knowledge.
- Write sight words.
- Follow three-step directions.

Dictation: Write Sentences

Use sentences to help students identify individual sounds in words.

1. Gather a pencil and the dictation notebook. Say the sentence, *Did the mum wilt?* Then give these directions to students:

   ▸ Repeat the sentence.
   ▸ Write the sentence in your notebook.
   ▸ Read the sentence aloud.

2. When students have finished, write the following sentence on your whiteboard: *Did the mum wilt?*

3. Have them compare their answer to your correct version.

4. Repeat this procedure with the sentence, *Help Nat get the belt.*

   ▸ If students make an error and don't see it, help them correct their mistake by having them finger stretch the sounds in the word they missed.
   ▸ If students are having difficulty selecting the correct letters or sounds, review those letters or sounds that are confusing them.
   ▸ If students have difficulty with first, middle, and last sounds, have them finger stretch the sounds in words.

 **20 minutes**

REVIEW: Ending Consonant Blend –*lt*

Students will work online independently to

- ▸ Practice the ending consonant blend –*lt*.
- ▸ Practice decoding text by reading a story.

Help students locate the online activities and provide support as needed.

Offline Alternative

No computer access? Have students point out and name things or words that contain the ending sound /lt/ (for example, *belt* or *felt*). You might also ask students to spell words that contain the ending consonant blend –*lt*.

Objectives

- Identify and use the blend –*lt*.
- Identify ending sounds in words.
- Read aloud grade-level text with appropriate automaticity, prosody, accuracy, and rate.
- Decode words by applying grade-level word analysis skills.

Practice Ending Consonant Blends
–lp and –lt

Lesson Overview

Offline	**FOCUS:** Practice Ending Consonant Blends –lp and –lt	**30** minutes

Sight Words	Sight Word Fun
Practice	Simon Says
	Sing "Old MacDonald's Farm"
	Review the Ending Consonant Blend –lp
	Review the Ending Consonant Blend –lt
Try It	"Walt's Gift"

Online	**REVIEW:** Ending Consonant Blends –lp and –lt	**20** minutes

Materials

Supplied
- *K¹² PhonicsWorks Readers Advanced 1*, pp. 19–24
- whiteboard, Learning Coach
- whiteboard, student
- Tile Kit

Also Needed
- sight words box

Advance Preparation

Place lowercase letter tiles in alphabetical order on your whiteboard.

 **30 minutes**

FOCUS: Practice Ending Consonant Blends –*lp* and –*lt*

Work **together** with students to complete offline Sight Words, Practice, and Try It activities.

Sight Words

Sight Word Fun

Help students learn the sight words *again*, *out*, and *pull*, and up to two additional sight word cards they have yet to master.

1. Gather the sight word cards for *again*, *out*, and *pull*, and up to two additional sight word cards.

2. Choose one sight word card to begin.

   Say: Look at this word and take a picture of it in your mind. When you think you can spell the word yourself, turn the card over and use your letter tiles to spell the word.

3. After students spell the word, have them check the card to see if they spelled the word correctly.

   Say: Read aloud the word you spelled with the letter tiles.

4. Repeat the activity with the remaining sight words.

TIP Sight words can be very difficult for some students. Let them work at their own pace and really master these words.

> **Objectives**
> - Read sight words.
> - Spell sight words.

Practice

Simon Says

Play a game with students to help them recognize words that rhyme.

1. **Say:** We're going to play a Simon Says sound game. Listen carefully for words that rhyme with the Simon Says word. Today the Simon Says word is *melt*. Say *melt*.

   - I'm going to say a word and do something. You will repeat the word.
   - If the word rhymes with *melt*, you will copy the action I make.
   - If the word doesn't rhyme with *melt*, then you will be still. We'll do two together.

2. Touch your nose as you say *felt*.

3. **Say:** We both say *felt* and touch our nose because *felt* rhymes with *melt*.

4. Stomp your feet as you say *soup*.

> **Objectives**
> - Identify words that rhyme.
> - Given the sound, identify the most common letter or letters.
> - Identify beginning sounds in words.
> - Identify and use the blend –*lp*.
> - Identify and use the blend –*lt*.
> - Identify ending sounds in words.

5. **Say:** The word is *soup*. Repeat the word.

   ▸ We won't stomp our feet when we say *soup* because *soup* doesn't rhyme with *melt*.

   ▸ Let's begin. Remember, the Simon Says word is *melt*. The new word is *pelt*.

6. Repeat the procedure with each of the following words and actions:

   ▸ *pelt*   touch your nose
   ▸ *welt*   rub your head
   ▸ *friend*   stomp your feet
   ▸ *belt*   rub your head
   ▸ *mill*   stomp your feet

Sing "Old MacDonald's Farm"

To review digraphs and the letters of the alphabet, have students sing "Old MacDonald's Farm." Grab your whiteboard with all letters in alphabetical order.

1. Place the digraph tiles *ch, sh, th,* and *wh* at the bottom of your whiteboard.

2. **Say:** Do you remember "Old MacDonald's Farm"? Get ready to sing the song. Think of an animal you want to have on the farm. When you reach that part of the song ("... and on that farm he had a _____"), point to the beginning letter of that word.

3. Repeat the song until students have named all of the animals they know. When they have finished, you may sing the song and let students point to the first letter of the animals you name.

Review the Ending Consonant Blend –*lp*

Help students recognize and use the ending consonant blend –*lp*.

1. Place the following letters on students' whiteboard: *g, l, p,* and *u*.

2. Make the word *gulp* and point to it.

3. **Say:** Touch and say this word.

   ▸ How many sounds are in the word? four
   ▸ How many letters are in the word? four
   ▸ The last sound /lp/ at the end of this word is called a blend because each of those letters keeps its own sound while the two sounds blend together.

Review the Ending Consonant Blend –*lt*

Help students recognize and use the ending consonant blend –*lt*.

1. Place the following letters on students' whiteboard: *i, l, qu, t,* and *w*.

2. Make the word *wilt* and point to it.

3. **Say:** Touch and say this word.

   ▶ How many sounds are in the word? four
   ▶ How many letters are in the word? four
   ▶ The last sound /lt/ at the end of this word is called a blend because each of those letters keeps its own sound while the two sounds blend together.

4. Practice with another word with this blend. Make the word *quilt* and point to it.

5. **Say:** Touch and say the sounds in *quilt*.

   ▶ How many sounds are in the blend /lt/? two
   ▶ How many letters are in the blend /lt/? two
   ▶ Where is the blend? at the end
   ▶ We know that the letters *l* and *t* at the end of this word are called a blend because each of those letters keeps its own sound while the two sounds blend together.

6. Provide additional guidance if students have difficulty with blends. Take the last letter off the word students are struggling with.

   Say: I have taken the last letter off this word. Touch and say the word without the last sound. What sound do you make at the end of the word? Answers will vary.
   Say: Now I am going to put the last letter back on the word. Touch and say. Now what is the sound you make at the end of the word? What two sounds are heard in the blend at the end of the word? Answers will vary.

Try It

"Walt's Gift"

Have students read "Walt's Gift" on page 19 of *K¹² PhonicsWorks Readers Advanced 1.*

Students should read the story silently once or twice before reading the story aloud. When students miss a word that can be sounded out, point to it and give them three to six seconds to try the word again. If students still miss the word, tell them the word so the flow of the story isn't interrupted.

After reading the story, make a list of all the words students missed, and go over those words with them. You may use tiles to show students how to read the words.

Objectives

- Read aloud grade-level text with appropriate automaticity, prosody, accuracy, and rate.
- Decode words by applying grade-level word analysis skills.

 **20 minutes**

REVIEW: Ending Consonant Blends –*lp* and –*lt*

Students will work online independently to

▶ Practice the ending consonant blends –*lp* and –*lt*.

Help students locate the online activities and provide support as needed.

Offline Alternative

No computer access? Have students point out and name things or words that contain the ending sounds /lp/ and /lt/ (for example, *kelp* and *colt*). You might also ask students to spell words that contain the ending consonant blends –*lp* and –*lt*.

⭐ **Objectives**

• Identify and use the blend –*lp*.

• Identify and use the blend –*lt*.

• Identify ending sounds in words.

Unit Checkpoint

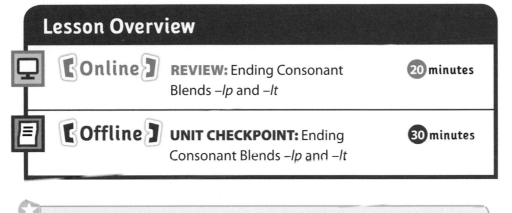

Lesson Overview

Online	REVIEW: Ending Consonant Blends –*lp* and –*lt*	**20** minutes
Offline	UNIT CHECKPOINT: Ending Consonant Blends –*lp* and –*lt*	**30** minutes

Materials

Supplied
- *K¹² PhonicsWorks Advanced Assessments,* pp. PH 31–36

Objectives

- Identify and use the blend –*lp*.
- Identify and use the blend –*lt*.
- Read, write, and spell words containing the blend –*lp*.
- Read, write, and spell words containing the blend –*lt*.
- Identify individual sounds in words.
- Write words by applying grade-level phonics knowledge.
- Read instructional-level text with 90% accuracy.
- Given the letter, identify the most common sound.
- Given the sound, identify the most common letter or letters.
- Read sight words.
- Write sight words.
- Read aloud grade-level text with appropriate automaticity, prosody, accuracy, and rate.

 **20** minutes

REVIEW: **Ending Consonant Blends –*lp* and –*lt***

Students will review the ending consonant blends –*lp* and –*lt* for the Unit Checkpoint. Help students locate the online activities and provide support as needed.

⟦ Offline ⟧ 🕥 minutes

UNIT CHECKPOINT: Ending Consonant Blends –*lp* and –*lt*

Explain that students are going to show what they have learned about sounds, letters, and words.

1. Give students the Unit Checkpoint pages for the Ending Consonant Blends –*lp* and –*lt* unit and print the Unit Checkpoint Answer Key, if you'd like.

2. Use the instructions below to help administer the Checkpoint to students. On the Answer Key or another sheet of paper, note student answers to oral response questions to help with scoring the Checkpoint later.

3. Use the Answer Key to score the Checkpoint, and then enter the results online.

Part 1. Read Words and Word Parts Moving left to right, have students say the sounds of each word or word part. Note any words or word parts they say incorrectly.

Part 2. Finger Stretching Say each word to students. Have them say each word aloud and finger stretch the sounds. Note any words they finger stretch incorrectly.

16. *milk*	19. *gulp*
17. *belt*	20. *and*
18. *wilt*	21. *quilt*

Part 3. Dictation Say each word to students. Have them repeat and write the word.

22. *help*	25. *belt*
23. *felt*	26. *yelp*
24. *end*	27. *and*

Part 4. Writing Read each sentence to students. Have them repeat and write the sentence.

28. *Can I help?*

29. *The quilt is soft.*

Part 5. Read Aloud Listen to students read the sentences aloud. Count and note the number of words they read correctly.

Part 6. Say Letters Say each sound. Have students say the letter or letters that make that sound. Note any incorrect responses.

31. /ĭ/

32. /ĕ/

33. /ŏ/

34. /ă/

35. /ŭ/

36. /ch/

37. /w/

38. /sh/

39. /th/

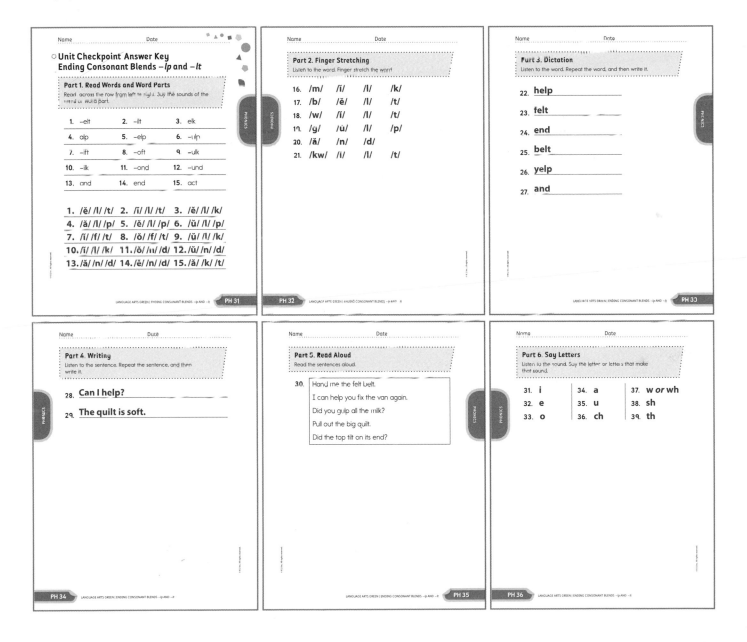

Name _____ Date _____

Unit Checkpoint Answer Key
Ending Consonant Blends – lp and – lt

Part 1. Read Words and Word Parts
Read across the row from left to right. Say the sounds of the word or word part.

1. –elt 2. –ilt 3. elk
4. alp 5. –elp 6. –ulp
7. –ift 8. –oft 9. –ulk
10. –ilk 11. –ond 12. –und
13. and 14. end 15. act

1. /ĕ/ /l/ /t/ 2. /ĭ/ /l/ /t/ 3. /ĕ/ /l/ /k/
4. /ă/ /l/ /p/ 5. /ĕ/ /l/ /p/ 6. /ŭ/ /l/ /p/
7. /ĭ/ /f/ /t/ 8. /ŏ/ /f/ /t/ 9. /ŭ/ /l/ /k/
10. /ĭ/ /l/ /k/ 11. /ŏ/ /n/ /d/ 12. /ŭ/ /n/ /d/
13. /ă/ /n/ /d/ 14. /ĕ/ /n/ /d/ 15. /ă/ /k/ /t/

Name _____ Date _____

Part 2. Finger Stretching
Listen to the word. Finger stretch the word.

16. /m/ /ĭ/ /l/ /k/
17. /b/ /ĕ/ /l/ /t/
18. /w/ /ĭ/ /l/ /t/
19. /g/ /ŭ/ /l/ /p/
20. /ă/ /n/ /d/
21. /kw/ /ĭ/ /l/ /t/

Name _____ Date _____

Part 3. Dictation
Listen to the word. Repeat the word, and then write it.

22. help _____
23. felt _____
24. end _____
25. belt _____
26. yelp _____
27. and _____

Name _____ Date _____

Part 4. Writing
Listen to the sentence. Repeat the sentence, and then write it.

28. Can I help? _____
29. The quilt is soft. _____

Name _____ Date _____

Part 5. Read Aloud
Read the sentences aloud.

30. Hand me the felt belt.
I can help you fix the van again.
Did you gulp all the milk?
Pull out the big quilt.
Did the top tilt on its end?

Name _____ Date _____

Part 6. Say Letters
Listen to the sound. Say the letter or letters that make that sound.

31. i
32. e
33. o
34. a
35. u
36. ch
37. w or wh
38. sh
39. th

Introduce Ending Consonant Blend –*mp*

Unit Overview

In this unit, students will
- ▸ Review the letters and sounds of the alphabet.
- ▸ Review the ending consonant blends –*nd*, –*ft*, –*lk*, and –*ct*.
- ▸ Review sight words.
- ▸ Identify beginning, middle, and ending sounds in words.
- ▸ Learn the ending consonant blends –*mp* and –*sp*.

Lesson Overview

[Offline] FOCUS: Introduce Ending Consonant Blend –*mp*		**30** minutes
Sight Words	Review Sight Words	
Get Ready	Face-Down Letters	
	Scrambled Letters	
	Signal Ending Sounds	
	Disappearing Blends	
	Review the Ending Consonant Blend –*nd*	
Learn	Introduce the Ending Consonant Blend –*mp*	
Try It	The Amazing Alphabet	
	Dictation: Write Sentences	
[Online] REVIEW: Ending Consonant Blend –*mp*		**20** minutes

Materials

Supplied
- K[12] *PhonicsWorks Advanced Activity Book*, p. PH 13
- whiteboard, Learning Coach
- whiteboard, student
- Tile Kit

Also Needed
- sight words box
- dictation notebook

Advance Preparation

Place lowercase letter tiles in alphabetical order on your whiteboard.

Offline 🕧 **30 minutes**

FOCUS: Introduce Ending Consonant Blend –*mp*

Work **together** with students to complete offline Sight Words, Get Ready, Learn, and Try It activities.

Sight Words

Review Sight Words

Help students learn to recognize sight words.

1. Gather all the sight word cards students have yet to master from their sight words box. Stack the cards on the table face down.

2. Have students pick a card and read it to you.

3. If they read it quickly and correctly, put the card in one stack. If they hesitate or do not read the word correctly, put it in another stack. The second stack should have words that that they will review again.

4. Take the stack of words that students read correctly and dictate each word to them. They may choose to either write the word or spell it aloud.

5. If students spell the word correctly, they have mastered the word. If they misspell the word, add it to the stack of cards to review again.

6. Chart students' progress on the back of each card.

   ► Divide the back of the card into two columns.
   ► Label the first column "Read" and the second column "Spell."
   ► Record the dates that students read or spell the word correctly. When students can read and spell the word correctly three times in a row, they have mastered the word. You may want to put a star or sticker on their card when they have mastered that word.

TIP Even if students can read and spell all the words correctly, it is still beneficial for them to review sight words. Choose as many additional words as you would like for each subsequent activity.

> **Objectives**
> • Read sight words.
> • Spell sight words.
> • Write sight words.

Get Ready

Face-Down Letters

To help students master the letters of the alphabet, have them practice identifying and naming letters. Grab your whiteboard with letters placed in alphabetical order.

1. Lay your whiteboard down on a flat surface and flip over the following letter tiles so they are face down on the whiteboard: *b, c, k, l, n, o, v,* and *w.*

2. **Say:** These letters are face down. We are looking at the back of them. Name each letter and then turn it over to see if you were right.

TIP If students miss any of the letters, have them turn over the missed ones and try again.

> **Objectives**
> • Identify letters of the alphabet.
> • Identify ending sounds in words.
> • Identify individual sounds in words.
> • Identify and use the blend –*nd.*

Scrambled Letters

To help students master the alphabet, have them practice identifying and naming the letters.

1. Place the following letter tiles in random order on students' whiteboard: *b, k, m*, and *z*.

2. Have students arrange the letters in alphabetical order.

   TIP Students may find this activity easier if they slowly sing "The Alphabet Song" to themselves as they work.

Signal Ending Sounds

Use a special signal to help students identify **ending sounds** in words.

1. **Say:** I'm going to tell you a special sound to listen for, and then I'll say some words. Repeat each word I say and make a special signal to tell me where the sound is. If the sound is at the end of the word, clap your hands. If the special sound is **not** at the end of the word, just smile at me. For example,

   ▶ If I ask you to listen for the sound /nd/ and I say the word *sand*, you'll repeat the word *sand* and clap your hands because *sand* has the sound /nd/ at the end.
   ▶ If I say the word *drum*, you'll repeat the word *drum* and smile at me because *drum* has the sound /m/, not the sound /nd/, at the end.

2. Say each consonant blend and group of words. Have students make the special signal to identify the ending sound.

   ▶ /lp/: *help, soon, pull, gulp, play* clap: *help, gulp*
   ▶ /lk/: *book, milk, elk, pump, drink* clap: *milk, elk*
   ▶ /nd/: *cream, sand, lend, cry, wall* clap: *sand, lend*
   ▶ /ft/: *raft, eye, print, shift, silk* clap: *raft, shift*

Disappearing Blends

Help students identify different sounds in a word.

1. **Say:** We're going to make parts of words disappear.

   ▶ First I will say a word. Then I will say part of the word that we are going to make disappear.
   ▶ Today the disappearing part of the word is the **ending blend**. To make the ending sounds of the word disappear, you will only say the part of the word that is left after you take the ending blend away.

2. **Say:** Let's try one. The word is *fact*. The sound I want you to make disappear is /kt/. What is the sound of the word without /kt/? /f/ . . . /ă/ . . . /kt/. The sound /fă/ is left when we take away the sound /kt/.

3. Repeat this procedure with the rest of the words in the list.

sand	What is the sound of the word without /nd/? /să",
bind	What is the sound of the word without /nd/? /bī/
band	What is the sound of the word without /nd/? /bă/
mind	What is the sound of the word without /nd/? /mī/
quilt	What is the sound of the word without /lt/? /kwĭ/

Review the Ending Consonant Blend *–nd*

Help students recognize and use the ending consonant blend *–nd*.

1. Make the word *hand* on students' whiteboard and point to it.

2. **Say:** Touch and say this word.

   ‣ How many sounds are in the word? four
   ‣ How many letters are in the word? four
   ‣ The sound /nd/ at the end of this word is called a blend because each of those letters keeps its own sound while the two sounds blend together.

Learn

Introduce the Ending Consonant Blend *–mp*

Help students recognize and use the ending consonant blend *–mp*.

1. Place the following letters on students' whiteboard: *b, j, m, p,* and *u*.

2. Make the word *bump* and point to it.

3. **Say:** Touch and say this word.

   ‣ How many sounds are in the word? four
   ‣ How many letters are in the word? four
   ‣ The sound /mp/ at the end of this word is called a blend because each of the letters, *m* and *p,* keeps its own sound while the two sounds blend together.

4. Redirect students if they have difficulty with the ending consonant blend *–mp*.

   Say: Those two letters are often together at the end of a word. When they are together, they blend into the sound /mp/, as in *jump*. Can you say the word *jump*? When you say *jump*, don't stop between the last two sounds, /m/ and /p/. Try saying the word again.

5. Make the word *jump* and point to it.

Objectives

- Identify and use the blend *–mp*.
- Identify ending sounds in words.
- Identify the number of sounds within words.

6. **Say:** Touch and say the sounds in *jump*.

   ► How many sounds are in the word? four
   ► How many letters are in the word? four
   ► Where is the blend? at the end

7. Provide additional guidance if students have difficulty with blends. Take the last letter off the word students are struggling with.

   Say: I have taken the last letter off of the word. Touch and say the word without the last sound. What sound do you make at the end of the word?
   Answers will vary.

   Say: Now I am going to put the last letter back on the word. Touch and say the word. When you read the word, be sure to say the sound that comes before the last letter. Which two sounds are heard in the blend at the end of the word?
   Answers will vary.

Try It

The Amazing Alphabet

Have students complete page PH 13 in *K¹² PhonicsWorks Advanced Activity Book* for more practice with words that end with the letters *–mp*. First have students say the name of each picture. Then have them circle the correct ending sound and write the letters.

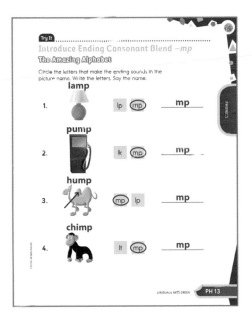

Objectives
- Identify and use the blend *–mp*.
- Identify ending sounds in words.
- Write words by applying grade-level phonics knowledge.

Dictation: Write Sentences

Use sentences to help students identify individual sounds in words.

1. Gather a pencil and the dictation notebook. Say the sentence, *Jump in the sand.* Then give these directions to students:

   ▸ Repeat the sentence.
   ▸ Write the sentence in your notebook.
   ▸ Read the sentence aloud.
   ▸ When students have finished, write the following sentence on your whiteboard: *Jump in the sand.*

2. Have them compare their answer to your correct version.

3. Repeat this procedure with the sentence, *Set up the camp.*

   ▸ If students make an error and don't see it, help them correct their mistake by having them finger stretch the sounds in the word they missed.
   ▸ If students are having difficulty selecting the correct letters or sounds, review those letters or sounds that are confusing them.
   ▸ If students have difficulty with first, middle, and last sounds, have them finger stretch the sounds in words.

 **20 minutes**

REVIEW: Ending Consonant Blend *–mp*

Students will work online independently to

▸ Practice the ending consonant blend *–mp.*
▸ Practice decoding text by reading a story.

Help students locate the online activities and provide support as needed.

Offline Alternative

No computer access? Have students point out and name things or words that contain the ending sound /mp/ (for example, *thump* or *bump*). You might also ask students to spell words that end with the consonant blend *–mp.*

Objectives

- Identify and use the blend *–mp.*
- Identify ending sounds in words.
- Read aloud grade-level text with appropriate automaticity, prosody, accuracy, and rate.
- Decode words by applying grade-level word analysis skills.

Practice Ending Consonant Blend −*mp*

Lesson Overview

[Offline] **FOCUS:** Practice Ending Consonant Blend −*mp* **30** minutes

Sight Words	Use Words in Sentences
Practice	Search Sentences for Blends
	Pick Up Letters
	Sort Blends
	Onset and Rime
	Word Chains
	What's the Word?
Try It	"Camp Champ"
	Dictation: Write Words

[Online] **REVIEW:** Ending Consonant Blend −*mp* **20** minutes

[Materials]

Supplied
- *K¹² PhonicsWorks Readers Advanced 1*, pp. 25–30
- whiteboard, Learning Coach
- whiteboard, student
- Tile Kit

Also Needed
- sight words box
- dictation notebook
- index cards (8)

Advance Preparation

For Sort Blends, print each of the following words on index cards, using one card per word: *bump, lamp, lump, camp, melt, fuzz, lend,* and *lift*.

 **30** minutes

FOCUS: Practice Ending Consonant Blend *–mp*

Work **together** with students to complete offline Sight Words, Practice, and Try It activities.

Sight Words

Use Words in Sentences

Help students use sight words in sentences.

1. Gather all the sight word cards students have yet to master from their sight words box. Spread the sight word cards on the table.

2. **Say:** Let's use sight words in sentences.

3. Have students

   ► Touch each card and read the word on it.
   ► Make up a sentence using the word.
   ► Put the card in a pile after using the word in a sentence.
   ► Go through the pile of cards and read each sight word again.
   ► Spell each word.

TIP If students have difficulty with any of the sight words, place those word cards in a pile to review later in the week.

> **Objectives**
> - Read sight words.
> - Spell sight words.

Practice

Search Sentences for Blends

Have students practice identifying **ending blends** in words that are in a sentence.

1. **Say:** I'm going to say an ending blend that is in a word. You will repeat the sound and the word. The first blend is /ft/, as in the word *left*.

2. Have students say the ending blend /ft/ and the word *left*.

3. **Say:** Now I will read a sentence. Repeat the sentence and tell me the word that has the same ending blend. The first sentence is, "Get on the raft." Which word in the sentence has the special ending blend? *raft*

4. Have students repeat the sentence and say the word.

5. Follow the same procedure with the words and sentences below to help students recognize ending blends in words.

   ► /kt/, as in *fact*   Pam and Ross like to act. *act*
   ► /lk/, as in *elk*   Pour the milk for Susie. *milk*
   ► /nd/, as in *lend*   The sand is on the beach. *sand*
   ► /mp/, as in *bump*   Bill skates down the ramp. *ramp*
   ► /lp/, as in *gulp*   Kerri likes to help her mom. *help*

> **Objectives**
> - Identify ending sounds in words.
> - Identify letters of the alphabet.
> - Given the sound, identify the most common letter or letters.
> - Identify beginning sounds in words.
> - Identify and use the blend *–mp*.
> - Identify a word when given the onset and rime.

Pick Up Letters

Help students master the letters of the alphabet by having them practice naming letters and making words.

1. Place the following letter tiles on students' whiteboard: *b, f, l, m, n, p, r, s,* and *sh.*

2. **Say:** We're going to play a game with these letters.
   - ▸ I will go first. I choose the letter(s) [target letter(s)].
   - ▸ The sound is [target sound]. A word that starts with the sound [target sound] is [word].
   - ▸ A sentence using that word is [sentence with the word].

3. Now it's your turn. Choose a tile.
   - ▸ What is (are) the letter(s)?
   - ▸ What is the sound?
   - ▸ What is a word that starts with that sound?
   - ▸ Make up a sentence that has that word.

4. Continue taking turns until all the letter tiles have been chosen.

5. Redirect students if they name a word that starts with the sound, but not the letter(s) (such as *knob*).

   Say: That is a word that doesn't follow the rules that we know for spelling; we will learn it later. Try another word.

6. Help students if they choose a word that starts with the sound but not the letter(s). Let them use the word. When they finish with their sentences,

   Say: You did a great job of finding a word that starts with the [target sound]. But I want you to know that the word is spelled with a [target letter(s)] as its first letter(s)."

7. Redirect students who are having trouble matching the sounds with words. Give them prompts. For example,

   Say: That's /j/ as in *jelly.* Can you think of another word that starts with that sound?

   If students are unable to say the sounds, they may need to review those sounds. You can go back to the lesson in which the sound was introduced and go through the procedure again.

Sort Blends

Help students identify words that have the **ending sound /mp/**.

1. Gather the index cards that you prepared and place them in random order in front of students.

2. **Say:** Some of these words have the sound /mp/ at the end. Your job is to find those words and make a pile of them. First touch and say each word. Then put the cards ending with the blend /mp/ in a pile.

(TIP) To extend this activity, scramble the cards when students have finished and then read the words aloud. Have them put their hands on their heads when they hear a word with the blend /mp/ at the end.

Onset and Rime

In a word, the part of the syllable before the first vowel sound is the **onset**. The part of the syllable after the first vowel sound is the **rime**. For example, in *dog*, /d/ is the onset and *og* is the rime. Help students put together words that are broken down into parts by onset and rime.

1. **Say:** I'm going to break a word into two parts. Your job is to put the parts back together and say the word. If the first part of a word is /b/ and the last part of the word is *ump*, then the whole word is *bump*: /b/ . . . *ump* . . . *bump*.

2. Say the following pairs of word parts. Have students tell you the word that each pair forms.

   ▸ /l/ . . . *amp lamp*   ▸ /k/ . . . *amp camp*
   ▸ /h/ . . . *ump hump*   ▸ /d/ . . . *amp damp*
   ▸ /d/ . . . *ump dump*

Word Chains

Have students build words by adding and changing letters to help them recognize and use individual sounds in words.

1. Place the following letters at the top of students' whiteboard: *b, d, h, j, l, m, p,* and *u*.

2. **Say:** I am going to build the first word in a chain. The word is *bump*.

   ▸ I will pull down the letters for the sounds /b/, /ŭ/, /m/, and /p/ to spell the word *bump*.
   ▸ Next I will touch and say *bump*. To change *bump* to *dump*, I will think about which sound changes from the word *bump* to *dump*. I will need to replace the letter *b* with the letter *d*.
   ▸ Touch and say the word *dump*. Now it's your turn to change *dump* to *lump*. You can spell *lump* by making only one change. Touch and say the new word.

3. Redirect students if they select the incorrect letter for any sound.

   Say: That letter is for the sound [incorrect sound]. We want the letter for the sound [target sound]. What letter makes that sound? Answers will vary.

4. Redirect students if they name the incorrect sound.

   Say: To change the word [first word] to [target word], we need the letter for the sound [target sound].

   Show students how to make the change. Have them touch and say the new word after they move the letters.

5. Follow this procedure to make the following words: *jump* and *hump*.

6. For every new word, have students add, replace, or remove only one letter.

TIP If students struggle, review the sounds and letters that are confusing them.

What's the Word?

Play a game with students to help improve phonological awareness.

1. **Say:** We're going to play a game. I will give you some clues, and you will guess the word. Listen closely. I am thinking of a word that starts with the sound /d/. It is something you play with. The last sound is /l/. What could the word be? *doll*

2. If students struggle, give them more clues.

    ▸ Tell them what vowel sound follows the beginning sound.
    ▸ Tell them the ending blend.
    ▸ Tell them how many syllables are in the word.
    ▸ Tell them a rhyming a word.

3. Continue this procedure with words such as *milk, lamp, shed,* and *book.*

TIP If students continue having trouble with this activity, go over the sounds they are having difficulty with.

Try It ●●

"Camp Champ"

Have students read "Camp Champ" on page 25 of *K¹² PhonicsWorks Readers Advanced 1.*

Students should read the story silently once or twice before reading the story aloud. When they miss a word that can be sounded out, point to it and give them three to six seconds to try the word again. If they still miss the word, tell them the word so the flow of the story isn't interrupted.

After reading the story, make a list of all the words the students missed, and go over those words with them. You may use letter tiles to show them how to read the words.

Dictation: Write Words

Have students practice identifying sounds and writing words.

1. Gather a pencil and the dictation notebook. Say the word *chimp.* Then give these directions to students:

    ▸ Repeat the word.
    ▸ Write the word in your notebook.
    ▸ Read the word aloud.

2. When students have finished, write the following word on your whiteboard: *chimp.*

3. Have them compare their answer to your correct version.

4. Repeat this procedure with the words *lump* and *chomp.*

    ▸ If students make an error and don't see it, help them correct their mistake by having them finger stretch the sounds in the word they missed.
    ▸ If students are having difficulty selecting the correct letters or sounds, review those letters or sounds that are confusing them.
    ▸ If students have difficulty with first, middle, and last sounds, have them finger stretch the sounds in words.

Objectives
- Read aloud grade-level text with appropriate automaticity, prosody, accuracy, and rate.
- Decode words by applying grade-level word analysis skills.
- Write words by applying grade-level phonics knowledge.
- Follow three-step directions.

 **20 minutes**

REVIEW: Ending Consonant Blend *–mp*

Students will work online independently to

▶ Practice the ending consonant blend *–mp*.

Help students locate the online activities and provide support as needed.

Offline Alternative

No computer access? Have students point out and name things or words that end with the consonant blend *–mp* (for example, *jump* or *bump*). You might also ask students to spell words that end with the consonant blend *–mp*.

> **Objectives**
> - Identify and use the blend *–mp*.
> - Identify ending sounds in words.

Introduce Ending Consonant Blend –*sp*

Lesson Overview

Materials

[Offline] **FOCUS:** Introduce Ending Consonant Blend –*sp*	**30** minutes

Sight Words	Sight Word Concentration
Get Ready	Finger Stretching
	Place That Name
	Review the Ending Consonant Blend –*mp*
Learn	Introduce the Ending Consonant Blend –*sp*
	Build Words
Try It	Dissect It

[Online] **REVIEW:** Ending Consonant Blend –*sp*	**20** minutes

Materials

Supplied
- *K¹² PhonicsWorks Advanced Activity Book*, p. PH 14
- whiteboard, student
- Tile Kit

Also Needed
- sight words box
- index cards (7)
- tape, clear

Advance Preparation

Gather two sets of all the sight word cards you have used to date.

For Place That Name, print on index cards the names of seven items that may be located nearby, using one card per word. Be sure the words are words that students can read independently, such as *milk, pan, hat, pen, fan, dish,* and *sack.*

 **30 minutes**

FOCUS: Introduce Ending Consonant Blend –*sp*

Work **together** with students to complete offline Sight Words, Get Ready, Learn, and Try It activities.

Sight Words

Sight Word Concentration

Help students review sight words.

1. Gather the two sets of all sight word cards.

2. Scramble both sets of sight word cards and place them face down on the table or floor.

3. Have students turn over two cards at a time; take turns with students. If the cards match, the person turning over the matching cards reads the word and uses it in a sentence. If the cards don't match, the person turns them back over.

4. Remove and save the matching cards.

5. Continue the activity until all the cards are paired.

6. Have students read all the words.

7. Take the stack of words that students read correctly and dictate each word to them.

8. Have students write each word or spell it aloud.

TIP If students have difficulty with any sight words, let them work at their own pace to really master these words.

Objectives
- Read sight words.
- Spell sight words.

Get Ready

Finger Stretching

Use finger stretching to help students identify individual sounds in words.

1. **Say:** We can finger stretch the sounds in a word to count how many sounds there are in that word. Let's finger stretch the sounds in *mend*. The first sound is /m/, the second sound is /ĕ/, the third sound is /n/, and the last sound is /d/. I will finger stretch each sound as I say it. Then I'll say the word *mend*, while pulling my fist toward my body.

2. Finger stretch the word *mend*.

Objectives
- Identify individual sounds in words.
- Given the letter, identify the most common sound.
- Read aloud grade-level text with appropriate automaticity, prosody, accuracy, and rate.
- Identify and use the blend –*mp*.
- Identify ending sounds in words.
- Identify beginning sounds in words.

3. **Say:** I'm going to say words with several sounds in them. You'll say each word and then finger stretch it while you say each sound in the word.

4. Say the following words and have students finger stretch them. After they finger stretch each word, ask them the question for that word.

   ▸ *rack* /r/ /ă/ /k/   What is the first sound? /r/
   ▸ *pill* /p/ /ĭ/ /l/   What is the middle sound? /ĭ/
   ▸ *gift* /g/ /ĭ/ /f/ /t/   What is the first sound? /g/
   ▸ *fan* /f/ /ă/ /n/   What is the last sound? /n/
   ▸ *band* /b/ /ă/ /n/ /d/   What is the first sound? /b/
   ▸ *lift* /l/ /ĭ/ /f/ /t/   What is the first sound? /l/
   ▸ *wax* /w/ /ă/ /ks/   What is the middle sound? /ă/

TIP Refer to the *K¹² PhonicsWorks* DVD for a demonstration of finger stretching.

Place That Name

Play a game with students to help them identify names of common objects.

1. Gather the index cards that you prepared with names of nearby objects. Place the cards face down in one pile.

2. **Say:** We're going to play a game called Place That Name.

   ▸ First you will choose a card and read the word on it. Then you will find that object nearby. You will tape the card to the object as a label, or tell me where the object is.
   ▸ I'll try first. Choose a card from the pile and say the word.

3. **Say:** I know where there is a [word on the card]. Let's put a label on it.

   ▸ It's your turn. Choose a card and read it to me.
   ▸ Now find that object and tape the card to it, or say where the object is.

4. Repeat Step 3 until students have used all cards. Remind students that all of the objects are somewhere nearby.

TIP If students stumble over any words, have them touch and say the words. Touch and say these words along with them.

Review the Ending Consonant Blend –mp

Help students recognize and use the ending consonant blend –mp.

1. Make the word *bump* on students' whiteboard and point to it.

2. **Say:** Touch and say this word.

   ▸ How many sounds are in the word? four
   ▸ How many letters are in the word? four
   ▸ The sound /mp/ at the end of this word is called a blend because each of the letters, *m* and *p*, keeps its own sound while the two sounds blend together.

Learn

Introduce the Ending Consonant Blend *–sp*

Help students recognize and use the ending consonant blend *–sp*.

1. Place the following letters on students' whiteboard: *a, g, p, r,* and *s.*

2. Make the word *gasp* and point to it.

3. **Say:** Touch and say this word.

   ▸ How many sounds are in the word? four
   ▸ How many letters are in the word? four
   ▸ We know that the letters *s* and *p* at the end of this word are called a blend because each of the letters keeps its own sound while the two sounds blend together.

4. Redirect students if they have difficulty with the ending consonant blend *–sp.*

   Say: Those two letters are often together at the end of a word. When they are together, they blend into the sound /sp/, as in *rasp.* Can you say the word *rasp*? When you say *rasp,* don't stop between the last two sounds, /s/ and /p/. Try saying the word again.

5. Make the word *rasp* and point to it.

6. **Say:** Touch and say the sounds in *rasp.*

   ▸ How many sounds are in the word? four
   ▸ How many letters are in the word? four
   ▸ Where is the blend? at the end

7. Provide additional guidance if students have difficulty with blends. Take the last letter off the word students are struggling with.

   Say: I have taken the last letter off this word. Touch and say the word without the last sound. What sound do you make at the end of the word? Answers will vary.

   Say: Now I am going to put the last letter back on the word. Touch and say. Now what is the sound you make at the end of the word? What two sounds are heard in the blend at the end of the word? Answers will vary.

Objectives

- Identify and use the blend *sp.*
- Identify ending sounds in words.
- Identify the number of sounds within words.

Build Words

Help students use letters and sounds to build words.

1. Place the following letter tiles at the top of students' whiteboard: *a, g, i, p, r, s,* and *w*.

2. Draw four horizontal lines across the middle of their whiteboard to represent the sounds in a word.

3. **Say:** Let's use letters and sounds to build the word *gasp*.

4. Have students finger stretch the sounds in *gasp*.

5. Have students

   ▸ Identify the individual sounds in *gasp*.
   ▸ Choose the corresponding letter for each of the sounds.
   ▸ Move the letters to the correct lines on their whiteboard.

6. Guide students with these questions:

   ▸ What is the first sound in *gasp*? /g/
     Which line does the letter for that sound go on? the first one
   ▸ What is the next sound in *gasp*? /ă/
     Which line does the letter for that sound go on? the second one
   ▸ What is the next sound in *gasp*? /s/
     Which line does the letter for that sound go on? the third one
   ▸ What's the last sound in *gasp*? /p/
     Which line does the letter for that sound go on? the last one

7. Have students touch and say the word.

8. Redirect students if they select the incorrect letter.

   Say: That sound is in the word [word], and it is the [first, second, third] sound. We want the sound [target sound].

   Continue until students select the correct letter.

9. Repeat the activity to build the following words:

   ▸ *rasp* /r/ /ă/ /s/ /p/
   ▸ *wisp* /w/ /ĭ/ /s/ /p/

Try It

Dissect It

Have students complete page PH 14 in *K¹² PhonicsWorks Advanced Activity Book* for more practice with words that end with the consonant blend *–sp*. Have students read each word aloud. Then have them draw a square around the ending blend and a circle around the vowel. Finally have students read the sentence aloud.

⟦ Online ⟧ ⟨20⟩ minutes

REVIEW: Ending Consonant Blend *–sp*

Students will work online independently to

▶ Practice the ending consonant blend *–sp*.
▶ Practice decoding text by reading sentences.

Help students locate the online activities and provide support as needed.

Offline Alternative

No computer access? Have students point out and name things or words that end with the sound /sp/ (for example, *wasp* or *clasp*). You might also ask students to spell words that end with the consonant blend *–sp*.

Practice Ending Consonant Blends
–*mp* and –*sp*

Lesson Overview

[Offline] **FOCUS:** Practice Ending
Consonant Blends –*mp* and –*sp*

30 minutes

Sight Words	Pick a Pair
Practice	**Signal Ending Sounds**
	I Spy
	Review Sounds
	Review the Ending Consonant Blend –*mp*
	Review the Ending Consonant Blend –*sp*
Try It	**"Ed the Chimp"**
	Dictation: Write Sentences

[Online] **REVIEW:** Ending Consonant
Blends –*mp* and –*sp*

20 minutes

Materials

Supplied
- *K12 PhonicsWorks Readers Advanced 2*, pp. 1–6
- whiteboard, Learning Coach
- whiteboard, student
- Tile Kit

Also Needed
- sight words box
- dictation notebook

 30 minutes

FOCUS: Practice Ending Consonant Blends –*mp* and –*sp*

Work **together** with students to complete offline Sight Words, Practice, and Try It activities.

Sight Words

Pick a Pair

Play a card game with students for more practice with sight words.

1. Gather the sight word cards that students are reviewing. Choose two words and place the cards on the table.

2. Ask questions to help students identify each word. For example, if the words are *or* and *one*, you could ask, "Which word names a number?" If the words are *on* and *but*, you could ask, "Which word is the opposite of *off*?"

3. Continue the activity until students identify all the words.

4. Take the stack of words that students read correctly and dictate each word to them.

5. Have students write each word or spell it aloud.

> **Objectives**
> - Read sight words.
> - Spell sight words.

Practice

Signal Ending Sounds

Use a special signal to help students identify **ending sounds** in words.

1. **Say:** I'm going to tell you some sounds to listen for. Repeat each word I say and make a special signal to tell me where the sound is. If the sound is at the end of the word, clap your hands. If the special sound is not at the end of the word, just smile at me. For example,

   ▸ If I ask you to listen for the sound /lp/ and I say the word *help*, you'll repeat the word *help* and clap your hands because *help* has the sound /lp/ at the end.

   ▸ If I say the word *mop*, you'll repeat the word *mop* and smile at me because *mop* has the sound /p/, not /lp/, at the end.

2. Say each sound and group of words. Have students make the special signal to identify the ending sound.

   ▸ /s/: *will, pass, miss, find* clap: *pass, miss*
   ▸ /d/: *pat, dad, rod, did, friend* clap: *dad, rod, did, friend*
   ▸ /ft/: *lift, hold, raft, sleep, gift* clap: *lift, raft, gift*
   ▸ /mp/: *bull, play, lamp, nail, jump* clap: *lamp, jump*

> **Objectives**
> - Identify ending sounds in words.
> - Identify beginning sounds in words.
> - Identify and use the blend –*mp*.
> - Identify and use the blend *sp*.
> - Identify the number of sounds within words.

I Spy

Have students name and use common objects to help them recognize beginning sounds in words.

1. Explain to students that you will be playing I Spy, and show them how to use the thumb and index finger to make a circle, simulating a spyglass.

2. **Say:** I say, "I spy, with my little eye, something that starts with the sound /l/." Your job is to guess what I spy. What I had in mind was the *light. Light* begins with the sound /l/.

3. Repeat Step 2 with a different object in the room.

4. **Say:** Are you ready to begin? I spy, with my little eye, something that starts with the sound [target sound]. Can you guess what it is?

5. After students have guessed the object, repeat Step 4 until you have spied six objects, or until students tire of the game. Possible words to use are *pencil, window, door, dog, television, radio, telephone, dish, hair, bowl, table, floor, book, paper, computer, cup,* and *rug.*

6. Redirect students if they name an object with an incorrect sound.

   Say: The sound that begins the word [word] is [sound]. We're looking for the sound [target sound]. What is a word that begins with that sound? Now look around the room. What do you see that begins with that sound?

7. Narrow down the search to a certain part of the room if students become frustrated. If students continue to have trouble, narrow down the search to two objects.

   Say: What is the beginning sound of [target word]? What is the beginning sound of [another word]? Which one starts with the sound [target sound]?

Review Sounds

Review sounds with students.

1. Place the following letter tiles at the top of students' whiteboard: *d, f, k, l, n,* and *t.*

2. Place the following letter tiles at the bottom of students' whiteboard: *a, e, g, i, l, m, o, r,* and *s.*

3. **Say:** I'm going to say some words. Your job is to find the letters that make the **beginning** and **ending sounds** of the word.

4. **Say:** First you will repeat the word I say. Then you will find the letters for the ending sound, and move them to the middle of the whiteboard. For example, if I say *sand*, you would repeat the word and move the letter tiles for *n* and *d* to the middle of the board because *n* and *d* blend together to make the sound /nd/.

5. **Say:** Finally you would move the letters *s* and *a* in front of the letters *n* and *d* because *s* and *a* make the sound /să/.

6. Have students touch and say the word. Repeat the procedure with the following words:

- ▸ *land*
- ▸ *milk*
- ▸ *gift*
- ▸ *elk*
- ▸ *send*

- ▸ *left*
- ▸ *soft*
- ▸ *raft*
- ▸ *silk*

Review the Ending Consonant Blend –mp
Help students recognize and use the ending consonant blend –*mp*.

1. Place the following letters on students' whiteboard: *b, m, l, p,* and *u*.

2. Make the word *bump* and point to it.

3. **Say:** Touch and say this word.

- ▸ How many sounds are in the word? four
- ▸ How many letters are in the word? four
- ▸ The sound /mp/ at the end of this word is called a blend because each of the letters, *m* and *p*, keeps its own sound while the two sounds blend together.

4. Redirect students if they have difficulty with the ending consonant blend –*mp*.

Say: Those two letters are often together at the end of a word, and when they are together, they blend into the sound /mp/, as in *lump*. Can you say the word *lump*? When you say the word *lump*, you don't stop between the last two sounds, /m/ and /p/, at the end of the word.

5. Make the word *lump* and point to it.

6. **Say:** Touch and say the sounds in *lump*.

- ▸ How many sounds are in the word? four
- ▸ How many letters are in the word? four
- ▸ Where is the blend? at the end
- ▸ We know that the letters *m* and *p* at the end of this word are called a blend because each of those letters keeps its own sound while the two sounds blend together.

7. Provide additional guidance if students have difficulty with blends. Take the last letter off the word students are struggling with.

   Say: I have taken the last letter off this word. Touch and say the word without the last sound. What sound do you make at the end of the word? Answers will vary.

   Say: Now I am going to put the last letter back on the word. Touch and say. Now what is the sound you make at the end of the word? What two sounds are heard in the blend at the end of the word? Answers will vary.

Review the Ending Consonant Blend –sp

Help students recognize and use the ending consonant blend –sp.

1. Place the following letters on students' whiteboard: *a, g, i, p, s,* and *w*.

2. Make the word *gasp* and point to it.

3. **Say:** Touch and say this word.

   - How many sounds are in the word? four
   - How many letters are in the word? four
   - The sound /sp/ at the end of this word is called a blend because each of those letters keeps its own sound while the two sounds blend together.

4. Make the word *wisp* and point to it.

5. **Say:** Touch and say the sounds in *wisp*.

   - How many sounds are in the word? four
   - How many letters are in the word? four
   - Where is the blend? at the end
   - We know that the letters *s* and *p* at the end of this word are called a blend because each of those letters keeps its own sound while the two sounds blend together.

6. Provide additional guidance if students have difficulty with blends. Take the last letter off the word students are struggling with.

   Say: I have taken the last letter off this word. Touch and say the word without the last sound. What sound do you make at the end of the word? Answers will vary.

   Say: Now I am going to put the last letter back on the word. Touch and say. Now what is the sound you make at the end of the word? What two sounds are heard in the blend at the end of the word? Answers will vary.

Try It ···

"Ed the Chimp"

Have students read "Ed the Chimp" on page 1 of *K¹² PhonicsWorks Readers Advanced 2*.

Students should read the story silently once or twice before reading the story aloud. When they miss a word that can be sounded out, point to it and give them three to six seconds to try the word again. If students still miss the word, tell them the words so the flow of the story isn't interrupted.

After reading the story, make a list of all the words students missed, and go over those words with them. You may use tiles to show how to read the words.

Dictation: Write Sentences

Use sentences to help students identify individual sounds in words.

1. Gather a pencil and the dictation notebook. Say the sentence, *Jack got the lamp.* Then give these directions to students:

   ▸ Repeat the sentence.
   ▸ Write the sentence in your notebook.
   ▸ Read the sentence aloud.

2. When students have finished, write the following sentence on your whiteboard: *Jack got the lamp.*

3. Have them compare their answer to your correct version.

4. Repeat this procedure with the sentence, *Did Mom gasp?*

   ▸ If students make an error and don't see it, help them correct their mistake by having them finger stretch the sounds in the word they missed.
   ▸ If they are having difficulty selecting the correct letters or sounds, review those letters or sounds that are confusing them.
   ▸ If students have difficulty with first, middle, and last sounds, have them finger stretch the sounds in words.

Objectives

- Read aloud grade-level text with appropriate automaticity, prosody, accuracy, and rate.
- Decode words by applying grade-level word analysis skills.
- Write words by applying grade-level phonics knowledge.
- Follow three-step directions.
- Write sight words.
- Read, write, and spell words containing the blend –*mp*.
- Read, write, and spell words containing the blend *sp*.

 **20 minutes**

REVIEW: Ending Consonant Blends *–mp* and *–sp*

Students will work online independently to

▸ Practice the ending consonant blends *–mp* and *–sp*.

Help students locate the online activities and provide support as needed.

Offline Alternative

No computer access? Have students point out and name things or words that contain the ending sounds /mp/ and /sp/ (for example, *jump* and *wasp*). You might also ask students to spell words that end with the consonant blends *–mp* and *-sp*.

Objectives

- Identify and use the blend *sp*.
- Identify and use the blend *–mp*.
- Identify ending sounds in words.

Unit Checkpoint

Lesson Overview

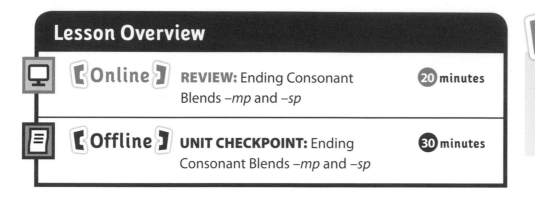

Online   **REVIEW:** Ending Consonant Blends *–mp* and *–sp*   **20** minutes

Offline   **UNIT CHECKPOINT:** Ending Consonant Blends *–mp* and *–sp*   **30** minutes

Materials

Supplied
- *K¹² PhonicsWorks Advanced Assessments,* pp. PH 37–42

Objectives

- Identify and use the blend *–mp*.
- Identify and use the blend *sp*.
- Read, write, and spell words containing the blend *–mp*.
- Read, write, and spell words containing the blend *sp*.
- Identify individual sounds in words.
- Given the letter, identify the most common sound.
- Given the sound, identify the most common letter or letters.
- Read aloud grade-level text with appropriate automaticity, prosody, accuracy, and rate.
- Read instructional-level text with 90% accuracy.
- Read sight words.
- Write sight words.
- Write words by applying grade-level phonics knowledge.

Online   **20** minutes

REVIEW: Ending Consonant Blends *–mp* and *–sp*

Students will review sounds, letters, and consonant blends to prepare for the Unit Checkpoint. Help students locate the online activities and provide support as needed.

[Offline] 🕥 minutes

UNIT CHECKPOINT: Ending Consonant Blends –*mp* and –*sp*

Explain that students are going to show what they have learned about sounds, letters, and words.

1. Give students the Unit Checkpoint pages for the Ending Consonant Blends –*mp* and –*sp* unit and print the Unit Checkpoint Answer Key, if you'd like.

2. Use the instructions below to help administer the Checkpoint to students. On the Answer Key or another sheet of paper, note student answers to oral response questions to help with scoring the Checkpoint later.

3. Use the Answer Key to score the Checkpoint, and then enter the results online.

Part 1. Read Word Parts Moving left to right, have students say the sounds of each word part. Note any word parts they say incorrectly.

Part 2. Finger Stretching Say each word to students. Have them say each word aloud and finger stretch the sounds. Note any words they finger stretch incorrectly.

16. *jump*
17. *asp*
18. *chimp*
19. *wisp*

20. *lamp*
21. *hasp*
22. *thump*
23. *chomp*

Part 3. Dictation Say each word to students. Have them repeat and write the word.

24. *pump*
25. *camp*
26. *limp*

27. *rasp*
28. *gasp*
29. *ramp*

Part 4. Writing Read each sentence to students. Have them repeat and write the sentence.

30. *The chimp can jump.*
31. *An asp can hiss.*

Part 5. Read Aloud Listen to students read the sentences aloud. Count and note the number of words they read correctly.

Part 6. Say Letters Say each sound. Have students say the letter or letters that make that sound. Note any incorrect responses.

33. /ĕ/

34. /ĭ/

35. /kw/

36. /ă/

37. /w/

38. /ch/

39. /th/

40. /ŏ/

41. /ŭ/

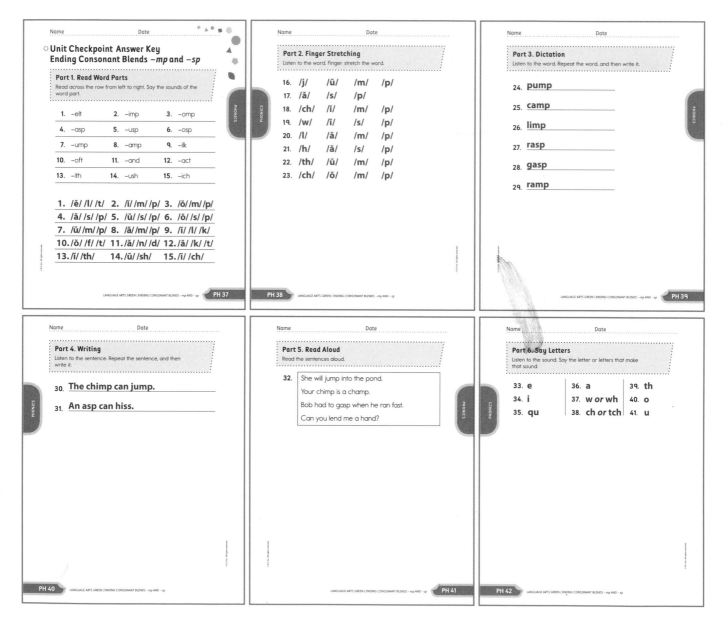

Name _____ **Date** _____

☉ Unit Checkpoint Answer Key
Ending Consonant Blends –mp and –sp

Part 1. Read Word Parts
Read across the row from left to right. Say the sounds of the word part.

1. –elt	2. –imp	3. –omp
4. –asp	5. –usp	6. –osp
7. –ump	8. –amp	9. –ilk
10. –oft	11. –and	12. –act
13. –ith	14. –ush	15. –ich

1. /ĕ/ /l/ /t/   2. /ĭ/ /m/ /p/   3. /ŏ/ /m/ /p/
4. /ă/ /s/ /p/   5. /ŭ/ /s/ /p/   6. /ŏ/ /s/ /p/
7. /ŭ/ /m/ /p/   8. /ă/ /m/ /p/   9. /ĭ/ /l/ /k/
10. /ŏ/ /f/ /t/   11. /ă/ /n/ /d/   12. /ă/ /k/ /t/
13. /ĭ/ /th/   14. /ŭ/ /sh/   15. /ĭ/ /ch/

Name _____ **Date** _____

Part 2. Finger Stretching
Listen to the word. Finger stretch the word.

16. /j/   /ŭ/   /m/   /p/
17. /ă/   /s/   /p/
18. /ch/   /ĭ/   /m/   /p/
19. /w/   /ĭ/   /s/   /p/
20. /l/   /ă/   /m/   /p/
21. /h/   /ă/   /s/   /p/
22. /th/   /ŭ/   /m/   /p/
23. /ch/   /ŏ/   /m/   /p/

Name _____ **Date** _____

Part 3. Dictation
Listen to the word. Repeat the word, and then write it.

24. **pump** _____

25. **camp** _____

26. **limp** _____

27. **rasp** _____

28. **gasp** _____

29. **ramp** _____

Name _____ **Date** _____

Part 4. Writing
Listen to the sentence. Repeat the sentence, and then write it.

30. **The chimp can jump.** _____

31. **An asp can hiss.** _____

Name _____ **Date** _____

Part 5. Read Aloud
Read the sentences aloud.

32. She will jump into the pond.
Your chimp is a champ.
Bob had to gasp when he ran fast.
Can you lend me a hand?

Name _____ **Date** _____

Part 6. Say Letters
Listen to the sound. Say the letter or letters that make that sound.

33. e	36. a	39. th
34. i	37. w or wh	40. o
35. qu	38. ch or tch	41. u

Ending Consonant Blend –sk

Unit Overview

In this unit, students will
- ► Review the letters and sounds of the alphabet.
- ► Learn the ending consonant blends *–sk*, *–st*, *–nt*, and *–nch*.
- ► Review sight words.
- ► Identify beginning, middle, and ending sounds in words.

Lesson Overview

[Offline] FOCUS: Ending Consonant Blend *–sk*　　**30** minutes

Sight Words	Introduce Sight Words
Get Ready	Alphabet Awareness
	Review the Ending Consonant Blend *–mp*
Learn	Introduce the Ending Consonant Blend *–sk*
	Build Words
Try It	The Amazing Alphabet
	Dictation: Write Sentences

[Online] REVIEW: Ending Consonant Blend *–sk*　　**20** minutes

Materials

Supplied
- K¹² *PhonicsWorks Advanced Activity Book,* p. PH 15
- whiteboard, Learning Coach
- whiteboard, student
- Tile Kit

Also Needed
- sight words box
- dictation notebook

Advance Preparation

Place lowercase letter tiles in alphabetical order on your whiteboard.

[Offline] 30 minutes

FOCUS: Ending Consonant Blend –*sk*

Work **together** with students to complete offline Sight Words, Get Ready, Learn, and Try It activities.

Sight Words ···

Introduce Sight Words

Help students learn the sight words *next*, *my*, and *friend*.

1. Gather the sight word cards *next*, *my*, and *friend*.

2. Show students the *next* card.

3. **Say:** This is the word *next*. We see this word so often that we want to be able to read and spell it quickly without thinking about it. Look closely at the word *next*. Spell the word *next* aloud. Take a picture of the word *next* in your mind. When you think you can spell *next* yourself, turn the card over and use your letter tiles to spell the word *next*. Check the card to see if you spelled the word *next* correctly. Read aloud the word you spelled with the letter tiles.

4. Repeat the activity with the remaining sight words.

5. Chart students' progress on the back of each card.

   ► Divide the back of the card into two columns.
   ► Label the first column "Read" and the second column "Spell."
   ► Record the dates that students read or spell the word correctly. When students can read and spell the word correctly three times in a row, they have mastered the word. You may want to put a star or sticker on their card when they have mastered that word.

6. Add the cards to students' sight words box.

TIP Sight words can be very difficult for some students. It's important to let them work at their own pace and really master these words, as they occur frequently in reading and writing.

Objectives
- Read sight words.
- Spell sight words.

Get Ready ···

Alphabet Awareness

To help students master the letters of the alphabet, have them practice identifying and naming letters. Grab your whiteboard with letters placed in alphabetical order.

1. For each letter, have students

   ► Touch the tile.
   ► Say the name of the letter.
   ► Say the sound the letter makes.
   ► Say the name of something that begins with that sound.

Objectives
- Identify letters of the alphabet.
- Given the letter, identify the most common sound.
- Identify the number of sounds within words.
- Identify ending sounds in words.
- Identify and use the blend –*mp*.

2. **Say:** I'll do the first one. The first letter is *a*. Its sound can be the sound /ă/. *Apple* starts with /ă/. Now it's your turn. What letter comes after *a*? Touch that letter as you tell me the letter and the sound it makes. Then tell me a word that starts with that sound.

Review the Ending Consonant Blend –*mp*

Help students recognize and use the ending consonant blend –*mp*.

1. Make the word *lump* on students' whiteboard and point to it.

2. **Say:** Touch and say this word.

   ▸ How many sounds are in the word? four
   ▸ How many letters are in the word? four
   ▸ We know that the letters *m* and *p* at the end of this word are called a blend because each letter keeps its own sound while the two sounds blend together.

Learn •••

Introduce the Ending Consonant Blend –*sk*

Help students recognize and use the ending consonant blend –*sk*.

1. Place the following letters on students' whiteboard: *a, k, m,* and *s*.

2. Make the word *ask* and point to it.

3. **Say:** Touch and say this word.

   ▸ How many sounds are in the word? three
   ▸ How many letters are in the word? three
   ▸ We know that the letters *s* and *k* at the end of this word are called a blend because each letters keep its own sound while the two sounds blend together.

4. Redirect students if they have difficulty with the blended sound /sk/.

   Say: Those two letters are often together at the end of a word. When they are together, they blend into the sound /sk/, as in *task*. Can you say the word *task*? When you say *task*, don't stop between the last two sounds /s/ and /k/. Try saying the word again.

5. Make the word *mask* and point to it.

6. **Say:** Touch and say the sounds in *mask*.

   ▸ How many sounds are in the word? four
   ▸ How many letters are in the word? four
   ▸ Where is the blend? at the end

Objectives

- Identify and use the blend *sk*.
- Identify the number of sounds within words.
- Identify ending sounds in words.
- Identify individual sounds in words.

7. Provide additional guidance if students have difficulty with blends. Take the last letter off the word students are struggling with.

   Say: I have taken the last letter off this word. Touch and say the word without the last sound. What sound do you make at the end of the word? Answers will vary.

   Say: Now I am going to put the last letter back on the word. Touch and say the word. Which two sounds do you hear in the blend at the end of the word? Answers will vary.

Build Words

Help students use letters and sounds to build words.

1. Place the following letter tiles at the top of students' whiteboard: *a, d, e, i, k, r, s,* and *t*.

2. Draw four horizontal lines across the middle of students' whiteboard to represent the sounds in a word.

3. **Say:** Let's use letters and sounds to build the word *desk*.

4. Have students finger stretch the sounds in *desk*.

5. Have students

   ▸ Identify the first, next, and last sounds in *desk*.
   ▸ Choose the corresponding letter for each of the sounds.
   ▸ Move the letters to the correct lines on their whiteboard.

6. Guide students with these questions:

   ▸ What is the first sound in *desk*? /d/
     Which line does the letter for that sound go on? the first one
   ▸ What is the next sound in *desk*? /ĕ/
     Which line does the letter for that sound go on? the second one
   ▸ What is the next sound in *desk*? /s/
     Which line does the letter for that sound go on? the third one
   ▸ What's the last sound in *desk*? /k/
     Which line does the letter for that sound go on? the last one

7. Have students touch and say the word.

8. Redirect students if they select the incorrect letter.

   Say: That sound is in the word [word], and it is the [first, second, third, fourth] sound. We want the sound [target sound].

   Continue until students select the correct letter.

9. Repeat the activity to build the following words:

   ▸ *risk* /r/ /ĭ/ /s/ /k/
   ▸ *task* /t/ /ă/ /s/ /k/

Try It

The Amazing Alphabet

Have students complete page PH 15 in *K¹² PhonicsWorks Advanced Activity Book* for more practice with words that end with the ending consonant blend *–sk*. Have students say the name of each picture and circle the letters that complete the word. Have them write the letters in the box.

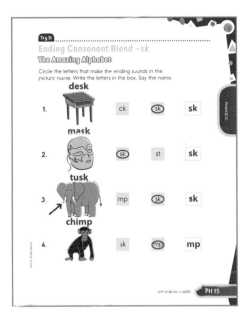

Dictation: Write Sentences

Use sentences to help students identify individual sounds in words.

1. Gather a pencil and the dictation notebook. Say the sentence, *Ask him for milk.* Then give these directions to students:

   ▸ Repeat the sentence.
   ▸ Write the sentence in your notebook.
   ▸ Read the sentence aloud.

2. When students have finished, write the following sentence on your whiteboard: *Ask him for milk.*

3. Have them compare their answer to your correct version.

4. Repeat this procedure with the sentence, *Pam had a fun mask.*

   ▸ If students make an error and don't see it, help them correct their mistake by having them finger stretch the sounds in the word they missed.
   ▸ If students are having difficulty selecting the correct letters or sounds, review those letters or sounds that are confusing them.
   ▸ If students have difficulty with first, middle, and last sounds, have them finger stretch the sounds in words.

 **20 minutes**

REVIEW: Ending Consonant Blend *–sk*

Students will work online independently to

▸ Practice the ending consonant blend *–sk*.

▸ Practice decoding text by reading a story.

Help students locate the online activities and provide support as needed.

Offline Alternative

No computer access? Have students point out and name things or words that end with the consonant blend *–sk* (for example, *task* or *mask*). You might also ask students to spell words that end with the consonant blend *–sk*.

⭐ **Objectives**

- Identify ending sounds in words.
- Identify and use the blend *sk*.
- Read aloud grade-level text with appropriate automaticity, prosody, accuracy, and rate.
- Decode words by applying grade-level word analysis skills.

Ending Consonant Blend –*st*

Lesson Overview

Offline FOCUS: Ending Consonant Blend –*st*   30 minutes

Sight Words	Sight Word Fun
Get Ready	Listen for Beginning Sounds
	Sort Blends
	Review the Ending Consonant Blend –*sk*
Learn	Introduce the Ending Consonant Blend –*st*
	Word Chains
	Make More Words: Beginning Blends
Try It	"The Best Nest"

Online REVIEW: Ending Consonant Blend –*st*   20 minutes

Materials

Supplied
- *K¹² PhonicsWorks Readers Advanced 2*, pp. 7–12
- whiteboard, student
- Tile Kit

Also Needed
- sight words box
- index cards (12)

Advance Preparation

For Sort Blends, print each of the following words on index cards, using one card per word: *risk, lump, husk, rash, desk, match, mask, dims, disk, ball, ask,* and *fuss.*

[Offline] **30** minutes

FOCUS: Ending Consonant Blend *–st*
Work **together** with students to complete offline Sight Words, Get Ready, Learn, and Try It activities.

Sight Words ···

Sight Word Fun
Help students learn the sight words *next*, *my*, and *friend*, and up to two additional sight words students have yet to master.

1. Gather the sight word cards *next*, *my*, and *friend*, and up to two additional sight word cards.

2. Choose one sight word card to begin.

   Say: Look at this word and take a picture of it in your mind. When you think you can spell the word yourself, turn the card over and use your letter tiles to spell the word.

3. After students spell the word, have them check the card to see if they spelled the word correctly.

   Say: Read aloud the word you spelled with the letter tiles.

4. Repeat the activity with the remaining sight words.

(TIP) Sight words can be very difficult for some students. Let students work at their own pace and really master these words.

> **Objectives**
> - Read sight words.
> - Spell sight words.

Get Ready ···

Listen for Beginning Sounds
Help students identify **beginning sounds** in words.

1. **Say:** I'm going to say a word. Listen for the beginning sound. Then tell me the sound.

   ▸ For example, if I say *mop*, you will say /m/ because the first sound you hear in *mop* is /m/.
   ▸ Now it's your turn. Listen to the word I say. You repeat the word, and then tell me the first sound in the word.

> **Objectives**
> - Identify beginning sounds in words.
> - Identify ending sounds in words.
> - Identify the number of sounds within words.
> - Identify and use the blend *sk*.

2. Repeat the process, using the following words to help students recognize beginning sounds:

- *forward* /f/
- *daily* /d/
- *then* /<u>th</u>/
- *check* /ch/

- *shelf* /sh/
- *play* /p/
- *rocket* /r/
- *west* /w/

Sort Blends

Help students identify words that have the **ending sound /sk/**.

1. Gather the index cards that you prepared, and place them in random order in front of students.

2. **Say:** Some of these words have the sound /sk/ at the end. Your job is to find those words and make a pile of them.

- First touch and say each word.
- Then put the cards ending with /sk/ in a pile.

TIP To extend this activity, scramble the cards when students have finished and then read the words to them. Have them put their hands on their head when they hear a word with the ending consonant blend –*sk*.

Review the Ending Consonant Blend –*sk*

Help students recognize and use the ending consonant blend –*sk*.

1. Make the word *mask* on students' whiteboard and point to it.

2. **Say:** Touch and say this word.

- How many sounds are in the word? four
- How many letters are in the word? four
- We know that the letters *s* and *k* at the end of this word are called a blend because each letter keeps its own sound while the two sounds blend together.

Learn

Introduce the Ending Consonant Blend –*st*

Help students recognize and use the ending consonant blend –*st*.

1. Place the following letters on students' whiteboard: *b, e, r, s,* and *t*.

2. Make the word *best* and point to it.

3. **Say:** Touch and say this word.

   ▸ How many sounds are in the word? four
   ▸ How many letters are in the word? four
   ▸ We know that the letters *s* and *t* at the end of this word are called a blend because each letter keeps its own sound while the two sounds blend together.

4. Redirect students if they have difficulty with the blended sound /st/.

   Say: Those two letters are often together at the end of a word. When they are together, they blend into the sound /st/, as in *lost*. Can you say the word *lost*? When you say *lost*, don't stop between the last two sounds /s/ and t/. Try saying the word again.

5. Make the word *rest* and point to it.

6. **Say:** Touch and say the sounds in *rest*.

   ▸ How many sounds are in the word? four
   ▸ How many letters are in the word? four
   ▸ Where is the blend? at the end

7. Provide additional guidance if students have difficulty with blends. Take the last letter off the word students are struggling with.

   Say: I have taken the last letter off this word. Touch and say the word without the last sound. What sound do you make at the end of the word? Answers will vary.

   Say: Now I am going to put the last letter back on the word. Touch and say the word. Which two sounds are heard in the blend at the end of the word? Answers will vary.

Word Chains

Have students build words by adding and changing letters to help them recognize and use individual sounds in words.

1. Place the following letters at the top of students' whiteboard: *b, e, n, qu, r, s, t, t,* and *w*.

2. **Say:** I am going to build the first word in a chain. The word is *rest*.

   ▸ I will pull down the letters for the sounds /r/, /ĕ/, /s/, and /t/ to spell the word *rest*.
   ▸ I will touch and say *rest*. To change *rest* to *test*, I will think about which sound changes from the word *rest* to *test*. I will need to replace the letter *r* with the letter *t*.
   ▸ Touch and say the word *test*. Now it's your turn to change *test* to *west*. You can spell *west* by making only one change. Touch and say the new word.

3. Redirect students if they select the incorrect letter for any sound.

   Say: That letter is for the sound [incorrect sound]. We want the letter for the sound [target sound]. What letter makes that sound? Answers will vary.

4. Redirect students if they select the wrong sound.

   Say: To change the word [first word] to [target word], we need the letter for the sound [target sound].

   Show students how to make the change. Have them touch and say the new word after they move the letters.

5. Follow this procedure to make the following words: *quest* and *best*.

6. For every new word, students should add, replace, or remove only one letter tile.

Make More Words: Beginning Blends

Have students add letters to and remove letters from words to make new words.

1. Place the following letters on students' whiteboard: *a, b, d, e, f, h, l, n, o, p,* and *s*.

2. Build the following word in the center of the board, with room to add a letter in front: *and*.

3. **Say:** When I put the letter *h* before the word *and*, I make a new word, *hand*. See how many new **real words** you can make by putting the letters on your whiteboard in front of *and*. *land, sand, band*

4. Continue this activity with the following combinations:

   ▸ letters *s, b,* and *l* and the ending *–end send, bend, lend*
   ▸ letters *p, b,* and *f* and the ending *–ond pond, bond, fond*

Try It ....

"The Best Nest"

Have students read "The Best Nest" on page 7 of *K¹² PhonicsWorks Readers Advanced 2.*

Students should read the story silently once or twice before reading the story aloud. When they miss a word that can be sounded out, point to it and give them three to six seconds to try the word again. If students still miss the word, tell them the word so the flow of the story isn't interrupted.

After reading the story, make a list of all the words students missed, and go over those words with them. You may use letter tiles to show them how to read the words.

Objectives

- Read aloud grade-level text with appropriate automaticity, prosody, accuracy, and rate.
- Decode words by applying grade-level word analysis skills.

 **20 minutes**

REVIEW: Ending Consonant Blend *–st*

Students will work online independently to

▸ Practice the ending consonant blend *–st.*

Help students locate the online activities and provide support as needed.

Objectives

- Identify individual sounds in words.
- Identify and use the blend *st.*

Offline Alternative

No computer access? Have students point out and name things or words that end with the consonant blend *–st* (for example, *post* or *last*). You might also ask students to spell words that end with the consonant blend *–st.*

Ending Consonant Blend –nt

Lesson Overview

[Offline] **FOCUS:** Ending Consonant Blend –nt — **30** minutes

Sight Words	Sight Word Fun
Get Ready	Review Vowel Sounds and Letters
	Questions About Letters and Sounds
	I Spy
	Review the Ending Consonant Blend –st
Learn	Introduce the Ending Consonant Blend –nt
Try It	Sorting Day
	Dictation: Write Sentences

[Online] **REVIEW:** Ending Consonant Blend –nt — **20** minutes

Materials

Supplied
- *K¹² PhonicsWorks Advanced Activity Book,* p. PH 16
- whiteboard, Learning Coach
- whiteboard, student
- Tile Kit

Also Needed
- sight words box
- dictation notebook
- crayons

Advance Preparation

Place lowercase letter tiles in alphabetical order, including the digraphs and trigraph, on your whiteboard.

[Offline] 30 minutes

FOCUS: Ending Consonant Blend –nt

Work **together** with students to complete offline Sight Words, Get Ready, Learn, and Try It activities.

Sight Words ●

Sight Word Fun

Help students learn the sight words the words *next*, *my*, and *friend*, and up to two additional sight words they have yet to master.

1. Gather the sight word cards *next*, *my*, and *friend*, and up to two additional sight word cards.

2. Choose one sight word card to begin.

   Say: Look at this word and take a picture of it in your mind. When you think you can spell the word yourself, turn the card over and use your letter tiles to spell the word.

3. After students spell the word, have them check the card to see if they spelled the word correctly.

   Say: Read aloud the word you spelled with the letter tiles.

4. Repeat the activity with the remaining sight words.

   TIP Sight words can be very difficult for some students. Let students work at their own pace and really master these words.

> **Objectives**
> - Read sight words.
> - Spell sight words.

Get Ready ●

Review Vowel Sounds and Letters

Help students review vowel sounds and letters.

1. Place the following letter tiles on students' whiteboard: *a, i, o,* and *u,* plus any letters that are confusing for students.

2. **Say:** I am going to point to each letter. Tell me the sound for that letter.

3. **Say:** I am going to say each sound. Repeat the sound and touch its letter.

4. Point to some letters two or three times, so students don't think that once they have named a sound they are finished with it.

5. Redirect students if they name the letter and not its sound.

   Say: You are right that the name of the letter is [letter]. We want the sound for this letter. What is the sound?

6. Redirect students if they name the sound incorrectly.

   Say: That is the sound of another letter.

> **Objectives**
> - Identify and use vowels and vowel sounds.
> - Identify letters of the alphabet.
> - Given the letter, identify the most common sound.
> - Identify beginning sounds in words.
> - Identify and use the blend *st.*
> - Identify ending sounds in words.

7. Provide additional guidance if students touch the wrong letter during the review.

   Say: That is the letter for the sound [sound of touched letter]. We are looking for the letter for the sound [target sound].

8. If students touch the wrong letter again, point to the correct letter.

   Say: This is the letter for the sound [target sound]. Touch this letter and say its sound.

Questions About Letters and Sounds

To help students master the letters and sounds of the alphabet, digraphs, and trigraphs, have them practice identifying and naming them.

1. Grab your whiteboard with letters placed in alphabetical order, including the digraphs and trigraph.

2. **Say:** What letter is always followed by a *u*? *q*

3. Have students touch all the letters that spell the sound /k/. *c, k*

4. Have students touch all the digraphs and say their sounds. *ch, /ch/; sh, /sh/; th, /th/ or /th/; wh, /w/*

5. Have students touch the trigraph and say its sound. *tch, /ch/*

I Spy

Have students name and use common objects to help them recognize individual sounds in words.

1. Explain to students that you will be playing I Spy, and show them how to use the thumb and index finger to make a circle, simulating a spyglass.

2. **Say:** I say, "I spy, with my little eye, something that starts with the sound /l/." Your job is to guess what I spy. What I had in mind was the *light. Light* begins with the sound /l/.

3. Repeat Step 2 with a different object in the room.

4. **Say:** Are you ready to begin? I spy, with my little eye, something that starts with the sound [target sound]. Can you guess what it is?

5. After students have guessed the object, repeat Step 4 until you have spied six objects, or until students tire of the game. Possible words to use are *pencil, window, pen, table, lamp, light, television, book, radio, paper, telephone, computer, fork, cup, hair,* and *rug.*

6. Redirect students if they name an object with an incorrect sound.

   Say: The sound that begins the word [word] is [sound]. We're looking for the sound [target sound]. What is a word that begins with that sound? Now look around the room. What do you see that begins with that sound?

7. Narrow down the search to a certain part of the room if students become frustrated. If students continue to have trouble, narrow down the search to two objects.

   Say: What is the beginning sound of [target word]? What is the beginning sound of [another word]? Which one starts with the sound [target sound]?

Review the Ending Consonant Blend –st
Help students recognize and use the ending consonant blend –st.

1. Place the following letters on students' whiteboard: *a, c, e, l, o, r, s, t,* and *u.*

2. Make the word *rest* and point to it.

3. **Say:** Touch and say this word.

   ▸ How many sounds are in the word? four
   ▸ How many letters are in the word? four
   ▸ We know that the letters *s* and *t* at the end of this word are called a blend because each letter keeps its own sound while the two sounds blend together.

4. Repeat this procedure with the following words:

   ▸ *last*
   ▸ *cost*
   ▸ *rust*

Learn

Introduce the Ending Consonant Blend –nt
Help students recognize and use the ending consonant blend –nt.

1. Place the following letters on students' whiteboard: *e, i, n, s, t,* and *w.*

2. Make the word *went* and point to it.

3. **Say:** Touch and say this word.

   ▸ How many sounds are in the word? four
   ▸ How many letters are in the word? four
   ▸ We know that the letters *n* and *t* at the end of this word are called a blend because each letter keeps its own sound while the two sounds blend together.

4. Redirect students if they have difficulty with the blended sound /nt/.

   Say: Those two letters are often together at the end of a word. When they are together, they blend into the sound /nt/, as in *mint.* Can you say the word *mint*? When you say *mint,* don't stop between the last two sounds /n/ and/t/. Try saying the word again.

5. Make the word *sent* and point to it.

Objectives
- Identify and use the blend –nt.
- Identify ending sounds in words.
- Identify the number of sounds within words.

6. **Say:** Touch and say the sounds in *sent*.

   ▸ How many sounds are in the word? four
   ▸ How many letters are in the word? four
   ▸ Where is the blend? at the end

7. Provide additional guidance if students have difficulty with blends. Take the last letter off the word students are struggling with.

   Say: I have taken the last letter off this word. Touch and say the word without the last sound. What sound do you make at the end of the word? Answers will vary.

   Say: Now I am going to put the last letter back on the word. Touch and say the word. Which two sounds do you hear in the blend at the end of the word? Answers will vary.

Try It

Sorting Day

Have students complete page PH 16 in *K¹² PhonicsWorks Advanced Activity Book* for more practice with words that end with consonant blends. Have students say each word aloud. Have them color words that are things yellow, and words that are ways to speak pink.

Try It
Ending Consonant Blend –*nt*
Sorting Day

Color the words that name things yellow.
Color the words that name ways to speak pink.

tell	hint **pink**	tent	mask **yellow**
chant **pink**	desk **yellow**	vest **yellow**	ask **pink**
yell **pink**	chest **yellow**	quilt **yellow**	nest **yellow**

PH 16   LANGUAGE ARTS GREEN

Objectives

- Identify ending sounds in words.
- Identify and use the blend –*nt*.
- Write words by applying grade-level phonics knowledge.
- Write sight words.
- Follow three-step directions.

Dictation: Write Sentences

Use sentences to help students identify individual sounds in words.

1. Gather a pencil and the dictation notebook. Say the sentence, *I had to ask if Pat went last.* Then give these directions to students:

   ▸ Repeat the sentence.
   ▸ Write the sentence in your notebook.
   ▸ Read the sentence aloud.

2. When students have finished, write the following sentence on your whiteboard: *I had to ask if Pat went last.*

3. Have them compare their answer to your correct version.

4. Repeat this procedure with the sentence, *I sent Jim to rent a big tent.*

   ▸ If students make an error and don't see it, help them correct their mistake by having them finger stretch the sounds in the word they missed.
   ▸ If students are having difficulty selecting the correct letters or sounds, review those letters or sounds that are confusing them.
   ▸ If students have difficulty with first, middle, and last sounds, have them finger stretch the sounds in words.

 **20 minutes**

REVIEW: Ending Consonant Blend *–nt*

Students will work online independently to

▸ Practice the ending consonant blend *–nt*.
▸ Practice decoding text by reading sentences.

Help students locate the online activities and provide support as needed.

Offline Alternative

No computer access? Have students point out and name things or words that end with the consonant blend *–nt* (for example, *went* or *tent*). You might also ask students to spell words that end with the consonant blend *–nt*.

Objectives

- Identify and use the blend *–nt*.
- Identify ending sounds in words.
- Read aloud grade-level text with appropriate automaticity, prosody, accuracy, and rate.
- Decode words by applying grade-level word analysis skills.

Ending Consonant Blend –nch

Lesson Overview

[Offline] **FOCUS:** Ending Consonant Blend –nch — **30** minutes

Sight Words	Sight Word Fun
Get Ready	Create Rhyming Words
	Climb the Ladder
	Review the Ending Consonant Blend –nt
Learn	Introduce the Ending Consonant Blend –nch
	Build Words
Try It	"Quinn and Kent Have a Friend"

[Online] **REVIEW:** Ending Consonant Blend –nch — **20** minutes

Materials

Supplied
- *K¹² PhonicsWorks Readers Advanced 2*, pp. 13–18
- whiteboard, student
- Tile Kit

Also Needed
- sight words box

[Offline] ⏱ 30 minutes

FOCUS: Ending Consonant Blend –*nch*

Work **together** with students to complete offline Sight Words, Get Ready, Learn, and Try It activities.

Sight Words

Sight Word Fun

Help students learn the sight words the words *next*, *my*, and *friend*, and up to two additional sight words they have yet to master.

1. Gather the sight word cards *next*, *my*, and *friend*, and up to two additional sight word cards.

2. Choose one sight word card to begin.

   Say: Look at this word and take a picture of it in your mind. When you think you can spell the word yourself, turn the card over and use your letter tiles to spell the word.

3. After students spell the word, have them check the card to see if they spelled the word correctly.

   Say: Read aloud the word you spelled with the letter tiles.

4. Repeat the activity with the remaining sight words.

TIP Sight words can be very difficult for some students. Let students work at their own pace and really master these words.

> **Objectives**
> - Read sight words.
> - Spell sight words.

Get Ready

Create Rhyming Words

Have students combine word parts and make words that rhyme.

1. **Say:** I'm going to break a word into two parts. Your job is to put the parts back together and say the word. For example,

   ▸ If the first part of the word is /b/ and the last part is /ĕnt/, then you'll say *bent*: /b/ . . . /ĕnt/ . . . *bent*.
   ▸ Next you'll add a new **beginning sound** to make a word that rhymes. You'll use the same last part, /ĕnt/, and a new first sound, /r/. That rhyming word is /r/ . . . /ĕnt/ . . . *rent*.

> **Objectives**
> - Identify words that rhyme.
> - Identify beginning sounds in words.
> - Identify individual sounds in words.
> - Identify ending sounds in words.
> - Identify and use the blend –*nt*.

2. Have students add a new beginning sound to the last part of the word and make a rhyming word. Continue with this procedure until students have made all the words in the list.

> ▸ /w/ . . . /ĕnt/ *went*; Possible rhyming words: *dent, tent, sent*
> ▸ /m/ . . . /ĭnt/ *mint*; Possible rhyming words: *lint, hint, tint*

TIP Students do not need to know the terms *onset* and *rime*. Instead, use the phrases *first part* and *last part*, or *rest of the word*, with students.

Climb the Ladder

Help students use letters to build words.

1. On students' whiteboards or a sheet of paper, draw a ladder with five or more rungs.

2. Write the word *bent* on the bottom rung.

3. Point to the word *bent*.

   Say: I can make the word *rent* by changing one letter in this word.

4. Write the word *rent* on the second rung of the ladder.

   Say: Think of a word that you can make by changing only one letter in *rent*. Tell me the word and write it on the next step on the ladder.

5. If students struggle, coach them to change the first letter in each word.

   Say: Read the word on the bottom rung. What sound do you hear at the beginning of the word? What letter has that sound?

   Say: Name a word that rhymes with the word at the bottom. What sound do you hear at the beginning of the rhyming word? What letter has that sound? Make a new word by using the new letter. Read the new word.

6. Continue the process until students reach the top of the ladder. Remind students that they may change only one sound: the beginning, second, third, or last sound.

7. Redirect students if they select a word that changes more than one letter.

   Say: How many letters changed from the last word to your new word? Try to think of a word that has only one letter change.

8. Redirect students if they spell a word incorrectly, but the sounds they spell are correct (such as *ruf* for *rough*).

   Say: You have the sounds and letters right, but that word doesn't follow our spelling rules. We will learn how to spell it later. Try another word.

TIP If students have difficulty thinking of real words, have them use nonsense words.

Review the Ending Consonant Blend –nt

Help students recognize and use the ending consonant blend –nt.

1. Make the word *bent* on students' whiteboard and point to it.

2. **Say:** Touch and say this word.

   ▶ How many sounds are in the word? four
   ▶ How many letters are in the word? four
   ▶ We know that the letters *n* and *t* at the end of this word are called a blend because each letter keeps its own sound while the two sounds blend together.

Learn

Introduce the Ending Consonant Blend –nch

Help students recognize and use the ending consonant blend –nch.

1. Place the following letter tiles on students' whiteboard: *b, c, ch, e, n,* and *u.*

2. Make the word *bench* and point to it.

3. **Say:** Touch and say this word.

   ▶ How many sounds are in the word? four
   ▶ How many letters are in the word? five
   ▶ We know that the letters *n* and *ch* at the end of this word are called a blend because the letter *n* and the digraph *ch* each keeps its own sound while the two sounds blend together.

4. Redirect students if they have difficulty with the blended sound /nch/.

   Say: Those three letters are often together at the end of a word. When they are together, they blend into the sound /nch/, as in *lunch.* Can you say the word *lunch?* When you say *lunch,* don't stop between the last two sounds /n/ and /ch/. Try saying the word again.

5. Make the word *bunch* and point to it.

6. **Say:** Touch and say the sounds in *bunch.*

   ▶ How many sounds are in the word? four
   ▶ How many letters are in the word? five
   ▶ Where is the blend? at the end

7. Provide additional guidance if students have difficulty with blends. Take the last two letters off the word students are struggling with.

   Say: I have taken the last two letters off this word. Touch and say the word without the last sound. What sound do you make at the end of the word? Answers will vary.

   Say: Now I am going to put the last two letters back on the word. Touch and say. Now what is the sound you make at the end of the word? What two sounds are heard in the blend at the end of the word? Answers will vary.

Objectives

- Identify and use the blend –nch.
- Identify ending sounds in words.
- Identify the number of sounds within words.
- Identify individual sounds in words.

Build Words

Help students use letters and sounds to build words.

1. Place the following letter tiles at the top of students' whiteboard: *a, ch, i, l, n, p, r,* and *u*.

2. Draw four horizontal lines across the middle of students' whiteboard to represent the sounds in a word.

3. **Say:** Let's use letters and sounds to build the word *ranch*.

4. Have students finger stretch the sounds in *ranch*.

5. Have students

    ▸ Identify the first, next, and last sounds in *ranch*.
    ▸ Choose the corresponding letter or letters for each of the sounds.
    ▸ Move the letters to the correct lines on their whiteboard.

6. Guide students with these questions:

    ▸ What is the first sound in *ranch*? /r/
      Which line does the letter for that sound go on? the first one
    ▸ What is the next sound in *ranch*? /ă/
      Which line does the letter for that sound go on? the second one
    ▸ What's the third sound in *ranch*? /n/
      Which line does the letter for that sound go on? the third one
    ▸ What's the last sound in *ranch*? /ch/
      Which line do the letters for that sound go on? the last one

7. Have students touch and say the word.

8. Redirect students if they select the incorrect letter or letters.

    Say: That sound is in the word [word], and it is the [first, second, third, fourth] sound. We want the sound [target sound].

    Continue until students select the correct letter or letters.

9. Redirect students if they have difficulty blending sounds into a word.

    ▸ Position the letters in the word about two inches apart.
    ▸ Place students' fingers on the first letter and have them say the sound of the first letter while moving the tile to touch the second letter.
    ▸ When the first letter touches the second letter, have students immediately say the sound of that letter.
    ▸ When the first two letters touch the next letter, have students immediately say the sound of that letter.
    ▸ When the first three letters touch the last letters, have them say the last sound. In this way, students blend the sounds into a word in a multisensory way.

10. Repeat the activity to build the following words:

    ▸ *punch* /p/ /ŭ/ /n/ /ch/
    ▸ *lunch* /l/ /ŭ/ /n/ /ch/
    ▸ *pinch* /p/ /ĭ/ /n/ /ch/

TIP If students don't know the sounds for the letters, review the sounds and letters again.

Try It •

"Quinn and Kent Have a Friend"

Have students read "Quinn and Kent Have a Friend" on page 13 of *K¹² PhonicsWorks Readers Advanced 2*.

Students should read the story silently once or twice before reading the story aloud. When students miss a word that can be sounded out, point to it and give them three to six seconds to try the word again. If students still miss the word, tell them the word so the flow of the story isn't interrupted.

After reading the story, make a list of all the words students missed, and go over those words with them. You may use letter tiles to show students how to read the words.

> **Objectives**
> - Read aloud grade-level text with appropriate automaticity, prosody, accuracy, and rate.
> - Decode words by applying grade-level word analysis skills.

 **Online** **20** minutes

REVIEW: Ending Consonant Blend *–nch*

Students will work online independently to

▸ Practice the ending consonant blend *–nch*.

Help students locate the online activities and provide support as needed.

> **Objectives**
> - Identify ending sounds in words.
> - Identify and use the blend *–nch*.

Offline Alternative

No computer access? Have students point out and name things or words that end with the consonant blend *–nch* (for example, *bench* or *munch*). You might also ask students to spell words that end with the consonant blend *–nch*.

Unit Checkpoint

Lesson Overview

🖥	**【Online】**	**REVIEW:** Ending Consonant Blends –*sk*, –*st*, –*nt*, and –*nch*	**20** minutes
📄	**【Offline】**	**UNIT CHECKPOINT:** Ending Consonant Blends –*sk*, –*st*, –*nt*, and –*nch*	**30** minutes

【Materials】

Supplied
- *K¹² PhonicsWorks Advanced Assessments*, pp. PH 43–48

★ Objectives

- Identify and use the blend *sk*.
- Identify and use the blend *st*.
- Identify and use the blend –*nt*.
- Identify and use the blend –*nch*.
- Read, write, and spell words containing the blend *sk*.
- Read, write, and spell words containing the blend *st*.
- Read, write, and spell words containing the blend –*nt*.
- Read, write, and spell words containing the blend –*nch*.
- Identify individual sounds in words.
- Identify the number of sounds within words.
- Given the letter, identify the most common sound.
- Given the sound, identify the most common letter or letters.
- Read aloud grade-level text with appropriate automaticity, prosody, accuracy, and rate.
- Read instructional-level text with 90% accuracy.
- Write words by applying grade-level phonics knowledge.
- Read sight words.
- Write sight words.
- Spell sight words.

【Online】 **20** minutes

REVIEW: : Ending Consonant Blends –*sk*, –*st*, –*nt*, and –*nch*

Students will review sounds, letters, and the ending consonant blends –*sk*, –*st*, –*nt*, and –*nch* to review for the Unit Checkpoint. Help students locate the online activities and provide support as needed.

[Offline] 🕥 minutes

UNIT CHECKPOINT: Ending Consonant Blends –sk, –st, –nt, and –nch

Explain that students are going to show what they have learned about sounds, letters, and words.

1. Give students the Unit Checkpoint pages for the Ending Consonant Blends –sk, –st, –nt, and –nch unit and print the Unit Checkpoint Answer Key, if you'd like.

2. Use the instructions below to help administer the Checkpoint to students. On the Answer Key or another sheet of paper, note student answers to oral response questions to help with scoring the Checkpoint later.

3. Use the Answer Key to score the Checkpoint, and then enter the results online.

Part 1. Read Word Parts Moving left to right, have students say the sounds of each word part. Note any word parts they say incorrectly.

Part 2. Finger Stretching Say each word to students. Have them say each word aloud and finger stretch the sounds. Note any words they finger stretch incorrectly.

16. *desk*	20. *ask*
17. *just*	21. *west*
18. *tent*	22. *lunch*
19. *went*	23. *bench*

Part 3. Dictation Say each word to students. Have them repeat and write the word.

24. *task*	27. *dust*
25. *pinch*	28. *rent*
26. *sent*	29. *bunch*

Part 4. Writing Read each sentence to students. Have them repeat and write the sentence.

30. *I must rest.*

31. *He lost his mask.*

Part 5. Read Aloud Listen to students read the sentences aloud. Count and note the number of words they read correctly.

Part 6. Say Letters Say each sound. Have students say the letter or letters that make that sound. Note any incorrect responses.

33. /ŏ/
34. /th/
35. /y/
36. /ă/
37. /w/

38. /ch/
39. /ĕ/
40. /ĭ/
41. /ŭ/

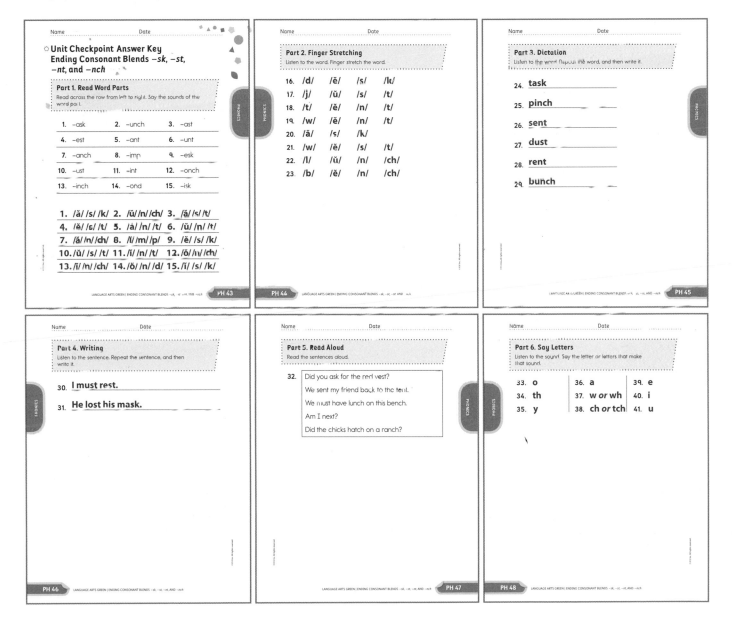

Name _____ Date _____

○ **Unit Checkpoint Answer Key**
Ending Consonant Blends –*sk*, –*st*, –*nt*, and –*nch*

Part 1. Read Word Parts
Read across the row from left to right. Say the sounds of the word part.

1. –ask   2. –unch   3. –ast
4. –est   5. –ant   6. –unt
7. –anch   8. –imp   9. –esk
10. –ust   11. –int   12. –onch
13. –inch   14. –ond   15. –isk

1. /ă/ /s/ /k/ 2. /ŭ/ /n/ /ch/ 3. /ă/ /s/ /t/
4. /ĕ/ /s/ /t/ 5. /ă/ /n/ /t/   6. /ŭ/ /n/ /t/
7. /ă/ /n/ /ch/ 8. /ĭ/ /m/ /p/ 9. /ĕ/ /s/ /k/
10. /ŭ/ /s/ /t/ 11. /ĭ/ /n/ /t/ 12. /ŏ/ /n/ /ch/
13. /ĭ/ /n/ /ch/ 14. /ŏ/ /n/ /d/ 15. /ĭ/ /s/ /k/

LANGUAGE ARTS GREEN | ENDING CONSONANT BLENDS –sk, –st, –nt, and –nch   PH 43

Name _____ Date _____

Part 2. Finger Stretching
Listen to the word. Finger stretch the word.

16. /d/   /ĕ/   /s/   /k/
17. /j/   /ŭ/   /s/   /t/
18. /t/   /ĕ/   /n/   /t/
19. /w/   /ĕ/   /n/   /t/
20. /ă/   /s/   /k/
21. /w/   /ĕ/   /s/   /t/
22. /l/   /ŭ/   /n/   /ch/
23. /b/   /ĕ/   /n/   /ch/

PH 46   LANGUAGE ARTS GREEN | ENDING CONSONANT BLENDS –sk, –st, –nt AND –nch

---

Name _____ Date _____

Part 3. Dictation
Listen to the word. Repeat the word, and then write it.

24. task _____
25. pinch _____
26. sent _____
27. dust _____
28. rent _____
29. bunch _____

LANGUAGE ARTS GREEN | ENDING CONSONANT BLENDS –sk, –st, –nt, AND –nch   PH 45

Name _____ Date _____

Part 4. Writing
Listen to the sentence. Repeat the sentence, and then write it.

30. I must rest. _____
31. He lost his mask. _____

PH 46   LANGUAGE ARTS GREEN | ENDING CONSONANT BLENDS –sk, –st, –nt, AND –nch

---

Name _____ Date _____

Part 5. Read Aloud
Read the sentences aloud.

32.
Did you ask for the red vest?
We sent my friend back to the tent.
We must have lunch on this bench.
Am I next?
Did the chicks hatch on a ranch?

LANGUAGE ARTS GREEN | ENDING CONSONANT BLENDS –sk, –st, –nt, AND –nch   PH 47

Name _____ Date _____

Part 6. Say Letters
Listen to the sound. Say the letter or letters that make that sound.

33. o   36. a   39. e
34. th   37. w *or* wh 40. i
35. y   38. ch *or* tch 41. u

PH 48   LANGUAGE ARTS GREEN | ENDING CONSONANT BLENDS –sk, –st, –nt, AND –nch

Beginning Consonant Blend *bl*–

Unit Overview

In this unit, students will

- ▸ Review sight words.
- ▸ Review ending consonant blends.
- ▸ Learn the beginning consonant blends *bl*–, *cl*–, *fl*–, *gl*–, *pl*–, and *sl*–.
- ▸ Practice identifying sounds in words.

Materials

Supplied

- *K¹² PhonicsWorks Advanced Activity Book*, p. PH 17
- whiteboard, Learning Coach
- whiteboard, student
- Tile Kit

Also Needed

- sight words box
- dictation notebook

Lesson Overview

[Offline] **FOCUS:** Beginning Consonant Blend *bl*– **30** minutes

Sight Words	Introduce Sight Words
Get Ready	Signal Ending Blends
	Finger Stretching
	Review the Ending Consonant Blend –*sk*
Learn	Introduce the Beginning Consonant Blend *bl*–
Try It	Word Parts
	Dictation: Write Sentences

[Online] **REVIEW:** Beginning Consonant Blend *bl*– **20** minutes

[Offline] 30 minutes

FOCUS: Beginning Consonant Blend *bl–*

Work **together** with students to complete offline Sight Words, Get Ready, Learn, and Try It activities.

Sight Words •

Introduce Sight Words

Help students learn the sight words *goes*, *anything*, and *begin*.

1. Gather the sight word cards *goes*, *anything*, and *begin*.

2. Show students the *goes* card.

3. **Say:** This is the word *goes*. We see this word so often that we want to be able to read and spell it quickly without thinking about it. Look closely at the word *goes*. Spell the word *goes* aloud. Take a picture of the word *goes* in your mind. When you think you can spell *goes* yourself, turn the card over and use your letter tiles to spell the word *goes*. Check the card to see if you spelled the word *goes* correctly. Read aloud the word you spelled with the letter tiles.

4. Repeat the activity with the remaining sight words.

5. Chart students' progress on the back of each card.

   ▸ Divide the back of the card into two columns.
   ▸ Label the first column "Read" and the second column "Spell."
   ▸ Record the dates that students read or spell the word correctly. When students can read and spell the word correctly three times in a row, they have mastered the word. You may want to put a star or sticker on their card when they have mastered that word.

6. Add the cards to students' sight words box.

TIP Sight words can be very difficult for some students. Let students work at their own pace and really master these words.

Get Ready •

Signal Ending Blends

Use a special signal to help students identify **ending blends** in words.

1. **Say:** I'm going to tell you a sound to listen for. Repeat each word I say and make a special signal to tell me where the sound is. If the sound is at the end of the word, clap your hands. If the sound is not at the end of the word, just smile at me. For example,

   ▸ If I ask you to listen for the sound /lp/ and I say the word *gulp*, you'll repeat the word *gulp* and clap your hands because *gulp* has the sound /lp/ at the end.
   ▸ If I say the word *tail*, you'll repeat the word *tail* and smile at me because *tail* has the sound /l/, not /lp/, as the end.

Objectives

- Read sight words.
- Spell sight words.

Objectives

- Identify ending sounds in words.
- Identify individual sounds in words.
- Identify the number of sounds within words.
- Identify and use the blend *sk*.

2. Say each consonant blend and group of words. Have students make the special signal to identify the ending sound.

- ▸ /lp/: *help, pulp, gets, free, yelp* clap: *help, pulp, yelp*
- ▸ /sk/: *dress, mask, whisk, cob, trap, ask* clap: *mask, whisk, ask*
- ▸ /ft/: *lift, puff, spin, left, raft* clap: *lift, left, raft*
- ▸ /mp/: *camp, lip, champ, stop, dump* clap: *camp, champ, dump*
- ▸ /st/: *gasp, rest, sick, jack, rust* clap: *rest, rust*

Finger Stretching

Use finger stretching to help students identify individual sounds in words.

1. **Say:** Let's review finger stretching. In the word *fact*, the first sound is /f/, the next sound is /ă/, the third sound is /k/, and the last sound is /t/. I will finger stretch each sound as I say it. Then I'll say the word, while pulling my fist toward my body.

2. Finger stretch the word *fact*.

3. **Say:** I'm going to say words with several sounds in them. You'll say each word and then finger stretch it while you say each sound in the word.

4. Say the following words and have students finger stretch them. After they finger stretch each word, ask them the question for that word.

- ▸ *hump* /h/ /ŭ/ /m/ /p/   What is the ending blend? /mp/
- ▸ *silk* /s/ /ĭ/ /l/ /k/   What is the ending blend? /lk/
- ▸ *chest* /ch/ /ĕ/ /s/ /t/   What is the ending blend? /st/
- ▸ *whiff* /w/ /ĭ/ /f/   What is the last sound? /f/
- ▸ *rasp* /r/ /ă/ /s/ /p/   What is the first sound? /r/
- ▸ *gift* /g/ /ĭ/ /f/ /t/   What is the first sound? /g/

TIP Refer to the *K¹² PhonicsWorks* DVD for a demonstration of finger stretching.

Review the Ending Consonant Blend –*sk*

Help students recognize and use the ending consonant blend –*sk*.

1. Make the word *desk* on students' whiteboard and point to it.

2. **Say:** Touch and say this word.

- ▸ How many sounds are in the word? four
- ▸ How many letters are in the word? four
- ▸ We know that the letters *s* and *k* at the end of this word are called a blend because each letter keeps its own sound while the two sounds blend together.

Learn

Introduce the Beginning Consonant Blend *bl–*

Help students recognize and use the beginning consonant blend *bl–*.

1. Place the following letters on students' whiteboard: *b*, *b*, *l*, *o*, and *t*.

2. Make the word *blot* and point to it.

3. **Say:** Touch and say this word.

   ▸ How many sounds are in the word? four
   ▸ How many letters are in the word? four
   ▸ We know that the letters *b* and *l* at the beginning of this word are called a blend because each letter keeps its own sound while the two sounds blend together.

4. Redirect students if they have difficulty with the beginning consonant blend *bl–*.

   Say: Those two letters are often together at the beginning of a word. When they are together, they blend into the sound /bl/, as in *blue*. Can you say the word *blue*? When you say *blue*, don't stop between the two sounds /b/ and /l/. Try saying the word again.

5. Make the word *blob* and point to it.

6. **Say:** Touch and say the sounds in *blob*.

   ▸ How many sounds are in the word? four
   ▸ How many letters are in the word? four
   ▸ Where is the blend? at the beginning

7. Provide additional guidance if students have difficulty with blends. Take the first letter off the word.

   Say: I have taken the first letter off of the word. Touch and say the word without the first sound. What sound do you make at the beginning of the word? Answers will vary.

   Say: Now I am going to put the first letter back on the word. Touch and say the word. Which two sounds do you hear in the blend at the beginning of the word? Answers will vary.

Objectives

- Identify and use the blend *bl–*.
- Identify the number of sounds within words.
- Identify beginning sounds in words.
- Identify ending sounds in words.

Try It

Word Parts

Have students complete page PH 17 in *K¹² PhonicsWorks Advanced Activity Book* for more practice with words that begin with the consonant blend *bl–*. Have students read the word aloud, underline the consonant blend, and circle the vowel. Have them read the sentence aloud.

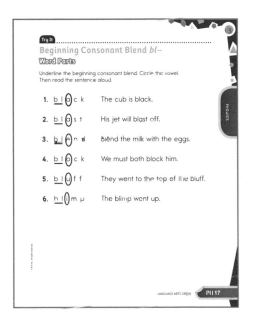

Dictation: Write Sentences

Use sentences to help students identify individual sounds in words.

1. Gather a pencil and the dictation notebook. Say the sentence, *Blend the milk for Dad.* Then give these directions to students:

   ▶ Repeat the sentence.
   ▶ Write the sentence in your notebook.
   ▶ Read the sentence aloud.

2. When students have finished, write the following sentence on your whiteboard: *Blend the milk for Dad.*

3. Have them compare their answer to your correct version.

4. Repeat this procedure with the sentence, *Hunt for the lost black duck.*

   ▶ If students make an error and don't see it, help them correct their mistake by having them finger stretch the sounds in the word they missed.
   ▶ If students are having difficulty selecting the correct letters or sounds, review those letters or sounds that are confusing them.
   ▶ If students have difficulty with first, middle, and last sounds, have them finger stretch the sounds in words.

 **20 minutes**

REVIEW: Beginning Consonant Blend *bl–*

Students will work online independently to

▶ Practice the beginning consonant blend *bl–*.

▶ Practice decoding text by reading a story.

Help students locate the online activities and provide support as needed.

Offline Alternative

No computer access? Have students point out and name things or words that begin with the consonant blend *bl–* (for example, *black* or *blue*). You might also ask students to spell words that begin with the blend *bl–*.

> **Objectives**
>
> • Identify beginning sounds in words.
>
> • Identify and use the blend *bl–*.
>
> • Read aloud grade-level text with appropriate automaticity, prosody, accuracy, and rate.
>
> • Decode words by applying grade-level word analysis skills.

Beginning Consonant Blend *cl–*

Lesson Overview

Offline FOCUS: Beginning Consonant Blend *cl–* **30** minutes

Sight Words	Sight Word Fun
Get Ready	Review Sounds
	Search Sentences for Blends
	Review the Beginning Consonant Blend *bl–*
Learn	Introduce the Beginning Consonant Blend *cl–*
	Build Words
	Listen for Beginning Blends
	Sort Beginning Blends
Try It	"The Best Club on the Block"

Online REVIEW: Beginning Consonant Blend *cl–* **20** minutes

Materials

Supplied
- *K¹² PhonicsWorks Readers Advanced 2*, pp. 20–24
- whiteboard, student
- Tile Kit

Also Needed
- sight words box

 **30 minutes**

FOCUS: Beginning Consonant Blend *cl–*

Work **together** with students to complete offline Sight Words, Get Ready, Learn, and Try It activities.

Sight Words

Sight Word Fun

Help students learn the sight words *goes*, *anything*, and *begin*, and up to two additional sight words they have yet to master.

1. Gather the sight word cards *goes*, *anything*, and *begin*, and up to two additional sight word cards.

2. Choose one sight word card to begin.

   Say: Look at this word and take a picture of it in your mind. When you think you can spell the word yourself, turn the card over and use your letter tiles to spell the word.

3. After students spell the word, have them check the card to see if they spelled the word correctly.

   Say: Read aloud the word you spelled with the letter tiles.

4. Repeat the activity with the remaining sight words.

TIP Sight words can be very difficult for some students. Let students work at their own pace and really master these words.

> **Objectives**
> - Read sight words.
> - Spell sight words.

Get Ready

Review Sounds

Help students practice identifying sounds, letters, and digraphs.

1. Place the following letter tiles on students' whiteboard: *ck, p, s, sh, t, th,* and *wh.*

2. **Say:** Let's review the sounds for these letters and digraphs.

3. Touch each tile and say the sound. Repeat in random order several times.

4. Have students touch each tile and say the sound. Do this several times.

5. Redirect students if they name the letter and not the sound.

   Say: You're right that the name of the letter is [letter]. What's the sound for this letter?

6. Redirect students if they name the sound incorrectly.

   Say: That is the sound for another letter. We want the sound for [target sound].

> **Objectives**
> - Given the sound, identify the most common letter or letters.
> - Given the letter, identify the most common sound.
> - Identify ending sounds in words.
> - Identify the number of sounds within words.
> - Identify beginning sounds in words.
> - Identify and use the blend *bl–*.

7. Provide additional guidance if students touch the wrong letter tile during the review.

   Say: That is the sound [sound for touched letter tile]. We are looking for the sound [target sound].

Search Sentences for Blends

Have students practice identifying **ending blends** in words that are in a sentence.

1. **Say:** I'm going to say an ending blend that is in a word. You will repeat that sound and the word. The first sound is /mp/, as in the word *bump*.

2. Have students say the target sound /mp/ and the word *bump*.

3. **Say:** Now I will read a sentence. Repeat the sentence and tell me the word that has the same ending sound. The first sentence is "Ross likes to run and jump."

   ▸ What is the sound of the special ending blend? /mp/
   ▸ What is the word that has the special ending blend? *jump*

4. Have students repeat the sentence and say the word.

5. Redirect students if they don't name the correct word.

   Say: Let me say the sentence again. Remember, you're listening for the sound [target ending blend].

6. Guide students if they have difficulty. Say two words from the sentence and have them choose the one with the target ending blend.

7. Follow the same procedure with the following words and sentences to help students recognize ending blends in words.

   ▸ /ft/, as in *left*   *Help him lift the box.* lift
   ▸ /nt/, as in *hunt*   *We sent Bob to get the ice cream.* sent
   ▸ /nch/, as in *lunch*   *He gave me a bunch of flowers.* bunch
   ▸ /kt/, as in *fact*   *Do you like to dance and act?* act
   ▸ /st/, as in *nest*   *You are my best friend.* best
   ▸ /mp/, as in *bump*   *Turn on the lamp so we can see.* lamp
   ▸ /sp/, as in *gasp*   *I see a wisp of smoke from the fire.* wisp

---

Review the Beginning Consonant Blend *bl–*

Help students recognize and use the beginning consonant blend *bl–*.

1. Make the word *black* on students' whiteboard and point to it.

2. **Say:** Touch and say this word.

   ▸ How many sounds are in the word? four
   ▸ How many letters are in the word? five
   ▸ We know that the letters *b* and *l* at the beginning of this word are called a blend because each letter keeps its own sound while the two sounds blend together.

Learn

Introduce the Beginning Consonant Blend *cl–*

Help students recognize and use the beginning consonant blend *cl–*.

1. Place the following letters on students' whiteboard: *a*, *c*, *i*, *l*, and *p*.

2. Make the word *clip* and point to it.

3. **Say:** Touch and say this word.

   ▸ How many sounds are in the word? four
   ▸ How many letters are in the word? four
   ▸ We know that the letters *c* and *l* at the beginning of this word are called a blend because each letter keeps its own sound while the two sounds blend together.

4. Redirect students if they have difficulty with the beginning consonant blend *cl–*.

   Say: Those two letters are often together at the beginning of a word. When they are together, they blend into the sound /kl/, as in *clown*. Can you say the word *clown*? When you say *clown*, don't stop between the two sounds /k/ and /l/. Try saying the word again.

5. Make the word *clap* and point to it.

6. **Say:** Touch and say the sounds in *clap*.

   ▸ How many sounds are in the word? four
   ▸ How many letters are in the word? four
   ▸ Where is the blend? at the beginning

7. Provide additional guidance if students have difficulty with blends. Take the first letter off the word.

   Say: I have taken the first letter off of the word. Touch and say the word without the first sound. What sound do you make at the beginning of the word? Answers will vary.

   Say: Now I am going to put the first letter back on the word. Touch and say the word. Which two sounds do you hear in the blend at the beginning of the word? Answers will vary.

⭐ Objectives

- Identify and use the blend *cl–*.
- Blend sounds to create words.
- Identify individual sounds in words.
- Identify the number of sounds within words.
- Identify beginning sounds in words.

Build Words

Help students use letters and sounds to build words.

1. Place the following letter tiles at the top of students' whiteboard: *a, b, c, ck, l, m, o, sh,* and *u.*

2. Draw four horizontal lines across the middle of students' whiteboard to represent the sounds in a word.

3. **Say:** Let's use letters and sounds to build the word *black.*

4. Have students finger stretch the sounds in *black.*

5. Have students

   ▸ Identify the first, next, and last sounds in *black.*
   ▸ Choose the corresponding letter for each sound.
   ▸ Move the letters to the correct lines on their whiteboard.

6. Guide students with these questions:

   ▸ What is the first sound in *black?* /b/
     Which line does the letter for that sound go on? the first one
   ▸ What is the next sound in *black?* /l/
   ▸ Which line does the letter for that sound go on? the second one
   ▸ What is the next sound in *black?* /ă/
     Which line does the letter for that sound go on? the third one
   ▸ What's the last sound in *black?* /k/
     Which line do the letters for that sound go on? the last one

7. Have students touch and say the word.

8. Redirect students if they select the incorrect letter.

   Say: That sound is in the word [word], and it is the [first, second, third, fourth] sound. We want the sound [target sound].

   Continue until students select the correct letter.

9. Repeat the activity to build the following words:

   ▸ *blush* /b/ /l/ /ŭ/ /sh/
   ▸ *clam* /k/ /l/ /ă/ /m/
   ▸ *clock* /k/ /l/ /ŏ/ /k/

Listen for Beginning Blends

Help students identify **beginning blends** in words.

1. **Say:** I'm going to say a word. Listen for the beginning blend. Then tell me the sound.

   ▸ For example, if I say *clap,* you will say /kl/ because the first sound you hear in *clap* is the blend /kl/.
   ▸ Now it's your turn. Listen to the word I say. You repeat the word, and then tell me the first sound in the word.

2. Repeat the process, using the following words to help students recognize beginning sounds:

- ▸ *black* /bl/
- ▸ *cliff* /kl/
- ▸ *cloth* /kl/
- ▸ *class* /kl/
- ▸ *blast* /bl/
- ▸ *blend* /bl/
- ▸ *clamp* /kl/

Sort Beginning Blends

Have students practice making words by adding letters to the end of beginning consonant blends.

1. At the top of students' whiteboard, use the tiles to set up the blends *cl* and *bl* as headings, with room to add letters after them to form words.

2. Under the blends, randomly place the letter tiles *a, ck, d, i, n, o, p, s,* and *t.*

3. **Say:** I'm going to say some words to you. You will repeat the words after me and find the letters on the whiteboard that make the **beginning blends** and **ending sounds** of the word. For example,

   - ▸ If I say the word *block*, you would say *block*, and then find the letters that make the beginning sound /bl/ on the whiteboard and point to those letters.
   - ▸ Then you will find the letters that make the sounds /ŏ/ and /k/ and move them after the letters *bl* to make the word *block*.
   - ▸ Finally I want you to touch and say the word by saying each sound while running a finger under the word from the first letter to the last letter. Now you try it.

4. Guide students if they form a word incorrectly.

   Say: Let's say the word, then finger stretch the sounds in the word together. Now you try to finger stretch the sounds in that word. Look for the letter that makes each of the sounds we finger stretched, beginning with the first sound.

5. Provide additional help if students continue to be confused. Remove all the letters from the board except for the ones forming the first word, *black*. Place the letters together to make *black*.

   Say: Touch and say the letters that make the sounds for *black*.

6. Repeat the process using the following words. (Pronounce the words very clearly, making sure that you pronounce both beginning sounds in the consonant blend words—and that students are watching your mouth.)

- ► *black*
- ► *clock*
- ► *click*
- ► *clap*
- ► *blast*
- ► *block*
- ► *clan*

TIP If students need more help, scramble the letters on the whiteboard, placing the blend *bl* at the top of the whiteboard. Then go through the steps of the activity, letting students show you how the sounds go together to form the word *black*.

"The Best Club on the Block"
Have students read "The Best Club on the Block" on page 20 of *K¹² PhonicsWorks Readers Advanced 2*.

Students should read the story silently once or twice before reading the story aloud. When students miss a word that can be sounded out, point to it and give them three to six seconds to try the word again. If students still miss the word, tell them the word so the flow of the story isn't interrupted.

After reading the story, make a list of all the words students missed, and go over those words with them. You may use letter tiles to show students how to read the words.

Objectives
- Read aloud grade-level text with appropriate automaticity, prosody, accuracy, and rate.
- Decode words by applying grade-level word analysis skills.

[Online] 20 minutes

REVIEW: Beginning Consonant Blend *cl–*
Students will work online independently to

- ► Practice the beginning consonant blend *cl–*.

Help students locate the online activities and provide support as needed.

Objectives
- Identify beginning sounds in words.
- Identify and use the blend *cl–*.

___

Offline Alternative

No computer access? Have students point out and name things or words that begin with the consonant blend *cl–* (for example, *claw* or *clap*). You might also ask students to spell words that begin with the blend *cl–*.

Beginning Consonant Blends *fl–* and *gl–*

Lesson Overview

[Offline] FOCUS: Beginning Consonant Blends *fl–* and *gl–*	**30** minutes

Sight Words	Sight Word Fun
Get Ready	Finger Stretching
	Climb the Ladder
	Review the Beginning Consonant Blend *cl–*
Learn	Introduce the Beginning Consonant *fl–*
	Introduce the Beginning Consonant *gl–*
Try It	Make Connections
	Dictation: Write Sentences

[Online] REVIEW: Beginning Consonant Blends *fl–* and *gl–*	**20** minutes

[Materials]

Supplied
- *K¹² PhonicsWorks Advanced Activity Book,* p. PH 18
- whiteboard, Learning Coach
- whiteboard, student
- Tile Kit

Also Needed
- sight words box
- dictation notebook

〔Offline〕 **30** minutes

FOCUS: Beginning Consonant Blends *fl–* and *gl–*

Work **together** with students to complete offline Sight Words, Get Ready, Learn, and Try It activities.

Sight Words •

Sight Word Fun

Help students learn the sight words *goes*, *anything*, and *begin*, and up to two additional sight words students have yet to master.

1. Gather the sight word cards *goes*, *anything*, and *begin*, and up to two additional sight word cards.

2. Choose one sight word card to begin.

   Say: Look at this word and take a picture of it in your mind. When you think you can spell the word yourself, turn the card over and use your letter tiles to spell the word.

3. After students spell the word, have them check the card to see if they spelled the word correctly.

   Say: Read aloud the word you spelled with the letter tiles.

4. Repeat the activity with the remaining sight words.

   TIP Sight words can be very difficult for some students. Let students work at their own pace and really master these words.

> **Objectives**
> - Read sight words.
> - Spell sight words.

Get Ready •

Finger Stretching

Use finger stretching to help students identify individual sounds in words.

1. **Say:** Let's review finger stretching. In the word *bland*, the first sound is /b/, the next sound is /l/, the next sound is /ă/, the fourth sound is /n/, and the last sound is /d/. I will finger stretch each sound as I say it. Then I'll say the word, while pulling my fist toward my body.

2. Finger stretch the word *bland*.

3. **Say:** I'm going to say words with several sounds in them. You'll say each word and then finger stretch it while you say each sound in the word.

> **Objectives**
> - Identify individual sounds in words.
> - Identify the number of sounds within words.
> - Blend sounds to create words.
> - Identify beginning sounds in words.
> - Identify and use the blend *cl–*.

4. Say the following words and have students finger stretch them. After they finger stretch each word, ask them the question for that word.

 ▸ *click* /k/ /l/ /ĭ/ /k/   How many sounds are in the word? four
 ▸ *blot* /b/ /l/ /ŏ/ t/   How many sounds are in the word? four
 ▸ *must* /m/ /ŭ/ /s/ /t/   How many sounds are in the word? four
 ▸ *champ* /ch/ /ă/ /m/ /p/   How many sounds are in the word? four
 ▸ *rack* /r/ /ă/ /k/   How many sounds are in the word? three
 ▸ *bluff* /b/ /l/ /ŭ/ /f/   How many sounds are in the word? four
 ▸ *send* /s/ /ĕ/ /n/ /d/   How many sounds are in the word? four

TIP Refer to the *K¹² PhonicsWorks* DVD for a demonstration of finger stretching.

Climb the Ladder

Help students use letters to build words.

1. On students' whiteboard or a sheet of paper, draw a ladder with five or more rungs.

2. Write the word *nest* on the bottom rung.

3. Point to the word *nest*.

   Say: I can make the word *best* by changing one letter in this word.

4. Write the word *best* on the second rung of the ladder.

   Say: Think of a word that you can make by changing only one letter in *best*. Tell me the word and write it on the next step on the ladder.

5. If students struggle, coach them to change the first letter in each word.

   Say: Read the word on the bottom rung. What sound do you hear at the beginning of the word? What letter has that sound?

   Say: Name a word that rhymes with the word at the bottom. What sound do you hear at the beginning of the rhyming word? What letter has that sound? Make a new word by using the new letter. Read the new word.

6. Continue the process until students reach the top of the ladder. Remind students that they may change only one sound: the beginning, middle, or ending sound.

7. Redirect students if they select a word that changes more than one letter.

   Say: How many letters changed from the last word to your new word? Try to think of a word that has only one letter change.

8. Redirect students if they spell a word incorrectly, but the sounds they spell are correct (such as *ruf* for *rough*).

   Say: You have the sounds and letters right, but that word doesn't follow our spelling rules. We will learn how to spell it later. Try another word.

TIP If students have difficulty thinking of real words, have them use nonsense words.

Review the Beginning Consonant Blend *cl–*

Help students recognize and use the beginning consonant blend *cl–*.

1. Make the word *clap* on students' whiteboard and point to it.

2. **Say:** Touch and say this word.

   ▸ How many sounds are in the word? four
   ▸ How many letters are in the word? four
   ▸ We know that the letters *c* and *l* at the beginning of this word are called a blend because each letter keeps its own sound while the two sounds blend together.

Learn

Introduce the Beginning Consonant Blend *fl–*

Help students recognize and use the beginning consonant blend *fl–*.

1. Make the word *flap* on students' whiteboard and point to it.

2. **Say:** Touch and say this word.

   ▸ How many sounds are in the word? four
   ▸ How many letters are in the word? four
   ▸ We know that the letters *f* and *l* at the beginning of this word are called a blend because each letter keeps its own sound while the two sounds blend together.

> **Objectives**
> - Identify and use the blend *fl–*.
> - Identify and use the blend *gl–*.
> - Identify the number of sounds within words.
> - Identify beginning sounds in words.

Introduce the Beginning Consonant Blend *gl–*

Help students recognize and use the beginning consonant blend *gl–*.

1. Make the word *glad* on students' whiteboard and point to it.

2. **Say:** Touch and say this word.

   ▸ How many sounds are in the word? four
   ▸ How many letters are in the word? four
   ▸ Where is the blend? at the beginning

3. Redirect students if they have difficulty with the beginning consonant blend *gl–*.

   Say: Those two letters are often together at the beginning of a word. When they are together, they blend into the sound /gl/, as in *glue*. Can you say the word *glue*? When you say *glue*, don't stop between the two sounds /g/ and /l/. Try saying the word again.

4. Provide additional guidance if students have difficulty with blends. Take the first letter off the word.

Say: I have taken the first letter off of the word. Touch and say the word without the first sound. What sound do you make at the beginning of the word? Answers will vary.

Say: Now I am going to put the first letter back on the word. Touch and say the word. Which two sounds do you hear in the blend at the beginning of the word? Answers will vary.

Try It

Make Connections

Have students complete page PH 18 in *K¹² PhonicsWorks Advanced Activity Book* for more practice with words that begin with consonant blends. Have students draw a line to connect the beginning and ending sounds to make words. Have them write the word and say each word.

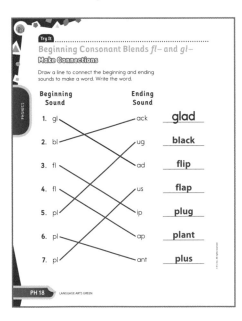

Objectives
- Blend sounds to create words.
- Identify beginning sounds in words.
- Identify ending sounds in words.
- Read aloud grade-level text with appropriate automaticity, prosody, accuracy, and rate.
- Write words by applying grade-level phonics knowledge.
- Write sight words.
- Follow three-step directions.

Dictation: Write Sentences

Use sentences to help students identify individual sounds in words.

1. Gather a pencil and the dictation notebook. Say the sentence, *That is a flat clam.* Then give these directions to students:
   - ▸ Repeat the sentence.
   - ▸ Write the sentence in your notebook.
   - ▸ Read the sentence aloud.

2. When students have finished, write the following sentence on your whiteboard: *That is a flat clam.*

3. Have them compare their answer to your correct version.

4. Repeat this procedure with the sentence, *Jim is glad to help Cliff.*

   ▸ If students make an error and don't see it, help them correct their mistake by having them finger stretch the sounds in the word they missed.
   ▸ If students are having difficulty selecting the correct letters or sounds, review those letters or sounds that are confusing them.
   ▸ If students have difficulty with first, middle, and last sounds, have them finger stretch the sounds in words.

20 minutes

REVIEW: Beginning Consonant Blends *fl–* and *gl–*

Students will work online independently to

▸ Practice the beginning consonant blends *fl–* and *gl–*.
▸ Practice decoding text by reading a story.

Help students locate the online activities and provide support as needed.

Offline Alternative

No computer access? Have students point out and name things or words that begin with the consonant blends *fl–* and *gl–* (for example, *flup* or *glad*). You might also ask students to spell words that begin with the blends *fl–* and *gl–*.

Objectives

- Identify and use the blend *fl–*.
- Identify and use the blend *gl–*.
- Identify beginning sounds in words.
- Read aloud grade-level text with appropriate automaticity, prosody, accuracy, and rate.
- Decode words by applying grade-level word analysis skills.

Beginning Consonant Blends *pl–* and *sl–*

Lesson Overview

Offline	FOCUS: Beginning Consonant Blends *pl–* and *sl–*	30 minutes

Sight Words	Sight Word Fun
Get Ready	Review Sounds and Letters
	Review the Beginning Consonant Blend *gl–*
Learn	Introduce the Beginning Consonant Blend *pl–*
	Introduce the Beginning Consonant Blend *sl–*
Try It	"Quinn and Kent Have a Sled"

Online	REVIEW: Beginning Consonant Blends *pl–* and *sl–*	20 minutes

Materials

Supplied
- *K¹² PhonicsWorks Readers Advanced 2*, pp. 25–30
- whiteboard, student
- Tile Kit

Also Needed
- sight words box

[Offline] **30** minutes

FOCUS: Beginning Consonant Blends *pl–* and *sl–*

Work **together** with students to complete offline Sight Words, Get Ready, Learn, and Try It activities.

Sight Words

Sight Word Fun

Help students learn the sight words *goes, anything,* and *begin,* and up to two additional sight words students have yet to master.

1. Gather the sight word cards *goes, anything,* and *begin,* and up to two additional sight word cards.

2. Choose one sight word card to begin.

   Say: Look at this word and take a picture of it in your mind. When you think you can spell the word yourself, turn the card over and use your letter tiles to spell the word.

3. After students spell the word, have them check the card to see if they spelled the word correctly.

   Say: Read aloud the word you spelled with the letter tiles.

4. Repeat the activity with the remaining sight words.

   TIP Sight words can be very difficult for some students. Let students work at their own pace and really master these words.

> **Objectives**
> - Read sight words.
> - Spell sight words.

Get Ready

Review Sounds and Letters

Help students review sounds for the letters and digraphs *b, i, m, o, qu, sh, th,* and *wh,* plus any letters that are confusing for them.

1. Place the following letter tiles in random order on students' whiteboard: *b, i, m, o, qu, sh, th,* and *wh,* plus any letters that are confusing.

2. **Say:** Let's go over some letters and sounds.

3. Point to each letter tile and have students say a sound that letter or digraph makes.

   - ► *sh* /sh/
   - ► *o* /ŏ/ or /ō/
   - ► *i* /ĭ/ or /ī/
   - ► *qu* /kw/
   - ► *th* /th/ or /<u>th</u>/
   - ► *m* /m/
   - ► *b* /b/
   - ► *wh* /w/

> **Objectives**
> - Given the sound, identify the most common letter or letters.
> - Given the letter, identify the most common sound.
> - Identify beginning sounds in words.
> - Identify and use the blend *gl–*.
> - Identify the number of sounds within words.

4. Say each of the following sounds. Have students repeat the sound and touch the corresponding letter tile.

- ► /sh/ *sh*
- ► /ŏ/ *o*
- ► /ĭ/ *i*
- ► /kw/ *qu*
- ► /th/ *th*
- ► /m/ *m*
- ► /b/ *b*
- ► /w/ *wh*

5. As you do the activity, point to some letter tiles two or three times so that students don't think they are finished with a sound after they have named it.

6. Redirect students if they say an incorrect sound when you point to a letter tile.

   Say: That's the sound of another letter. What is the sound for this letter?

7. Help students if they touch the wrong letter tile after they repeat a sound.

   Say: That letter tile goes with the sound [sound for touched letter tile]. We're looking for the letter tile that goes with the sound [target sound].

Review the Beginning Consonant Blend *gl*–

Help students recognize and use the beginning consonant blend *gl*–.

1. Make the word *glad* on students' whiteboard and point to it.

2. **Say:** Touch and say this word.

   - ► How many sounds are in the word? four
   - ► How many letters are in the word? four
   - ► We know that the letters *g* and *l* at the beginning of this word are called a blend because each letter keeps its own sound while the two sounds blend together.

3. Redirect students if they have difficulty with the beginning consonant blend *gl*–.

   Say: Those two letters are often together at the beginning of a word. When they are together, they blend into the sound /gl/, as in *glitter*. Can you say the word *glitter*? When you say *glitter*, don't stop between the two sounds /g/ and /l/. Try saying the word again.

4. Provide additional guidance if students have difficulty with blends. Take the first letter off the word.

   Say: I have taken the first letter off of the word. Touch and say the word without the first sound. What sound do you make at the beginning of the word? Answers will vary.

   Say: Now I am going to put the first letter back on the word. Touch and say the word. Which two sounds do you hear in the blend at the beginning of the word? Answers will vary.

Learn ••

Introduce the Beginning Consonant Blend *pl–*

Help students recognize and use the beginning consonant blend *pl–*.

1. Make the word *plan* on students' whiteboard and point to it.

2. **Say:** Touch and say this word.

   ‣ How many sounds are in the word? four
   ‣ How many letters are in the word? four
   ‣ We know that the letters *p* and *l* at the beginning of this word are called a blend because each letter keeps its own sound while the two sounds blend together.

3. Redirect students if they have difficulty with the beginning consonant blend *pl–*.

   Say: Those two letters are often together at the beginning of a word. When they are together, they blend into the sound /pl/, as in *place*. Can you say the word *place*? When you say *place*, don't stop between the two sounds /p/ and /l/. Try saying the word again.

Introduce the Beginning Consonant Blend *sl–*

Help students recognize and use the beginning consonant blend *sl–*.

1. Make the word *slip* on students' whiteboard and point to it.

2. **Say:** Touch and say this word.

   ‣ How many sounds are in the word? four
   ‣ How many letters are in the word? four
   ‣ We know that the letters *s* and *l* at the beginning of this word are called a blend because each letter keeps its own sound while the two sounds blend together.

3. Redirect students if they have difficulty with the beginning consonant blend *sl–*.

   Say: Those two letters are often together at the beginning of a word. When they are together, they blend into the sound /sl/, as in *slide*. Can you say the word *slide*? When you say *slide*, don't stop between the two sounds /s/ and /l/. Try saying the word again.

4. Provide additional guidance if students have difficulty with blends. Take the first letter off the word.

   Say: I have taken the first letter off of the word. Touch and say the word without the first sound. What sound do you make at the beginning of the word? Answers will vary.

   Say: Now I am going to put the first letter back on the word. Touch and say the word. Which two sounds do you hear in the blend at the beginning of the word? Answers will vary.

> **Objectives**
> - Identify beginning sounds in words.
> - Identify and use the blend *pl–*.
> - Identify and use the blend *sl–*.
> - Identify the number of sounds within words.

Try It

"Quinn and Kent Have a Sled"

Have students read "Quinn and Kent Have a Sled" on page 25 of *K¹² PhonicsWorks Readers Advanced 2*.

Students should read the story silently once or twice before reading the story aloud. When students miss a word that can be sounded out, point to it and give them three to six seconds to try the word again. If students still miss the word, tell them the word so the flow of the story isn't interrupted.

After reading the story, make a list of all the words students missed, and go over those words with them. You may use letter tiles to show students how to read the words.

Objectives

- Read aloud grade-level text with appropriate automaticity, prosody, accuracy, and rate.
- Decode words by applying grade-level word analysis skills.

 **20 minutes**

REVIEW: Beginning Consonant Blends *pl–* and *sl–*

Students will work online independently to

▶ Practice the beginning consonant blends *pl–* and *sl–*.

Help students locate the online activities and provide support as needed.

Objectives

- Identify beginning sounds in words.
- Identify and use the blend *pl–*.
- Identify and use the blend *sl–*.

Offline Alternative

No computer access? Have students point out and name things or words that begin with the consonant blends *pl–* and *sl–* (for example, *plant* or *slow*). You might also ask students to spell words that begin with the consonant blends *pl–* and *sl–*.

Unit Checkpoint

Lesson Overview

〖Online〗 REVIEW: Beginning Consonant Blends *bl–*, *cl–*, *fl–*, *gl–*, *pl–*, and *sl–* **20** minutes

〖Offline〗 UNIT CHECKPOINT: Beginning Consonant Blends *bl–*, *cl–*, *fl–*, *gl–*, *pl–*, and *sl–* **30** minutes

〖Materials〗

Supplied
- *K¹² PhonicsWorks Advanced Assessments*, pp. PH 49–54

Objectives
- Identify and use the blend *bl–*.
- Identify and use the blend *cl–*.
- Identify and use the blend *fl–*.
- Identify and use the blend *gl–*.
- Identify and use the blend *pl–*.
- Identify and use the blend *sl–*.
- Read, write, and spell words containing *bl*.
- Read, write, and spell words containing *cl*.
- Read, write, and spell words containing *fl*.
- Read, write, and spell words containing *gl*.
- Read, write, and spell words containing *pl*.
- Read, write, and spell words containing *sl*.
- Identify individual sounds in words.
- Given the letter, identify the most common sound.
- Given the sound, identify the most common letter or letters.
- Read aloud grade-level text with appropriate automaticity, prosody, accuracy, and rate.
- Read instructional-level text with 90% accuracy.
- Write sight words.
- Write words by applying grade-level phonics knowledge.

〖Online〗 **20** minutes

REVIEW: Beginning Consonant Blends *bl–*, *cl–*, *fl–*, *gl–*, *pl–*, and *sl–*

Students will review the beginning consonant blends *bl–*, *cl–*, *fl–*, *gl–*, *pl–*, and *sl–* to prepare for the Unit Checkpoint. Help students locate the online activities and provide support as needed.

【 Offline 】 🕥 minutes

UNIT CHECKPOINT: Beginning Consonant Blends *bl–*, *cl–*, *fl–*, *gl–*, *pl–*, and *sl–*

Explain that students are going to show what they have learned about letters, sounds, and words.

1. Give students the Unit Checkpoint pages for the Beginning Consonant Blends *bl–*, *cl–*, *fl–*, *gl–*, *pl–*, and *sl–* unit and print the Unit Checkpoint Answer Key, if you'd like.

2. Use the instructions below to help administer the Checkpoint to students. On the Answer Key or another sheet of paper, note student answers to oral response questions to help with scoring the Checkpoint later.

3. Use the Answer Key to score the Checkpoint, and then enter the results online.

Part 1. Read Nonsense Words Moving left to right, have students say the sounds of each nonsense word. Note any nonsense words they say incorrectly.

Part 2. Finger Stretching Say each word to students. Have them say each word and finger stretch the sounds. Note any words they finger stretch incorrectly.

16. *block*	19. *clip*
17. *glam*	20. *plan*
18. *slop*	21. *flesh*

Part 3. Dictation Say each word to students. Have them repeat and write the word.

22. *black*	25. *class*
23. *slip*	26. *flash*
24. *glad*	27. *plum*

Part 4. Writing Read each sentence to students. Have them repeat and write the sentence.

28. *Did you flip your sled?*

29. *The block is red.*

Part 5. Read Aloud Listen to students read the sentences aloud. Count and note the number of words they read correctly.

Part 6. Say Letters Say each sound. Have students say the letter or letters that make that sound. Note any incorrect responses.

31. /ŭ/

32. /sh/

33. /th/

34. /ă/

35. /ks/

36. /y/

37. /ĭ/

38. /ĕ/

39. /ŏ/

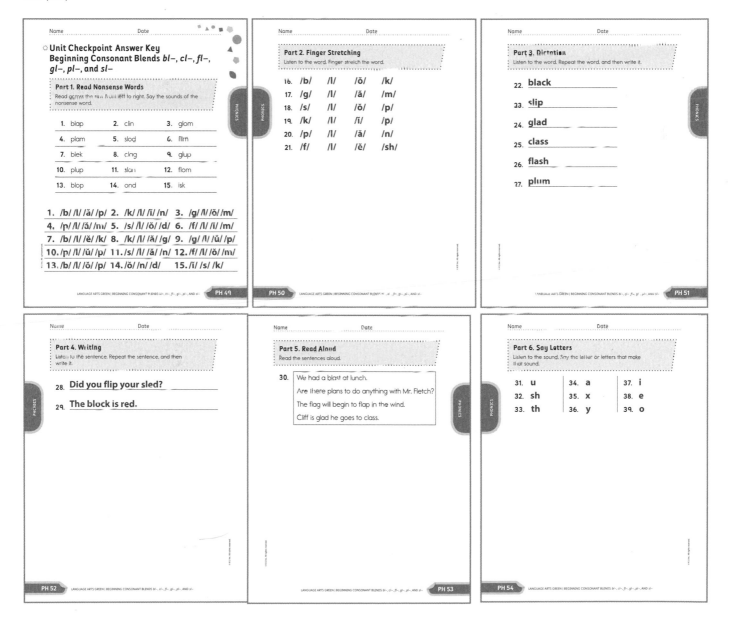

Name _____ Date _____

○ **Unit Checkpoint Answer Key**
Beginning Consonant Blends *bl–, cl–, fl–, gl–, pl–,* and *sl–*

Part 1. Read Nonsense Words
Read across the row from left to right. Say the sounds of the nonsense word.

1. blap	2. clin	3. glom
4. plam	5. slod	6. flim
7. blek	8. clng	9. glup
10. plup	11. slan	12. flom
13. blop	14. ond	15. isk

1. /b/ /l/ /ă/ /p/ 2. /k/ /l/ /ĭ/ /n/ 3. /g/ /l/ /ŏ/ /m/
4. /p/ /l/ /ă/ /m/ 5. /s/ /l/ /ŏ/ /d/ 6. /f/ /l/ /ĭ/ /m/
7. /b/ /l/ /ĕ/ /k/ 8. /k/ /l/ /ă/ /g/ 9. /g/ /l/ /ŭ/ /p/
10. /p/ /l/ /ŭ/ /p/ 11. /s/ /l/ /ă/ /n/ 12. /f/ /l/ /ŏ/ /m/
13. /b/ /l/ /ŏ/ /p/ 14. /ŏ/ /n/ /d/ 15. /ĭ/ /s/ /k/

Name _____ Date _____

Part 2. Finger Stretching
Listen to the word. Finger stretch the word.

16. /b/ /l/ /ŏ/ /k/
17. /g/ /l/ /ă/ /m/
18. /s/ /l/ /ŏ/ /p/
19. /k/ /l/ /ĭ/ /p/
20. /p/ /l/ /ă/ /n/
21. /f/ /l/ /ĕ/ /sh/

Name _____ Date _____

Part 3. Dictation
Listen to the word. Repeat the word, and then write it.

22. black _____
23. slip _____
24. glad _____
25. class _____
26. flash _____
27. plum _____

Name _____ Date _____

Part 4. Writing
Listen to the sentence. Repeat the sentence, and then write it.

28. Did you flip your sled? _____

29. The block is red. _____

Name _____ Date _____

Part 5. Read Aloud
Read the sentences aloud.

30. We had a blast at lunch.
    Are there plans to do anything with Mr. Fletch?
    The flag will begin to flap in the wind.
    Cliff is glad he goes to class.

Name _____ Date _____

Part 6. Say Letters
Listen to the sound. Say the letter or letters that make that sound.

31. u	34. a	37. i
32. sh	35. x	38. e
33. th	36. y	39. o

Beginning Consonant Blend *br–*

Unit Overview

In this unit, students will
- ▶ Review sight words.
- ▶ Learn the beginning consonant blends *br–*, *cr–*, *dr–*, *fr–*, *gr–*, *pr–*, and *tr–*.
- ▶ Practice identifying sounds in words.
- ▶ Build words.

〖Materials〗

Supplied
- *K¹² PhonicsWorks Advanced Activity Book*, p. PH 19
- whiteboard, Learning Coach
- whiteboard, student
- Tile Kit

Also Needed
- sight words box
- dictation notebook

Lesson Overview

〖Offline〗 FOCUS: Beginning Consonant Blend *br–*   **30** minutes

Sight Words	Review Sight Words
Get Ready	Review Sounds and Letters
	Review the Beginning Consonant Blend *sl–*
Learn	Introduce the Beginning Consonant Blend *br–*
	Make More Words: Beginning Blends
Try It	Careful Counting
	Dictation: Write Sentences

〖Online〗 REVIEW: Beginning Consonant Blend *br–*   **20** minutes

Offline **30** minutes

FOCUS: Beginning Consonant Blend *br–*

Work **together** with students to complete offline Sight Words, Get Ready, Learn, and Try It activities.

Sight Words

Review Sight Words

Help students learn to recognize sight words.

1. Gather all the sight word cards students have yet to master from their sight words box. Stack the cards on the table face down.

2. Have students pick a word and read it to you.

3. If students read it quickly and correctly, put the card in one stack. If they hesitate or do not read the word correctly, put it in another stack. The second stack should have words that they will review again.

4. Take the stack of words that students read correctly and dictate each word to them. They may choose to either write the word or spell it aloud.

5. If students spell the word correctly, put the card in the first stack because they have mastered the word. If they misspell the word, add it to the stack of cards to review again.

6. Chart students' progress on the back of each card.
   - ▸ Divide the back of the card into two columns.
   - ▸ Label the first column "Read" and the second column "Spell."
   - ▸ Record the dates that students read or spell the word correctly. When students can read and spell the word correctly three times in a row, they have mastered the word. You may want to put a star or sticker on their card when they have mastered that word.

TIP Even if students can read and spell all the words correctly, it is still beneficial for students to review sight words. Choose as many additional words as you would like for each subsequent activity.

Objectives
- Read sight words.
- Spell sight words.
- Write sight words.
- Write words by applying grade-level phonics knowledge.

Get Ready

Review Sounds and Letters

Help students review the sounds for the letters and digraphs *ch, e, f, l, m, qu, th,* and *u,* plus any letters that are confusing for them.

1. Place the following letter tiles in random order on students' whiteboard: *ch, e, f, l, m, qu, th,* and *u,* plus any letters that are confusing.

2. **Say:** Let's go over some letters and sounds.

3. Point to each letter tile and have students say a sound that letter or letters make.
   - *e* /ĕ/ or /ē/
   - *ch* /ch/
   - *u* /ŭ/ or /ū/
   - *l* /l/
   - *qu* /kw/
   - *th* /th/ or /<u>th</u>/
   - *m* /m/
   - *f* /f/

4. Say each of the following sounds. Have students repeat the sound and touch the corresponding letter tile.
   - /ĕ/ *e*
   - /ch/ *ch*
   - /ŭ/ *u*
   - /l/ *l*
   - /kw/ *qu*
   - /th/ *th*
   - /m/ *m*
   - /f/ *f*

5. As you do the activity, point to some letter tiles two or three times so that students don't think they are finished with a sound after they have named it.

6. Redirect students if they say an incorrect sound when you point to a letter tile.

   Say: That's the sound of another letter. What is the sound for this letter?

7. Help students if they touch the wrong letter tile after they repeat a sound.

   Say: That letter tile goes with the sound [sound for touched letter tile]. We're looking for the letter that goes with the sound [target sound].

Objectives
- Given the sound, identify the most common letter or letters.
- Given the letter or letters, identify the most common sound.
- Identify beginning sounds in words.
- Identify the number of sounds within words.
- Identify and use the blend *sl–*.

Review the Beginning Consonant Blend *sl*–

Help students recognize and use the beginning consonant blend *sl*–.

1. Make the word *slim* on students' whiteboard and point to it.

2. **Say:** Touch and say this word.

   ‣ How many sounds are in the word? four
   ‣ How many letters are in the word? four
   ‣ We know that the letters *s* and *l* at the beginning of this word are called a blend because each letter keeps its own sound while the two sounds blend together.

Learn ••

Introduce the Beginning Consonant Blend *br*–

Help students recognize and use the beginning consonant blend *br*–.

1. Place the following letters on students' whiteboard: *a, b, g, i, m,* and *r.*

2. Make the word *brim* and point to it.

3. **Say:** Touch and say this word.

   ‣ How many sounds are in the word? four
   ‣ How many letters are in the word? four
   ‣ We know that the letters *b* and *r* at the beginning of this word are called a blend because each letter keeps its own sound while the two sounds blend together.

4. Redirect students if they have difficulty with the beginning consonant blend *br*–.

   Say: Those two letters are often together at the beginning of a word. When they are together, they blend into the sound /br/, as in *bright.* Can you say the word *bright*? When you say *bright*, don't stop between the two sounds /b/ and /r/. Try saying the word again.

5. Make the word *brag* and point to it.

6. **Say:** Touch and say the sounds in *brag.*

   ‣ How many sounds are in the word? four
   ‣ How many letters are in the word? four
   ‣ Where is the blend? at the beginning

7. Provide additional guidance if students have difficulty with blends. Take the first letter off the word.

   Say: I have taken the first letter off of the word. Touch and say the word without the first sound. What sound do you make at the beginning of the word? Answers will vary.

   Say: Now I am going to put the first letter back on the word. Touch and say the word. Which two sounds do you hear in the blend at the beginning of the word? Answers will vary.

> **Objectives**
> - Identify and use the blend *br*–.
> - Identify the number of sounds within words.
> - Identify beginning sounds in words.
> - Identify individual sounds in words.
> - Blend sounds to create words.

Make More Words: Beginning Blends

Have students add and remove letters to make new words.

1. Place the following letter tiles on students' whiteboard: *a, ck, d, g, i, m, n, o, p, p, s, sh, th,* and *u.*

2. To make the blends *pl–* and *br–,* place the following letter tiles at the top of the whiteboard, with room to add letters after each blend: *p, l* and *b, r.*

3. **Say:** When I put the letters *u* and *sh* after the blend *br–,* I make a new word, *brush.* See how many new **real words** you can make by putting the letters on your whiteboard after the blends *br–* and *pl–.*

4. Continue this activity to make the following words:

   ► *brag*
   ► *plan*
   ► *plop*
   ► *brand*
   ► *plum*
   ► *broth*
   ► *brick*
   ► *plus*

Try It

Careful Counting

Have students complete page PH 19 in *K¹² PhonicsWorks Advanced Activity Book* for more practice with syllables. Have them count the number of syllables they hear in the word and write that number.

> **Try It**
> **Beginning Consonant Blend *br–***
> **Careful Counting**
>
> Count the number of sounds in the word and write the number.
>
> Examples: chip = 3   dock = 3   vest = 4   bless = 4   crunch = 5
>
> | 1. bat | 3 | 8. ship | 3 |
> | 2. brick | 4 | 9. brim | 4 |
> | 3. tent | 4 | 10. sand | 4 |
> | 4. ask | 3 | 11. chimp | 4 |
> | 5. blimp | 5 | 12. cluck | 4 |
> | 6. bran | 4 | 13. brush | 4 |
> | 7. brat | 4 | 14. brand | 5 |
>
> LANGUAGE ARTS GREEN   PH 19

Objectives

- Identify letters of the alphabet.
- Write words by applying grade-level phonics knowledge.
- Write sight words.
- Follow three-step directions.
- Read, write, and spell words containing the blend *br–.*

Dictation: Write Sentences

Use sentences to help students identify individual sounds in words.

1. Gather a pencil and the dictation notebook. Say the sentence, *Brad put the flag in his hands*. Then give these directions to students:

   ▶ Repeat the sentence.
   ▶ Write the sentence in your notebook.
   ▶ Read the sentence aloud.

2. When students have finished, write the following sentence on your whiteboard: *Brad put the flag in his hands*.

3. Have them compare their answer to your correct version.

4. Repeat this procedure with the sentence, *Jim can sip the glass of broth*.

   ▶ If students make an error and don't see it, help them correct their mistake by having them finger stretch the sounds in the word they missed.
   ▶ If students are having difficulty selecting the correct letters or sounds, review those letters or sounds that are confusing them.
   ▶ If students have difficulty with first, middle, and last sounds, have them finger stretch the sounds in words.

 **20 minutes**

REVIEW: Beginning Consonant Blend *br–*

Students will work online independently to

▶ Practice the beginning consonant blend *br–*.
▶ Practice decoding text by reading a story.

Help students locate the online activities and provide support as needed.

___

Offline Alternative

No computer access? Have students point out and name things or words that begin with the consonant blend *br–* (for example, *bran* or *broke*). You might also ask students to spell words that begin with the consonant blend *br–*.

Objectives

- Identify beginning sounds in words.
- Identify and use the blend *br–*.
- Read, write, and spell words containing the blend *br–*.
- Read aloud grade-level text with appropriate automaticity, prosody, accuracy, and rate.
- Decode words by applying grade-level word analysis skills.

Beginning Consonant Blends *cr–* and *dr–*

Lesson Overview

Offline **FOCUS:** Beginning Consonant Blends *cr–* and *dr–* **30** minutes

Sight Words	Use Words in Sentences
Get Ready	Finger Stretching
	What's in the Box!
	Review the Beginning Consonant Blend *br–*
Learn	Introduce the Beginning Consonant Blend *cr–*
	Introduce the Beginning Consonant Blend *dr–*
	Build Words
Try It	"Brett and Brad"

Online **REVIEW:** Beginning Consonant Blends *cr–* and *dr–* **20** minutes

Materials

Supplied
- *K¹² PhonicsWorks Readers Advanced 3*, pp. 1–6
- whiteboard, student
- Tile Kit

Also Needed
- sight words box
- household objects – different-sized boxes, small objects (such as dolls, marbles, pens, pencils, rings, paper, forks, napkins, or quarters)

Advance Preparation

For What's in the Box, find boxes of different sizes. Find objects that will fit inside the boxes, such as dolls, marbles, pens, pencils, rings, paper, forks, napkins, or quarters.

 **Offline** ⏱ 30 minutes

FOCUS: Beginning Consonant Blends *cr–* and *dr–*

Work **together** with students to complete offline Sight Words, Get Ready, Learn, and Try It activities.

Sight Words

Use Words in Sentences

Help students use sight words in sentences.

1. Gather all the sight word cards students have yet to master from their sight words box. Spread the sight word cards on the table.

2. **Say:** Let's use sight words in sentences.

3. Have students

   ▸ Touch each card and read the word on it.
   ▸ Make up a sentence using the word.
   ▸ Put the card in a pile after using the word in a sentence.
   ▸ Go through the pile of cards and read each sight word again.
   ▸ Spell each word.

TIP If students have difficulty with any of the sight words, place those cards in a pile to review again.

> **Objectives**
> • Read sight words.
> • Spell sight words.

Get Ready

Finger Stretching

Use finger stretching to help students identify individual sounds in words.

1. **Say:** Let's review finger stretching. In the word *brim*, the first sound is /b/, the next sound is /r/, the third sound is /ĭ/, and the last sound is /m/. I will finger stretch each sound as I say it. Then I'll say the word, while pulling my fist toward my body.

2. Finger stretch the word *brim*.

3. **Say:** I'm going to say words with several sounds in them. You'll say each word and then finger stretch it while you say each sound in the word.

4. Say the following words and have students finger stretch them. After they finger stretch each word, ask them the question for that word.

   ▸ *glass* /g/ /l/ /ă/ /s/   What is the first sound? /g/
   ▸ *cloth* /k/ /l/ /ŏ/ /th/   What is the middle sound? /ŏ/
   ▸ *brush* /b/ /r/ /ŭ/ /sh/   What is the first sound? /b/
   ▸ *clap* /k/ /l/ /ă/ /p/   What is the last sound? /p/
   ▸ *plant* /p/ /l/ /ă/ /n/ /t/   What is the first sound? /p/
   ▸ *flock* /f/ /l/ /ŏ/ /k/   What is the first sound? /f/

TIP Refer to the *K¹² PhonicsWorks* DVD for a demonstration of finger stretching.

> **Objectives**
> • Identify individual sounds in words.
> • Identify the number of sounds within words.
> • Identify beginning sounds in words.
> • Identify ending sounds in words.
> • Identify and use the blend *br–*.

What's in the Box?

Play a game with students to help them identify beginning sounds in words.

1. Gather the boxes and small household objects.

2. Place an object, such as a doll, in a box.

3. **Say:** Now we're going to play a game with boxes. I will give you the beginning sound of the word, and you have to guess what is in the box. Close your eyes and feel the object in the box. The beginning sound is /d/. What could be in the box?

4. Continue until students have discovered all the objects in the boxes.

5. Redirect students if they need more hints. Give them the ending sound.

   ► Tell them how many syllables are in the word or what vowel sound follows the beginning sound.
   ► If students continue having trouble with this activity, go over the sounds they are having difficulty with.

Review the Beginning Consonant Blend *br–*

Help students recognize and use the beginning consonant blend *br* -.

1. Make the word *brim* on students' whiteboard and point to it.

2. **Say:** Touch and say this word.

   ► How many sounds are in the word? four
   ► How many letters are in the word? four
   ► We know that the letters *b* and *r* at the beginning of this word are called a blend because each letter keeps its own sound while the two sounds blend together.

Learn

Introduce the Beginning Consonant Blend *cr–*

Help students recognize and use the beginning consonant blend *cr–*.

1. Place the following letters on students' whiteboard: *b, c, i, o, p,* and *r*.

2. Make the word *crib* and point to it.

3. **Say:** Touch and say this word.

   ► How many sounds are in the word? four
   ► How many letters are in the word? four
   ► We know that the letters *c* and *r* at the beginning of this word are called a blend because each letter keeps its own sound while the two sounds blend together.

4. Make the word *crop* and point to it.

> **Objectives**
> - Identify beginning sounds in words.
> - Identify and use the blend *cr–*.
> - Identify and use the blend *dr–*.
> - Identify the number of sounds within words.
> - Blend sounds to create words.

5. **Say:** Touch and say the sounds in *crop*.

   ▸ How many sounds are in the word? four
   ▸ How many letters are in the word? four
   ▸ Where is the blend? at the beginning

6. Provide additional guidance if students have difficulty with blends. Take the first letter off the word.

   Say: I have taken the first letter off of the word. Touch and say the word without the first sound. What sound do you make at the beginning of the word? Answers will vary.

   Say: Now I am going to put the first letter back on the word. Touch and say the word. Which two sounds do you hear in the blend at the beginning of the word? Answers will vary.

Introduce the Beginning Consonant Blend *dr–*

Help students recognize and use the beginning consonant blend *dr–*.

1. Place the following letters on students' whiteboard: *d, i, m, o, p, r,* and *u*.

2. Make the word *drop* and point to it.

3. **Say:** Touch and say this word.

   ▸ How many sounds are in the word? four
   ▸ How many letters are in the word? four
   ▸ We know that the letters *d* and *r* at the beginning of this word are called a blend because each letter keeps its own sound while the two sounds blend together.

4. Redirect students if they have difficulty with the beginning consonant blend *dr–*.

   Say: Those two letters are often together at the beginning of a word. When they are together, they blend into the sound /dr/, as in *drum*. Can you say the word *drum*? When you say *drum*, don't stop between the two sounds /d/ and /r/. Try saying the word again.

5. Make the word *drip* and point to it.

6. **Say:** Touch and say the sounds in *drip*.

   ▸ How many sounds are in the word? four
   ▸ How many letters are in the word? four
   ▸ Where is the blend? at the beginning

7. Provide additional guidance if students have difficulty with blends. Take the first letter off the word.

   Say: I have taken the first letter off of the word. Touch and say the word without the first sound. What sound do you make at the beginning of the word? Answers will vary.

   Say: Now I am going to put the first letter back on the word. Touch and say the word. Which two sounds do you hear in the blend at the beginning of the word? Answers will vary.

Build Words

Help students use letters and sounds to build words.

1. Place the following letter tiles at the top of students' whiteboard: *a, b, c, d, f, i, l, m, p, r, s, t,* and *u.*

2. Draw four horizontal lines across the middle of students' whiteboard to represent the sounds in a word.

3. **Say:** Let's use letters and sounds to build the word *drift.*

4. Have students finger stretch the sounds in *drift.*

5. Have students

   ► Identify the first, next, and last sounds in *drift.*
   ► Choose the corresponding letter for each sound.
   ► Move the letters to the correct lines on the whiteboard.

6. Guide students with these questions:

   ► What is the first sound in *drift*? /d/
     Which line does the letter for that sound go on? the first one
   ► What is the next sound in *drift*? /r/
     Which line does the letter for that sound go on? the second one
   ► What is the next sound in *drift*? /ĭ/
     Which line does the letter for that sound go on? the third one
   ► What's the next sound in *drift*? /f/
     Which line does the letter for that sound go on? the fourth one
   ► What's the last sound in *drift*? /t/
   ► Which line does the letter for that sound go on? the last one

7. Have students touch and say the word.

8. Redirect students if they select the incorrect letter.

   Say: That sound is in the word [word], and it is the [first, second, third, fourth] sound. We want the sound [target sound].

   Continue until students select the correct letter.

9. Repeat the activity to build the following words:

   ► *crust* /k/ /r/ /ŭ/ /s/ /t/
   ► *blast* /b/ /l/ /ă/ /s/ /t/
   ► *cramp* /k/ /r/ /ă/ /m/ /p/

Try It ···

"Brett and Brad"

Have students read "Brett and Brad" on page 1 of *K¹² PhonicsWorks Readers Advanced 3.*

Students should read the story silently once or twice before reading the story aloud. When students miss a word that can be sounded out, point to it and give them three to six seconds to try the word again. If students still miss the word, tell them the word so the flow of the story isn't interrupted.

After reading the story, make a list of all the words students missed, and go over those words with them. You may use letter tiles to show students how to read the words.

Objectives
- Read aloud grade-level text with appropriate automaticity, prosody, accuracy, and rate.
- Decode words by applying grade-level word analysis skills.

 **20 minutes**

REVIEW: Beginning Consonant Blends *cr–* and *dr–*

Students will work online independently to

▸ Practice the beginning consonant blends *cr–* and *dr–*.

Help students locate the online activities and provide support as needed.

Objectives
- Identify beginning sounds in words.
- Identify and use the blend *cr–*.
- Identify and use the blend *dr–*.

Offline Alternative

No computer access? Have students point out and name things or words that begin with the consonant blends *cr–* and *dr–* (for example, *crab* or *drag*). You might also ask students to spell words that begin with the consonant blends *cr–* and *dr–*.

Beginning Consonant Blends *fr–* and *gr–*

Lesson Overview

Offline **FOCUS:** Beginning Consonant Blends *fr–* and *gr–* — **30** minutes

Sight Words	Sight Word Concentration
Get Ready	Search Sentences for Short Vowels
	Rhyme and Read
	Review the Beginning Consonant Blend *dr–*
Learn	Introduce the Beginning Consonant Blend *fr–*
	Introduce the Beginning Consonant Blend *gr–*
	Word Chains
Try It	Finish the Job
	Dictation: Write Sentences

Online **REVIEW:** Beginning Consonant Blends *fr–* and *gr–* — **20** minutes

Supplied
- *K¹² PhonicsWorks Advanced Activity Book,* p. PH 20
- whiteboard, Learning Coach
- whiteboard, student
- Tile Kit

Also Needed
- sight words box
- dictation notebook

Advance Preparation

Gather two sets of all the sight word cards you have used to date.

 **30 minutes**

FOCUS: Beginning Consonant Blends *fr–* and *gr–*

Work **together** with students to complete offline Sight Words, Get Ready, Learn, and Try It activities.

Sight Words

Sight Word Concentration

Help students review sight words.

1. Gather the two sets of all sight word cards.

2. Scramble both sets of sight word cards and place them face down on the table or floor.

3. Have students turn over two cards at a time; take turns with students. If the cards match, the person turning over the matching cards reads the word and uses it in a sentence. If the cards don't match, the person turns them back over.

4. Remove and save the matching cards.

5. Continue the activity until all the cards are paired.

6. Have students read all the words.

7. Take the stack of words that students read correctly and dictate each word to them.

8. Have students write each word or spell it aloud.

TIP If students have difficulty with any sight words, let them work at their own pace to really master these words.

Objectives
- Read sight words.
- Spell sight words.
- Write sight words.

Get Ready

Search Sentences for Short Vowels

Have students practice identifying vowel sounds in words that are in a sentence.

1. **Say:** I'm going to say a special sound that is in a word. You will repeat that sound and the word. The first sound is /ŭ/, as in the word *up*.

2. Have students say the target sound /ŭ/ and the word *up*.

3. **Say:** I will read a sentence. Repeat the sentence and tell me the word that has the same sound. The first sentence is, "Ross likes to run and play." Which word in the sentence has the special sound? *run*

4. Have students repeat the sentence and say the word.

5. Redirect students if they don't name the correct word.

    Say: Let me say the sentence again. Remember, you're listening for the sound [special sound].

Objectives
- Identify short vowel sounds.
- Identify and use vowels and vowel sounds.
- Identify words that rhyme.
- Identify beginning sounds in words.
- Identify the number of sounds within words.
- Identify and use the blend *dr–*.

6. Guide students if they have difficulty. Say two words from the sentence and have them choose the one with the target vowel sound.

7. Follow the same procedure with the following words and sentences:

   ► /ŏ/, as in *hot*   *Pam got a pet pig. got*
   ► /ĕ/, as in *let*   *Set that box down. set*
   ► /ŭ/, as in *up*   *Can you hum? hum*
   ► /ĭ/, as in *pin*   *Sharks have fins. fins*
   ► /ă/, as in *at*   *Pat set it down. Pat*
   ► /ŭ/, as in *jump*   *Climb up the hill. up*

Rhyme and Read

Help students practice words that rhyme.

1. Have students say the words *sand* and *land*.

2. Have them tell how the words are alike. They rhyme.

3. Write the following word on students' whiteboard and have them read it: *hand*.

4. Change the *h* to *b*.

5. Have students read the new word. *band*

6. Repeat this procedure until students have spelled and read the following words:

   ► *bland*
   ► *brand*
   ► *strand*

Review the Beginning Consonant Blend *dr–*

Help students recognize and use the beginning consonant blend *dr–*.

1. Make the word *drum* on students' whiteboard and point to it.

2. **Say:** Touch and say this word.

   ► How many sounds are in the word? four
   ► How many letters are in the word? four
   ► We know that the letters *d* and *r* at the beginning of this word are called a blend because each letter keeps its own sound while the two sounds blend together.

Learn

Introduce the Beginning Consonant Blend *fr–*

Help students recognize and use the beginning consonant blend *fr–*.

1. Place the following letters on students' whiteboard: *ck, f, g, o,* and *r*.

2. Make the word *frog* and point to it.

3. **Say:** Touch and say this word.

   ▸ How many sounds are in the word? four
   ▸ How many letters are in the word? four
   ▸ We know that the letters *f* and *r* at the beginning of this word are called a blend because each letter keeps its own sound while the two sounds blend together.

4. Make the word *frock* and point to it.

5. **Say:** Touch and say the sounds in *frock*.

   ▸ How many sounds are in the word? four
   ▸ How many letters are in the word? five
   ▸ What is the beginning blend? *fr–*

6. Provide additional guidance if students have difficulty with blends. Take the first letter off the word.

   Say: I have taken the first letter off of the word. Touch and say the word without the first sound. What sound do you make at the beginning of the word? Answers will vary.

   Say: Now I am going to put the first letter back on the word. Touch and say the word. Which two sounds do you hear in the blend at the beginning of the word? Answers will vary.

Objectives

- Identify beginning sounds in words.
- Identify and use the blend *fr–*.
- Identify and use the blend *gr–*.
- Identify the number of sounds within words.
- Identify the new word when one sound is changed in a word.

Introduce the Beginning Consonant Blend *gr–*

Help students recognize and use the consonant blend *gr–*.

1. Place the following letters on students' whiteboard: *a, b, g, i, p,* and *r*.

2. Make the word *grip* and point to it.

3. **Say:** Touch and say this word.

   ▸ How many sounds are in the word? four
   ▸ How many letters are in the word? four
   ▸ Where is the blend? at the beginning

4. Redirect students if they have difficulty with the beginning consonant blend *gr–*.

   Say: Those two letters are often together at the beginning of a word. When they are together, they blend into the sound /gr/, as in *grape*. Can you say the word *grape*? When you say *grape*, don't stop between the two sounds /g/ and /r/. Try saying the word again.

5. Make the word *grab* and point to it.

6. **Say:** Touch and say this word.

   ▸ How many sounds are in the word? four
   ▸ How many letters are in the word? four
   ▸ Where is the blend? at the beginning

7. Provide additional guidance if students have difficulty with blends. Take the first letter off the word.

   Say: I have taken the first letter off of the word. Touch and say the word without the first sound. What sound do you make at the beginning of the word? Answers will vary.

   Say: Now I am going to put the first letter back on the word. Touch and say the word. Which two sounds do you hear in the blend at the beginning of the word? Answers will vary.

Word Chains

Have students build words by adding and changing letters to help them recognize and use individual sounds in words.

1. Place the following letters at the top of students' whiteboard: *a, c, d, g, i, n, o, p, r,* and *t.*

2. **Say:** I am going to build the first word in a chain. The word is *grin.*

   ▸ I will pull down the letters for the sounds /g/, /r/, /ĭ/, and /n/ to spell the word *grin.*
   ▸ I will touch and say *grin.* To change *grin* to *grip,* I will think about which sound changes from the word *grin* to *grip.* I will need to replace the letter *n* with the letter *p.*
   ▸ Touch and say the word *grip.* Now it's your turn to change *grip* to *trip.* You can spell *trip* by making only one change. Touch and say the new word.

3. Redirect students if they select the incorrect letter for any sound.

   Say: That letter is for the sound [incorrect sound]. We want the letter for the sound [target sound]. What letter makes that sound? Answers will vary.

4. Redirect students if they select the wrong sound.

   Say: To change the word [first word] to [target word], we need the letter for the sound [target sound]. Show students how to make the change. Have them touch and say the new word after they move the letters.

5. Follow this procedure to make the following words: *drip, drop, crop, cop, top, tap, trap, trip.*

6. For every new word, have students add, replace, or remove only one letter.

Try It

Finish the Job

Have students complete page PH 20 in *K¹² PhonicsWorks Advanced Activity Book* for more practice making sentences. Have them choose the word that best completes the sentence and read the sentence aloud.

Dictation: Write Sentences

Use sentences to help students identify individual sounds in words.

1. Gather a pencil and the dictation notebook. Say the sentence, *Watch the frog jump.* Then give these directions to students:

   ▸ Repeat the sentence.
   ▸ Write the sentence in your notebook.
   ▸ Read the sentence aloud.

2. When students have finished, write the following sentence on your whiteboard: *Watch the frog jump.*

3. Have them compare their answer to your correct version.

4. Repeat this procedure with the sentence, *Brad can nap on the grass.*

   ▸ If students make an error and don't see it, help them correct their mistake by having them finger stretch the sounds in the word they missed.
   ▸ If students are having difficulty selecting the correct letters or sounds, review those letters or sounds that are confusing them.
   ▸ If students have difficulty with first, middle, and last sounds, have them finger stretch the sounds in words.

 **20 minutes**

REVIEW: Beginning Consonant Blends *fr–* and *gr–*

Students will work online independently to

- ▸ Practice the beginning consonant blends *fr–* and *gr–*.
- ▸ Practice decoding text by reading a story.

Help students locate the online activities and provide support as needed.

Offline Alternative

No computer access? Have students point out and name things or words that begin with the consonant blends *fr–* and *gr–* (for example, *frog* or *grab*). You might also ask students to spell words that begin with the consonant blends *fr–* and *gr–*.

Objectives

- Identify and use the blend *fr–*.
- Identify and use the blend *gr–*.
- Identify beginning sounds in words.
- Read aloud grade-level text with appropriate automaticity, prosody, accuracy, and rate.
- Decode words by applying grade-level word analysis skills.

Beginning Consonant Blends *pr–* and *tr–*

Lesson Overview

Offline	**FOCUS:** Beginning Consonant Blends *pr–* and *tr–*	**30** minutes

Sight Words	Pick a Pair
Get Ready	Recognize Words and Syllables
	Sound Workout
	Review the Beginning Consonant Blend *gr–*
Learn	Introduce the Beginning Consonant Blend *pr–*
	Introduce the Beginning Consonant Blend *tr–*
	Build Words
Try It	"Trish and Fred"

Online	**REVIEW:** Beginning Consonant Blends *pr–* and *tr–*	**20** minutes

Materials

Supplied
- *K¹² PhonicsWorks Readers Advanced 3*, pp. 7–12
- whiteboard, student
- Tile Kit

Also Needed
- sight words box
- dictation notebook

 **30 minutes**

FOCUS: Beginning Consonant Blends *pr–* and *tr–*

Work **together** with students to complete offline Sight Words, Get Ready, Learn, and Try It activities.

Sight Words

Pick a Pair

Play a card game with students for more practice with sight words.

1. Gather the sight word cards that students are reviewing. Choose two words and place the cards on the table.

2. Ask questions to help students identify each word. For example, if the words are *or* and *one*, you could ask, "Which word names a number?" If the words are *on* and *but*, you could ask, "Which word is the opposite of *off*?"

3. Continue the activity until students identify all the words.

4. Take the stack of words that students read correctly and dictate each word.

5. Have students write each word or spell it aloud.

Get Ready

Recognize Words and Syllables

Review the concept of syllables with students.

1. **Say:** When we talk, we make words by pushing air out of our mouths. Each push of air in a word is called a **syllable**. Each word has one or more syllables. You can think of syllables as chunks of words.

2. **Say:** Let's break some words into syllables.

   ▶ I'll say a word. I'll repeat the word.
   ▶ You'll say the word after me, and you'll break it into syllables by saying the separate chunks of the word and tapping your fist on the table as you say each chunk.
   ▶ For example, I'll say *hammer,* and then I'll say it again.
   ▶ You'll say *ham / mer* and tap your fist on the table as you say each syllable.

3. Say each word and repeat it. Have students fist tap on the table as they say the syllables in each word.

   ▶ *basket bas / ket*
   ▶ *window win / dow*
   ▶ *counting count / ing*
   ▶ *rocket rock / et*
   ▶ *elephant el / e /phant*

TIP Have students name items in the room and fist tap the syllables with you. For example, have them name and fist tap words such as *ta / ble* and *win / dow*. Challenge students to name and fist tap something with several syllables, such as *tel / e / vi / sion*.

Sound Workout

Help students practice identifying ending sounds in words.

1. **Say:** I'll say a pair of words. Listen for the **ending sound** in the words. One of the words will have an ending blend and the other will not. Tell me which word ends in a blend.

   ▸ For example, if I say the words *dish* and *pond*, you'll repeat both words. Then you'll tell me that the word *pond* has an ending blend made up of the sounds /n/ and /d/.
   ▸ Now it's your turn. First repeat the pair of words I say, and then tell me which word has the ending blend and what two sounds are in the blend.

2. Use these pairs of words. (Pronounce the words very clearly, making sure you pronounce both sounds in the consonant blend words and students are watching your mouth as you do so.)

   ▸ *quick* and *raft raft,* /f/ /t/
   ▸ *risk* and *him risk,* /s/ /k/
   ▸ *chimp* and *nut chimp,* /m/ /p/
   ▸ *cap* and *silk silk,* /l/ /k/

3. Redirect students if they seem confused.

   Say: Listen for the ending in [word]. What is the ending? Does it have one or two sounds?

4. Provide additional guidance if students cannot distinguish between the ending sounds the second time. Have them finger stretch the sounds in the word. Then have them put the letter tiles on the board for that word, and have them touch and say.

Review the Beginning Consonant Blend *gr–*

Help students recognize and use the beginning consonant blend *gr–*.

1. Make the word *grin* on students' whiteboard and point to it.

2. **Say:** Touch and say this word.

   ▸ How many sounds are in the word? four
   ▸ How many letters are in the word? four
   ▸ We know that the letters *g* and *r* at the beginning of this word are called a blend because each letter keeps its own sound while the two sounds blend together.

Learn

Introduce the Beginning Consonant Blend *pr–*

Help students recognize and use the beginning consonant blend *pr–*.

1. Place the following letters on students' whiteboard: *e, o, p, p, r,* and *ss.*

2. Make the word *press* and point to it.

3. **Say:** Touch and say this word.

   ▸ How many sounds are in the word? four
   ▸ How many letters are in the word? five
   ▸ Where is the blend? at the beginning

4. Make the word *prop* and point to it.

5. **Say:** Touch and say this word.

   ▸ How many sounds are in the word? four
   ▸ How many letters are in the word? four
   ▸ We know that the letters *p* and *r* at the beginning of this word are called a blend because each letter keeps its own sound while the two sounds blend together.

Introduce the Beginning Consonant Blend *tr–*

Help students recognize and use the beginning consonant blend *tr–*.

1. Place the following letters on student whiteboard: *a, i, p, r,* and *t.*

2. Make the word *trip* and point to it.

3. **Say:** Touch and say this word.

   ▸ How many sounds are in the word? four
   ▸ How many letters are in the word? four
   ▸ Where is the blend? at the beginning

4. Make the word *trap* and point to it.

5. **Say:** Touch and say this word.

   ▸ How many sounds are in the word? four
   ▸ How many letters are in the word? four
   ▸ We know that the letters *t* and *r* at the beginning of this word are called a blend because each letter keeps its own sound while the two sounds blend together.

6. Provide additional guidance if students have difficulty with blends. Take the first letter off the word.

   Say: I have taken the first letter off of the word. Touch and say the word without the first sound. What sound do you make at the beginning of the word? Answers will vary.

   Say: Now I am going to put the first letter back on the word. Touch and say the word. Which two sounds do you hear in the blend at the beginning of the word? Answers will vary.

Objectives

- Identify and use the blend *pr–*.
- Identify and use the blend *tr–*.
- Identify beginning sounds in words.
- Identify the number of sounds within words.
- Identify individual sounds in words.

Build Words

Help students use letters and sounds to build words.

1. Place the following letter tiles at the top of students' whiteboard: *ck, f, i, m, o, p, r, t, u,* and *zz.*

2. Draw four horizontal lines across the middle of students' whiteboard to represent the sounds in a word.

3. **Say:** Let's use letters and sounds to build the word *frizz.*

4. Have students finger stretch the sounds in *frizz.*

5. Have students

   ▸ Identify the first, next, and last sounds in *frizz.*
   ▸ Choose the corresponding letter tile for each sound.
   ▸ Move the letters to the correct lines on the whiteboard.

6. Guide students with these questions:

   ▸ What is the first sound in *frizz*? /f/
     Which line does the letter for that sound go on? the first one
   ▸ What is the next sound in *frizz*? /r/
     Which line does the letter for that sound go on? the second one
   ▸ What is the next sound in *frizz*? /ĭ/
     Which line does the letter for that sound go on? the third one
   ▸ What's the last sound in *frizz*? /z/
     Which line do the letters for that sound go on? the last one

7. Have students touch and say the word.

8. Redirect students if they select the incorrect letter.

   Say: That sound is in the word [word], and it is the [first, second, third, fourth] sound. We want the sound [target sound]. Continue until students select the correct letter.

9. Repeat the activity to build the following words:

   ▸ *truck* /t/ /r/ /ŭ/ /k/
   ▸ *prim* /p/ /r/ /ĭ/ /m/
   ▸ *trim* /t/ /r/ /ĭ/ /m/

Try It ···

"Trish and Fred"

Have students read "Trish and Fred" on page 7 of *K¹² PhonicsWorks Readers Advanced 3*.

Students should read the story silently once or twice before reading the story aloud. When students miss a word that can be sounded out, point to it and give them three to six seconds to try the word again. If students still miss the word, tell them the word so the flow of the story isn't interrupted.

After reading the story, make a list of all the words students missed, and go over those words with them. You may use letter tiles to show students how to read the words.

Objectives

- Read aloud grade-level text with appropriate automaticity, prosody, accuracy, and rate.
- Decode words by applying grade-level word analysis skills.

 **20 minutes**

REVIEW: Beginning Consonant Blends *pr–* and *tr–*

Students will work online independently to

► Practice the beginning consonant blends *pr–* and *tr–*.

Help students locate the online activities and provide support as needed.

Objectives

- Identify beginning sounds in words.
- Identify and use the blend *pr–*.
- Identify and use the blend *tr–*.

Offline Alternative

No computer access? Have students point out and name things or words that begin with the consonant blends *pr–* and *tr–* (for example, *press* or *trash*). You might also ask students to spell words that begin with the consonant blends *pr–* and *tr–*.

Unit Checkpoint

Lesson Overview

🖥	**[Online]**	**REVIEW:** Beginning Consonant Blends *br–*, *cr–*, *dr–*, *fr–*, *gr–*, *pr–*, and *tr–*	**20** minutes
📄	**[Offline]**	**UNIT CHECKPOINT:** Beginning Consonant Blends *br–*, *cr–*, *dr–*, *fr–*, *gr–*, *pr–*, and *tr–*	**30** minutes

Materials

Supplied

- *K¹² PhonicsWorks Advanced Assessments,* pp. PH 55–60

Objectives

- Identify and use the blend *br–*.
- Identify and use the blend *cr–*.
- Identify and use the blend *dr–*.
- Identify and use the blend *fr–*.
- Identify and use the blend *gr–*.
- Identify and use the blend *pr–*.
- Identify and use the blend *tr–*.
- Read, write, and spell words containing *br*.
- Read, write, and spell words containing *cr*.
- Read, write, and spell words containing *dr*.
- Read, write, and spell words containing *fr*.
- Read, write, and spell words containing *gr*.
- Read, write, and spell words containing *pr*.
- Read, write, and spell words containing *tr*.
- Identify individual sounds in words.
- Given the letter or letters, identify the most common sound.
- Given the sound, identify the most common letter or letters.
- Read instructional-level text with 90% accuracy.
- Read aloud grade-level text with appropriate automaticity, prosody, accuracy, and rate.
- Write sight words.
- Write words by applying grade-level phonics knowledge.

[Online] 20 minutes

REVIEW: Beginning Consonant Blends *br–*, *cr–*, *dr–*, *fr–*, *gr–*, *pr–*, and *tr–*

Students will review the beginning consonant blends *br–*, *cr–*, *dr–*, *fr–*, *gr–*, *pr–*, and *tr–* to prepare for the Unit Checkpoint. Help students locate the online activities and provide support as needed.

[Offline] ⓴ minutes

UNIT CHECKPOINT: Beginning Consonant Blends *br–*, *cr–*, *dr–*, *fr–*, *gr–*, *pr–*, and *tr–*

Explain that students are going to show what they have learned about sounds, letters, and words.

1. Give students the Unit Checkpoint pages for the Beginning Consonant Blends *br–*, *cr–*, *dr–*, *fr–*, *gr–*, *pr–*, and *tr–* unit and print the Unit Checkpoint Answer Key, if you'd like.

2. Use the instructions below to help administer the Checkpoint to students. On the Answer Key or another sheet of paper, note student answers to oral response questions to help with scoring the Checkpoint later.

3. Use the Answer Key to score the Checkpoint, and then enter the results online.

Part 1. Read Nonsense Words Moving left to right, have students say the sounds of each nonsense word. Note any nonsense words they say incorrectly.

Part 2. Finger Stretching Say each word to students. Have them say each word and finger stretch the sounds. Note any words they finger stretch incorrectly.

16. *brush*	19. *crack*
17. *dress*	20. *frog*
18. *grill*	21. *press*

Part 3. Dictation Say each word to students. Have them repeat and write the word.

22. *brick*	25. *cross*
23. *drip*	26. *fresh*
24. *grab*	27. *trick*

Part 4. Writing Read each sentence to students. Have them repeat and write the sentence.

28. *Trap the crab.*

29. *Is that a frog?*

Part 5. Read Aloud Listen to students read the sentences aloud. Count and note the number of words they read correctly.

Part 6. Say Letters Say each sound. Have students say the letter or letters that make that sound. Note any incorrect responses.

31. /ŏ/

32. /ch/

33. /th/

34. /ŭ/

35. /r/

36. /kw/

37. /ĭ/

38. /ĕ/

39. /ă/

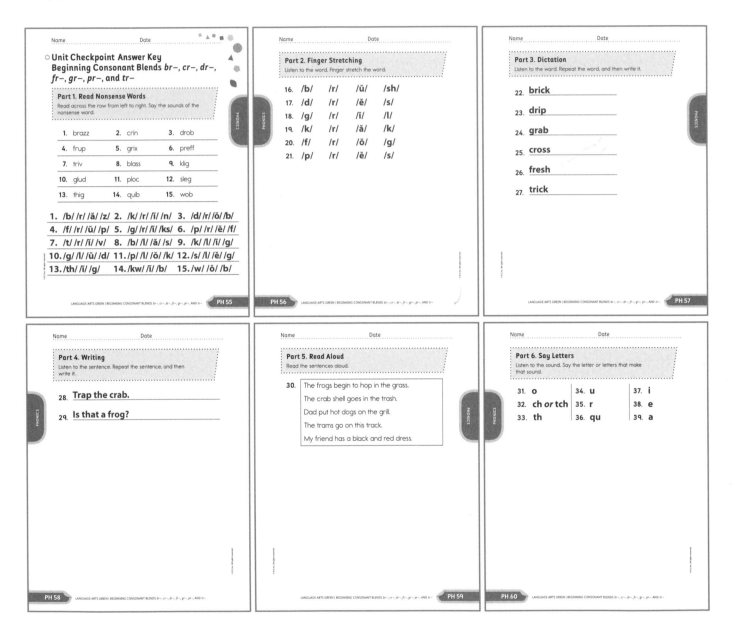

Name _____ Date _____

Unit Checkpoint Answer Key
Beginning Consonant Blends *br–, cr–, dr–, fr–, gr–, pr–,* and *tr–*

Part 1. Read Nonsense Words
Read across the row from left to right. Say the sounds of the nonsense word.

1. brazz	2. crin	3. drob
4. frup	5. grix	6. preff
7. triv	8. blass	9. klig
10. glud	11. ploc	12. sleg
13. thig	14. quib	15. wob

1. /b/ /r/ /ă/ /z/ 2. /k/ /r/ /ĭ/ /n/ 3. /d/ /r/ /ŏ/ /b/
4. /f/ /r/ /ŭ/ /p/ 5. /g/ /r/ /ĭ/ /ks/ 6. /p/ /r/ /ĕ/ /f/
7. /t/ /r/ /ĭ/ /v/ 8. /b/ /l/ /ă/ /s/ 9. /k/ /l/ /ĭ/ /g/
10. /g/ /l/ /ŭ/ /d/ 11. /p/ /l/ /ŏ/ /k/ 12. /s/ /l/ /ĕ/ /g/
13. /th/ /ĭ/ /g/ 14. /kw/ /ĭ/ /b/ 15. /w/ /ŏ/ /b/

LANGUAGE ARTS GREEN | BEGINNING CONSONANT BLENDS *br–, cr–, dr–, fr–, gr–, pr–,* AND *tr–*   **PH 55**

PH 56   LANGUAGE ARTS GREEN | BEGINNING CONSONANT BLENDS *br–, cr–, dr–, fr–, gr–, pr–,* AND *tr–*

Name _____ Date _____

Part 2. Finger Stretching
Listen to the word. Finger stretch the word.

16. /b/   /r/   /ŭ/   /sh/
17. /d/   /r/   /ĕ/   /s/
18. /g/   /r/   /ĭ/   /l/
19. /k/   /r/   /ă/   /k/
20. /f/   /r/   /ŏ/   /g/
21. /p/   /r/   /ĕ/   /s/

Name _____ Date _____

Part 3. Dictation
Listen to the word. Repeat the word, and then write it.

22. **brick** _____

23. **drip** _____

24. **grab** _____

25. **cross** _____

26. **fresh** _____

27. **trick** _____

LANGUAGE ARTS GREEN | BEGINNING CONSONANT BLENDS *br–, cr–, dr–, fr–, gr–, pr–,* AND *tr–*   **PH 57**

Name _____ Date _____

Part 4. Writing
Listen to the sentence. Repeat the sentence, and then write it.

28. **Trap the crab.** _____

29. **Is that a frog?**

PH 58   LANGUAGE ARTS GREEN | BEGINNING CONSONANT BLENDS *br–, cr–, dr–, fr–, gr–, pr–,* AND *tr–*

Name _____ Date _____

Part 5. Read Aloud
Read the sentences aloud.

30.

> The frogs begin to hop in the grass.
> The crab shell goes in the trash.
> Dad put hot dogs on the grill.
> The trams go on this track.
> My friend has a black and red dress.

LANGUAGE ARTS GREEN | BEGINNING CONSONANT BLENDS *br–, cr–, dr–, fr–, gr–, pr–,* AND *tr–*   **PH 59**

Name _____ Date _____

Part 6. Say Letters
Listen to the sound. Say the letter or letters that make that sound.

31. o	34. u	37. i
32. ch *or* tch	35. r	38. e
33. th	36. qu	39. a

PH 60   LANGUAGE ARTS GREEN | BEGINNING CONSONANT BLENDS *br–, cr–, dr–, fr–, gr–, pr–,* AND *tr–*

Introduce Beginning Digraph Blend *shr*–

Unit Overview

In this unit, students will
- ▸ Learn the sight words *down*, *know*, and *after*.
- ▸ Review sight words.
- ▸ Learn the beginning digraph blends *shr*– and *thr*–.
- ▸ Identify individual sounds in words.

Materials

Supplied
- *K¹² PhonicsWorks Advanced Activity Book*, p. PH 21
- whiteboard, Learning Coach
- whiteboard, student
- Tile Kit

Also Needed
- sight words box
- dictation notebook

Lesson Overview

〖 Offline 〗 FOCUS: Introduce Beginning Digraph Blend *shr*– **30 minutes**

Sight Words	Introduce Sight Words
Get Ready	Review Sounds and Letters
Learn	Introduce the Beginning Digraph Blend *shr*–
	Build Words
Try It	Match It
	Dictation: Write Sentences

〖 Online 〗 REVIEW: Beginning Digraph Blend *shr*– **20 minutes**

 **30 minutes**

FOCUS: Introduce Beginning Digraph Blend *shr–*

Work **together** with students to complete offline Sight Words, Get Ready, Learn, and Try It activities.

Sight Words

Introduce Sight Words

Help students learn the sight words *down, know,* and *after.*

1. Gather the sight word cards *down, know,* and *after.*

2. Show students the *down* card.

3. **Say:** This is the word *down.* We see this word so often that we want to be able to read and spell it quickly without thinking about it. Look closely at the word *down.* Spell the word *down* aloud. Take a picture of the word *down* in your mind. When you think you can spell *down* yourself, turn the card over and use your letter tiles to spell the word *down.* Check the card to see if you spelled the word *down* correctly. Read aloud the word you spelled with the letter tiles.

4. Repeat the activity with the remaining sight words.

5. Chart students' progress on the back of each card.

   ▸ Divide the back of the card into two columns.
   ▸ Label the first column "Read" and the second column "Spell."
   ▸ Record the dates that students read or spell the word correctly. When students can read and spell the word correctly three times in a row, they have mastered the word. You may want to put a star or sticker on their card when they have mastered that word.

6. Add the cards to students' sight words box.

(TIP) Sight words can be very difficult for some students. Let them work at their own pace and really master these words.

> **Objectives**
> - Read sight words.
> - Spell sight words.

Get Ready

Review Sounds and Letters

Help students review sounds for the letters and digraphs *ch, f, h, k, l, o, p, qu, r, sh, u, v,* and *wh,* plus any letters that are confusing for them.

1. Place the following letter tiles in random order on students' whiteboard: *ch, f, h, k, l, o, p, qu, r, sh, u, v,* and *wh,* plus any letters that are confusing.

2. **Say:** Let's go over some letters and sounds.

> **Objectives**
> - Given the letter, identify the most common sound.
> - Given the sound, identify the most common letter or letters.

3. Point to each letter tile and have students say a sound that letter or digraph makes.

- ▸ *o* /ŏ/ or /ō/
- ▸ *sh* /sh/
- ▸ *u* /ŭ/ or /ū/
- ▸ *l* /l/
- ▸ *qu* /kw/
- ▸ *wh* /w/
- ▸ *k* /k/ or /ck/

- ▸ *r* /r/
- ▸ *v* /v/
- ▸ *ch* /ch/
- ▸ *p* /p/
- ▸ *h* /h/
- ▸ *f* /f/

4. Say each of the following sounds. Have students repeat the sound and touch the corresponding letter tile.

- ▸ /ŏ/ *o*
- ▸ /sh/ *sh*
- ▸ /ŭ/ *u*
- ▸ /l/ *l*
- ▸ /kw/ *qu*
- ▸ /w/ *wh*
- ▸ /k/ *k*

- ▸ /r/ *r*
- ▸ /v/ *v*
- ▸ /ch/ *ch*
- ▸ /p/ *p*
- ▸ /h/ *h*
- ▸ /f/ *f*

5. As you do the activity, point to some letter tiles two or three times so that students don't think they are finished with a sound after they have named it.

6. Redirect students if they say an incorrect sound when you point to a letter tile.

   Say: That's the sound of another letter. What is the sound for this letter?

7. Help students if they touch the wrong letter tile after they repeat a sound.

   Say: That letter tile goes with the sound [sound for touched letter tile]. We're looking for the letter tile that goes with the sound [target sound].

Learn

Introduce the Beginning Digraph Blend *shr–*
Help students recognize and use the beginning digraph blend *shr–*.

1. Place the following letters on students' whiteboard: *b, g, r, sh,* and *u*.

2. Make the word *rug* and point to it.

3. **Say:** Touch and say this word.

   - ▸ How many sounds are in the word? three
   - ▸ How many letters are in the word? three
   - ▸ Where is the blend? There isn't one, but we can use the word to make a special blend.

4. Make the word *shrug* and point to it.

5. **Say:** Touch and say the sounds in *shrug*.

   - ▸ How many sounds are in the word? four
   - ▸ How many letters are in the word? five
   - ▸ Where is the blend? at the beginning

> **Objectives**
> - Identify and use the blend *shr–*.
> - Identify the number of sounds within words.
> - Identify beginning sounds in words.
> - Blend sounds to create words.

6. Redirect students if they have difficulty with the beginning digraph blend *shr–*.

   Say: Those three letters are often together at the beginning of a word. When they are together, they blend into the sound /shr/, as in *shrimp*. Can you say the word *shrimp*? When you say *shrimp*, don't stop between the two sounds /sh/ and /r/. Try saying the word again.

7. **Say:** When the letters *s*, *h*, and *r* are together at the beginning of a word, the digraph *sh–* keeps its sound and the letter *r* keeps its sound. That's why we use two tiles—because the digraph *sh–* and the letter *r* keep their own sounds.

8. Make the word *shrub* and point to it.

9. **Say:** Touch and say this word.

   ▸ How many sounds are in the word? four
   ▸ How many letters are in the word? five
   ▸ Where is the blend? at the beginning

Build Words

Help students use letters and sounds to build words.

1. Place the following letter tiles on students' whiteboard: *d, e, g, i, ll, m, p, r, sh,* and *u*.

2. Draw five horizontal lines across the middle of students' whiteboard to represent the sounds in a word.

3. **Say:** Let's use letters and sounds to build the word *shrimp*.

4. Have students finger stretch the sounds in *shrimp*.

5. Have students

   ▸ Identify the first, next, and last sounds in *shrimp*.
   ▸ Choose the corresponding letter for each of the sounds.
   ▸ Move the letters to the correct lines on their whiteboard.

6. Guide students with these questions:

   ▸ What is the first sound in *shrimp*? /sh/
     Which line do the letters for that sound go on? the first one
   ▸ What is the next sound in *shrimp*? /r/
     Which line does the letter for that sound go on? the second one
   ▸ What is the next sound in *shrimp*? /ĭ/
     Which line does the letter for that sound go on? the third one
   ▸ What is the next sound in *shrimp*? /m/
     Which line does the letter for that sound go on? the fourth one
   ▸ What's the last sound in *shrimp*? /p/
     Which line does the letter for that sound go on? the last one

7. Have students touch and say the word.

8. Redirect students if they select the incorrect letter.

   Say: That sound is in the word [word], and it is the [first, second, third] sound. We want the sound [target sound].

   Continue until students select the correct letter.

9. Repeat the activity, using four horizontal lines, to build the following words:

   ▸ *shred* /sh/ /r/ /ĕ/ /d/
   ▸ *shrill* /sh/ /r/ /ĭ/ /l/
   ▸ *shrug* /sh/ /r/ /ŭ/ /g/

Try It

Match It

Have students complete page PH 21 in *K¹² PhonicsWorks Advanced Activity Book* for more practice with words that begin with the digraph blend *shr–*. Have students read each sentence aloud and draw a line to the picture that matches the sentence.

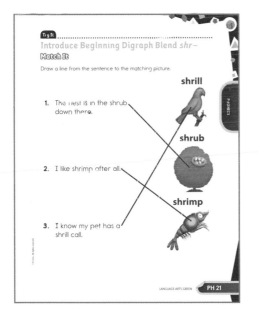

Dictation: Write Sentences

Use sentences to help students identify individual sounds in words.

1. Gather a pencil and the dictation notebook. Say the sentence, *Meg and Fran had shrimp for lunch.* Then give these directions to students:

   ▸ Repeat the sentence.
   ▸ Write the sentence in your notebook.
   ▸ Read the sentence aloud.

2. When students have finished, write the following sentence on your whiteboard: *Meg and Fran had shrimp for lunch.*

3. Have them compare their answer to your correct version.

4. Repeat this procedure with the sentence, *Fred will plant the shrub.*

   ▸ If students make an error and don't see it, help them correct their mistake by having them finger stretch the sounds in the word they missed.
   ▸ If students are having difficulty selecting the correct letters or sounds, review those letters or sounds that are confusing them.
   ▸ If students have difficulty with first, middle, and last sounds, have them finger stretch the sounds in words.

 **20 minutes**

REVIEW: Beginning Digraph Blend *shr–*

Students will work online independently to

▸ Practice the beginning digraph blend *shr–*.
▸ Practice decoding text by reading a story.

Help students locate the online activities and provide support as needed.

Offline Alternative

No computer access? Have students name things or words that begin with the digraph blend *shr–* (for example, *shrink* or *shrunk*). You might also have students spell words that have the beginning digraph blend *shr–*.

> **Objectives**
> - Identify and use the blend *shr–*.
> - Identify beginning sounds in words.
> - Read aloud grade-level text with appropriate automaticity, prosody, accuracy, and rate.
> - Decode words by applying grade-level word analysis skills.

Practice Beginning Digraph Blend *shr–*

Lesson Overview

Offline **FOCUS:** Practice Beginning Digraph Blend *shr–* **30** minutes

Sight Words	Sight Word Fun
Practice	Quick Last Sounds
	Word Walk
	Search Sentences for Blends
	Finger Stretching
Try It	"Trent"

Online **REVIEW:** Beginning Digraph Blend *shr–* **20** minutes

Materials

Supplied
- *K¹² PhonicsWorks Readers Advanced 3,* pp. 13–18
- whiteboard, Learning Coach
- whiteboard, student
- Tile Kit

Also Needed
- sight words box

Offline 30 minutes

FOCUS: Practice Beginning Digraph Blend *shr–*

Work **together** with students to complete offline Sight Words, Practice, and Try It activities.

Sight Words

Sight Word Fun

Help students learn the sight words *down, know,* and *after,* and up to two additional sight words they have yet to master.

1. Gather the sight word cards *down, know,* and *after,* and up to two additional sight word cards.

2. Choose one sight word card to begin.

   Say: Look at this word and take a picture of it in your mind. When you think you can spell the word yourself, turn the card over and use your letter tiles to spell the word.

3. After students spell the word, have them check the card to see if they spelled the word correctly.

   Say: Read aloud the word you spelled with the letter tiles.

4. Repeat the activity with the remaining sight words.

   TIP Sight words can be very difficult for some students. Let them work at their own pace and really master these words.

> **Objectives**
> - Read sight words.
> - Spell sight words.

Practice

Quick Last Sounds

Help students name words that have the same ending sound.

1. **Say:** I'm going to say a sound that ends a word. Your job is to think of as many words as you can that end with that same sound. Let's see how many you can name.

   ▸ The last sound is /f/, as in *laugh*. How many words can you say that end with that sound? Answers will vary.

2. Continue this procedure with the following sounds:

   ▸ /m/, as in *ham*
   ▸ /sh/, as in *wish*
   ▸ /k/, as in *pack*
   ▸ /d/, as in *sad*

> **Objectives**
> - Identify ending sounds in words.
> - Identify and use the blend *shr–*.
> - Identify beginning sounds in words.
> - Identify individual sounds in words.
> - Identify the number of sounds within words.

3. Redirect students if they have trouble thinking of words.

   ▸ Have them look around the room and find objects that end with that sound. You could also get a book and find pictures of things that end with that sound.
   ▸ If students continue to have trouble thinking of words, have them rhyme words, such as *ram, Sam, tam,* and *clam.*

Word Walk

Help students recognize words for things that are found outdoors.

1. **Say:** We're going to take a walk outside to see what we can find. You will help me write a list of things that we may find.

2. Help students write things they might see outdoors.

   Say: If you think we will see something, write it on your list. Remember, when we take our walk, check off each thing you see.

   TIP If the weather is bad, create a list of words that students are likely to see indoors, and add those words to the list before you do a word walk inside.

Search Sentences for Blends

Help students practice identifying the **beginning digraph blend *shr–*** in words that are in a sentence.

1. **Say:** I'm going to say the beginning digraph blend *shr–* that is in a word. You will repeat that sound and the word. The beginning digraph blend is *shr–,* as in the word *shred.*

2. Have students say the target sound /shr/ and the sample word *shred.*

3. **Say:** I will read a sentence. Repeat the sentence and tell me the word that has the same beginning digraph blend. The first sentence is, "Mark's dog has a shrill bark."

   ▸ What is the special beginning digraph blend? *shr–*
   ▸ What is the word that has the special beginning digraph blend? *shrill*

4. Have students repeat the sentence and say the word.

   ▸ If students don't name the correct word, repeat the sentence slowly, clearly pronouncing the beginning of the words. Remind them of the special beginning sound.
   ▸ If students have difficulty, say two words from the sentence and have them choose the one with the target beginning sound.

5. Follow the same procedure with the following words and sentences to help students recognize the beginning digraph blend *shr–.*

   ▸ /shr/, as in *shred*   *That shrub has grown.* shrub
   ▸ /shr/, as in *shrill*   *Do you like shrimp?* shrimp
   ▸ /shr/, as in *shrub*   *I shrank my pants.* shrank
   ▸ /shr/, as in *shred*   *I shrug my shoulders.* shrug

Finger Stretching

Use finger stretching to help students identify individual sounds in words.

1. **Say:** Let's review finger stretching. In the word *shred*, the first sound is /sh/, the next sound is /r/, the third sound is /ĕ/, and the last sound is /d/. I will finger stretch each sound as I say it. Then I'll say the word and while pulling my fist toward my body.

2. Finger stretch the word *shred*.

3. **Say:** I'm going to say words with several sounds in them. You'll say each word and then finger stretch it while you say each sound in the word.

4. Say the following words and have students finger stretch them. After they finger stretch each word, ask them the question for that word.

   ▸ *shrug* /sh/ /r/ /ŭ/ /g/   What is the first sound? /sh/
   ▸ *shrub* /sh/ /r/ /ŭ/ /b/   What is the vowel sound? /ŭ/
   ▸ *shrill* /sh/ /r/ /ĭ/ /l/   What is the first sound? /sh/
   ▸ *shrimp* /sh/ /r/ /ĭ/ /m/ /p/   What is the last sound? /p/

TIP Refer to the *K¹² PhonicsWorks* DVD for a demonstration of finger stretching.

Try It ••

"Trent"

Have students read "Trent" on page 13 of *K¹² PhonicsWorks Readers Advanced 3*.

Students should read the story silently once or twice before reading the story aloud. When students miss a word that can be sounded out, point to it and give them three to six seconds to try the word again. If students still miss the word, tell them the word so the flow of the story isn't interrupted.

After reading the story, make a list of all the words students missed and go over those words with them. You may use letter tiles to show them how to read the words.

> **Objectives**
> • Read aloud grade-level text with appropriate automaticity, prosody, accuracy, and rate.
> • Decode words by applying grade-level word analysis skills.

Online ⏱ **20** minutes

REVIEW: Beginning Digraph Blend *shr–*

Students will work online independently to

▸ Practice the beginning digraph blend *shr–*.

Help students locate the online activities and provide support as needed.

> **Objectives**
> • Identify and use the blend *shr–*.
> • Identify beginning sounds in words.

Offline Alternative

No computer access? Have students name things or words that begin with the digraph blend *shr–* (for example, *shrill* or *shrug*). You might also have students spell words that have the beginning digraph blend *shr–*.

Introduce Beginning Digraph Blend *thr*–

Lesson Overview

Offline **FOCUS:** Introduce Beginning Digraph Blend *thr*–   **30** minutes

Sight Words	Sight Word Fun
Get Ready	Secret Sound
	Review Sounds and Letters
	Review the Beginning Digraph Blend *shr*–
Learn	Introduce the Beginning Digraph Blend *thr*–
Try It	Finish the Job
	Dictation: Write Sentences

Online **REVIEW:** Beginning Digraph Blend *thr*–   **20** minutes

Materials

Supplied
- *K¹² PhonicsWorks Advanced Activity Book*, p. PH 22
- whiteboard, Learning Coach
- whiteboard, student
- Tile Kit

Also Needed
- dictation notebook
- sight words box

 **30 minutes**

FOCUS: Introduce Beginning Digraph Blend *thr–*

Work **together** with students to complete offline Sight Words, Get Ready, Learn, and Try It activities.

Sight Words

Sight Word Fun

Help students learn the sight words *down, know,* and *after* and up to two additional sight words the student has yet to master.

1. Gather the sight word cards *down, know,* and *after* and up to two additional sight word cards.

2. Choose one sight word card to begin.

   Say: Look at this word and take a picture of it in your mind. When you think you can spell the word yourself, turn the card over and use your letter tiles to spell the word.

3. After students spell the word, have them check the card to see if they spelled the word correctly.

   Say: Read aloud the word you spelled with the letter tiles.

4. Repeat the activity with the remaining sight words.

TIP Sight words can be very difficult for some students. Let students work at their own pace and really master these words.

> **Objectives**
> - Read sight words.
> - Spell sight words.

Get Ready

Secret Sound

Say groups of words that end with the same blend to help students recognize **ending sounds** in words.

1. **Say:** I am going to say some groups of words. Listen for a secret blend at the end of each word. Then tell me the sound of the blend you hear at the end of each group of words.

2. Say each of the following groups of words. Have students identify the sound of the ending blend in each group.

   ► *cost, fast, just* /st/
   ► *send, land, bond* /nd/
   ► *ant, bent, hunt* /nt/
   ► *help, pulp, gulp* /lp/
   ► *lunch, inch, bench* /nch/

TIP If students can't identify the secret sound, have them listen while you say each word again. Have students repeat each word and say the sound of the blend they hear at the end of each word.

> **Objectives**
> - Identify ending sounds in words.
> - Given the letter, identify the most common sound.
> - Given the sound, identify the most common letter or letters.
> - Identify and use the blend *shr–*.
> - Identify beginning sounds in words.

Review Sounds and Letters

Help students review sounds for the letters and digraph *b, c, h, j, p, qu, u, wh,* and *x,* plus any letters that are confusing for them.

1. Place the following letter tiles in random order on students' whiteboard: *b, c, h, j, p, qu, u, wh,* and *x,* plus any letters that are confusing.

2. **Say:** Let's go over some letters and sounds.

3. Point to each letter tile and have students say a sound that letter or letters make.

   - *p* /p/
   - *j* /j/
   - *qu* /kw/
   - *c* /k/ or /s/
   - *h* /h/

   - *wh* /w/
   - *u* /ŭ/ or /ū/
   - *b* /b/
   - *x* /ks/

4. Say each of the following sounds. Have students repeat the sound and touch the corresponding letter tile.

   - /p/ *p*
   - /j/ *j*
   - /kw/ *qu*
   - /k/ *c*
   - /h/ *h*

   - /w/ *wh*
   - /ü/ *u*
   - /b/ *b*
   - /ks/ *x*

5. As you do the activity, point to some letter tiles two or three times so that students don't think they are finished with a sound after they have named it.

6. Redirect students if they say an incorrect sound when you point to a letter tile.

   Say: That's the sound of another letter. What is the sound for this letter?

7. Help students if they touch the wrong letter tile after they repeat a sound.

   Say: That letter tile goes with the sound [sound for touched letter tile]. We're looking for the letter that goes with the sound [target sound].

Review the Beginning Digraph Blend *shr–*

Help students recognize and use the beginning digraph blend *shr–*.

1. Build the word *shrill* on students' whiteboard and point to it.

2. **Say:** Touch and say this word.

   ▶ How many sounds are in the word? four
   ▶ How many letters are in the word? six
   ▶ Where is the blend? at the beginning
   ▶ We know that the *sh–* and *r* at the beginning of this word are called a digraph blend because the digraph *sh–* and the letter *r* keep their own sounds while the two sounds blend together.

Learn ....

Introduce the Beginning Digraph Blend *thr–*

Help students recognize and use the beginning digraph blend *thr–*.

1. Build the word *thrill* on students' whiteboard and point to it.

2. **Say:** Touch and say this word.

   ▶ How many sounds are in the word? four
   ▶ How many letters are in the word? six
   ▶ We know that the *th–* and *r* at the beginning of this word is called a digraph blend because the digraph *th–* and the letter *r* each keep its own sound while the two sounds blend together.

3. Make the word *throb* and point to it.

4. **Say:** Touch and say the sounds in *throb*.

   ▶ How many sounds are in the word? four
   ▶ How many letters are in the word? five
   ▶ Where is the blend? at the beginning

5. Redirect students if they have difficulty with the digraph blend *thr–*.

   Say: Those two letters are often together at the beginning of a word. When they are together, they blend into the sound /thr/ as in *thrush*. Can you say the word *thrush*? When you say *thrush*, don't stop between the sounds /th/ and /r/. Try saying the word again.

6. **Say:** Touch and say this word.

   ▶ How many sounds are in the word? four
   ▶ How many letters are in the word? five
   ▶ Where is the blend? at the beginning

Objectives

- Identify and use the blend *thr–*.
- Identify the number of sounds within words.
- Identify beginning sounds in words.

Practice Beginning Digraph Blends *shr–* and *thr–*

Lesson Overview

[Offline] **FOCUS:** Practice Beginning Digraph Blends *shr–* and *thr–*   **30** minutes

Sight Words	Sight Word Fun
Practice	Review Sounds and Letters
	Sing "Old MacDonald's Farm"
	Word Chains
	Pick Up Letters
	Make More Words
Try It	"The Thrush and the Finch"

[Online] **REVIEW:** Beginning Digraph Blends *shr–* and *thr–*   **20** minutes

Materials

Supplied
- *K¹² PhonicsWorks Reader Advanced 3*, pp. 19–24
- whiteboard, Learning Coach
- whiteboard, student
- Tile Kit

Also Needed
- sight words box
- dictation notebook

Advance Preparation

Place lowercase letter tiles in alphabetical order on your whiteboard, including the digraph tiles *ch*, *sh*, and *th*.

[Offline] (30) minutes

FOCUS: Practice Beginning Digraph Blends *shr–* and *thr–*

Work **together** with students to complete offline Sight Words, Practice, and Try It activities.

Sight Words

Sight Word Fun

Help students learn the sight words *down, know,* and *after,* and up to two additional sight words they have yet to master.

1. Gather the sight word cards *down, know,* and *after,* and up to two additional sight word cards.

2. Choose one sight word card to begin.

   Say: Look at this word and take a picture of it in your mind. When you think you can spell the word yourself, turn the card over and use your letter tiles to spell the word.

3. After students spell the word, have them check the card to see if they spelled the word correctly.

   Say: Read aloud the word you spelled with the letter tiles.

4. Repeat the activity with the remaining sight words.

(**TIP**) Sight words can be very difficult for some students. Let them work at their own pace and really master these words.

> **Objectives**
> * Read sight words.
> * Spell sight words.

Get Ready

Review Sounds and Letters

Help students review sounds for the letters and digraphs *ch, h, i, o, p, r, sh,* and *v,* plus any other letters that are confusing for them.

1. Place the following letter tiles in random order on students' whiteboard: *ch, h, i, o, p, r, sh,* and *v,* plus any letters that are confusing.

2. **Say:** Let's go over some letters and sounds.

3. Point to each letter tile and have students say a sound that letter or digraph makes.

   ► *r* /r/
   ► *p* /p/
   ► *sh* /sh/
   ► *v* /v/
   ► *h* /h/
   ► *i* /ĭ/ or /ī/
   ► *o* /ŏ/ or /ō/
   ► *ch* /ch/

> **Objectives**
> * Given the sound, identify the most common letter or letters.
> * Given the letter, identify the most common sound.
> * Identify beginning sounds in words.
> * Identify individual sounds in words.
> * Identify and use the blend *thr–*.
> * Identify and use the blend *shr–*.
> * Write words by applying grade-level phonics knowledge.

4. Say each of the following sounds. Have students repeat the sound and touch the corresponding letter tile.

   - /r/ *r*
   - /p/ *p*
   - /sh/ *sh*
   - /v/ *v*
   - /h/ *h*
   - /ĭ/ *i*
   - /ŏ/ *o*
   - /ch/ *ch*

5. As you do the activity, point to some letter tiles two or three times so that students don't think they are finished with a sound after they have named it.

6. Redirect students if they say an incorrect sound when you point to a letter tile.

   Say: That's the sound of another letter. What is the sound for this letter?

7. Help students if they touch the wrong letter tile after they repeat a sound.

   Say: That letter tile goes with the sound [sound for the touched letter tile]. We're looking for the letter that goes with the sound [target sound].

Sing "Old MacDonald's Farm"

To review digraphs and the letters of the alphabet, have students sing the song "Old MacDonald's Farm." Grab your whiteboard with letters and digraphs.

1. **Say:** Do you remember "Old MacDonald's Farm"? Get ready to sing the song. Think of an animal you want to have on the farm. When you reach that part of the song ("... and on that farm he had a _____"), point to the beginning letter of that word.

2. Repeat the song until students have named all of the animals they know, or as time permits. When they have finished, you may sing the song and let them point to the first letter of the animals you name.

3. Redirect students if they point to a letter that could be the sound, but isn't, such as the letter *k* for *cow*.

   Say: The letter *k* does stand for the sound /k/, but the word *cow* starts with the letter *c*.

Word Chains

Have students build words by adding and changing letters to help them recognize and use individual sounds in words.

1. Place the following letters at the top of students' whiteboard: *c, d, g, i, l, o, p, p, r, s,* and *t*.

2. **Say:** I am going to build the first word in a chain. The word is *trip*.

   ▸ I will pull down the letters for the sounds /t/, /r/, /ĭ/, and /p/ to spell the word *trip*.

   ▸ Next I will touch and say *trip*. To change *trip* to *grip*, I will think about which sound changes from the word *trip* to *grip*. I will need to replace the letter *t* with the letter *g*.

   ▸ Touch and say the word *grip*. Now it's your turn to change *grip* to *drip*. You can spell *drip* by making only one change. Touch and say the new word.

3. Redirect students if they select the incorrect letter for any sound.

   Say: That letter is for the sound [incorrect sound]. We want the letter for the sound [target sound]. What letter makes that sound? Answers will vary.

4. Redirect students if they name the sound incorrectly.

   Say: To change the word [first word] to [target word], we need the letter for the sound [target sound].

5. Follow this procedure to make the following words: *drop, crop, prop, plop, plot, lot, slot, slit, slip, flip, flap, flat, flab, flag, lag, rag, brag*.

6. For every new word, students should add, replace, or remove only one letter.

TIP If students struggle, review the sounds and letters that are confusing.

Pick Up Letters

Help students use letters and sounds to make words and sentences.

1. Place the following letter tiles on students' whiteboard: *b, d, f, l, r, sh, t,* and *th.*

2. **Say:** Let's play a game with these letters.

3. Use the letter tiles for *b* and *l* to make the blend *bl–.*

4. **Say:** I chose the letters *bl.* The sound is /bl/. A word that starts with the sounds /bl/ is *black.* A sentence using that word is, "My favorite kitty is black." Now it's your turn.

5. Continue this activity taking turns until the following letter or letter combinations have been chosen: *t, r, f, dr–, fl–, sh–, shr–, th–,* and *thr–.*

6. Have students answer the following questions for each letter or group of letters:

   ▸ What is (are) the letter(s)?
   ▸ Is it a single sound or blend?
   ▸ What is the sound?
   ▸ What is a word that starts with that sound?
   ▸ What sentence can you make with that word?

7. Redirect students if they name a word that starts with the sound but not the letter (such as *knob*).

   Say: That is a word that doesn't follow the rules that we know for spelling. Try another word.

Make More Words

Have students add letters to and remove letters from words to make new words.

1. Make the following blends at the top of students' whiteboard: *shr–* and *thr–.*

2. Place the following letters on the bottom of students' whiteboard: *a, b, e, g, h, i, ll, m, o, p, r, s, sh, t,* and *u.*

3. **Say:** When I put the letters *ill* after the letters *shr,* I make the word *shrill.* See how many new **real words** you can make by putting the letters on your whiteboard after the letters *shr* and *thr.* Answers will vary.

4. Have students write each word in their dictation notebook.

5. When students finish making words, have them read each word aloud.

Try It ●

"The Thrush and the Finch"

Have students read "The Thrush and the Finch" on page 19 of *K¹² PhonicsWorks Readers Advanced 3.*

Students should read the story silently once or twice before reading the story aloud. When they miss a word that can be sounded out, point to it and give them three to six seconds to try the word again. If students still miss the word, tell them the word so the flow of the story isn't interrupted.

After reading the story, make a list of all the words students missed, and go over those words with them. You may use letter tiles to show them how to read the words.

Objectives

- Read aloud grade-level text with appropriate automaticity, prosody, accuracy, and rate.
- Decode words by applying grade-level word analysis skills.

 **20** minutes

REVIEW: Beginning Digraph Blends *shr–* and *thr–*

Students will work online independently to

▸ Practice the beginning digraph blends *shr–* and *thr–*.

Help students locate the online activities and provide support as needed.

___

Offline Alternative

No computer access? Have students point out and name things or words that begin with the digraph blends *shr–* and *thr–* (for example, *shrimp* or *thrush*). You might also have students spell words that have the beginning digraph blend *shr–* or *thr–*.

Objectives

- Identify and use the blend *shr–*.
- Identify and use the blend *thr–*.
- Identify beginning sounds in words.

Unit Checkpoint

Lesson Overview

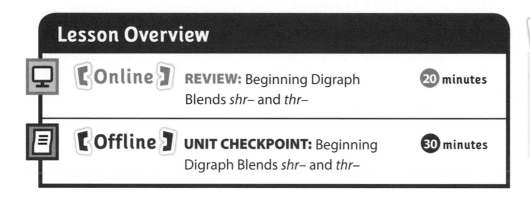

〔Online〕 **REVIEW:** Beginning Digraph Blends *shr–* and *thr–* — **20** minutes

〔Offline〕 **UNIT CHECKPOINT:** Beginning Digraph Blends *shr–* and *thr–* — **30** minutes

〔Materials〕

Supplied
- *K¹² PhonicsWorks Advanced Assessments,* pp. PH 61–66

★ Objectives

- Identify and use the blend *shr–*.
- Identify and use the blend *thr–*.
- Read, write, and spell words containing *shr*.
- Read, write, and spell words containing *thr*.
- Identify individual sounds in words.
- Given the letter, identify the most common sound.
- Given the sound, identify the most common letter or letters.
- Read instructional-level text with 90% accuracy.
- Read aloud grade-level text with appropriate automaticity, prosody, accuracy, and rate.
- Read sight words.
- Write sight words.
- Write words by applying grade-level phonics knowledge.

〔Online〕 **20** minutes

REVIEW: Beginning Digraph Blends *shr–* and *thr–*

Students will review the beginning digraph blends *shr–* and *thr–* to prepare for the Unit Checkpoint. Help students locate the online activities and provide support as needed.

 **30** minutes

UNIT CHECKPOINT: Beginning Digraph Blends *shr–* and *thr–*

Explain that students are going to show what they have learned about sounds, letters, and words.

1. Give students the Unit Checkpoint pages for the Beginning Digraph Blends *shr–* and *tr–* unit and print the Unit Checkpoint Answer Key, if you'd like.

2. Use the instructions below to help administer the Checkpoint to students. On the Answer Key or another sheet of paper, note student answers to oral response questions to help with scoring the Checkpoint later.

3. Use the Answer Key to score the Checkpoint, and then enter the results online.

Part 1. Read Nonsense Words Moving left to right, have students say the sounds of each nonsense word. Note any nonsense words they say incorrectly.

Part 2. Finger Stretching Say each word to students. Have them say each word aloud and finger stretch the sounds. Note any words they finger stretch incorrectly.

16. *shrub*	18. *shrimp*
17. *thrill*	19. *throb*

Part 3. Dictation Say each word to students. Have them repeat and write the word.

20. *shred*	23. *shrug*
21. *thrust*	24. *throb*
22. *shrub*	25. *thrill*

Part 4. Writing Read each sentence to students. Have them repeat and write the sentence.

26. *A thrush is in the nest.*

27. *This shrimp is hot.*

Part 5. Read Aloud Listen to students read the sentences aloud. Count and note the number of words they read correctly.

Part 6. Say Letters Say each sound. Have students say the letter or letters that make that sound. Note any incorrect responses.

29. /shr/

30. /thr/

31. /ă/

32. /ŭ/

33. /ĕ/

34. /ŏ/

35. /ĭ/

36. /r/

37. /kw/

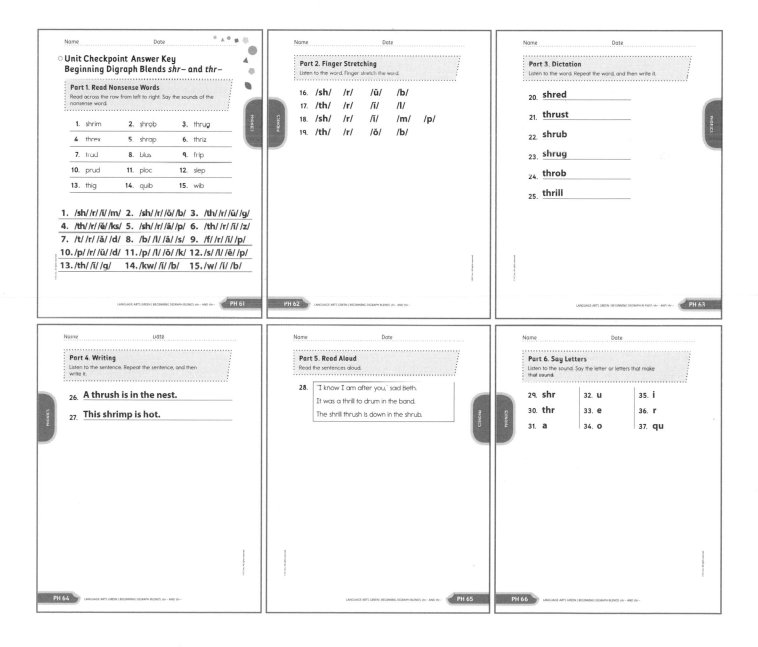

Unit Checkpoint Answer Key
Beginning Digraph Blends _shr–_ and _thr–_

Part 1. Read Nonsense Words
Read across the row from left to right. Say the sounds of the nonsense word.

1. shrim	2. shrob	3. thrug
4. threx	5. shrap	6. thriz
7. trud	8. blus	9. frip
10. prud	11. ploc	12. slep
13. thig	14. quib	15. wib

1. /sh/ /r/ /ĭ/ /m/ 2. /sh/ /r/ /ŏ/ /b/ 3. /th/ /r/ /ŭ/ /g/
4. /th/ /r/ /ĕ/ /ks/ 5. /sh/ /r/ /ă/ /p/ 6. /th/ /r/ /ĭ/ /z/
7. /t/ /r/ /ă/ /d/ 8. /b/ /l/ /ă/ /s/ 9. /f/ /r/ /ĭ/ /p/
10. /p/ /r/ /ŭ/ /d/ 11. /p/ /l/ /ŏ/ /k/ 12. /s/ /l/ /ĕ/ /p/
13. /th/ /ĭ/ /g/ 14. /kw/ /ĭ/ /b/ 15. /w/ /ĭ/ /b/

LANGUAGE ARTS GREEN | BEGINNING DIGRAPH BLENDS shr– and thr–　PH 61

PH 62　LANGUAGE ARTS GREEN | BEGINNING DIGRAPH BLENDS shr– AND thr–

Part 2. Finger Stretching
Listen to the word. Finger stretch the word.

16. /sh/　/r/　/ŭ/　/b/
17. /th/　/r/　/ĭ/　/l/
18. /sh/　/r/　/ĭ/　/m/　/p/
19. /th/　/r/　/ŏ/　/b/

Part 3. Dictation
Listen to the word. Repeat the word, and then write it.

20. **shred**

21. **thrust**

22. **shrub**

23. **shrug**

24. **throb**

25. **thrill**

LANGUAGE ARTS GREEN | BEGINNING DIGRAPH BLENDS shr– AND thr–　PH 63

Part 4. Writing
Listen to the sentence. Repeat the sentence, and then write it.

26. **A thrush is in the nest.**

27. **This shrimp is hot.**

PH 64　LANGUAGE ARTS GREEN | BEGINNING DIGRAPH BLENDS shr– AND thr–

Part 5. Read Aloud
Read the sentences aloud.

28. "I know I am after you," said Beth.
It was a thrill to drum in the band.
The shrill thrush is down in the shrub.

LANGUAGE ARTS GREEN | BEGINNING DIGRAPH BLENDS shr– AND thr–　PH 65

Part 6. Say Letters
Listen to the sound. Say the letter or letters that make that sound.

29. shr	32. u	35. i
30. thr	33. e	36. r
31. a	34. o	37. qu

PH 66　LANGUAGE ARTS GREEN | BEGINNING DIGRAPH BLENDS shr– AND thr–

Beginning Consonant Blends
sc– and *sp–*

Unit Overview

In this unit, students will
- ► Learn the sight words *mother*, *father*, and *only*.
- ► Review letters and sounds of the alphabet.
- ► Learn the beginning consonant blends *sc–*, *sp–*, *st–*, *sw–*, *sk–*, *sm–*, *sn–*, and *tw–*.
- ► Identify individual sounds in words.
- ► Blend sounds to build words.

【Materials】

Supplied
- *K¹² PhonicsWorks Advanced Activity Book*, p. PH 23
- whiteboard, student
- Tile Kit

Also Needed
- sight words box

Lesson Overview

【Offline】 **FOCUS:** Beginning Consonant Blends *sc–* and *sp–*	**30** minutes

Sight Words	Introduce Sight Words
Get Ready	Listen for Ending Blends
	Simon Says
	Review Sounds and Letters
	Review the Beginning Consonant Blend *dr–*
Learn	Introduce the Beginning Consonant Blend *sc–*
	Introduce the Beginning Consonant Blend *sp–*
	Build Nonsense Words
Try It	Match It

【Online】 **REVIEW:** Beginning Consonant Blends *sc–* and *sp–*	**20** minutes

 **30 minutes**

FOCUS: Beginning Consonant Blends *sc–* and *sp–*

Work **together** with students to complete offline Sight Words, Get Ready, Learn, and Try It activities.

Sight Words

Introduce Sight Words

Help students learn the sight words *mother*, *father*, and *only*.

1. Gather the sight word cards *mother*, *father*, and *only*.

2. Show students the *mother* card.

3. **Say:** This is the word *mother*. We see this word so often that we want to be able to read and spell it quickly without thinking about it. Look closely at the word *mother*. Spell the word *mother* aloud. Take a picture of the word *mother* in your mind. When you think you can spell *mother* yourself, turn the card over and use your letter tiles to spell the word *mother*. Check the card to see if you spelled the word *mother* correctly. Read aloud the word you spelled with the letter tiles.

4. Repeat the activity with the remaining sight words.

5. Chart students' progress on the back of each card.

   ▸ Divide the back of the card into two columns.
   ▸ Label the first column "Read" and the second column "Spell."
   ▸ Record the dates that students read or spell the word correctly. When students can read and spell the word correctly three times in a row, they have mastered the word. You may want to put a star or sticker on their card when they have mastered that word.

6. Add the cards to students' sight words box.

TIP Sight words can be very difficult for some students. Let them work at their own pace and really master these words.

> **Objectives**
> • Read sight words.
> • Spell sight words.

Get Ready ....

Listen for Ending Blends

Present pairs of words to help students recognize ending sounds.

1. **Say:** I'm going to say a word. Listen for the **ending blend**, and then tell me what it is. For example, if I say *camp*, you'll say /mp/ because /mp/ is the ending blend in *camp*.

2. Say each word. Have students say the word and identify the ending blend.

   - ▶ *help* /lp/
   - ▶ *lump* /mp/
   - ▶ *left* /ft/
   - ▶ *fact* /kt/
   - ▶ *lunch* /nch/

Simon Says

Play a game with students to help them recognize words that rhyme.

1. **Say:** We're going to play a Simon Says sound game. Listen carefully for words that rhyme with the Simon Says word. Today the Simon Says word is *blast*. Say *blast*.

   - ▶ I'm going to say a word and do something. You will repeat the word.
   - ▶ If the word rhymes with *blast*, you will copy the action I made.
   - ▶ If the word doesn't rhyme with *blast*, then you will be still. We'll do two together.

2. Touch your ear as you say *last*.

3. **Say:** We both say *last* and touch our ears because *last* rhymes with *blast*.

4. Stomp your feet as you say *blue*.

5. **Say:** The word is *blue*. Repeat the word.

   - ▶ We won't stomp our feet when we say *blue* because *blue* doesn't rhyme with *blast*.
   - ▶ Let's begin. Remember, the Simon Says word is *blast*. The new word is *past*.

6. Repeat the procedure with each word and action on the list.

   - ▶ *past*   clap your hands
   - ▶ *soup*   pull your ear
   - ▶ *zoo*   clap your hands
   - ▶ *mast*   pat your cheek
   - ▶ *melt*   touch your knee
   - ▶ *fast*   pull your ear

(**TIP**) If students cannot tell which words rhyme, break each word into its onset and rime (for example, /p/ . . . *itch* and /st/ . . . *itch*).

Objectives

- Identify ending sounds in words.
- Identify words that rhyme.
- Given the letter, identify the most common sound.
- Given the sound, identify the most common letter or letters.
- Identify and use the blend *dr–*.
- Identify the number of sounds within words.
- Identify beginning sounds in words.

Review Sounds and Letters

Help students review sounds for the letters and digraph *b*, *ck*, *e*, *g*, *h*, *s*, *y*, and *z*, plus any letters that are confusing for them.

1. Place the following letter tiles in random order on students' whiteboard: *b*, *ck*, *e*, *g*, *h*, *s*, *y*, and *z*, plus any letters that are confusing.

2. **Say:** Let's go over some letters and sounds.

3. Point to each letter tile and have students say a sound that letter or digraph makes.

   - *e* /ĕ/ or /ē/
   - *b* /b/
   - *ck* /k/
   - *g* /g/

   - *h* /h/
   - *s* /s/
   - *z* /z/
   - *y* /y/

4. Say each of the following sounds. Have students repeat the sound and touch the corresponding letter tile.

   - /ĕ/ *e*
   - /b/ *b*
   - /k/ *ck*
   - /g/ *g*

   - /h/ *h*
   - /s/ *s*
   - /z/ *z*
   - /y/ *y*

5. As you do the activity, point to some letter tiles two or three times so that students don't think they are finished with a sound after they have named it.

6. Redirect students if they say an incorrect sound when you point to a letter tile.

   Say: That's the sound of another letter. What is the sound for this letter?

7. Help students if they touch the wrong letter after they repeat a sound.

   Say: That letter tile goes with the sound [sound for touched letter tile]. We're looking for the letter that goes with the sound [target sound].

Review the Beginning Consonant Blend *dr–*

Help students recognize and use the beginning consonant blend *dr–*.

1. Make the word *dress* on students' whiteboard, and point to it.

2. **Say:** Touch and say this word.

   - How many sounds are in the word? four
   - How many letters are in the word? five
   - Where is the blend? at the beginning

3. **Say:** We know that the letters *d* and *r* at the beginning of this word are called a blend because each of those letters keeps its own sound, and the two sounds blend together.

4. Redirect students if they have difficulty with the beginning consonant blend *dr–*.

Say: Those two letters are often together at the beginning of a word. When they are together, they blend into the sound /dr/, as in *drum*. Can you say the word *drum*? When you say *drum*, don't stop between the two sounds /d/ and /r/. Try saying the word again.

Learn

Introduce the Beginning Consonant Blend *sc–*
Help students recognize and use the beginning consonant blend *sc–*.

1. Make the word *scuff* on students' whiteboard and point to it.

2. **Say:** Touch and say this word.

   ▸ How many sounds are in the word? four
   ▸ How many letters are in the word? five
   ▸ Where is the blend? at the beginning

3. Redirect students if they have difficulty with the beginning consonant blend *sc–*.

Say: Those two letters are often together at the beginning of a word. When they are together, they blend into the sound /sk/, as in *scab*. Can you say the word *scab*? When you say *scab*, don't stop between the two sounds /s/ and /k/. Try saying the word again.

Introduce the Beginning Consonant Blend *sp–*
Help students recognize and use the beginning consonant blend *sp–*.

1. Place the following letters on students' whiteboard: *i, n, o, p, s,* and *t*.

2. Make the word *spin* and point to it.

3. **Say:** Touch and say this word.

   ▸ How many sounds are in the word? four
   ▸ How many letters are in the word? four
   ▸ Where is the blend? at the beginning

4. Make the word *spot* and point to it.

5. **Say:** Touch and say this word.

   ▸ How many sounds are in the word? four
   ▸ How many letters are in the word? four
   ▸ Where is the blend? at the beginning

6. Redirect students if they have difficulty with the beginning consonant blend *sp–*.

Say: Those two letters are often together at the beginning of a word. When they are together, they blend into the sound /sp/, as in *sponge*. Can you say the word *sponge*? When you say *sponge*, don't stop between the two sounds /s/ and /p/. Try saying the word again.

Objectives
- Identify and use the blend *sc–*.
- Identify and use the blend *sp*.
- Identify the number of sounds within words.
- Identify beginning sounds in words.
- Blend sounds to create words.

Build Nonsense Words

Help students use letters and sounds to build nonsense words.

1. Place the following letter tiles at the top of students' whiteboard: *g, i, n, o, p, s, th,* and *u.*

2. Draw four horizontal lines across the middle of students' whiteboard to represent the sounds in a word.

3. **Say:** Some words don't have any meaning. We call these **nonsense words**. Even though we don't know what a word means, we can still read it. Nonsense words will be very important when we read longer words. When we break longer words into parts, sometimes the parts are nonsense words.

4. **Say:** Let's use letters and sounds to build the word *sputh.*

5. Have students finger stretch the sounds in *sputh.*

6. Have students

   ▸ Identify the first, next, and last sounds in *sputh.*
   ▸ Choose the corresponding letter for each of the sounds.
   ▸ Move the letters to the correct lines on their whiteboard.

7. Guide students with these questions:

   ▸ What is the first sound in *sputh*? /s/
     Which line does the letter for that sound go on? the first one
   ▸ What is the next sound in *sputh*? /p/
     Which line does the letter for that sound go on? the second one
   ▸ What is the next sound in *sputh*? /ŭ/
     Which line does the letter for that sound go on? the third one
   ▸ What's the last sound in *sputh*? /th/
     Which line do the letters for that sound go on? the last one

8. Have students say the word as they use a dry-erase marker to write the word on the whiteboard.

9. Have students touch and say the word.

10. Redirect students if they select the incorrect letter.

    Say: That sound is in the word [word], and it is the [first, second, third, fourth] sound. We want the sound [target sound].

    Continue until students select the correct letter.

11. Repeat the activity to build the following words:

    ▸ *spon* /s/ /p/ /ŏ/ /n/
    ▸ *spig* /s/ /p/ /ĭ/ /g/

Try It •••

Match It

Have students complete page PH 23 in *K¹² PhonicsWorks Advanced Activity Book* for more practice with words that begin with the consonant blends *sc–* and *sp–*. Have them read each sentence aloud and draw a line to the picture that matches the sentence.

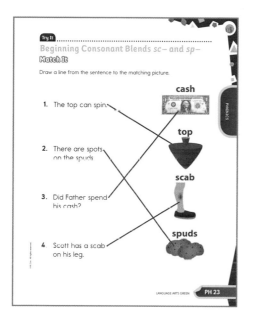

> ### Objectives
> - Read aloud grade-level text with appropriate automaticity, prosody, accuracy, and rate.
> - Identify and use the blend *sc–*.
> - Identify and use the blend *sp*.

[Online] 20 minutes

REVIEW: Beginning Consonant Blends *sc–* and *sp–*

Students will work online independently to

▸ Practice the beginning consonant blends *sc–* and *sp–*.
▸ Practice decoding text by reading a story.

Help students locate the online activities and provide support as needed.

Offline Alternative

No computer access? Have students name things or words that begin with the consonant blends *sc–* and *sp–* (for example, *scam* or *spill*). You might also have students spell words that have the consonant blends *sc–* and *sp–*.

> ### Objectives
> - Identify and use the blend *sc–*.
> - Identify and use the blend *sp*.
> - Identify beginning sounds in words.
> - Read aloud grade-level text with appropriate automaticity, prosody, accuracy, and rate.
> - Decode words by applying grade-level word analysis skills.

Beginning Consonant Blends *st–* and *sw–*

Lesson Overview

Offline   **FOCUS:** Beginning Consonant   **30** minutes
Blends *st–* and *sw–*

Sight Words	Sight Word Fun
Get Ready	Build Words
	Make Riddle Rhymes
	Review the Beginning Consonant Blend *sp–*
Learn	Introduce the Beginning Consonant Blend *st–*
	Introduce the Beginning Consonant Blend *sw–*
	Word Chains
Try It	"Stan's Stuff"
	Dictation: Write Sentences

Online   **REVIEW:** Beginning Consonant   **20** minutes
Blends *st–* and *sw–*

Materials

Supplied

- *K¹² PhonicsWorks Readers Advanced 3*, pp. 25–30
- whiteboard, Learning Coach
- whiteboard, student
- Tile Kit

Also Needed

- sight words box
- dictation notebook

[Offline] 🕥 minutes

FOCUS: Beginning Consonant Blends *st–* and *sw–*

Work **together** with students to complete offline Sight Words, Get Ready, Learn, and Try It activities.

Sight Words •••

Sight Word Fun

Help students learn the sight words *mother*, *father*, and *only*, and up to two additional sight words they have yet to master.

1. Gather the sight word cards *mother*, *father*, and *only*, and up to two additional sight word cards.

2. Choose one sight word card to begin.

   Say: Look at this word and take a picture of it in your mind. When you think you can spell the word yourself, turn the card over and use your letter tiles to spell the word.

3. After students spell the word, have them check the card to see if they spelled the word correctly.

   Say: Read aloud the word you spelled with the letter tiles.

4. Repeat the activity with the remaining sight words.

   TIP Sight words can be very difficult for some students. Let them work at their own pace and really master these words.

Objectives
- Read sight words.
- Spell sight words.

Get Ready •••

Build Words

Help students use letters and sounds to build words.

1. Place the following letter tiles at the top of students' whiteboard: *a, d, e, g, i, ll, m, n, o, p, r, s, ss,* and *t.*

2. Draw four horizontal lines across the middle of students' whiteboard to represent the sounds in a word.

3. **Say:** Let's use letters and sounds to build the word *drop.*

4. Have students finger stretch the sounds in *drop.*

5. Have students
   - ▸ Identify the sounds in *drop.*
   - ▸ Choose the corresponding letter for each of the sounds.
   - ▸ Move the letters to the correct lines on their whiteboard.

Objectives
- Blend sounds to create words.
- Identify individual sounds in words.
- Given the letter, identify the most common sound.
- Given the sound, identify the most common letter or letters.
- Identify words that rhyme.
- Identify and use the blend *sp.*
- Identify the number of sounds within words.
- Identify beginning sounds in words.

6. Guide students with these questions:

   ▸ What is the first sound in *drop*? /d/
     Which line does the letter for that sound go on? the first one
   ▸ What is the next sound in *drop*? /r/
     Which line does the letter for that sound go on? the second one
   ▸ What is the next sound in *drop*? /ŏ/
     Which line does the letter for that sound go on? the third one
   ▸ What's the last sound in *drop*? /p/
     Which line does the letter for that sound go on? the last one

7. Have students touch and say the word.

8. Redirect students if they select the incorrect letter.

   Say: That sound is in the word [word], and it is the [first, second, third, fourth] sound. We want the sound [target sound].

   Continue until students select the correct letter.

9. Repeat the activity to build the following words:

   ▸ *dress* /d/ /r/ /ĕ/ /s/   ▸ *drill* /d/ /r/ /ĭ/ /l/
   ▸ *drum* /d/ /r/ /ŭ/ /m/   ▸ *spot* /s/ /p/ /ŏ/ /t/
   ▸ *drip* /d/ /r/ /ĭ/ /p/   ▸ *spit* /s/ /p/ /ĭ/ /t/
   ▸ *drag* /d/ /r/ /ă/ /g/   ▸ *spun* /s/ /p/ /ŭ/ /n/

Make Riddle Rhymes

Have students identify words that rhyme by playing a riddle game.

1. **Say:** We are going to play a riddle game. I will think of a word and give you some clues. You guess the word and solve the riddle.

   ▸ It rhymes with *mend*. You do this with money when you want to buy something. It starts with the blend *sp–*. *spend*

2. Give students clues to words. Have them name each word, and then say and write it. Use these clues and words:

   ▸ You play it by hitting it with sticks. It starts with the blend *dr–*. It rhymes with *crumb*. *drum*
   ▸ It has four wheels, but it is bigger than a car. It starts with the blend *tr–*. It rhymes with *luck*. *truck*
   ▸ It says, "Ribbit!" and lives in a pond. It starts with the blend *fr–*. It rhymes with *log*. *frog*

Review the Beginning Consonant Blend *sp–*

Help students recognize and use the beginning consonant blend *sp–*.

1. Make the word *spot* on students' whiteboard and point to it.

2. **Say:** Touch and say this word.

   ▸ How many sounds are in the word? four
   ▸ How many letters are in the word? four
   ▸ Where is the blend? at the beginning

3. **Say:** We know that the letters *s* and *p* at the beginning of this word are called a blend because each of those letters keeps its own sound, and the two sounds blend together.

Learn

Introduce the Beginning Consonant Blend *st–*

Help students recognize and use the beginning consonant blend *st–*.

1. Make the word *stop* on students' whiteboard and point to it.

2. **Say:** Touch and say this word.

   ▸ How many sounds are in the word? four
   ▸ How many letters are in the word? four
   ▸ Where is the blend? at the beginning

3. **Say:** We know that the letters *s* and *t* at the beginning of this word are called a blend because each of those letters keeps its own sound, and the two sounds blend together.

4. Redirect students if they have difficulty with the beginning consonant blend *st–*.

   Say: Those two letters are often together at the beginning of a word. When they are together, they blend into the sound /st/, as in *stamp*. Can you say the word *stamp*? When you say *stamp*, don't stop between the two sounds /s/ and /t/. Try saying the word again.

Objectives

- Identify and use the blend *st*.
- Identify and use the blend *sw–*.
- Identify beginning sounds in words.
- Identify the number of sounds within words.
- Blend sounds to create words.
- Identify individual sounds in words.

Introduce the Beginning Consonant Blend *sw–*

Help students recognize and use the beginning consonant blend *sw–*.

1. Place the following letter tiles on students' whiteboard: *e, i, ll, m, s,* and *w.*

2. Make the word *swim* and point to it.

3. **Say:** Touch and say this word.

   ▸ How many sounds are in the word? four
   ▸ How many letters are in the word? four
   ▸ Where is the blend? at the beginning

4. Follow the same procedure to make the word *swell.*

5. Redirect students if they have difficulty with the blended sound /sw/.

   Say: Those two letters are often together at the beginning of a word. When they are together, they blend into the sound /sw/, as in *swamp*. Can you say the word *swamp*? When you say *swamp*, don't stop between the two sounds /s/ and /w/. Try saying the word again.

Word Chains

Have students build words by adding and changing letters to help them recognize and use individual sounds in words.

1. Place the following letter tiles at the top of students' whiteboard: *a, ck, g, i, l, m, s, sh, t, u,* and *w.*

2. **Say:** I am going to build the first word in a chain. The word is *swig.*

   ▸ I will pull down the letters for the sounds /s/, /w/, /ĭ/, and /g/ to spell the word *swig.*
   ▸ I will touch and say *swig.* To change *swig* to *swish,* I will think about which sound changes from the word *swig* to *swish.* I will need to replace the letter *g* with the digraph *sh.*
   ▸ Touch and say the word *swish.* Now it's your turn to change *swish* to *swim.* You can spell *swim* by making only one change. Touch and say the new word.

3. Redirect students if they select the incorrect letter for any sound.

   Say: That letter is for the sound [incorrect sound]. We want the letter for the sound [target sound]. What letter makes that sound? Answers will vary.

4. Help students if they select the wrong sound.

   Say: To change the word [first word] to [target word], we need the letter for the sound [target sound].

   Show students how to make the change. Have them touch and say the new word after they move the letters.

5. Follow this procedure to make the following words: *swam, swum, slum, slim, slick, stick, stuck, stack, sack, tack, lack, slack.*

6. For every new word, students should add, replace, or remove only one letter tile.

Try It ••

"Stan's Stuff"

Have students read "Stan's Stuff" on page 25 of *K¹² PhonicsWorks Readers Advanced 3*.

Students should read the story silently once or twice before reading the story aloud. When the they miss a word that can be sounded out, point to it and give them three to six seconds to try the word again. If they still miss the word, tell them the word so the flow of the story isn't interrupted.

After reading the story, make a list of all the words students missed, and go over those words with them. You may use tiles to show students how to read the words.

———————————————————————————————

Dictation: Write Sentences

Use sentences to help students identify individual sounds in words.

1. Gather a pencil and the dictation notebook. Say the sentence, *Cross the path to the pond.* Then give these directions to students:

   ▸ Repeat the sentence.
   ▸ Write the sentence in your notebook.
   ▸ Read the sentence aloud.

2. When students have finished, write the following sentence on your whiteboard: *Cross the path to the pond.*

3. Have them compare their answer to your correct version.

4. Repeat this procedure with the sentence, *Stick the stuff in the big bag.*

   ▸ If students make an error and don't see it, help them correct their mistake by having them finger stretch the sounds in the word they missed.
   ▸ If students are having difficulty selecting the correct letters or sounds, review those letters or sounds that are confusing them.
   ▸ If students have difficulty with first, middle, and last sounds, have them finger stretch the sounds in words.

Objectives

- Read aloud grade-level text with appropriate automaticity, prosody, accuracy, and rate.
- Decode words by applying grade-level word analysis skills.
- Write words by applying grade-level phonics knowledge.
- Write sight words.
- Follow three-step directions.

 **20 minutes**

REVIEW: Beginning Consonant Blends *st–* and *sw–*

Students will work online independently to

▸ Practice the beginning consonant blends *st–* and *sw–*.

Help students locate the online activities and provide support as needed.

Offline Alternative

No computer access? Have students name things or words that begin with the consonant blends *st–* and *sw–* (for example, *stem* or *swan*). You might also have students spell words that have the beginning consonant blends *st–* and *sw–*.

Beginning Consonant Blends *sk*– and *sm*–

Lesson Overview

[Offline] FOCUS: Beginning Consonant Blends *sk*– and *sm*–   30 minutes

Sight Words	Sight Word Fun
Get Ready	Signal Beginning Sounds
	Secret Sound
	Review the Beginning Consonant Blend *sw*–
Learn	Introduce the Beginning Consonant Blend *sk*–
	Introduce the Beginning Consonant Blend *sm*–
	Make Up a Sentence
Try It	Match It

[Online] REVIEW: Beginning Consonant Blends *sk*– and *sm*–   20 minutes

[Materials]

Supplied
- *K¹² PhonicsWorks Advanced Activity Book*, p. PH 24
- whiteboard, student
- Tile Kit

Also Needed
- sight words box
- dictation notebook
- index cards (7)

Advance Preparation

For Make Up a Sentence, print each of the following words on index cards, using one card per word: *sketch, swim, smell, skin, small, smack,* and *scab*.

[Offline] 30 minutes

FOCUS: Beginning Consonant Blends *sk–* and *sm–*

Work **together** with students to complete offline Sight Words, Get Ready, Learn, and Try It activities.

Sight Words ••

Sight Word Fun

Help students learn the sight words *mother*, *father*, and *only*, and up to two additional sight words they have yet to master.

1. Gather the sight word cards *mother*, *father*, and *only*, and up to two additional sight word cards.

2. Choose one sight word card to begin.

   Say: Look at this word and take a picture of it in your mind. When you think you can spell the word yourself, turn the card over and use your letter tiles to spell the word.

3. After students spell the word, have them check the card to see if they spelled the word correctly.

   Say: Read aloud the word you spelled with the letter tiles.

4. Repeat the activity with the remaining sight words.

   TIP Sight words can be very difficult for some students. Let them work at their own pace and really master these words.

> **Objectives**
> - Read sight words.
> - Spell sight words.

Get Ready ••

Signal Beginning Sounds

Use a special signal to help students identify **beginning sounds** in words.

1. **Say:** I'm going to tell you a special sound, and then I'll say some words. Repeat each word I say and make a special signal to tell me where the special sound is. If the special sound is at the beginning of the word, turn around. If the special sound is **not** at the beginning of the word, just smile at me. For example,

   ▸ If I ask you to listen for the sound /ă/ and I say the word *apple*, you'll repeat the word *apple* and turn around because *apple* has the sound /ă/ at the beginning.
   ▸ If I say the word *dog*, you'll repeat the word *dog* and smile at me because *dog* has the sound /d/, not /ă/, at the beginning.

> **Objectives**
> - Identify beginning sounds in words.
> - Identify and use the blend *sw–*.
> - Identify the number of sounds within words.

2. Say each sound and group of words. Have students make the special signal to identify the beginning sound.

  - /ă/: *apple, under, actor, over, after* turn around: *apple, actor, after*
  - /ĕ/: *ever, echo, silk, Edward, pretend* turn around: *ever, echo, Edward*
  - /ĭ/: *why, isn't, stop, ill, paper* turn around: *isn't, ill*
  - /ŏ/: *honey, Oliver, mug, oxen, camp* turn around: *Oliver, oxen*
  - /ŭ/: *upset, apple, us, tree, umbrella* turn around: *upset, us, umbrella*

TIP Guide students if they can't identify the beginning sound of each word. Say the word again and emphasize the beginning sound by repeating it three times (for example, *taste* /t/ /t/ /t/). You can also draw out the beginning sound when you say the word (for example, *mmmmmommy*). If necessary, have students look at your mouth while you repeat the sounds.

Secret Sound

Say groups of words to help students recognize **beginning sounds** in words.

1. **Say:** I am going to say a special sound and then I will read a sentence. Listen for the special sound at the beginning of a word that is used in the sentence. For example, if I say /d/ and I read the sentence "I have a doll," you will repeat the sentence and say the word *doll*, because *doll* has the beginning sound /d/.

2. Say each of the following groups of words. Have students identify the secret sound in each group.

  - /sh/, *What is that shape? shape*
  - /k/, *Kick the ball. kick*
  - /p/, *Use that pan. pan*
  - /r/, *You ride the bus. ride*
  - /t/, *What is the time? time*

TIP If students can't identify the secret sound, have them listen while you say each word again, and then have them repeat each word. Have them say the sound they hear at the beginning of each word.

Review the Beginning Consonant Blend *sw–*
Help students recognize and use the beginning consonant blend *sw–*.

1. Make the word *swim* on students' whiteboard and point to it.

2. **Say:** Touch and say this word.

   ▸ How many sounds are in the word? four
   ▸ How many letters are in the word? four
   ▸ Where is the blend? at the beginning
   ▸ We know that the letters *s* and *w* at the beginning of this word are called a blend because those letters keep their own sounds while the two sounds blend together.

Learn

Introduce the Beginning Consonant Blend *sk–*
Help students recognize and use the beginning consonant blend *sk–*.

1. Place the following letters on students' whiteboard: *i, k, n, p,* and *s.*

2. Make the word *skip* and point to it.

3. **Say:** Touch and say this word.

   ▸ How many sounds are in the word? four
   ▸ How many letters are in the word? four
   ▸ We know that the letters *s* and *k* at the beginning of this word are called a blend because each of those letters keeps its own sound while the two sounds blend together.

4. Make the word *skin* and point to it.

5. **Say:** Touch and say this word.

   ▸ How many sounds are in the word? four
   ▸ How many letters are in the word? four
   ▸ Where is the blend? at the beginning

6. Redirect students if they have difficulty with the beginning consonant blend *sk–*.

   Say: Those two letters are often together at the beginning of a word. When they are together, they blend into the sound /sk/, as in *skip*. Can you say the word *skip*? When you say *skip*, don't stop between the sounds /s/ and /k/. Try saying the word again.

Introduce the Beginning Consonant Blend *sm–*
Help students recognize and use the beginning consonant blend *sm–*.

1. Place the following letter tiles on students' whiteboard: *a, e, ll, m,* and *s.*

2. Make the word *small* and point to it.

> **Objectives**
> - Identify and use the blend *sk.*
> - Identify and use the blend *sm–.*
> - Identify the number of sounds within words.
> - Identify beginning sounds in words.
> - Read aloud grade-level text with appropriate automaticity, prosody, accuracy, and rate.

3. **Say:** Touch and say this word.

   - How many sounds are in the word? four
   - How many letters are in the word? five
   - We know that the letters *s* and *m* at the beginning of this word are called a blend because each of those letters keeps its own sound while the two sounds blend together.

4. Make the word *smell* and point to it.

   Say: Touch and say this word.

   - How many sounds are in the word? four
   - How many letters are in the word? five
   - Where is the blend? at the beginning

5. Redirect students if they have difficulty with the blended sound /sm/.

   Say: Those two letters are often together at the beginning of a word. When they are together, they blend into the sound /sm/, as in *small*. Can you say the word *small*? When you say *small*, don't stop between the sounds /s/ and /m/. Try saying the word again.

Make Up a Sentence

Help students use words to make sentences.

1. Gather the word cards you prepared.

2. Place the cards face down on the table in a pile.

3. Have students

   - Select a card.
   - Read the word.
   - Use the word in an interesting, fun, or silly sentence.

TIP If students read a word incorrectly, have them finger stretch the sounds in the word.

Try It ••

Match It

Have students complete page PH 24 in *K¹² PhonicsWorks Advanced Activity Book* for more practice with words that begin with the beginning consonant blends *sk–* and *sm–*. Have them read each sentence aloud and draw a line to the picture that matches the sentence.

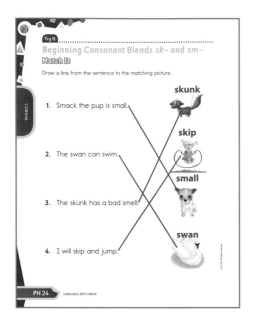

 **⟦Online⟧** ㉚ **minutes**

REVIEW: Beginning Consonant Blends *sk–* and *sm–*

Students will work online independently to

▶ Practice the beginning consonant blends *sk–* and *sm–*.
▶ Practice decoding text by reading a story.

Help students locate the online activities and provide support as needed.

Offline Alternative

No computer access? Have students point out and name things or words that begin with the consonant blends *sk–* and *sm–* (for example, *skull* or *smog*). You might also have students spell words that have the beginning consonant blends *sk–* and *sm–*.

Beginning Consonant Blends *sn–* and *tw–*

Lesson Overview

📄 **[Offline]** **FOCUS:** Beginning Consonant Blends *sn–* and *tw–*   **30** minutes

Sight Words	Sight Word Fun
Get Ready	Review Sounds and Letters
	From Words to Sentences
	Review the Beginning Consonant Blend *sm–*
Learn	Introduce the Beginning Consonant Blend *sn–*
	Introduce the Beginning Consonant Blend *tw–*
Try It	"The Smiths' Camp"
	Dictation: Write Sentences

🖥 **[Online]** **REVIEW:** Beginning Consonant Blends *sn–* and *tw–*   **20** minutes

[Materials]

Supplied

- *K¹² PhonicsWorks Readers Advanced 4*, pp. 1–6
- whiteboard, Learning Coach
- whiteboard, student
- Tile Kit

Also Needed

- sight words box
- dictation notebook

 **30** minutes

FOCUS: Beginning Consonant Blends *sn–* and *tw–*

Work **together** with students to complete offline Sight Words, Get Ready, Learn, and Try It activities.

Sight Words

Sight Word Fun

Help students learn the sight words *mother, father,* and *only,* and up to two additional sight words they have yet to master.

1. Gather the sight word cards *mother, father,* and *only,* and up to two additional sight word cards.

2. Choose one sight word card to begin.

   Say: Look at this word and take a picture of it in your mind. When you think you can spell the word yourself, turn the card over and use your letter tiles to spell the word.

3. After students spell the word, have them check the card to see if they spelled the word correctly.

   Say: Read aloud the word you spelled with the letter tiles.

4. Repeat the activity with the remaining sight words.

TIP Sight words can be very difficult for some students. Let them work at their own pace and really master these words.

Objectives
- Read sight words.
- Spell sight words.

Get Ready

Review Sounds and Letters

Help students review sounds for the letters *e, f, h, i, j, l, o, p,* and *s,* plus any letters that are confusing to them.

1. Place the following letter tiles in random order on students' whiteboard: *e, f, h, i, j, l, o, p,* and *s,* plus any letters that are confusing.

2. **Say:** Let's go over some letters and sounds.

3. Point to each letter tile and have students say a sound that letter makes.

   - *s* /s/
   - *l* /l/
   - *i* /ĭ/ or /ī/
   - *e* /ĕ/ or /ē/
   - *j* /j/

   - *h* /h/
   - *p* /p/
   - *o* /ŏ/ or /ō/
   - *f* /f/

4. Say each of the following sounds. Have students repeat the sound and touch the corresponding letter tile.

   - /s/ *s*
   - /l/ *l*
   - /ĭ/ *i*
   - /ĕ/ *e*
   - /j/ *j*

   - /h/ *h*
   - /p/ *p*
   - /ŏ/ *o*
   - /f/ *f*

5. As you do the activity, point to some letter tiles two or three times so that students don't think they are finished with a sound after they have named it.

6. Redirect students if they say an incorrect sound when you point to a letter tile.

   Say: That's the sound of another letter. What is the sound for this letter?

7. Help students if they touch the wrong letter tile after they repeat a sound.

   Say: That letter tile goes with the sound [sound for the touched letter tile]. We're looking for the letter that goes with the sound [target sound].

Objectives

- Given the sound, identify the most common letter or letters.
- Given the letter, identify the most common sound.
- Write words by applying grade-level phonics knowledge.
- Read aloud grade-level text with appropriate automaticity, prosody, accuracy, and rate.
- Identify and use the blend *sm−*.
- Identify beginning sounds in words.
- Identify the number of sounds within words.

From Words to Sentences

Have students practice writing words and sentences.

1. **Say:** Name three of your favorite letters. I will write those letters on my whiteboard.

   Write the letters on the whiteboard.

2. **Say:** Think of a word that starts with the sound for each letter and write it on your paper. Use each word in a sentence and write them on your paper.

3. Help students if they make a spelling mistake. Write the correct spelling above the word and have them make the correction.

   Say: That was a good try, but the word is spelled like this.

4. Guide students if they have trouble thinking of or writing sentences.

TIP To help students with writing words that are unfamiliar words, give them the word and help them spell it so that writing becomes a pleasure for students rather than a chore.

Review the Beginning Consonant Blend *sm–*

Help students recognize and use the beginning consonant blend *sm–*.

1. Make the word *smell* on students' whiteboard and point to it.

2. **Say:** Touch and say this word.

   - ▸ How many sounds are in the word? four
   - ▸ How many letters are in the word? five
   - ▸ Where is the blend? at the beginning
   - ▸ We know that the letters *s* and *m* at the beginning of this word are called a blend because those letters keep their own sounds while the two sounds blend together.

Learn

Introduce the Beginning Consonant Blend *sn–*

Help students recognize and use the beginning consonant blend *sn–*.

1. Place the following letter tiles on students' whiteboard: *a, i, n, p,* and *s.*

2. Make the word *snap* and point to it.

3. **Say:** Touch and say this word.

   ▸ How many sounds are in the word? four
   ▸ How many letters are in the word? four
   ▸ We know that the letters *s* and *n* at the beginning of this word are called a blend because each of those letters keeps its own sound while the two sounds blend together.

4. Make the word *snip* and point to it.

5. **Say:** Touch and say this word.

   ▸ How many sounds are in the word? four
   ▸ How many letters are in the word? four
   ▸ Where is the blend? at the beginning

6. Redirect students if they have difficulty with the beginning consonant blend *sn–*.

   Say: Those two letters are often together at the beginning of a word. When they are together, they blend into the sound /sn/, as in *snack*. Can you say the word *snack*? When you say *snack*, don't stop between the sounds /s/ and /n/. Try saying the word again.

Introduce the Beginning Consonant Blend *tw–*

Help students recognize and use the beginning consonant blend *tw–*.

1. Place the following letter tiles on students' whiteboard: *g, i, n, t,* and *w.*

2. Make the word *twin* and point to it.

3. **Say:** Touch and say this word.

   ▸ How many sounds are in the word? four
   ▸ How many letters are in the word? four
   ▸ We know that the letters *t* and *w* at the beginning of this word are called a blend because each of those letters keeps its own sound while the two sounds blend together.

4. Make the word *twig* and point to it.

5. **Say:** Touch and say this word.

   ▸ How many sounds are in the word? four
   ▸ How many letters are in the word? four
   ▸ Where is the blend? at the beginning

Objectives

- Identify and use the blend *sn–*.
- Identify and use the blend *tw–*.
- Identify the number of sounds within words.
- Identify beginning sounds in words.

6. Redirect students if they have difficulty with the beginning consonant blend *tw–*.

Say: Those two letters are often together at the beginning of a word. When they are together, they blend into the sound /tw/, as in *twitch*. Can you say the word *twitch*? When you say *twitch*, don't stop between the sounds /t/ and /w/. Try saying the word again.

Try It

"The Smiths' Camp"

Have students read "The Smiths' Camp" on page 1 of *K¹² PhonicsWorks Readers Advanced 4*.

Students should read the story silently once or twice before reading the story aloud. When the they miss a word that can be sounded out, point to it and give them three to six seconds to try the word again. If they still miss the word, tell them the word so the flow of the story isn't interrupted.

After reading the story, make a list of all the words students missed, and go over those words with them. You may use tiles to show students how to read the words.

***

Dictation: Write Sentences

Use sentences to help students identify individual sounds in words.

1. Gather a pencil and the dictation notebook. Say the sentence, *Scott snaps the twig.* Then give these directions to students:

   ▶ Repeat the sentence.
   ▶ Write the sentence in your notebook.
   ▶ Read the sentence aloud.

2. When students have finished, write the following sentence on your whiteboard: *Scott snaps the twig.*

3. Have them compare their answer to your correct version.

4. Repeat this procedure with the sentence, *The twins snap the lids shut.*

   ▶ If students make an error and don't see it, help them correct their mistake by having them finger stretch the sounds in the word they missed.
   ▶ If students are having difficulty selecting the correct letters or sounds, review those letters or sounds that are confusing them.
   ▶ If students have difficulty with first, middle, and last sounds, have them finger stretch the sounds in words.

Objectives

- Read aloud grade-level text with appropriate automaticity, prosody, accuracy, and rate.
- Decode words by applying grade-level word analysis skills.
- Write words by applying grade-level phonics knowledge.
- Write sight words.
- Follow three-step directions.

 **20 minutes**

REVIEW: Beginning Consonant Blends *sn*– and *tw*–

Students will work online independently to

▸ Practice the beginning consonant blends *sn*– and *tw*–.

Help students locate the online activities and provide support as needed.

Offline Alternative

No computer access? Have students point out and name things or words that begin with the consonant blends *sn*– and *tw*– (for example, *snack* or *twist*). You might also have students spell words that have the beginning consonant blends *sn*– and *tw*–.

Objectives

- Identify and use the blend *sn*–.
- Identify and use the blend *tw*–.
- Identify beginning sounds in words.

Unit Checkpoint

Lesson Overview

Online   **REVIEW:** Beginning Consonant Blends *sc–, sp–, st–, sw–, sk–, sm–, sn–,* and *tw–*   **20** minutes

Offline   **UNIT CHECKPOINT:** Beginning Consonant Blends *sc–, sp–, st–, sw–, sk–, sm–, sn–,* and *tw–*   **30** minutes

Materials

Supplied

- *K¹² PhonicsWorks Advanced Assessments,* pp. PH 67–72

Objectives

- Identify and use the blend *sc–*.
- Identify and use the blend *sp*.
- Identify and use the blend *st*.
- Identify and use the blend *sw–*.
- Identify and use the blend *sk*.
- Identify and use the blend *sm–*.
- Identify and use the blend *sn–*.
- Identify and use the blend *tw–*.
- Identify individual sounds in words.
- Given the letter, identify the most common sound.
- Given the sound, identify the most common letter or letters.
- Read instructional-level text with 90% accuracy
- Read sight words.
- Write sight words.
- Write words by applying grade-level phonics knowledge.

Online   **20** minutes

REVIEW: Beginning Consonant Blends *sc–, sp–, st–, sw–, sk–, sm–, sn–,* and *tw–*

Students will review the beginning consonant blends *sc–, sp–, st–, sw–, sk–, sm–, sn–,* and *tw–* to prepare for the Unit Checkpoint. Help students locate the online activities and provide support as needed.

⟦ Offline ⟧ 🕥 minutes

UNIT CHECKPOINT: Beginning Consonant Blends *sc–*, *sp–*, *st–*, *sw–*, *sk–*, *sm–*, *sn–*, and *tw–*

Explain that students are going to show what they have learned about sounds, letters, and words.

1. Give students the Unit Checkpoint pages for the Beginning Consonant Blends *sc–*, *sp–*, *st–*, *sw–*, *sk–*, *sm–*, *sn–*, and *tw–* unit and print the Unit Checkpoint Answer Key, if you'd like.

2. Use the instructions below to help administer the Checkpoint to students. On the Answer Key or another sheet of paper, note student answers to oral response questions to help with scoring the Checkpoint later.

3. Use the Answer Key to score the Checkpoint, and then enter the results online.

Part 1. Read Nonsense Words Moving left to right, have students say the sounds of each nonsense word. Note any nonsense words they say incorrectly.

Part 2. Finger Stretching Say each word to students. Have them say each word aloud and finger stretch the sounds. Note any words they finger stretch incorrectly.

11. *scab*		15. *speck*	
12. *stamp*		16. *switch*	
13. *sketch*		17. *smash*	
14. *twist*		18. *snug*	

Part 3. Dictation Say each word to students. Have them repeat and write the word.

19. *scat*		23. *spell*	
20. *stop*		24. *swim*	
21. *skill*		25. *small*	
22. *snap*		26. *twin*	

Part 4. Writing Read each sentence to students. Have them repeat and write the sentence.

27. *Spin the small top.*

28. *His twin had a snack.*

29. *Scott can swim and skip.*

Part 5. Read Aloud Listen to students read the sentences aloud. Count and note the number of words they read correctly.

Part 6. Say Letters Say each sound. Have students say the letter that makes that sound. Note any incorrect responses.

31. /ŏ/

32. /ă/

33. /ĭ/

34. /ĕ/

35. /ŭ/

36. /ŏ/

37. /ĭ/

38. /ĕ/

39. /ŭ/

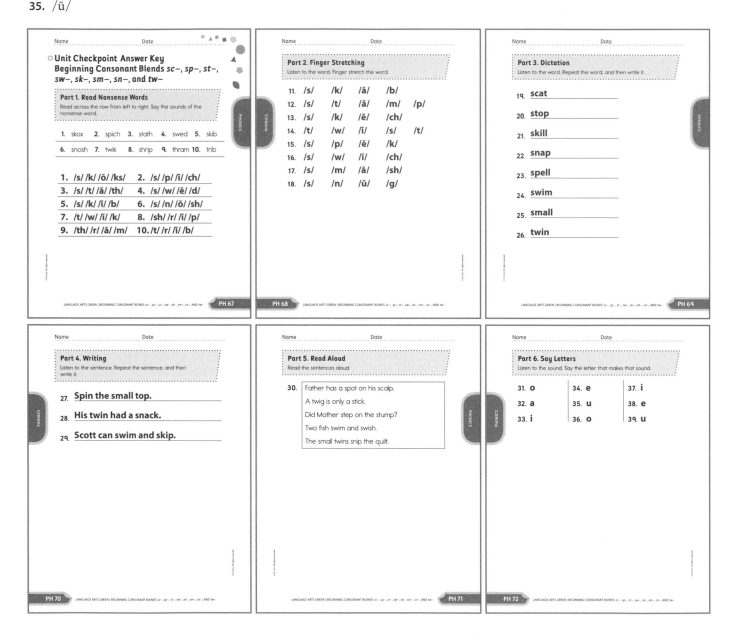

Name_____ Date_____

○ **Unit Checkpoint Answer Key**
Beginning Consonant Blends *sc–, sp–, st–, sw–, sk–, sm–, sn–,* **and** *tw–*

Part 1. Read Nonsense Words
Read across the row from left to right. Say the sounds of the nonsense word.

1. skox 2. spich 3. stath 4. swed 5. skib

6. snosh 7. twik 8. shrip 9. thram 10. trib

1. /s/ /k/ /ŏ/ /ks/   2. /s/ /p/ /ĭ/ /ch/
3. /s/ /t/ /ă/ /th/   4. /s/ /w/ /ĕ/ /d/
5. /s/ /k/ /ĭ/ /b/   6. /s/ /n/ /ŏ/ /sh/
7. /t/ /w/ /ĭ/ /k/   8. /sh/ /r/ /ĭ/ /p/
9. /th/ /r/ /ă/ /m/ 10. /t/ /r/ /ĭ/ /b/

LANGUAGE ARTS GREEN | BEGINNING CONSONANT BLENDS sc–, sp–, st–, sw–, sk–, sm–, sn–, AND tw–   **PH 67**

PH 68   LANGUAGE ARTS GREEN | BEGINNING CONSONANT BLENDS sc–, sp–, st–, sw–, sk–, sm–, sn–, AND tw–

Name_____ Date_____

Part 2. Finger Stretching
Listen to the word. Finger stretch the word.

11. /s/   /k/   /ă/   /b/
12. /s/   /t/   /ă/   /m/   /p/
13. /s/   /k/   /ĕ/   /ch/
14. /t/   /w/   /ĭ/   /s/   /t/
15. /s/   /p/   /ĕ/   /k/
16. /s/   /w/   /ĭ/   /ch/
17. /s/   /m/   /ă/   /sh/
18. /s/   /n/   /ŭ/   /g/

Name_____ Date_____

Part 3. Dictation
Listen to the word. Repeat the word, and then write it.

19. scat_____
20. stop_____
21. skill_____
22. snap_____
23. spell_____
24. swim_____
25. small_____
26. twin_____

LANGUAGE ARTS GREEN | BEGINNING CONSONANT BLENDS sc–, sp–, st–, sw–, sk–, sm–, sn–, AND tw–   **PH 69**

Name_____ Date_____

Part 4. Writing
Listen to the sentence. Repeat the sentence, and then write it.

27. Spin the small top.

28. His twin had a snack.

29. Scott can swim and skip.

PH 70   LANGUAGE ARTS GREEN | BEGINNING CONSONANT BLENDS sc–, sp–, st–, sw–, sk–, sm–, sn–, AND tw–

Name_____ Date_____

Part 5. Read Aloud
Read the sentences aloud.

30.
Father has a spot on his scalp.
A twig is only a stick.
Did Mother step on the stump?
Two fish swim and swish.
The small twins snip the quilt.

LANGUAGE ARTS GREEN | BEGINNING CONSONANT BLENDS sc–, sp–, st–, sw–, sk–, sm–, sn–, AND tw–   **PH 71**

Name_____ Date_____

Part 6. Say Letters
Listen to the sound. Say the letter that makes that sound.

31. o   34. e   37. i
32. a   35. u   38. e
33. i   36. o   39. u

PH 72   LANGUAGE ARTS GREEN | BEGINNING CONSONANT BLENDS sc–, sp–, st–, sw–, sk–, sm–, sn–, AND tw–

Beginning Consonant Blend *spr–*

Unit Overview

In this unit, students will
- ▶ Review sight words.
- ▶ Review letters and sounds of the alphabet.
- ▶ Learn the beginning consonant blends *spr–*, *str–*, *squ–*, *scr–*, and *spl–*.
- ▶ Identify individual sounds in words.
- ▶ Blend sounds to build words.

Materials

Supplied
- *K¹² PhonicsWorks Advanced Activity Book*, p. PH 25
- whiteboard, student
- Tile Kit

Also Needed
- sight words box

Lesson Overview

☰	**[Offline]** **FOCUS:** Beginning Consonant Blend *spr–*	**30** minutes

Sight Words	Review Sight Words
Get Ready	Pairs of Ending Sounds
	Search Sentences for Blends
	Review Sounds and Letters
	Review the Beginning Consonant Blend *sp–*
Learn	Introduce the Beginning Consonant Blend *spr–*
	Build Nonsense Words
Try It	Dissect It

🖥	**[Online]** **REVIEW:** Beginning Consonant Blend *spr–*	**20** minutes

Big Ideas

Working with nonsense words allows students to apply and practice letter–sound knowledge. As readers mature, the ability to quickly and accurately apply letter–sound knowledge is key to comprehending a variety of texts.

 **30** minutes

FOCUS: Beginning Consonant Blend *spr–*

Work **together** with students to complete offline Sight Words, Get Ready, Learn, and Try It activities.

Sight Words

Review Sight Words

Help students learn to recognize sight words.

1. Gather all the sight word cards students have yet to master from their sight words box. Stack the cards on the table face down.

2. Have students pick up a word and read it to you.

3. If they read it quickly and correctly, put the card in one stack. If they hesitate or do not read the word correctly, put it in another stack. The second stack should have words that that will be reviewed again.

4. Take the stack of words that students read correctly and dictate each word to them. They may choose to either write the word or spell it aloud.

5. If students spell the word correctly, they have mastered the word. If they misspell the word, add it to the stack of cards to review again.

6. Chart students' progress on the back of each card.

   ▸ Divide the back of the card into two columns.
   ▸ Label the first column "Read" and the second column "Spell."
   ▸ Record the dates that students read or spell the word correctly. When students can read and spell the word correctly three times in a row, they have mastered the word. You may want to put a star or sticker on their card when they have mastered that word.

TIP Even if students can read and spell all the words correctly, it is still beneficial for them to review sight words. Choose as many additional words as you would like for each subsequent activity.

Objectives
- Read sight words.
- Write sight words.
- Spell sight words.

....

Pairs of Ending Sounds

Help students recognize the difference between words that end with one sound or two sounds.

1. **Say:** Digraphs are two letters that make one sound. A blend is two letters, each of which keeps its own sound.

2. **Say:** I am going to say a pair of words. Repeat the pair of words I say and listen for the ending sounds. One word will end with a single digraph sound and the other will end with a consonant blend that has two sounds. When you hear a word with one ending sound, clap once. When you hear a word with two sounds that blend at the end, clap twice. For example,

   ▸ I will say *dish* and *pond*.
   ▸ You will repeat the word *dish* and clap once, since the word *dish* has one ending sound, /sh/.
   ▸ Then you will repeat the word *pond* and clap twice, since the word *pond* has two ending sounds, /n/ and /d/.

3. **Say:** Now it's your turn. The first pair of words is *dash* and *lump*. Students should repeat the words *dash* and *lump*, clapping once for *dash* and twice for *lump*.

   ▸ Which word has an ending blend? *lump*
   ▸ What two sounds make up the blend? /m/, /p/

4. Repeat Step 3 with these pairs of words. (Pronounce the words very clearly, making sure you pronounce both sounds in the consonant blend words and students are watching your mouth as you do so.

   ▸ *fact* and *rack* clap once: *rack,* clap twice: *fact*
      Which word has an ending blend? *fact,* /k/ and /t/
   ▸ *lunch* and *laugh* clap once: *laugh,* clap twice: *lunch*
      Which word has an ending blend? *lunch,* /n/ and /ch/
   ▸ *path* and *gift* clap once: *path,* clap twice: *gift*
      Which word has an ending blend? *gift,* /f/ and /t/

(TIP) If students have difficulty with first, middle, and last sounds, have them finger stretch the sounds in the word.

Search Sentences for Blends

Have students practice identifying **beginning blends** in words that are in a sentence.

1. **Say:** I'm going to say a beginning blend that is in a word. You will repeat the sound of the beginning blend and the word. The first sound is /br/, as in the word *brush*.

2. Have students say the target sound /br/ and the word *brush*.

3. **Say:** Then I will read a sentence. Repeat the sentence and tell me the word that has the same beginning blend. The first sentence is, "The dog is brown." Which word in the sentence has the special beginning sound /br/? *brown*

Objectives

- Identify ending sounds in words.
- Given the letter, identify the most common sound.
- Given the sound, identify the most common letter or letters.
- Identify the number of sounds within words.
- Identify beginning sounds in words.
- Identify and use the blend *sp*.

4. Have students repeat the sentence and say the word.

5. Redirect students if they don't name the correct word.

   Say: Let me say the sentence again. Remember, you're listening for the sound [special sound].

6. Guide students if they have difficulty. Say two words from the sentence and have them choose the one with the target beginning sound.

7. Follow the same procedure with the words and sentences below to help students recognize beginning blends in words.

   - /sk/, as in *scat*   *Scott is my friend. Scott*
   - /sn/, as in *snip*   *Can you snap your fingers? snap*
   - /tw/, as in *twist*   *His twin is Dave. twin*
   - /shr/, as in *shrimp*   *That noise is shrill. shrill*

Review Sounds and Letters

Help students review sounds for the letters *a, b, k, l, m, o, r, w,* and *y,* plus any letters that are confusing for them.

1. Place the following letter tiles in random order on students' whiteboard: *a, b, k, l, m, o, r, w,* and *y,* plus any additional letters that are confusing.

2. **Say:** Let's go over some letters and sounds.

3. Point to each letter tile and have students say a sound that letter makes.

   - *o* /ŏ/ or /ō/
   - *m* /m/
   - *r* /r/
   - *y* /y/
   - *w* /w/
   - *k* /k/
   - *b* /b/
   - *l* /l/
   - *a* /ă/ or /ā/

4. Say each of the following sounds. Have students repeat the sound and touch the corresponding letter tile.

   - /ŏ/ *o*
   - /m/ *m*
   - /r/ *r*
   - /y/ *y*
   - /w/ *w*
   - /k/ *k*
   - /b/ *b*
   - /l/ *l*
   - /ă/ *a*

5. As you do the activity, point to some letter tiles two or three times so that students don't think they are finished with a sound after they have named it.

6. Redirect students if they say an incorrect sound when you point to a letter tile.

   Say: That's the sound of another letter. What is the sound for this letter?

7. Help students if they touch the wrong letter tile after they repeat a sound.

   Say: That letter tile goes with the sound [sound for touched letter tile]. We're looking for the letter that goes with the sound [target sound].

Review the Beginning Consonant Blend *sp–*

Help students recognize and use the beginning consonant blend *sp–*.

1. Make the word *spot* on students' whiteboard and point to it.

2. **Say:** Touch and say this word.

   ‣ How many sounds are in the word? four
   ‣ How many letters are in the word? four
   ‣ Where is the blend? at the beginning
   ‣ We know that the letters *s* and *p* at the beginning of this word are called a blend because each of those letters keeps its own sound, and the two sounds blend together.

3. Redirect students if they have difficulty with the beginning consonant blend *sp–*.

   Say: Those two letters are often together at the beginning of a word. When they are together, they blend into the sound /sp/, as in *speak*. Can you say the word *speak*? When you say *speak*, don't stop between the two sounds /s/ and /p/. Try saying the word again.

Learn

Introduce the Beginning Consonant Blend *spr–*

Help students recognize and use the beginning consonant blend *spr–*.

1. Place the following letters on students' whiteboard: *g, i, n, p, r, s,* and *t*.

2. Make the word *sprig* and point to it.

3. **Say:** Touch and say this word.

   ‣ How many sounds are in the word? five
   ‣ How many letters are in the word? five
   ‣ Where is the blend? at the beginning

4. Make the word *sprint* and point to it.

5. **Say:** Touch and say this word.

   ‣ How many sounds are in the word? six
   ‣ How many letters are in the word? six
   ‣ Where is the blend? at the beginning

6. Redirect students if they have difficulty with the beginning consonant blend *spr–*.

   Say: Those three letters are often together at the beginning of a word. When they are together, they blend into the sound /spr/, as in *sprout*. Can you say the word *sprout*? When you say *sprout*, don't stop between the three sounds /s/, /p/, and /r/. Try saying the word again.

Objectives

- Identify and use the blend *spr–*.
- Identify beginning sounds in words.
- Identify the number of sounds within words.
- Blend sounds to create words.

Build Nonsense Words

Help students use letters and sounds to build words.

1. Place the following letter tiles at the top of students' whiteboard: *b, e, f, i, n, o, p, r, s, t,* and *u.*

2. Draw five horizontal lines across the middle of students' whiteboard to represent the sounds in a word.

3. **Say:** Some words don't have any meaning. We call these **nonsense words**. Even though we don't know what a word means, we can still read it. Nonsense words will be very important when we read longer words. When we break longer words into parts, sometimes the parts are nonsense words.

4. **Say:** Let's use letters and sounds to build the word *spret.*

5. Have students finger stretch the sounds in *spret.*

6. Have students

   ▸ Identify the first, next, and last sounds in *spret.*
   ▸ Choose the corresponding letter for each of the sounds.
   ▸ Move the letters to the correct lines on their whiteboard.

7. Guide students with these questions:

   ▸ What is the first sound in *spret?* /s/
     Which line does the letter for that sound go on? the first one
   ▸ What is the next sound in *spret?* /p/
     Which line does the letter for that sound go on? the second one
   ▸ What is the next sound in *spret?* /r/
     Which line does the letter for that sound go on? the third one
   ▸ What's the fourth sound in *spret?* /ĕ/
     Which line does the letter for that sound go on? the fourth one
   ▸ What's the last sound in *spret?* /t/
     Which line does the letter for that sound go on? the last one

8. Have students touch and say the word.

9. Redirect students if they select the incorrect letter:

   Say: That sound is in the word [word], and it is the [first, second, third, forth, fifth] sound. We want the sound [target sound].

   Continue until students select the correct letter.

10. Repeat the activity to build the following words:

    ▸ *spron* /s/ /p/ /r/ /ŏ/ /n/
    ▸ *sprib* /s/ /p/ /r/ /ĭ/ /b/
    ▸ *spruf* /s/ /p/ /r/ /ŭ/ /f/

Try It ....

Dissect It

Have students complete page PH 25 in *K¹² PhonicsWorks Advanced Activity Book* for more practice with words that begin with the consonant blend *spr–*. Have students read each sentence aloud and find the word that beings with the blend *spr–*. Have them write the word and read the sentence aloud again.

⟦Online⟧ ⓴ minutes

REVIEW: Beginning Consonant Blend *spr–*

Students will work online independently to

▸ Practice the beginning consonant blend *spr–*.
▸ Practice decoding text by reading a story.

Help students locate the online activities and provide support as needed.

Offline Alternative

No computer access? Have students name things or words that begin with the consonant blend *spr–* (for example, *sprig* or *sprint*). You might also have students spell words that have the beginning consonant blend *spr–*.

Beginning Consonant Blend *str–*

Lesson Overview

[Offline] **FOCUS:** Beginning Consonant Blend *str–* **30** minutes

Sight Words	Use Words in Sentences
Get Ready	Climb the Ladder
	I Spy
	Review the Beginning Consonant Blend *spr–*
Learn	Introduce the Beginning Consonant Blend *str–*
	Correct the Sentence
	Questions About Letters and Sounds
Try It	"Tess and Her Mother"
	Dictation: Write Sentences

[Online] **REVIEW:** Beginning Consonant Blend *str–* **20** minutes

Materials

Supplied

- *K¹² PhonicsWorks Readers Advanced 4*, pp. 7–12
- whiteboard, Learning Coach
- whiteboard, student
- Tile Kit

Also Needed

- sight words box
- dictation notebook
- index cards (4)

Advance Preparation

Place lowercase letter tiles in alphabetical order and digraphs on your whiteboard.

For Correct the Sentence, print each of the following sentences on index cards, using one card per sentence:

- ▶ *sprint to the end,*
- ▶ *the strap is on the watch,*
- ▶ *Who struck the drum*
- ▶ *I will stretch to the top?*

[Offline] 🕧 minutes

FOCUS: Beginning Consonant Blend *str–*

Work **together** with students to complete offline Sight Words, Get Ready, Learn, and Try It activities.

Sight Words ·······································

Use Words in Sentences

Help students use sight words in sentences.

1. Gather all the sight word cards students have yet to master from their sight words box. Spread the sight word cards on the table.

2. **Say:** Let's use sight words in sentences.

3. Have students

   ▸ Touch each card and read the word on it.
   ▸ Make up a sentence using the word.
   ▸ Put the card in a pile after using the word in a sentence.
   ▸ Go through the pile of cards and read each sight word again.
   ▸ Spell each word.

   TIP If students have difficulty with any of the sight words, place those word cards in a pile to review again.

> **Objectives**
> - Read sight words.
> - Spell sight words.

Get Ready ·······································

Climb the Ladder

Help students use letters to build words.

1. On students' whiteboard or on a sheet of paper, draw a ladder with five or more rungs.

2. Write the word *stick* on the bottom rung.

3. Point to the word *stick*.

   Say: I can make the word *stack* by changing one letter in this word.

4. Write the word *stack* on the second rung of the ladder.

   Say: Think of a word that you can make by changing only one letter in *stack*. Tell me the word and write it on the next step on the ladder.

5. If students struggle, coach them to change the first letter in each word.

   Say: Read the word on the bottom rung. What sound do you hear at the beginning of the word? What letter has that sound?

   Say: Name a word that rhymes with the word at the bottom. What sound do you hear at the beginning of the rhyming word? What letter has that sound? Make a new word by using the new letter. Read the new word.

> **Objectives**
> - Blend sounds to create words.
> - Identify and use the blend *st*.
> - Identify individual sounds in words.
> - Identify the number of sounds within words.
> - Identify ending sounds in words.
> - Identify beginning sounds in words.
> - Identify and use the blend *spr–*.

6. Continue the process until students reach the top of the ladder. Remind students that they may change only one sound: the beginning, middle, or last sound.

7. Consider having students name a word that rhymes with the word at the bottom.

   Say: What sound do you hear at the beginning of the rhyming word? What letter has that sound? Make a new word by using the new letter. Read the new word.

8. Redirect students if they select a word that changes more than one letter.

   Say: How many letters changed from the last word to your new word? Try to think of a word that has only one letter change.

9. Redirect students if they spell a word incorrectly, but the sounds they spell are correct (such as *ruf* for *rough*).

   Say: You have the sounds and letters right, but that word doesn't follow our spelling rules. Try another word.

   (TIP) If students have difficulty thinking of real words, have them use nonsense words.

I Spy

Have students name and use common objects to help them recognize individual sounds in words.

1. Explain to students that you will be playing "I Spy," and show them how to use their thumb and index finger to make a circle, simulating a spyglass.

2. **Say:** I say, "I spy, with my little eye, something that starts with the sound /l/." Your job is to guess what I spy. What I had in mind was the *light*. *Light* begins with the sound /l/.

3. Repeat Step 2 with a different object in the room.

4. **Say:** Are you ready to begin? I spy, with my little eye, something that starts with the sound [target sound]. Can you guess what it is?

5. After students have guessed the object, repeat Step 4 until you have spied six objects, or as time permits. Possible words to use are *pencil, window, door, television, radio, telephone, dish, hair, bowl, table, floor, book, paper, computer, cup,* and *rug.*

6. Redirect students if they name an object with an incorrect sound.

   Say: The sound that begins the word [word] is [sound]. We're looking for the sound [target sound]. What is a word that begins with that sound? Now look around the room. What do you see that begins with that sound?

7. Narrow down the search to a certain part of the room if students become frustrated. If they continue to have trouble, narrow down the search to two objects.

   Say: What is the beginning sound of [target word]? What is the beginning sound of [another word]? Which one starts with the sound [target sound]?

Review the Beginning Consonant Blend *spr*–
Help students recognize and use the beginning consonant blend *spr*–.

1. Make the word *sprig* on students' whiteboard and point to it.

2. **Say:** Touch and say this word.

   ▸ How many sounds are in the word? five
   ▸ How many letters are in the word? five
   ▸ Where is the blend? at the beginning

   Say: We know that the letters *s*, *p*, and *r* at the beginning of this word are called a blend because each of those letters keeps its own sound, and the three sounds blend together.

Learn

Introduce the Beginning Consonant Blend *str*–
Help students recognize and use the beginning consonant blend *str*–.

1. Place the following letters on students' whiteboards: *a*, *i*, *p*, *r*, *s*, and *t*.

2. Make the word *strip* and point to it.

3. **Say:** Touch and say this word.

   ▸ How many sounds are in the word? five
   ▸ How many letters are in the word? five
   ▸ Where is the blend? at the beginning

4. Make the word *strap* and point to it.

5. Redirect students if they have difficulty with the beginning blend *str*–.

   Say: Those three letters are often together at the beginning of a word. When they are together, they blend into the sound /str/, as in *strong*. Can you say the word *strong*? When you say *strong*, don't stop between the sounds /s/, /t/, and /r/. Try saying the word again.

Objectives
- Identify and use the blend *str*–.
- Identify beginning sounds in words.
- Identify the number of sounds within words.
- Use correct capitalization and punctuation.
- Identify letters of the alphabet.
- Given the letter, identify the most common sound.

Correct the Sentence
Help students learn more about writing sentences and identifying the correct capitalization and punctuation.

1. Gather the index cards you prepared.

2. Have students pick the first group of words and read the words.

3. **Say:** What is wrong with this sentence? It is missing a capital letter at the beginning and a period at the end.

4. Have students make the corrections to the sentence on the index card.

5. **Say:** Now read the sentence again.

   ▸ How do you know this sentence is correct? It has a capital letter at the beginning and a period at the end.

6. Have students pick another index card and repeat the procedure until they have capitalized and punctuated all the word groups correctly.

   ▸ sprint to the end Sprint to the end.
   ▸ the strap is on the watch The strap is on the watch.
   ▸ Who struck the drum Who struck the drum?
   ▸ I will stretch to the top? I will stretch to the top.

7. If students don't recognize what is wrong with the sentence, ask these questions:

   ▸ What is special about the first word in a sentence?
   ▸ Does the first word in this sentence start with a capital letter?
   ▸ How can you change the sentence so it begins with a capital letter?
   ▸ What is special about the mark at the end of a sentence?
   ▸ Is the last word in this sentence followed by a period or a question mark?
   ▸ What kind of sentence is it, a telling sentence or an asking sentence?
   ▸ What mark do you put at the end of a telling (asking) sentence?
   ▸ How can you change the sentence so it ends with the correct mark?

Questions About Letters and Sounds

To help students master digraphs and blends, have them practice identifying and naming them. Grab your whiteboard with letters placed in alphabetical order and digraphs.

1. Touch all the digraphs.

2. **Say:** These are tiles that have two letters that spell one sound. Tell me the sounds for each.

3. Ask the following questions:

   ▸ Which letters make the beginning blend /pl/, as in *plan*? *p* and *l*
   ▸ Which letters make the beginning blend /str/, as in *stretch*? *s, t,* and *r*
   ▸ Which letters make the beginning blend /shr/, as in *shrimp*? *s, h,* and *r*

Try It

"Tess and Her Mother"

Have students read "Tess and Her Mother" on page 7 of *K¹² PhonicsWorks Readers Advanced 4.*

Students should read the story silently once or twice before reading the story aloud. When students miss a word that can be sounded out, point to it and give them three to six seconds to try the word again. If students still miss the word, tell them the word so the flow of the story isn't interrupted.

After reading the story, make a list of all the words students missed, and go over those words with them. You may use tiles to show the student how to read the words.

Dictation: Write Sentences

Use sentences to help students identify individual sounds in words.

1. Gather a pencil and the dictation notebook. Say the sentence, *Stretch to see the sun.* Then give these directions to students:

   ▸ Repeat the sentence.
   ▸ Write the sentence in your notebook.
   ▸ Read the sentence aloud.

2. When students have finished, write the following sentence on your whiteboard: *Stretch to see the sun.*

3. Have them compare their answer to your correct version.

4. Repeat this procedure with the sentence, *He sprints to the wall.*

   ▸ If students make an error and don't see it, help them correct their mistake by having them finger stretch the sounds in the word they missed.
   ▸ If students are having difficulty selecting the correct letters or sounds, review those letters or sounds that are confusing them.
   ▸ If students have difficulty with first, middle, and last sounds, have them finger stretch the sounds in words.

Objectives

- Read aloud grade-level text with appropriate automaticity, prosody, accuracy, and rate.
- Decode words by applying grade-level word analysis skills.
- Write words by applying grade-level phonics knowledge.
- Write sight words.
- Follow three-step directions.

Online 20 minutes

REVIEW: Beginning Consonant Blend *str–*

Students will work online independently to

▸ Practice the beginning consonant blend *str–*.

Help students locate the online activities and provide support as needed.

Offline Alternative

No computer access? Have students name things or words that begin with the consonant blend *str–* (for example, *string* or *straw*). You might also have students spell words that have the beginning consonant blend *str–*.

Objectives

- Identify and use the blend *str–*.
- Identify beginning sounds in words.

Beginning Consonant Blends *squ–* and *scr–*

Lesson Overview

Offline — **FOCUS:** Beginning Consonant Blends *squ–* and *scr–*   **30** minutes

Sight Words	Sight Word Concentration
Get Ready	Finger Stretching
	Disappearing Sounds
	Review the Beginning Consonant Blend *str–*
Learn	Introduce the Beginning Consonant Blend *squ–*
	Introduce the Beginning Consonant Blend *scr–*
	Build Words
Try It	Hunt for Information

Online — **REVIEW:** Beginning Consonant Blends *squ–* and *scr–*   **20** minutes

Materials

Supplied
- *K¹² PhonicsWorks Advanced Activity Book,* p. PH 26
- whiteboard, student
- Tile Kit

Also Needed
- dictation notebook
- sight words box

Advance Preparation

Gather two sets of all the sight word cards you have used to date.

【 Offline 】 ⏱ 30 minutes

FOCUS: Beginning Consonant Blends *squ–* and *scr–*

Work **together** with students to complete offline Sight Words, Get Ready, Learn, and Try It activities.

Sight Words

Sight Word Concentration

Help students review sight words.

1. Gather the two sets of sight word cards.

2. Scramble both sets of sight word cards and place them face down on the floor or a table.

3. Turn over two cards at a time; take turns with students. If the cards match, the person turning over the matching cards reads the word and uses it in a sentence. If the cards don't match, the person turns them back over.

4. Remove and save the matching cards.

5. Continue the activity until all the word cards are paired.

6. Have students read all the words.

7. Take the stack of words that students read correctly and dictate each word to them.

8. Have students write each word or spell it aloud.

TIP If students have difficulty with any of the sight words, let them work at their own pace and really master these words.

> **Objectives**
> - Read sight words.
> - Write sight words.
> - Spell sight words.

Get Ready

Finger Stretching

Have students use finger stretching to represent the sounds in words.

1. **Say:** We can finger stretch the sounds in a word to count how many sounds there are in that word. Start by holding up your hand with your palm facing you and make a loose fist. Each time you say a sound in a word, extend a finger, starting with your thumb.

> **Objectives**
> - Identify and use the blend *str–*.
> - Identify individual sounds in words.
> - Identify the number of sounds within words.
> - Identify beginning sounds in words.
> - Identify ending sounds in words.

2. **Say:** Let's finger stretch the sounds in *stretch*.

> ▸ Say the first sound in the word *stretch*, /s/, and move your thumb out. Keep your thumb out.
> ▸ Say the second sound, /t/, and move your index finger out. Keep your finger stretched out.
> ▸ Say the next sound in the word *stretch*, /r/, and move your middle finger out. Keep your fingers out.
> ▸ Say the next sound in the word *stretch*, /ĕ/, and move your ring finger out. Keep your fingers out.
> ▸ Say the last sound, /ch/, and move your pinkie finger out. Your fingers are stretched out; you have finger stretched the word *stretch*.

3. **Say:** Let's count the number of sounds in the word *stretch*.

> ▸ How many fingers are out? five
> ▸ How many sounds are in *stretch*? five
> ▸ How many letters are in *stretch*? seven

4. **Say:** To finish finger stretching a word, put your fingers back into a fist and pull your fist toward your body as you say the word. When you finger stretch, you always say the word after you count the sounds with your fingers.

5. Have students finger stretch the following words. Remind them to say each word after finger stretching it.

> ▸ *sprig* /s/ /p/ /r/ /ĭ/ /g/   What is the first sound? /s/
> ▸ *watch* /w/ /ă/ /ch/   What is the third sound? /ch/
> ▸ *strand* /s/ /t/ /r/ /ă/ /n/ /d/   What is the first sound? /s/
> ▸ *drum* /d/ /r/ /ŭ/ /m/   What is the last sound? /m/
> ▸ *strap* /s/ /t/ /r/ /ă/ /p/   What is the second sound? /t/
> ▸ *sprint* /s/ /p/ /r/ /ĭ/ /n/ /t/   What is the first sound? /s/
> ▸ *crunch* /k/ /r/ /ŭ/ /n/ /ch/   What is the third sound? / ŭ /

TIP Refer to the K¹² *PhonicsWorks* DVD for a demonstration of finger stretching.

Disappearing Sounds

Have students practice identifying sounds by having them remove beginning blends in words.

1. **Say:** We're going to make parts of words disappear. First I will say a word. Then I will say part of the word that we are going to make disappear. Today the disappearing part of the word is the beginning sound. To make the beginning sound of the word disappear, you will only say the part of the word that is left after you take the beginning blend away.

2. **Say:** Let's try one. The word is *swam*. The sound I want you to make disappear is /sw/. What is the sound of the word without /sw/? /ă/ . . . /m/ . . . /am/ is left when we take away /sw/.

3. Repeat this procedure with the rest of the words in the list.

brand   What is the sound of the word without /br/? /and/
tramp   What is the sound of the word without /tr/? /amp/
scat   What is the sound of the word without /sk/? /at/
twin   What is the sound of the word without /tw/? /in/
crash   What is the sound of the word without /kr/? /ash/
trash   What is the sound of the word without /tr/? /ash/
switch   What is the sound of the word without /sw/? /itch/

TIP If students cannot figure out the part of the word that is left after taking away the target sounds, use the letter tiles to show them what sounds are left when the sounds are taken away. You might also have them finger stretch the word, then finger stretch only the sounds that are left after the target sound disappears.

TIP If students have difficulty or do not appear to enjoy an activity, it may be an indication that the activity is too difficult for them. In that case, pay special attention to the sounds students are having trouble with and review those sounds.

Review the Beginning Consonant Blend *str–*

Help students recognize and use the beginning consonant blend *str–*.

1. Make the word *strap* on students' whiteboard and point to it.

2. **Say:** Touch and say this word.

   ▸ How many sounds are in the word? five
   ▸ How many letters are in the word? five
   ▸ Where is the blend? at the beginning
   ▸ We know that the letters *s*, *t*, and *r* at the beginning of this word are called a blend because those letters keep their own sounds while the sounds blend together.

Learn

Introduce the Beginning Consonant Blend *squ–*

Help students recognize and use the beginning consonant blend *squ–*.

1. Place the following letter tiles on students' whiteboard: *d, i, s, sh,* and *qu.*

2. Make the word *squid* and point to it.

   Say: Touch and say this word.

   ▸ How many sounds are in the word? four
   ▸ How many letters are in the word? five
   ▸ Where is the blend? at the beginning

3. Redirect students if they have difficulty with the beginning consonant blend *squ–*.

   Say: Those three letters are often together at the beginning of a word. When they are together, they blend into the sound /skw/, as in *square*. Can you say the word *square*? When you say *square*, don't stop between the sounds /s/ and /kw/. Try saying the word again.

> **Objectives**
> - Identify and use the blend *squ–*.
> - Identify and use the blend *scr–*.
> - Identify the number of sounds within words.
> - Identify beginning sounds in words.
> - Blend sounds to create words.

4. Make the word *squish* and point to it.

5. **Say:** Touch and say this word.

  ▸ How many sounds are in the word? four
  ▸ How many letters are in the word? six
  ▸ Where is the blend? at the beginning

Introduce the Beginning Consonant Blend *scr–*

Help students recognize and use the beginning consonant blend *scr–*.

1. Place the following letters on students' whiteboard: *a, b, c, p, r, s,* and *u*.

2. Make the word *scrap* and point to it.

3. **Say:** Touch and say this word.

  ▸ How many sounds are in the word? five
  ▸ How many letters are in the word? five
  ▸ Where is the blend? at the beginning

4. Redirect students if they have difficulty with the beginning consonant blend *scr–*.

  Say: Those three letters are often together at the beginning of a word. When they are together, they blend into the sounds /s/, /k/, and /r/, as in *scribble*. Can you say the word *scribble*? When you say *scribble*, don't stop between the sounds /s/, /k/, and /r/. Try saying the word again.

5. Make the word *scrub* and point to it.

6. **Say:** Touch and say this word.

  ▸ How many sounds are in the word? five
  ▸ How many letters are in the word? five
  ▸ Where is the blend? at the beginning

Build Words

Help students use letters and sounds to build words.

1. Place the following letter tiles at the top of students' whiteboard: *a, b, c, i, m, n, qu, r, s, sh, t,* and *u*.

2. Draw five horizontal lines across the middle of students' whiteboard to represent the sounds in a word.

3. **Say:** Let's use letters and sounds to build the word *squint*.

4. Have students finger stretch the sounds in *squint*.

5. Have students
   - ► Identify the first, next, and last sounds in *squint*.
   - ► Choose the corresponding letter or letters for each of the sounds.
   - ► Move the letters to the correct lines on their whiteboard.

6. Guide students with these questions:
   - ► What is the first sound in *squint*? /s/
     Which line does the letter for that sound go on? the first one
   - ► What is the next sound in *squint*? /kw/
     Which line do the letters for that sound go on? the second one
   - ► What is the next sound in *squint*? /ĭ/
     Which line does the letter for that sound go on? the third one
   - ► What is the next sound in *squint*? /n/
     Which line does the letter for that sound go on? the fourth one
   - ► What's the last sound in *squint*? /t/
     Which line does the letter for that sound go on? the last one

7. Redirect students if they select the incorrect letter.

   Say: That sound is in the word [word], and it is the [first, second, third, forth, fifth] sound. We want the sound [target sound].

   Continue until students select the correct letter.

8. Have students touch and say the word.

9. Draw horizontal lines across the middle of students' whiteboard that represent the number of sounds in each word. Repeat the activity to build the following words:
   - ► *scrub* /s/ /k/ /r/ /ŭ/ /b/
   - ► *squish* /s/ /kw/ /ĭ/ /sh/
   - ► *scram* /s/ /k/ /r/ /ă/ /m/

Try It

Hunt for Information

Have students complete page PH 26 in *K¹² PhonicsWorks Advanced Activity Book* for more practice with words that begin with the consonant blends *squ–* and *scr–*. Have students read the story aloud. Have them choose a word from the story that best completes the sentence and read the sentence aloud.

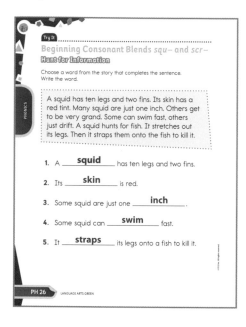

Online · 20 minutes

REVIEW: Beginning Consonant Blends *squ–* and *scr–*

Students will work online independently to

- ▶ Practice the beginning consonant blends *squ–* and *scr–*.
- ▶ Practice decoding text by reading a story.

Help students locate the online activities and provide support as needed.

Offline Alternative

No computer access? Have students point out and name things or words that begin with the consonant blends *squ–* and *scr–* (for example, *squish* or *scratch*). You might also have students spell words that have the beginning consonant blend *sqr–* or *scr–*.

Objectives

- Identify and use the blend *squ–*.
- Identify and use the blend *scr–*.
- Identify beginning sounds in words.
- Read aloud grade-level text with appropriate automaticity, prosody, accuracy, and rate.
- Decode words by applying grade-level word analysis skills.

Beginning Consonant Blend *spl–*

Lesson Overview

[Offline] FOCUS: Beginning Consonant Blend *spl–*   **30** minutes

Sight Words	Pick a Pair
Get Ready	Practice Blends and Sounds
	Place That Name
	Review the Beginning Consonant Blend *scr–*
Learn	Introduce the Beginning Consonant Blend *spl–*
	Sentence Scramble
	Make More Words
Try It	"The Splash Ball"
	Dictation: Write Sentences

[Online] REVIEW: Beginning Consonant Blend *spl–*   **20** minutes

Materials

Supplied
- *K¹² PhonicsWorks Readers Advanced 4*, pp. 13–18
- whiteboard, Learning Coach
- whiteboard, student
- Tile Kit

Also Needed
- sight words box
- dictation notebook
- index cards (36)

Advance Preparation

For Place That Name, print on index cards the names of several items that may be located nearby, using one card per word. Be sure the words are words that students can read independently, such as *lamp, belt, wall, quilt, rock, sack, sock, hat, can, map, pan, gum, tub, nut, pup, rug, brick, brush, dress, grass, branch, shrub, stamp,* and *twig.*

For Sentence Scramble, print the following words on index cards, using one index card for each word: *can, splash, he, scrub, the, dog, sprint, squid, stretch, Dan, scratch,* and *big.*

 **30 minutes**

FOCUS: Beginning Consonant Blend *spl–*

Work **together** with students to complete offline Sight Words, Get Ready, Learn, and Try It activities.

Sight Words

Pick a Pair

Play a card game with students for more practice with sight words.

1. Gather the sight word cards that students are reviewing. Choose two words and place the cards on the table.

2. Ask questions to help students identify each word. For example, if the words are *or* and *one*, you could ask, "Which word names a number?" If the words are *on* and *but*, you could ask, "Which word is the opposite of *off*?"

3. Continue the activity until students identify all the words.

4. Take the stack of words that students read correctly and dictate each word to them.

5. Have students write each word or spell it aloud.

> **Objectives**
> * Read sight words.
> * Write sight words.
> * Spell sight words.

Get Ready

Practice Blends and Sounds

Work with students to help them identify single sounds and blends.

1. Place the following letter tiles at the top of students' whiteboard: *c, d, m, n, p, r, s, t,* and *w*.

2. **Say:** We're going to play a game to practice letters, blends, and words.

3. Make the blend *dr–* on students' whiteboard.

4. **Say:** I'll go first. These are the letters *dr*. A word that starts with *dr* is *drum* and a sentence using that word is *I can bang a drum*. Now it's your turn.

5. Pull down the letter *m* on students' whiteboard and guide them with these questions:

   ▸ What is/are the letter(s)?
   ▸ Is it a blend?
   ▸ What is a word that starts with that/those letter(s)?
   ▸ Make up a sentence that has that word in it.

6. Continue the activity with the following letters and blends: *s, sc–, sn–, spr–, t, tr–,* and *w*.

> **Objectives**
> * Read aloud grade-level text with appropriate automaticity, prosody, accuracy, and rate.
> * Given the letter, identify the most common sound.
> * Given the sound, identify the most common letter or letters.
> * Identify and use the blend *scr–*.
> * Identify beginning sounds in words.
> * Identify the number of sounds within words.

Place That Name

Play a game with students to help them identify names of common objects.

1. Gather the index cards you prepared with names of nearby objects. Place the cards face down in one pile.

2. **Say:** We're going to play a game called Place That Name.

   ► First you will choose a card and read the word on it. Then you will find that object nearby and tape the card to it as a label or tell me where the object is.
   ► I'll try first. Choose a card from the pile and say the word.

3. **Say:** I know where there is a [word on the card]. Let's put a label on it.

   ► It's your turn. Choose a card and read it to me.
   ► Now find that object and tape the card to it, or say where the object is.

4. Repeat Step 3 until students have used all the cards. Remind students that all of the objects are somewhere nearby.

TIP If students stumble over any words, have them touch and say the words. Touch and say these words along with them.

Review the Beginning Consonant Blend *scr–*

Help students recognize and use the beginning consonant blend *scr–*.

1. Make the word *scrub* on students' whiteboard and point to it.

2. **Say:** Touch and say this word.

   ► How many sounds are in the word? five
   ► How many letters are in the word? five
   ► Where is the blend? at the beginning
   ► We know that the letters *s, c,* and *r* at the beginning of this word are called a blend because those letters keep their own sounds while the three sounds blend together.

Learn

Introduce the Beginning Consonant Blend *spl–*

Help students recognize and use the beginning consonant blend *spl–*.

1. Place the following letters on students' whiteboard: *a, i, l, p, s, sh,* and *t*.

2. Make the word *split* and point to it.

3. **Say:** Touch and say this word.

   ▸ How many sounds are in the word? five
   ▸ How many letters are in the word? five
   ▸ We know that the letters *s, p,* and *l* at the beginning of this word are called a blend because each of those letters keeps its own sound while the three sounds blend together.

4. Redirect students if they have difficulty with the beginning consonant blend *spl–*.

   Say: Those three letters are often together at the beginning of a word. When they are together, they blend into the sound /spl/, as in *splash*. Can you say the word *splash*? When you say *splash*, don't stop between the sounds /s/, /p/, and /l/. Try saying the word again.

5. Make the word *splash* and point to it.

6. **Say:** Touch and say this word.

   ▸ How many sounds are in the word? five
   ▸ How many letters are in the word? six
   ▸ Where is the blend? at the beginning

Sentence Scramble

Have students build sentences by rearranging words to help them learn the meaning of words and phrases.

1. Gather the index cards you prepared, a pencil, and the dictation notebook.

2. Place the index cards in front of students.

3. Point to each word and have students read it aloud with you.

4. Arrange three of the cards as follows: *can he splash*.

5. Have students say if the words make sense. Tell them that the words make an asking sentence.

6. Write the words as a sentence on students' whiteboard.

7. Point out the capital letter and the question mark in the sentence.

8. Read the sentence together.

Objectives

- Identify and use the blend *spl–*.
- Identify the number of sounds within words.
- Identify beginning sounds in words.
- Read aloud grade-level text with appropriate automaticity, prosody, accuracy, and rate.
- Decode words by applying grade-level word analysis skills.
- Use context and sentence structure to determine meaning of words, phrases, and/or sentences.
- Identify complete sentences.
- Identify and use the blend *spr–*.
- Identify and use the blend *str–*.
- Identify and use the blend *scr–*.
- Identify and use the blend *squ–*.
- Write words by applying grade-level phonics knowledge.

9. **Say:** I am going to mix these words back with the others. Choose some word cards and put them together to make a different sentence. Read the words in the order you put them.

   ▸ Does your sentence make sense? Is it an asking or a telling sentence?
   ▸ Now write the sentence. Be sure to start with a capital letter. Remember to put a period or a question mark at the end.

10. Return the words to the original group, and repeat the steps so that students can create and write one or more sentences.

11. Help students if they have difficulty in arranging the words correctly to make a sentence.

   Say: Read the sentence aloud. Does it make sense?

12. Point to any word that seems out of place and state the following:

   ▸ What is this word?
   ▸ Find a word that would make better sense.
   ▸ Switch the words. Now read the sentence.
   ▸ Does it make sense now?

Make More Words

Have students make new words by adding and removing letters to base words.

1. Use the letter tiles to create the following blends at the top of the students' whiteboard: *spr–, str–, scr–, squ–,* and *spl–.*

2. Place the following letter tiles randomly on the bottom of student's whiteboard: *a, d, i, m, p, sh, t,* and *u.*

3. **Say:** When I put the letters *ash* after the letters *spl–,* I make the word *splash.* See how many new **real words** you can make by putting the letters on your whiteboard after the letters *spr–, str–, scr–, squ–,* and *spl–.* Answers will vary.

4. Have the student write each word in the dictation notebook.

5. When students finish making words, have them read each word aloud.

Try It

"The Splash Ball"

Have students read "The Splash Ball" on page 13 of *K¹² PhonicsWorks Readers Advanced 4*.

Students should read the story silently once or twice before reading the story aloud. When students miss a word that can be sounded out, point to it and give them three to six seconds to try the word again. If students still miss the word, tell them the word so the flow of the story isn't interrupted.

After reading the story, make a list of all the words students missed, and go over those words with them. You may use tiles to show them how to read the words.

Dictation: Write Sentences

Use sentences to help students identify individual sounds in words.

1. Gather a pencil and the dictation notebook. Say the sentence, *Scrub the big tub.* Then give these directions to students:

   ▸ Repeat the sentence.
   ▸ Write the sentence in your notebook.
   ▸ Read the sentence aloud.

2. When students have finished, write the following sentence on your whiteboard: *Scrub the big tub.*

3. Have them compare their answer to your correct version.

4. Repeat this procedure with the sentence, *Can you see him squint?*

   ▸ If students make an error and don't see it, help them correct their mistake by asking them to finger stretch the sounds in the word they missed.
   ▸ If students are having difficulty selecting the correct letters or sounds, review those letters or sounds that are confusing them.
   ▸ If students have difficulty with first, middle, and last sounds, have them finger stretch the sounds in words.

Objectives

- Read aloud grade-level text with appropriate automaticity, prosody, accuracy, and rate.
- Decode words by applying grade-level word analysis skills.
- Write words by applying grade-level phonics knowledge.
- Write sight words.
- Follow three-step directions.

 **20 minutes**

REVIEW: : Beginning Consonant Blend *spl–*

Students will work online independently to

▸ Practice the beginning consonant blend *spl–*.

Help students locate the online activities and provide support as needed.

Offline Alternative

No computer access? Have students point out and name things or words that begin with the consonant blend *spl–* (for example, *splash*). You might also have students spell words that have the beginning consonant blend *spl–*.

Objectives

- Identify and use the blend *spl–*.
- Identify beginning sounds in words.

Unit Checkpoint

Lesson Overview

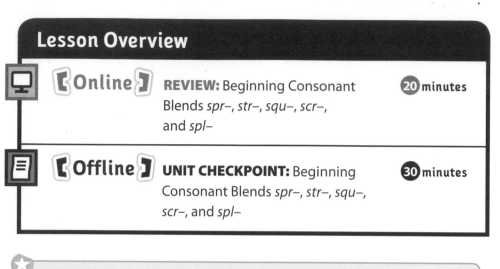

Online	**REVIEW:** Beginning Consonant Blends *spr–*, *str–*, *squ–*, *scr–*, and *spl–*	**20** minutes
Offline	**UNIT CHECKPOINT:** Beginning Consonant Blends *spr–*, *str–*, *squ–*, *scr–*, and *spl–*	**30** minutes

Materials

Supplied

- *K¹² PhonicsWorks Advanced Assessments,* pp. PH 73–78

Objectives

- Identify and use the blend *spr–*.
- Identify and use the blend *str–*.
- Identify and use the blend *squ–*.
- Identify and use the blend *scr–*.
- Identify and use the blend *spl–*.
- Identify individual sounds in words.
- Given the letter, identify the most common sound.
- Given the sound, identify the most common letter or letters.

- Read instructional-level text with 90% accuracy.
- Read aloud grade-level text with appropriate automaticity, prosody, accuracy, and rate.
- Write words by applying grade-level phonics knowledge.
- Write sight words.
- Read sight words.

 **Online** **20** minutes

REVIEW: Beginning Consonant Blends *spr–*, *str–*, *squ–*, *scr–*, and *spl–*

Students will review the beginning consonant blends *spr–*, *str–*, *squ–*, *scr–*, and *spl–* to prepare for the Unit Checkpoint. Help students locate the online activities and provide support as needed.

[Offline] **30** minutes

UNIT CHECKPOINT: Beginning Consonant Blends *spr–*, *str–*, *squ–*, *scr–*, and *spl–*

Explain that students are going to show what they have learned about sounds, letters, and words.

1. Give students the Unit Checkpoint pages for the Beginning Consonant Blends *spr–*, *str–*, *squ–*, *scr–*, and *spl–* unit and print the Unit Checkpoint Answer Key, if you'd like.

2. Use the instructions below to help administer the Checkpoint to students. On the Answer Key or another sheet of paper, note student answers to oral response questions to help with scoring the Checkpoint later.

3. Use the Answer Key to score the Checkpoint, and then enter the results online.

Part 1. Read Nonsense Words Moving left to right, have students say the sounds of each nonsense word. Note any nonsense words they say incorrectly.

Part 2. Finger Stretching Say each word to students. Have them say each word aloud and finger stretch the sounds. Note any words they finger stretch incorrectly.

11. *splash*

12. *scrub*

13. *squid*

14. *strip*

Part 3. Dictation Say each word to students. Have them repeat and write the word.

15. *sprint*   19. *scrap*

16. *squint*   20. *split*

17. *splash*   21. *strap*

18. *stretch*   22. *sprig*

Part 4. Writing Read each sentence to students. Have them repeat and write the sentence.

23. *Pick a sprig.*

24. *He can sprint fast.*

25. *Put the strap on your lap.*

Part 5. Read Aloud Listen to students read the sentences aloud. Count and note the number of words they read correctly.

Part 6. Say Letters Say each sound. Have students say the letter that makes that sound. Note any incorrect responses.

27. /ŏ/

28. /ă/

29. /ĭ/

30. /ĕ/

31. /ŭ/

32. /ŏ/

33. /ĭ/

34. /ĕ/

35. /ŭ/

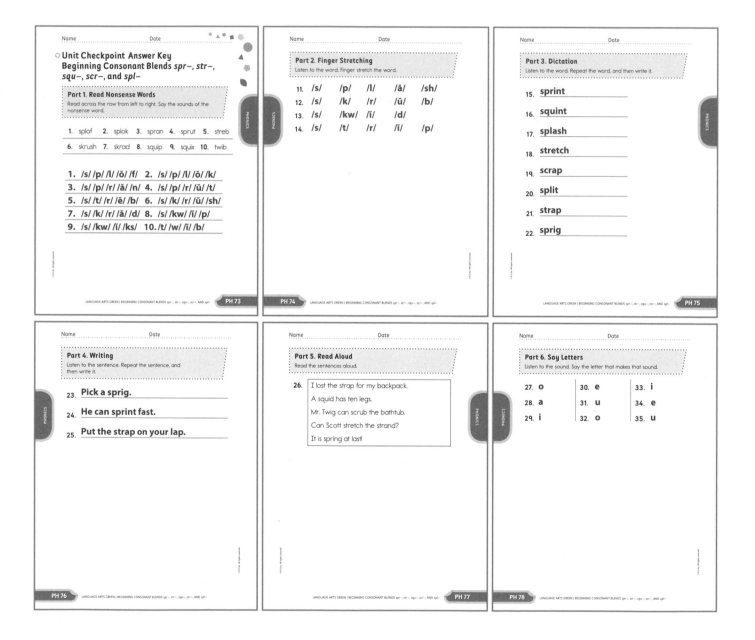

Name _____ Date _____

○ **Unit Checkpoint Answer Key**
Beginning Consonant Blends *spr–*, *str–*,
squ–, *scr–*, and *spl–*

Part 1. Read Nonsense Words
Read across the row from left to right. Say the sounds of the nonsense word.

1. splof 2. splok 3. spran 4. sprut 5. streb

6. skrush 7. skrad 8. squip 9. squix 10. twib

1. /s/ /p/ /l/ /ŏ/ /f/ 2. /s/ /p/ /l/ /ŏ/ /k/
3. /s/ /p/ /r/ /ă/ /n/ 4. /s/ /p/ /r/ /ŭ/ /t/
5. /s/ /t/ /r/ /ĕ/ /b/ 6. /s/ /k/ /r/ /ŭ/ /sh/
7. /s/ /k/ /r/ /ă/ /d/ 8. /s/ /kw/ /ĭ/ /p/
9. /s/ /kw/ /ĭ/ /ks/ 10. /t/ /w/ /ĭ/ /b/

Name _____ Date _____

Part 2. Finger Stretching
Listen to the word. Finger stretch the word.

11. /s/   /p/   /l/   /ă/   /sh/
12. /s/   /k/   /r/   /ŭ/   /b/
13. /s/   /kw/ /ĭ/   /d/
14. /s/   /t/   /r/   /ĭ/   /p/

Name _____ Date _____

Part 3. Dictation
Listen to the word. Repeat the word, and then write it.

15. **sprint** _____
16. **squint** _____
17. **splash** _____
18. **stretch** _____
19. **scrap** _____
20. **split** _____
21. **strap** _____
22. **sprig** _____

Name _____ Date _____

Part 4. Writing
Listen to the sentence. Repeat the sentence, and then write it.

23. **Pick a sprig.** _____
24. **He can sprint fast.** _____
25. **Put the strap on your lap.** _____

Name _____ Date _____

Part 5. Read Aloud
Read the sentences aloud.

26. I lost the strap for my backpack.
    A squid has ten legs.
    Mr. Twig can scrub the bathtub.
    Can Scott stretch the strand?
    It is spring at last!

Name _____ Date _____

Part 6. Say Letters
Listen to the sound. Say the letter that makes that sound.

27. o   30. e   33. i
28. a   31. u   34. e
29. i   32. o   35. u

Words Ending in *–ank*

Unit Overview

In this unit, students will
- ▶ Review sight words.
- ▶ Review letters and sounds of the alphabet.
- ▶ Learn words that end with *–ank*, *–ink*, *–onk*, and *–unk*.
- ▶ Identify individual sounds in words.
- ▶ Blend sounds to build words.

Materials

Supplied
- *K¹² PhonicsWorks Advanced Activity Book,* p. PH 27
- whiteboard, Learning Coach
- whiteboard, student
- Tile Kit

Also Needed
- sight words box
- index cards (4)
- scissors, adult

Lesson Overview

[Offline] FOCUS: Words Ending in *–ank* **30** minutes

Sight Words	Introduce Sight Words
Get Ready	Alphabet Awareness
Learn	Introduce the Oddball Sound /ank/
	Build Words
Try It	Match It
	Make and Read Sentences

[Online] REVIEW: Words Ending in *–ank* **20** minutes

Advance Preparation

Place lowercase letter tiles in alphabetical order on your whiteboard.

For Make and Read Sentences, print each of the following sentences on index cards, using one card per sentence:

- ▶ *Hank went to the bank.*
- ▶ *That plank is not flat.*
- ▶ *Frank went to the pond to fish.*
- ▶ *The tank sank fast.*

 **30 minutes**

FOCUS: Words Ending in *–ank*

Work **together** with students to complete offline Sight Words, Get Ready, Learn, and Try It activities.

Sight Words

Introduce Sight Words

Help students learn the sight words *even*, *look*, and *gone*.

1. Gather the sight word cards *even*, *look*, and *gone*.

2. Show students the *even* card.

3. **Say:** This is the word *even*. We see this word so often that we want to be able to read and spell it quickly without thinking about it. Look closely at the word *even*. Spell the word *even* aloud. Take a picture of the word *even* in your mind. When you think you can spell *even* yourself, turn the card over and use your letter tiles to spell the word *even*. Check the card to see if you spelled the word *even* correctly. Read aloud the word you spelled with the letter tiles.

4. Repeat the activity with the remaining sight words.

5. Chart students' progress on the back of each card.

   ▶ Divide the back of the card into two columns.
   ▶ Label the first column "Read" and the second column "Spell."
   ▶ Record the dates that students read or spell the word correctly. When students can read and spell the word correctly three times in a row, they have mastered the word. You may want to put a star or sticker on their card when they have mastered that word.

6. Add the cards to students' sight words box.

TIP Sight words can be very difficult for some students. It's important to let them work at their own pace and really master these words, as they occur frequently in reading and writing.

Objectives
- Read sight words.
- Spell sight words.

Get Ready

Alphabet Awareness

To help students master the letters of the alphabet, have them practice identifying and naming letters. Grab your whiteboard with letters placed in alphabetical order.

1. Place the the following letter tile on students' whiteboard: *g*, plus any letters that are confusing.

2. Draw a short horizontal line before and after the letter *g*.

3. Have students write the letters that come before and after the letter *g* on their whiteboard.

4. Redirect students if they write an incorrect letter.

   Say: That's the letter [letter students wrote]. Check my whiteboard to see if the letter [letter students wrote] comes right before [or after] the letter *g*. Point to the letters on my whiteboard and say their names.

5. Allow students to correct themselves when they read the letter names aloud. If they do not correct themselves, have them stop and review the letter when they get to it on their whiteboard.

6. For each letter on your whiteboard, have students

   ▸ Say the name of the letter.
   ▸ Say the sound the letter makes.
   ▸ Say the name of something that begins with that sound.

Objectives
- Identify letters of the alphabet.

Learn

Introduce the Oddball Sound /ank/

Help students recognize and use the oddball sound /ank/.

1. Place the following letter tiles on students' whiteboard: *ank, b, s, t, th,* and *y*.

2. Point to the –*ank* tile.

3. **Say:** When these three letters *ank* appear together, they aren't pronounced the way we expect them to be pronounced. They have an "oddball" sound, so we call the sound /ank/ an **oddball sound**. That's why all the letters are on one tile. When we see the letters *ank* together, we say /ank/.

4. **Say:** I am going to spell the word *bank* on your whiteboard. I will need only two tiles to do this: *b* and *ank*. When I touch and say, I am going to say /b/ ... /ank/.

5. Make the word *bank* and point to it.

6. **Say:** Touch and say this word.

   ▸ How many sounds are in the word? two
   ▸ How many letters are in the word? four

7. Make the word *sank* and point to it.

8. **Say:** Touch and say the sounds in *sank*.

   ▸ How many sounds are in the word? two
   ▸ How many letters are in the word? four

Objectives
- Identify ending sounds in words.
- Blend sounds to create words.
- Identify individual sounds in words.
- Identify and use –*ank*.

9. Provide additional guidance if students have difficulty understanding that the letters *ank* do not make separate sounds. Take the first letter off the word.

   Say: I have taken the first letter off the word. Touch and say the word without the first sound. The letters *ank* blend together to make the sound /ank/. When we finger stretch a word with an oddball sound, we stretch only one finger for the sounds on this tile.

10. Repeat this procedure for the following sounds and words:

   ► /t/ . . . /ank/ *tank*
   ► /y/ . . . /ank/ *yank*
   ► /th/ . . . /ank/ *thank*

Build Words

Help students use letters and sounds to build words.

1. Place the following letters tiles at the top of students' whiteboard: *ank, b, c, d, l, p,* and *r.*

2. Draw three horizontal lines across the middle of students' whiteboard to represent the sounds in a word.

3. **Say:** Let's use letters and sounds to build the word *blank.*

4. Have students finger stretch the sounds in *blank.*

5. Have students

   ► Identify the first, next, and last sounds in *blank.*
   ► Choose the corresponding letter tile for each of the sounds.
   ► Move the letter tiles to the correct lines on their whiteboard.

6. Guide students with these questions:

   ► What is the first sound in *blank*? /b/
     Which line does the letter for that sound go on? the first one
   ► What is the next sound in *blank*? /l/
     Which line does the letter for that sound go on? the second one
   ► What's the last sound in *blank*? /ank/
     Which line do the letters for that sound go on? the last one

7. Have students touch and say the word.

8. Redirect students if they select the incorrect letter tile:

   Say: That sound is in the word [word], and it is the [first, second, third] sound. We want the sound [target sound].

   Continue until students select the correct letter tile.

9. Repeat the activity to build the following words:

   ► *crank* /k/ /r/ /ank/
   ► *drank* /d/ /r/ /ank/
   ► *prank* /p/ /r/ /ank/

Try It ....

Match It

Have students complete page PH 27 in *K¹² PhonicsWorks Advanced Activity Book* for more practice with words that end with the oddball sound /ank/. Have students read each word aloud and draw a line to match the words that begin with the same letter.

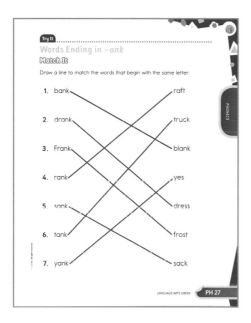

Make and Read Sentences

Have students practice reading and rearranging words to form complete sentences.

1. Gather the index cards you prepared and have students read them.

2. Cut each sentence into words, and put all the words on the table.

   Say: Here are the words that make up the sentences you just read. Touch and say each word that I point to.

3. Point to the words in a sentence, but not in the correct order to form the sentence.

   Say: Put the words in order to make a sentence. Remember that every sentence has a capital letter at the beginning and a period at the end. Read the sentence to me.

   Students should be able to recognize if the sentence does not make sense.

4. Remind students that the beginning of a sentence must be a capital letter and the ending must have a period. They can use these as clues to decide where to place words.

5. Have students read the sentence again. Touch and say any words that are difficult for them.

6. Scramble the words of the sentence again.

7. Continue this procedure, trying and discarding words, until they have formed a new sentence. When students have constructed another sentence, have them read the sentence to you.

TIP To get students started with this exercise, you may begin with two shorter sentences.

 **20 minutes**

REVIEW: Words Ending in –*ank*

Students will work online independently to

▸ Practice words that end with –*ank*.

▸ Practice decoding text by reading a story.

Help students locate the online activities and provide support as needed.

Offline Alternative

No computer access? Have students name things or words that end with –*ank* (for example, *tank* or *bank*). You might also have students spell words that end with –*ank*.

Objectives

- Identify and use –*ank*.
- Identify ending sounds in words.
- Read aloud grade-level text with appropriate automaticity, prosody, accuracy, and rate.
- Decode words by applying grade-level word analysis skills.

Words Ending in –*ink*

Lesson Overview

Offline FOCUS: Words Ending in –*ink*   30 minutes

Sight Words	Sight Word Fun
Get Ready	Review Sounds and Letters
Learn	Introduce the Oddball Sound /ink/
	Build Words
	Make More Words
Try It	"Ted and Frank"
	Dictation: Write Sentences

Online REVIEW: Words Ending in –*ink*   20 minutes

Materials

Supplied
- *K¹² PhonicsWorks Readers Advanced 4*, pp. 19–24
- whiteboard, Learning Coach
- whiteboard, student
- Tile Kit

Also Needed
- sight words box
- dictation notebook

【 Offline 】 30 minutes

FOCUS: Words Ending in *–ink*

Work **together** with students to complete offline Sight Words, Get Ready, Learn, and Try It activities.

Sight Words

Sight Word Fun

Help students learn the sight words *even*, *look*, and *gone*, and up to two additional sight words they have yet to master.

1. Gather the sight word cards *even*, *look*, and *gone*, and up to two additional sight word cards.

2. Choose one sight word card to begin.

   Say: Look at this word and take a picture of it in your mind. When you think you can spell the word yourself, turn the card over and use your letter tiles to spell the word.

3. After students spell the word, have them check the card to see if they spelled the word correctly.

   Say: Read aloud the word you spelled with the letter tiles.

4. Repeat the activity with the remaining sight words.

TIP Sight words can be very difficult for some students. Let them work at their own pace and really master these words.

Objectives
- Read sight words.
- Spell sight words.

Get Ready

Review Sounds and Letters

Help students review sounds for the letters *all*, *e*, *ff*, *g*, *i*, *n*, *o*, *p*, *t*, and *u*, plus any letters that are confusing for them.

1. Place the following letter tiles in random order on students' whiteboard: *all*, *e*, *ff*, *g* , *i*, *n*, *o*, *p*, and *t*, plus any additional letters that are confusing.

2. **Say:** Let's go over some letters and sounds.

Objectives
- Given the letter, identify the most common sound.
- Given the sound, identify the most common letter or letters.

3. Point to each letter tile and have students say a sound that letter or letters make.

- ▸ *o* /ŏ/ or /ō/
- ▸ *u* /ŭ/ or /ū/
- ▸ *ff* /f/
- ▸ *e* /ĕ/ or /ē/
- ▸ *p* /p/

- ▸ *all* /all/
- ▸ *i* /ĭ/ or /ī/
- ▸ *n* /n/
- ▸ *t* /t/
- ▸ *g* /g/

4. Say each of the following sounds. Have students repeat the sound and touch the corresponding letter tile.

- ▸ /ŏ/ *o*
- ▸ /ŭ/ *u*
- ▸ /f/ *ff*
- ▸ /ĕ/ *e*
- ▸ /p/ *p*

- ▸ /all/ *all*
- ▸ /ĭ/ *i*
- ▸ /n/ *n*
- ▸ /t/ *t*
- ▸ /g/ *g*

5. As you do the activity, point to some letter tiles two or three times so that students don't think they are finished with a sound after they have named it.

6. Redirect students if they say an incorrect sound when you point to a letter tile.

    Say: That's the sound of another letter. What is the sound for this letter?

7. Help students if they touch the wrong letter tile after they repeat a sound.

    Say: That letter tile goes with the sound [sound for touched letter tile]. We're looking for the letter that goes with the sound [target sound].

Learn

Introduce the Oddball Sound /ink/
Help students recognize and use the oddball sound /ink/.

1. Place the following letter tiles on students' whiteboard: *ank, ink, p, s, th,* , and *w*.

2. Point to the *–ink* tile.

3. **Say:** When these three letters *ink* appear together, they aren't pronounced the way we expect them to be pronounced. They have an "oddball" sound, so we call the sound /ink/ an **oddball sound**. That's why all the letters are on one tile. When we see the letters *ink* together, we say /ink/.

4. **Say:** I am going to spell the word *sink* on your whiteboard. I will need only two tiles to do this: *s* and *ink*. When I touch and say, I am going to say /s/ . . . /ink/.

5. Make the word *sink* and point to it.

6. **Say:** Touch and say this word.

    - ▸ How many sounds are in the word? two
    - ▸ How many letters are in the word? four

7. Make the word *wink* and point to it.

8. **Say:** Touch and say the sounds in *wink*.

    - ▸ How many sounds are in the word? two
    - ▸ How many letters are in the word? four

Objectives
- Identify ending sounds in words.
- Identify and use *–ink*.
- Blend sounds to create words.
- Identify individual sounds in words.
- Identify the new word when one sound is changed in a word.

9. Provide additional guidance if students have difficulty understanding that the letters *ink* do not make separate sounds. Take the first letter off the word.

   Say: I have taken the first letter off the word. Touch and say the word without the first sound. The letters *ink* blend together to make the sound /ink/. When we finger stretch a word with an oddball sound, we stretch only one finger for the sounds on this tile.

10. Repeat this procedure for the following sounds and words:

    ▸ /p/ . . . /ink/ *pink*
    ▸ /th/ . . . /ink/ *think*
    ▸ /th/ . . . /ank/ *thank*
    ▸ /s/ . . . /ank/ *sank*

Build Words

Help students use letters and sounds to build words.

1. Place the following letter tiles at the top of students' whiteboard: *b, d, ink, l, r,* and *sh.*

2. Draw three horizontal lines across the middle of students' whiteboard to represent the sounds in a word.

3. **Say:** Let's use letters and sounds to build the word *drink.*

4. Have students finger stretch the sounds in *drink.*

5. Have students

   ▸ Identify the first, next, and last sounds in *drink.*
   ▸ Choose the corresponding letter tile for each of the sounds.
   ▸ Move the letters to the correct lines on their whiteboard.

6. Guide students with these questions:

   ▸ What is the first sound in *drink*? /d/
     Which line does the letter for that sound go on? the first one
   ▸ What is the next sound in *drink*? /r/
     Which line does the letter for that sound go on? the second one
   ▸ What's the last sound in *drink*? /ink/
     Which line do the letters for that sound go on? the last one

7. Have students touch and say the word.

8. Redirect students if they select the incorrect letter tile:

    Say: That sound is in the word [word], and it is the [first, second, third] sound. We want the sound [target sound].

    Continue until students select the correct letter tile.

9. Repeat the activity to build the following words:

    ► *blink* /b/ /l/ /ink/
    ► *shrink* /sh/ /r/ /ink/

Make More Words

Have students make new words by adding and removing letters.

1. Place the letter tile *ink* at the top of students' whiteboard.

2. Place the following letter tiles randomly on the bottom of students' whiteboard: *b, l, m, p, r, s, sh, th,* and *w.*

3. **Say:** When I put the letter *m* before the letters *–ink,* I make the word *mink.* See how many new **real words** you can make by putting the letters on your whiteboard before the letters *–ink.* Answers will vary.

4. Continue this activity with the following combinations: *ank, b, f, th, r, s, t, l,* and *sh.*

5. Have students write each word in the dictation notebook. Answers will vary.

6. When students finish making words, have them read each word aloud.

Try It

"Ted and Frank"

Have students read "Ted and Frank" on page 19 of *K¹² PhonicsWorks Readers Advanced 4.*

Students should read the story silently once or twice before reading the story aloud. When students miss a word that can be sounded out, point to it and give them three to six seconds to try the word again. If students still miss the word, tell them the word so the flow of the story isn't interrupted.

After reading the story, make a list of all the words students missed, and go over those words with them. You may use tiles to show the student how to read the words.

Objectives
- Read aloud grade-level text with appropriate automaticity, prosody, accuracy, and rate.
- Decode words by applying grade-level word analysis skills.
- Read, write, and spell words containing the letters *ink.*
- Write words by applying grade-level phonics knowledge.
- Write sight words.
- Follow three-step directions.

Dictation: Write Sentences

Use sentences to help students identify individual sounds in words.

1. Gather a pencil and the dictation notebook. Say the sentence, *Frank drank the drink.* Then give these directions to students:

    ▸ Repeat the sentence.
    ▸ Write the sentence in your notebook.
    ▸ Read the sentence aloud.

2. When students have finished, write the following sentence on your whiteboard: *Frank drank the drink.*

3. Have them compare their answer to your correct version.

4. Repeat this procedure with the sentence, *What will Hank think?*

    ▸ If students make an error and don't see it, help them correct their mistake by having them finger stretch the sounds in the word they missed.
    ▸ If students are having difficulty selecting the correct letters or sounds, review those letters or sounds that are confusing them.
    ▸ If students have difficulty with first, middle, and last sounds, have them finger stretch the sounds in words.

 **20 minutes**

REVIEW: Words Ending in *–ink*

Students will work online independently to

▸ Practice words that end with *–ink.*

Help students locate the online activities and provide support as needed.

⭐ **Objectives**

- Identify and use *–ink.*
- Identify ending sounds in words.

Offline Alternative

No computer access? Have students name things or words that end with the letters *–ink* (for example, *drink* or *mink*). You might also have students spell words that end with *–ink.*

Words Ending in *–onk* and *–unk*

Lesson Overview

[Offline] **FOCUS:** Words Ending in *–onk* and *–unk*   **30** minutes

Sight Words	Sight Word Fun
Get Ready	Pairs of Ending Sounds
Learn	Introduce the Oddball Sound /onk/
	Introduce the Oddball Sound /unk/
	Build Words
Try It	To the Rescue

[Online] **REVIEW:** Words Ending in *–onk* and *unk*   **20** minutes

Materials

Supplied
- *K¹² PhonicsWorks Advanced Activity Book,* p. PH 28
- whiteboard, student
- Tile Kit

Also Needed
- sight words box
- crayons

[Offline] 30 minutes

FOCUS: Words Ending in *–onk* and *–unk*

Work **together** with students to complete offline Sight Words, Get Ready, Learn, and Try It activities.

Sight Words

Sight Word Fun

Help students learn the sight words *even*, *look*, and *gone*, and up to two additional sight words they have yet to master.

1. Gather the sight word cards *even*, *look*, and *gone*, and up to two additional sight word cards.

2. Choose one sight word card to begin.

   Say: Look at this word and take a picture of it in your mind. When you think you can spell the word yourself, turn the card over and use your letter tiles to spell the word.

3. After students spell the word, have them check the card to see if they spelled the word correctly.

   Say: Read aloud the word you spelled with the letter tiles.

4. Repeat the activity with the remaining sight words.

(TIP) Sight words can be very difficult for some students. Let them work at their own pace and really master these words.

> **Objectives**
> - Read sight words.
> - Spell sight words.

Get Ready

Pairs of Ending Sounds

Help students recognize the difference between words that end with one sound or two sounds.

1. **Say:** Digraphs are two letters that make one sound. A blend is two letters, each of which keeps its own sound.

2. **Say:** I am going to say a pair of words. Repeat the pair of words I say and listen for the ending sounds. One word will end with a single sound and the other will end with two sounds. When you hear a word with one ending sound, clap once. When you hear a word with two sounds at the end, clap twice. For example,

   ▸ I will say *wash* and *hand*.
   ▸ You will repeat the word *wash* and clap once, since the word *wash* has one ending sound, /sh/.
   ▸ Then you will repeat the word *hand* and clap twice, since the word *hand* has two ending sounds, /n/ and /d/.

> **Objectives**
> - Identify individual sounds in words.
> - Identify the number of sounds within words.
> - Identify ending sounds in words.

3. **Say:** Now it's your turn. The first pair of words is *much* and *raft*. Students should repeat the words *much* and *raft*, clapping once for *much* and twice for *raft*.

4. Repeat Step 3 with these pairs of words. (Pronounce the words very clearly, making sure you pronounce both sounds in the consonant blend words and students are watching your mouth as you do so).

   ▸ *fact* and *push* clap once: *push*, clap twice: *fact*
   ▸ *help* and *both* clap once: *both*, clap twice: *help*
   ▸ *just* and *dash* clap once: *dash*, clap twice: *just*

TIP If students have difficulty with first, middle, and last sounds, have them finger stretch the sounds in the word.

Learn

Introduce the Oddball Sound /onk/
Help students recognize and use the oddball sound /onk/.

1. Place the following letter tiles on students' whiteboard: *b, h, onk,,* and *t*.

2. Point to the *onk* tile.

3. **Say:** When these three letters *onk* appear together, they aren't pronounced the way we expect them to be pronounced. They have an "oddball" sound, so we call the sound /onk/ an **oddball sound**. That's why all the letters are on one tile. When we see the letters *onk* together, we say /onk/.

4. **Say:** I am going to spell the word *honk* on your whiteboard. I will need only two tiles to do this: *h* and *onk*. When I touch and say, I am going to say /h/ . . . /onk/.

5. Make the word *honk* and point to it.

6. **Say:** Touch and say this word.

   ▸ How many sounds are in the word? two
   ▸ How many letters are in the word? four

7. Make the word *tonk* and point to it.

8. **Say:** Touch and say the sounds in *tonk*.

   ▸ How many sounds are in the word? two
   ▸ How many letters are in the word? four

9. Provide additional guidance if students have difficulty understanding that the letters *onk* do not make separate sounds. Take the first letter off the word.

   Say: I have taken the first letter off the word. Touch and say the word without the first sound. The letters *onk* blend together to make the sound /onk/. When we finger stretch a word with an oddball sound, we stretch only one finger for the sounds on this tile.

10. Repeat this procedure for the following sounds and word: /b/ . . . /onk/ *bonk*.

Objectives
- Identify and use –*onk*.
- Read, write, and spell words containing the letters *onk*.
- Identify and use –*unk*.
- Read, write, and spell words containing the letters *unk*.
- Identify ending sounds in words.
- Blend sounds to create words.
- Identify individual sounds in words.

Introduce the Oddball Sound /unk/

Help students recognize and use the ending sound /unk/.

1. Place the following letter tiles on students' whiteboard: *b, ch, f, h, j, k, l, s,* and *unk*.

2. Make the word *junk* and point to it.

3. **Say:** Touch and say this word. Say and write the word.

   ▸ How many sounds are in the word? two
   ▸ How many letters are in the word? four
   ▸ What is the oddball sound in the word? /unk/

4. Make the word *sunk* and point to it.

5. **Say:** Touch and say the sounds in *sunk*.

   ▸ How many sounds are in the word? two
   ▸ How many letters are in the word? four
   ▸ What is the oddball sound in the word? /unk/

6. Provide additional guidance if students have difficulty understanding that the letters *unk* do not make separate sounds. Take the first letter off the word.

   Say: I have taken the first letter off the word. Touch and say the word without the first sound. The letters *unk* blend together to make the sound /unk/. When we finger stretch a word with an oddball sound, we stretch only one finger for the sounds on this tile.

7. Repeat this pattern with the following sounds and words:

   ▸ /b/ ... /unk/ *bunk,* /unk/
   ▸ /h/ ... /unk/ *hunk,* /unk/
   ▸ /ch/ ... /unk/ *chunk,* /unk/
   ▸ /fl/ ... /unk/ *flunk,* /unk/
   ▸ /sk/ ... /unk/ *skunk,* /unk/

Build Words

Help students use letters and sounds to build words.

1. Place the following letter tiles at the top of students' whiteboard: *k, l, p, r, s, t,* and *unk*.

2. Draw three horizontal lines across the middle of students' whiteboard to represent the sounds in a word.

3. **Say:** Let's use letters and sounds to build the word *skunk*.

4. Have students finger stretch the sounds in *skunk*.

5. Have students

   ▸ Identify the first, next, and last sounds in *skunk*.
   ▸ Choose the corresponding letter for each of the sounds.
   ▸ Move the letters to the correct lines on their whiteboard.

6. Guide students with these questions:

   ▸ What is the first sound in *skunk*? /s/
     Which line does the letter for that sound go on? the first one
   ▸ What is the next sound in *skunk*? /k/
     Which line does the letter for that sound go on? the second one
   ▸ What's the last sound in *skunk*? /unk/
     Which line do the letters for that sound go on? the last one

7. Have students touch and say the word.

8. Redirect students if they select the incorrect letter tile.

   Say: That sound is in the word [word], and it is the [first, second, third] sound.
   We want the sound [target sound].

   Continue until students select the correct letter tile.

9. Repeat the activity to build the following words:

   ▸ *plunk* /p/ /l/ /unk/
   ▸ *trunk* /t/ /r/ /unk/

Try It ●

To the Rescue

Have students complete page PH 28 in *K¹² PhonicsWorks Advanced Activity Book* for
more practice with words that end with *–ink*, *–onk*, and *–unk*. Have them read each
word aloud and color the real words to find the path to the log.

> **Try It** ....
> ## Words Ending in *–onk* and *–unk*
> ### To the Rescue
> Help the rabbit find the path to the log.
> Color the boxes that name real words.
>
> | honk | nink | lonk |
> | junk | pink | sunk |
> | kull | dup | junk |
> | epp | drink | stink |
> | kimp | dunk | thag |
> | tilk | ink | zank |
>
> PH 28   LANGUAGE ARTS GREEN

★ **Objectives**
- Read aloud grade-level text with appropriate automaticity, prosody, accuracy, and rate.
- Read, write, and spell words containing the letters *unk*.
- Identify and use *–unk*.
- Read, write, and spell words containing the letters *onk*.
- Identify and use *–onk*.
- Identify ending sounds in words.

 **20 minutes**

REVIEW: Words Ending in *–onk* and *–unk*

Students will work online independently to

▶ Practice words that end with *–onk* and *–unk*.

▶ Practice decoding text by reading a story.

Help students locate the online activities and provide support as needed.

Offline Alternative

No computer access? Have students name things or words that end with the sound *–onk* or *–unk* (for example, *honk* or *skunk*). You might also have students spell words that end with *–onk* and *–unk*.

Practice Words Ending in –*ank*, –*ink*, –*onk*, and –*unk*

Lesson Overview

[Offline] **FOCUS:** Practice Words Ending in –*ank*, –*ink*, –*onk*, and –*unk* **30** minutes

Sight Words	Sight Word Fun
Get Ready	Guess the Word
	Practice the Oddball Sounds
	Word Chains
Try It	"Bonk the Skunk"

[Online] **REVIEW:** Words Ending in –*ank*, –*ink*, –*onk*, and –*unk* **20** minutes

[Materials]

Supplied
- *K¹² PhonicsWorks Readers Advanced 4*, pp. 25–30
- whiteboard, Learning Coach
- whiteboard, student
- Tile Kit

Also Needed
- sight words box

[Offline] 30 minutes

FOCUS: Practice Words Ending in *–ank*, *–ink*, *–onk*, and *–unk*

Work **together** with students to complete offline Sight Words, Get Ready, and Try It activities.

Sight Words

Sight Word Fun

Help students learn the sight words *even*, *look*, and *gone*, and up to two additional sight words they have has yet to master.

1. Gather the sight word cards *even*, *look*, and *gone*, and up to two additional sight word cards.

2. Choose one sight word card to begin.

   Say: Look at this word and take a picture of it in your mind. When you think you can spell the word yourself, turn the card over and use your letter tiles to spell the word.

3. After students spell the word, have them check the card to see if they spelled the word correctly.

   Say: Read aloud the word you spelled with the letter tiles.

4. Repeat the activity with the remaining sight words.

TIP Sight words can be very difficult for some students. Let students work at their own pace and really master these words.

Objectives
- Read sight words.
- Spell sight words.

Get Ready

Guess the Word

Have students use word meaning and sentence structure to choose a word that best completes a sentence.

1. Write the following words on students' whiteboard: *blink*, *honk*, *sank*, *skunk*, *drank*, and *thank*. Make sure students know the meaning of all the words on their whiteboard before you do this activity.

2. Have students underline the oddball sounds *–ank*, *–ink*, *–onk*, and *–unk* at the end of each word.

Objectives
- Read aloud grade-level text with appropriate automaticity, prosody, accuracy, and rate.
- Identify and use *–ank*.
- Identify and use *–ink*.
- Identify and use *–onk*.
- Identify and use *–unk*.
- Identify the new word when one sound is changed in a word.

3. **Say:** We're going to play a guessing game. I'm going to read a sentence with a word missing. Your job is to look at the words on your whiteboard and decide which one is the right word to complete the sentence.

   ▸ Listen to this sentence: "If you know the answer, _____ your eyes."
   ▸ Next you will tell me what word makes sense in the blank of the sentence. This time the word would be *blink*.
   ▸ The complete sentence would be, "If you know the answer, *blink* your eyes." Now you try it.

4. Continue the procedure with the following sentences:

   ▸ *I _____ my milk at lunch. drank*
   ▸ *As the geese flew away you could hear them _____ . honk*
   ▸ *The _____ is an animal that can smell very bad. skunk*
   ▸ *The boat _____ to the bottom of the lake. sank*
   ▸ *It is good manners to say _____ you when someone gives you a gift. thank*

Practice the Oddball Sounds

Help students recognize and use words with the oddball endings *–ank*, *–ink*, *–onk*, and *–unk*.

1. Place the following letter tiles at the top of students' whiteboard: *ank*, *ink*, *onk*, and *unk*.

2. Place the following letter tiles at the bottom of students' whiteboard: *b, b, ch, h, r, s, th,* and *w*.

3. **Say:** I'm going to say some words. Repeat each word, and then find the letters on the whiteboard that make its ending sound. Then find the beginning letters on the whiteboard and spell the word.

4. **Say:** Let's practice. The first word is *bank*.

   ▸ Repeat the word *bank*.
   ▸ Point to the tile with the oddball sound in that word. *ank*
   ▸ Point to the letter that goes in front of the oddball sound in that word. *b*
   ▸ Use the tiles to spell the word. *bank*
   ▸ Touch and say the word.

5. Repeat the procedure with the following words:

   ▸ *think*
   ▸ *honk*
   ▸ *chunk*
   ▸ *rank*
   ▸ *sunk*
   ▸ *sink*
   ▸ *thank*

TIP Make sure students say the name of the letter at the same time they touch the letter tiles.

Word Chains

Have students build words by adding and changing letters to help them recognize and use individual sounds in words.

1. Place the following letters on students' whiteboard: *a, d, h, i, j, k, n, o, r, s,* and *u.*

2. **Say:** I am going to build the first word in a chain. The word is *drink.*

   ▸ I will pull down the letters for the sounds /d/, /r/, and /ink/ to spell the word *drink.*

   ▸ Next I will touch and say *drink.* To change *drink* to *drank,* I will think about what sound is changed from the word *drink* to *drank.* We will need to change the letter *i* in the middle of the word *drink* to the letter *a.*

   ▸ Touch and say the word *drank.* Let's make another word. Change *drank* to *sank.* You can spell *sank* by making only one change. Touch and say the new word.

3. Redirect students if they select the incorrect letter for any sound.

   Say: That letter is for the sound [incorrect sound]. We want the letter for the sound [target sound]. What letter makes that sound? Answers will vary.

4. Redirect students if they name the sound incorrectly.

   Say: To change the word [first word] to [target word], we need the letter for the sound [target sound].

   Show students how to make the change. Have them touch and say the new word after they move the letters.

5. Follow this procedure to make the following words: *sink, sunk, junk, hunk, honk.*

6. For every new word, have students add, replace, or remove only one letter.

"Bonk the Skunk"

Have students read "Bonk the Skunk" on page 25 of *K¹² PhonicsWorks Readers Advanced 4.*

   Students should read the story silently once or twice before reading the story aloud. When students miss a word that can be sounded out, point to it and give them three to six seconds to try the word again. If students still miss the word, tell them the word so the flow of the story isn't interrupted.

   After reading the story, make a list of all the words students missed, and go over those words with them. You may use tiles to show students how to read the words.

Objectives

- Read aloud grade-level text with appropriate automaticity, prosody, accuracy, and rate.
- Decode words by applying grade-level word analysis skills.

 **20 minutes**

REVIEW: Words Ending in *–ank, –ink, –onk,* and *–unk*

Students will work online independently to

▸ Practice words that end with *–ank, –ink, –onk,* and *–unk.*

Help students locate the online activities and provide support as needed.

Objectives

- Identify and use *–ank.*
- Identify and use *–ink.*
- Identify and use *–onk.*
- Identify and use *–unk.*
- Identify ending sounds in words.

Offline Alternative

No computer access? Have students name things or words that end with the sounds *–ank, –ink, –onk,* and *–unk* (for example, *bank, rink, bonk,* or *skunk*). You might also have students spell words that end with *–ank, –ink, –onk,* and *–unk.*

Unit Checkpoint

Lesson Overview

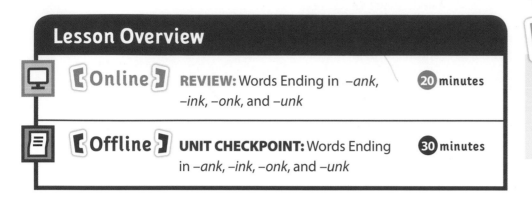

🖥	**Online** REVIEW: Words Ending in –*ank*, –*ink*, –*onk*, and –*unk*	**20** minutes
📄	**Offline** UNIT CHECKPOINT: Words Ending in –*ank*, –*ink*, –*onk*, and –*unk*	**30** minutes

Materials

Supplied

- *K¹² PhonicsWorks Advanced Assessments,* pp. PH 79–83

Objectives

- Identify and use –*ank*.
- Read, write, and spell words containing the letters *ank*.
- Identify and use –*ink*.
- Read, write, and spell words containing the letters *ink*.
- Identify and use –*onk*.
- Read, write, and spell words containing the letters *onk*.
- Identify and use –*unk*.
- Read, write, and spell words containing the letters *unk*.
- Identify ending sounds in words.
- Given the letter, identify the most common sound.
- Given the sound, identify the most common letter or letters.
- Read instructional-level text with 90% accuracy.
- Read aloud grade-level text with appropriate automaticity, prosody, accuracy, and rate.
- Read sight words.
- Write sight words.
- Write words by applying grade-level phonics knowledge.

Online **20** minutes

REVIEW: **Words Ending in –*ank*, –*ink*, –*onk*, and –*unk***

Students will review the ending sounds –*ank*, –*ink*, –*onk*, and –*unk* to prepare for the Unit Checkpoint. Help students locate the online activities and provide support as needed.

⟦ Offline ⟧ 🕙 minutes

UNIT CHECKPOINT: Words Ending in *–ank*, *–ink*, *–onk*, and *–unk*

Explain that students are going to show what they have learned about sounds, letters, and words.

1. Give students the Unit Checkpoint pages for the Words Ending in *–ank*, *–ink*, *–onk*, and *–unk* unit and print the Unit Checkpoint Answer Key, if you'd like.

2. Use the instructions below to help administer the Checkpoint to students. On the Answer Key or another sheet of paper, note student answers to oral response questions to help with scoring the Checkpoint later.

3. Use the Answer Key to score the Checkpoint, and then enter the results online.

Part 1. Read Word Parts and Nonsense Words Moving left to right, have students read the sound or sounds of each word part or nonsense word. Note any word parts or nonsense words they say incorrectly.

Part 2. Finger Stretching Say each word to students. Have them say each word aloud and finger stretch the sounds. Note any words they finger stretch incorrectly.

11. *bank*	15. *pink*
12. *ink*	16. *blink*
13. *bonk*	17. *sunk*
14. *junk*	18. *thank*

Part 3. Dictation Say each word to students. Have them repeat and write the word.

19. *sank*	23. *think*
20. *tank*	24. *blank*
21. *honk*	25. *rink*
22. *skunk*	26. *chunk*

Part 4. Writing Read each sentence to students. Have them repeat and write the sentence.

27. *He drank his milk.*

28. *She has your trunk.*

29. *The raft sank.*

Part 5. Read Aloud Listen to students read the sentences aloud. Count and note the number of words they read correctly.

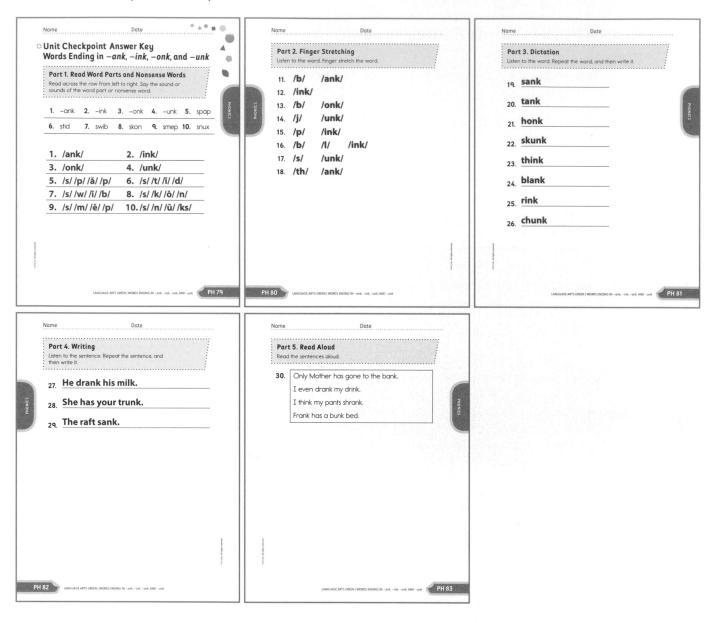

Unit Checkpoint Answer Key
Words Ending in *–ank*, *–ink*, *–onk*, **and** *–unk*

Part 1. Read Word Parts and Nonsense Words
Read across the row from left to right. Say the sound or sounds of the word part or nonsense word.

1. –ank 2. –ink 3. –onk 4. –unk 5. spap
6. stid 7. swib 8. skon 9. smep 10. snux

1. /ank/   2. /ink/
3. /onk/   4. /unk/
5. /s/ /p/ /ă/ /p/   6. /s/ /t/ /ĭ/ /d/
7. /s/ /w/ /ĭ/ /b/   8. /s/ /k/ /ŏ/ /n/
9. /s/ /m/ /ĕ/ /p/   10. /s/ /n/ /ŭ/ /ks/

Part 2. Finger Stretching
Listen to the word. Finger stretch the word.

11. /b/   /ank/
12. /ink/
13. /b/   /onk/
14. /j/   /unk/
15. /p/   /ink/
16. /b/   /l/   /ink/
17. /s/   /unk/
18. /th/   /ank/

Part 3. Dictation
Listen to the word. Repeat the word, and then write it.

19. sank
20. tank
21. honk
22. skunk
23. think
24. blank
25. rink
26. chunk

Part 4. Writing
Listen to the sentence. Repeat the sentence, and then write it.

27. He drank his milk.
28. She has your trunk.
29. The raft sank.

Part 5. Read Aloud
Read the sentences aloud.

30. Only Mother has gone to the bank.
I even drank my drink.
I think my pants shrank.
Frank has a bunk bed.

Words Ending in *–ang*

Unit Overview

In this unit, students will
- ► Review sight words.
- ► Learn words ending in *–ang, –ing, –ong,* and *–ung.*
- ► Practice identifying individual sounds in words.
- ► Build words.

[Materials]

Supplied
- *K¹² PhonicsWorks Advanced Activity Book*, p. PH 29
- whiteboard, student
- Tile Kit

Also Needed
- sight words box
- crayons

Lesson Overview

[Offline] **FOCUS:** Words Ending in *–ang*   **30** minutes

Sight Words	Introduce Sight Words
Get Ready	Finger Stretching
	Review Sounds and Letters
Learn	Introduce the Oddball Sound /ang/
	Build Words
Try It	Go Fish!

[Online] **REVIEW:** Words Ending in *–ang*   **20** minutes

[Offline] ⏱ 30 minutes

FOCUS: Words Ending in –*ang*

Work **together** with students to complete offline Sight Words, Get Ready, Learn, and Try It activities.

Sight Words ●●●

Introduce Sight Words

Help students learn the sight words *love*, *very*, and *some*.

1. Gather the sight word cards *love*, *very*, and *some*.

2. Show students the *love* card.

3. **Say:** This is the word *love*. We see this word so often that we want to be able to read and spell it quickly without thinking about it. Look closely at the word *love*. Spell the word *love* aloud. Take a picture of the word *love* in your mind. When you think you can spell *love* yourself, turn the card over and use your letter tiles to spell the word *love*. Check the card to see if you spelled the word *love* correctly. Read aloud the word you spelled with the letter tiles.

4. Repeat the activity with the remaining sight words.

5. Chart students' progress on the back of each card.

   ▸ Divide the back of the card into two columns.
   ▸ Label the first column "Read" and the second column "Spell."
   ▸ Record the dates that students read or spell the word correctly. When students can read and spell the word correctly three times in a row, they have mastered the word. You may want to put a star or sticker on their card when they have mastered that word.

6. Add the cards to students' sight words box

TIP Sight words can be very difficult for some students. Let students work at their own pace and really master these words, as they occur frequently in reading and writing.

> **Objectives**
> - Read sight words.
> - Spell sight words.

Get Ready ●●

Finger Stretching

Use finger stretching to help students identify individual sounds in words.

1. **Say:** Let's review finger stretching. In the word *rock*, the first sound is /r/, the next sound is /ŏ/, and the last sound is /k/. I will finger stretch each sound as I say it. Then I'll say the word while pulling my fist toward my body.

2. Finger stretch the word *rock* for students.

3. **Say:** I'm going to say words with several sounds in them. You'll say each word and then finger stretch it while you say each sound in the word.

> **Objectives**
> - Identify individual sounds in words.
> - Identify the number of sounds within words.
> - Given the sound, identify the most common letter or letters.
> - Given the letter, identify the most common sound.

4. Say the following words and have students finger stretch them. After they finger stretch each word, ask them the question for that word.

  ▶ *sink* /s/ /ink/   How many sounds are in the word? two
  ▶ *lift* /l/ /ĭ/ /f/ /t/   How many sounds are in the word? four
  ▶ *skunk* /s/ /k/ /unk/   How many sounds are in the word? three
  ▶ *bank* /b/ /ank/   How many sounds are in the word? two
  ▶ *kept* /k/ /ĕ/ /p/ /t/   How many sounds are in the word? four
  ▶ *box* /b/ /ŏ/ /ks/   How many sounds are in the word? three

TIP Refer to the *K¹² PhonicsWorks* DVD for a demonstration of finger stretching.

Review Sounds and Letters

Help students review the sounds for the letters *all, ank, f, ink, m, onk, r,* and *unk,* plus any letters that are confusing for them.

1. Place the following letter tiles in random order on students' whiteboard: *all, ank, f, ink, m, onk, r ,* and *unk,* plus any letters that are confusing.

2. **Say:** Let's go over some letters and sounds.

3. Point to each letter tile and have students say a sound that letter or letters make.

  ▶ *all* /all/   ▶ *f* /f/
  ▶ *m* /m/   ▶ *unk* /unk/
  ▶ *r* /r/   ▶ *onk* /onk/
  ▶ *ink* /ink/   ▶ *ank* /ank/

4. Say each of the following sounds. Have students repeat the sound and touch the corresponding letter tile.

  ▶ /all/ *all*   ▶ /f/ *f*
  ▶ /m/ *m*   ▶ /unk/ *unk*
  ▶ /r/ *r*   ▶ /onk/ *onk*
  ▶ /ink/ *ink*   ▶ /ank/ *ank*

5. As you do the activity, point to some letter tiles two or three times so that students don't think they are finished with a sound after they have named it.

6. Redirect students if they say an incorrect sound when you point to a letter tile.

  Say: That's the sound of another letter. What is the sound for this letter?

7. Help students if they touch the wrong letter tile after they repeat a sound.

  Say: That letter tile goes with the sound [sound for incorrect letter tile]. We're looking for the letter that goes with the sound [target sound].

Learn •

Introduce the Oddball Sound /ang/

Help students recognize and use the oddball sound /ang/.

1. Place the following letter tiles on students' whiteboard: *ang, b, f, h, r,* and *s.*

2. Point to the *ang* tile.

3. **Say:** When these three letters *ang* appear together, they aren't pronounced the way we expect them to be pronounced. They have an "oddball" sound, so we call the sound /ang/ an **oddball sound**. That's why all the letters are on one tile. When we see the letters *ang* together, we say /ang/.

4. **Say:** I am going to spell the word *bang* on your whiteboard. I will need only two tiles to do this: *b* and *ang.* When I touch and say, I am going to say /b/ . . . /ang/.

5. Make the word *bang* and point to it.

6. **Say:** Touch and say this word.

   ▸ How many sounds are in the word? two
   ▸ How many letters are in the word? four

7. Make the word *sang* and point to it.

8. **Say:** Touch and say the sounds in *sang.*

   ▸ How many sounds are in the word? two
   ▸ How many letters are in the word? four

9. Provide additional guidance if students have difficulty understanding that the letters *ang* do not make separate sounds. Take the first letter off the word.

   Say: I have taken the first letter off the word. Touch and say the word without the first sound. The letters *ang* blend together to make the sound /ang/. When we finger stretch a word with an oddball sound, we stretch only one finger for the sounds on this tile.

10. Repeat this procedure for the following sounds and words:

    ▸ /r/ . . . /ang/ *rang*
    ▸ /h/ . . . /ang/ *hang*
    ▸ /f/ . . . /ang/ *fang*

Build Words

Help students use letters and sounds to build words.

1. Place the following letter tiles at the top of students' whiteboard: *ang, ank, c, d, ink, l, r, s,* and *t.*

2. Draw three horizontal lines across the middle of students' whiteboard to represent the sounds in words.

3. **Say:** Let's use letters and sounds to build the word *clang.*

4. Have students finger stretch the sounds in *clang.*

5. Have students
   ▸ Identify the first, next, and last sounds in *clang*.
   ▸ Choose the corresponding letter for each of the sounds.
   ▸ Move the letters to the correct lines on their whiteboard.

6. Guide students with these questions:
   ▸ What is the first sound in *clang*? /k/
     Which line does the letter for that sound go on? the first one
   ▸ What is the next sound in *clang*? /l/
     Which line does the letter for that sound go on? the second one
   ▸ What's the last sound in *clang*? /ang/
     Which line do the letters for that sound go on? the last one

7. Have students touch and say the word.

8. Redirect students if they select the incorrect letter.

   Say: That sound is in the word [word], and it is the [first, second, third] sound. We want the sound [target sound].

   Continue until students select the correct letter.

9. Repeat the activity to build the following words:
   ▸ *slang* /s/ /l/ /ang/
   ▸ *drank* /d/ /r/ /ank/
   ▸ *stink* /s/ /t/ /ink/

Try It

Go Fish!

Have students complete page PH 29 in *K¹² PhonicsWorks Advanced Activity Book* for more practice with words that end with the letters *ang* and *ank*. Have students read each word aloud. Then have them color the fish that have the sound /ang/ yellow and the fish with the sound /ank/ pink.

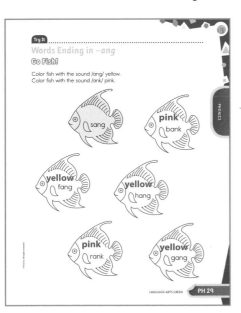

Objectives
- Identify ending sounds in words.
- Identify the sound, given the letters *ang*.
- Identify the letters, given the sound /ang/.

 **20** minutes

REVIEW: Words Ending in *–ang*

Students will work online independently to

- ► Practice words ending in the letters *ang*.
- ► Practice decoding text by reading a story.

Help students locate the online activities and provide support as needed.

Offline Alternative

No computer access? Have students point out and name things or words that end in the letters *ang* (for example, *gang* or *sang*). You might also ask students to spell words that contain the sound /ang/.

Words Ending in –*ing*

Lesson Overview

📋 [Offline] FOCUS: Words Ending in –*ing* — **30** minutes

Sight Words	Sight Word Fun
Get Ready	Search Sentences for Beginning Sounds
	Review Sounds and Letters
Learn	Introduce the Oddball Sound /ing/
	Build Words
Try It	"Quinn Loves the Spring"

🖥 [Online] REVIEW: Words Ending in –*ing* — **20** minutes

[Materials]

Supplied
- *K¹² PhonicsWorks Readers Advanced 5,* pp 1–6
- whiteboard, student
- Tile Kit

Also Needed
- sight words box

 **30 minutes**

FOCUS: Words Ending in –*ing*

Work **together** with students to complete offline Sight Words, Get Ready, Learn, and Try It activities.

Sight Words

Sight Word Fun

Help students learn the sight words *love*, *very*, and *some,* and up to two additional sight words they have yet to master.

1. Gather the sight word cards *love*, *very*, and *some,* and up to two additional sight word cards.

2. Choose one sight word card to begin.

   Say: Look at this word and take a picture of it in your mind. When you think you can spell the word yourself, turn the card over and use your letter tiles to spell the word.

3. After students spell the word, have them check the card to see if they spelled the word correctly.

   Say: Read aloud the word you spelled with the letter tiles.

4. Repeat the activity with the remaining sight words.

   TIP Sight words can be very difficult for some students. Let students work at their own pace and really master these words.

Objectives
- Read sight words.
- Spell sight words.

Get Ready

Search Sentences for Beginning Sounds

To help students learn to recognize the **beginning sound** in a word, have them practice identifying a target sound.

1. **Say:** I'm going to say a beginning sound that is in a word. You will repeat that sound and the word. For example, the beginning sound is /sw/, as in the word *swing*.

2. Have students say the target sound /sw/ and the word *swing*.

3. **Say:** Now I will read a sentence. Repeat the sentence and tell me the word that has the same beginning sound as *swing*. The first sentence is, "Ted and Jen like to swim."

   ▸ What is the special beginning sound? /sw/
   ▸ What is the word that has the special beginning sound? *swim*

Objectives
- Identify beginning sounds in words.
- Identify individual sounds in words.
- Given the sound, identify the most common letter or letters.
- Given the letter, identify the most common sound.

4. Follow the same procedure with the words and sentences below to help students recognize beginning sounds in words.

- ▸ /sp/, as in *spell*   *The top can spin. spin*
- ▸ /sn/, as in *snow*   *The snack I like best is a banana. snack*
- ▸ /fl/, as in *flat*   *Is the flag red or blue? flag*
- ▸ /gl/, as in *glove*   *Ken put the glass in the sink. glass*
- ▸ /dr/, as in *drop*   *Jill's new dress is pink. dress*

(TIP) If students don't name the correct word, repeat the sentence slowly, clearly pronouncing the beginnings of words. Remind them of the special beginning sound. If they have difficulty, say two words from the sentence and ask them to choose the one with the target beginning sound.

Review Sounds and Letters

Help students review sounds for the letters *all, ang, ank, c, ck, ink, k, onk, unk,* and *w,* plus any letters that are confusing for them.

1. Place the following letter tiles in random order on students' whiteboard: *all, ang, ank, c, ck, ink, k, onk, unk,* and *w,* plus any letters that are confusing.

2. **Say:** Let's go over some letters and sounds.

3. Point to each letter tile and have students say a sound that letter or letters make.

- ▸ *ang* /ang/
- ▸ *k* /k/
- ▸ *w* /w/
- ▸ *all* /all/
- ▸ *ink* /ink/
- ▸ *unk* /unk/
- ▸ *ck* /k/
- ▸ *ank* /ank/
- ▸ *c* /k/
- ▸ *onk* /onk/

4. Say each of the following sounds. Have students repeat the sound and touch a corresponding letter tile.

- ▸ /ang/ *ang*
- ▸ /k/ *c, k,* and *ck*
- ▸ /w/ *w*
- ▸ /all/ *all*
- ▸ /ink/ *ink*
- ▸ /unk/ *unk*
- ▸ /ank/ *ank*
- ▸ /onk/ *onk*

5. As you do the activity, point to some letter tiles two or three times so that students don't think they are finished with a sound after they have named it.

6. Redirect students if they say an incorrect sound when you point to a letter tile.

   Say: That's the sound of another letter. What is the sound for this letter?

7. Help students if they touch the wrong letter tile after they repeat a sound.

   Say: That letter goes with the sound [sound for incorrect letter tile]. We're looking for the letter that goes with the sound [target sound].

Learn

Introduce the Oddball Sound /ing/

Help students recognize and use the oddball sound /ing/.

1. Place the following letter tiles on students' whiteboard: *c, ing, k, l, r, s, th,* and *w.*

2. Point to the *ing* tile.

3. **Say:** When the three letters *ing* appear together, they aren't pronounced the way we expect them to be pronounced. They have an "oddball" sound, so we call the sound /ing/ an **oddball sound**. That's why all the letters are on one tile. When we see the letters *ing* together, we say /ing/.

4. **Say:** I am going to spell the word *sing* on your whiteboard. I will need only two tiles to do this: *s* and *ing*. When I touch and say, I am going to say /s/ . . . /ing/.

5. Make the word *sing* and point to it.

6. **Say:** Touch and say this word.

   ▶ How many sounds are in the word? two
   ▶ How many letters are in the word? four

7. Make the word *wing* and point to it.

8. **Say:** Touch and say the sounds in *wing.*

   ▶ How many sounds are in the word? two
   ▶ How many letters are in the word? four

9. Provide additional guidance if students have difficulty understanding that the letters *ing* do not make separate sounds. Explain that these letters blend together to make the sound /ing/.

   Say: You can hear the sound /ing/ in the word *ring*. Finger stretch the sounds with me. There are two sounds: /r/ and /ing/. Now try saying the word again.

10. Repeat this procedure for the following sounds and words:

    ▶ /kl/ . . . /ing/ *cling*
    ▶ /k/ . . . /ing/ *king*
    ▶ /th/ . . . /ing/ *thing*

Build Words

Help students use letters and sounds to build words.

1. Place the following letter tiles at the top of students' whiteboard: *b, ing, ink, l, p, r,* and *s.*

2. Draw three horizontal lines across the middle of students' whiteboard to represent the sounds in a word.

3. **Say:** Let's use letters and sounds to build the word *bring.*

4. Have students finger stretch the sounds in *bring*.

5. Have students

   ▸ Identify the first, next, and last sounds in *bring*.
   ▸ Choose the corresponding letter for each of the sounds.
   ▸ Move the letters to the correct lines on their whiteboard.

6. Guide students with these questions:

   ▸ What is the first sound in *bring*? /b/
     Which line does the letter for that sound go on? the first one
   ▸ What is the next sound in *bring*? /r/
     Which line does the letter for that sound go on? the second one
   ▸ What's the last sound in *bring*? /ing/
     Which line do the letters for that sound go on? the last one

7. Have students touch and say the word.

8. Redirect students if they select the incorrect letter.

   Say: That sound is in the word [word], and it is the [first, second, third] sound. We want the sound [target sound].

   Continue until students select the correct letter.

9. Draw horizontal lines across the middle of students' whiteboard that represent the number of sounds in each word. Repeat the activity to build the following words:

   ▸ *sling* /s/ /l/ /ing/
   ▸ *spring* /s/ /p/ /r/ /ing/
   ▸ *sink* /s/ /ink/

Try It

"Quinn Loves the Spring"
Have students read "Quinn Loves the Spring" on page 1 of *K¹² PhonicsWorks Readers Advanced 5*.

   Students should read the story silently once or twice before reading it aloud. When students miss a word that can be sounded out, point to it and give students three to six seconds to try the word again. If students still miss the word, tell them the word so the flow of the story isn't interrupted.

   After reading the story, make a list of all the words students missed, and go over those words with them. You may use letter tiles to show students how to read the words.

Objectives
- Read aloud grade-level text with appropriate automaticity, prosody, accuracy, and rate.
- Decode words by applying grade-level word analysis skills.

 **20 minutes**

REVIEW: Words Ending in *–ing*

Students will work online independently to

▸ Practice words ending in the letters *ing*.

Help students locate the online activities and provide support as needed.

Offline Alternative

No computer access? Have students point out and name things or words that end in the letters *ing* (for example, *wing* or *swing*). You might also ask students to spell words that contain the sounds /ing/.

⭐ **Objectives**

- Identify the sound, given the letters *ing*.
- Identify the letters, given the sound /ing/.
- Identify ending sounds in words.

Words Ending in *–ong* and *–ung*

Lesson Overview

Offline **FOCUS:** Words Ending in *–ong* and *–ung* **30** minutes

Sight Words	Sight Word Fun
Get Ready	Review Sounds and Letters
	Correct the Sentence
Learn	Introduce the Oddball Sound /ong/
	Introduce the Oddball Sound /ung/
	Build Words
Try It	Best Pick

Online **REVIEW:** Words Ending in *–ong* and *–ung* **20** minutes

Materials

Supplied
- *K¹² PhonicsWorks Advanced Activity Book*, p. PH 30
- whiteboard, student
- Tile Kit

Also Needed
- sight words box
- index cards (4)

Advance Preparation

For Correct the Sentence, print the following sentences on index cards, using one index card for each sentence:

- ► *the king has a ring*
- ► *can you bring it*
- ► *his dad can sing*
- ► *who can hang it*

 **Offline** **30** minutes

FOCUS: Words Ending in *–ong* and *–ung*

Work **together** with students to complete offline Sight Words, Get Ready, Learn, and Try It activities.

Sight Words

Sight Word Fun

Help students learn the sight words *love, very,* and *some,* and up to two additional sight words they have yet to master.

1. Gather the sight word cards *love, very,* and *some,* and up to two additional sight word cards.

2. Choose one sight word card to begin.

   Say: Look at this word and take a picture of it in your mind. When you think you can spell the word yourself, turn the card over and use your letter tiles to spell the word.

3. After students spell the word, have them check the card to see if they spelled the word correctly.

   Say: Read aloud the word you spelled with the letter tiles.

4. Repeat the activity with the remaining sight words.

TIP Sight words can be very difficult for some students. Let students work at their own pace and really master these words.

> **Objectives**
> * Read sight words.
> * Spell sight words.

Get Ready

Review Sounds and Letters

Help students review the sounds for the letters *all, ang, ank, ch, ing, ink, onk, sh, th,* and *unk,* plus any letters that are confusing for them.

1. Place the following letter tiles in random order on students' whiteboard: *all, ang, ank, ch, ing, ink, onk, sh, th,* and *unk,* plus any letters that are confusing.

2. **Say:** Let's go over some letters and sounds.

3. Point to each letter tile and have students say a sound that letter or letters make.

   ▶ *unk* /unk/
   ▶ *all* /all/
   ▶ *sh* /sh/
   ▶ *ank* /ank/
   ▶ *ink* /ink/

   ▶ *ing* /ing/
   ▶ *th* /th/ or /<u>th</u>/
   ▶ *ang* /ang/
   ▶ *ch* /ch/
   ▶ *onk* /onk/

> **Objectives**
> * Given the sound, identify the most common letter or letters.
> * Given the letter, identify the most common sound.
> * Capitalize the first word in a sentence.
> * Use periods to end telling sentences.
> * Use question marks to end asking sentences.

4. Say each of the following sounds. Have students repeat the sound and touch the corresponding letter tile.

- ▸ /unk/ *unk*
- ▸ /all/ *all*
- ▸ /sh/ *sh*
- ▸ /ank/ *ank*
- ▸ /ink/ *ink*

- ▸ /ing/ *ing*
- ▸ /th/ *th*
- ▸ /ang/ *ang*
- ▸ /ch/ *ch*
- ▸ /onk/ *onk*

5. As you do the activity, point to some letter tiles two or three times so that students don't think they are finished with a sound after they have named it.

6. Redirect students if they say an incorrect sound when you point to a letter tile.

   Say: That's the sound of another letter. What is the sound for this letter?

7. Help students if they touch the wrong letter tile after they repeat a sound.

   Say: That letter goes with the sound [sound for incorrect letter tile]. We're looking for the letter that goes with the sound [target sound].

Correct the Sentence

Have students correct sentences.

1. Gather the index cards you prepared.

2. Have students pick an index card and read it aloud.

   Say: What is wrong with this sentence? It is missing a capital letter at the beginning and punctuation at the end.

3. Have students make the corrections on the index card to the sentence.

   Say: Now read the sentence again. How do you know this sentence is correct? It has a capital letter at the beginning and a period or question mark at the end.

4. Have students pick another index card and repeat the procedure until they have capitalized and punctuated all the sentences correctly.

5. Guide students if they do not recognize what is wrong with the sentence. Ask them the following questions:

   - ▸ What is special about the first word in a sentence?
   - ▸ Does the first word in this sentence start with a capital letter?
   - ▸ How can you change the sentence so it begins with a capital letter?
   - ▸ What is special about the mark at the end of a sentence?
   - ▸ Is the last word in this sentence followed by a period or a question mark?
   - ▸ What kind of sentence is it, a telling sentence or an asking sentence?
   - ▸ What mark do you put at the end of a telling (asking) sentence?
   - ▸ How can you change the sentence so it ends with the correct mark?

Learn

Introduce the Oddball Sound /ong/

Help students recognize and use the oddball sound /ong/.

1. Place the following letters tiles on students' whiteboard: *g, ong, l, p, r, s,* and *t.*

2. Point to the *ong* tile.

3. **Say:** When the three letters *ong* appear together, they aren't pronounced the way we expect them to be pronounced. They have an "oddball" sound, so we call the sound /ong/ an **oddball sound**. That's why all the letters are on one tile. When we see the letters *ong* together, we say /ong/.

4. **Say:** I am going to spell the word *long* on your whiteboard. I will need only two tiles to do this: *l* and *ong.* When I touch and say, I am going to say /l/ . . . /ong/.

5. Make the word *long* and point to it.

6. **Say:** Touch and say this word.

   ▸ How many sounds are in the word? two
   ▸ How many letters are in the word? four

7. Make the word *song* and point to it.

8. **Say:** Touch and say the sounds in *song.*

   ▸ How many sounds are in the word? two
   ▸ How many letters are in the word? four

9. Provide additional guidance if students have difficulty understanding that the letters *ong* do not make separate sounds. Explain that these letters blend together to make the sound /ong/.

   Say: You can hear the sound /ong/ in the word *long.* Finger stretch the sounds with me. There are two sounds: /l/ and /ong/. Now try saying the word again.

10. Repeat this procedure for the following sounds and words:
    ▸ /g/ . . . /ong/ *gong*
    ▸ /p/ /r/ . . . /ong/ *prong*
    ▸ /s/ /t/ /r/ . . . /ong/ *strong*

Introduce the Oddball Sound /ung/

Help students recognize and use the oddball sound /ung/.

1. Place the following letter tiles on students' whiteboard: *h, l, r, s,* and *ung.*

2. Make the word *sung* and point to it.

3. **Say:** Touch and say this word.

   ▸ How many sounds are in the word? two
   ▸ How many letters are in the word? four
   ▸ What is the oddball sound in the word? /ung/

4. Make the word *hung* and point to it.

5. **Say:** Touch and say the sounds in *hung*.

   ► How many sounds are in the word? two
   ► How many letters are in the word? four
   ► What is the oddball sound in the word? /ung/

6. Repeat this procedure for the following sounds and words:

   ► /l/ . . . /ung/ *lung*
   ► /r/ . . . /ung/ *rung*

Build Words

Help students use letters and sounds to build words.

1. Place the following letter tiles at the top of students' whiteboard: *ang, c, b, f, ing, l, ung, p, r, s, t,* and *ung*.

2. Draw three horizontal lines across the middle of students' whiteboard to represent the sounds in a word.

3. **Say:** Let's use letters and sounds to build the word *flung*.

4. Have students finger stretch the sounds in *flung*.

5. Have students

   ► Identify the first, next, and last sounds in *flung*.
   ► Choose the corresponding letter for each of the sounds.
   ► Move the letters to the correct lines on their whiteboard.

6. Guide students with these questions:

   ► What is the first sound in *flung*? /f/
     Which line does the letter for that sound go on? the first one
   ► What is the next sound in *flung*? /l/
     Which line does the letter for that sound go on? the second one
   ► What is the last sound in *flung*? /ung/
     Which line do the letters for that sound go on? the last one

7. Have students touch and say the word.

8. Redirect students if they select the incorrect letter.

   Say: That sound is in the word [word], and it is the [first, second, third] sound. We want the sound [target sound].

   Continue until students select the correct letter.

9. Repeat the activity to build the following words:

   ▸ *stung* /s/ /t/ /ung/
   ▸ *prong* /p/ /r/ /ong/
   ▸ *clang* /k/ /l/ /ang/
   ▸ *bring* /b/ /r/ /ing/

Try It

Best Pick

Have students complete page PH 30 in *K¹² PhonicsWorks Advanced Activity Book* for more practice with words ending in the letters *ong* and *ung*. Have students read the sentence aloud and circle the word that best completes it. Then have students write the word and read the completed sentence aloud to determine if it makes sense.

Try It
Words Ending in – *ong* and – *ung*
Best Pick

Read the sentence aloud and circle the word that best completes it. Then write the word.

1. She loves to sing a ___**song**___ .   sung (song)
2. An inch is not so ___**long**___ .   (long) lung
3. She ___**hung**___ up the wet cloth.   hang (hung)
4. Will the bell ___**ring**___ ?   thing (ring)

PH 30   LANGUAGE ARTS GREEN

Objectives

- Identify the sound, given the letters *ong*.
- Identify the letters, given the sound /ong/.
- Identify the sound, given the letters *ung*.
- Identify the letters, given the sound /ung/.
- Identify ending sounds in words.
- Read aloud grade-level text with appropriate automaticity, prosody, accuracy, and rate.

 **20 minutes**

REVIEW: Words Ending in *–ong* and *–ung*

Students will work online independently to

▶ Practice words ending in the letters *ong* and *ung.*

▶ Practice decoding text by reading a story.

Help students locate the online activities and provide support as needed.

Offline Alternative

No computer access? Have students point out and name things or words that end in the letters *ong* and *ung* (for example, *song* or *sung*). You might also ask students to spell words that end with the sounds /ong/ and /ung/.

> ### Objectives
>
> - Identify the sound, given the letters *ong.*
> - Identify the letters, given the sound /ong/.
> - Identify the sound, given the letters *ung.*
> - Identify the letters, given the sound /ung/.
> - Identify ending sounds in words.
> - Read aloud grade-level text with appropriate automaticity, prosody, accuracy, and rate.
> - Decode words by applying grade-level word analysis skills.

Practice Words Ending in –*ang*, –*ing*, –*ong*, and –*ung*

Lesson Overview

[Offline] **FOCUS:** Practice Words Ending in –*ang*, –*ing*, –*ong*, and –*ung*		**30** minutes
Sight Words	Sight Word Fun	
Get Ready	Guess the Word	
	Practice the Oddball Sounds	
	Word Chains	
Try It	"Bess Loves to Sing"	
[Online] **REVIEW:** Words Ending in –*ang*, –*ing*, –*ong*, and –*ung*		**20** minutes

[Materials]

Supplied
- *K¹² PhonicsWorks Readers Advanced 5*, pp. 7–12
- whiteboard, student
- Tile Kit

Also Needed
- sight words box

〖 Offline 〗 ③⓪ minutes

FOCUS: Practice Words Ending in *–ang*, *–ing*, *–ong*, and *–ung*

Work **together** with students to complete offline Sight Words, Get Ready, and Try It activities.

Sight Words ···

Sight Word Fun

Help students learn the sight words *love*, *very*, and *some*, and up to two additional sight words they have yet to master.

1. Gather the sight word cards *love*, *very*, and *some*, and up to two additional sight word cards.

2. Choose one sight word card to begin.

   Say: Look at this word and take a picture of it in your mind. When you think you can spell the word yourself, turn the card over and use your letter tiles to spell the word.

3. After students spell the word, have them check the card to see if they spelled the word correctly.

   Say: Read aloud the word you spelled with the letter tiles.

4. Repeat the activity with the remaining sight words.

TIP Sight words can be very difficult for some students. Let students work at their own pace and really master these words.

Objectives
- Read sight words.
- Spell sight words.

Get Ready

Guess the Word

Have students use word meaning and sentence structure to choose a word that best completes a sentence.

1. Write the following words on students' whiteboard: *string, rang, hung, long,* and *bring*. Make sure students know the meaning of all the words on their whiteboards before you do this activity.

2. **Say:** We're going to play a guessing game. I'm going to read a sentence with a word missing. Your job is to look at the words on your whiteboard and decide which one is the right word to complete the sentence.

   ▸ Listen to this sentence: "I will use the scissors to cut the _____."
   ▸ Next you will tell me what word makes sense in the blank in the sentence. This time the word would be *string*.
   ▸ The complete sentence would be, "I will use the scissors to cut the *string*." Now you try it.

3. Continue the procedure with the following sentences:

   ▸ *When the doorbell _____, I went to see who was there. rang*
   ▸ *The neck of the giraffe is very _____. long*
   ▸ *If you _____ the book to me, I will read it to you. bring*
   ▸ *Mom _____ my picture on the wall. hung*

Practice the Oddball Sounds

Have students recognize and use words that end with the oddball sounds *–ang, –ing, –ong,* and *–ung*.

1. Place the following letter tiles at the top of students' whiteboard: *ang, ing, ong,* and *ung*.

2. Place the following letter tiles at the bottom of students' whiteboard: *b, d, f, k, l, r, s, t,* and *th*.

3. **Say:** I am going to say some words. Repeat each word, and then find the letter tile on your whiteboard that makes the ending sound for the word. Then find the beginning letters on your whiteboard and spell the word.

4. **Say:** Let's practice. The first word is *king*.

   ▸ Repeat the word *king*.
   ▸ Point to the tile with the oddball sound in that word. *ing*
   ▸ Point to the letter that goes in front of the oddball sound in that word. *k*
   ▸ Use the tiles to spell the word. *king*
   ▸ Touch and say the word.

5. Repeat this procedure with the following words:

- ► *song*
- ► *stung*
- ► *fang*
- ► *bring*
- ► *flung*
- ► *thing*
- ► *dong*

Word Chains

Have students build words by adding and changing letters to help them recognize and use individual sounds in words.

1. Place the following letter tiles at the top of students' whiteboard: *ang, h, ing, l, ong, s, th,* and *ung.*

2. **Say:** I am going to build the first word in a chain. The word is *thing.*

   - ► I will pull down the letters for the sounds /th/ and /ing/ to spell the word *thing.*
   - ► Next I will touch and say *thing.* To change *thing* to *sing,* I will think about what sound is changed from the word *thing* to *sing.* I will need to replace the letter tile *th* with the letter tile *s.*
   - ► Touch and say the word *sing.* Now it's your turn to change *sing* to *sang.* You can spell *sang* by making only one change. Touch and say the new word.

3. Redirect students if they select the incorrect letter for any sound.

   Say: That letter is for the sound [incorrect sound]. We want the letter for the sound [target sound]. What letter makes that sound? Answers will vary.

4. Redirect students if they name the sound incorrectly.

   Say: To change the word [first word] to [target word], we need the letter for the sound [target sound].

   Show students how to make the change. Have them touch and say the new word after they move the letters.

5. Follow this procedure to make the following words: *hang, hung, lung, long, song.*

6. For every new word, have students add, replace, or remove only one letter tile.

   (TIP) If students struggle, review the sounds and letters that are confusing them.

Try It •

"Bess Loves to Sing"

Have students read "Bess Loves to Sing" on page 7 of *K¹² PhonicsWorks Readers Advanced 5.*

Students should read the story silently once or twice before reading the story aloud. When students miss a word that can be sounded out, point to it and give students three to six seconds to try the word again. If students still miss the word, tell them the word so the flow of the story isn't interrupted.

After reading the story, make a list of all the words students missed, and go over those words with them. You may use letter tiles to show students how to read the words.

 **20 minutes**

REVIEW: Words Ending in *–ang*, *–ing*, *–ong*, and *–ung*

Students will work online independently to

▸ Practice words ending in the letters *ang, ing, ong,* and *ung.*

Help students locate the online activities and provide support as needed.

_____

Offline Alternative

No computer access? Have students point out and name things or words that end with the letters *ang, ing, ong,* and *ung* (for example, *sang, string, swung,* and *song*). You might also ask students to spell words that end with the sounds /ang/, /ing/, /ong/, and /ung/.

Unit Checkpoint

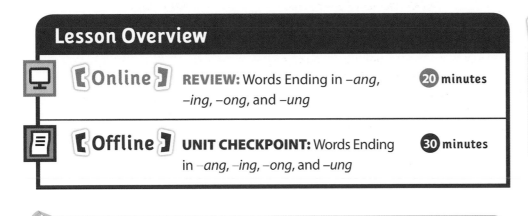

Lesson Overview

🖥️	**⟦ Online ⟧** REVIEW: Words Ending in –*ang*, –*ing*, –*ong*, and –*ung*	**20** minutes
📄	**⟦ Offline ⟧** UNIT CHECKPOINT: Words Ending in –*ang*, –*ing*, –*ong*, and –*ung*	**30** minutes

⟦ Materials ⟧

Supplied
- *K12 PhonicsWorks Advanced Assessments,* pp. PH 85–90

⭐ Objectives

- Identify the sound, given the letters *ang*.
- Identify the letters, given the sound /ang/.
- Read, write, and spell words containing –*ang*.
- Identify the sound, given the letters *ing*.
- Identify the letters, given the sound /ing/.
- Read, write, and spell words containing –*ing*.
- Identify the sound, given the letters *ong*.
- Identify the letters, given the sound /ong/.
- Read, write, and spell words containing –*ong*.
- Identify the sound, given the letters *ung*.
- Identify the letters, given the sound /ung/.
- Read, write, and spell words containing –*ung*.
- Identify individual sounds in words.
- Given the letter, identify the most common sound.
- Given the sound, identify the most common letter or letters.
- Read instructional-level text with 90% accuracy.
- Read aloud grade-level text with appropriate automaticity, prosody, accuracy, and rate.
- Write words by applying grade-level phonics knowledge.
- Write sight words.
- Read sight words.

⟦ Online ⟧ **20** minutes

REVIEW: **Words Ending in –*ang*, –*ing*, –*ong*, and –*ung***

Students will review words ending in –*ang*, –*ing*, –*ong*, and –*ung* to prepare for the Unit Checkpoint. Help students locate the online activities and provide support as needed.

⟦ Offline ⟧ ⏱ 30 minutes

UNIT CHECKPOINT: Words Ending in *–ang, –ing, –ong,* and *–ung*

Explain that students are going to show what they have learned about sounds, letters, and words.

1. Give students the Unit Checkpoint pages for the Words Ending in *–ang, –ing, –ong,* and *–ung* unit and print the Unit Checkpoint Answer Key, if you'd like.

2. Use the instructions below to help administer the Checkpoint to students. On the Answer Key or another sheet of paper, note student answers to oral response questions to help with scoring the Checkpoint later.

3. Use the Answer Key to score the Checkpoint, and then enter the results online.

Part 1. Read Word Parts and Nonsense Words Moving left to right, have students say the sound or sounds of each word part or nonsense word. Note any word parts or nonsense words they say incorrectly.

Part 2. Finger Stretching Say each word to students. Have them say each word aloud and finger stretch the sounds. Note any words they finger stretch incorrectly.

13. *sing*

14. *long*

15. *fang*

16. *hung*

Part 3. Dictation Say each word to students. Have them repeat and write the word.

17. *king*   21. *thing*

18. *rang*   22. *bang*

19. *song*   23. *long*

20. *stung*   24. *hung*

Part 4. Writing Read each sentence to students. Have them repeat and write the sentence.

25. *She can sing a song.*

26. *An inch is not long.*

27. *The bell has rung.*

Part 5. Read Aloud Listen to students read the sentences aloud. Count and note the number of words they read correctly.

Part 6. Say Letters Say each sound. Have students say the letters that make that sound. Note any incorrect responses.

29. /ong/

30. /ing/

31. /ung/

32. /ang/

33. /kw/

34. /ank/

35. /sh/

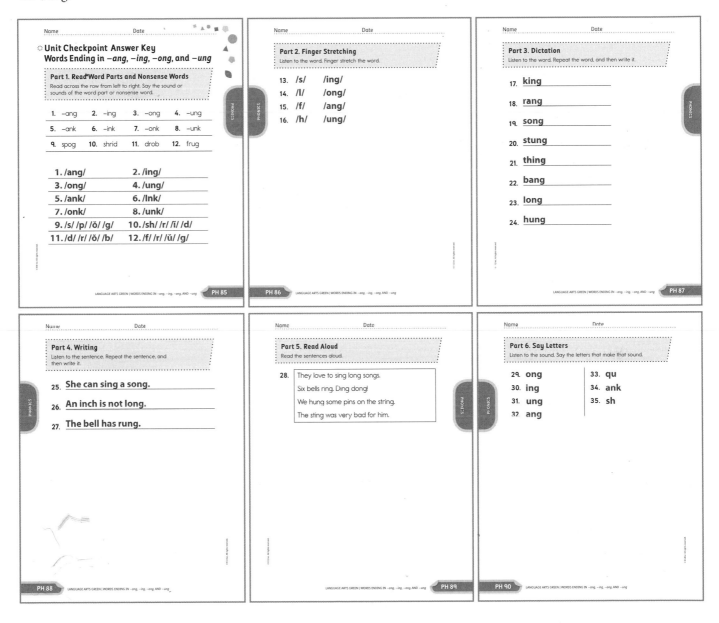

Unit Checkpoint Answer Key
Words Ending in –*ang*, –*ing*, –*ong*, and –*ung*

Part 1. Read Word Parts and Nonsense Words
Read across the row from left to right. Say the sound or sounds of the word part or nonsense word.

1. –ang	2. –ing	3. –ong	4. –ung
5. –ank	6. –ink	7. –onk	8. –unk
9. spog	10. shrid	11. drob	12. frug

1. /ang/	2. /ing/
3. /ong/	4. /ung/
5. /ank/	6. /lnk/
7. /onk/	8. /unk/
9. /s/ /p/ /ŏ/ /g/	10. /sh/ /r/ /ĭ/ /d/
11. /d/ /r/ /ŏ/ /b/	12. /f/ /r/ /ŭ/ /g/

LANGUAGE ARTS GREEN | WORDS ENDING IN –ang, –ing, –ong, AND –ung   PH 85

Part 2. Finger Stretching
Listen to the word. Finger stretch the word.

13. /s/ /ing/
14. /l/ /ong/
15. /f/ /ang/
16. /h/ /ung/

PH 86   LANGUAGE ARTS GREEN | WORDS ENDING IN –ang, –ing, –ong, AND –ung

Part 3. Dictation
Listen to the word. Repeat the word, and then write it.

17. king
18. rang
19. song
20. stung
21. thing
22. bang
23. long
24. hung

LANGUAGE ARTS GREEN | WORDS ENDING IN –ang, –ing, –ong, AND –ung   PH 87

Part 4. Writing
Listen to the sentence. Repeat the sentence, and then write it.

25. She can sing a song.
26. An inch is not long.
27. The bell has rung.

PH 88   LANGUAGE ARTS GREEN | WORDS ENDING IN –ang, –ing, –ong, AND –ung

Part 5. Read Aloud
Read the sentences aloud.

28. They love to sing long songs.
Six bells ring. Ding dong!
We hung some pins on the string.
The sting was very bad for him.

LANGUAGE ARTS GREEN | WORDS ENDING IN –ang, –ing, –ong, AND –ung   PH 89

Part 6. Say Letters
Listen to the sound. Say the letters that make that sound.

29. ong
30. ing
31. ung
32. ang

33. qu
34. ank
35. sh

PH 90   LANGUAGE ARTS GREEN | WORDS ENDING IN –ang, –ing, –ong, AND –ung

Silent *e* Spelling for Sound /ā/

Unit Overview

In this unit, students will

- ▶ Review sight words.
- ▶ Learn the silent *e* spelling for the sounds /ā/, /ī/, /ō/, and /ē/.
- ▶ Practice identifying individual sounds in words.
- ▶ Build words.

Materials

Supplied

- *K¹² PhonicsWorks Advanced Activity Book*, p. PH 31
- whiteboard, Learning Coach
- whiteboard, student
- Tile Kit

Also Needed

- sight words box
- dictation notebook

Lesson Overview

[Offline] FOCUS: Silent *e* Spelling for Sound /ā/   **30** minutes

Sight Words	Review Sight Words
Get Ready	Recognize Words and Syllables
	Vowel Sounds
Learn	Introduce Silent *e* and /ā/
	Build Words
Try It	Alphabet Addition
	Dictation: Write Words

[Online] REVIEW: Silent *e* Spelling for Sound /a/   **20** minutes

Advance Preparation

Refer to Super *e* on the *K¹² PhonicsWorks* DVD for a demonstration of how to do the touch and say for the silent *e*.

[Offline] 30 minutes

FOCUS: Silent *e* Spelling for Sound /ā/

Work **together** with students to complete offline Sight Words, Get Ready, Learn, and Try It activities.

Sight Words ....

Review Sight Words

Help students learn to recognize sight words.

1. Gather all the sight word cards students have yet to master from their sight words box. Stack the cards on the table face down.

2. Have students pick a word and read it to you.

3. If they read it quickly and correctly, put the card in one stack. If they hesitate or do not read the word correctly, put it in another stack. The second stack should have words that they will review again.

4. Take the stack of words that students read correctly and dictate each word to them. They may choose to either write the word or spell it aloud.

5. If students spell the word correctly, they have mastered the word. If they misspell the word, add it to the stack of cards to review again.

6. Chart students' progress on the back of each card.

   ▸ Divide the back of the card into two columns.
   ▸ Label the first column "Read" and the second column "Spell."
   ▸ Record the dates that students read or spell the word correctly. When students can read and spell the word correctly three times in a row, they have mastered the word. You may want to put a star or sticker on their card when they have mastered that word.

TIP Even if students can read and spell all the words correctly, it is still beneficial for them to review sight words. Choose as many additional words as you would like for each subsequent activity.

> **Objectives**
> * Read sight words.
> * Spell sight words.

Get Ready ···

Recognize Words and Syllables

Practice syllables with students.

1. **Say:** When we talk, we make words by pushing air out of our mouths. Each push of air in a word is called a **syllable**. Each word has one or more syllables. You can think of syllables as chunks of words.

2. **Say:** Let's break some words into syllables.

   ► I'll say a word. I'll repeat the word.
   ► You'll say the word after me, and you'll break it into syllables by saying the separate chunks of the word while tapping your fist on the table as you say each chunk.
   ► For example, I'll say *hammer,* and then I'll say it again.
   ► You'll say *ham / mer* and tap your fist on the table as you say each syllable.

3. Say each word and repeat it. Have students fist tap on the table as they say the syllables in each word.

   ► *cartoon car / toon*
   ► *play play*
   ► *lullaby lul / la / by*
   ► *computer com / pu / ter*

TIP Have students name items in a category, such as foods, furniture, or animals, and fist tap the syllables with you. For example, have them name and fist tap words such as *ta / ble* and *win / dow*. Challenge students to name and fist tap something with several syllables (for example, *tel / e / vi / sion*).

Vowel Sounds

Have students compare pairs of words to identify the word with the sound /ā/.

1. **Say:** I am going to say a pair of words. Your job is to identify the word with the special vowel sound /ā/. Repeat the pair of words I say and listen for the sound /ā/. For example, if I say the words *make* and *mat,* you will repeat the words and say *make* because *make* has the special sound /ā/.

2. Say the following pairs of words and have students identify the word with sound /ā/.

   ► *shape* and *ship shape*
   ► *fade* and *fad fade*
   ► *grin* and *grace grace*
   ► *plate* and *pet plate*
   ► *snack* and *snake snake*
   ► *chase* and *chug chase*

Learn

Introduce Silent *e* and /ā/

Help students recognize and use the silent *e* spelling for the sound /ā/.

1. Place the *a-e* tile at the top of students' whiteboard.

   Say: Today we will learn about silent *e*. When the silent *e* comes after a vowel and a consonant, it makes the vowel say its name.

2. Point to the *a-e* tile.

   Say: This tile reminds us that when the *a* [point to *a*] is followed by any single consonant [point to dash] and a silent *e* [point to *e*], the *a* says /ā/.

3. Return the *a-e* tile. Then place the following letter tiles on students' whiteboard: *a, e, f, m, n,* and *t*.

4. Make the word *mat*. Touch and say the word.

5. Place the letter *e* at the end of the word *mat* to create the word *mate*. Using your index and middle fingers, touch the *a* and *e* letter tiles at the same time.

   Say: We are going to learn one way to read and spell the sound /ā/. When the letter *e* comes at the end of a word and after a consonant, it works together with the vowel to make the vowel say its name. The letter *e* is silent and changes the sound of the vowel to the sound of its name.

6. **Say:** Touch and say the word *mate*. Touch the first letter and say its sound. Then touch the *a* and *e* at the same time with two fingers, saying /ā/. Touch the third letter and say its sound.

   ‣ How many sounds are in the word? three
   ‣ How many letters are in the word? four
   ‣ What two letters spell the sound /ā/? *a* and *e*

7. Redirect students if they name the letter and not its sound.

   Say: You are right that the name of the letter is [letter]. We want the sound for this letter. What is the sound?

8. Redirect students if they name the sound incorrectly.

   Say: That is the sound of another letter.

9. Guide students if they touch only the letter *a* tile.

   Say: That is one of the letters you need to make the sound /ā/. What is the other letter you need?

10. Repeat this procedure for the following words:

    ‣ *fat*
    ‣ *man*

Objectives

- Identify and use /ā/ spelling patterns.
- Identify and use the sound /ā/.
- Identify the letters, given the sound /ā/.
- Identify the number of sounds within words.
- Blend sounds to create words.

Build Words

Help students use letters and sounds to build words.

1. Place the following letter tiles at the top of students' whiteboard: *a, e, g, k, m, p, s, sh,* and *v.*

2. Draw three horizontal lines across the middle of students' whiteboard to represent the sounds in a word. Note that when building words with the silent *e* on the end, there is no line on which to place the *e,* which reinforces the fact that the *a* and the *e* work together to make the sound /ā/. The *e* does not make a sound on its own.

3. **Say:** Let's use letters and sounds to build the word *make.* Remember, the silent *e* works with the letter *a* to make the sound /ā/.

4. Have students finger stretch the sounds in *make.*

5. Have students

   ▸ Identify the first, next, and last sounds in *make.*
   ▸ Choose the corresponding letter for each sound.
   ▸ Move the letters to the correct lines on their whiteboard.

6. Guide students with these questions:

   ▸ What is the first sound in *make?* /m/
     Which line does the letter for that sound go on? the first one
   ▸ What is the next sound in *make?* /ā/
     Which line does the letter for that sound go on? the second one
   ▸ What's the last sound in *make?* /k/
     Which line does the letter for that sound go on? the third one
   ▸ What letter is silent in the word *make?* e
     Where does the silent letter go? at the end of the word

7. Have students touch and say the word. Be sure to check that students are using their index and middle fingers to touch the *a* and *e* at the same time before they touch and say the last letter and sound.

8. Redirect students if they select the incorrect letter.

   Say: That sound is in the word [word], and it is the [first, second, third,] sound. We want the sound [target sound].

   Continue until students select the correct letter.

9. Repeat the activity to build the following words:

   ▸ *game* /g/ /ā/ /m/
   ▸ *shape* /sh /ā/ /p/
   ▸ *save* /s/ /ā/ /v/

Try It

Alphabet Addition

Have students complete page PH 31 in *K¹² PhonicsWorks Advanced Activity Book* for more practice on making words that have the silent *e* spelling for the sound /ā/. First have students add the parts of the word together to make a new word. Then have them write the word and read it aloud.

> **Try It**
>
> #### Silent *e* Spelling for Sound /ā/
> #### Alphabet Addition
>
> Add the letters to make a word. Write the word, and then read it aloud.
>
> 1. cap + e = **cape**
> 2. can + e = **cane**
> 3. mat + e = **mate**
> 4. fat + e = **fate**
> 5. rat + e = **rate**
> 6. Sam + e = **same**
>
> **Just for Fun**
> Read the sentence aloud.
>
> Kate made pink capes for Kim and Jane.
>
> LANGUAGE ARTS GREEN   PH 31

Dictation: Write Words

Have students practice identifying sounds and writing words.

1. Gather a pencil and the dictation notebook. Say the word *case*. Then give these directions to students:

   - ► Repeat the word.
   - ► Write the word in your notebook.
   - ► Read the word aloud.

2. When students have finished, write the following word on your whiteboard: *case*.

3. Have them compare their answer to your correct version.

4. Repeat this procedure with the following words: *tame, wave, date, gaze*.

   - ► If students make an error and don't see it, help them correct their mistake by having them finger stretch the sounds in the word they missed.
   - ► If students are having difficulty selecting the correct letters or sounds, review those letters or sounds that are confusing them.
   - ► If students have difficulty with first, middle, and last sounds, have them finger stretch the sounds in words.

 **20 minutes**

REVIEW: Silent *e* Spelling for Sound /ā/

Students will work online independently to

▶ Practice the silent *e* spelling for the sound /ā/.

▶ Practice decoding text by reading a story.

Help students locate the online activities and provide support as needed.

Offline Alternative

No computer access? Have students point out and name things or words that contain the silent *e* spelling for the sound /ā/ (for example, *bake*). You might also ask students to spell words that contain the silent *e* spelling for the sound /ā/.

Objectives

- Identify and use /ā/ spelling patterns.
- Identify and use the sound /ā/.
- Identify the letters, given the sound /ā/.
- Identify individual sounds in words.
- Read aloud grade-level text with appropriate automaticity, prosody, accuracy, and rate.
- Decode words by applying grade-level word analysis skills.

Silent *e* Spelling for Sound /ī/

Lesson Overview

[Offline] FOCUS: Silent *e* Spelling for Sound /ī/ — 30 minutes

Sight Words	Use Words in Sentences
Get Ready	Silent *e* Words
Learn	Introduce Silent *e* and /ī/
	Build Words
	Word Chains
Try It	"A Cake for Mom"

[Online] REVIEW: Silent *e* Spelling for Sound /ī/ — 20 minutes

Materials

Supplied
- *K12 PhonicsWorks Readers Advanced 5*, pp. 13–18
- whiteboard, student
- Tile Kit

Also Needed
- sight words box
- index cards (25)

Advance Preparation

For Silent *e* Words, print each of the following words on index cards, using one index card per word: *cake, take, mane, sane, date, sap, rat, rate, vat, wax, wade, cat, Kate, Nate, gate, tame, game, quake, fate, late, lane, fat, get, man,* and *tan.*

Refer to Super *e* on the *K¹² PhonicsWorks* DVD for a demonstration of how to do the touch and say for the silent *e*.

[Offline] ⏱ 30 minutes

FOCUS: Silent *e* Spelling for Sound /ī/

Work **together** with students to complete offline Sight Words, Get Ready, Learn, and Try It activities.

Sight Words ••

Use Words in Sentences

Help students use sight words in sentences.

1. Gather all the sight word cards students have yet to master from their sight words box. Spread the sight word cards on the table.

2. **Say:** Let's use sight words in sentences.

3. Have students

   ▸ Touch each card and read the word on it.
   ▸ Make up a sentence using the word.
   ▸ Put the card in a pile after using the word in a sentence.
   ▸ Go through the pile of cards and read each sight word again.
   ▸ Spell each word.

TIP If students have difficulty with any of the sight words, place those cards in a pile to review again.

> **Objectives**
> • Read sight words.
> • Spell sight words.

Get Ready ••

Silent *e* Words

To help students learn to recognize words that use the silent *e* spelling, have them practice identifying words that have the silent *e* spelling for the sound /ā/.

1. Gather the index cards you prepared.

2. **Say:** We are going to use these cards to identify words with the silent *e* spelling for the sound /ā/. Take the top card from the stack and read the word. Is the word a silent *e* word?

3. Have students place the card in one of two piles: one with silent *e* words and one with words that are not silent *e* words.

4. Follow this procedure, taking turns with students until you have gone through all the words in the stack.

   ▸ **Silent *e* Words:** *cake, take, mane, sane, date, lane, late, rate, fate, quake, wade, tame, game, gate, Kate, Nate*
   ▸ **Nonsilent *e* Words:** *tan, man, get, fat, sap, rat, vat, wax, cat*

TIP If students have difficulty identifying which words have the silent *e*, remind them that the silent *e* helps the vowel say its name.

> **Objectives**
> • Identify and use /ā/ spelling patterns.
> • Identify and use the sound /ā/.
> • Identify the letters, given the sound /ā/.

Learn

Introduce Silent *e* and /ī/

Help students recognize and use the silent *e* spelling for the sound /ī/.

1. Place the *i-e* tile at the top of students' whiteboard.

   Say: Today we will learn about silent *e*. When the silent *e* comes after a vowel and a consonant, it makes the vowel say its name.

2. Point to the *i-e* tile.

   Say: This tile reminds us that when the *i* [point to *i*] is followed by any single consonant [point to dash] and a silent *e* [point to *e*], the *i* says /ī/.

3. Return the *i-e* tile. Then place the following letter tiles on students' whiteboard: *b, d, e, i, k, m, n, p,* and *t*.

4. Make the word *kit*. Touch and say the word.

5. Place the letter *e* at the end of the word *kit* to create the word *kite*. Using your index and middle fingers, touch the *i* and *e* letter tiles at the same time.

   Say: We are going to learn one way to read and spell the sound /ī/. When the letter *e* comes at the end of a word and after a consonant, it works together with the vowel to make the vowel say its name. The letter *e* is silent and changes the sound of the vowel to the sound of its name.

6. **Say:** Touch and say the word *kite*. Touch the first letter and say its sound. Then touch the *i* and *e* at the same time with two fingers, saying /ī/. Touch the third letter and say its sound.

   ▸ How many sounds are in the word? three
   ▸ How many letters are in the word? four
   ▸ What two letters spell the sound /ī/? *i* and *e*

7. Redirect students if they name the letter and not its sound.

   Say: You are right that the name of the letter is [letter]. We want the sound for this letter. What is the sound?

8. Redirect students if they name the sound incorrectly.

   Say: That is the sound of another letter.

9. Guide students if they touch only the letter *i* tile.

   Say: That is one of the letters you need to make the sound /ī/. What is the other letter you need?

10. Repeat this procedure for the following words:

    ▸ *dim*
    ▸ *pin*
    ▸ *bit*

Objectives

- Identify and use /ī/ spelling patterns.
- Identify and use the sound /ī/.
- Identify the letters, given the sound /ī/.
- Identify the number of sounds within words.
- Blend sounds to create words.
- Identify the new word when one sound is changed in a word.

Build Words

Help students use letters and sounds to build words.

1. Place the following letter tiles at the top of students' whiteboard: *ch, d, e, i, m, p, s,* and *w.*

2. Draw three horizontal lines across the middle of students' whiteboard to represent the sounds in a word. Note that when building words with the silent *e* on the end, there is no line on which to place the *e,* which reinforces the fact that the *i* and the *e* work together to make the sound /ī/. The *e* does not make a sound on its own.

3. **Say:** Let's use letters and sounds to build the word *wipe.* Remember, the silent *e* works with the letter *i* to make the sound /ī/.

4. Have students finger stretch the sounds in *wipe.*

5. Have students
   - ► Identify the first, next, and last sounds in *wipe.*
   - ► Choose the corresponding letter for each of the sounds.
   - ► Move the letters to the correct lines on their whiteboard.

6. Guide students with these questions:
   - ► What is the first sound in *wipe?* /w/
     Which line does the letter for that sound go on? the first one
   - ► What is the next sound in *wipe?* /ī/
     Which line does the letter for that sound go on? the second one
   - ► What's the last sound in *wipe?* /p/
     Which line does the letter for that sound go on? the third one
   - ► What letter is silent in the word *wipe? e*
     Where does the silent letter go? at the end of the word

7. Have students touch and say the word.

8. Redirect students if they select the incorrect letter.

   Say: That sound is in the word [word], and it is the [first, second, third] sound. We want the sound [target sound].

   Continue until students select the correct letter.

9. Repeat the activity to build the following words:
   - ► *side* /s/ /ī/ /d/
   - ► *chime* /ch/ /ī/ /m/

Word Chains

Have students build words by adding and changing letters to help them recognize and use individual sounds in words.

1. Place the following letters at the top of students' whiteboard: *a, b, d, e, f, i, k, l, m, n,* and *t.*

2. **Say:** I am going to build the first word in a chain. The word is *bake.*
   - ► I will pull down the letters for the sounds /b/, /ā/, and /k/ to spell the word *bake.*

- Next I will touch and say *bake*. To change *bake* to *bike*, I will think about what sound is changed from the word *bake* to *bike*. I will need to replace the letter *a* with the letter *i*.
  - Touch and say the word *bike*. Now it's your turn to change *bike* to *like*. You can spell *like* by making only one change. Touch and say the new word.

3. Redirect students if they select the incorrect letter for any sound.

   Say: That letter is for the sound [incorrect sound]. We want the letter for the sound [target sound]. What letter makes that sound? Answers will vary.

4. Redirect students if they name the sound incorrectly.

   Show students how to make the change. Have them touch and say the new word after they move the letters.

   Say: To change the word [first word] to [target word], we need the letter for the sound [target sound].

5. Follow this procedure to make the following words: *lake, make, Mike, like, line, fine, fin, din, dine, dime, dim, did, bid, bit, bite*.

6. For every new word, have students add, replace, or remove only one letter.

Try It

"A Cake for Mom"
Have students read "A Cake for Mom" on page 13 of *K¹² PhonicsWorks Readers Advanced 5.*
Students should read the story silently once or twice before reading the story aloud. When students miss a word that can be sounded out, point to it and give students three to six seconds to try the word again. If students still miss the word, tell them the word so the flow of the story isn't interrupted.
After reading the story, make a list of all the words students missed, and go over those words with them. You may use letter tiles to show students how to read the words.

> **Objectives**
> - Read aloud grade-level text with appropriate automaticity, prosody, accuracy, and rate.
> - Decode words by applying grade-level word analysis skills.

20 minutes

REVIEW: Silent *e* Spelling for Sound /ī/
Students will work online independently to

- Practice the silent *e* spelling for the sound /ī/.

Help students locate the online activities and provide support as needed.

> **Objectives**
> - Identify and use /ī/ spelling patterns.
> - Identify and use the sound /ī/.
> - Identify the letters, given the sound /ī/.
> - Identify individual sounds in words.

Offline Alternative

No computer access? Have students point out and name things or words that contain the silent *e* spelling for the sound /ī/ (for example, *dime* or *tire*). You might also ask students to spell words that contain the silent *e* spelling for the sound /ī/.

Silent *e* Spelling for Sound /ō/

Lesson Overview

Offline FOCUS: Silent *e* Spelling for Sound /ō/	**30** minutes

Sight Words	Sight Word Concentration
Get Ready	Silent *e* Words
Learn	Introduce Silent *e* and /ō/
	Build Words
	Rhyme Nonsense Words
Try It	Finish the Job

Online REVIEW: Silent *e* Spelling for Sound /ō/	**20** minutes

Materials

Supplied
- *K¹² PhonicsWorks Advanced Activity Book*, p. PH 32
- whiteboard, student
- Tile Kit

Also Needed
- sight words box
- index cards (38)

Advance Preparation

Gather two sets of all the sight word cards you have used to date.

For Silent *e* Words, print each of the following words on index cards, using one index card per word: *like, lick, kick, kite, white, yikes, pine, pin, hit, hot, cot, bite, wine, line, lime, nine, quite, vine, dine, hive, sip, mix,* and *win.* Also gather the set of silent *e* cards you have used to date.

For Rhyme Nonsense Words, print each of the following words on index cards, using one index card per word: *plake, hime, slame, gode, drave, crade, yine, pote, fide, gope, bine, pive, pome, spave,* and *quone.*

Refer to Super *e* on the *K¹² PhonicsWorks* DVD for a demonstration of how to do the touch and say for the silent *e.*

[Offline] 30 minutes

FOCUS: Silent *e* Spelling for Sound /ō/

Work **together** with students to complete offline Sight Words, Get Ready, Learn, and Try It activities.

Sight Words ....

Sight Word Concentration

Help students review sight words.

1. Gather the two sets of sight word cards.

2. Scramble both sets of sight word cards and place them face down on the table or floor.

3. Turn over two cards at a time; take turns with students. If the cards match, the person turning over the matching cards reads the word and uses it in a sentence. If the cards don't match, the person turns them back over.

4. Remove and save the matching cards.

5. Continue the activity until all the cards are paired.

6. Have students read all the words.

7. Take the stack of words that students read correctly and dictate each word to them.

8. Have students write each word or spell it aloud.

TIP If students have difficulty with any sight words, let them work at their own pace to really master these words.

> **Objectives**
> - Read sight words.
> - Spell sight words.
> - Write sight words.

Get Ready ....

Silent *e* Words

To help students learn to recognize words that use the silent *e* spelling, have them practice identifying words that have the silent *e* spelling for the sounds /ā/ and /ī/.

1. Gather the silent *e* cards you have used to date and the index cards you prepared with additional silent *e* words.

2. Shuffle the cards so that the sound /ā/ and sound /ī/ cards are well mixed.

3. **Say:** We are going to use these cards to identify words with the silent *e* spelling for the sounds /ā/ and /ī/. Take the top card from the stack and read the word. Is the word a silent *e* card?

4. Have students place the card in one of two piles: one with silent *e* words and one with words that are not silent *e* words.

> **Objectives**
> - Identify and use /ā/ spelling patterns.
> - Identify and use /ī/ spelling patterns.

5. Follow this procedure, taking turns with students until you have gone through all the words in the stack.

- ▶ **Silent *e* Words:** *cake, take, mane, sane, date, lane, late, rate, fate, quake, wade, tame, game, gate, Kate, Nate, like, kite, white, yikes, pine, bite, wine, line, lime, nine, quite, vine, dine, hive*
- ▶ **Nonsilent *e* Words:** *tan, man, get, fat, sap, rat, vat, wax, cat, lick, kick, pin, hit, hot, cot, sip, mix, win*

TIP If students have difficulty identifying which words have the silent *e*, remind them that the silent *e* helps the vowel say its name.

Learn

Introduce Silent *e* and /ō/

Help students recognize and use the silent *e* spelling for the sound /ō/.

1. Place the *o-e* tile at the top of students' whiteboard.

   Say: Today we will learn about silent *e*. When the silent *e* comes after a vowel and a consonant, it makes the vowel say its name.

2. Point to the *o-e* tile.

   Say: This tile reminds us that when the *o* [point to *o*] is followed by any single consonant [point to dash] and a silent *e* [point to *e*], the *o* says /ō/.

3. Return the *o-e* tile. Then, place the following letter tiles on students' whiteboard: *c, d, e, h, n, o, p, t,* and *t*.

4. Make the word *hop*. Touch and say the word.

5. Place the letter *e* at the end of the word *hop* to create the word *hope*. Using your index and middle fingers, touch the *o* and *e* letter tiles at the same time.

   Say: We are going to learn one way to read and spell the sound /ō/. When the letter *e* comes at the end of a word and after a consonant, it works together with the vowel to make the vowel say its name. The letter *e* is silent and changes the sound of the vowel to the sound of its name.

6. **Say:** Touch and say the word *hope*. Touch the first letter and say its sound. Then touch the *o* and *e* at the same time with two fingers, saying /ō/. Touch the third letter and say its sound.

   - ▶ How many sounds are in the word? three
   - ▶ How many letters are in the word? four
   - ▶ What two letters spell the sound /ō/? *o* and *e*

7. Redirect students if they name the letter and not its sound.

   Say: You are right that the name of the letter is [letter]. We want the sound for this letter. What is the sound?

8. Redirect students if they name the sound incorrectly.

   Say: That is the sound of another letter.

Objectives

- Identify and use /ō/ spelling patterns.
- Identify and use the sound /ō/.
- Identify the letters, given the sound /ō/.
- Identify the number of sounds within words.
- Identify individual sounds in words.
- Blend sounds to create words.
- Identify words that rhyme.

9. Guide students if they touch only the letter *o* tile.

   Say: That is one of the letters you need to make the /ō/ sound. What is the other letter you need?

10. Repeat this procedure for the following words:

    ▸ *nod*
    ▸ *cot*
    ▸ *tot*

Build Words

Help students use letters and sounds to build words.

1. Place the following letter tiles at the top of students' whiteboard: *b, ch, e, k, o, n, qu, t,* and *v*.

2. Draw three horizontal lines across the middle of students' whiteboard to represent the sounds in a word. Note that when building words with the silent *e* on the end, there is no line on which to place the *e*, which reinforces the fact that the *o* and the *e* work together to make the sound /ō/. The *e* does not make a sound on its own.

3. **Say:** Let's use letters and sounds to build the word *vote*. Remember, the silent *e* works with the letter *o* to make the sound /ō/.

4. Have students finger stretch the sounds in *vote*.

5. Have students

   ▸ Identify the first, next, and last sounds in *vote*.
   ▸ Choose the corresponding letter for each of the sounds.
   ▸ Move the letters to the correct lines on their whiteboard.

6. Guide students with these questions:

   ▸ What is the first sound in *vote*? /v/
     Which line does the letter for that sound go on? the first one
   ▸ What is the next sound in *vote*? /ō/
     Which line does the letter for that sound go on? the second one,
   ▸ What's the last sound in *vote*? /t/
     Which line does the letter for that sound go on? the third one
   ▸ What letter is silent in the word *vote*? e
     Where does the silent letter go? at the end of the word

7. Have students touch and say the word. Be sure to check that students are using their index and middle fingers to touch the *o* and *e* at the same time before they touch and say the last letter and sound.

8. Redirect students if they select the incorrect letter.

   Say: That sound is in the word [word], and it is the [first, second, third] sound. We want the sound [correct sound].

   Continue until students select the correct letter.

9. Repeat the activity to build the following words:

   ▸ *bone* /b/ /ō/ /n/
   ▸ *quote* /kw/ /ō/ /t/
   ▸ *choke* /ch/ /ō/ /k/

Rhyme Nonsense Words

Play a game with students to reinforce awareness of words that rhyme and the use of the silent *e*.

1. Gather the index cards you prepared with nonsense words.

2. **Say:** You're going to read nonsense words that are spelled with the silent *e*. Pick up a card and read the word. Remember, this is a nonsense word. When you're finished reading the word, put it face up on the table.

3. Have students read all the words in the stack.

4. After students finish reading all the cards, spread the cards out so that all the words can be seen.

5. **Say:** I'm going to choose a card. I want you to think of a real word to rhyme with the nonsense word. Now you choose a card and think of another rhyming word.

6. Continue Step 5 until students have chosen all the cards and thought of rhyming words.

TIP If students cannot read a word, use letter tiles to build the word and have them touch and say it. When rhyming a nonsense word, give students some choices for words that rhyme.

Try It

Finish the Job

Have students complete page PH 32 in *K¹² PhonicsWorks Advanced Activity Book* for more practice on making sentences. Have students choose the word that best completes the sentence. Have them write the word and read the sentence aloud.

[Online] 20 minutes

REVIEW: Silent *e* Spelling for Sound /ō/

Students will work online independently to

▶ Practice the silent *e* spelling for the sound /ō/.

▶ Practice decoding text by reading a story.

Help students locate the online activities and provide support as needed.

Offline Alternative

No computer access? Have students point out and name things or words that contain the silent *e* spelling for the sound /ō/ (for example, *home* or *rope*). You might also ask students to spell words that that contain the silent *e* spelling for the sound /ō/.

Silent *e* Spelling for Sound /ē/

Lesson Overview

[Offline] **FOCUS:** Silent *e* Spelling for Sound /ē/ — **30** minutes

Sight Words	Pick a Pair
Get Ready	Word Chains
Learn	Introduce Silent *e* and /ē/
	Build Words
	Word Chains
Try It	"Gene and Pete"
	Dictation: Write Sentences

[Online] **REVIEW:** Silent *e* Spelling for Sound /ē/ — **20** minutes

Materials

Supplied
- *K¹² PhonicsWorks Readers Advanced 5*, pp. 19–24
- whiteboard, Learning Coach
- whiteboard, student
- Tile Kit

Also Needed
- sight words box
- dictation notebook

Advance Preparation

Refer to Super *e* on the *K¹² PhonicsWorks* DVD for a demonstration of how to do the touch and say for the silent *e*.

[Offline] **30** minutes

FOCUS: Silent *e* Spelling for Sound /ē/

Work **together** with students to complete offline Sight Words, Get Ready, Learn, and Try It activities.

Sight Words ••

Pick a Pair

Play a card game with students for more practice with sight words.

1. Gather the sight word cards that students are reviewing. Choose two words and place the cards on the table.

2. Ask questions to help students identify each word. For example, if the words are *or* and *one*, you could ask, "Which word names a number?" If the words are *on* and *but*, you could ask, "Which word is the opposite of *off*?"

3. Continue the activity until students identify all the words.

4. Take the stack of words that students read correctly and dictate each word to them.

5. Have students write each word or spell it aloud.

> **Objectives**
> - Read sight words.
> - Write sight words.
> - Spell sight words.

Get Ready ••

Word Chains

Have students build words by adding and changing letters to help them recognize and use individual sounds in words.

1. Place the following letters at the top of students' whiteboard: *a, b, e, i, j, k, l, m, o, p, t,* and *w.*

2. **Say:** I am going to build the first word in a chain. The word is *kite.*

   ▸ I will pull down the letters for the sounds /k/, /ī/, and /t/ to spell the word *kite.*
   ▸ Next I will touch and say *kite.* To change *kite* to *bite,* I will think about what sound is changed from the word *kite* to *bite.* I will need to replace the letter *k* with the letter *b.*
   ▸ Touch and say the word *bite.* Now it's your turn to change *bite* to *bike.* You can spell *bike* by making only one change. Touch and say the new word.

3. Redirect students if they select the incorrect letter for any sound.

   Say: That letter is for the sound [incorrect sound]. We want the letter for the sound [target sound]. What letter makes that sound? **Answers will vary.**

> **Objectives**
> - Identify the new word when one sound is changed in a word.
> - Identify and use vowels and vowel sounds.
> - Identify and use /ā/ spelling patterns.
> - Identify and use the sound /ā/.
> - Identify the letters, given the sound /ā/.
> - Identify and use /ī/ spelling patterns.
> - Identify and use the sound /ī/.
> - Identify the letters, given the sound /ī/.
> - Identify and use /ō/ spelling patterns.
> - Identify and use the sound /ō/.
> - Identify the letters, given the sound /ō/.

4. Redirect students if they name the sound incorrectly.

    Say: To change the word [first word] to [target word], we need the letter for the sound [target sound].

    Show students how to make the change. Have them touch and say the new word after they move the letters.

5. Follow this procedure to make the following words: *bake, wake, woke, joke, poke, pole, mole, mile, male.*

6. For every new word, have students add, replace, or remove only one letter.

TIP If students struggle, review the sounds and letters that are confusing them.

Learn

Introduce Silent *e* and /ē/

Help students recognize and use the silent *e* spelling for the sound /e/.

1. Place the *e-e* tile at the top of students' whiteboard.

    Say: Today we will learn about silent *e*. When the silent *e* comes after a vowel and a consonant, it makes the vowel say its name.

2. Point to the *e-e* tile.

    Say: This tile reminds us that when the *e* [point to first *e*] is followed by any single consonant [point to dash] and a silent *e* [point to second *e*], the *e* says /ē/.

3. Return the *e-e* tile. Then place the following letters tiles on students' whiteboard: *e, e, g, h, n, p, P, r,* and *t.*

4. Make the word *pet.* Touch and say the word.

5. Place the letter *e* at the end of the word *pet* to create the word *Pete.* Using your index and middle fingers, touch the *e* and *e* letter tiles at the same time.

6. **Say:** We are going to learn one way to read and spell the sound /ē/. When the letter *e* comes at the end of a word and after a consonant, it works together with the vowel to make the vowel say its name. The letter *e* is silent and changes the sound of the vowel to the sound of its name.

7. **Say:** Touch and say the word *Pete.* Touch the first letter and say its sound. Then touch the *e* and *e* at the same time with two fingers, saying /ē/. Touch the third letter and say its sound.

    ▸ How many sounds are in the word? three
    ▸ How many letters are in the word? four
    ▸ What two letters spell the sound /ē/? *e* and *e*

8. Redirect students if they name the letter and not its sound.

    Say: You are right that the name of the letter is [letter]. We want the sound for this letter. What is the sound?

9. Redirect students if they name the sound incorrectly.

    Say: That is the sound of another letter.

Objectives
- Identify and use vowels and vowel sounds.
- Identify and use /ē/ spelling patterns.
- Identify and use the sound /ē/.
- Identify the letters, given the sound /ē/.
- Identify the number of sounds within words.
- Blend sounds to create words.
- Identify the new word when one sound is changed in a word.
- Identify the letters, given the sound /ā/.
- Identify the letters, given the sound /ī/.
- Identify the letters, given the sound /ō/.

10. Guide students if they touch only the letter *e* tile.

    Say: That is one of the letters you need to make the sound /ē/. What is the other letter you need?

11. Repeat this procedure for the following words:

    ▶ *gene*
    ▶ *here*

TIP For the proper name word, replace the lowercase letter with a capital letter. Remember to change back to the lowercase letter for the next word in the chain.

Build Words

Help students use letters and sounds to build words.

1. Place the following letter tiles at the top of students' whiteboard: *e*, *e*, and *v*.

2. Draw two horizontal lines across the middle of students' whiteboard to represent the sounds in a word. Note that when building words with the silent *e* on the end, there is no line on which to place the *e*, which reinforces the fact that the *e* and the *e* work together to make the sound /ē/. The *e* does not make a sound on its own.

3. **Say:** Let's use letters and sounds to build the word *eve*. Remember, the silent *e* works with the letter *e* to make the sound /ē/.

4. Have students finger stretch the sounds in *eve*.

5. Have students

    ▶ Identify the first and next sounds in *eve*.
    ▶ Choose the corresponding letter for each sound.
    ▶ Mmove the letters to the correct lines on the whiteboard.

6. Guide students with these questions:

    ▶ What is the first sound in *eve*? /ē/
      Which line does the letter for that sound go on? the first one
    ▶ What is the next sound in *eve*? /v/
      Which line does the letter for that sound go on? the second one
    ▶ What letter is silent in the word *eve*? e
      Where does the silent letter go? at the end of the word

7. Have students touch and say the word. Be sure to check that students are using their index and middle fingers to touch the *e* and *e* at the same time before they touch and say the last letter and sound.

8. Redirect students if they select the incorrect letter.

    Say: That sound is in the word [word], and it is the [first, second, third, fourth] sound. We want the sound [target sound].

    Continue until students select the correct letter.

Word Chains

Have students build words by adding and changing letters to help them recognize and use individual sounds in words.

1. Place the following letters at the top of students' whiteboard: *a, c, d, d, e, e, i, m, n, o, p, P, r, s,* and *t.*

2. **Say:** I am going to build the first word in a chain. The word is *Pete.*

   ▶ I will pull down the letters for the sounds /p/, /ē/, and /t/ to spell the word *Pete.*

   ▶ Next I will touch and say *Pete.* To change *Pete* to *pet,* I will think about what sound is changed from the word *Pete* to *pet.* I will need to remove the silent *e* at the end of the word *Pete* to make the word *pet.*

   ▶ Touch and say the word *pet.* Now it's your turn to change *pet* to *pat.* You can spell *pat* by making only one change. Touch and say the new word.

3. Redirect students if they select the incorrect letter for any sound.

   Say: That letter is for the sound [incorrect sound]. We want the letter for the sound [target sound]. What letter makes that sound? Answers will vary.

4. Redirect students if they name the sound incorrectly.

   Say: To change the word [first word] to [target word], we need the letter for the sound [target sound].

   Show students how to make the change. Have them touch and say the new word after they move the letters.

5. Follow this procedure to make the following words: *pot, not, note, nope, cope, code, rode, ride, rid, did, dim, dime, dome, dame, same, tame, tape, tap, tip, top, mop, mope.*

6. For every new word, have students add, replace, or remove only one letter.

TIP For the proper name word, replace the lowercase letter with a capital letter. Remember to change back to the lowercase letter for the next word in the chain.

Try It ●

"Gene and Pete"

Have students read "Gene and Pete" on page 19 of *K¹² PhonicsWorks Readers Advanced 5.*

Students should read the story silently once or twice before reading the story aloud. When students miss a word that can be sounded out, point to it and give students three to six seconds to try the word again. If students still miss the word, tell them the word so the flow of the story isn't interrupted.

After reading the story, make a list of all the words students missed, and go over those words with them. You may use letter tiles to show students how to read the words.

Objectives

- Read aloud grade-level text with appropriate automaticity, prosody, accuracy, and rate.
- Decode words by applying grade-level word analysis skills.
- Write words by applying grade-level phonics knowledge.
- Write sight words.
- Follow three-step directions.

Dictation: Write Sentences

Use sentences to help students identify individual sounds in words.

1. Gather a pencil and the dictation notebook. Say the sentence, *Can Zeke bake a cake?* Then give these directions to students:

   ▶ Repeat the sentence.
   ▶ Write the sentence in your notebook.
   ▶ Read the sentence aloud.

2. When students have finished, write the following sentence on your whiteboard: *Can Zeke bake a cake?*

3. Have them compare their answer to your correct version.

4. Repeat this procedure with the sentence, *I hope Kate is on time.*

   ▶ If students make an error and don't see it, help them correct their mistake by having them finger stretch the sounds in the word they missed.
   ▶ If students are having difficulty selecting the correct letters or sounds, review those letters or sounds that are confusing them.
   ▶ If students have difficulty with first, middle, and last sounds, have them finger stretch the sounds in words.

 **20 minutes**

REVIEW: Silent *e* Spelling for Sound /ē/

Students will work online independently to

▶ Practice the silent *e* spelling for the sound /ē/.

Help students locate the online activities and provide support as needed.

Offline Alternative

No computer access? Have students point out and name things or words that use the silent *e* spelling for the sound /ē/, (for example *here* or *gene*). You might also ask students to spell words that use the silent *e* spelling for the sound /ē/.

> **Objectives**
> - Identify and use /ē/ spelling patterns.
> - Identify and use the sound /ē/.
> - Identify the letters, given the sound /ē/.
> - Identify individual sounds in words.

Unit Checkpoint

Lesson Overview

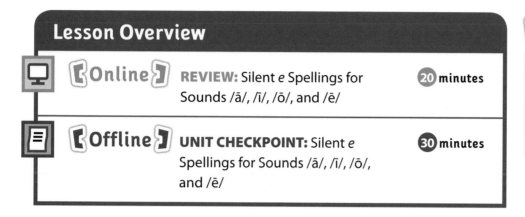

Online — **REVIEW:** Silent *e* Spellings for Sounds /ā/, /ī/, /ō/, and /ē/ — **20** minutes

Offline — **UNIT CHECKPOINT:** Silent *e* Spellings for Sounds /ā/, /ī/, /ō/, and /ē/ — **30** minutes

Materials

Supplied
- *K¹² PhonicsWorks Advanced Assessments,* pp. PH 91–96

Objectives
- Identify and use the sound /ā/.
- Identify and use /ā/ spelling patterns.
- Identify the letters, given the sound /ā/.
- Identify and use the sound /ē/.
- Identify and use /ē/ spelling patterns.
- Identify the letters, given the sound /ē/.
- Identify and use the sound /ī/.
- Identify and use /ī/ spelling patterns.
- Identify the letters, given the sound /ī/.
- Identify and use the sound /ō/.
- Identify and use /ō/ spelling patterns.
- Identify the letters, given the sound /ō/.
- Identify individual sounds in words.
- Given the letter, identify the most common sound.
- Given the sound, identify the most common letter or letters.
- Read instructional-level text with 90% accuracy.
- Read aloud grade-level text with appropriate automaticity, prosody, accuracy, and rate.
- Write words by applying grade-level phonics knowledge.
- Write sight words.
- Read sight words.

Online **20** minutes

REVIEW: **Silent *e* Spellings for Sounds /ā/, /ī/, /ō/, and /ē/**

Students will review the silent *e* spellings for the sounds /ā/, /ī/, /ō/, and /ē/ to prepare for the Unit Checkpoint. Help students locate the online activities and provide support as needed.

 **30 minutes**

UNIT CHECKPOINT: Silent *e* Spellings for Sounds /ā/, /ī/, /ō/, and /ē/

Explain that students are going to show what they have learned about sounds, letters, and words.

1. Give students the Unit Checkpoint pages for the Silent *e* Spellings for Sounds /ā/, /ī/, /ō/, and /ē/ unit and print the Unit Checkpoint Answer Key, if you'd like.

2. Use the instructions below to help administer the Checkpoint to students. On the Answer Key or another sheet of paper, note student answers to oral response questions to help with scoring the Checkpoint later.

3. Use the Answer Key to score the Checkpoint, and then enter the results online.

Part 1. Read Words and Words Parts Moving left to right, have students say the sounds of each word or word part. Note any word or word parts they say incorrectly.

Part 2. Finger Stretching Say each word to students. Have them say each word aloud and finger stretch the sounds. Note any words they finger stretch incorrectly.

13. *cake*

14. *kite*

15. *Pete*

16. *home*

Part 3. Dictation Say each word to students. Have them repeat and write the word.

17. *like*	21. *Gene*
18. *take*	22. *eve*
19. *name*	23. *home*
20. *hope*	24. *nine*

Part 4. Writing Read each sentence to students. Have them repeat and write the sentence.

25. *Mike can fix my bike.*

26. *The mole will dig a hole.*

27. *Pete will take a hike.*

Part 5. Read Aloud Listen to students read the sentences aloud. Count and note the number of words they read correctly.

Part 6. Say Letters Say each word part. Have students say the letters that make the sounds they hear in each word part. Note any incorrect responses.

29. /ā/ /t/

30. /ō/ /b/

31. /ī/ /f/

32. /ŏ/ /z/

33. /ē/ /v/

34. /ung/

35. /onk/

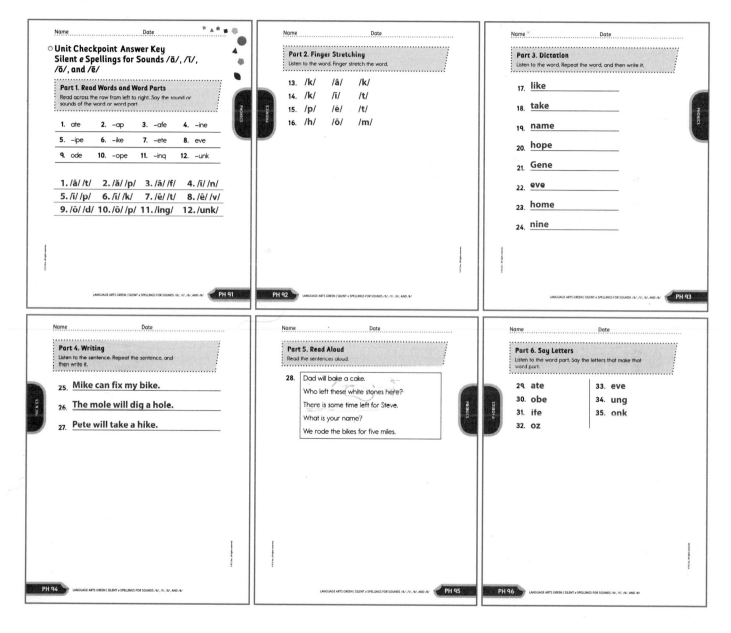

Name _____ Date _____

Unit Checkpoint Answer Key
Silent *e* Spellings for Sounds /ā/, /ī/, /ō/, and /ē/

Part 1. Read Words and Word Parts
Read across the row from left to right. Say the sound or sounds of the word or word part.

1. ate   2. –ap   3. –afe   4. –ine
5. –ipe   6. –ike   7. –ete   8. eve
9. ode   10. –ope 11. –inq   12. –unk

1. /ā/ /t/   2. /ă/ /p/   3. /ā/ /f/   4. /ī/ /n/
5. /ī/ /p/   6. /ī/ /k/   7. /ē/ /t/   8. /ē/ /v/
9. /ō/ /d/   10. /ō/ /p/ 11. /ing/   12. /unk/

Name _____ Date _____

Part 2. Finger Stretching
Listen to the word. Finger stretch the word.

13. /k/   /ā/   /k/
14. /k/   /ī/   /t/
15. /p/   /ē/   /t/
16. /h/   /ō/   /m/

Name _____ Date _____

Part 3. Dictation
Listen to the word. Repeat the word, and then write it.

17. like
18. take
19. name
20. hope
21. Gene
22. eve
23. home
24. nine

Name _____ Date _____

Part 4. Writing
Listen to the sentence. Repeat the sentence, and then write it.

25. Mike can fix my bike.
26. The mole will dig a hole.
27. Pete will take a hike.

Name _____ Date _____

Part 5. Read Aloud
Read the sentences aloud.

28. Dad will bake a cake.
    Who left these white stones here?
    There is some time left for Steve.
    What is your name?
    We rode the bikes for five miles.

Name _____ Date _____

Part 6. Say Letters
Listen to the word part. Say the letters that make that word part.

29. ate   33. eve
30. obe   34. ung
31. ife   35. onk
32. oz

Introduce Silent *e* Spelling for Sound /ū/

Unit Overview

In this unit, students will
- ▶ Learn the sight words *none, more,* and *held.*
- ▶ Learn the silent *e* spelling for the sounds /ū/ and long double *o.*
- ▶ Review beginning blends.
- ▶ Make and complete sentences.
- ▶ Practice reading and writing.

Materials

Supplied
- *K¹² PhonicsWorks Advanced Activity Book,* p. PH 33
- whiteboard, student
- Tile Kit

Also Needed
- sight words box
- index cards (36)

Lesson Overview

Offline FOCUS: Introduce Silent *e* Spelling for Sound /ū/ — **30** minutes

Sight Words	Introduce Sight Words
Get Ready	Word Practice
Learn	Introduce Silent *e* and /ū/
	Build Words
	Word Play
Try It	Alphabet Addition

Online REVIEW: Silent *e* Spelling for Sound /ū/ — **20** minutes

Advance Preparation

For Word Practice, print each of the following words on index cards, using one card per word: *bone, froze, choke, clove, code, cone, dome, vat, wax, doze, drove, globe, hole, smoke, spoke, stone, stove, throne, woke, chop, box, cob, cot, crop, dock, dot, frog, hot, hop, job, lot, pop, plot, shock, spot,* and *zone.*

Refer to Super *e* on the *K¹² PhonicsWorks* DVD for a demonstration of how to do the touch and say for the silent *e.*

[Offline] **30** minutes

FOCUS: Introduce Silent *e* Spelling for Sound /ū/

Work **together** with students to complete offline Sight Words, Get Ready, Learn, and Try It activities.

Sight Words ....

Introduce Sight Words

Help students learn the sight words *none, more,* and *held.*

1. Gather the sight word cards *none, more,* and *held.*

2. Show students the *none* card.

3. **Say:** This is the word *none.* We see this word so often that we want to be able to read and spell it quickly without thinking about it. Look closely at the word *none.* Spell the word *none* aloud. Take a picture of the word *none* in your mind. When you think you can spell *none* yourself, turn the card over and use your letter tiles to spell the word *none.* Check the card to see if you spelled the word *none* correctly. Read aloud the word you spelled with the letter tiles.

4. Repeat the activity with the remaining sight words.

5. Chart students' progress on the back of each card.

   ▸ Divide the back of the card into two columns.
   ▸ Label the first column "Read" and the second column "Spell."
   ▸ Record the dates that students read or spell the word correctly. When they can read and spell the word correctly three times in a row, they have mastered the word. You may want to put a star or sticker on their card when they have mastered that word.

6. Add the cards to students' sight words box.

(TIP) Sight words can be very difficult for some students. Let them work at their own pace and really master these words.

Objectives
- Read sight words.
- Spell sight words.

Get Ready ....

Word Practice

Have students practice reading words that use a silent *e.*

1. Gather the index cards you prepared, and place them face down in one pile.

2. **Say:** You are going to practice reading words that use a silent *e.*

   ▸ You will choose a card from the pile and read the word on it.
   ▸ You will tell me if the word is a silent *e* word.
   ▸ Then you will place the card in one of two piles: one for silent *e* words, and one for words that are not silent *e* words.

3. Choose a card from the pile and say the word. Tell students if the word is a silent *e* word.

   Say: Now it's your turn. Choose a card and read it to me.

Objectives
- Read aloud grade-level text with appropriate automaticity, prosody, accuracy, and rate.
- Identify and use silent *e.*

4. Follow this procedure, taking turns with students, until all of the words in the stack have been read.

   ▶ **Silent *e* Words:** *bone, froze, choke, clove, code, cone, dome, doze, drove, globe, hole, smoke, spoke, stone, stove, throne, woke, chop, zone*

   ▶ **Nonsilent *e* Words:** *vat, wax, chop, box, cob, cot, crop, dock, dot, frog, hot, hop, job, lot, pop, plot, shock, spot*

TIP If students stumble over any words, have them touch and say the words. Touch and say these words along with them.

Learn

Introduce Silent *e* and /ū/

Help students recognize and use the silent *e* spelling for sound /ū/.

1. Place the *u-e* tile at the top of the students' whiteboard.

   Say: Today we will learn about silent *e*. When the silent *e* comes after a vowel and a consonant, it makes the vowel say its name.

2. Point to the *u-e* tile.

   Say: This tile reminds us that when the *u* [point to *u*] is followed by any single consonant [point to dash] and a silent *e* [point to *e*], the *u* says /ū/.

3. Return the *u-e* tile. Then place the following letter tiles on students' whiteboard: *b, c, e, t,* and *u*.

4. Make the word *cut*. Touch and say the word.

5. Place the letter *e* after the word *cut* to create the word *cute*. Using your index and middle fingers, touch the *u* and *e* letter tiles at the same time.

   Say: We are going to learn one way to read and spell the sound /ū/. When the letter *e* comes at the end of a word and after a consonant, it works together with the vowel to make the vowel say its name. The letter *e* is silent and changes the sound of the vowel to the sound of its name.

6. **Say:** Touch and say the word *cute*. Touch the first letter, *c*, and say its sound, /k/. Then touch the *u* and *e* at the same time with two fingers, saying /ū/. Touch the third letter, *t*, and say its sound, /t/.

   ▶ How many sounds are in the word? three
   ▶ How many letters are in the word? four
   ▶ What two letters spell the sound /ū/? *u* and *e*

7. Redirect students if they name the letter and not its sound.

   Say: You are right that the name of the letter is [letter]. We want the sound for this letter. What is the sound?

8. Redirect students if they name the sound incorrectly.

   Say: That is the sound of another letter.

9. Guide students if they touch only the letter *u* tile.

   Say: That is one of the letters you need to make the sound /ū/. What is the other letter you need?

10. Repeat this procedure for the word *cube*.

Objectives

- Identify and use /ū/ spelling patterns.
- Identify and use the sound /ū/.
- Identify the letters, given the sound /ū/.
- Identify and use silent *e*.
- Identify the number of sounds within words.
- Blend sounds to create words.

Build Words

Help students use letters and sounds to build words.

1. Place the following letter tiles at the top of students' whiteboard: *e, f, l, m, t, s,* and *u*.

2. Draw three horizontal lines across the middle of students' whiteboard to represent the sounds in a word. Note that when building words with the silent *e* on the end, there is no line on which to place the *e*, which reinforces the fact that the *u* and the *e* work together to make the sound /ū/. The *e* does not make a sound on its own.

3. **Say:** Let's use letters and sounds to build the word *fume.* Remember, the silent *e* works with the letter *u* to make the sound /ū/.

4. Have students finger stretch the sounds in *fume.*

5. Have students

   ▸ Identify the first, next, and last sounds in *fume.*
   ▸ Choose the corresponding letter for each of the sounds.
   ▸ Move the letters to the correct lines on their whiteboard.

6. Guide students with these questions:

   ▸ What is the first sound in *fume*? /f/
     Which line does the letter for that sound go on? the first one
   ▸ What is the next sound in *fume*? /ū/
     Which lines does the letter for that sound go on? the second one
   ▸ What's the last sound in *fume*? /m/
     Which line does the letter for that sound go on? the third one
   ▸ What letter is silent in the word *fume*? e
     Where does the silent letter go? at the end of the word

7. Have students touch and say the word. Be sure to check that students are using their index and middle fingers to touch the *u* and *e* at the same time before they touch and say the last letter and sound.

8. Redirect students if they select the incorrect letter.

   Say: That sound is in the word [word], and it is the [first, second, third] sound. We want the sound [target sound].

   Continue until students select the correct letter.

9. Draw horizontal lines across the middle of students' whiteboard that represent the number of sounds in each word. Repeat the activity to build the following words:

   ▸ *mule* /m/ /ū/ /l/
   ▸ *mute* /m/ /ū/ /t/
   ▸ *use* /ū/ /z/

Word Play

Help students use letters and sounds to play with words that contain the silent *e*.

1. Place the following letter tiles at the top of students' whiteboard: *a-e, e-e, i-e, o-e*, and *u-e*.

2. Place the following letters at the bottom of students' whiteboard: *a, e, e, g, i, j, k, m, n, o, p, r, s, t*, and *u*.

3. **Say:** You are going to build words that have the silent *e*. I will say a word to you. First I want you to repeat the word after me. The first word is *tame*.

4. Have students say the word and find the letter tile at the top of the whiteboard that represents the silent *e* spelling of the long vowel sound /ā/. *a-e*

5. **Say:** Now find the letters that spell the word *tame*. Build the word *tame*.

   ▸ What is the beginning sound and letter in *tame*? /t/, *t*
   ▸ What is the middle sound in *tame*? /ā/
   ▸ What two letters work together to make that sound? *a-e*
   ▸ What is the last sound and letter in *tame*? /m/, *e*

6. Have students touch and say the word.

7. Redirect students if they select the incorrect letter.

   Say: That sound is in the word [word], and it is the [first, second, third, fourth] sound. We want the sound [target sound].

   Continue until students select the correct letter.

8. Repeat the activity to make the following words with silent *e*:

   ▸ *gene*
   ▸ *ripe*
   ▸ *joke*
   ▸ *muse*

Try It

Alphabet Addition

Have students complete page PH 33 in *K¹² PhonicsWorks Advanced Activity Book* for more practice with making words that have the silent *e* spelling for the sound /ū/. First have students add the parts of the word together to make a new word. Then have them write the word and read it aloud.

[Online] 20 minutes

REVIEW: Silent *e* Spelling for Sound /ū/

Students will work online independently to

▶ Practice the silent *e* spelling for the sound /ū/.
▶ Practice decoding text by reading a story.

Help students locate the online activities and provide support as needed.

Offline Alternative

No computer access? Have students point out and name things or words that contain the silent *e* spelling for the sound /ū/ (for example, *mule* or *cube*). You might also ask students to spell words that contain the silent *e* spelling for the sound /ū/.

Practice Silent *e* Spelling for Sound /ū/

Lesson Overview

Offline **FOCUS:** Practice Silent *e* Spelling for Sound /ū/ — **30** minutes

Sight Words	Sight Word Fun
Practice	Face-Down Letters
	Pairs of Vowel Sounds
	Word Chains
Try It	"Hope's Lunch"
	Dictation: Write Words

Online **REVIEW:** Silent *e* Spelling for Sound /ū/ — **20** minutes

Materials

Supplied
- *K¹² PhonicsWorks Readers Advanced 5*, pp. 25–30
- whiteboard, Learning Coach
- whiteboard, student
- Tile Kit

Also Needed
- sight words box
- dictation notebook

Advance Preparation

Place lowercase letter tiles in alphabetical order on your whiteboard.

 **30** minutes

FOCUS: Practice Silent *e* Spelling for Sound /ū/

Work **together** with students to complete offline Sight Words, Practice, and Try It activities.

Sight Words

Sight Word Fun

Help students learn the sight words *none, more,* and *held,* and up to two additional sight words they have yet to master.

1. Gather the sight word cards *none, more,* and *held,* and up to two additional sight word cards.

2. Choose one sight word card to begin.

   Say: Look at this word and take a picture of it in your mind. When you think you can spell the word yourself, turn the card over and use your letter tiles to spell the word.

3. After students spell the word, have them check the card to see if they spelled the word correctly.

   Say: Read aloud the word you spelled with the letter tiles.

4. Repeat the activity with the remaining sight words.

TIP Sight words can be very difficult for some students. Let students work at their own pace and really master these words.

> **Objectives**
> - Read sight words.
> - Spell sight words.

Practice

Face-Down Letters

Help students master the letters of the alphabet, have them practice identifying and naming letters. Grab your whiteboard with letters placed in alphabetical order.

1. Lay your whiteboard down on a flat surface and flip over the letter tiles *d, f, h, m, p, qu, s,* and *y* so they are face down on the whiteboard.

2. **Say:** These letters are face down. We are looking at the back of them. Name each letter and then turn it over to see if you were right.

TIP If students miss any of the letters, have them turn over the missed ones and try again.

Pairs of Vowel Sounds

Help students recognize vowel sounds in words.

1. **Say:** I am going to say a pair of words. Repeat the pair of words I say and listen for the special vowel sound. One word will have the special vowel sound /ū/, as in *use.* Your job is to identify the word with the sound /ū/. For example, if I say *cube* and *cut,* you will repeat both words and tell me the word *cube* because it has the special vowel sound /ū/.

2. **Say:** Now it's your turn. The first pair of words is *use* and *cheese.* Students should repeat the words *use* and *cheese* and then say *use.*

3. Say the following pairs of words:

   ► *hug* and *huge* huge
   ► *mitt* and *mute* mute
   ► *cat* and *cute* cute
   ► *muse* and *miss* muse
   ► *fume* and *fun* fume

Word Chains

Have students build words by adding and changing letters to help them recognize and use individual sounds in words.

1. Place the following letters at the top of students' whiteboard: *a, b, c, d, e, i, k, l, m, o, p, s, t,* and *u.*

2. **Say:** I am going to build the first word in a chain. The word is *mat.*

   ▶ I will pull down the letters for the sounds /m/, /ă/, and /t/ to spell the word *mat.*

   ▶ Next I will touch and say *mat.* To change *mat* to *mate,* I will think about which sound is changed from the word *mat* to *mate.* Because the middle sound changes from /ă/ to /ā/, we will need to add a silent *e* to the end of *mat.*

   ▶ Touch and say the word *mate.* Now it's your turn to change *mate* to *mute.* You can spell *mute* by making only one change. Touch and say the new word.

3. Redirect students if they select the incorrect letter for any sound.

   Say: That letter is for the sound [incorrect sound]. We want the letter for the sound [target sound]. What letter makes that sound? Answers will vary.

4. Redirect students if they select the wrong sound.

   Say: To change the word [first word] to [target word], we need the letter for the sound [target sound].

   Show students how to make the change. Have them touch and say the new word after they move the letters.

5. Follow this procedure to make the following words: *cute, cube, cub, cab, cap, cape, tape, take, lake, like, lime, dime, dome, dose.*

6. For every new word, have students add, replace, or remove only one letter.

(TIP) If students struggle, review the sounds and letters that are confusing them.

Try It

"Hope's Lunch"

Have students read "Hope's Lunch" on page 25 of *K¹² PhonicsWorks Readers Advanced 5.*

Students should read the story silently once or twice before reading the story aloud. When students miss a word that can be sounded out, point to it and give students three to six seconds to try the word again. If students still miss the word, tell them the word so the flow of the story isn't interrupted.

After reading the story, make a list of all the words students missed, and go over those words with them. You may use letter tiles to show students how to read the words.

Objectives

- Read aloud grade-level text with appropriate automaticity, prosody, accuracy, and rate.
- Decode words by applying grade-level word analysis skills.
- Write words by applying grade-level phonics knowledge.
- Follow three-step directions.

Dictation: Write Words
Have students practice identifying sounds and writing words.

1. Gather a pencil and the dictation notebook. Say the word *cube*. Then give these directions to students:

   ► Repeat the word.
   ► Write the word in your notebook.
   ► Read the word aloud.

2. When students have finished, write the following word on your whiteboard: *cube*.

3. Have them compare their answer to your correct version.

4. Repeat this procedure with the following words: *mute*, *snake*, and *smile*.

   ► If students make an error and don't see it, help them correct their mistake by having them finger stretch the sounds in the word they missed.
   ► If students are having difficulty selecting the correct letters or sounds, review those letters or sounds that are confusing them.
   ► If students have difficulty with first, middle, and last sounds, have them finger stretch the sounds in words.

 **20 minutes**

REVIEW: Silent *e* Spelling for Sound /ū/
Students will work online independently to

► Practice the silent *e* spelling for the sound /ū/.

Help students locate the online activities and provide support as needed.

Offline Alternative

No computer access? Have students point out and name things or words that contain the silent *e* spelling for the sound /ū/ (for example, *fume* or *cute*). You might also ask students to spell words that contain the silent *e* spelling for the sound /ū/.

> **Objectives**
> - Identify and use /ū/ spelling patterns.
> - Identify and use the sound /ū/.
> - Identify the letters, given the sound /ū/.
> - Identify and use silent *e*.
> - Identify individual sounds in words.

Introduce Silent *e* Spelling for Long Double *o*

Lesson Overview

Offline **FOCUS:** Introduce Silent *e* Spelling for Long Double *o*   **30** minutes

Sight Words	Sight Word Fun
Get Ready	Make Up a Sentence
Learn	Introduce Silent *e* and Long Double *o*
	Build Words
	Guess the Word
Try It	Fun with Long Double *o* Sound

Online **REVIEW:** Silent *e* Spelling for Long Double *o*   **20** minutes

Materials

Supplied
- *K¹² PhonicsWorks Advanced Activity Book,* p. PH 34
- whiteboard, student
- Tile Kit

Also Needed
- sight words box
- index cards (6)

Advance Preparation

For Make Up a Sentence, print each of the following words on index cards, using one card per word: *cube, joke, shine, blame, broke,* and *cute.*

Refer to Super *e* on the *K¹² PhonicsWorks* DVD for a demonstration of how to do the touch and say for the silent *e*.

[Offline] 30 minutes

FOCUS: Introduce Silent *e* Spelling for Long Double *o*

Work **together** with students to complete offline Sight Words, Get Ready, Learn, and Try It activities.

Sight Words

Sight Word Fun

Help students learn the sight words *none, more,* and *held,* and up to two additional sight words they have yet to master.

1. Gather the sight word cards *none, more,* and *held,* and up to two additional sight word cards.

2. Choose one sight word card to begin.

   Say: Look at this word and take a picture of it in your mind. When you think you can spell the word yourself, turn the card over and use your letter tiles to spell the word.

3. After students spell the word, have them check the card to see if they spelled the word correctly.

   Say: Read aloud the word you spelled with the letter tiles.

4. Repeat the activity with the remaining sight words.

   TIP Sight words can be very difficult for some students. Let students work at their own pace and really master these words.

> **Objectives**
> - Read sight words.
> - Spell sight words.

Get Ready

Make Up a Sentence

Help students use words to make sentences.

1. Gather the index cards you prepared, and place them face down on the table in one pile.

2. Have students
   - ► Select a card.
   - ► Read the word.
   - ► Use the word in an interesting, fun, or silly sentence.

   TIP If students read a word incorrectly, have them finger stretch the sounds in the word.

> **Objectives**
> - Read aloud grade-level text with appropriate automaticity, prosody, accuracy, and rate.
> - Identify complete sentences.

Learn

Introduce Silent *e* and Long Double *o*

Help students recognize and use the silent *e* spelling for the long double o sound, /o͞o/.

1. Place the *u-e* tile at the top of the students whiteboard.

   Say: Today we will learn about silent *e*. When the silent *e* comes after a vowel and a consonant, it makes the vowel say its name.

2. Point to the *u-e* tile.

   Say: This tile reminds us that when the *u* [point to *u*] is followed by any single consonant [point to dash] and a silent *e* [point to *e*], the *u* says /ū/.

3. Return the *u-e* tile. Then place the following letters tiles on students' whiteboard: *b, d, d, e, l, m, r, t,* and *u*.

4. Make the word *mule*. Touch and say the word.

5. Using your index and middle fingers, touch the *u* and *e* letter tiles at the same time.

   Say: When the letter *e* comes at the end of a word and after a consonant, it can work together with the vowel to make the vowel say its name. The letter *e* is silent and changes the sound of the vowel *u* to the sound of its name, /ū/.

6. Make the word *rule* on students' whiteboard. Touch and say the word.

   Say: Sometimes, though, the silent *e* makes the *u* say the sound /o͞o/, as in the word *rule*.

7. Using your index and middle fingers, touch the *u* and *e* letter tiles at the same time.

   Say: When there is a consonant between the *u* and the *e*, sometimes we read the sound /o͞o/. The *u* and the *e* are there to work together to make the sound /o͞o/. When we touch the letters for the sound /o͞o/, we touch both the *u* and the *e* at the same time.

8. Make the word *tube* on students' whiteboard. Touch and say the word.

9. **Say:** Touch and say the word *tube*. Touch the first letter and say its sound. Then touch the *u* and *e* at the same time with two fingers, saying the sound /o͞o/. Touch the third letter and say its sound.

   ▶ How many sounds are in the word? three
   ▶ How many letters are in the word? four
   ▶ What two letters spell the sound /o͞o/? *u* and *e*

10. Make the word *dude* on students' whiteboard. Touch and say the word.

    Say: Touch and say the word *dude*. Touch the first letter and say its sound. Then touch the *u* and *e* at the same time with two fingers, saying the sound /o͞o/. Touch the third letter and say its sound.

    ▶ How many sounds are in the word? three
    ▶ How many letters are in the word? four
    ▶ What two letters spell the sound /o͞o/? *u* and *e*

Objectives

- Identify and use the long double o sound.
- Identify the letters, given the long double o sound.
- Identify and use double o (oo) spelling patterns.
- Identify and use silent *e*.
- Identify the number of sounds within words.
- Blend sounds to create words.
- Identify complete sentences.

11. Redirect students if they name the letter and not its sound.

    Say: You are right that the name of the letter is [letter]. We want the sound for this letter. What is the sound?

12. Redirect students if they name the sound incorrectly.

    Say: That is the sound of another letter.

Build Words

Help students use letters and sounds to build words.

1. Place the following letter tiles at the top of students' whiteboard: *d, e, J, n, r, t,* and *u.*

2. Draw three horizontal lines across the middle of students' whiteboard to represent the sounds in a word. Note that when building words with the silent *e* on the end, there is no line on which to place the *e,* which reinforces the fact that the *u* and the *e* work together to make the sound /ū/. The *e* does not make a sound on its own.

3. **Say:** Let's use letters and sounds to build the word *June.*

4. Have students finger stretch the sounds in *June.*

5. Have students

   ▸ Identify the first, next, and last sounds in *June.*
   ▸ Choose the corresponding letter for each of the sounds.
   ▸ Move the letters to the correct lines on their whiteboard.

6. Guide students with these questions:

   ▸ What is the first sound in *June?* /j/
     Which line does the letter for that sound go on? the first one
   ▸ What is the next sound in *June?* /o͞o/
     Which line does the one for that sound go on? the second
   ▸ What's the last sound in *June?* /n/
     Which line does the letter for that sound go on? the third one
   ▸ What letter is silent in the word *June?* e
     Where does the silent letter go? at the end of the word

7. Have students touch and say the word. Be sure to check that students are using their index and middle fingers to touch the *u* and *e* at the same time before they touch and say the last letter and sound.

8. Redirect students if they select the incorrect letter.

   Say: That sound is in the word [word], and it is the [first, second, third] sound. We want the sound [target sound].

   Continue until students select the correct letter.

9. Repeat the activity to build the following words:

   ▸ *tune* /t/ /o͞o/ /n/
   ▸ *rude* /r/ /o͞o/ /d/

Guess the Word

Have students use word meaning and sentence structure to choose a word that best completes a sentence.

1. Write the following words on students' whiteboard: *dune, flute, prune, tune,* and *tube*. Make sure students know the meaning of all the words on their whiteboard before you do this activity.

2. **Say:** We're going to play a guessing game. I'm going to read a sentence with a word missing. Your job is to look at the words on your whiteboard and decide which one is the right word to complete the sentence.

   ▸ Listen to this sentence: "The wind blew the sand into a _____ ."
   ▸ Next you will tell me what word makes sense in the blank of the sentence. This time the word would be *dune*.
   ▸ The complete sentence would be, "The wind blew the sand into a *dune*." Now you try it.

3. Continue the procedure with the following sentences:

   ▸ *I had a _____ in my breakfast cereal.* prune
   ▸ *Be sure to put the cap on the _____ of the toothpaste.* tube
   ▸ *Ben wants to learn to play the _____ .* flute
   ▸ *I heard a _____ I knew on the radio.* tune

4. Redirect students if they have difficulty recognizing the vowel sound in any of the words. Display the red *u-e* tile and remind students of the silent *e*. Have students point to the word and touch and say. Ask students the following questions:

   ▸ How many sounds are in the word?
   ▸ How many letters are in the word?
   ▸ What does the silent *e* do?

Try It

Fun with Long Double *o* Sound

Have students complete page PH 34 in *K¹² PhonicsWorks Advanced Activity Book* for more practice with the silent *e* spelling for the sound /o͞o/. Have them read each word and sentence and circle the word with the sound /o͞o/.

Try It

Introduce Silent *e* Spelling for
Long Double *o* Sound

Fun with Long Double *o* Sound

Read the word aloud. Read the sentence aloud, and then circle the
word with the sound /o͞o/ in it. Read the sentence again.

1. plume   I see a (plume) of smoke.
2. June   It gets so hot in (June)
3. tune   None of them sang a (tune.)
4. tube   Put your (tube) in the water.
5. flute   I have a drum and she has a (flute.)
6. dune   See! That is a tall sand (dune)
7. rude   It is (rude) to stare at people.

PH 34   LANGUAGE ARTS GREEN

Objectives

- Read aloud grade-level text with appropriate automaticity, prosody, accuracy, and rate.
- Identify and use the long double *o* sound.
- Identify and use double *o* (oo) spelling patterns.
- Identify and use silent *e*.

Online   20 minutes

REVIEW: Silent *e* Spelling for Long Double *o*

Students will work online independently to

▶ Practice the silent *e* spelling for the sound /o͞o/.
▶ Practice decoding text by reading a story.

Help students locate the online activities and provide support as needed.

Offline Alternative

No computer access? Have students point out and name things or words that contain the silent *e* spelling for the sound /o͞o/ (for example, *rude* or *dude*). You might also ask students to spell words that that contain the silent *e* spelling for the sound /o͞o/.

Objectives

- Identify and use the long double *o* sound.
- Identify and use double *o* (oo) spelling patterns.
- Identify the letters, given the long double *o* sound.
- Identify and use silent *e*.
- Identify individual sounds in words.
- Read aloud grade-level text with appropriate automaticity, prosody, accuracy, and rate.
- Decode words by applying grade-level word analysis skills.

Practice Silent *e* Spelling for Long Double *o*

Lesson Overview

Materials

Offline — **FOCUS:** Practice Silent *e* Spelling for Long Double *o* — **30** minutes

Sight Words	Sight Word Fun
Practice	Sound Workout
	Identify Silent *e* Words
Try It	"Sue Makes a Note"

Online — **REVIEW:** Silent *e* Spelling for Long Double *o* — **20** minutes

Supplied
- *K¹² PhonicsWorks Readers Advanced 6*, pp. 1–6

Also Needed
- sight words box
- index cards (36)

Advance Preparation

For Identify Silent *e* Words, print each of the following words on index cards, using one card per word: *crude, flute, June, prune, rude, rule, tube, tune, cube, cute, fume, mule, mute, use, bun, fun, pun, sun, stun, gust, hush, jump, just, luck, lump, must, plum, plus, pump, tug, snug, shut, rub, pup, nut,* and *mud*.

[Offline] 30 minutes

FOCUS: Practice Silent *e* Spelling for Long Double *o*

Work **together** with students to complete offline Sight Words, Practice, and Try It activities.

Sight Words

Sight Word Fun

Help students learn the sight words *none, more,* and *held,* and up to two additional sight words they have yet to master.

1. Gather the sight word cards *none, more,* and *held,* and up to two additional sight word cards.

2. Choose one sight word card to begin.

   Say: Look at this word and take a picture of it in your mind. When you think you can spell the word yourself, turn the card over and use your letter tiles to spell the word.

3. After students spell the word, have them check the card to see if they spelled the word correctly.

   Say: Read aloud the word you spelled with the letter tiles.

4. Repeat the activity with the remaining sight words.

   TIP Sight words can be very difficult for some students. Let students work at their own pace and really master these words.

> **Objectives**
> - Read sight words.
> - Spell sight words.

Practice

Sound Workout

To help students learn to recognize the silent *e* spelling for the sound /o͞o/, have them practice identifying the sound in words.

1. **Say:** I'll say a pair of words. Listen for the special vowel sound /o͞o/, as in the word *rude* in one of the words. You will repeat both words and tell me the word with the special vowel sound /o͞o/.

   ▸ For example, if I say the words *dude* and *road*, you'll repeat both words. Then you will tell me which word has the sound /o͞o/. *dude*
   ▸ Now it's your turn. First repeat the pair of words I say. Then say the words again. Tell me which word has the special vowel sound /o͞o/.

2. Follow the same procedure with the pairs of words below.

   ▸ *dark* and *duke duke*
   ▸ *float* and *flute flute*
   ▸ *crude* and *crash crude*
   ▸ *prize* and *prune prune*
   ▸ *tune* and *tone tune*

> **Objectives**
> - Identify and use vowels and vowel sounds.
> - Identify and use silent *e*.
> - Identify and use double *o* (oo) spelling patterns.
> - Identify and use the long double *o* sound.
> - Identify the letters, given the long double *o* sound.
> - Identify and use the sound /ū/.
> - Identify and use /ū/ spelling patterns.

Identify Silent e Words

To help students learn to recognize words that use the silent *e* spelling, have them practice identifying words that have the silent *e* spelling for the sound /ū/ and the sound /o͞o/.

1. Gather the index cards you prepared.

2. **Say:** We are going to use these cards to identify words with a silent *e*. Take the top card from the stack and read the word. Is the word a silent *e* word?

3. Have students place the card in one of two piles: one for silent *e* words, and one for words that are not silent *e* words.

4. Follow this procedure, taking turns with the student, until you have gone through all the words in the stack.

   ▸ **Silent *e* words:** *crude, flute, June, prune, rude, rule, tube, tune, cube, cute, fume, mule, mute,* and *use.*

   ▸ **Nonsilent *e* words:** *bun, fun, pun, sun, stun, gust, hush, jump, just, luck, lump, must, plum, plus, pump, tug, snug, shut, rub, pup, nut,* and *mud.*

(TIP) If students have difficulty identifying which words have a silent *e*, remind them that the silent *e* helps the vowel say its name.

Try It
. . . .

"Sue Makes a Note"

Have students read "Sue Makes a Note" on page 1 of *K¹² PhonicsWorks Readers Advanced 6.*

Students should read the story silently once or twice before reading the story aloud. When students miss a word that can be sounded out, point to it and give students three to six seconds to try the word again. If students still miss the word, tell them the word so the flow of the story isn't interrupted.

After reading the story, make a list of all the words students missed, and go over those words with them. You may use letter tiles to show students how to read the words.

Objectives

- Read aloud grade-level text with appropriate automaticity, prosody, accuracy, and rate.
- Decode words by applying grade-level word analysis skills.

〔Online〕 **20** minutes

REVIEW: Silent *e* Spelling for Long Double *o*

Students will work online independently to

▶ Practice the silent *e* spelling for the sound /o͞o/.

Help students locate the online activities and provide support as needed.

Offline Alternative

No computer access? Have students point out and name things or words that use the silent *e* spelling for the sound /o͞o/ (for example, *tune* or *tube*). You might also ask students to spell words that use the silent *e* spelling for the sound /o͞o/.

⭐ **Objectives**

- Identify and use silent *e*.
- Identify and use double *o* (oo) spelling patterns.
- Identify and use the long double *o* sound.
- Identify and use the sound /ū/.
- Identify and use /ū/ spelling patterns.
- Identify individual sounds in words.

Unit Checkpoint

Lesson Overview

🖥️ **[Online]**	**REVIEW:** Silent *e* Spellings for Sounds /ū/ and Long Double *o*	**30** minutes
📄 **[Offline]**	**UNIT CHECKPOINT:** Silent *e* Spellings for Sounds /ū/ and Long Double *o*	**20** minutes

Materials

Supplied

• *K¹² PhonicsWorks Advanced Assessments,* pp. PH 97–102

⭐ Objectives

- Identify and use vowels and vowel sounds.
- Identify and use silent *e*.
- Identify and use /ū/ spelling patterns.
- Identify and use long double *o* (oo) spelling patterns.
- Identify the letters, given the long double *o* sound.
- Identify the letters, given the sound /ū/.
- Identify individual sounds in words.
- Given the letter, identify the most common sound.
- Given the sound, identify the most common letter or letters.
- Read instructional-level text with 90% accuracy.
- Read aloud grade-level text with appropriate automaticity, prosody, accuracy, and rate.
- Write words by applying grade-level phonics knowledge.
- Write sight words.
- Read sight words.

[Online] 20 minutes

REVIEW: Silent *e* Spellings for Sounds /ū/ and Long Double *o*

Students will review the silent *e* spellings for the sounds /ū/ and /o͞o/ to prepare for the Unit Checkpoint. Help students locate the online activities and provide support as needed.

[Offline] 30 minutes

UNIT CHECKPOINT: Silent *e* Spellings for Sounds /ū/ and Long Double *o*

Explain that students are going to show what they have learned about sounds, letters, and words.

1. Give students the Unit Checkpoint pages for the Silent *e* Spellings for Sounds /ū/ and Long Double *o* unit and print the Unit Checkpoint Answer Key, if you'd like.

2. Use the instructions below to help administer the Checkpoint to students. On the Answer Key or another sheet of paper, note student answers to oral response questions to help with scoring the Checkpoint later.

3. Use the Answer Key to score the Checkpoint, and then enter the results online.

Part 1. Read Words and Word Parts Moving left to right, have students say the sounds of each word or word part. Note any word or word parts they say incorrectly.

Part 2. Finger Stretching Say each word to students. Have them say each word aloud and finger stretch the sounds. Note any words they finger stretch incorrectly.

13. *cute*

14. *mule*

15. *use*

16. *rule*

Part 3. Dictation Say each word to students. Have them repeat and write the word.

17. *use*

18. *rule*

19. *cube*

20. *tube*

21. *mule*

22. *cute*

23. *tune*

24. *rude*

Part 4. Writing Read each sentence to students. Have them repeat and write the sentence.

25. *I have a mule.*

26. *Use your hands.*

27. *Sing a tune.*

Part 5. Read Aloud Listen to students read the sentences aloud. Count and note the number of words they read correctly.

Part 6. Say Letters Say each word part. Have students say the letters that make each word part. Note any incorrect responses.

29. /ā/ /t/

30. /ū/ /b/

31. /ī/ /f/

32. /ŏ/ /p/

33. /ē/ /t/

34. /ū/ /k/

35. /ŭ/ /sh/

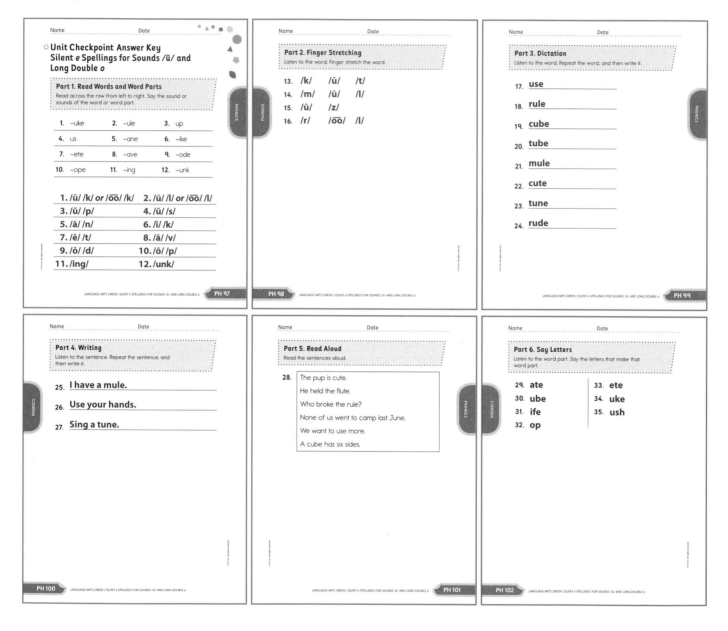

Unit Checkpoint Answer Key
Silent _e_ Spellings for Sounds /ū/ and Long Double _o_

Part 1. Read Words and Word Parts
Read across the row from left to right. Say the sound or sounds of the word or word part.

1. –uke   2. –ule   3. up

4. us   5. –ane   6. –ike

7. –ete   8. –ave   9. –ode

10. –ope   11. –ing   12. –unk

1. /ū/ /k/ or /ōō/ /k/   2. /ū/ /l/ or /ōō/ /l/
3. /ū/ /p/   4. /ū/ /s/
5. /ā/ /n/   6. /ī/ /k/
7. /ē/ /t/   8. /ā/ /v/
9. /ō/ /d/   10. /ō/ /p/
11. /ing/   12. /unk/

Part 2. Finger Stretching
Listen to the word. Finger stretch the word.

13. /k/   /ū/   /t/
14. /m/   /ū/   /l/
15. /ū/   /z/
16. /r/   /ōō/   /l/

Part 3. Dictation
Listen to the word. Repeat the word, and then write it.

17. use

18. rule

19. cube

20. tube

21. mule

22. cute

23. tune

24. rude

Part 4. Writing
Listen to the sentence. Repeat the sentence, and then write it.

25. I have a mule.

26. Use your hands.

27. Sing a tune.

Part 5. Read Aloud
Read the sentences aloud.

28. The pup is cute.
He held the flute.
Who broke the rule?
None of us went to camp last June.
We want to use more.
A cube has six sides.

Part 6. Say Letters
Listen to the word part. Say the letters that make that word part.

29. ate   33. ete
30. ube   34. uke
31. ife   35. ush
32. op

Introduce Sounds /ar/ and /or/

Unit Overview

In this unit, students will

- ▸ Learn the sight words *would*, *could*, and *should*.
- ▸ Learn the sounds /ar/ and /or/ and silent *e* spellings.
- ▸ Review words with blends.
- ▸ Practice reading and writing.

Materials

Supplied

- *K¹² PhonicsWorks Advanced Activity Book*, p. PH 35
- whiteboard, Learning Coach
- whiteboard, student
- Tile Kit

Also Needed

- sight words box
- dictation notebook
- index cards (36)
- household objects – small item (such as a key, button, or bean bag)

Lesson Overview

Offline	FOCUS: Introduce Sounds /ar/ and /or/	30 minutes
Sight Words	Introduce Sight Words	
Get Ready	Signal Ending Sounds	
Learn	Introduce *ar* and *or*	
	Build Words	
	Word Chains	
	Target Toss	
Try It	Match It	
	Dictation: Write Sentences	

Online	REVIEW: Sounds /ar/ and /or/	20 minutes

Advance Preparation

Go to Target Toss to view the lists of words. Print the words in each word list on index cards, using one index card per word.

[Offline] 30 minutes

FOCUS: Introduce Sounds /ar/ and /or/

Work **together** with students to complete offline Sight Words, Get Ready, Learn, and Try It activities.

Sight Words

Introduce Sight Words

Help students learn the sight words *would*, *could*, and *should*.

1. Gather the sight word cards *would*, *could*, and *should*.

2. Show students the *would* card.

3. **Say:** This is the word *would*. We see this word so often that we want to be able to read and spell it quickly without thinking about it. Look closely at the word *would*. Spell the word *would* aloud. Take a picture of the word *would* in your mind. When you think you can spell *would* yourself, turn the card over and use your letter tiles to spell the word *would*. Check the card to see if you spelled the word *would* correctly. Read aloud the word you spelled with the letter tiles.

4. Repeat the activity with the remaining sight words.

5. Chart students' progress on the back of each card.

   ▸ Divide the back of the card into two columns.
   ▸ Label the first column "Read" and the second column "Spell."
   ▸ Record the dates that students read or spell the word correctly. When students can read and spell the word correctly three times in a row, they have mastered the word. You may want to put a star or sticker on their card when they have mastered that word.

6. Add the cards to students' sight words box.

TIP Sight words can be very difficult for some students. Let them work at their own pace and really master these words.

> **Objectives**
> • Read sight words.
> • Spell sight words.

Get Ready

Signal Ending Sounds

Use a special signal to help students identify **ending sounds** in words.

1. **Say:** I'm going to tell you a special sound, and then I'll say some words. Repeat each word I say and make a special signal to tell me where the sound is. If the special sound is at the end of the word, clap your hands. If the special sound is **not** at the end of the word, just smile at me. For example,

   ▸ If I ask you to listen for the sound /kt/ and I say the word *fact*, you'll repeat the word *fact* and clap your hands because *fact* has the sound /kt/ at the end.
   ▸ If I say the word *fall*, you'll repeat the word *fall* and smile at me because *fall* has the sound /l/, not /kt/, at the end.

2. Say each consonant blend and group of words. Have students make special signals to identify the ending sounds.

   ▸ /lp/: *help, gulp, stiff, ring, pulp* clap: *help, gulp, pulp*
   ▸ /kt/: *end, act, fact, clown, tact* clap: *act, fact, tact*
   ▸ /lt/: *belt, spin, quilt, guess, wilt* clap: *belt, quilt, wilt*
   ▸ /m/: *soft, sum, ham, land, swim* clap: *sum, ham, swim*
   ▸ /lk/: *milk, mist, hulk, elk, stop* clap: *milk, hulk, elk*
   ▸ /ft/: *cake, left, soft, lip, shift, raft* clap: *left, soft, shift, raft*

TIP If students can't identify the ending sound of each word, say the word again and emphasize the ending sound by repeating it three times (for example, *sit* /t/ /t/ /t/). You can also draw out the ending sound when you say the word (for example, *kissssss*). If necessary, have students look at your mouth while you repeat the sounds.

Objectives

- Identify ending sounds in words.
- Identify individual sounds in words.
- Identify and use the blend *–lp*.
- Identify and use the blend *–ct*.
- Identify and use the blend *–lt*.
- Identify and use the blend *–lk*.
- Identify and use the blend *–ft*.

Learn

Introduce *ar* and *or*

Help students recognize and use sounds for the letters *ar* and *or*.

1. Place the following letter tiles on students' whiteboard: *ar, c, f, or,* and *t*.

2. Make the word *car*. Touch and say the word.

   Say: When we the touch and say the word *car*, we will touch the *c* tile for the sound /k/ and the *ar* tile for the sound /ar/.

3. Make the word *for*. Touch and say the word.

   Say: When we the touch and say the word *for*, we will touch the *f* tile for the sound /f/ and the *or* tile for the sound /or/.

4. **Say:** The letters *ar* and *or* are on one tile because when the letter *r* comes after a vowel sound, it changes how we would expect that vowel to sound.

   ▸ Point to each *r* tile and tell me the sound. /ar/ and /or/
   ▸ Which one of the *r* tiles is a word all by itself? *or*

Objectives

- Identify and use *–ar*.
- Identify and use *–or*.
- Identify and use vowels and vowel sounds.
- Blend sounds to create words.
- Identify individual sounds in words.
- Identify and use the blend *st*.
- Identify and use the blend *sk*.
- Identify and use the blend *–nd*.
- Identify and use the blend *–mp*.

Build Words

Help students use letters and sounds to build words.

1. Place the following letter tiles at the top of students' whiteboard: *ar, b, c, ch, d, f, m, n, or, p, sh,* and *t.*

2. Draw three horizontal lines across the middle of students' whiteboard to represent the sounds in a word.

3. **Say:** Let's use letters and sounds to build the word *torch.*

4. Have students finger stretch the sounds in *torch.*

5. Have students
   ▸ Identify the first, next, and last sounds in *torch.*
   ▸ Choose the corresponding letter for each of the sounds.
   ▸ Move the letters to the correct lines on their whiteboard.

6. Guide students with these questions:
   ▸ What is the first sound in *torch?* /t/
     Which line does the letter for that sound go on? the first one
   ▸ What is the next sound in *torch?* /or/
     Which line do the letters for that sound go on? the second one
   ▸ What's the last sound in *torch?* /ch/
     Which line do the letters for that sound go on? the last one

7. Have students touch and say the word.

8. Redirect students if they select the incorrect letter.

   Say: That sound is in the word [word], and it is the [first, second, third] sound. We want the sound [target sound].

   Continue until students select the correct letter.

9. Repeat the activity to build the following words:
   ▸ *port* /p/ /or/ /t/
   ▸ *card* /k/ /ar/ /d/
   ▸ *born* /b/ /or/ /n/
   ▸ *short* /sh/ /or/ /t/

Word Chains

Have students build words by adding and changing letters to help them recognize and use words that use *ar* and *or*.

1. Place the following letters at the top of students' whiteboard: *ar, b, ch, d, f, h, m, or, p, s, t,* and *y*.

2. **Say:** I am going to build the first word in a chain. The word is *art*.

   ▸ I will pull down the letters for the sounds /ă/, /r/, and /t/ to spell the word *art*.
   ▸ Next I will touch and say *art*. To change *art* to *art*, I will think about what sound is changed from the word *art* to *part*. Because the first sound changes from /ă/ to /p/, I will need to add the letter *p* to the beginning of the word *art*.
   ▸ Touch and say the word *part*. Now it's your turn to change *part* to *hart*. You can spell *hart* by making only one change. Touch and say the new word.

3. Redirect students if they select the incorrect letter for any sound.

   Say: That letter is for the sound [incorrect sound]. We want the letter for the sound [target sound]. What letter makes that sound? Answers will vary.

4. Redirect students if they select the wrong sound.

   Say: To change the word [first word] to [target word], we need the letter for the sound [target sound].

   Show students how to make the change. Have them touch and say the new word after they move the letters.

5. Follow this procedure to make the following words with the sound /ar/: *hard, yard*.

6. Follow this procedure to make the following words with the sound /or/: *for, form, fort, sort, port, sport*.

7. For every new word, have students add, replace, or remove only one letter tile.

   TIP If students struggle, review the sounds and letters that are confusing them.

Target Toss

Play a game with students to help them review letters and sounds. The following word lists will be used in this game:

▸ **List 1 (/ar/):** *barn, dog, chart, form, start, mark, card, nose, far*
▸ **List 2 (/st/):** *best, lost, sing, rest, stop, must, nest, past, chest*
▸ **List 3 (/sk/):** *ask, swim, desk, husk, bus, skip, whisk, came, risk*
▸ **List 4 (/or/):** *fine, or, form, milk, orb, pine, fork, stork, lamp*

1. Gather the word cards you created for list 1 and organize the cards face up in a rectangular grid that measures approximately 1½ feet on one side and 1 foot on the other side. Make the grid on a tabletop or on the floor.

2. Gather the small household object.

3. **Say:** I am going to say part of a word. The first sound is /ar/, as in *hard*. Try to toss this object onto a card that shows a word with the sound /ar/, as in *hard*.

4. Have students toss the small object onto a card on the grid and read the word on the card where it lands.

5. Give students one point for each word that the object lands on and that they can read that contains the target ending sound.

6. Keep track of students' points. When they score five points, replace the cards in the grid with the cards from list 2.

7. Repeat the activity using the cards from lists 2 through 4.

TIP This game can be played outdoors. Just use chalk to make the grid on the sidewalk or driveway and write the words inside the boxes.

Try It

Match It

Have students complete page PH 35 in *K¹² PhonicsWorks Advanced Activity Book* for more practice with words that have the sound /ar/ or /or/. Have students read each sentence aloud and draw a line to the picture that matches the sentence.

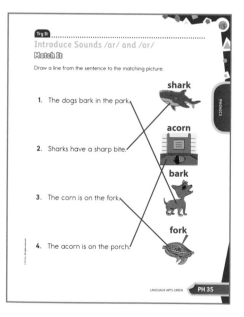

> **Try It**
> Introduce Sounds /ar/ and /or/
> **Match It**
> Draw a line from the sentence to the matching picture.
>
> **shark**
> 1. The dogs bark in the park.
>
> **acorn**
> 2. Sharks have a sharp bite.
>
> **bark**
> 3. The corn is on the fork.
>
> **fork**
> 4. The acorn is on the porch.
>
> LANGUAGE ARTS GREEN   PH 35

Objectives

- Read aloud grade-level text with appropriate automaticity, prosody, accuracy, and rate.
- Identify and use –*ar*.
- Identify and use –*or*.
- Write words by applying grade-level phonics knowledge.
- Write sight words.
- Follow three-step directions.

Dictation: Write Sentences

Use sentences to help students identify individual sounds in words.

1. Gather a pencil and the dictation notebook. Say the sentence, *This charm is for you.* Then give these directions to students:

    ▶ Repeat the sentence.
    ▶ Write the sentence in your notebook.
    ▶ Read the sentence aloud.

2. When students have finished, write the following sentence on your whiteboard: *This charm is for you.*

3. Have them compare their answer to your correct version.

4. Repeat this procedure with the sentence, *The corn fell off my fork.*

    ▶ If students make an error and don't see it, help them correct their mistake by having them finger stretch the sounds in the word they missed.
    ▶ If students are having difficulty selecting the correct letters or sounds, review those letters or sounds that are confusing them.
    ▶ If students have difficulty with first, middle, and last sounds, have them finger stretch the sounds in words.

 **20 minutes**

REVIEW: Sounds /ar/ and /or/

Students will work online independently to

▶ Practice spellings for the sounds /ar/ and /or/.
▶ Practice decoding text by reading a story.

Help students locate the online activities and provide support as needed.

Offline Alternative

No computer access? Have students point out and name things or words that contain the sounds /ar/ and /or/ (for example, *car* or *corn*). You might also ask students to spell words that contain the sounds /ar/ and /or/.

> **Objectives**
> - Identify and use *–ar*.
> - Identify and use *–or*.
> - Identify individual sounds in words.
> - Read aloud grade-level text with appropriate automaticity, prosody, accuracy, and rate.
> - Decode words by applying grade-level word analysis skills.

Practice Sounds /ar/ and /or/

Lesson Overview

[Offline] FOCUS: Practice Sounds /ar/ and /or/
30 minutes

Sight Words	Sight Word Fun
Practice	Search Sentences for the Middle Sound /or/
	Change Words with Silent *e*
	Write Rhyming Words
Try It	"Bart and Mark"
	Dictation: Write Sentences

[Online] REVIEW: Sounds /ar/ and /or/
20 minutes

[Materials]

Supplied
- *K¹² PhonicsWorks Readers Advanced 6*, pp. 7–12
- whiteboard, Learning Coach
- whiteboard, student
- Tile Kit

Also Needed
- sight words box
- dictation notebook

 **30** minutes

FOCUS: Practice Sounds /ar/ and /or/

Work **together** with students to complete offline Sight Words, Practice, and Try It activities.

Sight Words

Sight Word Fun

Help students learn the sight words *would, could,* and *should,* and up to two additional sight words they have yet to master.

1. Gather the sight word cards *would, could,* and *should,* and up to two additional sight word cards.

2. Choose one sight word card to begin.

   Say: Look at this word and take a picture of it in your mind. When you think you can spell the word yourself, turn the card over and use your letter tiles to spell the word.

3. After students spell the word, have them check the card to see if they spelled the word correctly.

   Say: Read aloud the word you spelled with the letter tiles.

4. Repeat the activity with the remaining sight words.

   TIP Sight words can be very difficult for some students. Let students work at their own pace and really master these words.

> **Objectives**
> - Read sight words.
> - Spell sight words.

Practice

Search Sentences for the Middle Sound /or/

To help students learn to recognize the **middle sound /or/** in a word, have them practice identifying the sound.

1. **Say:** I'm going to say a middle sound that is in a word. You will repeat that sound and the word. For example, the middle sound is /or/, as in the word *corn.*

2. Have students say the target sound /or/ and the word *corn.*

3. **Say:** Now, I will read a sentence. Repeat the sentence and tell me the word that has the same middle sound as *corn.* The first sentence is, "Do you have a fork and a spoon?"

   ▸ What is the special middle sound? /or/
   ▸ What is the word that has the special middle sound? *fork*

> **Objectives**
> - Identify and use –*or.*
> - Identify and use –*ar.*
> - Identify middle sounds in words.
> - Identify and use silent *e.*
> - Write words by applying grade-level phonics knowledge.
> - Identify words that rhyme.

4. Follow the same procedure with the words and sentences below to help students recognize the middle sound /or/ in words.

> ► *Have you ever seen a stork fly by? stork*
> ► *If it is hot, you can wear shorts. shorts*
> ► *I will take a short nap. short*
> ► *The page was torn right in half. torn*
> ► *Can you play the horn? horn*
> ► *I want to shorten my hair. shorten*
> ► *Did you forget the game? forget*

TIP If students don't name the correct word, repeat the sentence slowly, clearly pronouncing the middle sound of the words. You might remind them of the special middle sound or say two words from the sentence if they continue to have difficulty and have them choose the word with the target middle sound.

Change Words with Silent *e*

To help students learn words that use silent *e*, have them practice making words that end with silent *e*.

1. Dictate the following words to students, and have them write the words in their dictation notebook: *fin, pin, slim, bath, cod, slop, rip, pet, fad, plan, scrap, past, plum, tub.*

2. Have students add a silent *e* to the end of every word and read the new word aloud: *fine, pine, slime, bathe, code, slope, ripe, Pete, fade, plane, scrape, paste, plume, tube.*

Write Rhyming Words

Have students practice writing rhyming words that have the middle sound /ar/.

1. **Say:** You are going to write some words that rhyme. I will give you a word and the first letter or letters that make a rhyming word. You will think of the rhyming word that starts with the letter or letters I give you. You will write the rhyming word on your whiteboard and read it to me.

2. **Say:** For example, the word is *art*. I'll ask you to tell me the word that rhymes with *art* that has the beginning letter *p*. You'll write the word *part* because *part* rhymes with *art* and has the beginning letter *p*.

3. **Say:** Now it's your turn. The letter is *c*. Write the word and read aloud the word that starts with the sound /k/ and rhymes with *art*. *cart*

4. Follow the same procedure with the word *art* and the letter(s) below:

> ► *ch chart*
> ► *d dart*
> ► *t tart*
> ► *sm smart*
> ► *st start*

Try It ·

"Bart and Mark"

Have students read "Bart and Mark" on page 7 of *K¹² PhonicsWorks Readers Advanced 6.*

Students should read the story silently once or twice before reading the story aloud. When students miss a word that can be sounded out, point to it and give students three to six seconds to try the word again. If students still miss the word, tell them the word so the flow of the story isn't interrupted.

After reading the story, make a list of all the words students missed, and go over those words with them. You may use letter tiles to show students how to read the words.

Dictation: Write Sentences

Use sentences to help students identify individual sounds in words.

1. Gather a pencil and the dictation notebook. Say the sentence, *It is hard to march in a storm.* Then give these directions to students:

   ▸ Repeat the sentence.
   ▸ Write the sentence in your notebook.
   ▸ Read the sentence aloud.

2. When students have finished, write the following sentence on your whiteboard: *It is hard to march in a storm.*

3. Have them compare their answer to your correct version.

4. Repeat this procedure with the sentence, *Mark made a fort in the yard.*

   ▸ If students make an error and don't see it, help them correct their mistake by having them finger stretch the sounds in the word they missed.
   ▸ If students are having difficulty selecting the correct letters or sounds, review those letters or sounds that are confusing them.
   ▸ If students have difficulty with first, middle, and last sounds, have them finger stretch the sounds in words.

Objectives
- Read aloud grade-level text with appropriate automaticity, prosody, accuracy, and rate.
- Decode words by applying grade-level word analysis skills.
- Write words by applying grade-level phonics knowledge.
- Write sight words.
- Follow three-step directions.

 **20 minutes**

REVIEW: Sounds /ar/ and /or/

Students will work online independently to

► Practice spellings for the sounds /ar/ and /or/.

Help students locate the online activities and provide support as needed.

Offline Alternative

No computer access? Have students point out and name things or words that contain the sounds /ar/ and /or/ (for example, *bark* or *fort*). You might also ask students to spell words that contain the sounds /ar/ and /or/.

Review Beginning Blends

Lesson Overview

[Offline] **FOCUS:** Review Beginning Blends **30** minutes

Sight Words	Sight Word Fun
Practice	Quick Sounds
	Phonics Questions
	Build Words
	Word Chains
Try It	Match It

[Online] **REVIEW:** Beginning Blends **20** minutes

Materials

Supplied
- *K¹² PhonicsWorks Advanced Activity Book*, p. PH 36
- whiteboard, Learning Coach
- whiteboard, student
- Tile Kit

Also Needed
- sight words box

Advance Preparation

Place lowercase letter tiles in alphabetical order, plus digraphs *sh*, *ch*, *ck*, *th*, *th*, and *wh*; trigraph *tch*; and double-letter ending tiles *ff*, *ll*, *ss*, and *zz*, on your whiteboard.

[Offline] **30** minutes

FOCUS: Review Beginning Blends

Work **together** with students to complete offline Sight Words, Practice, and Try It activities.

Sight Words ....

Sight Word Fun

Help students learn the sight words *would*, *could*, and *should*, and up to two additional sight words they have yet to master.

1. Gather the sight word cards *would*, *could*, and *should*, and up to two additional sight word cards.

2. Choose one sight word card to begin.

   Say: Look at this word and take a picture of it in your mind. When you think you can spell the word yourself, turn the card over and use your letter tiles to spell the word.

3. After students spell the word, have them check the card to see if they spelled the word correctly.

   Say: Read aloud the word you spelled with the letter tiles.

4. Repeat the activity with the remaining sight words.

TIP Sight words can be very difficult for some students. Let students work at their own pace and really master these words.

> **Objectives**
> - Read sight words.
> - Spell sight words.

Practice ....

Quick Sounds

Help students name words with beginning blends that have the same **beginning sound**.

1. **Say:** I'm going to say some sounds that begin a word. Your job is to think of as many words as you can that begin with those same sounds. Let's see how many you can name. The first one is /sp/, as in *spill*. How many words can you say that begin with /sp/?

   If students have trouble thinking of words, have them look around the room and find objects that start with that sound.

2. Continue this procedure with the following sounds:

   ▶ /tw/, as in *twin*
   ▶ /st/, as in *stop*
   ▶ /sk/, as in *sky*
   ▶ /sn/, as in *snacks*

TIP You can get a book and find pictures of things that start with that sound.

> **Objectives**
> - Identify beginning sounds in words.
> - Identify and use blends.
> - Identify letters of the alphabet.
> - Given the letter, identify the most common sound.
> - Given the sound, identify the most common letter or letters.
> - Identify the new word when one sound is changed in a word.
> - Identify individual sounds in words.

Phonics Questions

To help students master the letters and the sounds of the alphabet, have them review and practice identifying and naming letters, digraphs, trigraphs, and double letter endings.

1. Grab your whiteboard with letters placed in alphabetical order, plus digraph, trigraph, and double-letter ending tiles.

2. Ask students the following questions:

   ▸ What letter is always followed by the letter *u*? *q*
   ▸ Touch and say the short sound for each vowel. /ă/, /ĕ/, /ĭ/, /ŏ/, /ŭ/
   ▸ Touch all the letters that have the sound /k/. *c, ck, k*
   ▸ Touch all the letters that have the sound /w/. *w, wh*
   ▸ Touch the two tiles that have *th* on them. What is the difference between the underlined <u>th</u> and the *th* without an underline? The digraph *th* makes two sounds instead of one. The sounds for the digraph *th* are /th/, as in *thin,* and /<u>th</u>/, as in *that.*
   ▸ Touch all the digraphs. These are tiles that have two letters to spell one sound. *sh, ch, ck, th,* <u>th</u>, *wh*
   ▸ Tell me the sounds for each digraph. /sh/, /ch/, /k/, /th/ /<u>th</u>/, and /w/
   ▸ Touch the trigraph. This is the tile that has three letters to spell one sound. What sound do the letters make? /ch/
   ▸ What letters are almost always doubled at the end of a one-syllable word if they follow a short vowel? the double letters *ff, ll, ss,* and *zz*
   ▸ Touch the double-letter ending tiles on the whiteboard.

Build Words

Help students use letters and sounds to build words that have beginning blends.

1. Place the following letter tiles at the top of students' whiteboard: *ank, b, c, ch, e, i, ing, k, l, n, o, p, r, s, t, u,* and *w.*

2. Draw four horizontal lines across the middle of students' whiteboard to represent the sounds in a word.

3. **Say:** Let's use letters and sounds to build the word *spring.*

4. Have students finger stretch the sounds in *spring.*

5. Have students

   ▸ Identify the first, second, next, and last sounds in *spring.*
   ▸ Choose the corresponding letter for each of the sounds.
   ▸ Move the letters to the correct lines on their whiteboard.

6. Guide students with these questions:

   ▸ What is the first sound in *spring*? /s/
   Which line does the letter for that sound go on? the first one
   ▸ What is the second sound in *spring*? /p/
   Which line does the letter for that sound go on? the second one
   ▸ What is the next sound in *spring*? /r/
   Which line does the letter for that sound go on? the third one
   ▸ What's the last sound in *spring*? /ing/
   Which line do the letters for that sound go on? the last one

7. Have students touch and say the word.

8. Redirect students if they select the incorrect letter.

   Say: That sound is in the word [word], and it is the [first, second, third, fourth] sound. We want the sound [target sound].

   Continue until students select the correct letter.

9. Draw horizontal lines across the middle of students' whiteboard that represent the number of sounds in each word. Repeat the activity to build the following words:

   ▸ *scrunch* /s/ /k/ /r/ /ŭ/ /n/ /ch/
   ▸ *twine* /t/ /w/ /ī/ /n/
   ▸ *blank* /b/ /l/ /ank/
   ▸ *broke* /b/ /r/ /ō/ /k/
   ▸ *prune* /p/ /r/ /ū/ /n/

Word Chains

Have students build words by adding and changing letters to help them recognize and use individual sounds and beginning blends in words.

1. Place the following letters at the top of students' whiteboard: *a, e, f, g, i, k, l, p, r, s, t,* and *t.*

2. **Say:** I am going to build the first word in a chain. The word is *ate.*

   ▸ I will pull down the letters for the sounds /ā/ and /t/ to spell the word *ate.*
   ▸ Next I will touch and say *ate.* To change *ate* to *late,* I will think about what sound is changed from the word *ate* to *late.* Because the sound /l/ is added to the beginning of the word, I will need to add the letter *l* to make the word *late.*
   ▸ Touch and say the word *Kate.* Now it's your turn to change *Kate* to *skate.* You can spell *skate* by making only one change. Touch and say the new word.

3. Redirect students if they select the incorrect letter for any sound.

   Say: That letter is for the sound [incorrect sound]. We want the letter for the sound [target sound]. What letter makes that sound? Answers will vary.

4. Redirect students if they name the sound incorrectly.

   Say: To change the word [first word] to [target word], we need the letter for the sound [target sound].

   Show students how to make the change. Have them touch and say the new word after they move the letters.

5. Follow this procedure to make the following words: *state, stat, slat, flat, flap, flip, slip, lip, lap, gap, gape, grape, grate, rate.*

6. For every new word, have students add, replace, or remove only one letter.

Try It ....

Match It

Have students complete page PH 36 in *K¹² PhonicsWorks Advanced Activity Book* for more practice with words that have beginning blends. Have students read each sentence aloud and draw a line to the picture that matches the sentence.

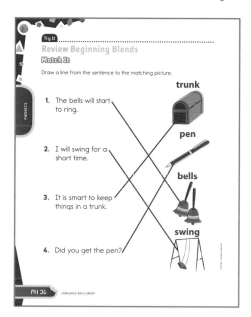

 **[Online]** **20** minutes

REVIEW: Beginning Blends

Students will work online independently to

- ▸ Practice beginning blends.
- ▸ Practice decoding text by reading a story.

Help students locate the online activities and provide support as needed.

Offline Alternative

No computer access? Have students point out and name things or words that contain beginning blends *sc–, sp–, st–, sw–, sk–, sm–, sn–, tw–, bl–, cl–, fl–, gl–, pl–, sl– br–, cr–, dr–, fr–, gr–, pr–,* and *tr–* (for example, *scab, spit, stash, swim, skip, smack, snack, twin, bled, clap, flap, glob, plug, slim, bran, cram, drip, frisk, grab, prop,* and *tram*).

Review Silent *e* Spellings

Lesson Overview

[Offline] **FOCUS:** Review Silent *e* Spellings   **30** minutes

Sight Words	Sight Word Fun
Practice	Word Chains
	Make Riddle Rhymes
	Word Walk
Try It	"Barb Is a Sports Star"

[Online] **REVIEW:** Silent *e* Spellings   **20** minutes

[Materials]

Supplied
- *K¹² PhonicsWorks Readers Advanced 6*, pp. 13–18
- whiteboard, student
- Tile Kit

Also Needed
- sight words box

 **30** minutes

FOCUS: Review Silent *e* Spellings

Work **together** with students to complete offline Sight Words, Practice, and Try It activities.

Sight Words

Sight Word Fun

Help students learn the sight words *would, could,* and *should,* and up to two additional sight words they have yet to master.

1. Gather the sight word cards *would, could,* and *should,* and up to two additional sight word cards.

2. Choose one sight word card to begin.

   Say: Look at this word and take a picture of it in your mind. When you think you can spell the word yourself, turn the card over and use your letter tiles to spell the word.

3. After students spell the word, have them check the card to see if they spelled the word correctly.

   Say: Read aloud the word you spelled with the letter tiles.

4. Repeat the activity with the remaining sight words.

   TIP Sight words can be very difficult for some students. Let students work at their own pace and really master these words.

> **Objectives**
> * Read sight words.
> * Spell sight words.

Practice

Word Chains

Have students build words by adding and changing letters to help them recognize and use individual sounds in words.

1. Place the following letters at the top of students' whiteboard: *a, d, e, f, g, i, l, m, n, o, p, r, s, t,* and *u*.

2. **Say:** I am going to build the first word in a chain. The word is *rim*.

   ▸ I will pull down the letters for the sounds /r/, /ĭ/, and /m/ to spell the word *rim*.
   ▸ Next I will touch and say *rim*. To change *rim* to *grim*, I will think about which sound is changed from the word *rim* to *grim*. Because the first sound changes from /r/ to /g/, I will need to add the letter *g* at the beginning of the word *rim* to make the word *grim*.
   ▸ Touch and say the word *grim*. Now it's your turn to change *grim* to *trim*. You can spell *trim* by making only one change. Touch and say the new word.

> **Objectives**
> * Identify the new word when one sound is changed in a word.
> * Identify individual sounds in words.
> * Identify words that rhyme.
> * Identify and use *–ar*.
> * Identify and use *–or*.
> * Identify and use vowels and vowel sounds.
> * Identify and use silent *e*.
> * Write words by applying grade-level phonics knowledge.

3. Redirect students if they select the incorrect letter for any sound.

   Say: That letter is for the sound [incorrect sound]. We want the letter for the sound [target sound]. What letter makes that sound? Answers will vary.

4. Redirect students if they name the sound incorrectly.

   Say: To change the word [first word] to [target word], we need the letter for the sound [target sound].

   Show students how to make the change. Have them touch and say the new word after they move the letters.

5. Follow this procedure to make the following words: *tram, ram, ran, run, fun, fan, pan, plan, plant, pant, punt, runt, rant, grant, grand, gland, land, and, sand, sane, lane, lone, lope, rope, ripe, gripe, grape, drape.*

6. For every new word, have students add, replace, or remove only one letter.

TIP If students struggle, review the sounds and letters that are confusing them.

Make Riddle Rhymes

Have students identify words that rhyme by playing a riddle game.

1. **Say:** We are going to play a riddle game. I will think of a word and give you some clues. You will guess the word and solve the riddle.

   ▶ It is the opposite of tall. It rhymes with *fort. short*

2. Give students clues to words. Have them name each word and then say and write it. Use these clues and words:

   ▶ It means when something has a rip in it. It rhymes with *born. torn*
   ▶ It is a small light that shines in the sky at night. It rhymes with *far. star*
   ▶ It swims in the ocean and has a lot of teeth. It rhymes with *park. shark*

Word Walk

Help students recognize words for things that are found outdoors.

1. **Say:** I am going to name some words that are spelled with a silent *e*. You will write each word. Then we're going to take a walk outside to see how many of the words we can find on the list.

2. Dictate five to seven words to students. Here are some possible silent *e* words for things students might see outdoors: *gate, rake, skate, vine, bike, kite, hole, stone, hose,* and *rope.*

3. **Say:** When we take our walk, check off each thing you see.

4. Redirect students if they have difficulty writing the silent *e* words. Have them spell the words using the letter tiles, and remind them how to touch and say the silent *e* words.

TIP If the weather is bad, create a list of words that students are likely to see indoors, and add those words to the list before you do a word walk inside.

Try It ●

"Barb Is a Sports Star"

Have students read "Barb Is a Sports Star" on page 13 of *K¹² PhonicsWorks Readers Advanced 6.*

Students should read the story silently once or twice before reading the story aloud. When students miss a word that can be sounded out, point to it and give students three to six seconds to try the word again. If students still miss the word, tell them the word so the flow of the story isn't interrupted.

After reading the story, make a list of all the words students missed, and go over those words with them. You may use letter tiles to show students how to read the words.

> **Objectives**
> - Read aloud grade-level text with appropriate automaticity, prosody, accuracy, and rate.
> - Decode words by applying grade-level word analysis skills.

 **20 minutes**

REVIEW: Silent *e* Spellings

Students will work online independently to

▸ Practice silent *e* spellings.

Help students locate the online activities and provide support as needed.

> **Objectives**
> - Identify and use silent *e*.
> - Identify individual sounds in words.

Offline Alternative

No computer access? Have students point out and name things or words that use the silent *e* spelling (for example, *bake* or *bite*). You might also ask students to spell words that use the silent *e* spelling.

Unit Checkpoint

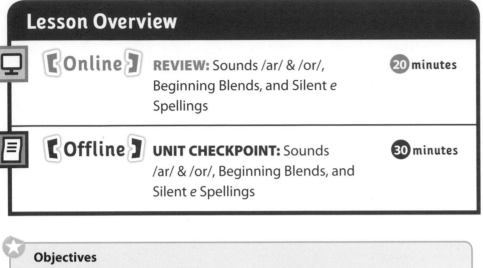

Lesson Overview

[Online] **REVIEW:** Sounds /ar/ & /or/, Beginning Blends, and Silent *e* Spellings — **20** minutes

[Offline] **UNIT CHECKPOINT:** Sounds /ar/ & /or/, Beginning Blends, and Silent *e* Spellings — **30** minutes

Materials

Supplied

- *K¹² PhonicsWorks Advanced Assessments,* pp. PH 103–108

Objectives

- Identify and use vowels and vowel sounds.
- Identify and use silent *e*.
- Identify and use *–ar*.
- Identify and use *–or*.
- Identify and use blends.
- Identify individual sounds in words.
- Given the letter, identify the most common sound.
- Given the sound, identify the most common letter or letters.
- Read instructional-level text with 90% accuracy.
- Read aloud grade-level text with appropriate automaticity, prosody, accuracy, and rate.
- Write words by applying grade-level phonics knowledge.
- Write sight words.
- Read sight words.

 **[Online]** **20** minutes

REVIEW: Sounds /ar/ & /or/, Beginning Blends, and Silent *e* Spellings

Students will review the sounds /ar/ & /or/, beginning blends, and silent *e* spellings to prepare for the Unit Checkpoint. Help students locate the online activities and provide support as needed.

[Offline] **30** minutes

UNIT CHECKPOINT: Sounds /ar/ & /or/, Beginning Blends, and Silent *e* Spellings

Explain that students are going to show what they have learned about sounds, letters, and words.

1. Give students the Unit Checkpoint pages for the Sounds /ar/ & /or/, Beginning Blends, and Silent *e* Spellings unit and print the Unit Checkpoint Answer Key, if you'd like.

2. Use the instructions below to help administer the Checkpoint to students. On the Answer Key or another sheet of paper, note student answers to oral response questions to help with scoring the Checkpoint later.

3. Use the Answer Key to score the Checkpoint, and then enter the results online.

Part 1. Read Word Parts Moving left to right, have students say the sounds of each word part. Note any word parts students say incorrectly.

Part 2. Finger Stretching Say each word to students. Have them say each word aloud and finger stretch the sounds. Note any words they finger stretch incorrectly.

13. *park*

14. *form*

Part 3. Dictation Say each word to students. Have them repeat and write the word.

15. *charm* 19. *bride*

16. *storm* 20. *trade*

17. *smart* 21. *clove*

18. *sport* 22. *scar*

Part 4. Writing Read each sentence to students. Have them repeat and write the sentence.

23. *Would Barb get us the forms?*

24. *Mark should have held the forks.*

25. *Clark could look for the snake.*

Part 5. Read Aloud Listen to students read the sentences aloud. Count and note the number of words they read correctly.

Part 6. Say Letters Say each word part. Have students say the letters that make the sounds they hear in each word part. Note any incorrect responses.

27. /ā/ /k/

28. /or/ /k/

29. /ī/ /f/

30. /ĭ/ /st/

31. /ar/ /p/

32. /ū/ /k/

33. /ung/

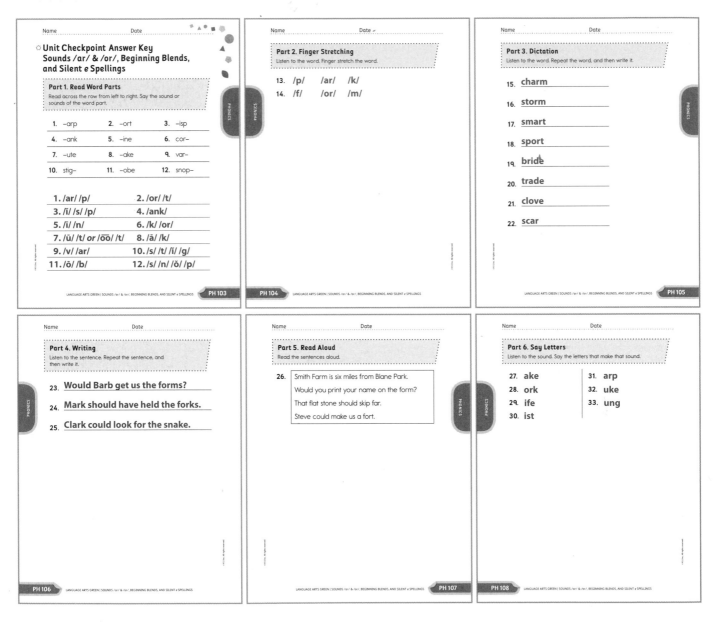

Name _____ Date _____

○ **Unit Checkpoint Answer Key**
Sounds /ar/ & /or/, Beginning Blends,
and Silent *e* Spellings

Part 1. Read Word Parts
Read across the row from left to right. Say the sound or sounds of the word part.

1. –arp	2. –ort	3. –isp
4. –ank	5. –ine	6. cor–
7. –ute	8. –ake	9. var–
10. stig–	11. –obe	12. snop–

1. /ar/ /p/	2. /or/ /t/
3. /ī/ /s/ /p/	4. /ank/
5. /ī/ /n/	6. /k/ /or/
7. /ū/ /t/ or /o͞o/ /t/	8. /ā/ /k/
9. /v/ /ar/	10. /s/ /t/ /ī/ /g/
11. /ō/ /b/	12. /s/ /n/ /ŏ/ /p/

Name _____ Date _____

Part 2. Finger Stretching
Listen to the word. Finger stretch the word.

13. /p/ /ar/ /k/

14. /f/ /or/ /m/

Name _____ Date _____

Part 3. Dictation
Listen to the word. Repeat the word, and then write it.

15. charm _____

16. storm _____

17. smart _____

18. sport _____

19. bride _____

20. trade _____

21. clove _____

22. scar _____

Name _____ Date _____

Part 4. Writing
Listen to the sentence. Repeat the sentence, and then write it.

23. **Would Barb get us the forms?** _____

24. **Mark should have held the forks.** _____

25. **Clark could look for the snake.** _____

Name _____ Date _____

Part 5. Read Aloud
Read the sentences aloud.

26.
Smith Farm is six miles from Blane Park.
Would you print your name on the form?
That flat stone should skip far.
Steve could make us a fort.

Name _____ Date _____

Part 6. Say Letters
Listen to the sound. Say the letters that make that sound.

27. ake

28. ork

29. ife

30. ist

31. arp

32. uke

33. ung

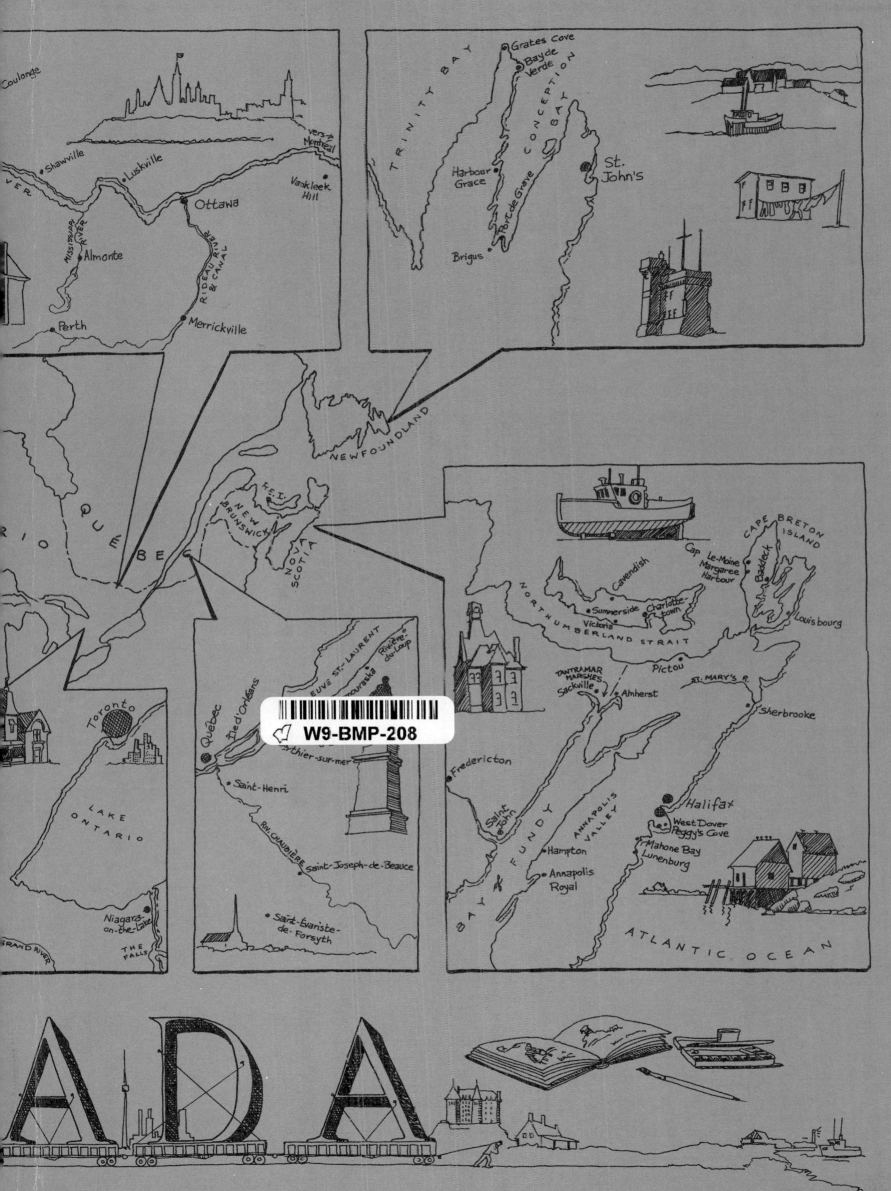

M. KLUCKNER '98

CANADA

CANADA
A Journey of
Discovery

Text and Watercolours by
Michael Kluckner

*The Château
Frontenac
from Québec
City's
Lower Town*

RAINCOAST BOOKS

Vancouver

First published in 1998 by

Raincoast Books
8680 Cambie Street
Vancouver, B.C.
V6P 6M9
(604) 323-7100

Web Site: www.raincoast.com

1 2 3 4 5 6 7 8 9 10

CANADIAN CATALOGUING IN PUBLICATION DATA

Kluckner, Michael.
Canada

ISBN 1-55192-204-5

1. Kluckner, Michael – Journeys. 2. Canada – Pictorial works. 3. Canada in art. 4. Canada – Description and travel. I. Title.

FC59.K58 1998   971.064'8'0222   C98-910443-5
F1017.K58 1998

Book Design: Hermani & Sorrentino Design

Printed in Italy

Raincoast Books gratefully acknowledges the support of the Government of Canada, through the Book Publishing Industry Development Program, the Canada Council for the Arts and the Department of Canadian Heritage. We also acknowledge the assistance of the Province of British Columbia, through the British Columbia Arts Council.

Contents

Men gathering firewood near Port de Grave, Newfoundland.

"The common people have no history:
persecuted by the present, they cannot
think of preserving the memory of the past."

— Jean-Henri Fabre

Foreword: Landscapes of Memory

WHERE CAN YOU FIND THE PAST OF A COUNTRY that wants to believe that it has no past? This is the paradox that lies beneath Michael Kluckner's quest, and it gives a rueful flavour to almost everything he tells and shows us in *Canada: A Journey of Discovery*. History exists on the fringes of Canada's collective consciousness and Kluckner wants to pull it back toward the centre, where it belongs. So he sets off, armed with insight and talent, in an ambitious and idealistic attempt to explore the historical sites where we can breathe "air infused with the magic elixir of memory."

In some countries, the way to such places is clearly marked. Canada is not such a country. The landscape of our history is hidden, confusing and contradictory. Most of us understand it, if we understand it at all, in ways that are local, regional, personal and idiosyncratic rather than national, shared and communal. For Canada, history is a series of problems that we never manage to solve and often prefer to ignore – for good reason. As we are often reminded, even the unveiling of a historical monument can produce more controversy than enlightenment.

In the spring of 1998 the Québec provincial government erected a monument commemorating the Québec City conferences at which Winston Churchill and Franklin Roosevelt plotted the course of the Second World War. A third participant in those talks, Mackenzie King, was simply ignored; as a federal prime minister, he was beneath the notice of a separatist Québec government. Naturally, federalists were infuriated, and in the end the monument taught only one historical lesson, a lesson already overfamiliar: Canadians can't begin to agree on their history, even when dealing with events of only half a century ago. Our past is unmastered, unsorted – and therefore dangerous.

Kluckner dreams of living in a Canada that is more aware of the past, more articulate about it, more attentive. He says that anyone who goes out and observes the lay of the land eventually asks, "Is anyone in charge out there?" The short answer is no. A longer answer would have to consider the diffusion of power and authority in Canada, and the absence of a coherent national purpose in that field. Kluckner yearns for something like the National Trust in England, which carefully curates the British past. In France, the national heritage is managed in an even more centralized way. In Japan, a national agency in Tokyo rates objects, buildings and even people on the basis of their status as National Treasures. But the authority of any such agency flows from a consensus about the past, and in Canada no such consensus exists.

Of course it's hyperbole to say that we have no past – after all, people have lived here for thousands of years, they have acted in noble or evil or quite ordinary ways and they have left records of various kinds. That's a past, certainly. But in another sense we are, or try to be, a pastless country. We have learned to wipe the slate clean with each generation and make a new beginning. We do not hesitate to alter our history, erase our historic symbols and deny many elements in our historic nature that seemed obvious and central to our parents and grandparents.

In Québec, only thirty years ago, it was commonplace to understand history since the 17th century through the role of the Roman Catholic Church; today, when Québecers discuss their past, the Church sounds almost marginal. Two generations ago, Canada's historic place under the British Crown was absolutely vital to the understanding of a huge part of the population; but we began to cease emphasizing it some decades ago, and today it appears almost inconsequential.

"The mystic chords of memory" – that was the phrase Abraham Lincoln used to describe the feelings evoked by words, monuments, buildings and battlefields of historic interest. He was explaining that

Americans needed more than logic and convenience as reasons for living together; they also needed shared memories and emotions, mutual feelings that could bring to life the words of their constitution and their laws. Canadians also need to hear those chords, but we can do so only with difficulty. Kluckner explores imagery as developed by the Group of Seven, searches out the physical origins of Anne of Green Gables, nimbly escorts us through the history of the railways as creators of identity and pauses to note more recent historic sites, such as Joni Mitchell's old hometown of Maidstone, Saskatchewan. Wherever he goes, ambivalence pursues him, as it must pursue everyone who searches for something as evanescent as the nature of Canada. Like a good Canadian he seems always to be asking himself whether he should take this project seriously; and he seems always to answer, yes, sort of.

Kluckner's enjoyable, evocative trip through the swamplands of national memory will leave each of us wondering whether the Canadian past is alive within us – and if it is, how we manage to keep it that way. My own answer is partly literary. I believe in written history more than in history spelled out by architecture and memorial art. Certainly there are days when I would give you any number of immaculately restored buildings for a good copy of a classic like O. D. Skelton's *Life and Letters of Sir Wilfrid Laurier*, in which Laurier comes alive and stays alive through his own words. And yet I think of Samuel de Champlain's monument at Orillia whenever I read his name, I love to walk around Francis Rattenbury's 1898 legislature in Victoria and even a glimpse of a Newfoundland outport can send me into excited imaginings of the first families who clung to those rocky shores centuries ago.

As I followed Kluckner across the country, I realized that – without quite being conscious of it – I have over the years organized my own part of the world historically. I know and cherish at least a little of what has happened near me. Five blocks southeast of my house in midtown Toronto is the site (unmarked) of Hangman's Hill, where rebels were executed after the Mackenzie uprising of 1837; three blocks east of me is a cemetery containing the graves of Catherine Faeley Hennessey and John Pickford Hennessey, maternal grandparents of the world's first movie star, Mary Pickford; two blocks east of me is the apartment where Glenn Gould lived for many years; two blocks to the west is Timothy Eaton Memorial Church, the only cathedral in the world named after a retail merchant; and just on the other side of my backyard fence is a public school once attended by the philosopher George Grant. Thinking all this through, spatially organizing my own neighbourhood's history, was one of my responses to Kluckner.

Many of us will enthusiastically support his plea for more careful attention to the remnants of our history, while realizing that no large-scale change is likely to arrive in the near future. The truth is that many sections of Canada have become far more responsive to their own past than they were a couple of generations ago, and no doubt we will continue to improve in this way. Even so, if we are to know our history, most of us must learn to imagine it and appreciate it for ourselves, in our own unique ways – much as Michael Kluckner has done.

Robert Fulford
MAY 1998

Acknowledgements

JOHN ATKIN BOUND THE FIRST SKETCHBOOK FOR ME. Claude Dubé and Christine Vallée were hospitable in Québec City, as were Shane and Maire O'Dea in St. John's and Brent and Meg Slobodin in Whitehorse. Brian Anthony, Pat Davis, Douglas Franklin, Hal Kalman, Leslie Langille, Pat Lusk, Ian Sacré and Marion Tucker provided information and direction. Graham Quint of the National Trust of Australia explained government policies to me. Brian Scrivener provided sound editorial input (and knew the Joseph Howe quotation). Mark Stanton of Raincoast Books clearly saw the value of the project through my confusing meanderings. And Christine Allen, my wife and partner, kept the home fires burning and the farm running while I looked for surviving evidence of the country I grew up in. My thanks to them all.

In Search of Canada

I WAS TRAVELLING IN QUÉBEC, along the south shore of the St. Lawrence River, on July 1, 1997, which I remembered as Dominion Day and now knew as Canada Day, but here I found it was known as *Fête de la Confédération* (Confederation Festival). It was a blazingly hot, humid day, the sky the grey-blue colour of a cheap revolver, the air almost opaque, with the north shore of the river barely visible through the haze. Late in the afternoon, after passing miles of long, narrow farm fields dating from the time of the old seigneuries, I decided to pull in for the night at a hotel in Montmagny. UN P'TIT COIN D'EUROPE, its sign said. A terrace dotted with tables and chairs separated it from the street; couples, all chattering *en français*, sat at the tables and drank beer. The hotel was a charming old building, in business since 1855, its thick stone walls festooned with ivy. While the desk clerk looked for the room key, I scanned the visitors' book and noted that most of the guests were from elsewhere in Québec. I had heard that Québec was its own best tourist market. The previous day's English-language Montréal *Gazette* shared a bin near the door with *Le Devoir* and a couple of local French-language papers.

I picked up the *Gazette* and carried it, with my bag, up the two flights of stairs to my garret room, unpacked the stuff I needed for the night and pushed open the casement windows. Pouring a glass of red wine from the bottle in my bag into one of the bathroom glasses, I picked up the paper and moved toward the single chair that was jammed into the corner of the room beneath the sloping ceiling. Suddenly, not far away, an amplifier squealed into life. A raucous, female voice, distorted by reverberation, shouted a salutation, then *"un, deux, trois, quatre. . . ."* and a band exploded into life. *Uh-oh,* I thought.

Great little band, if a bit loud. From what I could understand in the breaks between songs, they were "Coco Salsa," Latino beat with French lyrics. Ignoring the noise and concentrating on the paper, I skimmed the front page, which was mainly articles on the Montréal Jazz Festival, and turned the pages, reading a little here and there, before arriving at page A8.

"Young Canadians flunk history test," blared the headline. The article quoted historian Jack Granatstein, one of a group of academics who had designed the test, blaming the schools for graduating a generation of students lacking a national memory. "We have gone a huge distance in this country to pretend we don't have a past," he said. On average, students across the country got one question in three correct, but Québecers, unencumbered by knowledge of anything beyond the provincial borders, fared the worst. Interestingly, though, the Identity Machine had been effective at defining the enemy, as three-quarters of the Québec respondents knew that Britain had defeated France on the Plains of Abraham in 1759, compared with only 58 percent of those next door in Ontario. "What is happening, because we don't teach our history, is that we are letting American history and culture wash over our own people," Granatstein said.

Outside, the thundering Latino beat bounced around the walls of the little town, seeming to intensify the heat. I noticed from my window the number of people sitting outside, sweating quietly, drooping on their stoops, talking a little to neighbours who passed by.

My wine and the *Gazette* finished, I descended and walked along the street, drawn to the noise until, only a couple of doors past the hotel's terrace, I arrived at a vacant lot beside the town's tavern. Tables with umbrellas sporting the logo of Labatt 50 (CINQUANTE!) were set up, and about fifty people grooved and shimmied to the throbbing beat. Some bikers had arrived and were eyeing a bench lined with young women: classic Québecoises with little cat faces like Geneviève Bujold's – black haired, eyes painted so black they were like holes burned in a bedsheet, little red mouths pursed around cigarettes. Everybody, it seemed, smoked. *Ahh, a Québec moment,* I thought, on Confederation Day.

Back at the hotel's terrace, with *une bière blonde,* I reflected on the *Gazette's* history survey. At least the Battle of the Plains of Abraham has an advantage over other events in the historical record in that it has a great site that is still intact. It has been preserved and can be visited: as history, it is more tangible than, say, the extremely significant Reciprocity Election of 1911, or the 1917 federal election when women first voted, or the repeal of the Chinese Exclusion Act in 1947 or the Royal Commission on Health Services in 1961 that led to the establishment of universal medical care. A historical event is made tangible and relevant by the preservation and commemoration of its site, if it has one.

And historical characters are made real by the preservation of their homes. Some of these places become shrines or museums, while others are home to new people who go about their contemporary lives while taking some pride in the plaque on the wall outside. As I mulled this over, what popped into my mind was GEORGE WASHINGTON SLEPT HERE – the legendary plaques dotted around buildings in the eastern United States – evidence that Professor Granatstein's point about Canadians being the slice of processed cheese on the American Big Mac has validity.

My food came – Caesar salad with Cajun chicken. I ordered another *Cinquante.*

❨ ❨ ❨

Sometimes I feel I'm a nomad in a country with a winter as cold as charity. The old verities of hearth and home, neighbourhood and village, King and Country, have all but disappeared in this era of the global village. Nevertheless, Canadians have spent a lot of time trying to develop a collective identity and become a nation in more than a geographic sense. To do so, they try to put down roots, identify with a spirit of place, share experiences and agree upon their myths and legends. A famous quip, attributed to Voltaire, that "history is a pack of lies agreed upon," hints at the process of history-making that every country has to go through and suggests that historians ought to put the letters B.S., along with those signifying their other degrees, after their names.

Some countries, like the United States, take to the process of history-making with gusto and manage to flagellate themselves enthusiastically for perceived historical errors without ever questioning their under-lying unity. After all, we live in a revisionist age: as they say in the former USSR, "There is nothing more unpredictable in Russia than the past."

Much has been made, since the days a century ago of writer/philosophers like Goldwin Smith, of the notion that Canada is untenable – a marginal society in the shadow of the French, the British and now the American Empires. A century before Smith's heyday, yet another comment by Voltaire laid the foun-dation for a Canadian inferiority complex: "You know that these two nations [France and England] have been at war over a few acres of snow near Canada, and that they are spending on this fine struggle more than Canada itself is worth," he wrote in 1759 in *Candide*. The major battle in that final French and Indian War, as every schoolchild and tourist to Québec ought to know, took place on the Plains of Abraham on the edge of Québec's old walled city and inspired the lyrics of the song "The Maple Leaf Forever" that we sang patriotically as (English-Canadian) schoolchildren. It being Canada, some of us still dispute whether the battle on the night of September 13, 1759, was a victory or a defeat.

Evidently, though, the true defeat has been in education, as the Canadian history survey revealed, for youth, regardless of where they were born or what cultural baggage they carry, know little and care less about Canadian history. To be fair, they're profoundly ignorant of most things, but they seem to know even less of history than of their other academic subjects. History in the abstract just isn't cool.

☾ ☾ ☾

Although history and historic sites are important to a country, legends and myths have an equal ability to focus pride and national identity. When you can combine a myth with a site, you're well on your way to creating a national institution. Stewart Brand, in his book *How Buildings Learn*, dissects a classic example from south of the border: "As the nation approached its first centennial in 1875, the search was on for a female hero of the revolution. Philadelphia had two candidates – Lydia Darragh, an intrepid and effective spy, and Betsy Ross, who sewed American flags and *might* have sewed the first one. But Darragh's house on Second Street [had been] replaced by a hotel, so that left Ross. A campaign to save her house hustled pennies from the nation's schoolchildren. Darragh was forgotten by history. Betsy Ross entered legend." The little house on Arch Street in Philadelphia became a national shrine in 1937, and the remains of Elizabeth Ross Claypole, which had mouldered anonymously elsewhere for more than a century, were reinterred with great ceremony in the cleared lot next door.

A Canadian equivalent, perhaps, to Mrs. Claypole is Laura Ingersoll Secord, born in 1775, the year before the American Revolution, in Great Barrington, Massachusetts. At twenty she moved to Upper Canada with her father and settled just north of the international border along the Niagara River near Niagara-on-the-Lake. During the War of 1812, aware of an impending American attack, she walked nearly thirty kilometres to warn the nearest British commander. The plaque outside

Montmagny, Québec
July 1st — "Confederation Day"

The Observer   *The Observed.*

(Patriotic biker has fleur-de-lys tattoo on his arm!)

her simple frame house notes that THE COURAGE AND TENACITY DISPLAYED ON THIS OCCASION IN JUNE 1813 PLACES HER IN THE FOREFRONT OF THE PROVINCE'S HEROINES. Like Betsy Ross, Laura Secord passed much of the rest of her life in obscurity, but in her old age her story was revived during the visit to Canada of the Prince of Wales, later Edward VII, who was deeply impressed by the example she had set. In 1864, a cow and a milk pail were added to her legend in William F. Coffin's book *War of 1812 and Its Moral.*

Secord died a few years later, in 1868, but lived on as a hero and a patriot for the infant Canadian nation. A stone marker was placed in front of her house in 1901 by the Women's Literary Club of St. Catharines. Although Coffin's tale was summarily dismissed as "a fable" by Secord's niece, Emma Currie, in her 1913 book *The Story of Laura Secord,* as well as by other scholars, a school textbook published in 1923, *The Dominion Educator,* made the cow into a historical "bovinage": "As [James Secord, a wounded militia officer] was unable to warn the British commander, his wife undertook the dangerous mission. Driving a cow before her until she reached the woods, in order that the enemy might not suspect her purpose . . ." Perhaps the cow and the milk pail inspired Frank O'Connor, an Ontario businessman, to create a line of milk chocolates that he sold through his Laura Secord Candy Shops, beginning about 1915, in Canada. In the States, though, the same candy was available at his Fanny Farmer Candy Shops.

In a similar vein, there was the debate in Canada in the summer of 1997 over the actual land-fall of John Cabot. Did it happen in Newfoundland or on Cape Breton Island or somewhere else? Newfoundland was first out of the gate when the federal government announced it had some funds set aside for a 500th-anniversary celebration. As the controversy grew and the date approached, a Parks Canada spokesman was asked how the federal government felt it could endorse one site over another. "Nation building is about myth-making," he said. One exploration of the explorer's voyage is that of historian Peter E. Pope, a University of Toronto professor, in his book *The Many Landfalls of John Cabot*, which reflects on "how nationalists construct a nation's past by using and sometimes distorting historical events."

Just as real as Cabot, his crew and Laura Secord's cow are the characters in literature who have defined time and place for generations of Canadians. Some of these characters occupy imaginary places, like Stephen Leacock's Mariposa or Margaret Laurence's Manawaka, although these can easily be pinned to real towns. Others can be tied to a specific piece of turf, such as Mordecai Richler's St. Urbain Street in Montréal. Most familiar of all is the house known as "Green Gables" near Cavendish, Prince Edward Island, a place of pilgrimage for the fans of Lucy Maud Montgomery's Anne Shirley, mainly young women from all over the world. (As the local slogan has it, WE PUT THE ANNE IN JAPAN!) When Green Gables was badly damaged by fire in the spring of 1997, the potential impact on P.E.I. (and Canadian) tourism was serious. The federal government wasted no time in ensuring that the house was quickly repaired and reopened to keep the legend alive and the flow of tourists coming across the new

Japanese girls on pilgrimage to "Green Gables," Cavendish, Prince Edward Island.

Confederation Bridge from New Brunswick (a bridge that ought to have been named Span of Green Gables, according to local wits). Sam McGee's Yukon cabin, home of the namesake of poet Robert Service's most famous character, is a similar shrine, although it has lost its original site and now sulks behind a chain-link fence on the MacBride Museum grounds in downtown Whitehorse.

❨ ❨ ❨

Like literature, art has had a profound impact on our perception of *terra cognito*. The word "landscape" entered England from Holland at the end of the 16th century, adapted from a Germanic word signifying a unit of human habitation. Dutch landscape painting usually contained people and suggested a narrative about their lives, as did non-aboriginal North American painting before the 20th century.

English paintings, especially the 18th- and 19th-century watercolours that included cottage gardens, hedgerows and village churches, provide an excellent example of how selection and modification of images by artists helped to define a style of land*scaping*, in this case the rather cozy one we have of rural England, and make it a part of the national identity. As was the case in Japan, where the tortured rocks and trees in Zen brush-and-ink painting influenced, if not actually created, garden design and the art of bonsai, the perception of life in England began to imitate art.

Much of that familiar countryside sprang from a desire on the part of tastemakers such as John Ruskin and William Morris to return to a romantic, pre-industrial England. Advocates of picturesqueness, part of the Romantic Movement that dominated literature, art and music in the late 18th and 19th centuries, had insisted that cottages be designed to give pleasure to the spectator, regardless of whether they provided comfort and good health to the cottager. British watercolourists of the period often made up pretty, floral "cottage" gardens to go with the cottages' thatched roofs and whitewashed, half-timbered walls and included happy rustics, especially little girls in frilly frocks, to give human interest to the scene. Paintings in books such as Ruskin's *The Art of England* (1884) and *The Happy England of Helen Allingham* (1903), and on placemats, plates and mugs, postcards and giftwrap, spread this ideal of rural England around the world. As a visual theme it not only survived the upheaval of the 20th century but made the appearance of the English countryside one of the country's greatest national assets.

In Canada, a national landscape ideology evolved slowly during the 19th century. Apart from a handful of artists and wealthy collectors, most people were head down and slogging, trying to make a living, and soon after retirement, if they made it that far, they died. Few travelled any distance at all during their lifetimes, and nine out of ten of them were farmers, plough firmly in the furrow, or were otherwise involved with food production and sales. Printed images were scarce: the halftone process only became affordable following an 1892 patent. In order for photographs and paintings to be mass produced, they had to be hand-drawn onto etching plates.

Affordable artistic images made it into Canadian homes when popular newspapers published folios of reproduced artwork as supplements. My grandmother, at that time about twenty years old, purchased an 1893 set called "Masterpieces from the World's Art Galleries," a one-dollar supplement from the *Toronto Mail and Empire*. The paintings, reproduced as black-and-white engravings, are romantic and sentimental. There were no Canadian images, although many were similar to the narrative, allegorical painting being done at the time by artists such as George Agnew Reid (1860-1947) of Toronto, whose canvases bore such titles as *Mortgaging the Homestead* and *The Foreclosure of the Mortgage*.

One of the first large-scale publishers of Canadian images was the Canadian Pacific Railway, which, almost from the time its tracks were laid in the 1880s, sold sets of views of mountains, "Indians" and other subjects of interest, many photographed by the William Notman and Son studio of Montréal. They were marketed to tourists – a tiny, wealthy minority of the population, most of whom lived in England and the United States. A typical tourist book of the time was *Through Canada with a Kodak* by Lady Aberdeen, wife of the governor general. This book celebrated both Canadian scenery and the fad, created by George Eastman's 1888 easy-to-use box camera, for "kodaking" everything.

These books and pamphlets of Canada in the 1880s and 1890s shared common themes. First, the raves about scenery far exceeded in length the descriptions of the human-made *cultural* landscape (such as the Parliament Buildings in Ottawa). FIFTY SWITZERLANDS IN ONE became a common CPR slogan for the western mountains, directed primarily at the wealthy English travellers who had yodelled around the Alps since the 1860s. In addition to these attractions, booklets extolled Niagara Falls, usually mentioning how both the American and Canadian governments had seized the choice spots back from the hucksters and the speculators, and Bell Farm near Indian Head, Saskatchewan, touted as the largest and most progressive farm in the world. The scenery attracted the tourists, and the fertile Prairies attracted immigrant farmers – the two sides of the CPR's revenue coin.

Much of the natural landscape of this "curiously savage country" was foreign to the sensibilities of well-travelled foreigners. A later vice-regal consort, Lady Tweedsmuir, writing in the early years of the Second World War, observed: "In the winter the train passes through unending aisles of what appear to be Christmas trees"; in Northern Ontario, "in summer you see the vivid green of the treacherous muskegs, [with only] an occasional wooden shack, with a flutter of washing on a line, varying the monotony." Just a shack and washing on the line – a poor cousin to English villages and rustic cottages with pretty flower gardens.

Depictions of life in the countryside – that staple of English and French landscape painting – became the quest of many artists, including Cornelius Krieghoff and Marc-Aurèle de Foy Suzor-Côté in Québec, and Lucius O'Brien, Horatio Walker and Homer Watson in Ontario. Influenced by the Barbizon artists in France and the Hudson River School in the United States, the latter group painted and sketched out of doors *(en plein air)* in the well-settled parishes of Ontario and Québec, often reworking their images onto large canvases in their studios.

Lucius O'Brien's skill at painting the Canadian landscape dovetailed perfectly with the promotional needs of the Canadian Pacific Railway, which wanted to sell "our mountains," as general manager William Van Horne described the Rockies, to wealthy travellers. The CPR had decided in 1882 to cross the Prairies by a southern route and traverse the Rocky Mountains through the Kicking Horse Pass, instead of by the northerly Yellowhead route followed thirty years later by the Canadian Northern Railway and the Grand Trunk Pacific Railway, and had unwittingly stumbled upon a tourist gold mine. Needing images for high-quality tourist pamphlets and brochures, as well as original paintings for displays at fairs and ticket offices, Van Horne supported such artists as O'Brien, Frederick M. Bell-Smith and John Fraser, giving them railway passes and later buying some of their work. In his book *The Selling of Canada*, E. J. Hart wrote that "the CPR's requirements and its assistance played a key part in what may be called 'the Railway School,' Canada's first 'national' school of art." Most of these works showed dramatic scenery and usually contained indications of passing trains or distant, picturesque hotels such as the Banff Springs – puny human works next to awesome nature.

An international perception of Canada began to emerge from beneath the snow and ignorance. Through Van Horne's patronage of "the Railway School," Canadian art took a step away from the bucolic and the pastoral toward a vision of the country as a romantic wilderness. The final step, off the

English landscape painter authentically recording the countryside.

wilderness cliff into a new way of seeing Canada, happened soon after the turn of the 20th century. Prime Minister Sir Wilfrid Laurier had opined that it would be Canada's century, and in the Boer War the country had, for the first time, mounted its own military effort under its own name. Patriotism and nationalism were in the air, and the country was rapidly industrializing and urbanizing. In the art world, the trigger was an exhibition of Scandinavian landscapes in Buffalo, New York, in 1913 that galvanized the painter Lawren Harris into seeing Canada in a new way. His timing was perfect: Toronto was ascendant, and its aggressive media, especially the *Toronto Star* and its magazine the *Star Weekly*, reached out into the hinterland. Two years earlier, much as would happen in 1988, the country had divided on the matter of free trade with the Americans. In 1911, however, afraid of being gobbled up by the American beast, Canadians had voted for the Conservative party and protectionism. Radicalized and proudly Canadian, the public was ready to appreciate a new vision of their country.

According to an article by Gregory Clark in the *Star Weekly* on November 21, 1914, Harris and his associates, including A. Y. Jackson and J. E. H. MacDonald, were going to paint

> all the sunlight, the height of the sky, the freedom of windy space that is Canada. . . . Canada is all landscape so far – at least, landscape is all that is national yet. . . . Her people and her cities are not characteristic. . . . But Canada's physical appearance is distinctive and our artists are aiming to catch the illusive appearance of its face, to see in it what virtues, what natural qualities it has to breed into the Canadian people.

Their technique was descended from the French Impressionists and Post-Impressionists, filtered through the lens of the Scandinavian exhibition and given a Canadian twist through their articulate pronouncements.

Eventually dubbing themselves the Group of Seven, the artists congregated at the Arts and Letters Club on Elm Street in Toronto, where they could lick their wounds in a convivial atmosphere and recover from the savage attacks of some Toronto art critics, who fulminated at the sight of their brightly coloured, almost abstract canvases, usually devoid of people. They were the "Hot Mush School," according to one *Toronto Star* review. But through the years of the First World War they persevered and eventually began to succeed in creating what author Robert Fulford later described as a "Great Canadian Myth."

Their communion with nature in Algonquin Park north of Toronto, and the death by drowning there in July 1917 of the artist Tom Thomson (a kindred spirit who died before the Group named itself), added to the legend. Soldiering on, they became accepted in the 1920s; by the 1930s, theirs was the measure by which all paintings had come to be judged with regard to their "Canadianism." By then, among the art elite, a reaction had set in when it was believed that art development had frozen. "It is time," wrote Frank Underhill in 1936 "that we demand from our artists that they cease to be mere escapists and that they concentrate their gaze upon the life that is actually lived by our 10 million Canadians."

However, the Canadian public, who had slowly become aware of the Group of Seven's works through coloured reproductions that were widely distributed across the country, liked what they saw. The wilderness *did* seem distinctly Canadian. They also identified with the story of struggle and triumph. In 1965, the creation of the McMichael Canadian Art Collection at Kleinburg, north of Toronto, a bequest of 194 works of art consisting largely of the Group's paintings, added further respectability to the saga. Just as Sam McGee's cabin was moved to Whitehorse, so Tom Thomson's studio shack was moved from its original site in Toronto to the gallery's grounds.

Books spread the Group's theories as effectively as the popular reproductions spread their vision. *A Canadian Art Movement: The Story of the Group of Seven*, by Fred Housser, published in 1926, articulated an ideology that it

Tom Thomson's "The Jack Pine"

claimed was common to all the Group's members. A half-century later, Peter Mellen's *Landmarks of Canadian Art*, published in 1978, described the Group as exemplifying "The Canadian Spirit in Art." Although most of the Group's famous images were Ontarian, their paintings became archetypal for the entire country. "The remote northern landscape, where nature was still wild, pure, and unspoiled, became a romantic symbol for the unique qualities of Canada," Mellen wrote. Describing *The Jack Pine* and *The West Wind* – both paintings depicting solitary trees on a rocky outcrop with a lake and hills in the background – he wrote, "Surely there are no greater landmarks in Canadian art . . . both painted by Tom Thomson in the year of his death." The question of how Thomson died became the subject of much speculation. Had he just fallen out of his canoe, or was he murdered, or . . . ? For Canadians, Thomson's canoe could be added to critic Robert Hughes's three great icons of modern art – Van Gogh's ear, Dali's moustache and Picasso's testicles.

The Group's vision was further popularized by the book and exhibition entitled *The Group of Seven: Art for a Nation*, mounted by the National Gallery of Canada in 1995 and circulated to Toronto, Vancouver and Montréal during the subsequent year. Although the show exhibited many of the famous images depicting Canada as an unpeopled wilderness, it also included paintings of towns, villages, slums, factories and people, putting the lie to the idea that all the artists wanted to paint was nature rampant. Then came the lawsuits: in 1996, Robert and Signe McMichael sued the trustees of their eponymous gallery over whether it could acquire and exhibit art not in the style of the Group's landscapes. Perhaps, asked commentators, the McMichael Collection was less about art than it was about a Canadian mystique?

A more recent widely published art form has been wildlife painting, with Canadian Robert Bateman being the most talented of the many artists working in this genre. Its popularity might imply that what is created by people – the cultural landscape – is not an essential part of the Canadian heritage. You might conclude, after having seen a roomful of Group of Seven paintings or a wildlife art exhibit in a mall gallery, that our greatest contribution to a national identity would be to do nothing and leave the countryside alone. That's a far cry from the poetic tradition of *la douce France* which, in historian Simon Schama's words, is a geography as much as a history, depicting "the sweetness of a classically well-ordered place where rivers, cultivated fields, orchards, vineyards and woods are all in harmonious balance with each other." Human endeavour just doesn't seem to make it in the collective vision of Canada.

☾ ☾ ☾

"Well, it can't be all that bad," you're probably saying to yourself, and perhaps it isn't.

Indeed, there are Canadian historic sites, and buildings in cities, and towns with interesting histories and plaques to read. The more there are to find, such as in a Charlottetown or a Québec City, the richer the experience of living there or visiting can be. You can go and visit a place where some historical event took place, or at least is alleged to have taken place, and breathe air infused with the magic elixir of memory. This air also pervades the sites of non-colonial cultures, especially aboriginal ones, which have sprung from a world of traditions and beliefs very different from the linear, object-oriented culture I grew up in.

An example is X̱á:ytem, otherwise known as the Hatzic Rock Site, near the town of Mission in the Fraser Valley east of Vancouver, British Columbia. X̱á:ytem is the site of an ancient settlement occupied by the ancestors of the Stó:lo people between 4,000 and 9,000 years ago – before the Pyramids, before Stonehenge. Archaeologists from the Stó:lo Nation and the University of British

Columbia are carefully sifting through the remains of a pit house dating from about 5,000 to 6,000 years ago. Among the human-altered objects unearthed are obsidian tools traceable to southern Oregon, demonstrating the extent of trade across the 49th Parallel before Brian Mulroney's day. (Obsidian tools from the same quarry have been found in southeastern British Columbia, within sight of the Rocky Mountains.)

Xá:ytem itself is a large rock standing on a grassy bank that was purchased in 1993 by the B.C. Heritage Trust to ensure its preservation. It is one of the "stone people" sites, where the Xexá:ls (the creator) transformed the Si.yams (the chiefs) into stone for not teaching the people the written language that was given to them. Infused with the life force, the rock, in geological terms a "glacial erratic" left behind by the retreating glaciers, gives the place a powerful spirituality. A longhouse for interpreting Xá:ytem and Stó:lō culture was built nearby in 1994. One of the images used in the interpretive brochure is a painting from about 1850 by Paul Kane, depicting the interior of a Coast Salish dwelling – an inspiration to all us wanderers with sketchbooks.

Aboriginal and European heritage sites have some common threads. One is the Alexander Mackenzie Heritage Trail, following the route taken in 1793 by the fur trader and explorer from Montréal across the continent to the Pacific Ocean, more than a decade before the much-hyped traipse of Lewis and Clark across the continental United States. Parts of Mackenzie's route used aboriginal trails and local guides and followed the pathways of commerce – especially the "grease trails" running inland from the Pacific Ocean, along which coastal tribes carried oolichan oil to trade with interior tribes. At Dean Channel west of Bella Coola, Mackenzie recorded in his journal his arrival at tidewater: "I now mixed up some vermillion in melted grease and inscribed in large characters on the southeast face of the rock . . . Alexander Mackenzie, from Canada, by land. July 22, 1793." Not far away. in a shaded canyon, petroglyphs cut into a rock face mark the passage of different travellers.

There are similarities, then, in the heritage sites of the different cultures that make up Canada. Obviously there are differences, too, which is either Canada's great strength or its insurmountable weakness, depending on how you feel about multiculturalism. One of the more interesting aspects of the difference between Canadian cultural groups lies in their attitudes toward objects and their permanence. Aboriginal cultures tend to believe that everything should decay and return to the earth as part of a natural cycle, while European cultures tend to believe that objects themselves ought to be preserved – that there is little value in a copy. The non-European, non-aboriginal groups that make up so much of modern, urban Canada are slowly creating their own landmarks and sites, initially with distinctive religious temples (as was the case a lifetime ago with the Ukrainian churches on the Prairies). A rare example of ethnically influenced, non-religious architecture in Canada is the commercial buildings of Vancouver's Chinatown. However, immigrants usually get other groups' architectural castoffs in left-behind neighbourhoods, and much of their cultural imprint is temporary: paint colours and signage on old buildings. By the time they become established and prosperous, former immigrants usually build in the fashionable, international architectural styles that have made urban Canada look like everywhere else.

Aboriginal beliefs are well respected in the treatment of decaying totem poles at Ninstints on Anthony Island (also known as Sk'un'gwaii) at the southern tip of the Queen Charlotte Islands (Haida Gwaii) off the British Columbia mainland coast. Ninstints was recognized in 1981 as a World Heritage Site by the United Nations. Although the poles will eventually rot away, the only intervention has been to ensure that the rate of decay is minimized, largely by carefully managing the surrounding Sitka spruce rainforest to ensure that the poles are somewhat protected from the wind and from mechanical

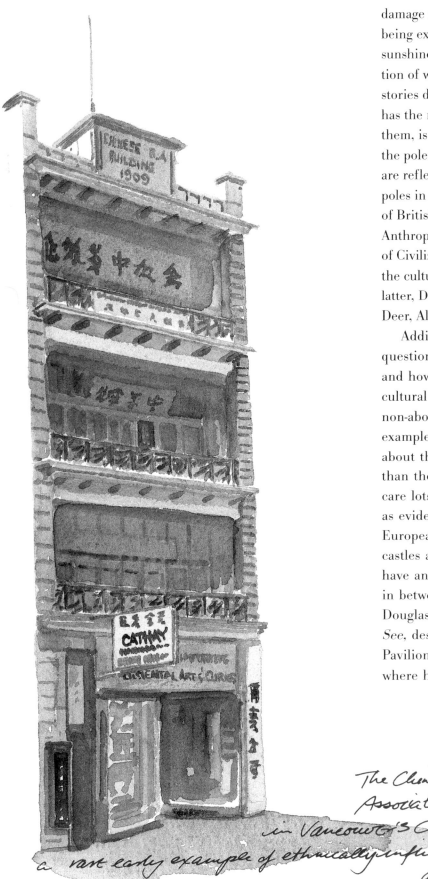

The Chinese Benevolent
Association building
in Vancouver's Chinatown —
a rare early example of ethnically influenced non-religious
architecture.

damage from the trees themselves, while being exposed, albeit rarely, to the sunshine. To the aboriginals, the question of who owns the crests and the stories depicted on the poles, and of who has the right to replicate them and adapt them, is more important than the fate of the poles themselves. European beliefs are reflected in the preservation of totem poles in museums, such as the University of British Columbia's Museum of Anthropology and the Canadian Museum of Civilization in Hull, Québec. Bridging the cultural gap is the architect of the latter, Douglas Cardinal, born in Red Deer, Alberta, to Métis parents.

Adding further complexity to the question of what constitutes a heritage and how you preserve it are the cultural beliefs of the non-European, non-aboriginal citizens of Canada. For example, while aboriginals care more about the spirituality of the object than the object itself, and Europeans care lots about the authentic object – as evidenced by the standard European package-tour itinerary of castles and artifacts – Oriental cultures have an attitude that fits somewhere in between. The English writer Douglas Adams, in *Last Chance to See*, described a visit to the Gold Pavilion Temple in Kyoto, Japan, where he was:

The evolution of the Québec farmhouse
La maison Drouin, near Sainte-Famille
on the Île d'Orléans – a very
simple little house for
an 'habitant' from about
1734.

← 19th century farmhouse
near Berthier-sur-Mer –
style probably influenced
key buildings such as the
Manoir Montmorency near
Québec City.

mildly surprised at quite how well it had weathered the passage of time since it was first built in the fourteenth century. I was told it hadn't weathered well at all, and had in fact been burnt to the ground twice in this century.

"So it isn't the original building?" I had asked my Japanese guide.

"But yes, of course it is," he insisted, rather surprised at my question.

"But it's been burnt down?"

"Yes."

"Twice."

"Many times."

"And rebuilt."

"Of course. It's an important and historic building."

"With completely new materials."

"But of course. It was burnt down."

"So how can it be the same building?"

"It is always the same building."

A brave step in this direction was taken when the Manoir Montmorency near Québec City burned down on May 13, 1993, more than 200 years after it was built. Located on a sublime site beside the Montmorency Falls, which are more than thirty metres higher than Niagara Falls, the manoir was the summer retreat of Sir Frederick Haldimand, the commander of the British forces occupying Québec after the Battle of the Plains of Abraham.

Erected around 1780, Manoir Montmorency differed from other Québec buildings, having been designed as a picturesque villa with Palladian elements surrounded by covered galleries or verandahs that were more typical of French buildings in Louisiana or of the architecture of British India. Writing about the manoir in the *Canadian Journal of the International Commission on Monuments and Sites (ICOMOS* Canada), David Mendel noted: "Indeed, it is probable that the later development of the typical 19th-century Québec farm house, with its curving roof extending out over a covered gallery, had its origin with the model provided by this residence built for a representative of the King of England."

The ownership of the building in the century after Sir Frederick's death in 1791 added to its Anglo patina. An occupant during the next few years was Prince Edward, later the Duke of Kent and future father of Queen Victoria. In 1815, a lumber merchant named Peter Patterson bought the site so he could harness the falls to power a lumber mill. In 1877, the Québec Railway Light and Power Company bought the property and managed to transmit electricity to Québec City, twelve kilometres away. The company employed the architects Staveley and Staveley to transform the house, by that time a century old, into a prestigious hotel they renamed Kent House. It soon came to be referred to as a "manoir," adding to its prestige by begging associations with the seigneuries of New France.

The Government of Québec bought the property in 1974, during a period of ascendant nationalism. Nearly twenty years later, during a project to upgrade the manoir and its surrounding park and the falls into a major recreational attraction, disaster struck when the structure burned. Soon after, architectural historian Luc Noppen advised the government to rebuild. According to Mendel, "the objective was to create a reconstruction that was close enough to the appearance of the original building to give the impression that the fire had never taken place." A new steel structure was dressed in the clothing of the Kent House Hotel as it had appeared at the beginning of the 20th century.

The saga of the Manoir Montmorency hints at a maturing of the Canadian culture, in spite of the ongoing Québec-versus-Canada *opéra bouffe,* that is a far cry from the situation in Montréal in the early 1970s. Cast your mind back to Montréal in those heady, post-Expo days. The city was shedding the vestiges of its gilded, Anglo-Scottish-dominated age, when it was indisputably the premier city of a provincial nation and, in its new wardrobe of glass and steel, it looked outward for approval. Millions of dollars of investment flowed to this international city with a French flavour, creating megaprojects like Place Ville Marie and Place Bonaventure. Along the way, blocks of historic buildings were razed: Place Guy Favreau destroyed the city's vintage Chinatown. According to one estimate, 70 percent of the residents of the downtown working-class east end had to relocate due to new construction. Also in the path of the bulldozers were the former homes of some historically significant Canadians, two of whom were key figures in the building of the Canadian Pacific Railway.

One mansion, the Drummond Street home of the financier George Stephen, honoured by Queen Victoria as Baron Mount Stephen, had been the Mount Stephen Club since 1926. Less lucky, yet perhaps more important historically, was the Sherbrooke Street home of Sir William Cornelius Van Horne, the CPR's general manager and later president.

Van Horne's house was a fifty-two-room, grey-stone mansion built in 1869 and bought by Van Horne twenty years later. It had an ornate interior of plaster and gilt made by Tiffany protégé Edward Colonna. This was thought to be the only complete example of his work in North America. But time and families move on, and Van Horne's descendants sold the mansion in 1973 to David Azrieli, a developer, who proposed to construct a high-rise complex on the site.

Under its charter, the City of Montréal could do nothing to halt the development, but the province of Québec could have used its Cultural Property Act, passed the year before, to classify the property and protect it from demolition. Initially François Cloutier, the Québec minister of culture, declared his support for classification, but in June 1973, he inexplicably withdrew it. Unless it were to purchase the mansion outright, a precedent it didn't want to set, the federal government's hands were tied. Under the legislation of the day, its only course of action was to declare the house a National Historic Site, and this was possible only if the province made the request. Under the British North America Act, since replaced by the Canada Constitution Act, provinces have sole jurisdiction over property.

Attempting to justify the Québec government's lack of support, the director-general of National Cultural Property, Marcel Junius, stated that the mansion was not "typically Québecois." Some years later, historian Pierre Berton reflected on the decision: "In those days, a building had to be 'significant' to be preserved – significant historically and significant architecturally. A [Université de] Laval professor proclaimed that, since Van Horne was a union buster, his mansion did not deserve designation. Only the homes of saints, it appeared, were worthy of consideration." So, by the afternoon of Saturday, September 8, 1973, after a hard day's work by the demolition crew, the Van Horne house was rubble.

☾ ☾ ☾

Politics aside, the demolition of the Van Horne house was out of character for the Québecois, who had been the first Canadians to commemorate sites from their past, beginning in 1860 when the St. Jean Baptiste Society erected a memorial column to mark the centenary of the last victory of French forces in the battle for New France. A dozen years later, following the lobbying efforts of the antiquarian and journalist Joseph-Octave Dion and the acquisition of funding from the federal Department of Public Works, restoration began on Fort Chambly on the Richelieu River southeast of Montréal, a 1665 bulwark against marauding Iroquois. Using language that has become common in recent pronouncements by Québec politicians, Dion called Fort Chambly "a sacred trust from the French-Canadian past." C. J. Taylor, in *Negotiating the Past*, described the fort as "a shrine to traditional Québec culture."

Around the time of Confederation in 1867, Ontarians began to rally around their United Empire Loyalist past, much as Québecois were finding common cause with the St. Jean Baptiste Society, and made their first moves to preserve and commemorate the battlefields of the War of 1812. The Lundy's Lane Historical Society, formed in 1887, convinced the federal Department of Militia and Defence to place a monument on the battlefield at Lundy's Lane, near Niagara Falls. (More than a century later, in 1996, Lundy's Lane was once again in the news, when Ruth Redmond, a ninety-four-year-old retired Niagara Falls schoolteacher, bequeathed a 1.2 hectare piece of the old battlefield site to the City of Niagara Falls as a historic park. She had been acquiring property connected with the battle since 1954 and, for her efforts, received the Gabrielle Léger Award from the Heritage Canada Foundation, its highest honour.)

Other War of 1812 battlefields – Crysler's Farm and Stoney Creek in Ontario and Châteauguay in Québec – also received commemorative monuments erected by the government. The English poet Rupert Brooke, *en voyage* across Canada in 1913 and very aware of its growing pains, noted: "And in this land, that is as yet hardly at all conscious of itself as a nation, Toronto and Ontario do their best in leading and realising national sentiments."

Meanwhile, as colonization proceeded westward along the path of the Canadian Pacific Railway, the federal government became involved in a different sort of preservation. In 1883, CPR general manager William Van Horne first visited the Rocky Mountains and, aware of the tourist value of Yellowstone National Park to the American Northern Pacific Railroad, suggested that the federal government cooperate with his company in the development of a Canadian national park system.

The discovery that year of the Cave and Basin Hot Springs near the future town of Banff by some railway workers, and their attempts at exploiting it, prompted the government in 1885 to consider creating a reservation to preserve the springs from commercialization. With advice from the CPR, the Canadian government looked at the example of Hot Springs, Arkansas, reserved for the public by the United States government in 1832, and Yellowstone, established in 1872, and decided in 1885 to create a reservation of about twenty-six square kilometres around the Cave and Basin Hot Springs. That tentative step led to legislation to incorporate the Hot Springs Reservation into Canada's first national park, the 676-square-kilometre Rocky Mountains Park (later Banff National Park). In 1911, the Parks Branch of the Department of the Interior, now known as Parks Canada, was established to create and maintain a national system of parks.

Centre Block.
Parliament
Buildings,
Ottawa.

Another branch of the federal government, the Department of Public Works, was intent on creating a national style of architecture. The earliest and most dramatic of all federal buildings actually predate Confederation: the Parliament Buildings in Ottawa, designed in a High Victorian Gothic style for the Province of Canada. Many lesser buildings were constructed in the Second Empire style, popular in France and the United States. Between Confederation in 1867 and the turn of the 20th century, the federal government erected about 300 buildings. One politician who

West Block.

Tower of the East Block.
Parliament Hill.
— the three buildings all variations on
Victorian Gothic styles. An attempt to create
a national style of architecture for Canada.

insisted on high standards was the minister of Public Works, Sir Hector-Louis Langevin, who, as architectural historian Harold Kalman wrote, "was determined to create an imposing government presence across the country, and felt that the Department of Public Works should set a good example that would encourage local developers to erect substantial buildings."

Langevin appointed Thomas Fuller as chief architect of the Department of Public Works in 1881; some twenty years earlier, Fuller and his partner Chilion Jones had won the competition to build the main Parliament Building. During Fuller's time as chief architect, from 1881 to 1897 – the year before his death at the age of seventy-six – he designed about eighty post offices and federal buildings in towns and cities across the country. Some of the survivors, such as the former post office in Baddeck, Nova Scotia, were abandoned by the Crown but have become beloved local landmarks, the subjects of spirited restoration campaigns using locally raised money and talent. In Baddeck, a committee of townsfolk even made notecards and fabric carry-bags with the stencilled image of the old building to raise money, a few dollars at a time, for the ongoing restoration project.

The federal government's attitude in the late 19th century seems like a far cry from what it is today, when most governments, fearing the wrath of taxpayers, erect the lowest-quality, most-invisible buildings possible. In Langevin's time, as the *Canadian Architect and Builder* magazine noted, Fuller's buildings were "an influence for good" and helped to "form the public taste." Winston Churchill expressed a similar sentiment in one of his most adroit quips: "We shape our buildings, and afterwards our buildings shape us."

To the casual glance, the best federal buildings of the 19th century look almost the same as the CPR's famous "railway chateau" hotels – the Banff Springs, the Château Frontenac and the Empress in Victoria. The other railways that amalgamated to form the CNR also completed a nationwide set of hotels with tall copper roofs and picturesque profiles, including the Château Laurier in Ottawa, the Fort Garry in Winnipeg, the Bessborough in Saskatoon, the Royal York in Toronto and the Hotel Vancouver. It is all rather a nice set, and very Canadian. The role of the aforementioned CPR general manager, later president, William Van Horne cannot be overemphasized: beginning in 1886, while developing a system of hotels exploiting the choicest views in the Rockies and the Selkirks, "he found recreation and delight in sketching, suggesting or modifying the elevations and plans of these structures," according to his biographer, Walter Vaughan. Wanting to make everything fit into a "Canadian Alps" theme, Van Horne directed his architects on the design of the early hotels, one of which was the Banff Springs (1888). For the Château Frontenac in Québec City (1892), he ensured that the designs and siting achieved the "broad effects" he wanted. As well, Van Horne supervised the production of immigration brochures and the idealized "commercial" art published in them to sell the Prairies to potential settlers from Europe and the United States. The first thing new immigrants saw was the local railway station, the early designs of which were influenced by Van Horne's sketches.

☾ ☾ ☾

Canada's heritage buildings began to gain a national focus due to the efforts of the Royal Society of Canada, which had been founded in the 1880s to support scholarship in the arts and sciences. Around 1900, members of the society became aware of the heritage movement in the United States, which had received a lot of public attention in the quarter-century following the American centennial, and of the National Trust for Places of Historic Interest or National Beauty in England, founded in 1895 by three disciples of the writer-artists John Ruskin and William Morris. The National Trust contacted the Royal Society of Canada in 1901, requesting donations to help it acquire *British* heritage sites. Preferring to focus on its own history, the Royal Society formed a subcommittee to promote the cause of heritage preservation, which in 1907 became a separate body called the Historic Landmarks Association.

Rather than use this association to advise it on heritage sites and commemoration, the federal government created the Historic Sites and Monuments Board of Canada (HSMBC) in 1919. The commissioner of Dominion Parks, James B. Harkin, had managed to persuade the government that a number of obsolete properties, such as fortifications and fur-trading posts, were of national significance. Under its first chair, Brigadier General E. A. Cruikshank, the HSMBC erected plaques at about 300 sites in its first twenty years of operation. Perhaps not surprisingly, a lot of the sites were significant to military history, such as the Fortress of Louisbourg on Cape Breton Island, Fort Beauséjour near Sackville, New Brunswick, and a string of North-West Mounted Police fortified posts across the west, leading to the comment in the Massey Commission report in 1951 (the Royal Commission on National Development in the Arts, Letters, and Sciences) that there was "a curious emphasis [on commemorating military history] in a country that boasts not infrequently of the longest undefended frontier in the world." Some of these identified sites could be restored, while others had to be rebuilt entirely. Politicians, explorers and other interesting personages made up the balance of the National Historic Site designations.

The Massey Commission included in its final report a recommendation from the Royal Architectural Institute of Canada that "the preservation of old houses of architectural merit" become a priority. In 1953, under the new Historic Sites and Monuments Act, the HSMBC was given increased resources and statutory authority, and in 1955 it was given the power to recommend national designation of buildings of great age or exemplary architectural design. However, because control of property is vested in the provinces, designation of properties did little more than commemorate them. Thus, by the late 1950s, the HSMBC was recommending that Ottawa create a national trust, like the English one. After fifteen years of internal debate, the federal government took a tentative first step when the Canadian Inventory of Historic Building project was launched in 1970. Thousands of buildings across the country were photographed and catalogued, initially from the pre-First World War period, later from pre-1945. That fifteen-year hiatus and the lack of action since suggest how low a priority a succession of federal governments has placed on preserving buildings as part of our country's cultural heritage.

☾ ☾ ☾

"Kluckner . . . Kluckner . . . Isn't that a German name?"

I used to get that a lot from people – from Canadians – of the generation before mine. Most had British surnames. Not that there was any implied superiority in the question, but it provoked from me a surly response.

"No, it's a *Canadian* name," I'd reply.

With its "ö" replaced by a "u," Kluckner had become a Canadian name – a hybrid – for a family that has been in this country for more than a century. My grandfather, born in England in 1867 to a German-born musician who conducted an oompah-pah band in towns along the Channel coast, had immigrated to Canada as a young man, married, lost his first wife (though not due to carelessness, we were assured), then remarried, in 1906, to one Carrie Hooper of Paris, Ontario. His work as a superintendent for the Canada Vinegar Works took him, over the ensuing twenty-five years, to plants in Goderich, Belleville, Hamilton and, finally, Winnipeg. In his sixties, with a promised thirty-five dollars a month from the company pension plan, he was launched into retirement and, with my grandmother, sought a gentler climate than that found in balmy Winnipeg. West they went and ended their days in Vancouver (named for Captain

Vancouver, a Royal Navy explorer of Dutch ancestry) in a shingle-covered bungalow typical of Southern California set a half-dozen blocks from English Bay (that's *English* Bay) in the Kitsilano neighbourhood (that's *Khahtsahlanough*, named by the Canadian Pacific Railway to honour a chief of the local First Nation).

Typical Canadian story, eh?

Grandfather was not a "hyphenated Canadian," and his children and grandchildren sure as hell weren't either. We were just folks in one of the suburbs of the nascent global village, and I grew up surrounded by the symbols of a rather confused nation. In Cubs, we learned which side was up on the Union Jack, and as schoolchildren we lustily sang:

Wolfe, the dauntless hero came
And planted firm, Britannia's flag
On Canada's fair domain . . .

Market on "Rue Somerset St."
in bilingual Ottawa — muggy
late-summer day, milky sky

Meanwhile, we were taught about ICBMs and fallout shelters and read *Life* and *Saturday Evening Post* magazines from the States and knew the names of President Kennedy's children before we knew the name of the prime minister's wife. In my recollection, the most memorable part of "Canada's national magazine," *Maclean's*, was a cartoon called "Jasper," about a bear, which we thought was Canadian because Jasper was a resort in the Rocky Mountains we had passed through once on a car trip.

On the walls in my school's art classroom, reproductions of Group of Seven paintings, featuring rocky outcroppings, lone pines and bright autumn colours, were the only depictions of Canada – yet they were of a place I had never seen. Out there it is all wilderness, said the paintings, unpeopled and pristine. Yet, on the wall of the den at home, there hung a small needlepoint tapestry of my mother's, showing a *habitant's* horse-drawn sleigh gliding along a narrow lane between high snowbanks toward a cheery stone farmhouse. Smoke curled from its massive chimney into a cobalt-blue sky. That image of a Québec winter may have been her childhood landscape, but outside my Vancouver window winter was green and misty.

Other images from schoolbooks confirmed that there was a distinctive *cultural* landscape to go with the unpeopled natural one. There were the farmhouses of *les habitants*, which I already knew about from the den wall, the shanties and dories of Maritime fishermen, vast Prairie farms and grain elevators, the ghost towns of the mountainous west, the settled hamlets of Ontario (like Stephen Leacock's Mariposa) and even igloos presided over by stolid "Eskimos," as Inuit were then called. And, of course, there were a few deluxe national symbols, especially the Parliament Buildings and the Peace Tower, and probably also Maple Leaf Gardens and the Montréal Forum. Everything was stitched together by railways (not rail*roads*, which were as American as the stitching on a baseball). The Canadian Pacific Railway employed a beaver on its logo, not one-half of the Stars and Stripes, and the Canadian National Railways used a maple leaf. It seems now that my childhood identification with Canada was based on such images, modified of course by my imagination – children had to imagine things then, as there were so few easily available pictures, and so few people travelled. In short, I felt Canadian because I believed I knew what the country *looked* like, even if I was somewhat confused about what it stood for. If I knew the lay of the land, surely I must be a citizen.

Those images of Canada were a select few that had become archetypes – perhaps merely visual clichés – but they were especially distinctive amidst what was a much more verbal culture than the current television-dominated one. Indeed, we lived in an era of visual innocence. Today, in the midst of the blizzard of images from around the world, Canadians have become obsessed with abstract, button-pushing concepts: words like "health care" and "heritage" and "rights" (as in the 1982 charter) have defined a new Canada which, compared with the nation of my childhood, is a virtual place with few physical symbols understood in common. "Heritage," for example, now means everything from a kindly, accepting multiculturalism (as in the federal government's Department of Canadian Heritage) to an atavistic yearning for a simpler time of "family values" and religion (as in the Christian Heritage Party). The English language has become as muddled and fuzzy as the country. In the heated debate in the early 1990s over whether Québec could be dubbed a distinct society, I was prepared to suggest a compromise: no new title for Québec, but the moniker "indistinct society" for the rest of us.

I first thought about the Canadian quicksilver landscape in the fall of 1991, as I sat near an abandoned orchard on Okanagan Lake in the interior of British Columbia and painted the view across an old farmstead to the distant mountains. Nothing evolves in this part of Canada, I said to myself; every generation or so the landscape is clearcut and the clock is reset to zero. We have no heritage. The landscape no longer says anything about the cultures that created it. All is transient.

Pretty gloomy stuff. True it may be for that part of British Columbia, but what about elsewhere? Was I just a sap, unwilling to accept the god's truth of constant change, the gospel according to technology? "As the complex nature of man-made existence of the modern world turns its machinery and its knowledge of science towards the comfort of humanity, it yet aggravates the discontent which is evident around us," wrote Group of Seven artist Arthur Lismer in 1927. "Our polluted cities, our mechanical fashion of living, our ugly squalid architecture, our commercial pride and foolishness, and cheap enticing entertainment, are all squeezing the beauty out of life, and making us a standardized disdainful people. We cut and slash our trees to make room for ugly buildings; we fill in and stamp out the natural beauty of our cities; we carry into the vast hinterland our city banalities, and prey upon its denizens." Perhaps his message was an anachronism even then?

Then came the Québec sovereignty referendum of 1995. The Québec government, who are masters at the Identity Game, had been working for decades preserving monuments and retaining and developing an encoded, magical landscape, redolent of myth and legend, of ancient settlement and the changing seasons, of roots and history, of the warmth of home and the deep snows of winter. The federal government's response, coordinated by the Department of Canadian Heritage, was to give away more than $20 million worth of Canadian flags, without any corresponding discount or tax rebate on flagpoles. They might as well have been grabbing at smoke.

In the aftermath of that referendum, I decided to see if *my* encoded Canadian landscape, cobbled together from the symbols, images and imaginings of my youth, actually existed. Was this dreamscape mere make-believe? Had economic and social change caused it to fade, while new development homogenized it, so that every part of the country looked like every other part? Had Canada become a virtual country, held together only by emotions and abstractions?

It had been years since I had travelled in Canada; every airplane I boarded seemed to be going over the pole to Europe or across the Pacific to Australia, and every car I drove was pointed at California. Did Canada still look like the old pictures I remembered from my school days? Since 1970 – arguably the end of my youth – the world has been turned upside down by social and political change. Had the stretches of bucolic countryside photographed for my school geography books survived or had it all become a gigantic strip mall, like Joel Garreau's *Edge City?* Were there still buildings and landscapes that everyone knew or had Canada become an illusion, tied together with phone lines and Internet connections rather than with railway tracks?

I had never been to the Maritimes and had seen the Prairies only through the dust on a train window. Somewhere I had read that Canada was the most urbanized nation on Earth, and I wondered whether the country's two solitudes were no longer Hugh MacLennan's English and French peoples but were, instead, country people and city people. The newspapers talked of modern urban Canada as an explosion of multiracial colour in what had once been a dour, Protestant place – this was the new Canada, they exclaimed. What had happened to the old one?

Notes from the Road

Maritimes

"Our main export is our children," said a friend who had grown up in Nova Scotia. She had left, too, following marriage to a navy man in Halifax and a transfer to the West Coast, but she still missed the friendliness of the Maritimers, their lack of the sort of keeping-up-with-the-Joneses materialism she saw all around her in British Columbia. "The sea holds back the arrival of winter," she said, "but it also holds back the arrival of spring." I'll go in October, I thought, to see the fall colours, and I won't have to take a snow shovel as carry-on baggage.

Although Halifax and Dartmouth have their charming neighbourhoods, they were too big-city for me when I got there, so I went south along the coast. Quicker than you can say "Jack Robinson" I was on a rocky coast of coves and peninsulas with little lighthouse-exclamation points, following a winding road past houses loosely strung together into villages. the paraphernalia of the owners' maritime lives strewn about their yards and along the shore. Ropes, traps, floats, nets and old dories planted with petunias splashed bright colour on the faded grass next to the white houses.

West Dover, Nova Scotia — the view from a fish & chip shop at the roadside. Houses dotted about without rhyme or reason along the rocky shore.

Pulled off and stopped at Peggy's Cove, determined to see whether it looked like the photos on the calendars sent by a real-estate agent who had once pestered me. I had heard it was overrun with tour buses but found it serene and almost deserted in the early autumn sunshine. Seagulls perched in lines of Morse code along the ridges of the shanties and boathouses. Gnarled characters in blue jeans and work shirts yarned while they patiently coiled ropes on the great plates of rock that make up most of the foreshore. With the Atlantic fishery a mess and these people members of the picturesque poor, I thought maybe they deserved a salary from the tour-bus companies.

When I resumed my southbound meander, a few kilometres of driving led me into a completely different landscape. The dotted houses perched on plates of granite and braced against the harsh winds on the shore at Peggy's Cove gave way to scenes reminiscent of Ontario or New England villages. Around Margaret's Bay, and just to the south at Mahone Bay, the coves are sheltered from the open sea, hardwood trees shade quiet streets, church steeples poke through the leafy canopy and pretty fretwork decorates the houses. Mahone Bay is a village from some arcadia. Farther south still is magical Lunenburg, recently declared a World Heritage Site by the United Nations.

Peggy's Cove, all blue
& tranquil in the
warm October sun.

Low tide
at Hampton,
Nova Scotia,
along the Bay
of Fundy.
Men fixing the
breakwater—

Mahone Bay fit Lady Tweedsmuir's deft description of Nova Scotia: "The soft landscape of the villages, each grouped round its church, suggests an England transplanted somehow into a clearer air." Other Maritime towns also date from English colonial times but, unlike Mahone Bay, they are planned on a grid. Traditional English villages were laid out around crooked lanes and streets "not made for hasty progress," as Thomas Hardy wrote, and reflected a time "when one-handed clocks sufficiently subdivided the day." The Imperial gridiron town plan imposed order and symmetry on a tangled world. Halifax and Lunenburg are relentlessly right-angled; at Lunenburg, there was hardly enough flat land for a parade ground, but they had one anyway, bordered on two sides by streets that descended steep and straight to the harbour.

But it was Annapolis Royal, on the Bay of Fundy side of Nova Scotia, that was my dream Atlantic village come to life. Stately homes lined a handful of streets, a little commercial area hugged the shore, a few colonial relics (in this case Fort Anne, dating from the early 1700s) and a historic garden competed discreetly for attention. Boats of all sizes and purposes tugged at their moorings and posed picturesquely on ways for scraping and painting. The tide rose and ebbed to an astonishing degree: on my morning's walk, all the boats were level with the top of the dock, while in the afternoon they sat indecorously on the muddy shore, tipped a bit to one side like fat old tabbies on their bums. In the evening there were some nice restaurants for tourists and a warm, inviting pub frequented by the local lobster fishermen,

Annapolis Royal.

Tavern at Annapolis Royal, N.S.

who bitched quietly about the state of their lives in the commercial breaks of the televised hockey game. And what team were the barflies rooting for, you may ask? The local one: Boston.

On my way into Annapolis Royal from the east, after crossing the province from the Atlantic shore, I came across two inns on opposite sides of the road. One, the Queen Anne, a grand example of the Second Empire style of architecture, stood fifty metres back from the road in the midst of a large lawn with some beautiful trees around it. The other, called Hillsdale House, was a more subtly ornamented and evidently older Georgian building, also set back from the road. I went to it.

Unlike the Queen Anne, which was a converted house, Hillsdale House had been a guesthouse since it was built in 1849 and had hosted two English kings as well as prime ministers and other dignitaries. The innkeeper, a man of about forty, was fond of conversation and told me while showing me to my room that he liked to sit and chat with guests in the evening in the parlour. After a quiet dinner down the road I returned to the inn and found him, true to his word, engaged in conversation with a couple from New Brunswick. They soon excused themselves, pleading an early start the next morning, and the owner turned his attention to me, willingly

Former New York stockbroker – no kidding! that's what he said he was – selling his first apple crop along the roadside in the Annapolis Valley, Nova Scotia.

(Also raising Jacob sheep & selling eggs.)

answering my questions about Annapolis Royal and his life there. He was a ninth-generation Nova Scotian and had turned his love of old houses into a career. As well as the Hillsdale, he owned one place in Lunenburg that he was restoring, a farmhouse on a hill in the countryside and the lavish Queen Anne Inn across the street.

"That one, too?" I asked, rather incredulously, forgetting how affordable property can be in Canada's economic backwaters.

"The Queen Anne's the money-maker," he replied. "The Americans like it best. It's their idea of a heritage building. But I prefer this one – even though it barely breaks even."

This gentle Maritime landscape of villages, sheltered seacoast and countryside extends northward along the Bay of Fundy, through the bucolic Annapolis Valley, past Wolfville and Sackville and around to the New Brunswick shore. Some villages are merely pretty, with their tree-lined streets; others, like St. Andrews, are beautifully restored and tarted up with boutiques for tourists; still others, like St. George, with its abandoned paper mill, survive precariously on the vestiges of their industrial pasts. Sackville and Wolfville are invigorated by their universities and bear a resemblance to American New England college towns; Fredericton, the capital of New Brunswick as well as a university town, is perhaps the best of the lot.

I arrived in Fredericton on the Friday evening of Thanksgiving weekend and booked into a large old house converted into an inn. Downtown, students from the university jammed the bus station, queueing for coaches to take them back to their hometowns for the holiday. I walked the streets of the old part of town, lined with fine old houses; many had their lights on but had no curtains drawn, displaying their

Queen-Anne style house at Amherst, Nova Scotia

interior woodwork and detailing to the curious passerby. The walls of some houses looming over the sidewalk bore signs reading: BEWARE OF FALLING ICE. On one an M had been added to ICE.

Saturday morning was market day, and local farmers had come to town, selling preserves, vegetables and corn stalks, still with the ears attached, for Hallowe'en decorations. That evening, the dining room at the inn was full of families, the children and even the teenagers well behaved and smart in dresses, jackets and ties, eating turkey dinner. At one table, father reposed in splendour at the end, while a younger daughter watched her sister, whose scrubbed boyfriend sat quietly next to her while mother discreetly observed them all. Almost a Norman Rockwell painting – damn! There's that American influence creeping in again!

The calm and settled Maritime ambience continues across the Northumberland Strait onto Prince Edward Island. In Charlottetown I located an inn, the former residence of the university president, a few blocks from Province House where the Charlottetown Conference of 1864 – which laid the groundwork for Confederation – took place. In my room there was a copy of a booklet on the city's old buildings that noted: "Progress, as it relates to the change or destruction of heritage resources, has been relatively slow in Charlottetown. Fire, it seems, has been the worst enemy, though on the whole, little disruption has occurred that would make way for newer, less worthy buildings. The only real and constant threat has been neglect and the passage of time."

Conversation around the breakfast table reflected on the island's slow pace and the relationship between the locals and the CFAs – the Come From Aways – those whom the Newfoundlanders called the Mainlanders or the Outlanders. One story concerned a P.E.I. potato farmer chugging home slowly in his old truck along a country road. Unbeknownst to him (because his rearview mirror had fallen off years before), he is being tailgated by an impatient CFA, probably from Halifax, hurrying to his summer place on the island so he can relax and get away from it all. Slowly, the truck grinds up a long hill, inexplicably moving over into the left lane. The CFA, seizing the opportunity to pass, floors it but, just as he is about to pull level, the old farm truck swings across his bow, narrowly missing him, and chugs into a driveway on the right. Shaking with rage, the CFA pursues the farm truck up the driveway. As the old farmer is getting out, the CFA accosts him.

"You could have killed me! You didn't signal you were turning right!"

"Why do I have to signal?" replies the farmer. "Everybody knows I live here."

A succinct variation on this story involves a tourist attempting to get directions to an ancestor's farm. The islander tells him: "Just go down to where the Anglican church used to be and turn left."

Whatever the topic, every conversation ended up on the subject of the new Confederation Bridge, then within months of completion, and the question of what impact it would have on the island lifestyle. The inn's owner talked of the reports in the newspapers of CFAs, especially Germans, buying up waterfront property. I wondered whether there would be more theme parks and amusement grounds, such as the one near Green Gables in Cavendish that features a replica of the Space Shuttle, along with other attractions reflecting the cultural richness of our modern age. Had there

Old café in St. John, New Brunswick with pressed-tin ceiling. The only place (other than Tim Hortons) open Sunday morning.

Cap le-Moine
on Cape Breton
Island.

been a spate of rezoning proposals for golf courses and resort properties, I asked? Could P.E.I. survive the onslaught? A former islander, who had brought his ailing old dad back to have a last look at the family homestead, gave short shrift to romantic notions of a vanishing lifestyle. "Island traditions," he scoffed. "You mean, like poverty and wife-beating?"

A regular feature at the inn, and in the Confederation Centre a few blocks away downtown where Lucy Maud Montgomery's original manuscripts and photographs were on display, were the young women who had made the pilgrimage to see the Montgomery home and Green Gables, the inspiration for the home of the fictional Anne Shirley. One woman, perhaps twenty-five years old, although of Chinese ancestry revealed her nationality by her broad Australian accent. Will you be spending long in Canada? I asked. No, she replied, it was hard to get much time away from her job, so she was only away for two weeks. Would she be spending the whole time on P.E.I.? No, she was going to see Canada. Really? Yes, she would be visiting Green Gables, Niagara Falls, Banff and Whistler. The essential Canada, I assured her.

Near Margaree Harbour,
Cape Breton.
One of a myriad little lighthouses
along the shore; breezy
late-summer day, grasses rippling

Mahone Bay, Nova Scotia, a village from a more pious age than this one. Although it's on the Atlantic coast, it's tucked into a narrow inlet & protected from the bleak winds that stunt the trees at Peggy's Cove, only a few miles away.

The Tantramar Marshes, looking from Fort Beauséjour toward Nova Scotia. Cold, mid-October day with a few snow flurries in the air & the wind blowing so hard it rocked the car.

My room at the Duffus Inn in Baddeck on
Cape Breton Island. Paused there for a few
days to "let my soul catch up." Baddeck could
be the archetype of the summer-cottage community,
a sleepy little place with the Alexander Graham
Bell home on a nearby hillside, & no shopping
mall! (I was in heaven).

*View from my room at Baddeck onto
Bras d'Or Lake — actually an arm of the sea.
Mid-October, town quiet, the summer people all gone
home.*

Gothic Revival church at Victoria,
P.E.I. — the field adjoining
crowded with round hay bales
ready for the winter.

All over P.E.I., the red potato-growing earth is deeply
furrowed for the winter.
♪ "I'm Bud the Spud, from the bright red mud" — Stompin'
Tom

Round bale with
grass seed sprouting
on top.

Town Hall.

Sunday
morning in
Summerside,
Prince Edward
Island.

The waterfront at West Dover,
Nova Scotia. Sat at a picnic table
outside the fish'n'chip shop ; packed looking
into the sun. Early October.

Coiling ropes at Peggy's Cove.

Painting the
'Bluenose II' from
the wharf at
Lunenburg, N·S.

Laundry on a line at Lunenburg, N·S.

Solar dryers are still very popular all over the
Maritimes & Newfoundland, although little used
in the more prosperous parts of the country.

Newfoundland

"WHY ARE YOU GOING TO NEWFOUNDLAND IN THE WINTER?" friends asked me. They were genuinely puzzled. "I mean, why not go in August or something?"

"Because," I declared, "all the colour will be stripped out of the landscape by the snow and . . . uhh, you know . . . and I hear the houses are brightly coloured so it should be good to paint!"

"Whatever . . ." they replied skeptically.

The flight from civilization, aka Toronto, was packed with chattering, tanned Newfoundlanders on their way home from Florida and other sunny spots. Several were wearing Hard Rock Café T-shirts, and I don't remember any of them carrying coats. One was carrying what looked like a case of rum and had some trouble getting it into the overhead locker. The three-hour flight was uneventful – except for an announcement that fog might thwart a landing and we would have to divert to Halifax. However, we did eventually land at St. John's airport after a descent so bumpy I wasn't sure when we actually touched down. It was two in the morning and so foggy you couldn't see across the road.

Second-Empire-style houses on Gower Street, looking
through into Willicott's Lane, St. John's, Newfoundland.

"Is t'is yar first time on t' Rock, t'en?" the cabbie asked, as we whipped through the icy streets toward downtown St. John's.

"Yup, never been here before."

"Ya should ha told me. I could ha taken ya on a bituva tour."

"Oh well, you've got work to do and, anyway, it's dark."

"Yar right about t'at! Can't see much now!"

Within a few minutes, we had gone through an old residential area, the tall wooden houses rising straight up from the edge of the sidewalk, and had arrived in the downtown. The fog had lifted a little, and I could see a cathedral on the hill; above some rooftops, a huge fixed spotlight shone into the darkness.

"Marks t'harbour entrance," the cabbie remarked. He paused a minute, listening to the crackling conversation on his radio. "I'll prab'ly be busy again in about 'alf an hour," he said.

"At this time of night?" I asked, surprised. "Another flight trying to come in?"

"Bars'll close," he replied, gesturing to his left toward a block of low buildings. "T'at's George Street. Every building's a bar, and t'ey don't close till tree."

Foggy day in St. John's, January. From Gower Street, looking down Cathedral Street with the harbour in the distance.

Grates Cove —
still some
relics from the
salt cod-fishing era, esp.
the flakes + stages (the flat platforms + the shacks)
on the steep hillside above the cove.

The following morning the fog had lifted somewhat by the time I emerged from the hotel. St. John's presented itself as a San Francisco without the palm trees. It is hilly and the buildings are wooden, albeit in different designs from San Francisco's. They are rather flat in the façade, usually without the pronounced bay windows that give San Francisco streetscapes their accordion look. Row houses in reds, greens and yellows brighten the streets even on dull days. Boys – some wearing sneakers, others roller blades – had set up nets and were playing road hockey a block from Duckworth Avenue, the main commercial street. Many roads intersect at odd angles or are only a block or two long. It is European, I thought, or . . . well, it's like its almost-namesake, St. John, New Brunswick, but St. John isn't as hilly and there aren't the fancy paint jobs on the houses. Or maybe it feels a little like Québec City, but . . . no. St. John's is like nowhere else.

In fact, Newfoundland itself is like nowhere else. Compared with the easygoing plenty of much of Canada, Newfoundland's culture revolves around images of survival – survival on the Rock against a hostile climate. Around its rim is the endless, unforgiving sea. (I must confess: to me, water is something that's fine in a glass or useful when accompanied by a bar of soap. As a child, engrossed in stories of the Second World War, I recoiled from the photographs of drowning men – one in particular of a German submariner who'd lost das boot and was pleading to be rescued from the icy North Atlantic.) In a shop, I skimmed an article in a Newfoundland magazine that noted that sailors favoured tattoos because they improved the chance of having their bodies identified after a prolonged float in the water. And of course there was the *Titanic* disaster: all that drowning, all that cold water. I shivered at the image of Newfoundlanders in their dories on the rolling sea, their freezing hands clutching ropes stiffened by icy spray; the women, at home in the outports, kerchiefs tied tightly over their hair, pushing baby carriages along the lanes and gazing out to sea. A grim people in a grim environment, tragedy riding around with them as comfortably as a parrot on a pirate's shoulder.

But everyone I met belied my thoughts. They were friendly, casual, self-deprecating and funny. "What'll ya have?" a waitress asked. "Cod 'n' chips, chicken 'n' chips or chips 'n' chips?" In Grates Cove, a woman came up to me to say hello because "I could tell you were a stranger and you might want to meet someone." I asked her how things were going. "No work yet this year," she replied cheerfully, "but the shrimp plant'll start up soon!" Their casual attitude reminded me of an observation of Thomas

"Burke's House" in the area called
Riverhead near Brigus, Newf. Built about
1840 in a sort of Georgian style. Tough to dig a
foundation into the rock, I suppose, so they build the
houses vertically — cheaper to heat, too.

Hardy's in *Tess of the D'Urbervilles* concerning people who were "a gay survival from Old Style days, when cheerfulness and Maytime were synonyms – days before the habit of taking long views had reduced emotions to a monotonous average."

There was another side to the story, though, as I had heard some months earlier when I was tooling along the road through another of Canada's economically depressed areas – in Saskatchewan – and listening to an item on the CBC about the Summit of the Sea conference being held in St. John's. The artist Christopher Pratt was talking about how the outports had disappeared; at least, he said, the isolation and subsistence that had made them unique no longer existed. Author E. Annie Proulx, whose most potent image in *The Shipping News* was of a house affixed by cables to the rocks to keep it from blowing away, talked of how the young people – those between eighteen and forty-five – were gone. Fathers no longer communicated the lore of fishing and the sea to their sons. There was no point, she implied, for that life and time had gone forever, like the rural England of Hardy's day, abandoned by farmers' sons who had gone to work in the factories.

North of St. John's, after a day spent drifting around the seashore near Brigus, I shipwrecked for the night at an inn at Harbour Grace. One of the owners was a longtime Newfoundlander who traced his roots back to 1812 and a couple of Irish brothers who had settled on an island in Placentia Bay. He talked about his grandparents who worked almost communally with their neighbours. His grandfather and his mates fished for cod from dories; his grandmother, the neighbour women and their children split, salted and dried the fish on flakes – wooden platforms exposed to the sun and wind. When you were a fisherman, you either had a credit with the merchants or else you were in debt to them: you never had any cash of your own. His grandparents saw the writing on the wall during the Depression of the 1930s and had left their island home in favour of some good farmland on the Burin Peninsula – the peninsula on the south shore to the west of the Avalon Peninsula where the capital, St. John's, stands.

They were prescient, as the salt-cod fishery faded after the Second World War, replaced by trawlers and draggers that employed some of the men and fish-packing plants that employed some of the women. A cash economy began, and following Confederation with Canada in 1949 the government began to resettle outport people into "growth centres," which were established where it believed there was a chance of diversifying the economy. "When you say resettle," I asked him, "they weren't forced to go?"

"No. They'd just say, you want a dock? You want medical care? Then move." From that period came one of the enduring images of outport Newfoundland: houses being floated across bays or dragged across the ice to new locations. Eventually, as everyone now knows, high-tech fishing helped kill off the cod that had been the mainstay of that way of life.

In some towns, the government built large, multicoloured apartment buildings nicknamed "jelly bean squares" and allocated housing to the new settlers by having them draw lots. In rural Newfoundland, families had lived a sort of communal existence, usually in clusters of houses, sharing cooking and babysitting and fishing duties. So what was intended as a humanitarian move – as a way of providing new opportunities and modern government services – in addition changed the social structure of the Newfoundland community. The young began to abandon their rural roots, and many left for industrial jobs on the mainland. "Newfoundlanders are quite eager to have Québec separate," quipped John Crosbie, the former politician, "because they think it'll take them less time to drive to Toronto."

Bay de Verde, a classic Newfoundland outpost. Little houses scattered about, a couple of big churches, a shrimp plant, & a couple of stores. Bright January day with a howling wind off the Atlantic – all the snow blown off the rocky barrens, but ice still clinging to the shady spots.

In Newfoundland, directions may confuse, but place names amuse. I went onto one long spit of land to see a town called Port de Grave and passed Blow Me Down Road near the village of Bareneed. Intrigued, I pulled out the map and looked for other strange names. There was Cupids, which had nothing to do with Valentine's Day but was historically significant as the site of the first English settlement in 1610. Also on the Avalon Peninsula are Witless Bay, the curious Upper Gullies, and the suggestive Dildo across the bay from Spread Eagle. Heart's Delight, Heart's Desire and Heart's Content are three villages on a stretch of coastline north of Dildo. Leading Tickles stands on Notre Dame Bay on the north shore of the island, not far from Lushes Bight. And there is even a Pasadena near Corner Brook.

"Where are you goin', then?" the owner of the inn asked me.

"I think I'll go up to Bay de Verde," I replied. "Up" because it was north – higher up on the map.

"Oh, you mean *down*," he exclaimed. "It's always 'down' when you're heading out to the end of a peninsula."

Being there in February, I missed seeing the pack ice that fills the bays in the spring and the huge 'bergs that drift south just off the coast. Another time, I thought.

The Cabot Tower (built 1897 to
commemorate the 400th anniversary of
Cabot's voyage) obscured by the fog.
enveloping Signal Hill. Just below
the tower. Marconi sent the first
↓ Trans-Atlantic wireless message
in 1901.

Fog rolling into St. John's herbour, January.

The day had dawned clear & blue, — a false spring — but late in the afternoon it turned into winter again. Dubious climate statistics: for major Canadian cities, Vancouver is the wettest, Winnipeg the coldest, Montreal the snowiest, + St. John's the foggiest.

(Lighthouse just past the harbour entrance painted earlier in the day)

Ontario

I HAVE LONG BELIEVED THAT ONTARIO IS THE ONLY CANADIAN PROVINCE where the citizens, en masse, have deep roots and a sense of contentment and permanence (in a bad mood, I'd call it smugness). Newfoundlanders and Maritimers have roots, too, but for many generations they've had too *little* change to instill contentment: the permanence there, reflected in such homilies as "our past is our future" and "the 20th century just about passed us by" have worn rather thin. The Québecois have roots, but there's been little contentment there in the political climate of the last thirty years. Ontario is different: not a frontier for nomads like the West and the North, it has an industry-based rather than a resource-based economy and, to the annoyance of virtually everyone else in the nation, sees itself as the centre of things. Not surprisingly, many of the people I've met across Canada who are involved in historical societies and heritage preservation have come from small-town Ontario, fanning out across the country as if to carry their message to the uninitiated.

In the past there was a bow-tied boosterism typical of Ontario, lampooned first in Stephen Leacock's 1912 masterpiece, *Sunshine Sketches of a Little Town.* "Ask any of its inhabitants if Mariposa isn't a

The Mississippi River, a tributary of the Ottawa River, at Almonte in eastern Ontario. Like Stephen Leacock's Ossawippi River, the Mississippi was the source of hydro-electricity for industries in the region until quite recently. A plaque nearby tells of the Mississippi River Improvement Company, founded in 1909 (3 years before Leacock wrote 'Sunshine Sketches'), which built & maintained dams, levied tolls & generated power. The company closed in 1991. Some of the old factory buildings in Almonte have been converted into shops, popular with Ottawa day trippers — one is the Victorian Woollen Mill; according to a plaque, in 1890 it employed 500 people. Main floor of the fine old Post Office building (a Thomas Fuller design) is now a pub.

busy, hustling, thriving town," he wrote. "Even the transcontinental railways, as any townsman will tell you, run through Mariposa. It is true that the trains mostly go through at night and don't stop." The fictional Mariposa's Main Street was laid out with "none of the short-sightedness which is seen in the cramped dimensions of Wall Street and Piccadilly."

The year after Leacock wrote his sketches, the patrician traveller Rupert Brooke recoiled at that boosterism, which he found everywhere except for Ottawa, where "Canada is more than the [extremely individualistic] Canadian. A man desiring to praise Ottawa would begin to do so without statistics of wealth and the growth of population, and this can be said of no other city in Canada except Quebec." He nevertheless liked the Ontario countryside: "After the States and after Quebec it is English. There are weather-beaten farmhouses, rolling country, thickets of trees, little hills green and grey in the distance, decorous small fields, orchards and, I swear, a hedge or two. Most of the towns we went through are a little too vivacious or too pert to be European." Brooke found Ontarians to be conscious of more than just their "Old-Country" roots. In Ontario, he wrote, "men have lived contentedly on this land and died where they were born, and so given it a certain sanctity." Beyond Toronto, the province was a mixture of prosperous farms, small cities and towns, and it exuded confidence in a *Canadian* future.

The old hydroelectric works at Almonte, Ontario.

Old Order Mennonites in the
countryside around Elmira, Ontario.

Two ways to spot one of their houses:
① no power lines ② the laundry on the line is all blacks &
purples, as if an urban "goth" lives there.

Today, Ontario is "the heartland," or perhaps "the industrial heartland," and when one thinks of industrial Ontario it is of sprawling factories and freeways along the lake from Toronto to Burlington and Hamilton. The modern economy has all but eliminated industries from the little towns that dot much of southern and eastern Ontario; usually built along rivers that provided them with their power, these towns today are often well preserved, their main streets lined with substantial, century-old buildings, and are surrounded by farmland and picturesque sugar bushes. Almonte on the Mississippi River near Ottawa, for example, was once the seat of the wool trade in Canada. A number of historic towns line the Trent-Severn and the Rideau canal-and-river systems in eastern Ontario – Perth and Merrickville being representative. West of Toronto along the Grand River are former industrial towns like Elora and Paris; in the adjoining countryside, especially near Elmira, live Old-Order Mennonites in their black and purple clothing, hats and bonnets, their horse-drawn buggies sharing the streets and highways with modern traffic. This is the closest approximation in Canada of historian Simon Schama's *la douce France* – the well-ordered landscape balanced between nature and culture.

Elora on the Grand still has an operating hydroelectric plant in the basement of the old mill, now a country inn. Almonte's hydroelectric works dominate the view of the river from the town. It is all so much from another era, when the only power grid linked Niagara to Toronto, and towns such as Elora, Almonte or Smiths Falls were worlds unto themselves, manufacturing or milling a product for a market huddled behind tariff walls. As Stephen Leacock wrote, by the time the electricity from the little plant on the Ossawippi rapids reached Mariposa, nineteen miles away, it had turned into coal oil again, so the electric light bulbs glowed "as yellow and bleared as ever."

I arrived on the Grand River at Fergus late on a Sunday afternoon in October, having fought the traffic out from Toronto, and dawdled along the road through beautiful countryside toward Elora. Oblivious to the line of sport utility vehicles behind me, I slowed almost to a crawl when passing Wellington County's dramatic House of Industry and Refuge, a shelter for "the deserving poor" from 1877 till 1971 and now a museum. In Elora, as evening fell, it was evident that most people had gone back to the big city for the week. I sat with my book in a quiet pub on the riverbank, the only sounds being the cash register printing its evening tally after a busy day and a baby in a bassinet quietly sobbing while its parents finished their dessert. Went back to the hotel and channel-surfed. The bathroom light made me look like my grandfather.

Taking this as a sign from above, I went to Paris – Ontario, that is – to seek the church where my grandparents were married in 1906 (Paris is the smallest of the three "capitals" in that part of Ontario, the others being London and Berlin, the latter changing its name to Kitchener in 1915). The church stood on the far side of the river from the downtown, set on a V-intersection at the top of a hill, with some old houses on the streets nearby. It didn't look much different from the photograph in my Aunt Lillian's living room. Lunchtime was approaching, so I returned to the downtown and walked along the main street, looking to grab a sandwich. In a café, I skimmed the local paper, which was from Brantford, a city a few kilometres to the southeast best known as Wayne Gretzky's hometown and once an industrial centre with a Massey-Ferguson factory, among others. Noted a couple of weddings, with photos of pretty brides and sallow grooms, the success of the local football team and a contract let for a new building. Near the back of the paper, on the editorial page, a letter described how the writer had travelled the world, visiting Stonehenge, the Acropolis and the ruins of abbeys and ancient towns. In all of them, he had stood in the rubble with other tourists and had had his picture taken. Perhaps, he suggested, Brantford could advertise the rubble of its downtown and become a world tourist destination, too? I finished my coffee and set my compass for Brantford.

Elora, Ontario — the old mill
building (now an Inn) on
the Grand River from the
Victoria Street bridge.

1877 stone church, now used
as a pottery studio.
Henderson Street, Elora.

From its outskirts, Brantford, like many small Canadian cities, appears to be a busy place: diggers digging, pavers paving and so on. Boy, I thought, summoning my best Leacockian verbiage, this place is a real going concern! According to the OPENING SOON signs, the construction was of the big-box type – automotive, home-improvement and discount places, emporia for people who want to buy a lifetime's supply of toilet paper all at once at the best possible price. Passing them by, I took the highway exit marked CITY CENTRE and a few minutes later found myself on Colburne Street. Some small machines were working on a piece of property, but it was hard to tell whether they were taking something down or putting something up. All around were vacant lots, some with the rubble alluded to in the letter. It looked like it had been bombed or perhaps shelled by artillery.

The two main streets, Colburne and Dalhousie, were lined with fine, substantial buildings, but paint had peeled and cornices sagged and most of the storefronts were vacant. It did not surprise me to find, a little bit further east, a mall to which most of the downtown commerce had fled. Called Eaton Market Square, it was evidently an object of civic pride – the interlocking pavers for a block or so around it and the enhanced street ambience of saplings, benches and waste bins were a dead giveaway. I parked and went to check it out, shouldering my way through the swarm of black-on-black, ball-capped, cigarette-smoking teenagers loitering around the doorway. Inside the Muzak played, the fountain burbled, the

Queen-Anne style house in
Paris, Ontario, pretty in
the October dapple.

Vacant   Vacant   Portu-guese fish shop   Vacant Vacant   International Fun House   Vacant...etc.   This way to the mall →

Brantford, Ontario, at the corner of Colburne & King.

cash registers in the chain stores rang and the NO LOITERING signs exhorted. But even there a lot of the storefronts were vacant, too.

Getting back into the car, and feeling the need of a psychological boost, I headed for Niagara-on-the-Lake, with a detour to see the Falls, just for old times' sake. After passing through kilometres of motels and souvenir shops of the most cheesy variety, I followed the road down the hill past Lundy's Lane and came in sight of the Falls, partly obscured by the huge new casino. However, along the river, where the landscaping and buildings are controlled by Parks Canada, Niagara Falls seemed Canadian in the best sense of the word: orderly and conservative.

Unlike the Australian woman at the inn in Charlottetown, I knew all about Niagara-on-the-Lake, several kilometres downstream from the Falls where the Niagara River flows quietly into Lake Ontario. A colonial-era town surrounded by historic sites and dubbed (by a Toronto magazine) CANADA'S MOST BEAUTIFUL TOWN, Niagara-on-the-Lake was the United Empire Loyalists' beachhead in the wilderness following their flight northward from the newly liberated United States of America more than two centuries ago. On a grid of quiet streets, these conservative settlers created the archetypal Ontario town, and over the years the UELs transformed themselves into FOOFs (Fine Old Ontario Families). Growing up as I did in a country dominated by Ontario and its media, I came to believe towns like this were typically Canadian, too – not just Ontarian.

Adjusting my traveller's eyes to absorb the dignified and settled quality of the town while screening out the twee boutiques, I wandered about. Sure, Queen Street was done up like a

Niagara Falls

—"from the sublime to the ...."

(Beaver with
a blue bow tie)

Martha Stewart TV special, but a half block on either side were fine Georgian houses, towering boulevard trees all gold and red in the autumn sunlight, dads and sons practising hockey in their driveways and . . . Okay, go ahead and laugh! It may not be representative of the rest of the country, but it was a nice little escape from the reality of modern life.

Slightly shabby after my days on the road, I walked into the Prince of Wales Hotel on Queen, looking for a room. From the outside, it had a rambling quaintness that I thought might match my budget, but once through the door I quickly realized I was in the wrong place. A few heads turned to look, the way I turn when I see a potential mugger on a city street. Undeterred, I made it to a brochure rack and found one that contained the room rates, the cheapest of which were well into the three digits. My suspicions confirmed, I beat a hasty retreat back to the street.

A couple of blocks away, on a side street, I came upon the Olde Angel Inn, established about 1825 and not much bigger than a house. Excuse for a bar, I thought to myself, but went in the side entrance and found its tiny registration desk. In an apologetic voice, the young concierge told me the only room they had available was a small one above the tavern. "I have to tell everyone that they might find it noisy," she said, "but there's no live music tonight so it shouldn't be too bad." How much? "Sixty." *Yes!* I thought, while outwardly looking skeptical. I climbed the creaking stairs, ducking at the top under a low beam, and made my way to the room. It was small, coloured in blues and yellows, with a couple of pieces of old furniture and a four-poster bed – an upscale version of Van Gogh's room at Arles. Two casement windows looked out onto the backs of the buildings lining Queen Street.

Descending to the bar at about eight o'clock, I ordered fish and chips and a mug of local beer and watched an enthusiastic darts match. Later, in the room, the dull roar from below increased for a time, then subsided, and I soon fell asleep. Much later, there was brief whooping and sport utility vehicle door-banging, then silence. I awoke once and looked out the window: snow was falling very lightly, visible only in the glow of the streetlights. There was little trouble in paradise.

I woke early and walked in the dawn light, eventually finding an old-fashioned café – one of the few latte-free zones in town – that served bottomless cups of flat coffee to a handful of regulars. The weather forecast said snow. I returned to the Angel in time to let in a group of marooned joggers who had inadvertently locked themselves out, grabbed my stuff, put it in the car and headed for Toronto. It was time to go back to reality.

The 1847 Court House, now the Town Hall, in Niagara-on-the-Lake on Queen Street. The clock tower in the median of the street was erected as a war memorial.

Room in the olde Angel Inn at Niagara-on-the-Lake.
Windows look out onto Market Street just off Queen, the
main drag. Mid-October, so darkness fell late afternoon,
lamps came on. Killed time by painting this while waiting to
descend to the tavern for dinner — have to ration the good
times, as I can't drink as much as I used to. ...

Corn drying in the autumn fields.

"Wellington Home." between
Elora & Fergus, Ontario — the
former House of Industry &
Refuge, now the museum &
archives for the
county.

(Economically disadvantaged Ontarian
— unable to afford a leaf blower.)

Everyone anthropomorphizes their pumpkins, well in advance of Hallowe'en. Like the scarecrows of summer.

The West Montrose covered bridge, built in 1880 is the last remaining one in Ontario. Known locally as "the Kissing Bridge," according to a heritage sign on the roadside.

January - farm near Merrickville, Ontario, the long purple
shadows stretching across the snow.

A stayed a couple of days in Merrickville at a nice inn.
One night after dinner, decided to go for a walk & could
hear from blocks away the sounds of a hockey game —
crack of sticks, shouts, the whack of the puck on the boards.
Walked toward it, the air so cold the snow squeaked under
my feet, so clear that the sound travelled effortlessly.
In the freezing night, the game looked something like this.

Lanark, Ontario, on the Clyde River—
all the names are from the "Old
Country." Not a gridiron Ontario
town. Area was settled in the 1820s.
mainly with unemployed
Scottish weavers.

Québec

ALTHOUGH QUÉBEC IS UNIQUE LINGUISTICALLY WITHIN CANADA, to an outsider the lifestyle there seems more North American than, say, Newfoundland's does. But anybody who travels through it cannot fail to see the unique way the land was settled and the villages were built. It is France transplanted, whereas in the Maritimes and Ontario the lay of the land and the design of the villages are only pale echoes of Mother England

I grew up with a few Québec images around the house because my mother was a third-generation Québec Anglo, born in Lennoxville in the Eastern Townships. Her needlepoint picture of a *habitant* riding his sled hung on the den wall at home; beside it was a painted tile, as colourful as faïence, with the refrain of the bizarre folk song "Alouette" (in which the singer plucks a skylark) printed around its edge. At school, I watched National Film Board educational movies featuring French Canadian lumberjacks, perhaps named Pierre and Ti-Jean, wearing toques and needing a shave; in stupid Hollywood films about Canada, ze bad guy he was always "Frenchie." Books added to my store of dubious knowledge: travellers'

Near Kamouraska, Québec, painted from the shore of the St. Lawrence River. The long, narrow hayfields stretch back from the river to the village.

accounts romanticized *les habitants* (the peasants) much as they did Canada's other "primitives" – the "Red Indians." Rupert Brooke expressed a typical opinion: the rural Québecois were "a jolly sight. They are like children in their noisy content. They are poor and happy, Roman Catholics; they laugh a great deal, and they continually sing. They do not progress at all." In her travel book, Lady Tweedsmuir claimed to know the cause: the policy of the Roman Catholic Church, she wrote, was "to promote contentment with rural life." Later, I became aware of Cornelius Krieghoff's 19th-century paintings of rural Québec, images that were popular with European collectors but hated by the Québec bourgeoisie, who felt they were patronizing and clichéd.

Unlike *les habitants* of Krieghoff's day, today's Québecois in their Levis and Benetton gear look like everybody else. Now it is the French villages that provide the unmistakable image of Québec, so different from Loyalist towns. In the former, the houses huddle around a huge, grey-stone Roman Catholic church – a symbol of protection and domination – while in the latter the churches of the many Protestant denominations are small and wooden and scattered about. (As Domenico Carracciolo remarked, the English have sixty different religions and only one sauce.) "The traveller who sails up the St. Lawrence River is struck by the way strips of cultivation run down to the edge of the water, and by the size of the churches compared to the smallness of the villages," wrote Lady Tweedsmuir. She noted how different the Roman Catholic churches were from the Gothic architecture favoured by the Protestant denominations: "their slim silvery spires reflect the sunshine in the winter, and they stand like jewels against the snow."

En route to Québec City, I passed through the Haute-Beauce region and found there, high and bright among the rolling hills, the little town of Saint-Évariste-de-Forsyth, its church spire as much a beacon in its day as radio and cell-phone towers are today. I returned there to paint and found myself late in the evening seeking accommodation at a nearby town, La Guadeloupe, which had the only local motel. It was a tough little place, with a poolroom and a bar; I took a room and was amused to find mirror tiles glued to the ceiling above the bed.

Evidently, in the years since La Révolution Tranquille of the early 1960s, the universal piety of Québec rural society has faded. An architectural specialty nowadays is the conversion of disused

Saint Évariste-de-Forsyth
in the Haute-Beauce, seen
from the roadside near
La Guadeloupe. The church
on the hill, protecting the
town & the farmers in their fields.

The 1906 presbytère & the 1887
church at Saint Évariste-de-Forsyth. Since 1980, the
presbytère has been used as the museum for the Haute-Beauce.

churches to other uses – one excellent example is in Lévis, the town across the river from Québec City, which has converted a fine old church into a library.

His first sight of Québec City from the deck of an approaching ship inspired Rupert Brooke to write: "And high and gray and serene above the morning lay the citadel of Québec." Brooke was just one of many travel writers impressed by the last fortified city in North America, now a United Nations World Heritage Site. When I first visited the city in 1981, I stayed in a little *pensione* across the street from the city hall in the heart of the old upper town. Some days I wandered the city streets, stopping to watch the street artists or the tourists sightseeing in horse-drawn *calèches*. One memorable day I went to Île d'Orléans to pick strawberries and returned with a large basket to share with the pensione's owners; supplementing the strawberries with some yoghurt and a bottle of chilled chablis, we sat on the roof terrace in the summer sunshine and gazed over the rooftops and chimney pots of the city, down into the Jardin des Ursulines – the garden of the convent which, according to a tourist booklet, preserves the relics of a missionary killed by Iroquois.

For the first time since that trip, I returned to the city in the sweltering heat of early July after several days on the road and booked into the Clarendon, a small hotel of very French character at the opposite end of the block from my earlier lodging. Below my window, on the lawn of the city hall, a large tent and some kiosks advertised the impending arrival of the Québec Jazz Festival. I had a couple of days to kill and the urge to be *touristique* but was thwarted by a violent summer thunderstorm that turned the streets into ankle-deep rivers and left cool, rainy weather in its wake. So I replaced the dim bulb in the desk lamp with the sixty-watter from the bathroom and spent the days painting quietly, finishing sketches from the Québec countryside and only emerging between rain showers to seek food and drink in the warren of old streets. And to look at real-estate ads ("Kluckner . . . Kluckner . . . *C'est un nom allemand, oui?"*).

❰ ❰ ❰

One January, after several days in the pretty towns between Ottawa and Perth, Ontario, I returned to Québec, journeying eastward to Van Kleek Hill, a town of curious flat-roofed houses. I crossed the Ottawa River at Hawkesbury, turned westward and, with the river on my left and the Gatineau Hills on my right, motored slowly through the area known as the Outaouais. Towns with names like Chelsea and Buckingham stood cheek-by-jowl with ones called Gatineau and Masson-Angers. Somewhere behind me, downstream toward Montréal, was a town called Hudson where my grandmother had spent her final years, a place familiar to me only from postmarks on letters forty years ago. I passed through Hull, saw Parliament Hill dramatic on the far side of the river, and was soon into a farming area where villages named Bristol, Portage-du-Fort, Bryson and Campbell's Bay were dotted along the road.

For much of the way, there were splendid vistas in the Ottawa River Valley. I pulled off the main road at Luskville to admire the farmland down the bluff to the river flats and, deciding to paint the view, stopped on the side of the road in front of a farmhouse. A sudden knock on the car window startled me – a woman of about sixty had approached. I rolled the window down.

"Lookit, sorry to bother you," she said, "but my old dad inside the house – he always sits where he can look out the window. He's all upset that a car's going to come along and run into you."

"I thought I was off to the side," I mumbled, instinctively looking both ways and seeing only a quiet little country road. Not a single car had passed in the time I'd been there.

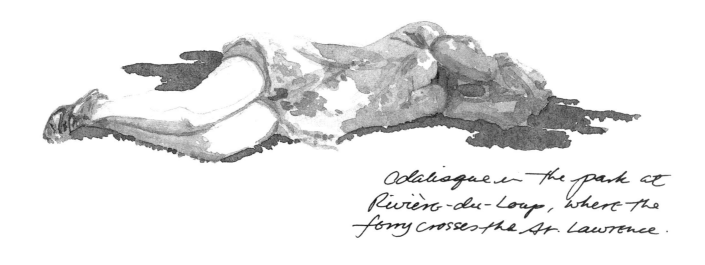

Odalisque in the park at Rivière-du-Loup, where the ferry crosses the St. Lawrence.

"You are . . . no, it's not that. He's just gone funny in the head," she continued, with an apologetic tone in her voice. "But he won't settle down until you're off the road, so can you move the car into the driveway? Please? Don't worry. Nobody's coming here. And come in for coffee."

"Well, ah, sure, if it's . . ."

"Don't mention it!" she exclaimed. "It'd be great to have the company! I'm Pat Lusk: we're the Lusks of Luskville."

So after a little while, once I had daubed away to my satisfaction, I walked up the driveway to the house, a low structure sheathed with white aluminum siding that glinted in the sun. A handful of small sheds and coops stood nearby, with a barn above on the hill. As was characteristic of the area, a herd of brown Hereford cattle lounged around in a feedlot. Some took turns at a large metal hay-feeder while others stood in the sun, blinking and chewing their cud.

Inside, a very old, frail man sat in a big leather chair, alternately smoking and coughing while his daughter brought him coffee and lit his cigarette when he couldn't manage it. "It's the only pleasure he gets now," she offered by way of explanation, perhaps sensing me recoil from the thick atmosphere. "You sit here and talk while I get you some coffee."

He told me that his family had come to the area more than a century earlier and for generations had taken grain and hay crops off the fields below. Great- and great-great-grandsons of the pioneers had since taken over the farming and gradually divided up the huge homestead while the old guy and his daughter lived on in the original family home.

"So this is the original home?" I asked, seizing a potential conversational gambit.

"Yeah, it's square-log, you know, a real heritage building. But we fixed 'er up!" he replied proudly.

After a few more minutes of struggling conversation, the old boy seemed tired and I took my coffee into the kitchen to talk with his daughter. She had the radio on and was intent on the weather report. "Where are you staying tonight?" she asked me. "They're predicting a blizzard." I told her I didn't know but was heading west toward the end of the road, where the highway crossed the Ottawa River back to the Ontario side near Pembroke.

Town in the Beauce, south of Québec City.
Sugar bushes, hayfields, dairy barns & farmhouses,
& all the houses of the village huddled around the
huge church. Churches in the area built 1905-10;
covered bridges, like the one nearby at Notre-Dame-
les-Pins, still being
built in the 1920s.
All the house
styles are
19th
century.

The presbytère at St. Joseph-de-Beauce.

The Ottawa Valley (Québec side) looking westward — upstream. Snowsqualls forecast on the car radio.

She seemed concerned. "There's not much open up here at this time of the year, but I'll see what I can find you."

Before I could say anything, she was dialling the phone and was soon exchanging pleasantries with a friend. Was that bed-and-breakfast open near Chichester, she asked. "No, well how about that other one – you know, the woman who lost her husband?" A faint voice came through from the receiver; she made notes on a piece of paper, then thanked her friend and hung up.

"Seems like this place here is open," she said, gesturing at the scribble. "It's a ways back into the hills but really pretty. My friend says you'll see a sign to it at the crossroads in Chichester."

I thanked her for her hospitality, moved quietly past the old boy who had fallen into a slumber and resumed my slow progress. Much later, after a lunch in Shawville, which was so defiantly Anglo that there wasn't a single French sign, and a coffee at Roy's Salle de Billard in Fort Coulonge, which was unilingually French, I arrived at what I thought were the appointed crossroads but couldn't find the sign. It was about three in the afternoon, with the sky to the north taking on a definitely stormy look. The motels I had seen were all closed for the winter, with a half-metre of untracked snow right up to their doors. An old postal van, converted into a mobile snack shop with a sign advertising FRITES – POUTINE attached to its roof, sat marooned off to the side of the road. Reluctantly I thought about crossing back into Ontario, but I really wanted to spend another day on the Québec side of the river.

A sideroad crossed onto Île aux Allumettes – Matchstick Island – and out of curiosity I followed it across a piece of flat land past a few houses and up a steep hill. Ahead, on the high point of land, stood a Roman Catholic church with its steeple soaring above the surrounding countryside. At the crest of the

View from the Lusks' driveway
of the fields of Luskville.
Ottawa River + Ontario in the
distance. January day,
about −5°.

Poker game at Roy's pool hall, Fort-Coulonge, Québec

hill a sign announced I'd arrived in Chapeau; just past the sign stood a large old two-story gabled building with covered balconies on its front and a small neon sign: HOTEL CHAPEAU. Just an excuse for a bar, I thought, the sort of place where hunters and out-of-work loggers might stay. I continued up the street, past the *presbytère*, which was the best house for many a mile, to the church, where I turned around and started back through the town.

A second look at the hotel suggested it had a dining room, and there were lights on in a couple of rooms upstairs. On impulse, I stopped and went in. The old front door opened onto a shabby hallway, with some plywood panelling on the walls and the sort of green paint on the ceiling that had often been on sale before it was discontinued in 1952. The closed door to the left had a handwritten sign: DINING ROOM OPENS 7; straight ahead, a narrow staircase ascended to a landing, while on the right another door opened onto a tavern, cluttered with dusty animal heads and sports pennants and illuminated mainly by the neon signs of beer brands and the glow from the Video Lotto terminals in the corner. Drawn by some unseen force, I found myself ordering a beer from the old bartender and sat down where I could observe him and a young guy in a ball cap transfixed by his Video Lotto game.

Outside it had begun to snow. The bartender came over. "Again?" he gestured at my glass. I said no, and then without really thinking about what I was doing asked him if he rented rooms. "Sure," he said, "gotta nice one on the back corner." "How much?" "Go see it first." He handed me a key and directed me up the stairs and around a couple of corners to Room 14 – the last door on the right.

I swung the door open, found the light switch and flipped on a bare bulb hanging by its electrical cord from the ceiling; the room was perhaps five metres by three; a narrow cot with patched blankets and darned sheets stood in one corner, a small dresser and a chair in the other. There were windows on two sides that looked out onto the village in the valley below, now obscured by

The Hotel Chapeau:
cheery tavern, good dining
room, &, uh, spartan &
affordable accommodation
for the wandering artist.

Only non-sociable people in
the tavern are the Video-Lotto
players. Transfixed, they sit
so still — very easy to draw.

the blowing snow and the rapidly fading light. There was no closet, but a door with a sliding bolt opened onto a small fly-spotted bathroom, the paint worn and discoloured. It was not so much unclean as old, really old. At the far end of the bathroom, which was as long as the tub, was another door, which I guessed went into my neighbour's room. A sign said LOCK DOOR WITH CHAIN: a chain attached to my door could be hooked over a clasp on the neighbour's door, holding them both shut and ensuring privacy! Never seen that one before, I thought.

Wondering whether to stay or to drive, maybe even walk, into the blizzard, I descended the stairs and went back into the tavern. "What'd you think?" the bartender asked.

"Well . . . how much is it?"

"Twelve dollars a night." Erasing from my mind an imaginary newspaper headline reading "Tourist Dies in Hotel Fire," I took it.

Sometime later, after a discreet check of the condition of the fire escapes, I descended to the dining room and found it had begun to fill with couples and families. On the wall was a photo of a middle-aged couple, one obviously the bartender many years younger. A sign said: FRED'S – ESTABLISHED 1941, and a clipping pinned to the wall from the local newspaper noted the hotel's fifty-fifth anniversary. The bartender-cum-owner came through the room, stopping at each table. "Wine?" he asked me. "Is the house wine okay?" He quickly produced a half-bottle of Mommesin, uncorked it with a flourish and filled my glass. A waitress arrived with a small basket containing slices, each at least an inch thick, of a homemade, hand-cut bread; beside it she put a small plate with a huge whack of yellow butter on it. Dinner was roast pork, followed by homemade apple pie, for twelve dollars. That was the evening's menu: it reminded me of the one-star "mum-and-pop" hotels in France, which offer travellers anything they want to eat as long as it's a *rôti* – a roast.

After dinner, I returned to the room and read for a while, only vaguely aware of the occasional thump and yell from the tavern below, and then slept soundly with the snow swirling around the windows outside. The snowplow clearing the street awoke me at dawn.

The Serenade.
(guy was singing Elton John's
"Your Song" in 'henglish')

Room 422,
Clarendon Hotel
7:30 a.m.
early
July.
Notre Dame Cathedral & the 'dreaming spires' of old Québec

Dairy farm near
Sainte-Famille on the
Île d'Orléans. Area of
farming & vineyards.
settled in the 17th century
& protected by
heritage legislation
since 1970.

Typical "bank barn"
on the "Île". Farmer
uses the bank & ramp
to get his hay & grain
into the storage floor.
The cows live in a byre
below. Easier to feed during
the long, snowy winter.
Mon pays c'est l'hiver, oui?

An English house in Québec, so different from the French rural styles: the house called "Les Rochers" near Rivière-du-Loup, the summer residence of Sir John A. Macdonald from 1872 till 1890. House established in 1850, but evidently built in 2 parts: the left side Second Empire style, the right side Victorian Gothic style like an Ontario farmhouse. Now run as a B & B by the organization "Canadian Heritage of Québec". Could have stayed & slept in Sir John A's bed, but didn't have a bottle of gin with me; as it was early in the day, decided to move on.

Near Cap-Saint-Ignace on the St. Lawrence River.

Prairies

At a party I ran into an old acquaintance who recently had driven across the country. He was regaling his audience with a story about crossing southern Saskatchewan, where he had spied on the map a little town called Cadillac and decided to make the detour to pay it a visit. On the main street there was a lone café. Inside, a woman in a T-shirt was wiping the counter; half a dozen men in work shirts and overalls sat with their coffee cups at one of a half-dozen tables. As he entered, conversation stopped and everyone turned to look at him. A fly buzzed in the shaft of sunlight coming through the window on the door.

He asked, "Could a person get a little lunch here?"

"Yup," said the woman. Dead silence.

"Well, can *I* get some lunch?"

"Sure. Sit over there," she said.

The regulars continued to stare at him, so he ventured an opinion: "For a town with a name like Cadillac, it's kinda small?"

"Keeps burnin' down," said one of the coffee-drinkers.

"Oh."

"Every time it looked like it was going to make something out of itself, there'd be a big fire."

"That's too bad."

"Yeah," he said, gesturing out to the main corner where a single gas station was the only occupant of the crossroads, "there used to be four gas stations there."

"So what happened?"

"Fire."

"What a shame."

"Yeah, but it keeps the competition down."

Sounded like the Prairies were full of characters like those found in the Maritimes or Newfoundland: black humour on the black soil, as it were.

(((

Jet flight from the West Coast, destination Calgary. After nearly an hour spent soaring over a landscape that from 10,000 metres up looked like a crumpled blue bedsheet, the jet crossed the Rockies, grey-brown in the late summer sunshine. Suddenly, the bedsheet smoothed out, as if pulled from its rumpled middle but not properly tucked, into rolling foothills. It flattened further with every minute travelled as we began the descent into Calgary airport.

International 4000 Raper on a lunch break.

Ranfurly, Alberta, one of the single-elevator towns between Vegreville & Vermilion east of Edmonton on the CN rail line. Town all but boarded up & abandoned, grain elevator no doubt soon to follow.

Gas station near Viking, Alberta, east of Camrose.

By the time the plane was on its final approach, the rolling ranchland had become a flat landscape divided into squares and rectangles. Grainfields recently harvested were delineated by the pattern made by combines; windrows of straw left from the harvesting lay in parallel lines awaiting bailing; a few fallow pastures, greener than the grainfields, were dotted with "dugouts" – little water holes – some with cattle socializing around their edges, while in a few fields iron ants bobbed tirelessly to extract the black, liquid gold. The only trees visible from the airplane were poplars, tall and columnar like the cypresses of Tuscan hillsides but planted tightly together to form windbreaks around the farmhouses and their outbuildings. The farmhouses were far apart, dotted along the straight roads: this was not a village land-scape like Québec's.

It was my third time on the Prairies. The first had been with the family, on an odyssey by car when I was a child, to pick up granny in Québec and bring her back to British Columbia. Although I remember most of the trip through my parents' reminiscences, crossing the Prairies in midsummer stuck in my young mind: standing up in the back of the '54 Chevy, my chin resting on the seat back, watching the odometer steadily move through the endless tenths of miles; for drinking cups, the thin paper cones in gas-station washrooms and the flat, harsh water in them, mother holding them to my lips. Most vivid is the memory of the smashed bugs, huge, strange and brightly coloured on the wire screen that my father had mounted on the front bumper to keep the precious radiator from plugging and overheating.

I made the second trip by train when I was fifteen, sitting up coach-class for three nights from Toronto to Vancouver. During the three decades since, I had read of Prairie droughts, abandoned rail lines, grain elevators coming down in every second hamlet and had smiled wryly at quips like, "Will the last person to leave Saskatchewan please turn off the lights?"

I decided to go north from Calgary to the Canadian National Railways line that runs through Edmonton and head east and south through the Parklands, then return westward across the Dry Belt following the Canadian Pacific line. On the road north, near Didsbury, an enormous thunderstorm formed in the tall sky above the prairie and the rain began to pelt down. So many Prairie stories are about the weather: storms you can see rollin' in from a hundred miles away, the wind full of 'hoppers, dust or bitter winter cold. In her travel book written in the 1940s, Lady Tweedsmuir saw only the vast space and reflected: "The prairie people rarely want to leave for other places in Canada. Everywhere else seems to them rather confined and cramping after the huge expanses to which they are accustomed."

The grid of properties, the long, straight roads, the fickle weather, the relentless work and the railways have all defined Prairie life since colonization began more than a century ago. To expedite settlement and farming, the Canadian government decided to adapt American homesteading legislation and, in 1872 – two years after it purchased the "North West" from the Hudson's Bay Company – passed the Dominion Lands Act, which divided the land into a pattern of squares oriented to points of the compass. Arable land was divided into townships, each made up of thirty-six sections, each section measuring one square mile (640 acres or 259 hectares). Farmers soon realized that the basic homestead of a quarter section was, because of the harsh Canadian climate and the lack of cheap labour, too small a unit to support a family.

Marshall, Saskatchewan – the first town east of
Lloydminster & the Alberta border. In Saskatchewan,
at least the rural parts, poverty hangs in the air
like the threat of an early frost.
   Orange "Pioneer" company elevator in background.
Striped building is the hotel/beer parlour, opposite
where the railway station once stood.
   Dirt streets, rusty pickups, cumulus clouds
      in the enormous prairie sky.

Early September —
worst time
of the year.
School's
back but
hockey
season hasn't
started
yet.

Windowshopping
on a Sunday
afternoon — town
shut up as tight
as a clam (though
not as tight as a
prairie oyster).

In the half-century since Lady Tweedsmuir's progress through the countryside, farming has become mechanized and farms have been consolidated. Fuel and borrowed capital for machinery have proven to be cheaper than labour. There was little work for wages and many settlers left with their families, prompting the collapse of many village economies. Surviving farmers have to truck their grain great distances to huge concrete elevator terminals. CN and CP practically tripped over themselves in their rush to abandon the branch-line railway system that had helped make them rich a couple of generations earlier. There was little passenger-train service anymore, and many villagers were forced to band together and protest just to keep their post offices. If the provincial government had built a hospital then a town had a fighting chance, although even that truism was challenged by the cost-cutting '90s. Sure, some of the abandoned branch lines were bought and reopened (by an Edmonton company called RaiLink and an American one called OmniTrax), but there was little to stem the flight from all those little farms and sweet Prairie towns.

Post office at Speers,
Saskatchewan, east
of North Battleford.

Car on a dirt road

Krydor, Sask., between Hafford & Blaine Lake, big
Ukrainian church on the outskirts of a typical CN town.

The Canadian railways had followed the lead of their American counterparts, which had spread gridiron planning across the U.S. plains. The gridiron town plan was "the natural tool of the land speculator," wrote historian John Reps. "No other plan was so easy to survey and no other system of planning yielded so many uniform lots, easy to describe in deeds or to sell from the auctioneer's block." As far as he was concerned, this had led to "an identical brand of uniformity and mediocrity in American cities from coast to coast." I found it hard to get upset about the grid: I liked the relentless horizontals of the prairie and the punctuation of the grain elevators, beacons across a sea of wheat like the fisherman's lighthouses, and the little towns focused on their raison d'être – the railway.

Rupert Brooke, passing through without stopping in 1913, expressed the opinion that "towns should be on hills or in valleys, however small. A town dumped down, apparently by chance, on a flat expanse, wears the same air of discomfort as a man trying to make his bed on a level, unyielding surface such as a lawn or pavement." He travelled east to west on the Canadian Pacific line and noted that "each village – I beg your pardon, 'town' – seems to be exactly like the next." To that I must add that they have a slightly different layout from the Parklands towns along the CN line. There is the same arrangement of grain elevators along the tracks on the opposite side from the downtown, with the railway station (now usually gone, sometimes replaced by a shopping mall) directly across the tracks from them. Behind the station, running parallel to the tracks, is a street usually called Railway Avenue; perpendicular to it and terminating at the station is, in CN towns, the commercial street, with angle parking and the hotel on the corner across from the station. In CP towns like Morden, Manitoba, the first street parallel with Railway Avenue is the main commercial street, although the old railway hotel with the bar is in the same spot as it is in a CN town.

The typical small town today has a handful of stores and services, such as those in Hafford, Saskatchewan, a CN town: a grain elevator or two, probably soon to be demolished, a hotel with a beverage room and a liquor store, two cafés, an insurance outlet that doubles as the Sears catalogue store, a beauty salon, a Lucky Dollar food store and a post office. Many people who come into town to get their mail angle-park along the main street and leave their pickups unattended with the engines running while they chat with acquaintances and do a bit of shopping. That's the winter habit, I guess: you get 'er warm and don't turn 'er off till she's back home with the block heater plugged in.

All these towns have lost their focus since the days, say, forty years ago, when the railway station was the centre of activity, a role now played in larger places by the mall (for some, the bar was the real centre of activity, but only for a certain class – men like Bram Shipley in Margaret Laurence's *The Stone Angel*). All along the line, people used to wander down to the station on summer evenings to check their watches and see who was leaving and who was arriving. That was an activity my brother and I loved: we would beg mother to let us go to the station to watch the

Late-summer thunderstorm.

"Dominion," the sister train to the more famous "Canadian," roll into little Salmon Arm on a summer's eve, bringing with it a whiff of adventure and distant places. Gosh, we thought, it was going to go all the way to *Toronto!* Young women in frocks, wearing white gloves and carrying small overnight cases, stepped off the train, helped down by the Negro porters, and anxiously scanned the crowd for . . . whom? A beau? Probably just parents. Families united and parted. Tears were shed. The platform was perfumed with the smell of hot wheel grease.

Travelling across the Prairies at the age of fifteen on the "Canadian," *sans* parents, I found it full of nuns and farmers and other ordinary folk, devoid of the spies and socialites who frequented the Orient Express in *From Russia with Love*, the James Bond film that had come out a couple of years earlier. It was the people's transport in unexotic Canada, except for those so poor they had to take the bus or hitchhike.

With the branch lines abandoned and the colourful old wooden grain elevators closed and awaiting demolition, the wind whistles along the dusty streets and the towns are bereft of life and vigour. A yellow school bus will come off the highway, drive along the main street past some boarded-up shop fronts and turn onto a side street; although there is no traffic, the bus will stop and, with full ritual, the flashers will flash, the red stop sign will swing out and sometimes just a lone child will alight. Just one to a town – now *that* is sad. Greyhound buses still stop in some places, but there are few trains, except for the long freights that roar through with their whistles blowin'.

You can tell when you've crossed the border into Saskatchewan because the streets are paved with dirt. Not far past the Alberta border, I saw a sign for Maidstone and could see it in the distance; just another Prairie town, I thought, and was about to pass it by when a distant song lyric swam up into my consciousness: "When we were kids in Maidstone, Sharon / I went to every wedding in that little town."

God, it's Joni Mitchell's hometown, I suddenly realized, and made a screeching left turn, narrowly missing a Greyhound bus full of Newfoundlanders on their way to Alberta, and in a minute was on the

Switch for the elevator siding & switcher's shack at Speers, Saskatchewan.

main street. One just like all the others. I parked near the bus depot and walked a ways, hands in pockets, sorta slow-like; round a corner there were some people standing around a couple of folding tables on the edge of the street outside a church. Smoke drifted up from a gas barbecue. In return for a two-dollar donation toward a trip for the schoolkids, a hot dog, jelly doughnut and coffee could be mine. I bit.

Silver Leaf Café
Canora,
Saskatchewan

I wolfed down the dog, exchanged a few pleasantries with the chef and took the doughnut and coffee back toward the car. A young guy, mid-twenties, with a sports bag at his feet was leaning against the wall outside the bus depot, gazing down the street toward the grain elevators. I stood across the street and watched him, imagining his sports bag was a guitar case. A Greyhound bus trailing dust like Rommel crossing the desert, SASKATOON on its signboard, pulled up. The driver emerged and spent a few minutes carrying parcels and boxes into the bus depot, which doubled as the Sears outlet. He returned to the bus, followed by a couple of elderly women from the waiting room; the "musician" joined them, the door closed and the bus pulled away.

Later that day, I was meditating on all this, sitting at the side of the road near Bresaylor, which was in danger of blowing away entirely, when a song by the band "Prairie Oyster" came on the car radio. The refrain was: "Every train that's leavin' a prairie town / Is runnin' on a one-way track." At Bresaylor, beside one house and an almost-collapsed church, there was a boarded-up wooden building with a sign on it:

COMMUNITY HALL WITH HARDWOOD FLOOR

FOR MOVING

OR DEMOLITION

– NO REASONABLE OFFER REFUSED –

Many miles farther along, after a couple of days in pretty Saskatoon and some time painting onion-domed Ukrainian churches and a Chinese café, I crossed the border into Manitoba and felt a bat-squeak of prosperity creep back into the air. It was going into evening at the end of a long day, and I hoped to make Neepawa for the night. Neepawa – Margaret Laurence's Manawaka in *The Stone Angel*. I wanted to see the inspiration for the town where Hagar Shipley had grown up and married. From the Saskatchewan border east the prairie was almost deserted, though not devoid of evidence of the human hand, for it was cultivated with grain in every direction. Mile after mile I went; occasionally a sign announced a town, but there was no gas, no coffee, no motel. Finally, with the tank near empty, I came upon a gas station and coffee shop and pulled in to refuel both me and the car. Darkness had replaced the dusk.

"How far to Neepawa?" I asked the waitress, who also cooked, pumped gas and ran the till.

"Oh, about three-quarters of an hour – it's real close."

By comparison with the rather barren prairie I'd passed through, Neepawa was a settled, lush, prosperous town – THE MOST BEAUTIFUL TOWN IN MANITOBA, according to a sign on its outskirts. The railway station, still painted in the classic CPR red "the colour of dried blood," as Laurence described it, stood on the edge of the town. The highway through town was intersected by the main street, quiet as a grave on a Sunday morning. A few women sold vegetables from the tail-gates of pickup trucks in a parking lot behind a community centre. A sign directed me a block off the main street to Laurence's birthplace, a substantial brick house on a tree-lined street just on the edge of the commercial district – kitty-corner was a large supermarket parking lot. Her house, and the nearby residential streets, looked very settled and calm, more suited to an Ontario town than a Prairie one. It was the sort of place where a girl couldn't wear makeup downtown for fear a

Margaret Laurence's birthplace, Neepawa, Manitoba.

Union Station,
Winnipeg — the hub
of the West.
Built 1908-11 by
the Grand Trunk
Pacific & the
Canadian Northern;
same architects as
Grand Central Station
in New York.

← The Exchange
District, often dubbed
the "Chicago of the
North," has a tremendous
collection of old
warehouses from before the
turn of the 20th century.
Recently named a
National Historic District.

friend of her mother might see her. In *The Stone Angel*, Hagar Shipley recalls "how small the town was, and how short a time it took to leave it, as we measure time."

From there, it is only a short drive to Winnipeg, as we now measure time. After a couple of days of urbanity, I went south, into the Red River Valley so recently flooded but, in the scalding heat of late August, showing little sign of water of any kind at all. Driving south into the sun at midday, on what must be one of the flattest places on the planet, I watched as the road ahead dissolved into mirages of rippling water; the telephone poles marched arrow-straight along the road ahead to the edge of the world and seemed to hang above the mirage. Out of my memory rose the same scene from my childhood trip across the Prairies long ago.

My quest was a hamlet called New Bergthal, west of the Red River near the American border. Here, the Dominion government – recognizing the difficulties of settling some of the poorer Prairie land – had actively solicited Mennonite farmers from Eastern Europe, who had a proven record for rendering poor land profitable. The government even bent its own rules to allow them, and other cultural groups, to settle into villages where they could retain some of their traditional ways. New Bergthal, which was recently declared a National Historic Site, has classic house-barn combinations on both sides of a single street, with long strip-fields extending behind them onto the prairie.

Heading west, back across the dry prairies of south Saskatchewan, I entered W. O. Mitchell country, Wallace Stegner country. "The superlative sun that shone down on us was Greek; the grass sea around us was our Aegean," Mitchell wrote of his boyhood home. It is a land of ranchers, cowboys, oil rigs and huge farms, stretching over miles, that are profitable for grain-growing in the good years. Cow-calf operations and feedlots occupy vast tracts of southern Alberta. After that come the foothills and, near Fort Macleod, Head-Smashed-In Buffalo Jump, where for millennia aboriginals stampeded bison over a cliff to their deaths. It is a profoundly spiritual place; one can walk along the cliff face and, looking to the high ground, imagine the awful climax to the hunt. In the other direction, past the cliff, the prairie stretches away to infinity. To me, Head-Smashed-In had a kinship with all the little abandoned Prairie towns, for time has passed it by, too.

Parkbeg in south Saskatchewan – a Dry Belt town along the CP Railway line.

↑ Puff of dust in the
distance — a combine
working

Bresaylor, Sask. — once a hamlet
with a church & a community hall,
now almost gone. Farm consolidations
due to technological change & high
labour costs = rural depopulation
= death of villages.

Bank of Commerce building
at Innisfree, Alberta—the
first town east of Ranfurly.
It is a pre-fab, built
by the B.C. Mills Timber
& Trading Company of
New Westminster, B.C.
about 1908 & shipped
here on a railcar.
The Bank of Commerce
was one of BC MT&T's
biggest customers all
over the west.

Another Bank of Commerce
at Kitscoty, Alberta—
this one a custom
design. Now used
by "Ye Olde Bank
Antiques". When I was painting it, an old guy came up
& asked: "What're you interested in that old wreck for?"
"Don't you like it?"
"It's old," he said. "Should'a
got rid of it years ago....."

Rainy morning—farmers killing time
at Kin's Café, Vermilion, Alberta.

Court House at Humboldt, Saskatchewan.
Crest says: "Honi Soit Qui Mal Y Pense"
— "Evil Be to
Him Who
Evil
Thinks?"

COURT HOUSE

SASKATCHEWAN
POOL
WROXTON
A

Old Humboldt Post Office —
built 1911, a fine building that
"represented the extension of federal
services across the West", says the
plaque near the door by Historic
Sites + Monuments Board.

Wroxton, Saskatchewan — grain elevator & the steeple of
the Ukrainian Church visible for miles. Most stores boarded up.

Red River Valley, heading south, near Dominion City —
telephone poles hanging above the mirages.

Combine working, tractor pulling a disc harrow.
Farmers finishing the harvest ; getting the land
ready for winter.
Incredibly prosperous farms, or at least incredibly
prosperous farm-equipment dealers....

Approaching New Berghal, a former Mennonite hamlet, from the west. Hamlet is bisected by the country road. The trees in the distance, perpendicular to the road, define the hamlet's street; lining the street on both sides are house-barn combinations that originally backed onto long strip fields. A village type of settlement very different from the standard isolated homesteader on a quarter-section.

West of Red River Valley, near Altona, Manitoba.

Southern
Prairies

Brick farmhouse
near Melita, Manitoba

Former Northern Bank
building, now post office,
in Manor, Sask.

Hillside with coulees —
Qu'Appelle Valley,
September.

Marieval, at the
east end of Crooked
Lake in the
Qu'Appelle Valley,
Saskatchewan

Former residential
school on the
Cowessess Reserve.
Marieval Mission School
is the last surviving Native residential school in
Saskatchewan.

Southern Alberta — almost a desert (the Pallicer Triangle).
Some scattered ranches, many using round haybales
as windbreaks around their corrals.

West of Calgary, near Cochrane, the prairie that has been so flat for 3 provinces suddenly heaves itself up into rolling foothills with, as a backdrop, the dramatic grey & brown castle walls of the Rocky Mountains. I first saw them on a westbound CPR train when I was 15 and, with my school lessons still fresh in my mind, thought of the explorers La Verendrye & Palliser & how the sight must have astounded them. The world was a much larger place then — 3 days on the train for me, 3 months on foot for them to get across the country.

The Far West

TOPOGRAPHICALLY SPEAKING, Canada's Far West is much more diverse than the "sea of mountains" an Ontario politician declared it to be in the 1870s to justify his claim that a transcontinental railway would be a waste of young Canada's treasure. It is more than just mountains, or desert, or rainforest, or coastline or flatland: all are there. My Far West comprises everything west of the Prairies; if I were in charge I'd give the Rocky Mountains, and especially the resorts of Banff and Jasper, to British Columbia. After all, Albertans have little experience with verticality beyond Calgary's skyline. In exchange, I would allow Alberta to annex the flat Peace River farming country adjoining their northwest border, where they would probably be welcomed with the enthusiasm the Dutch gave to their Canadian liberators at the end of the Second World War (what is it about modern Canada that makes all borders seem flexible?).

My earliest painting trips were into the narrow valleys of the British Columbia interior, where foolish settlers have attempted for a century and a half to establish farms and orchards. When Art Garfunkel sang of "shattered dreams and worthless years," he could have been describing this landscape. Of all the stories of crushed hopes, the most poignant is that of Walhachin, near Cache Creek in the arid southern interior, built by English remittance men in the decade before the

Ranch above the Thompson River in the desert
near Spences Bridge, British Columbia.
Sagebrush, bunch grass & a few scattered
pine trees. 15-20 cm. of rain some years.

August morning, a chill in the air & long blue
shadows, but promising to be a blistering day.

First World War and briefly renowned for its orchards and refined lifestyle. When the war began, the men of Walhachin responded to the call and returned to their British regiments; many died in action and the town died soon after. Other ghost towns, especially in the silver-mining Kootenay area in the southeast part of the province, were established in the wildest mountain fastnesses; they too enjoyed a fleeting prosperity before their lodes ran out.

☾ ☾ ☾

I was in Victoria on the sort of sweet January day that is dry and bright with the temperature about ten degrees (Celsius). Blossoms dotted the oriental cherry trees; crocuses, scilla and snowdrops brightened gardens; and in some yards winter-flowering rhododendrons made bold pink splashes against the blue shadows. The populace had emerged to take the sea air, some towed by enthusiastic hounds on leashes. For a time, I sat on the plinth of the war memorial in front of the Parliament Buildings and watched the passing parade. There were red double-decker buses and twee tourist shops, just like in an Olde English seaside town; fine public buildings as befits a capital; the Empress Hotel; and the traffic and street life of a modern, bustling city. I thought how much it resembled Québec City with its overlay of the French *ancien régime*. Both were annexed – okay, one was conquered – and I recalled the tale of Joseph Despard Pemberton, the former colonial surveyor of the Colony of Vancouver Island, who resisted Confederation with Canada in the late 1860s. Americans were no more foreign than Canadians, he wrote, and noted in a letter to a local newspaper that:

> True loyalty's to Motherland
> & Not to Canada.
> The love we bear is second-hand
> To any step-mama.

Something like it could have been written in Québec City at any time since 1759 or in St. John's 190 years later.

As I gazed at the Empress Hotel – which is so like the Château Frontenac – more prosaic thoughts entered my mind, and I found myself taking the path through the rose garden into the hotel's side entrance. All the profundity had made me thirsty. It was hard to imagine that this edifice had been so out of fashion in the early 1960s that Canadian Pacific, its builder and owner since 1908, seriously considered demolishing it and replacing it with a motor hotel; in recent years, they added a new lobby and spent millions on restoration and redecoration. I passed through the old lobby where high tea, so beloved by American tourists, was being served and continued along a back corridor to the Bengal Lounge, which had been, in the distant past – during the 1952-72 regime of Premier W. A. C. Bennett and his Social Credit government – one of the few refined watering holes in what was almost a teetotal town. By any standard, the Bengal Lounge was a curiosity – redolent of palm courts and Victorian-era first-class travel, with an enormous tiger skin on the wall above the fireplace. Twenty-five years ago, wastrels like me used to attempt to "liberate" the lounge by getting served there in blue jeans.

Victoria, B.C., on a bright January day — a good day to get out the tweeds & the walking shoes.

House of former premier John Robson (died 1895), typical of 1880s west coast of North America from San Francisco north. Narrow eaves + lots of tall bay windows to catch the light — these are houses designed for an era before electric light became common.

But now I found the Empress had liberated itself and that the high tea ceremony had shed its dress code. Most people wore jeans or chinos and the sort of casual windbreakers that pass for winter coats in Victoria. Only the tiger skin remained unchanged, and I drank a glass of Chardonnay to its health.

With a couple of days to spare, I chose to travel north from Victoria, following the only road along the east coast of Vancouver Island to the point where it crosses over to the west coast. I wanted to see what had become of Ucluelet, a fishing village where I had spent part of a summer when I was twenty-one. Vancouver Island is balkanized both climatically and culturally: Victoria, in the rainshadow of Washington State's Olympic Mountains, is dry, bright, elegant and urbane, while the west coast and the north of the island are rainforest dotted with tough logging towns, stupendous trees and the surf and whales at Long Beach – midway between Ucluelet and Tofino.

In my youth, Ucluelet was almost an outport in the Newfoundland sense – accessible more easily by sea, as the winding gravel road over the mountains was tricky to negotiate. Since then, Long Beach has become part of the Pacific Rim National Park and the road has been paved – helping the tourist industry, with whale watching now being one of the big attractions – but the salmon fishery has been devastated almost to the extent of the Atlantic cod fishery, and the ancient forest has become a battleground peopled by environmentalists versus loggers. Clayoquot and Carmanagh have become synonymous with the fight to preserve, on the one hand, old-growth forest, and, on the other, the loggers' jobs and the viability of their communities.

With a freshly minted university degree, but with hair too long and attitude too insouciant to impress a personnel department, I worked on a two-man salmon troller – a fish boat, similar to what the Maritimers would call a longliner – operating out of Ucluelet. That spring of 1972 we fished the bank off the coast for several days at a stretch, interspersing this activity with long walks on deserted Long Beach with the surf crashing in and the wind sweeping the scrubby shore pines back and away from the ocean

B.C.'s Parliament Buildings on Victoria's Inner Harbour.
Celebrated their 100th birthday in the spring of '98.

just as it did our stiff, unwashed hair. Rolling on the ocean swell, we awoke at dawn to a world all silvery grey and silent and spent our time counting the birds in the enormous sky and watching the whales and seals while awaiting the morning's salmon run. We would run out a line and catch a couple of fish, gut them and examine their entrails like soothsayers to see what they were eating, then choose our lures accordingly. It was a game of chance *and* skill, so different from the technique of the high-tech trawlers (draggers on the east coast) that scoop up everything and toss back the "bycatch" – the modern euphemism for the non-commercial species killed in the nets.

I hated it. It was hard, solitary work, dawn to dark: catch, kill, clean, pack in the ice, cook lunch, repeat all afternoon, cook the dinner, catch, kill, clean and pack again during the salmon's evening chow time, then on stormy nights wedge myself into the bunk, a foot braced on the opposite gunwale in the narrow cabin to keep myself from being pitched out onto the floor. My romantic notion of the *experience* of fishing couldn't sustain me. After a month, with every day so much like every other, I argued with the skipper and, on a return to Ucluelet, announced I was done and heading back to the mainland.

At that time, the place to look for a ride was the beer parlour. Typically, the sort of people who'd give you a ride loaded up with a few beers before starting the trip to Nanaimo, where the ferry crosses the Strait of Georgia for the mainland. There were several groups sitting at the round, terry cloth-covered tables characteristic of B.C. taverns, smoking and drinking and yarning. One guy, burly and bearded, sat alone. I approached him.

"You know anybody who's going over to Nanaimo?" I asked.

"Yeah," he said. "I'm goin'. You want a ride?"

"Sure – love one."

"Sit down and have a beer. I'll be ready to go soon." He was heading over to the bright lights to kill a bit of time while his boat's engine problems got sorted out. On his way out to the car he stopped at the bar and bought a six-pack for the road.

Now, in my conservative middle-age, I drove over the mountain pass that separates Alberni Inlet from the coast at Ucluelet, with vague recollections of that old station wagon fishtailing up the steep washboard hills, and marvelled at the fact I had survived. This trip it was winter, with rain at the Alberni end turning to snow near the pass, then changing back to rain as the road writhed down the steep mountainside to the coast. Ucluelet, a poor town at the best of times, seemed quiet and almost deserted; a few people who hadn't sold their fishing licences back to the government scraped their boats in the drizzly mist, preparing them for the next fishing season. Depressed, I drove the fifty-odd kilometres up the road to Tofino, headquarters of local ecotourism. There, the fishing fleet bobbed at anchor in the peaceful harbour, kayakers paddled across the horizon, bald eagles drifted over and the cafés sold cappuccino. Tofino had every likelihood of surviving the collapse of the fishery. As for Ucluelet . . .

View from in front of the Parliament Buildings of Victoria's Inner Harbour.
The Empress Hotel, opened in 1908, designed by F.M. Rattenbury, the same architect as for the Parliament Buildings 10 years earlier.

Union Club, also by Rattenbury

the business end
of a troller —
rather like the one
I worked on as a youth.

Harbour of Tofino, B.C., in February.
    Mild (about 12°C.), weather alternately raining
& about-to-rain, a myriad of fishboats bobbing,
seals in the harbour, eagles soaring overhead,
ecotourists in kayaks paddling about,
cappuccinos hissing in nearby cafés.
    The resource industries (fishing + logging)
may be dying in this part of the world, but
Tofino will reinvent itself & survive.

Banff railway station.

The view from the railway station looking along Lynx Street toward Banff, with the Banff Springs Hotel framed by the mountains in the distance like a magical castle. (I didn't paint the ugly RCMP Building that now obscures this view).

❨ ❨ ❨

Later in that summer many years ago, after surviving the beery drive from Ucluelet, I decided to go to the opposite end of my Far West to visit a girlfriend who had taken a summer job waitressing at the Banff Springs Hotel. Rather than compete with the throngs hitchhiking on the Trans-Canada Highway, I bought a one-way ticket on the ultimate slow boat – the transcontinental passenger train – which arrived in Banff five hours late on a bright mountain morning. With a handful of other passengers, I stumbled off the train and, having reclaimed my packsack, squinted toward the town. In the distance, perhaps a couple of kilometres away on a ridge framed by magnificent mountains, stood a fairy-tale castle – the hotel. It seemed utterly magical and, like the dreams of my childhood, impossibly remote from my experience. This was less a romantic thought than a practical one, for it was chic and expensive, while I was scruffy and broke.

In 1972, Banff was an easy place to get work if you weren't too particular. Influenced considerably by the proximity of the aforementioned girlfriend, I managed, by the end of that first morning, to obtain two jobs, both as dishwashers, in cafés along Banff Avenue. Both paid Alberta minimum wage – $1.55 an hour – so I took the one that offered a place to sleep in a backyard cabin behind the owner's house a few blocks away.

My former abode – employee quarters for the Mr. Steer Restaurant, with Cascade Mountain in the background. The ultimate shack-with-a-million-dollar-view.

When I returned to Banff in 1997, I went to the old CPR station and found that it was now used only by a privately operated tourist train – the "Rocky Mountaineer." The view from the spot on the platform where I had first espied the hotel was blocked by a new RCMP building. And Banff itself had become so urbane: the little laundromats and flophouses that had served Canada's vagabond hippies had been replaced by fine, new buildings designed along a relatively dignified alpine theme, most three or four stories high above a row of shops. Young tourists, many being newlywed couples from Japan, sauntered around, festooned with cameras and carrying shopping bags emblazoned with the logos of exotic clothing companies. I felt distinctly lost.

Worse was to come. I found that my old place of employment – a cafeteria-style steak house called Mr. Steer – had been demolished and replaced by a smart condo/retail complex. The other place to offer me a job – the Banff Café, a venerable business with its date of construction (1926) on the building's parapet – was gone, too. There were no HELP WANTED signs in the windows; probably all the staff were professional and permanent nowadays, for Banff had become a year-round resort. Walking along the lanes, I retraced my former route from Mr. Steer back to the old cabin, and to my immense surprise found it still standing; probably now used to store lawnmowers or inlaws, it was the last survivor of the group of little shacks that had housed the café's staff. Even the owner's house was gone, replaced by a big stucco duplex.

With the thought that, as a prosperous artist, I could now afford one night in the Banff Springs Hotel, I made the trek across the bridge over the Bow River and followed the curving drive along the river to the hotel. A young man of about twenty-one, wearing a smart uniform, directed my dusty rent-a-car to a parking spot near the entrance. Feeling like an imposter, I entered the lobby and mustered my confidence to stride across to the reception desk.

"Do you have any rooms available tonight?" I asked the desk clerk.

She stared into her computer screen, frowning and tapping occasionally on the scroll key with a long and well-polished fingernail. Looking up finally, she said, "Sorry, we're fully booked . . . but we'll have something tomorrow night!"

I mumbled something like, "Uhh, no, I won't be in town then," and walked away. Although I could have stayed another day, perhaps it was best to keep the Banff Springs just as a dream.

☾ ☾ ☾

Old Hazelton (not to be confused with New Hazelton, a stop on the Grand Trunk Pacific Railway a couple of hundred kilometres east of the terminus at Prince Rupert) is a river port at the head of navigation on the Skeena River. From about 1870 until it was bypassed by the railway in 1915, the town thrived as the supply point for the mines of the Omineca District. The last riverboat, the *Hazelton*, is permanently dry-docked just above the highwater mark and is now a fish and chip shop. I knew the town only from family legend: two cousins, both nurses, worked in a small hospital there in the early 1960s, tending to the sick of the local Native villages. Nearby are two Native villages – Gitanmaax and Hagwilget – in the shadow of Mount Rocher Déboulé. It is the heartland of

Banff
Springs
Hotel.

Japanese tourists
enjoying the
Canadian wilderness
experience.

Gitanyow (formerly
spelled as Kitwancool) –
the poles of 2 cultures across the street from each other

St. Paul's Anglican Church at Kitwanga, B.C.
in January. "Built in 1893 by the Gitksan people,"
according to a plaque on the door.

the Gitksan and Wet'suwet'en peoples, whose aboriginal land claim has, in recent years, never been far from the centre of B.C. political debate.

The modern highway follows the railway, now the Canadian National, so all the action – the motel, drive-in and lumberyard strip – is in New Hazelton, while the old town a few kilometres away is a collection of heritage buildings lining narrow streets and fronting the river. Ignoring the motels on the highway, I sought a hotel in the old town and found the Inlander, built in 1956 and probably the only Moderne building for about 500 miles. Although it appeared very shabby, the owner seemed a worthy sort and explained that she and her husband were gradually fixing it up, financing the project with the profits from the food store they owned next door. It was like the Hotel Chapeau in the Outaouais, except quieter: there were no hunters or ice fishermen boozing it up while waiting for a break in the weather. In fact, that Thursday evening there was almost nobody in town, and the price was twenty-five dollars: that's why I checked in.

Coming into town, I had spotted the B.C. Café in a little boomtown-front building about a block away, a typical mum-and-pop Chinese-and-Canadian-specialties operation, like something out of a Joni Mitchell song. I had my travel-eating down to a science: if I was in a part of the country that didn't have chicken Caesar salads, I always went for Chinese food. Accordingly, about seven, I left my room, had a beer downstairs while watching a couple of Native guys play pool, then set off up the street. In the couple of hours since the sun went down, the air had become much colder and it had begun to snow a little. The snow already on the streets was stiffening against the cold.

Hagwilget Indian village near Hazelton, B.C.
I came over the hill, driving on automatic pilot, saw
the brightly coloured, government issue houses & the
big Catholic church, & for a second thought I was back
in Newfoundland, looking at an outport.

Old Hazelton on the Skeena
River in northwestern
British Columbia.

The contrast between the
warm yellow light of
the indoors & the cold blue
light outdoors.

Logcabin
in
Old Hazelton

Mount Rocher Déboulé above the town

The café's interior had been modernized maybe thirty or forty years ago and furnished with the sort of chrome-legged chairs and Formica-topped tables with chrome edge-strips that are now all the rage among urban Gen-Xers. The space once occupied by the old counter and stools had been filled with a low screen and three tables for two. The owner, or the owner's aunt, or mum or whatever – a Chinese woman of indeterminate age – shuffled her slippers over to me with a menu.

"You want coffee?" she asked.

"No, tea – Chinese tea, please." She handed me the menu.

"You see specials?" she gestured across the room at a blackboard. Special "A" was a mushroom burger, fries and soup; "B" was chow mein, breaded almond chicken and sweet-and-sour spareribs.

"I'll have 'B,'" I replied.

While I waited, I watched the other diners: a large Native woman and her small son, and a table of three young Natives – two girls and a guy, dressed in black with ball caps turned backwards. My tea arrived. I opened Eric Newby's *A Traveller's Life*, my travel reading, and found myself with Mr. Newby en route by bicycle from England to Italy. He had made it into France and was camping in a field near

Rouen. After reflecting on how beautiful and infinitely varied the countryside was, he wrote: "Out there, too, are the French, a nation made up of Celts, Latins and people of Germanic origin: yet all of them regarding themselves, not as the Scots, Irish and Welsh tend to, and increasingly so, as separate, distinct nationalities within the British Isles, but as one people, wholly and utterly French." The old Chinese lady brought my plate of food. If Newby had written the same thing about Canada, I wondered, would she agree with him?

Ten minutes later she returned.

"Everything okay? You want something else?"

Her son – at least I presumed he was her son – had emerged from the kitchen, looking tired. He took off his apron, sat down at a table with a coffee and lit a cigarette. His mother took the soy sauce off my table and added it to a tray of bottles of ketchup.

"Just the bill, thanks."

☾ ☾ ☾

Prince Rupert is the western terminus of a transcontinental railway – the Grand Trunk, the second of the major railways (the Canadian Northern being the other) chartered by the government of Sir Wilfrid Laurier in the early years of the 20th century. Because it was 800 kilometres closer to the Orient than the Port of Vancouver, terminus of the Canadian Pacific Railway and the under-construction Canadian Northern, Prince Rupert seemed an ideal location to build a new metropolis. But it was not to be: Charles Hays, the visionary president of the Grand Trunk, drowned on the *Titanic* in 1912; concur-

rently, the world economy foundered as the European nations increasingly poured their money into armaments. Not long after Prince Rupert welcomed the first transcontinental train in April 1914 the railway declared bankruptcy; soon, the Canadian Northern followed suit. By 1917, the guarantor of the railways' bonds – the federal government – had become the effective owner. Both lines were amalgamated into the publicly owned Canadian National Railways system.

Fortune never smiled on Prince Rupert again, and it has remained a backwater, although the lumber and fishing industries have usually prospered and the CNR continues to use the harbour as a freight terminus. In the summer of 1997, before my trip there, Prince Rupert had been very much in the news due to the blockade of an Alaska State ferry by local fish boats, their skippers frustrated by the decline in the fishery and enraged by Alaskan fishermen allegedly intercepting too many fish. Not long after, the provincial government bailed out another major local employer – a pulp mill.

I took a room in a hotel with a view down the steep bluff to the waterfront that had been the subject of so many dreams a lifetime ago. Several sets of tracks ran across the abandoned ground. Visible among the weeds and brown grass were foundations of what must once have been freight sheds. A very small dock with a very big sign announced that cruise-ship lighters disembarked there. There was a maintenance shed with two sets of tracks disappearing through its front doors and a small railway station which, according to a brochure I read, had been moved to the Prince Rupert waterfront from a rural community to save it from demolition. And there was a square brick building with an awning, fronting onto the tracks. Was this the transcontinental railway terminus?

The North Pacific Cannery
at Port Edward, near the
mouth of the Skeena River
& Prince Rupert, B.C. Built
1889, closed 1969, the last survivor
of the dozen or so canneries operating in the
area at the turn of the 20th century. There
are a few other canneries on the coast — most
notably the huge Gulf of Georgia cannery at Steveston
near Vancouver — but this one is the last survivor with
its village intact.

Later that day, I went down to the waterfront to inspect. The station was filthy and dilapidated, its passenger canopy along the track held up by two-by-four struts. At one end, a VIA Rail sign said: WAITING ROOM. But the door was locked. A typed sign apologized for the inconvenience and promised that the station would reopen in time for the next train in a couple of days. A schedule noted arrivals and departures – three a week each. It was the "Skeena" service, according to a poster I could see through the grimy window: CANADA'S BEST-KEPT SCENIC SECRET! I couldn't have put it better.

The following morning when I was checking out of the hotel, I chatted to the owner while we waited for my credit-card payment to be processed somewhere in the virtual world. "I've been here for years," she said, "and I don't think we ever had a worse year than '97" – the machine finally began to spit out the receipt – "but I've been here long enough to know that, no matter how bad it gets, it always comes back." She has to be right; Charles Hays wasn't stupid, it was just that his timing was off.

The VIA Rail station on the waterfront at Prince Rupert,
B.C., the surviving vestige of what was to be a hotel /
rail terminus / docks complex for the Grand Trunk
Pacific Railway connecting the Orient with Canada's
commercial centres in Toronto & Montreal. Designed
by F.M. Rattenbury, who bought the GTP Ry's dream
& jumped in with both feet; he speculated in
Prince Rupert land & lost his shirt; as well, he
had alienated a former client — the Canadian Pacific —
for whom he had designed Victoria's Empress Hotel.
Later, he was murdered in England by his wife's
lover, who was also his chauffeur. Shattered
dreams....

Barn near Fruitvale, B.C.

Trip to the B.C.
Interior, February.

House in Nelson,
from the back
window of "Inn
the Garden."
Nelson's firehall,
made famous
by the movie
"Roxanne,"
is a few
blocks away
uphill.

The Silverledge Hotel, now
a museum, in Ainsworth
Hot Springs, an abandoned mining town
from the 1890s on
Kootenay Lake, B.C.

The steeple of
St. Andrews United
Church in Kaslo, built
in 1893; one of the oldest buildings
in the Kootenays.

House at
Sandon

Followed the snowplow into Sandon on a February day during the snowiest winter anyone could remember.

Fabulous silver strike at Sandon in the early 1890s — by 1898, town had a population of 5,000, but it is all gone — the silver to market & the town to fire & flood. Just a handful of diehards live there now.

Miners' house at Silverton on Slocan Lake, B.C., another of the Kootenay towns that boomed a century ago.

Summer trip
through
southern B.C.

Doukhobor
'double house'
near Grand
Forks, a house
style for communal
living devised in
Saskatchewan by
Peter Verigin.

Verigin moved about 6,000
Doukhobors to B.C. in 1908
after the feds decided to
enforce the land settlement
act & make each individual
settle on his 1/4 section.
(Thus, no more hamlets like
New Bergthal, Manitoba.)

Twin houses for communal
living.
Small house at back
of "U" for laundry, etc.

The North

I THINK I'M PART OF THE LAST GENERATION OF CANADIANS to have grown up with the concept of the frontier as a physical place. My daughter wouldn't know it: for her generation, the frontier is a virtual place, an intellectual construct, a brave new world not of real time and space. Like the word "clockwise" in this age of digital timekeeping, the word "frontier," as I knew it, has disappeared from common parlance (the expression "going on like a broken record," of which I am sometimes guilty, is about to meet the same fate). Also gone is the image of the end of the road, beyond which the unforgiving, infinite forest stretched, ruled perhaps by Kurt Vonnegut's "God the Supremely Indifferent." In Canada's time, the frontier has shifted from west to north and, now, after a brief flirtation with outer space, to cyberspace.

The frontier as I knew it also meant a place where you could start over again – where there was work as long as you could take the isolation and the rigour. In my day, United Keno Hill Mines at Faro in the Yukon, which always needed employees and paid high wages, was such a place. Friends who were trying to put together a grubstake – to travel the world, buy a house or start a business – trekked north and put

White Pass & Yukon Route Railway Station at the foot of Main Street in Whitehorse, from 1905 to 1982 the hub of transportation for the Yukon — connected to Skagway, Alaska, on the "panhandle" on the Pacific Coast. Railway doesn't run into the Yukon anymore — superseded by the roads.

in their year or so; a few came back with enough money to make a fresh start. I worked a couple of summers in similar camps populated by the frontiersmen of the 1960s – eccentric, aloof, hard men who had gone north to work on the DEW (Distant Early Warning) Line during the Cold War and had grown accustomed to camp life, with its good food and lack of responsibility. Today, that frontier isn't available to youth, who moon about in the cities working at McJobs and have little opportunity for the kind of personal reinvention a trip to the North used to guarantee.

Did the "end of the road" still exist in any tangible way? I went to the Yukon to find out. There, the holy grail is now usually defined as "opportunity," where once it had been a simple four-letter word: gold. Dawson City, the centre of the Gold Rush of '98, has been beautifully restored, but the hub of the modern Yukon is Whitehorse.

In Whitehorse, on a June evening at about ten o'clock, I wandered out into the sunshine and began to walk. There was a dusky amber quality to the light, for the sun had swung around into the northern sky and was dipping toward the horizon to make its 2 a.m. sunset. At one point I passed a tough tavern called The Brass Rail, full of bikers who were spilling out onto the street where they could fondle their Harleys when not swilling and spilling beer and fondling their babes; their party was well under way in the warm late evening. Crossing a couple of roadways and some waste ground, I soon found myself along the bank of the Yukon River. "Grandma's Burger Bus" stood beside a shack where you could make a reservation for rafting tours. After about an hour of wandering, I reached a little community of shacks and old vehicles. According to my guidebook, the area was variously known as Sleepy Hollow, Moccasin Flats or the Shipyards: it was the local squatters' town.

In the pale sunlight, I explored the sleeping little hamlet. Cabins were interspersed with a few substantial buildings, everything coexisting in cheerful disarray. All had yards full of *stuff* – scrap metal, barrels, cars, tools-of-the-trade – the signature of the North. A modern grader stood outside one small shack. The sun cast long, grey shadows up and over the various piles. Some penned huskies yipped and yowled as I came into sight.

An old school bus, its purple and pink paint job faded by the sun, caught my eye; the grass grew up around its flattened tires; a metal chimney poked out into the sky from a hole cut in its roof. All it lacked was a hand-painted sign on its side reading YUKON OR BUST. Someone had set off from somewhere in search of a new beginning and had kept going until the wheels fell off. Turned out it had happened at Whitehorse. As long as there is a squatters' community somewhere, the Canadian frontier must still exist.

Formerly mobile, now a home: the bus in the squatters' community – Whitehorse, Yukon. 11 pm near the summer solstice.

Carcross, Yukon — a little community on the White Pass
rail line near the B.C. border.

Good café in the hotel, & some nearby
cabins for rent .... Hmm.... With 10 cords of wood
& an Internet connection, I could make it through
the winter.

Drifters &
pensioners

Log skyscraper in
downtown Whitehorse,
built in 1947 to
help relieve a
rental housing
shortage.
(closest thing to a pagoda "north of 60")

The Quest for a National Trust

A wise nation preserves its records, gathers up its monuments, decorates the tombs of its illustrious dead, repairs its greatest structures and fosters national pride and love of country by perpetual references to the sacrifices and glories of the past.

– Joseph Howe (1804-1873), *Premier of Nova Scotia and Father of Confederation*

Canadian
Scenic Drive
(d'après R. Cobb)

ANYONE WHO TRAVELS THROUGH CANADA, as I have done during the past few years, and observes the lay of the land ends up asking himself: "Is anyone in charge out there?" Many places, especially the outskirts of towns and cities, are a wasteland of tacky new development accessible only by automobile, while other parts of the country, such as the Prairies, are dotted with abandoned villages. Some provinces seem to rejoice in their past, putting plaques on landmark buildings and erecting signposts on pioneer roadways, while others obscure the view of the countryside with billboards declaiming they're OPEN FOR BUSINESS! "Bring lots of money," they say, "and we won't impose any restrictions on you." While one town might have a restored main street with thriving, family-owned shops, the one in the next county might have a mall tenanted only by thriving chain stores with a parking lot the size of P.E.I. and, not far away, an old downtown where boarded-up storefronts have become the rule rather than the exception.

By comparison, wilderness and wildlife habitat have been treated consistently well and, especially during the past thirty or so years, have garnered increasing public support as the environmental movement has gained credibility. Canada was one of the first countries in the world to preserve and celebrate its *natural* treasures, first through its national park system and later through systems of provincial parks. But the other side of the conservation coin – the cultural landscape – has fallen victim to the sort of laissez-faire, do-as-you-please, lowest-common-denominator-sets-the-standards attitude of our time. Missing nowadays is the vision Joseph Howe expressed in that long-ago, nation-building phase when Canada was knitting itself together with shared symbols. Canada is not one of Joseph Howe's wise nations.

This country's biggest step toward a Joseph Howe-type of vision occurred in 1919 with the formation of the Historic Sites and Monuments Board of Canada but, as explained earlier, that body has lacked statutory authority to preserve Canada's "greatest structures" and has only been able to "foster national pride and love of country" through a modest program of plaquing historic sites. (Hands up everyone who knows what an HSMBC plaque looks like and where the nearest one is.) Although the government department currently known as Parks Canada has a higher profile than does the HSMBC and has restored and manages and interprets heritage sites across the country, it is hobbled by its duty to run its properties with well-paid staff and keep them open to the public. In short, Parks Canada's heritage places are expensive and are, by definition, frozen in the amber of a historical period rather than preserved through being sensitively used by people with modern lives and businesses. As anyone who has travelled to England will tell you, it's not like we've got a national trust here.

But it's not just England that has a national trust; that is, an independent body incorporated under an act of government with statutory authority to preserve properties in perpetuity. Although the English National Trust was the first, founded in 1895, since then there have been many others: Scotland (1931), Northern Ireland (1936), the Republic of Ireland (1948), the United States of America (1949), Barbados (1961), Australia (1965), Bermuda (1969), Fiji (1970), Greece (1972), New Zealand (1980) and the Philippines (1981). In recent years, even a number of Caribbean Islands, including Trinidad and Tobago,

People in Montreal — June

have passed national trust legislation. In other countries that combine highly centralized systems of government with a Joseph Howe-type of vision, most notably France, government departments perform the "Trust" role. (France has done an admirable job of juggling high culture [including preserving large numbers of buildings, villages, artwork and monuments] and high-tech [including the TGV train and the Mistral jet] and, in so doing, has defined itself as a nation. Its castoff children, the Québecois, have done almost the same thing. Perhaps it's genetic?)

Best known of the nongovernmental organizations is the English National Trust. Incorporated as the National Trust for Places of Historic Interest or Natural Beauty, it was founded during the last half of the 19th century, a period from which, as C. P. Snow observed in *The Masters*, "nine English traditions out of ten" date. Snow's list included the old school tie, the royal ceremonial, Gilbert and Sullivan, test-match cricket, Sherlock Holmes and bacon and eggs. We can add to that list the Trust and *Country Life* magazine (founded 1897), plus the continuation of a few other English traditions of a sort, including rural depopulation, urban overcrowding, extreme stratification of the social classes and the decline of English craftsmanship and industry.

The Trust's roots, then, were in a period of rapid change, anxiety and uncertainty – a period not unlike our own. Ironically, perhaps, the organization's structure developed from a trans-Atlantic cross-pollenization: an American, Charles Eliot, had observed the efforts of the Commons Preservation Society in England and, in 1891, established the Trustees of (Public) Reservations in Massachusetts; two active members of the Commons group, Octavia Hill and Sir Robert Hunter, were so impressed by Eliot's model that they resolved to use it as the basis for a national trust. Hill was a housing reformer radicalized by the grimness of slum life in London, and she came to the support of the Commons because she believed that access to the countryside was essential to the moral well-being of the working classes. Hunter had been the solicitor for the Commons Preservation Society and championed the rights of public access against the protests of aristocratic landlords. They were joined by Canon Rawnsley – an advocate of the preservation of the Lake

House-barn combination on a little farm on the Route-du-Président Kennedy near Saint Henri, south of Lévis, Québec. Wouldn't look out of place in western Canada, except for the galvanized metal roof & the wild paint job.

District "in all its Wordsworthian purity," as historian David Cannadine wrote in the introduction to *The National Trust: The Next Hundred Years.* Although they held different specific interests, all three were dyed-in-the-wool conservationists. Strange bedfellows, but, as Cannadine observed with reference to today's environmental activists, "conservation is a broad church."

In 1877, nearly twenty years before the National Trust was born, the artist William Morris, founder of the Society for the Protection of Ancient Buildings, wrote: "It has truly been said that these old buildings do not belong to us only; that they belonged to our forefathers and they will belong to our descendants unless we play them false. They are not in any sense our property, to do as we like with them. We are only trustees for those that come after us." The key word to Morris was "trusteeship." Nearly three-quarters of a century later, the founder of the National Trust for Australia (New South Wales), Mrs. I. B. Wyatt, well expressed this universal issue: "I used to lie awake and wonder desperately what could be done about the destruction. The great essential of course was permanence. That could not be found in either government or local government bodies, as however sincere the intentions of the members when they accepted trusteeship, *they have no power to control beyond their term of office.* It had to be some new organization pledged to perpetual responsibility. Moreover, it had to arise among the people themselves."

Most people, English or otherwise, who are aware of the National Trust think of it in terms of two words: country houses. Indeed, the fine old estates owned by the Trust and open to the public are the most publicized and popular aspect of its efforts (responsible certainly for a fair portion of its two-million-plus membership), but they are by no means the only one and are, in fact, a comparatively recent addition to the portfolio. The Trust is primarily a landowner, steward of nearly a quarter-million hectares, its holdings only surpassed by the Forestry Commission and the Ministry of Defence. It is trustee of more than 300 historic houses and gardens, 60 villages and hamlets, 466 sites of special scientific interest, 28 national nature reserves, 1,000 registered ancient monuments, 25 wind- and water-mills and 25 industrial sites as well as 8,000 paintings and a million books; it employs more than 2,700 people. Unlike the high-profile historic houses, which are on display and attract visitors to view their interiors and gardens, much of the Trust's property is leased and used for modern purposes, like farming and residency. Although protected by covenants against unsympathetic change, it is nonetheless productive. It evolves, in a slow and sustainable way.

In the century since its founding, the National Trust has passed through four major phases. As an infant organization, it spent the twenty years before the First World War preserving open spaces and ensuring access to them for the English public. It acquired a number of scenic properties and, in 1896, for the grand sum of ten pounds, bought its first building – a 14th-century clergy house in Sussex! In 1907, its acquisition through a bequest of a dilapidated country house coincided with the passage of the first National Trust Act, which empowered it "to preserve lands and tenements (including buildings) of beauty or historic interest" and to hold them as "inalienable" – in perpetuity for the English people. Nevertheless, nature remained the priority for the Trust's founders. "The national heritage which they sought to preserve was natural rather than manmade, rural rather than urban," wrote Cannadine. "Like many of their contemporaries, they believed that the essence of Englishness was to be found in the fields and hedgerows, not in the suburbs and slums." (It is rather like the prevailing attitude toward the Group of Seven's paintings and the national parks system – that they represent the essence of a wild, unpeopled, romantic Canada.)

The National Trust's second phase, which lasted through the Second World War, proclaimed "spiritual values" – country-worship, the sort of thing that lurks between the lines in the novels of Thomas Hardy, who lived until 1928. But it was the third phase – germinated by the First World War, fertilized by the disruptions of Prime Minister Ramsay MacDonald's tenure, the Great Depression and the Second World War and then harvested in 1945 through the election of Clement Atlee's Labour government – that made the National Trust into the household word it is today.

Amendments to the National Trust Act in 1931 and 1937 made it possible for the Trust to receive land and buildings and to exempt a donor from death duties. They also empowered local authorities to give buildings to the Trust and to contribute to their maintenance. In 1946, the Chancellor of the Exchequer established the National Land Fund and empowered it to compensate the treasury if it (or in its name the National Trust) accepted land, and subsequently houses and their contents, in lieu of death duties. The postwar era in England was characterized by high taxes and socialist legislation, and a bittersweet mood, caught evocatively in Evelyn Waugh's nostalgic *Brideshead Revisited* (published in 1945), set the stage for a major downsizing, as we might now describe it, in the expectations of the landed gentry. Almost in a stampede, minor aristocrats bequeathed their country houses: within thirty years, the National Trust acquired seventy-eight houses from the old landed gentry, and the core of the modern British tourist industry was born.

Since 1965, while not turning its back on any of its previous activities, the National Trust has refocused itself on the natural environment. Under the banner of Enterprise Neptune, the Trust systematically bought up unspoiled but threatened coastline and today owns nearly 900 kilometres of it. The Trust could almost be said to have come full circle, except that today it addresses environmental concerns in a more holistic way (including issues of sustainable agriculture and social change throughout its vast estates and numerous properties) than did its founders a century ago. The last time I was in England with only a few days to spare I joined the throngs and visited a number of the Trust's classic country houses, mainly those with famous gardens attached (such as Vita Sackville-West's Sissinghurst), but I noted in the shops that the Trust's current fundraising campaign was called the "Devil's Dyke Appeal" – a campaign to purchase a coastal property with historical associations dating to St. Cuthman and the Knights Templar. "To make the first payment to secure the purchase of [the property]," said the campaign brochure, "the National Trust has had to empty the 'fighting fund' of the South Downs Appeal. The National Trust has just 12 months to find the balance of payment to Brighton Borough Council." This sort of campaign – give us money in return for a tax receipt and we'll buy something important – reminded me of the efforts of the Nature Conservancy of Canada, which is described in some detail below.

But England is England is England, as Gertrude Stein might have said, and what does its having a national trust have to do with us and our situation? Well, the two countries most like Canada – the United States and Australia – also have national trusts.

Our neighbour to the south has always seemed, to me at least, to blend patriotism, culture and business into an especially heady brew. Their children absorb Americanness with their mothers' milk while Canadians, except during wartime, the Centennial year and the 1995 Québec-separation referendum, have been a bit too cool to effuse openly about their Canadianness. South of the border private philanthropy has always thrived, and it is not unusual to find, in any little ol' town, a handsome preserved building, with a wide front lawn and the Stars and Stripes flapping on a flagpole, that was proudly purchased as a gesture of citizenship by a local businessperson. Admittedly, the U.S. tax structure supports such seemingly magnanimous gestures, but as a Canadian it is hard not to be envious of Americans and embarrassed by our record.

City Hall in Kaslo, B.C.,
in the Kootenays. Built in
1898, it was to be replaced in
the 1970s by a modern structure,
but citizen protest saved it.
Recognized as a National
Historic Site in 1988.

Member of the counterculture,
generation #2, Kaslo.

I mentioned earlier the example of the Van Horne house in Montréal. Two other examples are illustrative. In Kelowna, British Columbia, the fine home and property of W. A. C. Bennett, the millionaire hardware merchant and premier of the province from 1952 to 1972 (he industrialized the province and made fortunes for many businesspeople as well as for his own family), languished vacant and deteriorating following his death in 1979. The family didn't donate it and no one came forward to purchase it, whether for a public purpose or even (American-style) as a shrine of capitalist virtue. Eventually, it was incorporated into a condominium development.

A second example involves the birthplace of Canadian prime minister John Diefenbaker in Neustadt, Ontario. No Abe Lincoln log cabin, Diefenbaker's 1890, yellow-brick Victorian-style home still had all its decorative masonry and wooden gingerbread in the gable, even after a twenty-year vacancy, when a Toronto lawyer named John Medcof bought it for the paltry sum of $60,000. Quoted in a Canadian Press story, Medcof fumed: "The government refused to acquire the house or even commemorate it – so I bought it. I think that it's important to encourage governments to promote Canadianism and take over historic sites and it shouldn't really be left to private citizens." According to the news story, Medcof was working with local service groups and historical societies to develop plans for the house. Perhaps it will become a museum, but it could always be rented out to a tenant: in my rural bailiwick, the local heritage society rents a former church to an avant-garde sculptor and potter who gives classes (and sometimes good parties); several former farmhouses to carefully chosen tenants who perform minor maintenance duties in return for reduced rent; a former Canadian National Railways station to a telegraphy society, the

Monument put to
a modern purpose –
Parliament Hill,
Ottawa

Chamber of Commerce and a group of painters; and a one-room school building with unisex outhouse to the local school district, which runs special classes, complete with a martinet of a schoolmarm, as part of the elementary history curriculum. In these cases, the historic sites are preserved while the buildings are given a practical modern use.

Anyway, back to the U.S.A. Chartered by the United States Congress in 1949, the National Trust for Historic Preservation, like its counterparts elsewhere, receives donations of sites, buildings and objects significant in American history and culture and preserves and administers them for public benefit. It has also been very active in promoting public pride and involvement in heritage and in lobbying for better legislation, even to the point of litigating enthusiastically to pursue its advocacy goals. Involved in about fifty lawsuits in the past twenty-five years, it has won some major victories, perhaps most notably the St. Bartholomew's case of 1989, in which a federal court rejected the premise that laws to preserve landmark buildings violated the Constitution by interfering with the free exercise of religion. The American National Trust is not a landowner on nearly the same scale as is the English National Trust, maintaining nineteen properties as historic house museums, but it enjoys broad public support, having about a quarter of a million members.

Although geographically remote, Australia has more similarities with Canada than does the United States. Both are former British colonies: the impetus to establish Australia as a penal colony occurred because, after 1776, the U.S. was no longer available as a dumping ground for miscreants; Canada was the loyalist holdout against rampant American republicanism and fought the War of 1812 to define the international boundary. Instead of sneering at the Americans, as many Canadians do, Australians have always united against those supercilious, superior "pommy bastards" – the English. Along with their Vegemite sandwiches, Australian children learn tales of British bias and incompetence at Gallipoli during the First World War and in the defence of Australia during the Second; "the ashes," as the England versus Australia test-match cricket is called, prompts a level of fervour usually reserved for holy wars.

Like the Americans, the Australians push all the available buttons to inculcate national identity and pride into the populace. One strategy involves their very active National Trust. In fact, it is a federation of state trusts, for Australia, like Canada, is a federal state with a division of powers not unlike ours. Control over land, for example, is vested in the Australian state legislatures, while control over taxation is a federal matter.

The first of the trusts was organized by a housewife, Mrs. I. B. Wyatt, who had cut her activist teeth protesting the loss of mature trees in the leafy suburb of Gordon, near Sydney, New South Wales. On a holiday one year, she spoke with a stonemason who had worked for the National Trust in England, and she became convinced that Australia needed just such a group to act as a trustee for the relics of its colonial past. Her group, founded in 1945, campaigned strenuously against the proposed demolition of historic buildings in downtown Sydney. As their campaign progressed, they received some unexpected support from none other than the actor Vivien Leigh who, during the 1948 antipodean season of the Old Vic Company, urged the preservation of the historic precinct around the old Parliament House. Their actions managed to forestall some of the demolitions-in-the-name-of-progress that were plaguing Sydney, and the group gained in strength and reputation; nevertheless, it took twelve years, until 1960, for the New South Wales parliament to pass the act making Mrs. Wyatt's little band a statutory body for the preservation of the state's heritage.

Slowly, the trust movement gathered strength throughout Australia. Between 1955 and 1963, all the states except the Northern Territory incorporated their own organizations, in most cases by an Act of

Parliament. In 1965, the groups came together as a federation through the incorporation of the Australian Council of National Trusts. Today, this National Trust owns or manages approximately 285 properties – mainly built-heritage but some natural, 180 of which are open to the public – has 78,000 members (in a country with a population of 18 million), employs more than 450 people and has a volunteer workforce of about 6,000. National Trust shops in the major cities sell guidebooks to the open properties, many of which are run as small museums, as well as books of advice for home owners wishing to authentically restore their own houses and gardens.

Through the Australian Heritage Commission and its Register of the National Estate, Australians have managed to consolidate their stewardship of the natural landscape, including a national parks system, with government preservation activities and the efforts of the National Trust. The term "the National Estate" was coined by the British architect William Clough Ellis and is probably defined as "the places we should keep." David Yencken, a former chair of the Australian Heritage Commission, wrote that the term "national estate" was "pleasantly neutral in its overtones. Heritage carries connotations of buildings and monuments; conservation suggests natural environment. The National Estate means both natural and cultural and both Aboriginal and white history without qualification or distinction."

The Register of the National Estate is an inventory of all the places in Australia that have "aesthetic, historic, scientific or social significance, or other special value" for present and future generations. Places that are evaluated and added to the list are published in the *Commonwealth Gazette* as a matter of law but have also been published in book form as a massive tome (which became a bestseller!) entitled *The Heritage of Australia*. For the private landowner, the Register is an information resource of moral, rather than of legal, authority; for the federal government, it imposes a code of procedure on all ministers and authorities. "For the most part," wrote Yencken, "this system has worked effectively. It has proved a good basis for intelligent discussions about development options. Very many projects have been adjusted to preserve National Estate values. No projects have, however, to our knowledge been entirely stopped."

The Register of the National Estate is probably most valuable because it sets a standard of stewardship: it says, "These are the things that are important to us, and this is how we propose to maintain them." The list is amended as new cultural values emerge, and occasionally properties that can't be incorporated into modern priorities get the chop. All in all, it is a nation-building exercise; to quote Yencken again: "Proud though Australians have always been of different aspects of their country, cultural attitudes have suffered from a sense of inferiority – understandable if misplaced – reflecting the attitudes of settlers who have brought their cultural baggage from other places." He could easily have been talking about Canadians, who have their own cultural baggage. Our well-travelled, multicultural populace perhaps compares the Canadian "national estate" with those of the United States, England or even Australia, or perhaps it remembers other homelands and watches televised historical dramas set elsewhere; it looks around at Canada and can't figure out whether anybody – especially the government – has a clue about what's important.

The impetus for a national Canadian heritage organization that would create a national trust and, in the spirit of Joseph Howe, "foster national pride and love of country," had gained momentum in the 1960s. Pierre Trudeau's Liberal government, elected in 1968, pledged to establish a comprehensive cultural policy, and Trudeau appointed his friend, Gérard Pelletier, who had entered federal politics with him in 1965, as his secretary of state. Like so many intellectual Québecois of his generation, Pelletier had been influenced by the cultural policy of France and considered the minister of culture there, André Malraux, who had passed laws on heritage preservation and the protection of historic districts, as a mentor.

However, the first practical legislative proposal came from the Liberal member of parliament for York-Simcoe, John Roberts, who was concerned that the Historic Sites and Monuments Board of Canada was "archival" rather than concerned with preservation "of what was good in the past not simply because it is unique or of museum value but because it is good." In October 1969, Roberts introduced a private member's bill, C-35, entitled "An Act to establish the Canadian Heritage Foundation," an organization he envisaged as being similar to the English National Trust. The new foundation would be funded by Parliament and administered by the Office of the Secretary of State; Roberts saw it as administering a revolving, interest-free loan program for heritage renovations and acquiring, restoring and reselling properties under restrictive covenants so that they could not subsequently be demolished.

Bill C-35 went the way of most private member's bills: it failed to receive second reading. However, Cabinet was not unsupportive of the *idea* of a national trust, as long as it remained in control, and so instructed Parks Canada to examine heritage trusts abroad. In 1970, Cabinet approved the concept of a Canadian national trust but, instead of following Roberts's proposal, decided it would be structured as a charitable foundation at arm's length from the government rather than be operated as a department of Parks Canada or of the Office of the Secretary of State. Thus, the new organization could easily establish its own policy, advocate preservation and criticize government (and, just as easily, be ignored, like most charitable organizations).

On September 12, 1972, the federal Department of Indian and Northern Affairs issued a press release from Vancouver:

> The Honourable Jean Chrétien, Minister of Indian Affairs and Northern Development, announced the setting up of a national trust, to be called Heritage Canada, with an initial endowment of $12 million in Government funds. The trust will expand the present program of preservation and protection of Canada's historical, architectural, natural and scenic heritage through citizen and corporate participation. "There is an urgent need in Canada today," said Mr. Chrétien, "for a new and more comprehensive program for the preservation of nationally significant sites and structures than is possible with the finances and staff resources presently available."

The concluding paragraph of the press release quoted Chrétien, who became Canada's prime minister twenty-one years later: "I am confident that Heritage Canada will attract the interest, the dedication, the voluntary labour of private citizens, Canadian organizations and corporations, thereby substantially supplementing and expanding the work that has been accomplished up to now by almost complete reliance upon government programs and funds." Some had thought it ought to be named the National Trust of Canada, but a financial organization had already registered that name. England, Scotland, the United States of America, New Zealand and Australia all had their major heritage conservation organizations called the National Trust, but in Canada the National Trust was a trust company. By early 1973, the government had drafted letters of incorporation and a set of proposed bylaws and had determined that the new organization would be overseen by a volunteer board of governors. R. A. J. Phillips, the former director-general of Information Canada and a heritage enthusiast, was named executive director, while the founding chair was Hartland Molson MacDougall, the executive vice-president of the Bank of Montréal; included on the first board was the country's best-known historian, Pierre Berton.

((((((

The Heritage Canada Foundation was launched during a period when the two Rs of the postwar world – Remove and Redevelop – had begun to be replaced in the public mind by the three Rs – Reduce, Reuse and Recycle. By the late 1960s, urban renewal was widely believed to have been a failure; the symbolic coup de grâce took place in St. Louis, Missouri, on the afternoon of July 15, 1972, with the dynamiting of the Pruitt-Igoe public housing project. A more humanistic version of city life began to emerge with the publication in 1964 of *The Death and Life of Great American Cities*, the magnum opus of Toronto writer Jane Jacobs. Conservation and reuse suddenly had a fashionable cachet and complemented the burgeoning environmental movement; small had become beautiful, and everyone began to notice that all the interesting social movements – whether artists in garrets or boutiques in storefronts – happened in old buildings.

More evidence in support of conservation drifted over the border along with the acid rain. As had been the case in Ontario and Québec during the 19th century, much of American preservation activity was spawned by patriotic sentiments. Beginning in 1850, for example, a series of George Washington's military headquarters from the American Revolutionary War were identified and preserved. Many historic sites gained official recognition, and many a little building became a museum. The first large-scale preservation effort in North America was the plan to restore Williamsburg, Virginia, to its colonial heyday, financed initially in the late 1920s by John D. Rockefeller. Another, more curious example from the 1920s was Henry Ford's Greenfield Village, a petting zoo of relocated and restored buildings in Dearborn, Michigan (Ford expressed his opinion on the past in a 1916 interview: "History is more or less bunk," he said). Charleston, South Carolina and New Orleans, Louisiana, passed historic-district zoning regulations in 1931 and 1937, respectively; some of the buildings there were historically significant and some were just old, but it was their visual consistency that made them a pleasing attraction. Other developments renovated industrial sites, like the old Ghirardelli chocolate buildings in San Francisco. Unlike the Williamsburg plan, most heritage developments in the States renovated and provided new uses for old buildings.

In *How Buildings Learn*, Stewart Brand extolled the virtues of this "low road" – the used, modest structures that had never been "magazine architecture." In a chapter entitled "Nobody Cares What You Do in There," he quoted the head of Apple Computers, John Sculley, on his preference for old buildings rather than new ones. "They are much more freeing," Sculley said. Indeed, the modern computer industry was created in the legendary garages of Silicon Valley: the garage in Palo Alto where William Hewlett and David Packard founded their electronics firm in 1939 is now a state historical monument; not far away, in 1973, Steve Wozniak worked with Steve Jobs in the latter's garage and created the

Apple, the world's first personal computer. In rock and roll, a "garage band" implies a state of mind as much as it does a place to practise.

It soon became evident that there were many advantages to the preservation of old buildings and old parts of towns. Renovation produced twice as many jobs per dollar invested as did new construction, according to the Canadian Construction Association. And fixed-up buildings attracted tourists: according to the 1971 Canadian Travel Study, sponsored by the federal government, nearly one-third of domestic tourist spending by Canadians was directly related to visiting historic and cultural sites. The federal government had already begun restoration and reconstruction of Fort Langley, British Columbia, in 1955; Louisbourg, the French fortress on Cape Breton Island in Nova Scotia, in 1961; and Lower Fort Garry, Manitoba, in 1965. The provinces were also in the act: in Ontario, the construction of the St. Lawrence Seaway in the 1950s prompted the creation of Upper Canada Village near Morrisburg, an assemblage of rural and town buildings rescued from the rising waters; a decade later in New Brunswick, King's Landing reused buildings in the path of a filling reservoir. Barkerville and Fort Steele in British Columbia were designated and developed as Provincial Historic Parks in 1959 and 1961, respectively; in Nova Scotia, the Sherbrooke Village Restoration Area was established in 1969. Tourists flocked to them all: to paraphrase W. P. Kinsella's truism, "If you restore it, they will come." (This aspect of tourism has grown since the 1971 travel study. Visits to cultural and heritage sites which, according to the federal way of keeping statistics, include parks and wilderness area, are worth $2.5 billion a year to the Canadian economy. Shortly after it was established in June 1993, the federal government's Department of Canadian Heritage launched a National Heritage Tourism Initiative.)

In addition to these initiatives, several provincial governments acted to control redevelopment in historic areas. Québec City received historic-district status in 1963, Old Montréal in 1964 and Île d'Orléans on the St. Lawrence River near Québec City in 1970. In Halifax in the late 1960s, a protest against a waterfront freeway led a private developer, with support from city council and financial assistance from Parks Canada, to restore and renovate a number of old warehouses along Lower Water Street; known as Historic Properties, the warehouses adjoin restored commercial buildings along Granville Street (a major occupant of which is the Nova Scotia College of Art and Design) and have become a centrepiece of the old downtown. In 1971, at the other end of the country in British Columbia, the provincial government responded to citizen outrage against a CPR-sponsored megadevelopment on the waterfront and yet another proposed freeway system by designating Gastown and Chinatown, the two areas that were to be destroyed, as historic districts. But it was a patchwork approach, and rarely was there due process or adequate follow-up: in the B.C. example, the Social Credit government used a piece of legislation intended to preserve archaeological and historic sites to prevent demolitions in Gastown and Chinatown, then turned the management of the districts, and the creation of zoning policy, over to the City of Vancouver. Property owners who went along with the heritage theme and improved their buildings were then nailed to the wall when their local taxes went up and were further hammered by federal income tax regulations that did not allow them to capitalize their restoration expenses; to add insult to injury, the City of Vancouver had recently helped an Eastern Canadian developer consolidate property and construct Pacific Centre, a huge underground mall a few blocks away that was in direct competition with the Gastown merchants. Many were not amused.

Nevertheless, in recent years heritage has gained a lot of prestige from some unlikely sources. One is global communications, which has helped to foster a sameness of design around the world. Toronto's modern downtown, for example, looks like Montréal's or Vancouver's to anybody but an expert in architecture. Regional differences are largely things of the past, and once something

1822 house

1840
triplex

Johnson Street, Niagara-on-the-Lake, in the
fullness of autumn

becomes successful it is soon copied everywhere. The concrete high-rise apartment buildings in the background of news clips from Beirut, Bosnia or Boston are alarmingly similar. Cars are an even better example of this axiom: they are all, with the possible exception of Citroëns, starting to look the same. So the law of supply and demand works in favour of the preservation of old buildings: they are from a time when there were local crafts and idioms, and there is value in their distinctiveness. Heritage buildings appear in modern advertising when there is something prestigious to sell – luxury cars, for example. The butler who takes the Lexus for a joyride does so with an ivy-covered stone mansion in the background. One bizarre juxtaposition saw the venerable Raffles Hotel make a cameo appearance in a Singapore advertising campaign. "Can a city of the future still let you sleep in the past?" the ad asked.

☾ ☾ ☾

In the twenty-five years since its founding, the Heritage Canada Foundation has a number of achievements to its credit, although the general public has remained largely unaware of its existence and has not understood its role. Reflecting the terms of its original mandate, in 1975 Heritage Canada made a stab at acquiring and restoring individual properties, in a manner similar to a Scottish National Trust program, through its Revolving Mortgage and Loan Program. The idea was to provide bridge financing to groups that wanted to purchase and restore heritage properties: the Halifax home of Sir Sandford Fleming, the CPR-era surveyor and inventor of Standard Time, was one property assisted by the

Along the St. Mary's River near Sherbrooke, Nova Scotia

program; Victoria Hall in Cobourg, Ontario, was another. Heritage Canada also purchased a number of properties but decided in 1982 to sell most of them, keeping only the ones that it had taken as a Crown trustee. Having decided in 1979 to discontinue the loan program, Heritage Canada refocused itself on community development and area conservation, implementing its own Main Street program.

It was only in the 1930s that the modern idea of area conservation emerged. In 1932, in Great Britain, the Town and Country Planning Act empowered local governments to preserve single buildings or groups of them. Five years later, the City of Bath Act began the protection of that 18th-century town from modern encroachment: Bath has since been declared a World Heritage Site by the United Nations. More legislation in the years following the Second World War ensured that buildings within conservation areas could not be destroyed or altered without approval. England now has almost 8,600 legally designated conservation areas, over a quarter of which have been established within the past decade (by comparison, Canada has about 120).

The Main Street idea that Heritage Canada adopted was less rigorous than the legal designation of a heritage district. "Main Street" originated in Norwich, England, in the late 1950s: Magdalen Street having lost much of its character to shoddy renovation and redevelopment, the Civic Trust, an organization wishing to improve municipal planning, approached Norwich City Council with a proposal to restore the old storefronts. Business owners were encouraged to paint and patch, to remove tacky additions and replace lost cornices and woodwork, and thus to reawaken their main street's small-town character; social benefits were sure to follow, including a larger tax base, more employment, less automobile use and perhaps a stable town population. Within a year, the project fixed up sixty-six properties, turned a parking lot into a park, removed some billboards and coordinated the design of bus shelters and lamp standards. The refit was so successful that Norwich council and property owners started to restore other parts of the city. The "Norwich Plan" became known in planning circles worldwide and gained a significant following throughout England.

In North America, main streets had begun to decline after the Second World War. The catalyst was the automobile, the most influential of the myriad of changes that had taken place during the previous quarter-century. Technological advancement had not only made people more mobile and able to live in suburbs separate from the old town centres, it had also made agriculture more efficient and spurred the creation of supermarkets, which needed parking lots and thrived best on cheap land on the outskirts of existing towns. A chain reaction set in: malls consolidated their advertising budgets and razzle-dazzled customers curious to try shopping the modern way; smaller businesses soon had to follow the supermarkets to the malls, abandoning buildings along the main streets. Many people bought the whole package and moved out to new suburbs, leaving the towns like doughnuts. The same thing happened in cities, whose cores were abandoned to the poor and the predators; in old city neighbourhoods, shops along the "streetcar strips" couldn't compete. More recently, small malls have fought for market share against huge, regional malls, and everyone has fought against the "category killers" – the big-box retailers that often locate near highway interchanges on the edges of cities.

Heritage Canada first became involved in attempting to resuscitate old districts in the mid-1970s in the Old Strathcona area of Edmonton. At about the same time, the U.S. National Trust for Historic Preservation launched its Main Street program, ironically named for the "Main Street, U.S.A." attraction in Disneyland, with three projects in towns in the American midwest. Offering more than just façade rehabilitation, the projects coordinated stores' marketing campaigns around a heritage theme, using the techniques that malls had invented. In 1979, Heritage Canada launched its own Main Street program, using Perth, Ontario, as the pilot project. Capitalizing on this success, the foundation solicited more than a million dollars from the federal government and undertook six more Main Street projects: Nelson, British Columbia, a revitalization already begun by the city in partnership with the provincial government; Bridgetown and Windsor, Nova Scotia; Cambridge, Ontario; Moose Jaw, Saskatchewan; and Fort Macleod, Alberta. Some provinces developed their own main-street schemes around the concept of downtown revitalization or the "BIA" (Business Improvement Area).

Viewing "Main Street" as a winning combination of community development and job creation, the federal Department of Regional Industrial Expansion in 1984 contributed $5 million to Heritage Canada, allowing projects to go ahead in some seventy communities across the country. Of all the provincial governments, Alberta became the most involved and ended up doing its own Main Street program; Québec, with its myriad of little towns and sense of common purpose, took to the program like *un canard* to water. According to one estimate, for every government dollar invested in a main street, the private sector invested eighteen. The federal government continued its involvement with a further $3 million in 1990. In total, about 130 communities across the country did some variation on the Main Street theme before the federal cosponsorship ended in 1994.

During this period, the Heritage Canada Foundation was also actively involved in lobbying governments for preservation legislation and was most dramatically successful when the Heritage Railway Stations Protection Act passed in 1988. It is the only federal act protecting heritage property; such protection is usually provided under provincial legislation, but the federal government was able to effect this legislation as it had control over many of the country's railways through the Railway Act. The act forces a railway company to apply to the minister of Canadian heritage to "alter, move, sell or destroy" a station that has been designated as historically significant. The act created an orderly process for dealing with railway stations, although many that have been preserved have had to be moved away from the tracks that gave them their original *raison d'être*.

Although the federal government, in the name of regional economic expansion, was a keen participant in "heritage" through the Main Street program, most other government departments were indifferent, if not actually antagonistic, to the aims of heritage conservation. In recent times, the only federal department waving the flag for heritage preservation was Parks Canada, whose mandate included the national parks system and the Historic Sites and Monuments Board of Canada. Its committee to oversee federally owned heritage buildings, the Federal Heritage Buildings Review Office (FHBRO), was established in 1982 but was created by a Cabinet directive rather than by an Act of Parliament and thus lacked the jurisdiction to deal with heritage buildings owned by crown corporations; in addition, it was underfunded and was able to move only slowly in classifying some of the country's built treasures. Branches of the government were evidently not speaking to each other when, in 1985 during a $22 million "renovation" of the Royal Canadian Mint, about two-thirds of the building was demolished. In a more recent example, a century-old cannery building on the Steveston waterfront near Vancouver, bought by the federal government in 1984 and officially recognized as a heritage building, was demolished in December 1997 before the public was able to comment and before the local business community had the opportunity to offer to restore the building. There is evidently no coordinated policy in the federal government regarding its heritage buildings: there are more than forty federal departments and agencies that have something to do with heritage buildings, but only one (Parks Canada) that is actively interested in preservation. What is needed, obviously, is a piece of legislation with the teeth of the Australian Heritage Commission Act.

The most negative of all the federal bureaucracies, and regrettably the one with the biggest impact, is the Department of Finance, responsible for establishing income-tax policy. The Income Tax Act treats the depreciation of revenue-producing buildings as a tax-deductible loss, but if a building is sold at a profit, then the government "recaptures" the depreciation; however, if the building is demolished rather than sold, then the act regards the building as a "terminal loss," and the owner not only recaptures its depreciation but can deduct from his taxable income most of its book value. No wonder so many buildings have bitten the dust, only to be replaced by parking lots.

The Manoir Mauvide-Genest at Saint Jean on the Île d'Orléans near Québec City. Built in 1734, it was named for the seigneur Jean Mauvide, who had taken over the seigneury of the Île. To my eyes, it is the most French building in Canada — to come upon it on its narrow lane is like a scene from Normandy.

Little restaurant on a terrace out back. Had lunch & listened to an American describing to the waiter how he was a Turcotte, a grandson of one of the pioneering families on the Île — his grandfather had moved to New England in the 1920s & found work in a carpet factory. The grandfather had never returned to Québec.

Toronto skyline from near the Parliament Street crossing — the first & the biggest of the modern Canadian skylines done with phallus afterthought.

They work in these ↱ but want to live in these ↘

Spruce Street Cabbagetown.

Another negative clause concerns the tax treatment of renovation expenses (about four times the amount spent on new construction in Canada in 1970) and has made it difficult for owners to fight their way through red tape and determine what can be deducted as a current expense as opposed to what has to be capitalized and written off over a period of years. According to lawyer and housing lobbyist Marc Denhez, "The entire governmental apparatus had been geared, over decades, to the destruction of older districts, not their renovation." It is a far cry from what happens in the United States, where the National Parks Service of the Department of the Interior administers a policy of preservation tax incentives for historic buildings; even owners who have "non-historic" buildings constructed before 1936 can receive a rehabilitation tax credit, at half the rate applicable to the certified heritage gems.

An analysis done for the Heritage Canada Foundation in 1997 estimated that there are 15,000 to 16,000 designated heritage buildings in Canada – buildings that have some form of covenant registered against their title prohibiting their demolition or unsympathetic renovation. As well, there are probably another 50,000 privately owned buildings of some historical or architectural merit recognized on the heritage lists and inventories of the various levels of government. Of these, probably about one-fifth, or 13,000 buildings, are revenue-producing and thus are affected by the federal Income Tax Act. According to a speech given in Ottawa in October 1997 by Douglas Franklin of the Heritage Canada Foundation, if 1,000 of these buildings were to be renovated in a single year, then "the total 'cost to government' of a modest program of tax incentives would be something in the order of what the federal government spent last year giving away flags. Seen another way, an initial tax incentive program for preservation would cost about 50 to 75 cents per year for each Canadian citizen." By way of comparison, Franklin pointed out that the government spends about twenty-five dollars per capita each year on broadcasting, and about five dollars on museum funding.

Evidently, then, the federal government's attitude toward heritage preservation under Prime Minister Chrétien is less sympathetic than it was under Minister of Indian and Northern Affairs Chrétien. Ironically, the Heritage Canada Foundation has had to labour harder to carve out its own identity under the Chrétien government than it had previously. The name Heritage Canada was said to be personally favoured by him when he founded the organization in 1973. Throughout the next two decades, although the foundation had a name that made it sound as though it were part of government – as in Agriculture Canada or Industry Canada – there was nevertheless no federal government department called "heritage" anything. However, shortly before the Liberals returned to power in 1993, a new ministry, the Department of Canadian Heritage, was created from an amalgamation of several smaller ones. Predictably, much of the media, and even some federal politicians, called the new federal ministry Heritage Canada.

(((

The provinces have not been idle in creating their own heritage trusts but, in the absence of a structure such as the National Trust of Australia, they have developed virtually independently. The oldest is in Nova Scotia, operating since 1960 as the Nova Scotia Museum under the Department of Education. The Ontario Heritage Foundation, established in 1968, is the second-oldest. British Columbia established its Heritage Trust in 1977; Alberta in 1980; Prince Edward Island in 1983; Newfoundland and Labrador in 1985; and Saskatchewan in 1991. To varying degrees, these trusts accept property, manage it and interpret it, run educational programs and give out grants to local organizations for heritage restoration activities. There are, in addition, a number of other nongovernmental heritage trusts in Canada and more are being formed all the time.

The idea of a "trust" or "foundation" has caught on throughout the country recently, providing a focus for donors who seek some assurance of permanent stewardship and – equally important – a tax deduction. Private foundations have an added appeal because many potential donors will do almost anything to avoid giving money to the government. Not surprisingly, perhaps, once again the federal Department of Finance discriminates against potential donors of immoveable property, forcing them to pay capital gains tax on most gifts of real estate to the Crown; in an odd twist, donations of *portable* capital property, such as artifacts or art, are exempt from capital gains tax. A donor could give his private residence to a trust, but any other property donation attracts the tax man, so it is not surprising that few people are able to follow the English example described earlier.

Nevertheless, people give cash to charitable foundations, which then buy property. One of the more interesting is Canadian Heritage of Québec. A registered charity incorporated in 1960 by a group of Montréal-area individuals led by Jack Molson, of the brewery family, it is funded by private donations and has managed to preserve about thirty sites in Québec, a number of which form a circuit of bed-and-breakfast accommodations. Other properties are rented to tenants, and a couple are locally curated museums. As an example, Bon Désir east of Tadoussac is a rustic property like those of the Landmark Trust in England or the national "gîte" system of holiday cottages in France: the farmhouse "can accommodate six persons occupying three bedrooms. Lighting is by coal oil lamp, heat is from the wood stove and there is an ice box for refrigeration. There is also a propane cooking stove and hot water heater. Potable water is piped from the guardian's house and water is also obtained by hand pump from a well."

The organization that bears the strongest resemblance to the English National Trust is the Nature Conservancy of Canada, a nonprofit corporation that is a registered charity. Unlike Canadian Heritage of Québec, its concern is natural land, and it fundraises systematically to buy ecologically sensitive and endangered properties. It also runs a conservation easement program, helping sympathetic landowners modify their land-title documents to preserve their land in perpetuity. Founded in 1962, it has about 15,000 members and has preserved 700 nature reserves comprising 542,326 hectares across the country. Its role is the natural side of the landscape coin, while the Heritage Canada Foundation's role is the cultural side.

Recent rumblings within the federal government indicate a reawakening of interest in creating a true national trust. It's funny the way these things happen: the Prince of Wales, on a visit to the Maritimes, mentioned in a casual conversation how good the English National Trust was for preservation, tourism, pride and so on. "You should get one," he reportedly quipped. Some federal politicians and officials in the room made notes.

If the federal government were interested in preserving its "national estate," it could look to several countries for models and procedures. Along with a national trust with statutory authority, it will have to come up with a comprehensive heritage policy that binds its myriad departments and Crown corporations into a preservation-oriented mindset. That, of course, includes the Department of Finance and the discriminatory tax treatment it doles out to the nation's individual custodians of heritage property. Only then will Canada be able to be one of Joseph Howe's wise nations – like England, the United States and Australia, all of which have made concerted efforts to retain their national identities in the face of rapid change and globalization.

People in Toronto — October.

Pictou, Nova Scotia
on an October day. The industrious
chap with the paintbrush is
demonstrating
Isaac Asimov's
axiom:
"Maintenance is
the foundation
of eternity."

Bibliography

The following books and papers were cited in the text or used as references.

Brand, Stewart. *How Buildings Learn: What Happens after They're Built.* New York: Viking-Penguin, 1994.

Denhez, Marc. *The Canadian Home: From Cave to Electronic Cocoon.* Toronto and Oxford: Dundurn Press, 1994.

Green, Dianne. *Exploring Old Whitehorse: Three Walking Tours of the Yukon's Capital.* Whitehorse: Yukon Historical and Museums Association, 1996.

Hart, E. J. *The Selling of Canada: The CPR and the Beginnings of Canadian Tourism.* Banff: Altitude Publishing, 1983.

Heritage Canada Foundation, Youth Services Programme. *Living Between Land and Sea: The People of Newfoundland and Labrador.* Ottawa: Heritage Canada Foundation, 1997.

Hill, Charles C. *The Group of Seven: Art for a Nation.* Ottawa: Publications Division, National Gallery of Canada, 1995.

Kalman, Harold. *A History of Canadian Architecture.* Toronto: Oxford University Press, 1994.

Kurelek, William. *Kurelek's Canada.* Toronto: Pagurian Press, 1978.

Lady Tweedsmuir. *Canada.* London: William Collins, 1941.

Laurence, Margaret. *The Stone Angel.* Toronto: McClelland and Stewart, 1968.

Leacock, Stephen. *Sunshine Sketches of a Little Town.* Toronto: Bell and Cockburn, 1912.

Martin, Sandra, and Roger Hall, eds. *Rupert Brooke in Canada.* Toronto: Peter Martin, 1978.

Mellen, Peter. *Landmarks of Canadian Art.* Toronto: McClelland and Stewart, 1978.

Mitchell, W. O. *How I Spent My Summer Holidays.* Toronto: McClelland and Stewart, 1981.

Newby, Eric. *A Traveller's Life.* London: Picador-Pan Books, 1983.

Newby, Howard, ed. *The National Trust: The Next Hundred Years.* London: The National Trust, 1995.

Pope, Peter E. *The Many Landfalls of John Cabot.* Toronto: University of Toronto Press, 1997.

Reps, John W. *The Making of Urban America: A History of City Planning in the United States.* Princeton: Princeton University Press, 1965.

Schama, Simon. *Landscape and Memory.* Toronto: Random House, 1995.

Stegner. Wallace. *Wolf Willow: A History, a Story and a Memory of the Last Prairie Frontier.*
    Toronto: Macmillan, 1955.

Stokes, Peter John. *Old Niagara on the Lake.* Toronto and Buffalo: University of Toronto Press, 1971.

Thorne, Steven. *Policies for Preservation: The Heritage Canada Foundation 1973-1993.* Waterloo: Research Group
    on Leisure and Cultural Development, University of Waterloo, 1994.

Wilson, Barry. *Beyond the Harvest: Canadian Grain at the Crossroads.* Saskatoon: Western Producer Prairie, 1981.

Heritage Organizations

The following organizations were cited in the text.

Australian Heritage Commission
GPO 1567
Canberra, A.C.T. 2601 Australia
<www.erin.gov.au/portfolio/ahc/ahc_site/html/ahc_home.htm>

Canadian Heritage/Parks Canada
Room 10H2, 25 Eddy Street
Hull, Québec K1A 0M5
<parkscanada.pch.gc.ca>

The Canadian Heritage of Québec
1181 Mountain Street
Montréal, Québec H3G 1Z2

Heritage Canada Foundation
P.O. Box 1358, Station B
Ottawa, Ontario K1P 5R4
(Some information is available from the Canadian Heritage Information Network,
sponsored by the Department of Canadian Heritage, at <www.chin.gc.ca>)

International Council on Monuments and Sites
ICOMOS Canada
P.O. Box 737, Station B
Ottawa, Ontario K1P 5R4
<www.icomos.org>

The National Trust
36 Queen Anne's Gate
London, England SW1H 9AS
<www.ukindex.co.uk/nationaltrust/>

The National Trust of Australia
P.O. Box 1002
Civic Square, A.C.T. 2608 Australia
<www.tandem.aust.com/nationaltrust/>

The National Trust for Historic Preservation
1785 Massachusetts Ave. N.W.
Washington, D.C. U.S.A. 200036
<www.nationaltrust.org>

The Nature Conservancy of Canada
110 Eglinton Avenue West, 4th Floor
Toronto, Ontario M4R 2G5

The UNESCO World Heritage Centre
7, place de Fontenoy
75352 Paris 07 SP
France
<www.unesco.org/whc/>
(The World Heritage List is at <www.cco.caltech.edu/%7Esaimon/world.heritage.html>)

List of Illustrations

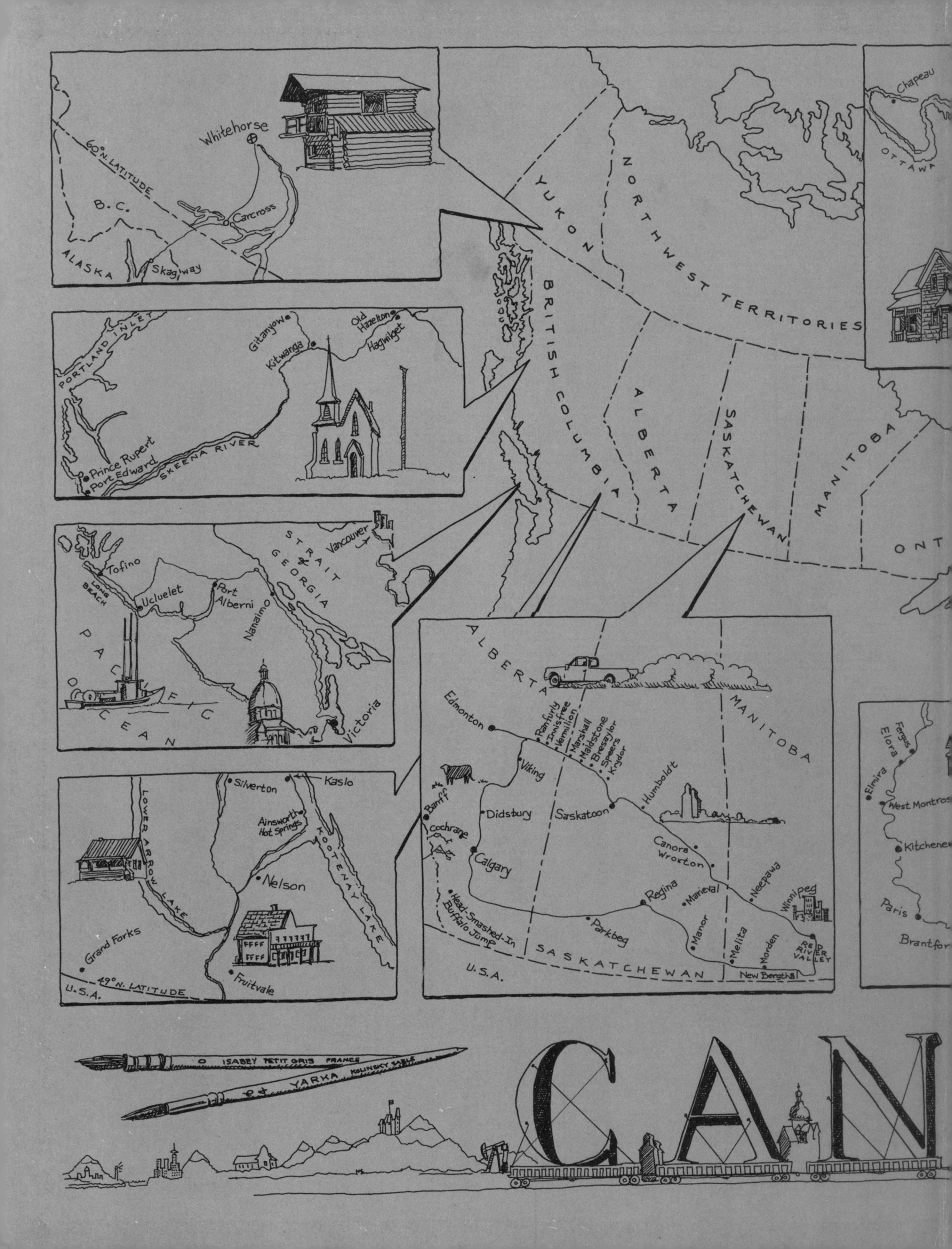